SURAS

LATEST

GENERAL

KNOWLEDGE

Fully Revised

By
V.V.K. Subburaj

EDITION
2008

SURA COLLEGE OF COMPETITION

An imprint of Sura Books (Pvt) Ltd.

(An ISO 9001:2000 Certified Company)

Chennai ● Ernakulam

Price: Rs.70.00

© PUBLISHERS

LGK

Updated upto 15th August, 2007

Price: Rs.70.00

ISBN : 81-7254-006-X

SURA COLLEGE OF COMPETITION
[An imprint of Sura Books (Pvt) Ltd.]

Head Office:
1620, 'J' Block,
16th Main Road,
Anna Nagar,
Chennai - 600040.
Phones: 26162173, 26161099.

Branch:
XXXII/2328, New Kalavath Road,
Opp. to BSNL, Near Chennoth Glass,
Palarivattom,
Ernakulam - 682025.
Phone: 0484-3205797

Printed at T.Krishna Press, Chennai - 600 012 and Published by
V.V.K.Subburaj for Sura College of Competition,
[An imprint of Sura Books (Pvt) Ltd.]
1620, 'J' Block, 16th Main Road, Anna Nagar, Chennai - 600 040.
Phones: 91-44-26162173, 26161099. Fax: (91) 44-26162173.
email: surabooks@eth.net, website: www.surabooks.com

08 07 3000

CONTENTS

		Pages
1.	Constitution of India	1
2.	Indian History	39
3.	History of Assam and History of South India	42
4.	Medieval India	43
5.	Mughal Rule in India	45
6.	Communal and Regional Uprising	47
7.	Modern India	48
8.	National Movement	50
9.	World Wars	60
10.	Upper Echelon of Indian Government	62
11.	Historical Dates and Events	63
12.	Geography of India	90
13.	Flora and Fauna	91
14.	Vital Statistics of the People	92
15.	National Symbols	93
16.	Planning	95
17.	Banking in India	100
18.	Defence	108
19.	Scientific Research	115
20.	Communications	118
21.	Transport	122
22.	Press	130
23.	Cultural Activities	136
24.	Arts in States	138
25.	Cinema	141
26.	National Awards	144
27.	International Awards	149
28.	UNO	151
29.	Geography – *The Universe*	153
30.	Geographical Terms	159
31.	Countries, Capitals, Currencies, Languages and Religions	175
32.	Terminology – *General*	184

		Pages
33.	Science	200
34.	Scientific Phenomena	220
35.	Inventions and Discoveries	230
36.	Scientific Instruments	236
37.	Biology and Medicine - *Important Events*	241
38.	Units of Measurement	242
39.	Human Body	243
40.	Vitamins	248
41.	Well-known Indian Scientists	249
42.	World's Prominent Scientists	251
43.	Important Personalities (Past)	257
44.	Books and Authors	290
45.	Important Places in India	306
46.	Towns and Industries	320
47.	Abbreviations	324
48.	Firsts in the World	346
49.	Firsts in India	346
50.	Persons and Places	349
51.	Popularly known as	349
52.	Symbols	351
53.	Names of Parliaments	351
54.	Independence Days of various countries	352
55.	Official Books and Papers, National Emblems and Flower Emblems	353
56.	Epithets	354
57.	Well-known Places in the World	356
58.	Important Sites in India	358
59.	Sanctuaries and Parks in India	359
60.	Major Ports in India	361
61.	Important Days	367
62.	Indian and Foreign Towns on Rivers	370
63.	Foreign Towns and Industries	371
64.	Names - *Old and New*	379
65.	Sports	380

CURRENT AFFAIRS

INDIAN POLITY

THE CONSTITUTION OF INDIA

The idea of Constituent Assembly for India was put forward for first time by M.N. Roy in 1934. M.N. Roy was a pioneer of Communist movement in India. In 1935, the Indian National Congress for the first time, officially demanded a Constituent Assembly to frame the Constitution of India.

Constituent Assembly was elected on the basis of Adult franchise. Total strength of the Constituent Assembly was to be 389. 296 seats were allotted to British India, and 93 seats to the princely states. Total number of members of Constituent Assembly was reduced from 389 to 299. 229 seats were allotted to British India and 70 seats to princely states.

The Constituent Assembly held its first meeting on December 9, 1946 under temporary President of Constituent Assembly, Dr. Sachchidanand Sinha. Later on December 11, 1946 Dr. Rajendraprasad and H.C. Mukherjee was elected as the President and Vice President of Assembly respectively. Sir B.N. Rau was appointed as the Constitutional Advisor to the Assembly.

Completion of Constituent Assembly took a period of 2 years, 11 months 18 days. The total expenditure incurred on making the Constitution Assembly amounted to Rs. 64 lakhs. The Constituent Assembly appointed 22 committees to deal with different tasks of Constitution making. Drafting committee was set up on August 29, 1947.

Drafting committee consisted of seven members. Dr. B.R. Ambedkar was one of the members and chairman of the Drafting Committee. Drafting Committee took 114 days to prepare its draft.

The Constitution as adopted on November 26, 1949 contained a preamble, 395 articles and 8 schedules. Objective resolution was given by Jawaharlal Nehru. It was adopted by Assembly on January 22, 1947. Objective resolution in modified version forms the preamble of our Constitution. The Constitution came into force on Jan. 26, 1950. At present Constitution of India contains a preamble, 444 articles and 12 schedules.

THE PREAMBLE

WE, THE PEOPLE OF INDIA, having solemnly resolved to constitute India into a SOVEREIGN SOCIALIST SECULAR DEMOCRATIC REPUBLIC and to secure to all its citizens –

JUSTICE,	social, economic and political,
LIBERTY	of thought, expression, belief, faith and worship,
EQUALITY	of status and of opportunity; and to promote among them all,
FRATERNITY	assuring the dignity of the individual and the unity and integrity of the nation,

IN OUR CONSTITUENT ASSEMBLY, this twentysixth day of November, 1949, do HEREBY ADOPT, ENACT AND GIVE TO OURSELVES THIS CONSTITUTION.

The Preamble of our Constitution emphasizes the ultimate sovereignty of the people and that the Constitution itself is founded on the authority of the people. India is a sovereign country because it does not act under the dictation of any foreign country. It is absolutely independent in its internal affairs, external relations and all transactions. In short, it is absolute within its own sphere.

India is a Democratic Republic. It has been argued that the word "Democratic" used before the word "Republic" is redundant and superfluous. But it is not so because Democracy does not necessarily establish the Republican form of Government. Though Britain, where there is a Hereditary Monarchy, is a Democracy, it is not a Republic. But India, where the President who is the Constitutional head, is elected by the representatives of the people for a period of five years is a republic.

The words SOVEREIGN SOCIALIST/SECULAR have been introduced by 42nd Amendment which came into force on 18th December 1976. It must be noted that the people of India give the Constitution of India to themselves.

Our Constitution has been divided into 24 parts. The first part deals with the Union and its Territories. The first Article says, *India, that is, Bharat, shall be a union of states.* Nowhere in our Constitution, we find the word Federation. It is generally said that *our Constitution is quasi-federal in nature designed to work as a federation in normal times and as an Unitary State in emergency.* But the best and correct interpretation is 'Union of States'. There are 28 States and 7 Union Territories. The 69th Amendment of 1991 states that Delhi should continue to be a Union Territory known as National Capital Territory and be provided with a Legislative Assembly (70 seats) and a Council of Ministers (7 ministers). National Capital Territory of Delhi and the Union Territory of Pondicherry though administered by the President through a Lt.Governor he is advised by a Council of Ministers, responsible to the Legislative Assembly headed by the Chief Minister. He carries on the administration directly. The Legislative Assembly of Pondicherry has 33 seats. The 70th Amendment states that the elected members of the Legislative Assemblies of Delhi and of Pondicherry form part of electoral college in electing the President.

The salient features of our Constitution are: Sovereignty of the people, adult franchise, abolition of Princely states, Supreme Court in place of Privy Council, abolition of untouchability, abolition of titles, equality, secular 'socialist' republic and making certain important provisions of the Constitution rigid while retaining the flexibility of the Constitution itself.

SOURCES OF OUR CONSTITUTION

Indian constitution borrowed from its many salient features from the constitutions of various countries. But Government of India Act of 1935 is the very basis of our constitution.

Sources :	Features borrowed :
British Constitution	Parliamentary government, Rule of law, Single citizenship, Cabinet system.

US Constitution	Fundamental rights, Judicial review, Independence of Judiciary, Impeachment of President, Removal of Supreme & High Court Judges
Russian Constitution	Fundamental duties and Ideal of Justice
Irish Constitution	Directive principles of state policy, Nomination of members of Rajya Sabha
Canadian Constitution	Federation with strong centre
Australian Constitution	Concurrent list, Joint sitting of two Houses of Parliament
Weimer Constitution of Germany	Suspension of Fundamental Rights during emergency.
French Constitution	Republic & Ideals of liberty, equality and fraternity in the Preamble
South African Constitution	Procedure for amendment of the Constitution
Japanese Constitution	Procedure established by law

CITIZENSHIP

India has two sets of people as (i) citizens (ii) aliens. Citizens are full members of Indian state. They enjoy all civil and political rights. Aliens do not enjoy all the civil and political rights.

Constitution deals with the citizenship from articles 5 to 11 under Part II. Accordingly the Parliament has enacted the citizenship act 1955, which has been amended in 1986 & 1992.

Acquisition of citizenship : The Citizenship Act of 1955 prescribes five ways of acquiring citizenship viz. birth, descent, registration, naturalization and incorporation of territory.

By Birth : The act amended in 1986 provides that a person is a citizen of India by birth (a) if he is born in India on or after 26, Jan. 1950 but before 1st July, 1987 (or) (b) if he is born in India on or after 1 July, 1987 but before 3rd December, 2004 is considered citizen of India by birth if either of his parents was a citizen of India. The second provision, added in 1986, makes the acquisition of Indian citizenship by the persons coming to India as refugees from Srilanka, Bangladesh and some African countries more difficult.

By Descent : Citizen of India by descent if at the time of his birth either of his parents was an Indian citizen. But before 1992, a person born outside India was entitled to Indian citizenship only if his father was an Indian citizen.

By Registration : Persons of Indian origin who are ordinarily resident in India for five years immediately before making an application for registration.

By naturalization : He has either resided in India or has been in Indian government service for 12 months before making an application for naturalization.

By incorporation of Territory : If any foreign territory becomes a part of India, the government of India specifies the persons who among the people of territory shall be citizens of India.

Loss of Citizenship : The citizenship Act 1955, prescribes three ways of losing citizenship whether acquired under the act or prior to it under the constitution, viz. renunciation, termination and deprivation.

Commonwealth Citizenship : The Citizenship Act 1955, recognizes formally the concept of Commonwealth Citizenship. Every person who is citizen of a Commonwealth country has the status of a Commonwealth Citizen in India.

Single Citizenship : Indian constitution is federal and envisages of dual polity (centre & state). It provides for only single citizenship, that is the Indian citizenship. The citizens in India owe allegiance only to the union. There is no separate state citizenship.

FUNDAMENTAL RIGHTS

The third and the most important part contains the Fundamental Rights. Fundamental Rights are granted to citizens under Articles 12 to 35 of the Constitution. Some of the provisions of the Fundamental Rights are of the nature of prohibitions and place Constitutional limitations on the authority of the state.

The object of the Fundamental Rights, Dr. Ambedkar said, is *two fold*. First that every citizen must be in a position to claim those rights. Secondly they must be binding upon every authority. They must be binding not only on Central Government but on the State Governments, districts, local bodies, municipalities, even Village Panchayats and Taluk Boards. But the Bill of Rights in the United States imposes limitations on the National Government alone.

Article 13 (2) of our Constitution says *The state shall not make any law which takes away or abridges the rights conferred by this part.* Any law made in contravention, is void. It has been much debated whether the word law includes Constitutional Amendment or not. The present opinion is that *law* does not include Constitutional Amendment. And according to the judgement given in the Keshavanand Bharathi's case in April 1973, this is made clear that the Parliament can amend the Fundamental Rights. So it implies that the word *law* does not include Constitutional amendment. Thus the Supreme court shifted back to its original position in the Gopalan case of 1950, that *Parliament is omnipotent.* The Golaknath case judgement has been overruled. It is apt here to discuss what is Golaknath case. The Supreme Court by a historic 6-5 ruling on February 27, 1967 reversing its earlier decision declared that Parliament had no power to abridge or take away Fundamental Rights guaranteed under the Constitution. The majority view was expressed in two separate judgements - one by the then Chief Justice Mr.K. Subba Rao for himself and for Justices S.C. Shah, J.M. Shelat and Vaidyalingam and the other by Mr. Justice Hidayathullah. The judges who gave dissenting judgement were Wanchoo, Bhargawat, Mitter and Ramasami. The Government's demand to abridge the Fundamental Rights was dubbed as "too extravagant". When such a contingency arises, the Parliament by exercising its residuary powers, might call the Constituent Assembly to frame a new Constitution or to change it radically. The article 368 which deals with the Amendment to our Constitution gives only the procedure and not the power to the Parliament. Here it can be argued, how can there be procedure without power? Moreover when the Parliament has no power to amend or abridge the Fundamental Rights, how can it give power to a Constituent Assembly which is to be created by the Parliament? A coin has always two sides.

Specific Fundamental Rights

Right to Equality (Art. 14-18): It guarantees equality to all persons before the law, thrashes out discrimination on grounds of religion, race, caste, sex or place of birth between citizens, grants equality of opportunity in the matter of public employment and abolishes untouchability and titles. Minorities may establish their own schools and Government cannot deny grants on the grounds of race, religion or language.

Exemptions: (First Amendment) The State may make special provisions to give preference to the socially and economically backward classes of citizens or for the Scheduled Castes and Tribes. The Parliament may confine employment under any state or local authority to residents. The state may also provide for the reservation of appointments or posts for members of backward classes which in the opinion of the state are not adequately represented in the services under the state. Offices connected with religious denominations may be reserved only to the adherents of that denomination.

Right to Freedom (Art. 19-22): These Articles deal with the right to freedom. Article 19 guarantees seven fundamental rights which are known as seven freedoms; namely *a) freedom of speech and expression, (b) freedom of assembly, (c) freedom of association, (d) freedom of movement, (e) freedom of residence and settlement, (f) freedom of profession, occupation, business or trade, (g) freedom of possession.*

Exemption: The reservations restricting this right are in the interests of the security of the state, friendly relations with foreign states, public order, decency, morality or relating to contempt of court, defamation or incitement to an offence. Freedom of assembly and of association is subject to restrictions in the interests of the public order. The freedom of movement is also restricted in the interest of the public and of any scheduled tribes. In times of emergency, every citizen cannot claim access to places considered to be of military or strategic importance. The freedom of movement may be restricted to the place where an epidemic spreads. Any person can be forbidden from entering into any part of the country for a particular period or can be detained on the sufficient grounds in the interest of public order. The right of carrying any trade or profession is subject to reasonable restrictions.

The Articles 20 to 22 which deal with the personal liberty, say that no one should be subjected to any punishment for any kind of offence under any law which is not in force at the time when the offence was committed.

No person can be deprived of life except by the procedure established by law. Similarly no person can be detained for more than 24 hours without the authority of the nearest magistrate. The Article 22 deals with the arrests made under the Preventive Detention Acts.

Right Against Exploitation (Art. 23 & 24): These articles prohibit the traffic in human beings and beggary and similar forms of forced labour. But regarding services, the state shall not make any discrimination on grounds of religion, race, caste or class. Nobody below the age of fourteen years shall be employed to work in any factory or mine or engaged in any other hazardous employment.

Right to Freedom of Religion (Art. 25-28): All persons are equally entitled to freedom of conscience and possess the right to profess freely, practise and propagate religion, subject to public order, morality and health. No one can be compelled to pay tax for propagation or maintenance of any religion. No school or college wholly maintained out of government revenues can impart religious instructions.

Cultural and Educational Rights (Art. 29 & 30): These articles guarantee to every minority or section of the citizens residing in the territory of India or any part thereof to have the right of having a distinct language script of culture of its own and of conserving the same. All minorities are given freedom to establish educational institutions of their choice. The state shall not discriminate in granting aid to educational institutions on the ground that it is under the management of a minority whether based on religion or language.

Right to Property (Art. 31): According to this Article no person shall be deprived of his property saved by authority of law. Further no property shall be compulsorily acquired or requisitioned save for public purpose and save by authority of law without paying adequate compensation. But the word compensation has been now replaced by the word 'amount' (25th Amendment). Further it was provided that if the Parliament or a State Legislature makes a law with the declaration that it is going to give effect to the 'Directive Principles of State Policy' it cannot be brought under 'Judicial Review'. But this part has been struck down by the Supreme Court. Now the Right to Property, contained in Part III - Fundamental Rights - of the Constitution, has been taken away as a fundamental right and made a legal right under art .300A by 44th Amendment 1978, with effect from June 20, 1979.

Right to Constitutional Remedies (Art. 32-35): Dr. B.R. Ambedkar denoted the right as Heart & Soul of our Constitution. These articles guarantee every person to move the Supreme Court for the enforcement of the fundamental rights. But while a proclamation of emergency is in operation, Fundamental Rights related to seven freedoms stand automatically suspended. The President, by an order may suspend the right to move the courts to enforce the Fundamental Rights. But such an order must be laid before the Parliament in accordance with the related provisions of the Constitution. Article 32 (1) allows moving the Supreme Court to issue directions or orders or writs in the nature of Habeas Corpus, Mandamus, Certiorari, Prohibition and Quo warranto.

DIRECTIVE PRINCIPLES OF STATE POLICY

Directive Principle State Policy are three principles, such as (1) Socio (or) Economical (2) Gandhian (3) Liberal.

Part IV of our Constitution contains Directive Principles of State Policy which are declared, according to Articles 36 to 51 - fundamental in the governance of the country. Dr.Ambedkar said in the Constituent Assembly that these declarations are not mere pious declarations. The future legislature and the executive should not merely pay lip-service but they must form the very basis of all legislative and executive action.

Distinction between Fundamental rights and Directive principles :

Fundamental rights	Directive principles
1. These are negative as they prohibit the state from doing certain things	They are positive as they require the state to do certain things
2. These are justiciable	These are non justiciable
3. They aim at establishing democracy in the country	They aim at establishing social, political democracy in the country
4. These have legal sanctions	These have moral and political sanctions
5. They promote the welfare of the individual	They promote the welfare of community
6. Can be suspended during emergency	No such provision
7. They are automatically enforced	They are not automatically enforced
8. The courts are bound to declare a law violative of any of the fundamental rights as unconstitutional and invalid	The courts cannot declare a law violative of any of the Directive principles as unconstitutional and invalid

Directive Principles: Articles 36 to 51 cover all the Directive Principles enshrined in our Constitution.

1. Definition of State (Art. 36)
2. Application of Directive Principles (Art. 37)
3. State to secure a social order for the promotion of welfare of the people (Art. 38)
4. Certain principles of policy to be followed by the State (Art. 39)
5. Equal justice and free legal aid (Art. 39A)
6. Organisation of village panchayats (Art. 40)
7. Right to work, to education and to public assistance in certain cases (Art. 41)
8. Provision for just and humane conditions for work and maternity relief (Art. 42)
9. Living wage etc. for workers (Art. 43)
10. Participation of workers in management of industries (Art. 43A)
11. Uniform civil code for the citizens (Art. 44)
12. Provision for early childhood care and education to children below age of six years (Art. 45)

13. Promotion of educational and economic interests of Scheduled Castes, Scheduled Tribes and other weaker sections (Art. 46)
14. Duty of the State to raise the level of nutrition and standard of living and to improve public health (Art. 47)
15. Organisation of Agriculture and Animal husbandry (Art. 48)
16. Protection and improvement of environment and safeguarding of forests and wild life (Art. 48A)
17. Protection of monuments and places and objects of national importance (Art. 49)
18. Seperation of judiciary from executive (Art. 50)
19. Promotion of international peace and security (Art. 51)

Mr. Chatterjee asserted "These solemn declarations (the Directive Principles) in the Constitution were not directives but only *decoratives* in the Constitution." Mr. B.N. Datar, the then Home Minister, replying to his criticism, said that these principles were like *Manifesto of Aims* and were not a matter of immediate achievement. They are the directives by which we have to go. They are trends and tendencies that have to be taken into account in laying down the policies of the government. The policies of the Government have been shaped in accordance to the principles. Every decision of the Planning Commission has been guided or coloured by the "Directive Principles". Our present government attaches increasing importance to these principles and thus tries to ensure economic democracy without undermining the political democracy. Political democracy without economic democracy is void.

THE PRESIDENT

Article 52 of our Constitution declares that "There shall be a President of India". The executive power of the Union and the Supreme Command of Defence Forces is vested with him. Our Constitution simply creates the office of the President of India. But it does not say anywhere that the President is either the Head of the State or the executive.

Qualifications of the President: The President of India must be a citizen of India, must have completed the age of 35 years and be qualified for election as a member of the Lok Sabha. At the time of the election, he should not hold an office of profit under any Government - union or state or local. However, he is not deemed to hold office of profit by reason only that he is the President or the Vice-President of India or the Governor of a state, or a minister either at the Centre or in the State. If he is a member of either House of Parliament or of a House of the Legislature of any State and elected to the office of the President, he is deemed to have vacated the membership, as soon as he enters upon his office as President. The superintendence, direction and control for the election of President is vested with the Election Commission. The decision on doubts and disputes relating to the election of the President rests with the Supreme Court and its decision is once for all final.

The salary and other emoluments of the President are determined by the Parliament. They cannot be increased or diminished during the term of his office. The Parliament has fixed a salary (see table in the coming pages). The President is entitled to use the official furnished residence without payment of any rent and he is permitted to spend a fixed sum of rupees per year on travel, entertainment, etc.

Term of Office: The President holds office for a period of five years and is eligible for re-election. He may resign. His resignation must forthwith be addressed to the Vice-President, who is required to communicate forthwith to the Speaker of the Lok Sabha. The President of India can be impeached for 'violation of Constitution'. But the 'violation of Constitution' has not been defined. The procedure of impeachment is covered by Article 61. When a President is to be impeached for violating the Constitution, the charge shall be preferred by either House of Parliament. The President must be given fourteen days notice in writing signed by not less than one fourth of the total number of members of the House to move such a resolution and such a resolution must be passed by a majority of not less than two thirds of the total membership of the House. When such a charge has been so preferred by either House of Parliament the other House shall investigate the charge and the President shall have the right to appear and to be represented at such investigation. As a result of the investigation a resolution is passed by a majority of not less than two thirds of total membership of the House by which the charge was investigated, the President shall forthwith be removed from office.

Mode of Election: The President of India is elected by the members of electoral college consisting of *(a) the elected members of both Houses of Parliament; and (b) the elected members of the Legislative Assemblies of the States in accordance with the proportional representation by means of single transferable vote.* Each Member of a State Legislature (MLA) has as many votes as are obtained by the formula:

$$\frac{\text{Total Population of state (ascertained at the last census)}}{\text{Total number of elected members of the Legislative Assembly}} \div 1000$$

Fractions exceeding half will be counted as one. For securing parity between the states as a whole and the Union, the votes of each Member of Parliament (MP) will be according to this formula:

Total number of votes assigned to elected members to the Legislative Assemblies of all states ÷ Total number of the elected member of both House of Parliaments

$$\text{Quota:} \frac{\text{Total number of votes polled}}{\text{Number of Candidates}} + 1$$

If at the first count no candidate is able to secure the requisite quota of votes, the candidate securing the least number of votes is eliminated and his votes are transferred among the other candidates according to the second preferences on the ballot papers of the voters who gave him first preferences. This process of elimination and transfer of votes continues till such a candidate is elected who has obtained the requisite quota of votes. Disputes, if any, about the election of the President are heard and decided by the Supreme Court.

Power and Duties of the President: Though all executive actions of the Union Government are expressed to be taken in the name of the President, his authority is formal. He has the right to be kept informed by the Prime Minister of all decisions taken by the Council of Ministers. He appoints the Prime Minister and other Ministers, the Attorney-General of India, the Comptroller and Auditor General of India, Judges of the Supreme Court and of the High Courts and the State Governors. The President has the power to remove his ministers, the Attorney-General of India and the Governors of the States. He has the power to appoint an interstate council, the Union Public Service Commission, the Election Commission, a commission to report on the administration of Scheduled Areas, Special Officer for Scheduled Castes and Scheduled Tribes, a commission to investigate into conditions of backward classes and a commission on languages. Union Territories are under the direct control of the President.

The Constitution vests the supreme command of the Armed forces in the President. But he has to exercise this power in conformity with law. Parliament has exclusive legislative powers, relating to the defence forces. The diplomatic business is conducted in the name of the President. All treaties and international agreements are negotiated and concluded in the name of the President. The election of a new President must be held within six months of the date of the occurrence of the vacancy. When the President is unable to perform his functions owing to absence, illness or any other cause, the Vice President discharges the functions of the President until the President resumes duties of his office.

Emergency Powers of the President: Three kinds of emergencies have been contemplated in India. The President of India can declare emergency arising due to *a) war, external aggression and armed rebellion; (b) failure of Constitutional machinery in a state; and (c) threat to financial stability or credit of India*. It is up to the President to determine whether the condition has been created to declare emergency. He cannot be questioned. According to article 352, 'If at any time the President of India is satisfied that there has arisen a grave emergency created by war or armed rebellion which threatens the security of India or any part of its territory, he can by declaration (i) give directions to the constituent states as to how their authority is to be exercised, and (ii) suspend from operation several Articles (268 to 280) of the constitution under which it is obligatory on the union government to make certain contributions to the states. However it is necessary to place the President's proclamation of emergency before the Parliament within 2 months for approval. The Parliament acquires the power to legislate on any matters enumerated in the State List during the period of operation of such emergency. Such proclamation of Emergency suspends automatically the Fundamental Rights guaranteed under Article 19. But the citizens right to move the court to enforce Fundamental Rights can be suspended only by a separate proclamation.

President's Rule: Under Article 356, the President can take over the administration of a state in the event of break-down of its Constitutional machinery in the state. The President can do so either on receipt of a report from the governor or when he is otherwise satisfied that a situation has arisen in which the government of the state cannot be carried on in accordance with the provisions of the Constitution.

Such a proclamation of the President must be laid down before the Parliament within two months. Even after the approval of the Parliament it cannot remain in force for more than one year. When such a proclamation is in operation, the concerned State Assembly can either be dissolved or kept in animated suspension.

Administration of Union Territories: Except as otherwise provided by law, the Union Territories are administered by the President.

The President can also appoint the Governor of a State as the administrator of an adjoining Union Territory and when a Governor is appointed, he will exercise his powers and function as administrator independently of his Council of Ministers.

VICE-PRESIDENT

The Vice-President of India is elected by all members of the Lok Sabha and Rajya Sabha in accordance with the system of proportional representation by a single transferable vote. His term of office is five years. He can be re-elected. He is the ex-officio Chairman of the Rajya Sabha. He acts as the President during the temporary absence of the President, or during a casual vacancy in the office of the President for a maximum six-month period.

To be eligible to become Vice-President, he must be an Indian citizen, he must have completed the age of 35 years and he must be qualified to be a member of the Rajya Sabha.

The Vice-President may be removed from his office by a resolution of the Rajya Sabha passed by a majority of all the then members and must be agreed to by the Lok Sabha. To move such a resolution, fourteen days notice must be given.

Unlike the Vice-President of USA, the Vice-President does not automatically become the President, on the latter's death, resignation or removal from office.

UNION COUNCIL OF MINISTERS

If the President is the constitutional Head of the State, the real executive is Council of Ministers. Article 74 (i) provides that there shall be a Council of Ministers with the Prime Minister at the head to aid and advise the President in the exercise of his functions. The President appoints the Prime Minister and the other Ministers are appointed by the President on the advice of the Prime Minister. The Ministers hold office during the pleasure of the President while the Council of Ministers are collectively responsible to the Lok Sabha. Before a Minister enters his office, the President shall administer to him the oath of office and secrecy according to the prescribed form in the third schedule. A minister must be a member of either House of Parliament. If he is not, he ceases to be a Minister after the expiry of six months of his appointment. Vote of no-confidence against any minister automatically leads to the resignation of the entire Council. The salaries and allowances are determined by law.

The major powers of the Council of Ministers are

(i)   It formulates the policy of the country on the basis of which the administration is carried on.

(ii)   It introduces all important bills and resolutions in the Parliament and pilots them through.

(iii)   It presents the budget of the country before the Parliament. Though Parliament can modify the budget, it is generally passed in the form in which it is presented.

(iv)   It determines the foreign policy of the country and the kind of relations it should have with other powers. All diplomatic appointments are made by the President on the recommendation of the Council of Ministers. The Council also approves the international agreements and treaties.

(v)   Cabinet members of the Council of Ministers render advice to the President regarding the proclamation of emergency on grounds of war, external aggression or armed rebellion.

PRIME MINISTER

The office of the Prime Minister in Britain is the result of accident of circumstances and growth. But in India, the office has been created by the Constitution itself. The Prime Minister heads the Council of Ministers which he or she forms. The Ministers are technically appointed by the President but in actual practice they are the nominees of the Prime Minister. The Prime Minister forms the Ministry but he can alter it or destroy it. But Constitution is silent on how the President appoints the Prime Minister. It does not say whether the Prime Minister must belong to the Lok Sabha or Rajya Sabha. When Mrs. Indira Gandhi was appointed the Prime Minister after the death of Mr. Sastri, she was a member of Rajya Sabha. The accepted convention is that the head of the State summons the leader of the party which has a majority in Lok Sabha if there is one, or such a person capable of commanding a majority in Legislature, when there is no single party having clear majority, and appoints him as the Prime Minister and commissions him to form the Ministry.

The Prime Ministership of India entails one of the heaviest burdens in the world. In India the Prime Minister is *Primus inter parus - first among equals*. He is rather a "sun around which planets revolve".

PARLIAMENT

The Constitution assigns the name Parliament (Sansad) to the Union Legislature. It consists of the President and two Houses - *Rajya Sabha* (Council of States) and *Lok Sabha* (House of the People). Thus *our Parliament is bicameral*. The House of the People represents people on the basis of population and Council of States gives representation to the Constituent States.

The Rajya Sabha is not exclusively the representative of the Constituent units of the Union. It also consists of 12 nominated members which by itself is a departure from the federal principle.

RAJYA SABHA (COUNCIL OF STATES)

The Constitution fixes the maximum strength of the Rajya Sabha at 250. Twelve are nominated by the President to represent literature, science, art and social services and not more than 238 members represent the States and the Union Territories. The representatives of a State are elected by the elected members of its legislative assembly in accordance with the system of proportional representation by means of single transferable vote. The method of election is thus indirect. In the case of Union Territories members are chosen in such a manner as the Parliament may, by law, determine.

The Rajya Sabha is a continuous body and is not subject to dissolution, one third of its members retiring after every two years.

Qualification for Members: To be qualified, a candidate for election to the Rajya Sabha must be *(a) a citizen of India (b) not less than thirty years of age and (c) possess such other qualifications as may be prescribed by Parliament.* By Representation of the Peoples Act, 1951, a candidate for election to the Rajya Sabha must be a Parliamentary elector in the State from which he seeks election.

The Vice-President of India is the ex-officio Chairman of the Rajya Sabha. But he is not a member of the Rajya Sabha. He has no right to vote except in the event of a tie. The Rajya Sabha elects a Deputy Chairman from among its own members who presides in the absence of the Chairman or during any period when the Vice-President may be removed by the resolution of the Rajya Sabha. The Deputy Chairman may also be removed by a resolution of the House supported by an absolute majority of the total membership.

Functions of the Rajya Sabha: In the process of law-making the Lok Sabha alone cannot do anything. All bills, except money bills can originate in either House of Parliament. In case of disagreement, the President is empowered to summon both Rajya Sabha and Lok Sabha in a joint sitting for deliberation and voting on the Bill. But at the joint sitting the will of the Lok Sabha is bound to prevail on account of its numerical strength.

Regarding money Bills, Rajya Sabha practically has no power. The Constituent function of the Rajya Sabha is equally important. A bill to amend the Constitution may originate in either House of the Parliament. And this bill must be passed by both the Houses of Parliament with requisite majority.

The Rajya Sabha has a share in the election of the President and the Vice-President and in their removal from office. A judge of the Supreme Court or a High Court may be removed for proven misbehaviour or incapacity on the address passed by both Houses of Parliament supported by requisite majorities. The approval of both the Rajya Sabha and Lok Sabha, is necessary for the continuance of the proclamation of Emergency beyond a period of two months.

LOK SABHA (HOUSE OF THE PEOPLE)

The Lok Sabha is the Lower House of Parliament. Maximum strength of the House envisaged by the Constitution is now 552 (530 members to represent the States, 20 to represent the Union Territories, and the President may, if he is of the opinion that the Anglo-Indian community is not adequately represented, nominate two members of that community).

Qualifications for Membership: A candidate for the membership of the Lok Sabha must be *(a) a citizen of India (b) not less than twenty five years of age and (c) possess such other qualifications as may be prescribed by Parliament by law.*

A person is disqualified to be chosen or to remain as a member of either House **(a)** if he holds any office of profit under the Union or the State other than an office declared by Parliament or the State Legislature not as disqualifying its holder **(b)** if he is declared unsound in mind by a competent court **(c)** if he is an undischarged insolvent **(d)** if he is not a citizen of India or has voluntarily accepted the citizenship of a foreign state or is under acknowledgment of allegiance or adherence to a foreign state and **(e)** if he is so disqualified by or under any law made by the Parliament. A member who has been absent without permission for sixty days may be disqualified to remain a member of the House and his seat is declared vacant.

Duration of the House: The Lok Sabha has a life of five years, unless sooner dissolved. But while a proclamation of Emergency is in operation the life of the House may be extended by the law of Parliament for a period not exceeding one year at a time and not exceeding in any case beyond a period of six months after the proclamation has ceased to operate. The strength of the thirteenth Lok Sabha is 545 consisting of 530 elected members from the states and 13 elected members from the Union Territories and the remaining 2 appointed by the President.

Functions of the Lok Sabha: Any Bill including money bill can originate in the Lok Sabha. The demands for grants are not submitted to the Rajya Sabha. The sanctioning of expenditure is the exclusive privilege of the Lok Sabha. The elected members of both Houses of Parliament form part of the Electoral College for the election of the President. The Lok Sabha enjoys equal power with the Rajya Sabha in the election of the Vice-President of India. The important function is that the Lok Sabha controls the executive. The Constitution makes the Council of Ministers collectively responsible to the Lok Sabha. The constituent functions of the Lok Sabha are the same as those of the Rajya Sabha. (Refer to Rajya Sabha).

The Parliament has the power to remove the judges of the Supreme Court, those of the High Courts, the Chief Election Commissioner, Comptroller and Auditor General, and the members of the Union Public Service Commission. Any of the two houses can prefer the charge for the impeachment of the President. The resolution to remove the Vice-President of India, passed by the Rajya Sabha must be ratified by the Lok Sabha. The approval of the Lok Sabha along with the Rajya Sabha is necessary for the continuance of various proclamations of Emergency issued by the President. The reports of the Union Public Service Commission, the Comptroller and Auditor General, the Scheduled Castes and Tribes Commission, the Finance Commission are placed before both the Houses for their consideration.

SPEAKER

The Speaker of Lok Sabha is elected by its members to preside over its sittings and conduct the proceedings. The Speaker vacates his office and ceases to be member of the House when he resigns at any time or he may be removed by a resolution by the majority of the members after giving 14 days notice. The Speaker does not vacate his office on the dissolution of the Lok Sabha. He continues in office until the next elected House meets.

The Constitution also provides for the office of the Deputy-Speaker and he performs the duties of the Speaker when the latter is absent or while the office of the Speaker is vacant. The Constitution gives to the Speaker only a casting vote in the case of a tie.

THE SUPREME COURT

The Supreme Court is the highest judicial organ in India. Situated in Delhi, it consists of one Chief Justice and Twenty Five other judges. There is no maximum number for Judges fixed by the Constitution. The number can be raised by an Act of Parliament. The Constitution says that no case involving a substantial question of law as to the interpretation of the Constitution or a reference under Article 143 shall be decided by less than five Judges.

Qualifications for Appointment of a Judge: A candidate for the appointment as a Judge of the Supreme Court shall not be qualified unless he is a citizen of India, and **(a)** has been for atleast five years a Judge of a High Court or of two or more such courts in succession or **(b)** has been for atleast ten years an advocate of a High Court or of two or more such courts in succession and **(c)** is in the opinion of the President a distinguished Jurist. Every Judge of the Supreme Court is appointed by the President.

A Judge holds the office until he attains the age of 65. He may resign from his office. He may be removed from his office after an address for removal is presented to the President by each House of Parliament. Such an address should be supported by a majority of not less than two-thirds of the members of that House present and voting in the same session. Removal can take place only on the ground of misbehaviour or incapacity investigated and proved in accordance with the Parliamentary procedure.

Powers of the Supreme Court: Constitution of India, vests the Supreme Court with the original and exclusive jurisdiction in any dispute **(a)** between the Government of India on one side and one or more States on the other side; or **(b)** between two or more States which involves a legal right. The Supreme Court is vested with special jurisdiction and responsibility in the matter of enforcement of Fundamental Rights.

The Supreme Court is the final appellate tribunal in the country. An appeal can be made in civil, criminal or other proceedings in which a Constitutional question is involved. The Supreme Court has advisory jurisdiction under which the President can refer any question of public importance.

AMENDING POWERS OF THE PARLIAMENT

The Indian Constitution can be characterised as partly flexible and partly rigid. It is said that Indian Constitution strikes a good balance between extreme rigidity and too much flexibility.

The Constitution of India prescribes three different methods for Amendment of the different provisions of the Constitution (See Article 368).

(1) Some parts of the Constitution can be amended by a simple majority in both Houses of Parliament. It must however be pointed out that there are a very few provisions which allow alterations by simple majority. By this, new states may be created and abolished. The provisions for the administration of Scheduled Areas and Scheduled Tribes may be altered. But these matters will not be treated as Amendments for the purpose of the Article 368.

(2) Certain specified subjects as Amendments affecting the method of electing the President, the extent of the Executive and Legislative powers of the Union or the States, the representation of the States in Parliament and the method of Amending the Constitution requires **(a)** a majority of the total membership in each House of Parliament; **(b)** a majority of not less than two thirds of the members present and voting in each House of the Parliament and **(c)** ratification by the Legislatures of one half of States.

(3) The remaining provisions of the Constitution can be amended by **(a)** a majority of the total membership in each House of the Parliament and **(b)** a majority of not less than two-thirds of the members present and voting in each House of the Parliament.

THE STATE EXECUTIVE - GOVERNOR

The Governor of a State is appointed by the President. His term of office is five years. He is removable from office at any time by the same authority.

Qualifications for Appointment as Governor: A governor must be a citizen of India and must have completed the age of thirty five years. He shall not be a member of either House of Parliament or of a House of the Legislature of any State. He shall not hold any other office of profit.

Powers and Functions of the Governor: The powers of the Governor can be conveniently divided into (a) Executive powers (b) Legislative powers (c) Financial powers and (d) Judicial powers.

The executive power of the State is vested with the Governor. All executive actions are expressed to be taken in the name of the Governor. The Governor appoints a Council of Ministers with the Chief Minister as the Head to aid and advise him in the exercise of his functions except in matters where the Governor acts in discretion. The discretionary power exercised by the Governor under Article 193 is unique, as the President has no discretionary power. He receives advice from the Council of Ministers. But his discretion either to accept or reject them is final. The advice tendered by the Council of Ministers cannot be questioned in a Court of law. It is the duty of the Chief Minister to keep the Governor informed of all the decisions of the Council of Ministers relating to administration of the affairs of the State and proposals for legislation. The Governor appoints the Advocate General of the State, the members of the State Public Service Commission, and Judges of High Court. The Ministers hold office during the pleasure of the Governor.

The sphere of the legislative powers of the Governor is wide. He is the part of the State Legislature. He can summon, prorogue any or both Houses of the State Legislature and dissolve the Legislative Assembly. He may address the House or both the Houses assembled together. A bill passed by the State Legislature with requisite majority becomes a law only after getting the assent of the Governor. He may assent or withhold or may reserve the bill for the consideration of the President. The Governor can promulgate ordinance during the recess of the Legislature. Ordinances have the same effect as law. The Ordinances so promulgated cease to operate after the expiry of six weeks from the reassembly of the Legislature or earlier.

The financial powers of the Governor resemble those of the President at the centre. No money bill or other Financial bills can be introduced in the Legislative Assembly except on the recommendations of the Governor. The Governor is empowered to ask for supplementary, additional or excess grants from the Legislature.

The Governor has the power to pardon, commute or suspend sentence of any person convicted of any offence against any law relating to matters to which the executive power of the State extends. But this power is not intended to be used arbitrarily. The Governor receives annual report of the State Public Service Commission. He deals with the report of the Auditor General regarding income and expenditure of the State.

STATE COUNCIL OF MINISTERS

The Constitution provides that there shall be a Council of Ministers with Chief Minister as the head to aid and advise the Governor in the exercise of his functions except in the cases where Governor acts in his own discretion. The Governor appoints the Chief Minister and other Ministers on the advice of the Chief Minister. The Minister holds office during the pleasure of the Governor. The number of Ministers is not fixed. It is for the Chief Minister to determine the size. The Council of ministers are collectively responsible to Legislative Assembly of the State.

THE CHIEF MINISTER

The Governor can appoint the leader of majority party as Chief Minister. But he must be an elected member of the Assembly. But the convention is that the Governor summons the leader of the majority party and commissions him to form the Ministry. The Constitution prescribes that it shall be the duty of the Chief Minister (a) to communicate to the Governor all the decisions of the Council of Ministers relating to the administration of the affairs of the State and proposals for legislation; (b) to furnish such other information relating to the administration of the affairs of the State and proposals for legislation as the Governor may call for and (c) if the Governor so requires to submit the consideration of Minister but which has not been considered by the Council.

THE STATE LEGISLATURE

The Legislature of a State consists of a Governor and a House or two Houses, as the case may be. The Upper House in the States having bicameral legislature is known as Legislative Assembly (Vidhan Sabha). In the States where there is only one chamber it is the Legislative Assembly. The Constitution provides for the abolition of the Legislative Council in a State which has one or for its creation in a State without one.

THE LEGISLATIVE ASSEMBLY

The Legislative Assembly is the popular chamber and the real centre of power in a State. It is composed of members directly elected by the people in territorial constituencies in which the State is divided. The suffrage is universal, that is every adult citizen of 18 and above irrespective of his race, caste, creed or sex has the right to vote provided he is not otherwise disqualified on the grounds of non-residence, unsoundness of mind, crime or corrupt or illegal practice.

It is provided in the Constitution that the maximum strength of a Legislative Assembly must not exceed 500 and its minimum strength shall not fall below 60. Term of an assembly is five years unless otherwise it is dissolved earlier.

Qualifications for Membership and Functions: Refer to Lok Sabha.

Legislative Council: The minimum strength of the Council is 40 and the maximum is one third of the total membership of the Legislative Assembly.

The election to the council is indirect. The members are elected by proportional representation by means of single transferable vote. A candidate for election to the Legislative Council must be a citizen of India, not less than thirty years of age and should possess such other qualifications as may be prescribed by Parliament.

It is a permanent body. One-third of its members retire every two years. The Council along with the Assembly must be summoned atleast twice a year. The intervening period between two sessions should not exceed six months. The Governor can prorogue the Legislative Council. The Legislative Council chooses its own Chairman and a Deputy Chairman.

Functions of the Council: Immunities and privileges enjoyed by members of State Legislature. In the Legislative Chamber, the members enjoy freedom of speech. They are not liable to any proceedings in any court of law in respect of anything said or any vote given by them in the legislature or a legislative committee.

THE STATE JUDICIARY - HIGH COURT

The High Court is the Highest Court in a State and stands at the apex of its judicial organisation.

A High Court consists of the Chief Justice and such other Judges as the President may from time to time deem it necessary to appoint. The President appoints the Chief Justice of a High Court by a warrant under his hand and seal after consultation with the Chief Justice of India and the Governor of the State. But in appointing other Puisne Judges, the President consults the Chief Justice of the High Court to which they are appointed.

A Judge of High Court must be a citizen of India and must have held for at least ten years a judicial office in a territory of India or must have been, for at least ten years an advocate of a High Court.

A Judge of a High Court holds his office until he attains the age of 62 years. But he may resign or may be removed by the President in the same manner as a Judge of the Supreme Court may be removed.

ATTORNEY GENERAL OF INDIA

The President will appoint a person who is qualified to be appointed a judge of the Supreme court as the Attorney General of India. The duty of the Attorney General is to advise the President on such legal matters and to perform such other duties of legal character, as may from time to time be referred or assigned to him by the President. He has the right of audience in all courts in the territory of India. The Attorney General will hold office during the pleasure of the President. He has the right to speak and take part in the proceedings of either House and to be a member of any Parliamentary Committee but is not entitled to vote (Article 88).

COMPTROLLER AND AUDITOR GENERAL OF INDIA

He is appointed by the President. He can be removed from the office in like manner and on like grounds as a Judge of the Supreme Court. He shall perform such duties and exercise such powers in relation to the accounts of the Union and of the States and of any other authority or body as may be prescribed by or under any law made by Parliament. The reports of the Comptroller and Auditor General of India relating to the accounts of the Union and to those of a State shall be submitted to the President and to the Governor respectively who in turn shall lay them before the Parliament and Legislature of the State respectively.

Salaries

1.	President of India	:	Rs.50,000 per month
2.	Vice-President of India	:	Rs.40,000 per month
3.	Governor of a State	:	Rs.36,000 per month
4.	Chief Justice of India	:	Rs.33,000 per month
5.	The Comptroller and Auditor General of India	:	Rs.30,000 per month
6.	Chief Justice of High Court and other Judges of Supreme Court	:	Rs.30,000 per month
7.	Other Judges of High Court	:	Rs.26,000 per month

Salary and Perks of M.Ps

Salary and D.A.: Rs.30,000 per month, **D.A.:** Rs.500 per day during sessions, **Constituency allowance:** Rs.10,000 pm, **Office expenses:** Rs.14,000 pm, **Travelling allowance:** Rs. 8 per km, **Free Electricity:** 50,000 units, **Free water:** upto Rs. 1,500, **Telephone calls:** upto 1,70,000 free calls, **Accommodation:** rent free huge bangalow or Rs. 35,000 pm, **Air Travel:** 32 air tickets, **Train Travel:** AC first class, **Foreign Travel:** First class air ticket with 5 star hotel accommodation, **Pension:** After a five-year term Rs.3,000 per month for life plus Rs.600 for every year completed as MP. **Computers:** One palm-top cell phone-cum-computer. One desktop or laptop computer with printer.

PUBLIC SERVICE COMMISSION

The Constitution provides for a Public Service Commission for the Union and a Public Service Commission for each State. The members of the Union Public Service Commission and of any joint Commission are appointed by the President, and the members of a State Public Service Commission by the Head of the Commission. Union or State members must have held office for atleast ten years either under the Government of India or under the Government of a State. A member holds office for six years or until he attains, in the case of the Union Commission the age of sixty-five and in the case of a State Commission the age of sixty- two years (41st Amendment) whichever is earlier. A member of a Public Service Commission, on the expiry of his term of office, is not eligible for reappointment to that office. A member of the Union Public Service Commission can be removed from office by order of the President on the grounds of misbehaviour.

Functions of the Public Service Commission:

(1) The Union and State Public Service Commissions shall conduct examinations for appointment to the Union and State services respectively.

(2) To assist the States in framing the operating schemes of joint recruitment for any services for which candidates possessing special qualifications are required if two or more states make such a request to the Union Public Service Commission.

(3) To give advice: **(a)** on any matter referred to them on methods and recruitment to civil service and for civil posts **(b)** on the principles to be followed in making appointments and in making promotions and transfers from one service to another **(c)** on disciplinary matters including petitions on such matters **(d)** on the claim made by any person that the costs of defending legal proceedings against him in respect of acts done or purported to be done in the execution of his duty, should be borne by the Government **(e)** on any claim for the award of a pension in respect of injuries sustained by a person while serving under the Government in a civil capacity and any question to the amount of any such award.

(4) Any other functions in respect of services referred to or conferred by Parliament in the case of the Union Commission and by the State Legislature in the case of State Commission.

ADVOCATE GENERAL

Every State shall have an Advocate General to advise the government on legal matters (Art. 165). His functions and duties can be more or less equated to those of Attorney General of India.

FINANCE COMMISSION

The Constitution (Article 280) provides for the appointment of a Finance Commission consisting of a Chairman and four other members within two years of the inauguration of the Republic, and thereafter at the expiry of every fifth year or earlier. The duties of the Commission are to recommend to the President the distribution of the taxes which are distributable between the Centre and the States, the principles on which grants should be made out of the Union revenues to the States and any other matter referred to the Commission by the President in the interest of sound finance. The Finance Commission is appointed by the President.

Finance Commission	Chairman	Date of Appointment
First	K.C.Neogy	Feb. 1953
Second	K.Santhanam	Sep. 1957
Third	K.K.Chanda	Dec. 1961
Fourth	Dr. P.V.Rajamannar	Sep. 1965
Fifth	Mahavir Tyagi	Nov. 1969
Sixth	Brahmananda Reddy	Dec. 1973
Seventh	J.M.Shelat	Oct. 1978
Eighth	Y.B.Chavan	Oct. 1983
Ninth	N.K.P.Salve	Oct. 1988
Tenth	K.C.Pant	June 1993
Eleventh	A.N. Khusro	July 1998
Twelfth	Dr. C. Rangarajan	2002

ELECTION COMMISSION

The Superintendence, direction and control and the preparation of the electoral rolls and the conduct of all elections to Parliament and to the Legislature of every State and of elections to the offices of President and Vice-President held under this Constitution shall be vested with the Election Commission. The Commission shall consist of one Chief Election Commissioner and a number of Election Commissioners appointed by the President.

The Chief Election Commissioner is assured of an independent status. To ensure independence of the Election Commission, the Chief Election Commissioner shall not be removed from his office except in like manner and on like grounds as a Judge of the Supreme Court and the conditions of service of the Chief Election Commissioner shall not be varied to his disadvantage after his appointment. (The present Chief Election Commissioner is Mr. N. Gopalsamy).

BUDGET: Budget is the Annual Financial Statement presented to Parliament normally on the last day of February each year in two parts-the Railway Budget and the General Budget. The Railway Budget exclusively deals with the receipts and expenditure of the Railways and it is separately presented by the Union Railway Minister. The General Budget deals with estimates of the Departments of the Government of India excluding Railways and it is presented by the Union Finance Minister.

We find nowhere in our Constitution, the Latin word, *Budget*. The Phrase, *Annual Financial Statement* is used instead of the word *Budget*.

PARLIAMENTARY COMMITTEES

The parliament is assisted by a number of Committees in the discharge of its duties. The Parliamentary Committees exercise effective control over government activity on a regular and continuing basis. These committees comprise representative of various groups and parties in the parliament. These groups and parties are given representation in proportion to their respective strengths in the parliament. Committee work in a more intimate and informal atmosphere on non-party lines.

Committee Name	Chairman	Number of Representative	Objectives
Business Advisory Committee	Speaker	15	It plans and regulates the business of the house and renders advice regarding the allocation of time for discussion of different matters.
Private member's bills and resolutions committee	Deputy Speaker	15	The committee classifies the bills submitted by members of the house according to their importance

Committee Name	Chairman	Number of Representative	Objectives
Committee on petitions	--	15	The committe examines the petitions submitted to it and suggests remedial measures
Rules Committee	Speaker	15	It considers matters of procedure and the conduct of the business in the House and make suggestions for the improvement of procedures
Committee on privileges	--	15	Regarding the violation of privileges of members of parliament and recommends appropriate action
Committee on welfare Scheduled Castes and Scheduled Tribes	--	30 (20 LS+10 RS)	The committee also ensures effective implementation of the constitutional safeguards for the backward communities
Committee on Government Assurances	--	15	It examines how far the assurances and undertakings given by the ministers on the floor of the house have been implemented within the stipulated period
Committee on absence of members	--	--	The committee examines the leave applications of members. It also looks into cases where members have been missing from the house without permission for more than six months. It can condone the absence of such members or declare the seat vacant and ask for a by-election to fill up the same.

Committee Name	Chairman	Number of Representative	Objectives
Estimates Committee	Deputy Speaker	30 (20 LS+10 RS)	The committee examines the annual estimates and suggests alternative policies to the government to ensure efficiency and economy in administration
Public Accounts Committee	Deputy Speaker	22 (15 LS+7 RS)	It ensures that expenditure has not exceeded the grants made by the Parliament and the money has been spent for the purpose for which it was sanctioned. Committee ensures regularity and economy in expenditure
Committee on public undertakings	--	15 (10 LS+5 RS)	This committee examines the working of public undertakings including their accounts and finances
Joint Committee on Salaries & Allowances	--	15 (10 nominated by the Speaker of Lok Sabha, 5 nominated by the Chairman of Rajya Sabha)	The committee frames rules for regulating of salaries and amenities like housing, telephone, postal, secretarial and medical facilities
Joint Committee on Offices of Profit	--	15 (10 LS+5 RS)	This committee examines the composition of various committes and bodies constituted by the Union and State governments, and recommends whether persons holding those offices should be disqualified from being elected as a member of Parliament or not.

Committee Name	Chairman	Number of Representative	Objectives
Select Committee	--	--	These committees are constituted for the consideration of different kinds of bills. These committes collect information and submit reports on bills refered to them.
Committee on subordinate legislation	--	--	This committee examines rules and regulations enacted by the executive to fill the gaps in the laws enacted by Parliament and ascertains how far these rules are within the limits prescribed in the main law.

Parliamentary subjects committee : Parliamentary subjects committees are its standing committees, six committees are constituted by the Chairman of the Rajya Sabha and 11 by the Speaker of Lok Sabha. Some of these committees are joint committees. Each standing committee comprises 45 members (30 from Lok Sabha and 15 from Rajya Sabha). These committees work during the recess of the Parliament and discuss individual demands for grants for each ministry (or) department and submit their report to the Parliament.

OFFICIAL LANGUAGE

Article 343 declares that official language of the Union shall be Hindi in Devanagari script but English shall continue to be used for all the official purposes of the Union for a period of fifteen years from the commencement of the Constitution. The official Language Act 1967, provides that English shall be used for communication between the Union and the States which do not have Hindi as official language.

ESSENTIAL SERVICES MAINTENANCE ACT

The Act defines the 'Essential Services' and authorises the Central Government to prohibit strikes in them and declare such strike as illegal and provides for penalising the people participating in or instigating and financing such strikes.

LEGISLATIVE AND CONSTITUTIONAL TERMS

Adjournment: When a sitting Assembly is discontinued to be resumed later, it is said that the Assembly is adjourned without prescribing date for reassemblage; it is said that the Assembly has been adjourned *sine die*. A sitting can be adjourned by the speaker on a resolution being passed by the Assembly.

Bicameral States: Those States which have two Houses of Legislature. Unicameral States have only one House.

By-Elections: Election held to fill a vacancy during the running term of an elected person. The vacancy may be caused either due to death or resignation or due to disqualification.

Caucus: A meeting of a group of politically interested people to work out a common action.

Climbing on the Bandwagon: Endorsing support to a person who is likely to be elected.

Crossing the Floor: When a legislator changes his party label, he is said to have crossed the floor.

Cross Voting: The voting by members breaking the barriers of the party.

Dissolution: Disbanding of the Assembly to hold fresh elections.

Filibuster: Indulgence in long-winded, unnecessary speeches to obstruct or delay the enactment of a measure under consideration.

Gallup Poll: Conduct of test poll to ascertain public opinion on topical subjects. It has been named after Dr.Gallup of U.S.A who introduced this poll.

Inner Cabinet: The most influential coterie surrounding the Prime Minister. Most important decisions are taken by this coterie. The full cabinet comes into the picture later.

Lame Duck Session: The last session of the old members of the Legislature before the completion of its term, though the new legislature has been elected.

Lobbying: To frequent the lobby of the legislature hall to influence the members on certain action.

Mid-Term Poll: Election held out of schedule as a result of dissolution of the legislature before it completes its normal term.

People Sniffer: Indictment of Government through unofficial media.

Prorogation: The discontinued sitting of the sitting of the Assembly is to be reassembled later. It is done by the Governor or the President on the advice of the Chief Minister or the Prime Minister respectively. Adjournment can be overruled by prorogation.

Question Hour: The legislature begins its day with question hour during which the members ask questions which are answered by Ministers in charge, either orally or in writing.

Shadow Cabinet: The persons who have been elected by the opposition party to assume portfolios in case the party is able to wrest the power.

Snap Vote: Voting unexpectedly recorded without the voters being informed in advance by party whip.

Starred and Unstarred Questions: Starred questions are answered orally and unstarred questions are answered in writing.

Zero Hour: The time allotted to various business items like call-attention motion.

CONSTITUTIONAL AMENDMENTS

Constitution (1st Amendment) Act, 1951: This amendment provided for several new grounds of restrictions to the right to freedom of speech and expression and the right to practise any profession or to carry on any trade or business as contained in Article 19 of the Constitution. These restrictions related to public order, friendly relations with foreign States or incitement to an offence in relation to the right to freedom of speech, and to the prescribing of professional or technical qualifications or the carrying on by the State, etc., of any trade, business, industry or service in relation to the right to carry on any trade or business. The amendment also inserted two new Articles, 31 A and 31 B and the Ninth Schedule to give protection from challenge to land reform laws.

Constitution (2nd Amendment) Act, 1952: Amended Article 81 with a view to readjusting the scale of representation in the House of the People, necessitated by the completion of the 1951 census.

Constitution (3rd Amendment) Act, 1954: Substituted entry 33 of the Concurrent List in the 7th Schedule by a new one including foodstuffs, cattle fodder, raw cotton and jute as additional items whose production and supply can be controlled by the government, if found expedient in the public interest.

Constitution (4th Amendment) Act, 1955: The Amendment provides that when the State compulsorily acquires private property for a public purpose, the scale of compensation prescribed by the authorising legislation could not be called in to question in a court. Another clause excludes the temporary taking over of a property by the State, either in public interest or to secure its better management, from the compensation clause. The amendment also operates as a saving clause for State monopolies. Seven new entries were also added to the 9th Schedule.

Constitution (5th Amendment) Act, 1955: Empowers the President to fix a time limit for State Legislatures to express their views on proposed Central laws affecting the area and boundaries, etc. of their respective States.

Constitution (6th Amendment) Act, 1956: Adds a new entry to the Union List in the Seventh Schedule relating to taxes on the sale and purchase of goods in the course of Inter State transactions.

Constitution (7th Amendment) Act, 1956: It was enacted by the Parliament in the Seventh year of the Republic. The amendment was necessitated by reorganisation of states. Part A, B, and C states were abolished. The maximum strength of Lok Sabha was fixed at 525.

Constitution (8th Amendment) Act, 1960: Article 334 was amended with a view to extending the period of reservation of seats for Scheduled Castes and Scheduled Tribes and to the Anglo-Indian community by nomination in Parliament and in the State Legislatures for a further period of ten years.

Constitution (9th Amendment) Act, 1960: This amended the first Schedule of the Constitution in order to give effect to the transfer of certain territories of Pakistan in pursuance of the agreements entered into between the Governments of India and Pakistan in Sept. 1958. This amendment was necessitated in view of the Judgement of Supreme Court in "In Re Berubari Union" by which it was held that any agreement to cede a territory to another country could not be implemented by a law made under Article 3 but would only be implemented by an amendment of the Constitution.

Constitution (10th Amendment) Act, 1961: Incorporated former Portuguese enclaves of Dadra and Nagar Haveli within India and provided for their administration by the President.

Constitution (11th Amendment) Act, 1961: Obviated the necessity of a joint meeting of the two Houses of Parliament by forming them into an electoral college for the election of Vice-President. It also amended Article 66 and 71 so as to make it clear that the election of the President or the Vice President shall not be challenged on the ground of any vacancy, for whatever reason, in the appropriate electoral college.

Constitution (12th Amendment) Act, 1962: The Twelfth Amendment was passed to include the territories of Goa, Daman and Diu as a Union Territory in the First Schedule to the Constitution and to empower the President to make, regulations for the peace, progress and good government of the areas.

Constitution (13th Amendment) Act, 1962: Created Nagaland as the sixteenth State in the Indian Union. By this amendment, a new Article 371A was added to make special provisions with respect to state of Nagaland in pursuance of an agreement between Government of India and Naga People's Convention.

Constitution (14th Amendment) Act, 1962: Conferred necessary legislative powers on Parliament to enact laws for the creation of Legislature and Council of Ministers in Union Territories. Former French establishments of Pondicherry, Karaikal, Mahe and Yanam were specified in the Constitution as the Union Territory of Pondicherry.

Constitution (15th Amendment) Act, 1963: It was a minor amendment empowering the President of India, in consultation with the Chief Justice of India to make final decisions on dispute about a High Court Judge's age. It also shortened the procedure for disciplinary action against State employees.

Constitution (16th Amendment) Act, 1963: It sought to impose reasonable restrictions on the fundamental rights "in the interest of the sovereignty and integrity of India".

Constitution (17th Amendment) Act, 1964: It protected many land reform Acts passed by many State Governments. It enlarged the definition of the term 'estate' to include Ryotwari lands. The enforcement of certain Directive Principles of State Policy was ensured.

Constitution (18th Amendment) Act, 1966: Provided for the linguistic reorganisation of the Punjab into a Punjabi speaking State called Punjab and a Hindi-speaking State called Haryana.

Constitution (19th Amendment) Act, 1966: Is a minor amendment clarifying the duties of the Election Commission. Article 324 was amended to effect a consequential change as a result of the decision to abolish Election Tribunals and to hear election petitions by High Courts.

Constitution (20th Amendment) Act, 1966: Validates the appointment of certain District Judges, irregularly appointed. A new Article 233A was added and the appointments made by Governor were validated.

Constitution (21st Amendment) Act, 1967: Provided for the inclusion of Sindhi in the Eighth Schedule to the Constitution.

Constitution (22nd Amendment) Act, 1969: Empowered Parliament to carve a new State. (Meghalaya out of Assam).

Constitution (23rd Amendment) Act, 1969: Provided for the extension of the reservation of seats for Scheduled Castes and Tribes and the nomination of members of the Anglo-Indian community for another 10 years.

Constitution (24th Amendment) Act, 1971: Was passed by Parliament in August 1971. According to it (i) "not withstanding any thing contained in the Constitution, the Parliament may, in the exercise of its constituent power, amend by way of addition, variation or repeal any part of the Constitution" (ii) that the President must give his assent to a Constitution Amendment Bill if it has been passed by both the Houses' and (iii) the Article 13 (which provides that the state shall not make any law which takes away or abridges fundamental rights) shall have no application to laws passed under 24th Amendment.

Constitution (25th Amendment) Act, 1971: Was passed by the Parliament in December 1971. It aimed at ensuring that the Fundamental Rights, particularly property rights, do not stand in the implementation of Directive Principles of State Policy as embodied in the Constitution of India. The amendment bars the jurisdiction of Courts over the acquisition of property or on the ground that any such law violates Article 19(1)(f) of fundamental rights. The rights of minority educational institutions guaranteed under Article 33 however, remain protected. The Amendment also inserts in the Constitution a new clause-3/C, to provide that any legislation passed in pursuance of the directive principles Article 39B and C (which concern the ownership and control of material resources and concentration of wealth and means of production) shall not be challenged in a Court on the grounds that it takes away or abridges any of the rights contained in Articles 14, 19 or 31.

Constitution (26th Amendment) Act, 1971: It contains three clauses, The first clause deletes the Articles 291 and 362 of our Constitution which thereto gave protection to the rights of ex-rulers to privy purses and other privileges. The second clause inserts Article 363 (A) which deprives the princes and their successors of presidential recognitions. The rights, obligations and other liabilities of the Government towards them are extinguished. The third clause, amending the Article 366, redefines the term 'ruler' as a person who was recognised by the President as the ruler of the Indian State before the commencement of the Constitution.

Constitution (27th Amendment) Act, 1971: Recognised North-Eastern Area Act, 1971 and established new states of Manipur, Tripura and Meghalaya and two new Union Territories of Mizoram and Arunachal Pradesh. The Act defined their territories and made necessary provision regarding representation in Paliament and in the Legislative Assemblies of States and other matters.

Constitution (28th Amendment) Act, 1972: Article 314 of the Constitution is deleted by this Amendment and a new Article 312-A has been inserted to give Parliament powers to vary or revoke by law the conditions of services of officers belonging to Indian Civil Service.

Constitution (29th Amendment) Act, 1972: This Amendment included the Kerala Land Reforms (Amendment) Act, 1969 and the Kerala Land Reforms (Amendment) Act, 1971, in the Ninth Schedule to the Constitution so as to protect these Acts from judicial review.

Constitution (30th Amendment) Act, 1972: It was introduced in the Lok Sabha on May 24, 1972. It implements the Law Commission's recommendation according to which there should be no valuation test prescribed for declaring a case fit for appeal to the Supreme Court. The Bill seeks to amend Article 133 of the Constitution which laid down that if the value of suit exceeded twenty thousand rupees, there was an almost unrestricted right of appeal to the Supreme Court on any judgement, decree or final order in Civil proceedings of a High Court.

Constitution (31st Amendment) Act, 1973: Increased the upper limit of elective seats in the Lok Sabha from 525 to 545.

Constitution (32nd Amendment) Act, 1973: Implemented the 6-point programme for Andhra Pradesh.

Constitution (33rd Amendment) Act, 1974: Invalidated the acceptance of resignations by members of the State Legislatures and Parliament, which were made under duress or coercion, or any other kind of involuntary resignations.

Constitution (34th Amendment) Act, 1974: Provided constitutional protection to 20 Land Reforms Acts passed by the various states, by including them in the 9th Schedule to the Constitution.

Constitution (35th Amendment) Act, 1974: Provided for Associate State status to Sikkim.

Constitution (36th Amendment) Act, 1975: Made Sikkim a State of the Indian Union-the 22nd State in fact.

Constitution (37th Amendment) Act, 1975: Provided for a Legislative Assembly and a Council of Ministers for the Union Territory of Arunachal Pradesh.

Constitution (38th Amendment) Act, 1975: The Amendment seeks to allot Sikkim one seat in the Lok Sabha and one seat in the Rajya Sabha. The amendment will confer on the Governor of Sikkim 'a special responsibility' for peace and an equitable arrangement for ensuring the social and economic advancement of different sections of the population of Sikkim. The provision says that in the discharge of his special responsibility under this clause "The Governor of Sikkim shall be subject to such directions as the President may give".

Constitution (39th Amendment) Act, 1975: By this Act, disputes relating to the election of President, Vice-President, Prime Minister and Speaker are to be determined by such authority as may be determined by Parliamentary Law. Certain Central enactments were also included in the Ninth Schedule by this Act.

Constitution (40th Amendment) Act, 1976: Amended Act 297th and declared that "all land, minerals and other things of value underlying the ocean within the territorial waters or the continental shelf or the exclusive economic zone of India shall vest in the Union and shall be held for the purpose of the Union".

"The limits of the territorial waters, the continental shelf, the exclusive marine zone or other maritime zones of India shall be such as may be specified from time to time by or under any law made by Parliament".

Constitution (41st Amendment) Act, 1976: Raised the retiring age of State Public Service Commission members from 60 to 62. This does not affect the members of the Union Public Service Commission who retire at the age of 65.

Constitution (42nd Amendment) Act, 1976: It is termed as mini constitution. The Amendment Act inserted a new chapter on the Fundamental Duties of citizens and made special provisions for dealing with anti-national activities. The Judiciary provisions were amended by providing minimum number of judges to decide the constitutional validity of law and for a special majority of not less than two-third majority for declaring any law to be Constitutionally invalid.

For the speedy disposal of the mounting arrears in the High Court this amendment provides a separate administrative and other tribunals to deal such matters and preserve the jurisdiction of Supreme Court in regard to such matters under Article 136.

Constitution (43rd Amendment) Act, 1977: It provides restoration of the jurisdiction of the Supreme Court and High Courts, earlier curtailed by the enactment of the Constitution (42nd Amendment) Act, 1976 and accordingly Articles 32A, 131A, 144A, 226A and 228A included in the Constitution by the 42nd Amendment, were deleted by this Act. It also deleted Article 31D which conferred special powers on Parliament to enact certain laws in respect of anti-national activities.

Constitution (44th Amendment) Act, 1978: This Amendment brought a lot of changes in many Articles. The preventive detention for a period of more than two months can be ordered only on the recommendations of an Advisory Board. The right to property was omitted as a fundamental right and made as a legal right. But minorities will have rights to establish or run their educational institutions as before.

Constitution (45th Amendment) Act, 1980: It aims to extend the reservation for scheduled castes and tribes as well as for the Anglo-Indians for ten more years from January 1, 1980 to December 31, 1989.

Constitution (46th Amendment) Act, 1982: The bill was introduced in the Lok Sabha on April 3, 1981 and the same was passed by Lok Sabha on July 14, 1982. It seeks to insert an entry in the Union List in the Seventh Schedule to enable Parliament to levy tax on inter-state consignment of goods.

Constitution (47th Amendment) Act, 1984: This amendment provides for the inclusion of certain land reforms acts in the Ninth Schedule to the Constitution with a view of obviating the scope of litigation hampering the implementation process of those acts.

Constitution (48th Amendment) Act, 1984: This was an Amendment to Clause 5 of Article 356 of the Constitution for the continuation of President's Rule in Punjab for one more year.

Constitution (49th Amendment) Act, 1984: The Government of Tripura recommended that the provisions of the Sixth Schedule to the Constitution may be made applicable to the tribal areas of that state. The amendment involved in the Act is intended to give a constitutional security to the autonomous District Councils functioning in the state.

Constitution (50th Amendment) Act, 1984: It brings, apart from the armed forces, other forces connected with the administration of public property, persons in the intelligence departments and telecommunication department connected with this duty into the ambit of Article 33 of the Constitution with a view to maintain discipline among these people and ensure proper discharge of their duties.

Constitution (51st Amendment) Act, 1984: Amendment for Article 330 provides reservation of seats for ST's in Meghalaya, Nagaland, Arunachal Pradesh and Mizoram in Parliament, and that of Article 332 for local tribal people for Nagaland and Meghalaya Legislative Assemblies.

Constitution (52nd Amendment) Act, 1985: The Amendment effected by a Bill popularly called Anti-Defection Bill, was to curb defection by disqualification.

Constitution (53rd Amendment) Act, 1986: Inserted a new article (371-G) conferring full statehood on Mizoram.

Constitution (54th Amendment) Act, 1986: Amended Part-D of the 2nd schedule giving effect to the increase of salaries of the Chief Justice and Judges of Supreme Court and High Courts. And enabling provision for changes in the salaries of judges in future by Parliament by law, was made in Articles 125 and 221.

Constitution (55th Amendment) Act, 1986: Conferred full statehood on Arunachal Pradesh and for this purpose, a new Article 371H has been inserted which, inter alia, confers, having regard to the sensitive location of Arunachal Pradesh to vest special responsibility on Governor. The new Article also provides that the new Legislative Assembly shall consist of not less than thirty members.

Constitution (56th Amendment) Act, 1987: With this Amendment a new state of Goa is created. Parts of Daman & Diu of the erstwhile Union Territory of Goa, Diu and Daman were separated and formed into the new Union Territory.

Constitution (57th Amendment) Act, 1987: As the 51st Amendment could not be implemented properly, 57th Amendment was introduced for special arrangement in the reservation for Scheduled Tribes in the State assemblies of Arunachal Pradesh, Nagaland, Mizoram and Meghalaya, until readjustment of seats on the basis of the first census after 2000 A.D.

Constitution (58th Amendment) Act, 1987: The Constitution has been amended to empower President of India to publish under his authority the translation of the Constitution in Hindi signed by the Members of the Constituent Assembly with such modification as may be necessary to bring it in conformity with the language, style and terminology adopted in the authoritative texts of Central Acts in Hindi language.

Constitution (59th Amendment) Act, 1988: Gives the power to declare emergency for a period upto 3 years in Punjab due to internal disturbance; but extended only for 2 years.

Constitution (60th Amendment) Act, 1988: The Act amends Clause (2) of Article 276 of the Constitution so as to increase the ceiling of taxes on professions, trades, callings and employment from two hundred and fifty rupees per annum to two thousand and five hundred rupees per annum. The upward revision of this tax will help the State Government in raising additional resources. The provision to Clause (2) has been omitted.

Constitution (61st Amendment) Act, 1989: It lowers the voting age from 21 to 18 to give wider representation and involve the present day literate youth, in the mainstream of political life of the nation.

Constitution (62nd Amendment) Act, 1989: It seeks to extend the privileges and reservation of seats in Lok Sabha and State assemblies for Scheduled Castes and Tribes for another 10 years from 31st December, 1989.

Constitution (63rd Amendment) Act, 1989: Repealed the 59th Amendment which gave special powers to the government to impose emergency in Punjab.

Constitution (64th Amendment) Act, 1989: President's Rule in Punjab was extended by another 6 months thus totalling it upto 3 years and 6 months.

Constitution (65th Amendment) Act, 1990: To set up a National Commission for Scheduled Castes and Tribes, with powers of a civil court, in the exercise of its duties.

Constitution (66th Amendment) Act, 1990: On 1st June, Parliament gave its approval to the Constitution (66th Amendment) Bill. It seeks to bring all land reforms laws enacted by different States into the Ninth Schedule and thus protecting them from litigation.

Constitution (67th Amendment) Act, 1990: Extension of President's Rule in Punjab by another 6 months.

Constitution (68th Amendment) Act, 1991: Extension of President's Rule in Punjab by one more year (Total 5 years).

Constitution (69th Amendment) Act, 1991: Delhi became a City State with a Legislative Assembly and a Council of Ministers getting a special status among the Union Territories.

Constitution (70th Amendment) Act, 1992: The elected members of Pondicherry and the National Capital of Delhi were included in the electoral college.

Constitution (71st Amendment) Act, 1992: To include Konkani, Manipuri and Nepali language in the 8th Schedule of the Constitution.

Constitution (72nd Amendment) Act, 1992: Provision was made to determine the number of seats reserved for ST's in the Assembly of the State of Tripura.

Constitution (73rd Amendment) Act, 1993: To add a new part for ensuring direct election to all seats in Panchayats, for the reservation of seats for SC's and ST's in proportion to their population and for the reservation of not less than 1/3 of the seats for women.

Constitution (74th Amendment) Act, 1993: To ensure effective functioning of the Urban Local Bodies, a new part IX-A relating to the Municipalities has been incorporated in the Constitution to provide for among other things; Constitution of three types of Municipalities, *i.e.*, Nagar Panchayats for areas in transition from a rural area to Urban area, Municipal Councils for smaller Urban areas and Municipal Corporations for larger urban areas.

Constitution (75th Amendment) Act, 1993: Provides for the establishment of State level tribunals to settle landlord-tenant cases and also provides for the reduction of tiers of all courts except Supreme Court relating to rent litigation.

Constitution (76th Amendment) Act, 1994: The government of Tamil Nadu reserves 18% to Scheduled Castes, 1% to Scheduled Tribes and 50% to Other Backward Castes (total 69%) in education institutions and public employments.

Constitution (77th Amendment) Act, 1995: Makes provision for reservation in matters of promotion in any class or classes of posts in services in State in favour of Scheduled Castes and Scheduled Tribes which in the opinion of the state are not adequately represented in the service in a state.

Constitution (78th Amendment) Act, 1995: Inserts certain state laws in respect of land reforms in the Ninth Schedule of the Constitution.

Constitution (80th Amendment) Act, 2000: Relates to the revenue sharing between the Centre and the States whereby States' over-all share was increased to 29% as per the Tenth Finance Commission's recommendation.

Constitution (81st Amendment) Act, 2000: Relates to carrying forward backlog vacancies of Scheduled Castes and Scheduled tribes.

Constitution (82nd Amendment) Act, 2000: Relates to relaxation in qualifying marks and reservation of posts in super speciality courses in Medical and Engineering disciplines, etc. for SC/ST etc.

Constitution (83rd Amendment) Act, 2000: Relates to the reservation of seats under Panchayati Raj in Arunachal Pradesh.

Constitution (84th Amendment) Act, 2000: Relates to the creation of new States of Jharkhand, Chhattisgarh and Uttaranchal.

Constitution (86th Amendment) Act, 2000: Compulsory education for all our children. By this amendment it is raised from 10 to 11 fundamental duties.

Constitution (89th Amendment) Bill, 2000: The Bill passed by Parliament on May 16, 2000, provides for the transfer of 29% share of net tax proceeds to States for a five-year period and seeks to bring several Central taxes and duties like Corporation Tax and Customs Duty at par with personal income-tax for the purpose of sharing with the States.

Constitution (93rd Amendment) Bill, 2001: It seeks to provide free and compulsory education for the children aged 6 to 14 across the country.

Contitution (94th Amendment) Bill, 2003: Lok Sabha passed the Constitution Bill (94th Amendment) paving the way for setting up a separate national commission for Scheduled Tribes (STs).

Constitution (95th Amendment) Bill, 2003: Empowering the Centre to levy service tax and allow both the Centre and the States to collect and appropriate service tax.

Constitution (96th Amendment) Bill, 2003: It seeks to provide for readjustment of electoral constituencies, including those reserved for Scheduled Castes and Scheduled Tribes on the basis of the population census for the year 2001 without affecting the number of seats allocated to States in the Legislative bodies.

Constitution (97th Amendment) Bill, 2003: It seeks to strengthen the Anti-Defection Law and limit the size of the Council of Ministers to 10 per cent of the respective strengths of Parliament and the State legislatures.

Constitution (98th Amendment) Bill, 2003: The Constitution 98th Amendment Bill seeks to constitute a National Judicial Commission (NJC) by including Chapter IV A in Part V of the Constitution which will be in charge of appointing judges to the higher judiciary and for transferring High Court Judges. The bill also seeks to empower the National Judicial Commission to draw up a code of ethics for judges, inquire into cases of misconduct or deviant actions of a judge other than those that are punishable with his or her removal, and advise the Chief Justice of India or Chief Justice of High Court appropriately after such inquiry.

Constitution (99th Amendment) Bill, 2003: It seeks to protect the rights of the non-tribals in the newly-elected Bodo Territorial Council (BTC) by keeping intact the existing representation of the Scheduled Tribes and non-Scheduled Tribes in the Assam Legislative Assembly from the Bodoland Territorial Council Areas district.

Constitution (100th Amendment) Bill, 2004: This amendment has inserted Bodo, Dogri, Maithli and Santhali in the 8th Schedule of the Constitution when this Act is enforced the 8th Schedule will have 22 languages. Jharkhand - Both are tribal language. Dogri is spoken in Jammu and Kashmir. Maithli is spoken in Bihar.

Constitution (104th Amendment) Bill, 2005: The Parliament passed the Constitution (104th) Amendment Bill proclaiming reservation for the socially and educationally backward classes, besides the Scheduled Castes and the Scheduled Tribes, in private unaided educational institutions.

SCHEDULES TO THE CONSTITUTION

First Schedule: (Under Articles 1 and 4) gives a list of the States and Territories comprising the Union.

States: 1. Andhra Pradesh 2. Assam 3. Bihar 4. Gujarat 5. Kerala 6. Madhya Pradesh 7. Tamil Nadu 8. Maharashtra 9. Karnataka 10. Orissa 11. Punjab 12. Rajasthan 13. Uttar Pradesh 14. West Bengal. 15. Jammu and Kashmir 16. Nagaland 17. Haryana 18. Himachal Pradesh 19. Manipur 20. Tripura 21. Meghalaya 22. Sikkim 23. Mizoram 24. Arunachal Pradesh 25. Goa 26. Chattisgarh 27. Uttarakhand and 28. Jharkhand. **Union Territories:** 1. Delhi 2. Andaman and Nicobar Islands 3. Lakshadweep 4. Dadra and Nagar Haveli 5. Daman and Diu 6. Puducherry and 7. Chandigarh.

Second Schedule: [Under Articles 59(3), 65(3), 75(6), 97, 125, 148(3) 158(3)] consists of 5 parts, A to E, and fixes the remuneration and emoluments payable to the President, Governors, Judges of the Supreme Court and High Courts and Comptroller and Auditor-General of India.

Third Schedule: [Under Articles 75(4), 99, 124(6), 148(2), 164(3), 188 and 219] contains forms of Oaths and Affirmations.

Fourth Schedule: [Under Articles 4(1) and 20] allocates seats for each State and Union Territory, in the Council of States.

Fifth Schedule: [Under Article 224(1)] provides for the administration and control of Scheduled Areas. This schedule provides for amendment by a simple majority of Parliament and takes it out of the ambit of Article 368 (Amendment of the Constitution).

Sixth Schedule: [Under Articles 214(2), and 275(1)] provides for the administration of Tribal Areas in Assam, Meghalaya and Mizoram. This is a lengthy schedule which goes into the details of the administration in the Tribal Areas concerned. This schedule can also be amended by a simple majority of the Parliament.

Seventh Schedule: [Under Article 246] gives three Lists: **(a)** Union List containing 99 subjects in which the Union Government has exclusive authority **(b)** State List containing 66 subjects which are under the exclusive authority of State Governments and **(c)** Concurrent List containing 52 subjects, where the Union and States have concurrent powers.

Eighth Schedule: [Under Articles 344(1) and 351(1)] gives a list of 22 languages recognised by the Constitution: 1. Assamese 2. Bengali 3. Gujarati 4. Hindi 5. Kannada 6. Kashmiri 7. Malayalam 8. Marathi 9. Oriya 10. Punjabi 11. Sanskrit 12. Sindhi 13. Tamil 14. Telugu 15. Urdu 16. Manipuri 17. Konkani 18. Nepali 19. Bodo 20. Dogri 21. Mythili and 22. Santhali, the four languages (19 to 22) are also included in this schedule by 100th Amendment.

Ninth Schedule: [Under Article 31(b)] was added by the Constitution (First Amendment) Act, 1951. It contains Acts and orders relating to land tenures, land tax, railways, industries, etc., passed by the State Governments and the Union Government which are beyond the jurisdiction of civil courts. Now it laws open to judicial review by the Supreme Court.

Tenth Schedule: [Under Articles 101, 102, 191, 192] It contains the Anti-defection Act.

Eleventh Schedule: [Under Article 243 G] It deals with Panchayat Raj system in India.

Twelfth Schedule: It mentions three types of municipalities - Nagar Panchayats for transitional areas, Municipal Councils for smaller urban areas and Municipal Corporation for large urban areas.

PARTY POLITICS IN INDIA

At the dawn of Independence, there were only two Political Parties - the Indian National Congress and the Communist Party of India. Soon came the proliferation that as many as 77 parties contested in the 1952 General Elections.

The Communist Party split up into two in 1964; namely, the Communist Party of India and the Communist Party (Marxist). The most important development occurred in 1969 was that the Congress Party split up into two - the party led by Mrs. Indira Gandhi and the party led by Mr. Nijalingappa. In the 1971 elections the Congress party under Mrs. Gandhi won a massive majority in the Lok Sabha with 356 seats. The Nijalingappa's party won only 16 seats.

In 1977 General Elections, the opposition United Front known as Janata Party won the elections with 296 seats. Mr. Morarji Desai became the Prime Minister on 24th March 1977. Mr. Charan Singh withdrew his support to Mr. Desai. So Mr.Desai was obliged to resign in July 1979. Charan Singh and his supporters formed a new party called Janata (Secular) and formed a new ministry. Mrs. Gandhi withdrew the support on 20th August 1979 and the Charan Singh ministry fell. In the 1980 elections, Mrs.Gandhi came back to power and her party became popularly known as Indira Congress or Congress (I). After the assassination of Mr. Rajiv Gandhi in 1991 Congress President Mr. Narasimha Rao came to power. After the fall of the Congress Party in the Eleventh General Election 1996, Mr. Kesari became the Congress President. Now Mrs. Sonia Gandhi has taken over the leadership.

The old Janata Party has split up with Mr. Chandrasekar as the President of the new Janata. The Lok Dal - the original splinter party started by Mr.Charan Singh was now split up into Lok Dal (A) and Lok Dal (D). Lok Dal (A) was led by Ajit Singh and the other one by Mr.Devi Lal. Lok Dal (A) merged with the Janata Party with Mr.Ajit Singh as the President of the party. The Jana Sangh has gathered strength under a new banner, the Bharatiya Janata Party with Mr. L.K.Advani as President. The BJP Party President Mr. L.K. Advani who has succeeded Mr. Venkaiah Naidu who resigned to accept the moral responsibility of the 14th General election in which their party defeated, while the Congress won the majority. Mr. Rajnath Singh became BJP Party President on 2-1-2006 succeeding Mr. L.K. Advani to end the controversy that started in June 2, 2005 in the Sang Parivar after Mr. Advani made the controversial remark that Pakistan founder Mohamed Ali Jinnah was secular. Mr. Rajnath Singh is reelected BJP president for a full term untill 2008.

GENERAL ELECTIONS

The General Elections to the Parliament as well as to State Assemblies were held simultaneously till 1970. In 1971, this policy was given up. The national and state elections were held separately.

First General Election, 1952: The First General Election was held in 1952. The Congress won with massive majority.

Second General Election, 1957: At the Second General Election, the Congress secured 371 out of 494 elective seats in the Lok Sabha.

Third General Election, 1962: Out of 494 Parliamentary seats, the Congress won 361.

Fourth General Election, 1967: At the Fourth General Election, the performance of Congress party was comparatively poor. It secured only 283 seats out of 520.

Fifth General Election, 1971: This was a mid-term election; the Lok Sabha having been dissolved on December 27, 1971 one year and two months before the expiry of the full period. The Ruling Congress, under Mrs. Indira Gandhi, swept the polls and came out with a massive majority of 350 out of 518 elective seats in the Lok Sabha.

Duration of the Fifth Lok Sabha: On 26th June 1975, the President declared an emergency. This emergency was lifted only after the results of the Sixth General Election were announced, namely on 22nd March, 1977.

Sixth General Election, 1977: The Sixth General Election (March 1977) brought the Janata to power. Janata won more than 296 seats in a total of 542, a clear majority while the Congress could muster only 153 seats.

Seventh General Election, 1980: The Seventh General Election (January 1980) returned Indira Gandhi to power again with a two- thirds majority in the Lok Sabha.

Eighth General Election, 1985: Polling was held on 24, 27 and 28th December 1984 in 508 constituencies. 401 seats were won by the Congress under Mr. Rajiv Gandhi.

Ninth General Election, 1989: The Ninth General Election was held on 24th and 27th November 1989 in 528 constituencies. The Ruling Congress (I) Party lost power. The Opposition alliance [The National Front composed of BJP, Janata Dal and CPI (M)] got the majority of 310 seats. The Janata Dal headed by V.P.Singh which won 141 seats formed the government with outside support of Bharatiya Janata Party, some regional parties, and leftist parties. Eventually it was voted out of power by a confidence motion in Parliament on 7th November, 1990. The rival faction of Janata Dal headed by Mr.Chandra Sekhar, formed the government with the Congress (I) promising outside support. On withdrawal of latter's support, the Chandra Sekhar government resigned on March 6, 1991. So inevitably, schedule for fresh poll was announced on 17th March, 1991.

Tenth General Election, 1991: In the polls the Congress (I) secured single party majority. In June, an elected government under Mr.P.V.Narasimha Rao was formed. Inspite of many trials and tribulations, his government continued to remain in power.

Eleventh General Election, 1996: The Eleventh Lok Sabha constituted on 15th May 1996 after the General Election to the Lok Sabha in which 590 million voters cast their vote to elect 543 members was a verdict against the Congress-I in power. None other parties, Bharatiya Janata Party or National Front, Left Front combine could reach anywhere near the striking distance of an absolute majority. As a result, a 21-member, five party coalition government of the United Front, headed by Mr. H.D.Deve Gowda was sworn in New Delhi on June 1996. But within a span of 10 months Mr.Deve Gowda had to vacate the Prime Ministerial post due to political friction and Mr. I.K.Gujral of United Front became the twelfth Prime Minister of India on 21st April 1997. Consequent upon the withdrawal of Congress support after the interim report of the Jain Commission was submitted, the President was advised to dissolve Lok Sabha and fresh elections were to be conducted in Feb/March 1998.

Twelfth General Election, 1998: The twelfth general elections which were unfortunately thrust upon the people who were already reeling under economic recession were held in three phases in February 1998. The back lustre attitude of the voters was reflected in the poor voter turnout of about 55%. The B.J.P. lost heavily in Maharashtra, Rajasthan, the ruling D.M.K. gave away to its arch rival AIADMK in Tamil Nadu, in Assam the ruling AGP lost its face. Even in West Bengal, Trinamul Congress fared better. The Congress could not win even a single seat in U.P., though it improved in Western region owing to Sonia factor. The final tally in the 543 member Lok Sabha was BJP and its allies could not cross 272 mark (251). The Congress and its allies scored 166, the United Front 95 and others 19. Again the elections paved the way for hung Parliament. However, the BJP formed the government in March 1998 with Mr. A.B. Vajpayee as Prime Minister with the support of its electoral allies and the issue based support offered by Telugu Desam of Mr. Chandrababu Naidu. The fate of much pressured coalition government headed by Mr. A.B. Vajpayee was sealed on 17th April, 1999 when it lost the confidence of Lok Sabha by one vote, after AIADMK withdrew its support. The President was left with no other alternative than dissolving the Lok Sabha and ordering elections for 13th Lok Sabha costing the government exchequer several crores of rupees.

13th General Election 1999: The13th General Election held from 5th September to 3rd October, 1999 in 5 phases. BJP and its allies (NDA-National Democratic Alliance) brought a clear victory by winning 294 seats. The Congress and its allies secured 131 seats, the Left Front and allies scored 42 and others 64. On 13th October 1999, Mr. A.B. Vajpayee, under his Prime Ministership formed the BJP Government. Assembly elections for Karnataka, Maharashtra, Arunachal Pradesh, Sikkim and Andhra Pradesh were also held.

14th General Election 2004: The 2004 elections proved to be a disaster for the NDA, with the BJP-led alliance falling short of the 200 mark. The Congress, with 145 seats, emerged as the single largest party, gaining ground across the country and staked its claim to form the next government. The Left parties also registered their best performance in recent elections. The elections were held between April 20 and May 10, 2004 in four phases. As per final results of 539 seats, the BJP alliance took 185 (BJP on its own got 138 seats), while Congress and its allies surged ahead in 217 seats, the Left in 60 and others in 77.

INDIAN HISTORY

Indus Valley Civilization: We could have drawn a blank about the rich and unparalleled civilization of Indus Valley people, but for the efforts of John Marshall, the well-known Archaeologist, who brought it to light in 1921. The excavations made in Mohanjodaro and Harappa - (both are in Pakistan) revealed the prestigious civilization of our ancient Indians. This civilization dates back between 3000 to 1500 BC. The other excavated sites are Lothal, Rupar, Rangpur, Chanhudaro, Amri, Lohumjo-duro, Ali Murad, Jhukar etc. From the available remains, we can conclude that the Indus Valley people had excelled their contemporaries in Mesopotamia, Egypt and Sumaria in architecture. They had constructed wide and straight roads. The drainage system ran along the sides of the roads. In the centre of the village, a swimming pool 'Great Bath' had been constructed. They used red burnt bricks. They had commercial contacts with the foreigners in Egypt and Sumaria. The Indus Valley people used gold, silver, copper, tin etc. But they did not know the use of iron. It is believed that their civilization might have been destroyed by the Aryans. **The Indus Valley people probably might have spoken Dravidian language.** The 'Pictographic' script of Indus Valley is not yet deciphered.

The Aryans: Though various theories have been advanced on the origin of the Aryans it is widely believed that the Aryans might have come from Central Asia. There might have been two divisions of Aryans - one settled in Punjab or called Sapta Sindhu region and the other settled in the south of Punjab or on the bank of Ganga and Jamuna by subduing the natives Dasas or Dasyus by force. The Aryans had advanced up to central India. During their period initially the Vedas came into being. They are Rig, Yajur, Sama and Atharvana Vedas. The Vedas are the main source to know the culture and civilization of the Aryans followed by Brahmanas and Aranyakas and the Upanishads. As the Aryans destroyed the Indus Valley Civilization, it is confirmed that the Aryans lived after the Dravidians. The Aryan Civilization is known as the Vedic Civilization. **Veda means knowledge.**

Jainism: Jainism came into existence in the sixth century B.C. Rishaba founded the religion. His son was Bharatha. India is known as Bharath after him only. Mahavira was 24th Thirthankara of Jainism. He was the son of Sidhartha, the king of Vaishali. He was born at Kundagrama near Vaishali in 539 B.C and lived till 467 B.C. His name was Vardhamana. Mahavira and Buddha were contemporaries. Mahavira propagated three ideals 'Triratna' or Three Jewels - Good faith, Good knowledge, Good conduct. God did not create the world and is not saviour of the world. Animal sacrifice and pronouncing of the Vedas were condemned by him. Attaining Nirvana is the last act of man. He preached Ahimsa. Jainism was widely followed. Jain temples were constructed. Most of these temples were destroyed later by Ajaya Bala of Arya dynasty and Alauddin Khilji. The Jains were perfect architects. The remains at Ellora in the North and Saravanabelagola in the South are standing examples. Because of the severe discipline and lack of support from the Kings, Jainism was followed by very few. Hence today it is a minority religion.

Buddhism: It was founded by Buddha who lived during 567-487 B.C. He attained enlightenment at the age of 35 under a Bodhi tree at Gaya. His first sermon was delivered at Sarnath. He spent about 45 years of his life in propagation of Buddhism. As it was patronised by the Kings like Ashoka, it soon became a world-wide religion. It is largely followed even today in China, Tibet, Japan, Korea and Sri Lanka. The principles of Buddhism talk about desire which is the origin for all ills and preach vegetarianism. The sacrifice of animals should be dispensed with. Four conferences were held on Buddhism. The first immediately after his death in Rajagraha, the second at Vaishali at his death centenary celebration. Third at Patalipura by Ashoka and the fourth at Kashmir or Jullundur during the rule of Kanishka. During the period of Kanishka, the two divisions of the Buddhism - **Hinayana and Mahayana** - emerged. The followers of Hinayana followed the principles of Buddhism and those of Mahayana worshipped Buddha as God. As there were no rival religions - either Islam or Christianity, Buddhism received the support of the people. In the later years, because of religious fanaticism of the Muslims, Buddhism remained as a minority religion.

Puranas: The Puranas give a clear picture of the Aryans. They are eighteen in number. They contain fables, discipline, religious rites, etc. Vishnu Purana, Bhagavatha Purana are some of the important Puranas.

Epics: The available epics are Ramayana and Mahabharatha. The former was written by Valmiki and the latter by Ved Vyas. Bhagavad Gita is part of Mahabharatha. The Gita is full of teachings to Arjuna by Lord Krishna. Ramayana was written much earlier than Mahabharatha.

Nandas: When Alexander invaded India, the Nandas ruled over Magadha which comprised of the Modern Patna and Gaya districts in Bihar. According to the Puranas, the Nandas ruled for 100 years and there were 9 kings. Hieun Tsang mentions about the last king of the Nanda as Dana Nanda. The Nanda rule came to an end when the Mauryans invaded.

Lichchavis: The Capital of the Lichchavis was Vaishali. It is believed that the mother of Mahavira belonged to Lichchavis. Chanakya mentions about the Lichchavis in his Arthasastra.

Alexander, the Great: He was the son of a great king of Macedonia, King Philip. Inspired by the teachings of Aristotle who was his teacher, Alexander wanted to bring India under his control so that he could become the Emperor of the whole world. He came to India in 326 B.C. and defeated Porus. As his soldiers desired to go back home, Alexander returned. On his way back, he died, at Babylon in 323 B.C at the age of 33.

Mauryas: After defeating the Nandas, Chandragupta Maurya established his kingdom with Pataliputra as his capital. He defeated Seleucus Nicator who came from Babylonia. Then Nicator sent Megasthanes as his ambassador. Indika of Megasthanes is a valuable source to picturize Mauryan history. Kautilya, the author of Arthasastra was Chandragupta's Minister. Kautilya was worked as minister of Chandragupta Maurya. He wrote Arthasastra. Arthasastra described as political system of Chandragupta Maurya. Chandragupta was succeeded by his son Bindusara, father of Ashoka. Ashoka ruled between 273 B.C. and 236 B.C. The war he waged with Kalinga changed his whole life. Then he became a Buddhist to propagate the ideals of Buddhism. Certain policies of Ashoka were responsible for the invasion of Sungas under Pushyamitra Sunga, who was commander-in-chief of the Mauryas and established the Sunga dynasty which overthrew the Mauryans and they ruled from 187-75 BC.

The Kanvas (75-30 B.C): Vasudeva was the founder of Kanva dynasty who slaughtered Devabhuh, the last ruler of the Surya dynasty. Altogether only four Kanva Kings - Vasudeva. Bhumimitra, Narayana and Susuman ruled till 30 B.C and was overruled by the Andhras.

The Kalingas: Kalinga was liberated immediately after the death of Ashoka. Nothing concrete is known about them except that Kharavela was the most popular ruler who ruled the territory.

The Satavahanas or Andhras: Simuka, the founder of the dynasty, started his reign in 230 B.C. Gautami Putra Satakarni, the famous Andhra ruler had Parthian as his capital near the bank of Godavari. He has been described as destroyer of Sakas, Yavanas and Pahlavas. After a few centuries of their rule, the Sakas made inroads into the territory of the Satavahanas. The stupas at Amaravat, bear eloquent testimony to the Graeco-Roman influence in Satavahanas. Prakrit language was patronised during the period.

Kushans: Though many petty dynasties rose and fell in the period after the Mauryas, the Kushana dynasty has made indelible history on the Indian soil. Though many theories have been forwarded about the origin of the Kushanas, it can be said that they came from Central Asia. Of the Kushana Kings, Kanishka's reign is well known. The beginning of Saka era on which the Indian calendar is based coincides with enthronement of Kanishka in 78 A.D. Gandhara Art, the fusion of Indo-Greek arts flourished during the period of Kushanas. The Gandhara art is famous for standing Buddha. The two branches of Buddhism emerged during the reign of Kanishka.

Guptas (320-540 A.D): The age of Guptas is known as **Golden Age** in the history of India for the reasons of revival of Hinduism, Art, Literature, etc. Kalidasa, the author of Sakunthala, Raguvamsam, Meghdhoot, etc., and Aryabhatta, the great mathematician and astronomer lived during this age. Fahien visited the court of Chandra Gupta II and stayed in India between 399 and 417 A.D. Though the founder of Gupta dynasty is not definitely known, we can well say that Chandra Gupta I, Samudra Gupta and Chandra Gupta II are well known great Kings. Because of his valiant conquest, Samudra Gupta is known as **Indian Napoleon**.

Vardhana Dynasty: After the Guptas, the well-known Hindu dynasty in the north was Vardhana dynasty of which Harsha Vardhana was a famous king.

Harsha was a great scholar. Hieun Tsang visited India in the 7th Century A.D. during Harsha's period. Hieun Tsang's accounts are a valuable source of information on Harsha's period. Nalanda University flourished and two conferences on Buddhism were held under Harsha - one at Kannauj under the religious leadership of Hieun Tsang and the second conference at Allahabad. He was defeated ultimately by Pulakesin II of Chalukya dynasty. Bana Bhatt wrote Harsha Charita. Harsha himself wrote three dramas Ratnavali, Priyadarsika and Nagananda in Sanskrit. Thus Harsha was not only a warrior but a scholar and good administrator also. The Vardhana dynasty was the last Hindu dynasty in the north.

HISTORY OF ASSAM

In the pre-christian era known as Praagjyotisha ruled by descendants of Naraka (legendary) born of embrace of Vishnu in the Boar form with Earth as the Nidhanpur copperplate of Bhaskaravarman (594 - 650) declared and confirmed by almost all the subsequent inscriptions. During Naraka's rule Praagjyotisha became known as Kaamarupa. When Naraka's descendants ceased to rule, Pushyavarman (355-80) establish the Bhaumavarman dynasty (355 - 650). During this dynasty's rule, five Aswamedha sacrifices were performed, which proves strong Brahmanic influences. As the last ruler of the preceding dynasty was unmarried, Saalastambha occupied the throne and began the Saalastambha dynasty (650-990). Last king of preceding dynasty was childless, the Prakriti selected Brahmapala (990-1010), a scion of the Bhauma dynasty and with him began the Pala dynasty (990-1138). When last king of preceding dynasty died, Vaidyadeva (1138-45) occupied the throne and his dynasty ruled for a small period (1138-1228). Kaamarupa broke into 6 kingdoms after 1228: (a) Bhuyan kingdom (1260-1497); (b) Kamala kingdom (1195-1498); (c) Chuliya kingdom (1187-1523); (d) Koch kingdom (1515-1613); (e) Ahom kingdom (1228-1826) and (f) Kachari kingdom (1187 - 1832). All the kingdoms later on merged with the Ahom kingdom and the East India Company occupied Assam in 1826. The name Assam originated from the Ahom rulers and later on used to mean the former Kaamarupa kingdom.

HISTORY OF SOUTH INDIA

Sangam Age: The word 'Sangam' in Sanskrit means 'an association of poets' who virtually made literary contribution during the Pandya Kings. The Roman records referring to the life depicted in the two epics Silappadikaram and Manimekalai and other corroborating evidences, point out that the period from 2nd century B.C to 2nd century A.D was the probable period of Sangam Age. This age is well known for its high meticulous literary and administrative advancement. Moreover women held a high position in the society.

The Kalabhras: Kalabhras emerged at the closing of 3rd century and lasted till the 6th century. The Cholas and the Pandyas were running under low profile which led to the upper hand of Kalabhras. Evidences are vague about the history of the Kalabhras.

The Pallavas: Pallavas dominated the areas between the river Krishna and Cauvery during the 6th century A.D., Kanchi was their capital city.

Mahendravarman I who was the popular Pallava ruler was drastically defeated by Pulakesin II of Chalukya dynasty. His son Narashima Varman I (695-722 A.D) defeated his father's rival and killed him and thus he got the title **'Mamallan'** or **'Great warrior'**. He became more popular due to his architectural achievements even now seen in Mahabalipuram or Mamallapuram named after him.

The Cholas: Chola Kingdom was founded by Vijayala the feudatory of Pallavas who captured Tanjore in 850 A.D. They dominated over the Indian peninsula, parts of Sri Lanka and Maldives. They ruled the very fertile delta of Cauvery basin which lies in the modern Trichy and Tanjore districts of Tamilnadu. Though their rule lasted for about 200 years, the rule of Raja Raja, the great and that of his son Rajendra Chola are marked for their administration and conquest. Raja Raja ruled between 985 A.D. and 1014 A.D. He built the Brihadeeswara Temple at Tanjore. His was a rule of democracy. He was a staunch Hindu. But he practised religious tolerance not known in those days. Raja Raja was succeeded by his son Rajendra who ruled between 1012 A.D. and 1044 A.D. During his time foreign trade flourished. Kulothunga Chola I introduced the **Kudavolai** system of elections.

The Pandyas: The presence of the Pandyas can be traced from the Sangam Age. They were the rulers of the modern districts of Madura, Ramnad and Tirunelveli with Madura as the capital. There was a gradual decline in the 9th century on the invasion of Kalabhras. But the survival of the Pandyas and their rise at the end of the 13th century under Maravarman Sundara Pandya I had made Pandyas prominent in the South Indian History. He defeated Raja Raja II of the Cholas and burnt the capital cities of Woraiyur and Tanjore. But the Pandyas were able to dominate for another century when they were routed out severely by Malik Kafur in 1311 during Sundara Pandya II and Vira Pandya. Later Ulughkhan the son of Ghiyas-ud-din Tughlaq captured Madura in 1323 A.D and annexed to the Muslim Province.

MEDIEVAL INDIA

During the period between 8th and 10th century A.D. a number of powerful empires emerged in India. Palas dominated the eastern and northern parts of India. The Prathihara empire extended over the western and parts of northern India. In the south the Rashtrakuta empire dominated the Deccan. Of these three the Rashtrakuta empire lasted the longest.

The Palas: Pala Kingdom was founded by Gopala in 750 A.D. The greatest among the Palas was Dharmapala, (770 to 810 A.D). The empire slowly disintegrated after the death of Devapala son of Dharmapala. Palas were great patrons of Buddhist religion and so Nalanda University became famous during the reign of Dharmapala and Vikramashila University at Magadha was founded by him.

The Pratiharas: Raja Bhoja was the founder of the Pratihara Kingdom or Gurjara Pratiharas had control over Kanauj by 836 A.D. After him Mahendrapala and Mahipala ruled. Mahipala was defeated by the Rashtrakuta King Indra III in 915 A.D. On the debris of the Pratiharas sprang the Rajput Kings, the Chauhans, the Paramaras and the Chandellas.

The Rashtrakutas: Rashtrakutas ruled the Deccan region whereas Palas ruled the eastern and Prathiharas ruled the northern and western parts. Rashtrakuta empire was founded by Dantidurga. Krishna I built Kailasanathar temple at Ellora. The greatest among the Rashtrakutas was Krishna III (939-965 A.D) who crunched all his opponents in south and north and captured Ujjain.

Arab Conquest of Sind: Mohammad Bin Qasim made a conquest of Sind in 712 A.D. But his dream to establish a Muslim rule in India did not come true, as Qasim was murdered at his early age. But the dream was realised by Mohammed Ghori. In 1175, Ghori brought Sind under his control. In 1186, Punjab came under his rule. But in 1191 Prithviraj Chauhan defeated him in the First Battle of Tarain. However, his victory at Kanauj in 1194, paved the way for the establishment of Muslim rule in India.

Slave Dynasty: (1196-1290 A.D.) Qutb-ud-din-Aibak was a slave purchased by Ghori. After the second Battle of Terrain in 1192, he was appointed by Ghori as governor of Lahore. After the death of Ghori, by the support of the people of Lahore, he proclaimed himself as a King. His period was between 1206-1212. A.D The famous Qutab Minar was built by him though he could not complete it before his death. Qutb-ud-din Aibak was succeeded by his son-in-law Iltutmish (1210-1236 A.D) who was once a slave of Aibak. He completed Qutb-Minar in 1232 A.D. Iltutmish was succeeded by his capable daughter Razia Sultana (1236-1240 A.D.) the first women ruler of India. The next important ruler worth mentioning was Giyasud-din-Balban (1266-1288 A.D) one of the nobles in the court of Iltutmish. The successors of Balban were weak, and thus slave dynasty came to an end.

Khilji Dynasty (1290-1320 A.D): Alauddin Khilji (1296-1316 A.D.) was the first Muslim ruler whose empire covered almost the whole of India up to its extrme South. He is well known for his administration and military system. Akbar's Mansabdari System was contemplative of what was introduced by Alauddin Khilji.

Tughlaq Dynasty (1320-1412 A.D): It lasted for about 100 years. Mohammad-bin-Tughlaq is well-known for his personal oddities. He was the King who introduced token currency system and who changed his capital from Delhi to Daulatabad and back to Delhi. Though his ideas were fantastic, they could not be implemented as they lacked practical imagination. The worst part of it was that he changed not only his capital but the entire populace. As a historian said, he *could have better been a Professor than a King*.

Lodi Dynasty (1451-1526 A.D.): This was the last Arab Muslim dynasty which ruled Delhi. Ibrahim Lodi ruled Delhi while Mohammed Lodi was in Gujarat. Including the rule of their predecessors, the Lodi rule lasted for about 75 years between 1451 A.D. and 1526 A.D. Because of fraternal factions and rivalries, Mohammed Lodi invited Babur to fight with his brother Ibrahim Lodi. It resulted in the First Battle of Panipat (1526 A.D.) which paved way for the Mughal rule in India.

Vijayanagara Empire : It was established by Harihara and Bukka on the banks of Tunghabadra in Andhra (1336 A.D.). Krishnadevaraya was a famous king who ruled between 1509 A.D. and 1530 A.D. He brought under his control, the modern Raichur, Bijapur, Gulbarga, etc., in Karnataka and Kondapalli and Kondaveedu in Andhra Pradesh. His period witnessed peace and prosperity. Krishnadevaraya, himself, was a scholar. His court room was adorned by Ashtadiggajas of whom Tenalirama is well-known for his witticism. Because of the weak successors and of the rise of Bahmani Kingdoms, Vijayanagara Empire vanished by Bhamini Kingdoms at Talikota on 1565.

Bahmini Kingdom (1347-1526 A.D.): The Deccan nobles of Muhammad bin Tughlak revolted against him and formed a Muslim Bahmini Kingdom in South. In 1347 A.D. Hasan-Abdul Muzaffar and Ala-ud-din Bahman Shah founded Bahmini Kingdom. Totally 18 rulers ruled for 175 years. They had constant wars with their Hindu neighbour Vijayanagar Empire. Muhamad Gawan minister of state for twenty years was the most popular person who had enriched the administration, organised finance, encouraged public education, and reformed revenue system. The Bahmini Kingdom declined with the death of Kalimullah in 1527 A.D.

The Bhakti Movement: The dominating Muslim society faced the Hindu revivalist movement headed by Shankaracharya a great thinker and a distinguished philosopher. He preached on the doctrine 'Advaita'. The second reviver of Hinduism was Ramanuja who preached Bhakti through Vaishnavism. Among later exponents of the Bhakti movement, the notable were Ramananda, Chaitanya, Kabir and Nanak. These saints had faith in one god. Their main aim was Bhakti (Devotion) the only means to salvation. Though Bhakti movement could not help to remove permanently the gulf between Islam and Hinduism it helped a good deal in creating harmony between the Hindus and Muslims.

Sufism: The terms Sufi, Wali, Durvesh and Faqir are used for Muslim saints who attempted to achieve intuitive faculties through ascetic exercises, contemplation, renunciation and self-denial. Sufism rebelled against all forms of religious formalism, orthodoxy, falsehood and hypocrisy and endeavoured to create a new world order in which spiritual bliss was the only and ultimate goal.

MUGHAL RULE IN INDIA

Babur (1526-1530 A.D.) : Babur who was driven out of his own country, was invited by Mohammed Lodi to invade India. After his failure thrice to get back Samarkhand, Babur locked himself and concentrated on his invasion on India. The first Battle of Panipat in 1526 A.D. with Ibrahim Lodi, led to the establishment of Mughal Rule in India. Babur ruled for only 4 years, hence he could not consolidate his gains. He was succeeded by a weak son Humayun. Babur has written his biography 'Baburnama'.

Humayun (1530-1556 A.D.) : Fraternal factions criss-crossed with a weak character of his own Humayun could not stand for a long time when he was driven out of the country by a native Sher Shah Suri. Humayun *tumbled through his life and tumbled out of it.* After trials and tribulations and wanderings for many years, he could stage a come back with some of his well-wishers. In the mean time Akbar was born at Amarkot in 1542 A.D.

Suri interregnum (1540-1545) : Sher Shah Suri, worth his name of tiger, could easily defeat the force of Humayun in many engagements. Though his rule lasted for only six years between 1539 A.D. and 1545 A.D., Sher Shah could pay much attention to the revenue administration and organise the army on scientific lines. During his time the Grand Trunk Road between Chennai and Calcutta was built. As he was succeeded by weak rulers, the Suri interregnum could linger on for a few years only.

Akbar (1556-1605 A.D.) : He came to power at the age of 14. Though he was illiterate, his vision of religious tolerance, revenue administration and military hierarchy had far-reaching consequences. He was adept to realise his position in a foreign land and hence he preached Hindu-Muslim Unity. He abolished *Jizya* tax imposed on Hindus by the Muslim rulers. He married Rajput ladies. He founded a religion, 'Din-i-Ilahi'. Though the religion had a few followers and died soon after the death of Akbar, we have to take into account the broad view Akbar had in the Sixteenth Century.

Jahangir (1605-1627 A.D.) : Akbar was succeeded by his son, Jahangir. Though no remarkable achievements were made by Jahangir, that the royal affairs were handled and the royalty dominated by a harem around his wife Noorjehan is worth mentioning. Jahangir used to consume 24 pegs of wine daily. Religious intolerance started surfacing and bankruptcy permeated.

Shah Jahan (1627-1658 A.D.) : More than his conquests and administration, his love for Mumtaz, art and architecture need mentioning. Because of lavish spending on art and architecture, the government coffers started drying and excessive doses of taxation year after year was the only remedy. Thus the people groaned under heavy and unbearable taxes. Taj Mahal, built of white marbles in memory of his wife Mumtaz, remains ever as a *tear drop on the cheek of Eternity*. In the construction of buildings and monuments white marbles replaced red stones used extensively by Akbar.

Aurangzeb (1658-1707 A.D.) : Though he is variedly branded as a heretic or a religious fanatic, Aurangzeb's personal character is beyond any kind of blemishes. He did not touch wine. He slept for only six hours a day. Under him the Mughal empire reached its zenith of expansion. However, it contributed negatively. His long absence at the capital and Deccan wars brought the fall of Mughal empire. As he was succeeded by weak rulers, the Mughal empire soon died. The last king of the Mughal line was Bahadur Shah-II who was executed in Rangoon in 1857 A.D. for his participation in the Sepoy Mutiny against the English.

Nadir Shah's Invasion: It was during the reign of Muhammad Shah that in 1739 A.D., Nadir Shah, a mighty King of Iran defeated the Mughal army at Karnal and plundered Delhi taking away with him immense wealth and Koh-i-Noor diamond and the Peacock throne of Shah Jahan.

CAUSES FOR THE DOWNFALL OF
THE MUGHAL EMPIRE

1. The Mughal Empire had become too big and complex to be governed from a single centre.

2. Aurangzeb's policy of Deccan occupied half of his life. His religious intolerance earned the wrath of the Hindus. His Government was a personal despotism and lacked popular support.

3. The successors of Aurangzeb were not competent. They were pleasure loving and dependent on unscrupulous ministers.

4. The attacks of Nadir Shah and Ahamed Shah Abdali left the Mughal Empire in shambles.

5. The internal rivalries and fratricidal wars dismembered the very fabric of administration and led to chaos.

6. The rise of Marathas was also a strong cause.

COMMUNAL AND REGIONAL UPRISING

The Sikh Power: Sikhism was founded by Guru Nanak Dev, in 1499 A.D. at the age of thirty. He travelled throughout India, went to Mecca, Baghdad and preached the Unity of God and brotherhood of man. Guru Nanak was the first Guru followed by ten other Gurus such as Guru Angad Dev, Guru Amar Das, Guru Ram Das, Guru Arjun Dev, Guru Hargobind, Guru Har Rai, Guru Harkishan, Guru Tezh Bahadur, Guru Govind Singh and Maharaja Ranjit Singh. Out of these Gurus, Guru Govind Singh and Maharaja Ranjit Singh who became the ruler of Punjab were quite popular. **Guru Granth Sahib** is regarded as the Guru or the spiritual guide of the Sikhs.

The Marathas: The Marathas during the reign of Mughal Emperor, Aurangzeb, developed into a challenging power under Shivaji and posed a great threat to the weak Kings of the later Mughal period. They stretched along the Western Ghats spilling over into the plains of Konkan and across the Deccan into Central India. They had a common language Marathi, a common religion Hinduism, a strong sense of belonging and national feeling. Shivaji, the great Maratha leader freed them from the Muslim yoke and made them a mighty power which dominated India in the 18th century and became the major factor for the decline of the Mughal Empire.

The founder of the Maratha Empire was Shivaji, the great, born in 1627 AD. His father was a fief holder of Bijapur and his mother, Jijabai was a highly religious person. Her teaching had so much influence on her son that from the very childhood Shivaji had a belief that his mission on earth was to liberate the Hindus and free his country from the Muslim yoke. He conquered some forts in Bijapur state and threw out the army general of the Sultan of Bijapur Afzal Khan in 1659. Mutual understanding between Aurangzeb and Shivaji proved to fail, inspite of the efforts of Rajput Raja Jai Singh and Shivaji was imprisoned from where he made his dramatic escape.

After his return from Agra he recaptured the forts he had surrendered to the Mughals. He coronated himself in 1674 as Chatrapati Shivaji, the ruler of Marathas in the Deccan. He died in 1680 at the age of 53 leaving behind the strong and dominating empire which flourished for another half a century.

The Peshwas: Peshwa was the title for the Prime Minister of the Maratha Kings. The Peshwas came to power during the reign of Shahu, grandson of Shivaji.

Peshwa Balaji Vishwanath (1713-20) who founded the Peshwa dynasty and launched the era of Maratha expansion. Followed by him was his son Baji Rao I (1720-40) an efficient statesman, a capable soldier and an able administrator. During his time the Marathas captured Malwa, Gujarat and Bundelkhand and strengthened their hold over the Deccan. He died at a very early age of 42 in 1740 and let his 18 year old son Balaji Baji Rao (1740-61) succeed him. Under him the Marathas captured Bihar and Orissa in the east and Punjab in the north. But in course of time, due to lack of good administration arose the five Peshwas at Poona, Gaekwad at Baroda, Bhonsle at Nagpur, Holkar at Indore and Scindia at Gwalior.

The Marathas developed a ruthless attitude of plunder which alienated them from other Indian rulers and the common names. So when Ahamed Shah Abdali, the successor of the Persian invader Nadir Shah invaded Punjab and came in direct conflict with the Marathas a decisive battle was fought at Panipat in 1761 where Abdali defeated them. Neither the Rajputs, Jats nor the Sikhs helped them in the war which routed the Maratha supremacy. Whatever power was left the third Battle of Panipat in 1761 drained it.

MODERN INDIA

The Portuguese were the first to discover a sea route to India, free from the Turkish attacks. Vasco-da-Gama in 1498 rounded the Cape of Good Hope and landed at Calicut. The Portuguese soon established a political power along the western coast. Albuqerque (1509-1515) was their ablest viceroy. Albuqerque conquered Goa from Bijapur dynasty in 1510. The first Viceroy was Francis Almeida (1505-1509). He developed Blue Water policy. The Dutch trading company came in 1602 but their power was not lasting. The French founded Pondicherry in 1674 and held power till 1763.

ADVENT OF THE EUROPEANS

The Portuguese were the first Europeans to enter into India and settle in Goa. After the victory of the English over the Spanish Armada in 1588, the English wanted to trade directly with India and Far East. In 1612, Captain Best defeated the Portuguese fleet off Swaily near Surat. By this victory the influence of English company increased. In 1615, General Thomas Roe came to the court of Jahangir and got some trade concessions. Other Europeans like the French also thought of trying their luck. In 1667, the first French factory was established at Surat. The French had their settlements at Chandra Nagore,

Balasore and Qasim Bazar. On the Malabar Coast, the French got Mahe in 1726. In 1739 they got Karaikkal on the Coromandal Coast. There had been many fights between the English and the French to establish their supremacy in India. However, because of certain advantages, the English and their sway firmly established in India. The naval supremacy can be attributed to the English victory. The English had control over three important naval bases in India namely Calcutta, Chennai and Mumbai. The French entered India from the wrong quarter. The Deccan was not fertile. But the English entered through Calcutta - "the fertile Gangetic Plain". Moreover Lord Clive was more than a match for Dupleix. The home Government in France was absolutely rotten at that time.

After many victories, the English under the Governorship of Lord Clive strengthened their administration in India. Lord Clive was followed by two inefficient people namely Vereist (1767-69) and Cartier (1770-72). Things were at their worst until Warren Hastings became the Governor of Bengal. After the passing of Regulating Act, he became the Governor-General.

THE BRITISH RULE IN INDIA

The Regulating Act, 1773: The purpose of the Act was to legalise the working Constitution of the East India Company. Governor-General Warren Hastings was appointed. Supreme Court was set up at Kolkatta.

Pitt's India Act, 1784: It ensured the centralisation of the company under the British Parliament. Creation of double government.

Permanent Settlement of Bengal, 1793: It was carried out by Cornwallis. It was an important revenue system. The settlement brought the revenue administration on scientific lines. Zamindhari system introduced during this period.

Subsidiary Alliance System of Wellesley: It paved the way for stationing of British troops in the territories of native princes. The princes had to pay for the stationing of troops. The troops took care of the defence of the territories. First subsidiary alliance with Nizam of Hyderabad.

Doctrine of Lapse: Lord Dalhousie's diplomatic Doctrine of Lapse laid down that on the death of a prince without direct descendants, the British will take over the territories of princes after declaring the dominion of the deceased as "lapsed" to the sovereign power by total failure of their natural heir. It abolished the adoption of heirs also. Satara - 1848, Sambalpur, Jaipur - 1849, Baghat - 1850, Udaipur - 1852, Jhansi - 1853, Nagpur - 1854, Oudh - 1856.

First War of Indian Independence: Dubbed by the British historians as 'Sepoy Mutiny', the First War of Indian Independence was a popular movement. It broke out in 1857. The increasing modernisation was construed by the Indian people as encroachment of their culture and civilisation. Jhansi Rani, Nana Sahib, and others participated in the movement. It did not affect South India. Because of lack of cohesion and popular support, it failed. After end of Sepoy mutiny, the administration of India directly ruled by British government due to Victoria Proclamation on 1858.

Indian Councils Act, 1861: It brought many administrative changes. Non-official Indians were taken in the Executive Council, the Government departments were decentralised and the portfolio system was introduced. The Act sought to bridge the gap between rulers and the ruled.

Ilbert Bill (1883): It is an important landmark in the history of British India. Mr. Ilbert, the law member of the Governor General's Executive Council introduced this bill known after his name to win the goodwill of the Indians. Until that time Indian Magistrates except in the Presidency towns of Mumbai, Calcutta and Chennai could not try the criminal cases in which the Englishmen were involved. The Ilbert Bill abolished this. The whole European Community opposed this bill. Hence a modification was brought in. An amendment that an European accused could claim to be tried by a jury atleast half of whose number were Europeans, was introduced. The Ilbert Bill actually aroused the feelings of the Indians and made them realise their humble position and degradation.

NATIONAL MOVEMENT

Our National Movement can conveniently be divided into three phases - the first being that of *Moderate Era* (1885-1905), the second that of *Extremist Era* (1905-1919), and the third that of *Gandhian Era* (1919-1947).

The year 1885 marks the beginning of a new epoch in Indian history, as by then the Indian mind became increasingly conscious of its political position. The Macaulayian system of education opened the new gates of European thought with the ideals of liberty, nationality and self-government.

S.N.Banerjee started the Indian Association to represent the view of the educated community and to inspire them with living interest in public life. In 1883 an All India National Conference was convened and it met for the second time in 1885 at Calcutta. In both the above Conferences representatives from all major towns of India attended. This awakening formed the ground for Mr.A.O.Hume. He decided to bypass this Indian National Conference and instead organise a loyal and innocuous political organisation. This indeed culminated into the formation of the Indian National Congress. This Congress was indeed not the voice of the masses.

First Phase (1885-1905): During this period, the object of the Congress was not the removal of British rule in India, but broadening of its base. The Congressmen believed that the obstacle in the path of India's progress was not British rule but the social and economic backwardness of the people and the reactionary rule of the bureaucracy. The Congress leaders believed that their prime duty was to represent the case before the British Government and the Government in turn would redress their grievances. Even the demands were in an apologetic language. Progressive leaders were dissatisfied with the progress and disliked the attitude adopted by pioneers, which led to the emergence of a new party within the Congress. The two factions were called as Moderate Party and Extremist Party. This split took place at Surat in 1907.

Second Phase (1905-1919): Extremists dominated this period, their aim was Swaraj through self-reliance and self-help. The process of rejuvenation was through love for one's own country, own religion and self-government. They lost all faith in the British sense of justice and fairplay. Lala Lajpat Rai exhorted the people that if they really cared for their country "they would have to strike a blow for freedom themselves". During his campaign Tilak was arrested. Government tried to stifle public opinion and suppress lawlessness. Tilak gave the slogan "Swaraj is my birthright and I shall have it". Extremists took recourse to boycott mainly foreign goods. Partition of Bengal was done during this period. Due to incessant agitation, it was annulled in 1911. The British Government introduced Minto-Morley reforms.

Home rule movement was started by Mrs. Annie Besant on July 1916 at Chennai. The Home Rule Movement was first started by Tilak at Mumbai on April 1916. Both worked in unison and aimed at the achievement of self-government. Montague-Chelmsford announced in 1917 "The policy of His Majesty's Government with which the Government of India is in complete accord is that of the increasing association of Indians in every branch of administration and gradual development of self-governing institutions with a view to the progressive realisation of responsible Government in India as an integral part of the British Empire".

Third Phase (1919-1947): The period was dominated by the personality of Mahatma Gandhi. Gandhiji deprecated the policy of violence and underground plots but preached open and active resistance to injustice. He advocated the adoption of the policy of Satyagraha i.e., non-violence and non-cooperation towards the Government. After the advent of Gandhiji, the Congress movement became a mass movement. The organisation was strengthened and its Constitution made democratic. The Congress party extended its support to the British Government in the First World War. Disillusioned by the events Gandhiji launched Civil disobedience movement and non-cooperation towards the unjust Government. The policy involved renunciation of Government titles, boycott of legislatures, law-courts, educational institutions, foreign goods and finally non-payment of taxes. Gandhiji toured the whole country to whip up enthusiasm of the people in support of the Swadeshi movement.

FIRST PHASE OF NATIONAL MOVEMENT

Founding of Indian National Congress: Indian National Congress was founded in Dec. 1885 by A.O. Hume, a retired English Civil Servant. The idea behind its foundation was to create a forum to ventilate the grievances and feelings of the mass movement in a strong and unified code. The first session was held at Mumbai under the Presidentship of W.C.Banerjee.

Era of Three Ps (1885-1905): The Congress was mainly an organisation of small minority of English Educated Indians and it was a moderate body. The known leaders of that time were Dadabhai Naoroji, Ferozeshah Mehta, Surendranath Banerji, Gopala Krishna Gokhale and Madan Mohan Malaviya. They were not only loyal well wishers of royal British Government but enamoured of British civilisation. Their Era popularly known as three Ps. (Petition, Prayer and Protest) witnessed their modest demands of extension of the Legislative Councils, separation of judiciary from executive, Indianisation of services, reduction of military expenditure, freedom of the press, etc. Their demands and calls did not receive the attention of the English rulers. But the spadework done by them is note-worthy.

SECOND PHASE OF NATIONAL MOVEMENT

Emergence of Extremists: A section of the Congress leaders felt that the peaceful means of attaining Independence would not do, unless stern methods were adopted to achieve the goal. The main contributory factors to the rise of extremists are defeat of a big European country, Russia by a tiny Asian neighbour Japan in the Russo-Japanese war in 1904 and the partition of Bengal by Lord Curzon in 1905. Against partition, there was agitation in Bengal. The leaders preached the boycott of British goods and the adoption of Swadeshi. We could witness discontent in the whole country. Though the end of both extremists and moderates was that of self-government the means adopted by them were different. The well-known extremist leaders were Lokmanya Bal Gangadhara Tilak from Maharashtra, Lala Lajpat Rai from Punjab and Bipin Chandra Pal from Bengal. This trio was called **Lal-Bal-Pal.**

Partition of Bengal (1905): Bengal which included Bihar and Orissa in those days was too big to be administered, so felt Lord Curzon who split it into two - one with Dacca as capital and other with Calcutta. The people were enraged at this act of Lord Curzon. As the underlying motive behind this move, the people presumed, was to weaken the Bengali nationalism and its solidarity.

Swadeshi Movement (1905): The agitation was aimed at the 'boycott of British goods' especially cotton goods. Sir Surendranath Banerji spearheaded the movement which speedily spread throughout India. Other eminent leaders of this movement were Shri Aurobindo Ghosh and Bipin Chandra Pal.

The Muslim League (1906): The Muslims in India grew suspicious of Hindu majority. The well-known policy of the English, 'Divide-et-impera' culminated in the formation of Muslim League in 1906 under the leadership of Sir Syed Ahmed Khan to promote the feeling of loyalty among the Muslims and advance the political rights and interests of the Muslims in India. Later, Mohd. Ali Jinnah became the President.

Surat Split (1907): The Surat session of the Congress in 1907 witnessed a row over the selection of the President. The moderates who outnumbered the extremists in Congress won the election. The extremists left the Congress. Now the object became the achievement of Dominion Status for India by peaceful means.

Minto-Morley Reforms (1909): Lord Minto, the then Viceroy introduced certain drastic laws to curb the extremist movement and please the moderates. The drastic measures were known as Minto-Morley Reforms - named after him and Morley, the then Secretary of State for India. According to this Act, the official majority was replaced by a majority of nominated members. However, elected members remained in minority. The reforms, can be said to have been introduced a sort of 'benevolent despotism'. The worst part of the reforms was that separate electorate was introduced for Muslims. Landlords, merchant class, etc. were given separate representation. Minto came to known as the father of communal electorate.

Revolutionary or Terrorist Movement : This movement was mainly contained to Punjab, Maharashtra, Bengal in the north and Pondicherry in the south. They believed in terrorising British officials and demoralising the entire official machinery. They made dacoities and looted arms. Even attempts were made on the lives of Lord Hardinge and Lord Minto. The terrorist movements were organised outside India also.

India League : The organisation, India League was founded in England to mobilise public opinion against the British Government and espouse the cause of Indian independence. Many well-known elites including Harold Lasky were members.

Bomb on Viceroy (Dec. 1912) : When Lord and Lady Hardinge II made the state entry into the new capital Delhi (Capital was shifted from Calcutta to Delhi in 1911) on a decorated elephant, a revolutionary threw a bomb at them when the procession was nearing Chandni Chowk. The Viceroy escaped with minor injuries.

The Ghadar Party (1913) : It was founded by the Indian revolutionaries living in Canada and America at Sanfrancisco. It had branches in other countries also. Important personalities were Rash Behari Bose, Madam Cama, Abdul Rehman, Raja Mahendra Pratap, Hardayal Sohan Singh Baghna and others. Many Sikhs were members. The Party had planned to send a shipload of arms to Punjab where some regiments were to revolt on 21st February 1916. However, the secret leaked out. The Regiments were disbanded and the ship was impounded.

Home Rule Movement (1916): Home Rule Movement was started by Mrs.Annie Besant in Chennai on July 1916 to secure home rule for the Indians. The movement vanished when Lord Montague, Secretary of State for India made his August Declaration in 1917 promising self-government in stages for India.

Lucknow Pact (1916): As a result of stronger growth of nationalism among the Indians during the First World War, the Congress and the Muslim League came closer to a pact known as Lucknow Pact in 1916. Their joint demand that a majority of the members of the Legislative Council be elected, that atleast half of the Viceroy's Council be filled with Indians and that more powers be given to the Legislative Council. Congress and League unitedly made plea for Swaraj. But the spirit was short-lived and both were kept separate.

August Declaration (1917): India rendered a great help to the Allies in the First World War. Hence in order to satisfy the demand of self-government, the British Government made an important declaration on 10th August, 1917 which stated that control over the Indian government would be gradually transferred to the Indian people and a responsible government would be set up gradually.

Montague-Chelmsford Reforms (1919): Following the August declaration, Mr.Edwin Montague, the then Secretary of State, paid a visit to India to have first hand information and he stayed in India for five months. Along with the then Viceroy Lord Chelmsford, he drew up a report called **Montague-Chelmsford report.** On the basis of this report was born the famous Montague-Chelmsford Reforms which introduced several reforms.

This act set up a bicameral legislature in New Delhi in the place of Imperial Legislative Council. A system of direct elections was introduced but franchise remained restricted. The law-making power of the central legislature was increased. The size of the provincial councils was enlarged. It introduced dyarchy in the provinces. Dyarchy meant sub-division of subjects in the state list into (i) reserved subjects to be dealt with by the Governor and his nominees and (ii) transferred subjects to be dealt with by the Governor and his ministers. However, the nationalists were not satisfied with the reforms.

Rowlatt Act (1919): In 1918, the Government appointed a Sedition Committee with Mr.Justice Rowlatt as its Chairman to study the nature and extent of the revolutionary movement in India and to suggest how to deal with it. On the basis of his recommendation, Rowlatt Act was passed in 1919. This Act gave extraordinary powers to the Government in dealing with the terrorists. According to the Act, the Government could detain the people in prison for an indefinite period without trial.

Jallianwalabagh Tragedy (1919): There was agitation against the Rowlatt Act. Intolerance of the British Government reached its height when General Dyer fired on unarmed peaceful gathering of protesters met on 13th April, 1919, the Baisakhi day. After this incident, martial law was declared in many parts of Punjab.

Satyagraha (1919) : To nullify the effect of the Rowlatt Act, Mahatma Gandhi launched his Satyagraha Movement to offer passive and peaceful resistance to the cruel and unjust laws so that the Government might be obliged to repeal the law. The Satyagraha Day was observed on Sunday, the 16th April, 1919, throughout India.

The period between 1919 and 1947 can rightly be called the GANDHIAN ERA of our National Movement. The end of this period saw the dawn of Independence.

Non-violent Non-cooperation Movement (1920-22): The ghastly events in Punjab in 1919 made Mahatma Gandhi launch the All India Non-violent Non-Cooperation Movement on 1st August 1920. This was the first important step in the Freedom Movement. This movement was not confined to the elite section but involved all the villagers. The Government decided to deal with the situation with an iron hand. About 30,000 people were imprisoned but the people stood undaunted and undivided.

The Khilafat Movement (1920) : After the First World War, the British Government imposed harsh terms on Turkey. The people looked upon the head of Turkey as the Khalifa or their religious head. The Muslims under the leadership of Ali Brothers, Maulana Mohammed Ali and Shaukat Ali started what is known as Khilafat Movement and the Congress adopted it as a part of the Non-Cooperation Movement. The Muslims actively participated in the movement and it became a popular movement. However, the office of Khalifa was abolished in Turkey itself and Turkey succeeded in securing much better terms. The Khilafat Movement thus withered away.

Chauri Chaura Incident (1922) : The Non-Cooperation Movement was at its height when Lord Reading arrived in India as Viceroy. Though this Movement was non-violent in character at some places the mob indulged in violence. At Chauri Chaura, processionists were infuriated and set fire to a police post and burnt 22 policemen to death on Feb. 5, 1922. Shocked at this incident, Gandhiji withdrew the non-cooperation struggle. Later on Gandhi himself called this step 'a Himalayan mistake'. Taking advantage of this move, Lord Reading arrested Gandhiji and other leaders. At the same time, the terms settled with Khalifa were considerably modified. Hence the cooperation from the Muslims was not forthcoming as before. A rift was created between the Hindus and the Muslims. It culminated in the partition of India.

The Swarajist Party (1923) : It dominated the scene from 1923 to 1925. The party believed in attaining Swaraj by putting obstacles on the way of Government. Its leaders were C.R.Das, Pt. Motilal Nehru and others. The party was well-known for its walkouts from legislatures. The party weakened after the death of C.R.Das in 1925.

Anti-Imperialist League (1927) : It was formed at Brussels in 1927 at the Congress of the Oppressed Nationalists. Its aim was to campaign for ending of Imperialism everywhere in the world. The conference was attended by Albert Einstein, Romain Rolland, Jawaharlal Nehru, etc. Indian National Congress was affiliated to it.

Simon Commission (1928) : The 1919 Act laid down after ten years a Commission would visit India to assess how far the 1919 reforms had been successful and what further reforms should be granted. However, the Indians pressed for reforms even earlier than 1929. Hence the Simon Commission visited India in February, 1928. The Commission was headed by Sir John Simon, a brilliant lawyer from England. All the seven members of the Commission were British. Hence the slogan 'Simon go back'. Wherever the Commission went, it was greeted by black flags. Lala Lajpat Rai was beaten up mercilessly when he was leading a demonstration at Lahore Railway Station and as a result he died on 30th October 1928. Exactly, one month after, the police officer, Saunders, who beat Lalaji, was shot dead in England by Sardar Bhagat Singh.

Nehru Report (1928) : The All Parties Conference met at Calcutta in 1928. It appointed a committee under the chairmanship of Motilal Nehru to draft a Constitution for India. It recommended that India should be a secular state. There should be joint electorates for minorities in accordance with population with the right to contest additional seats. It recommended Dominion Status to India. Jinnah rejected this report.

Meerut Conspiracy Case (1929) : About 32 labour leaders including three Britishers were arrested and tried at Meerut for conspiracy to overthrow the British Government. Many were sentenced to long imprisonment. This case came to be known as Meerut Conspiracy case.

Lahore Conspiracy Case (1929) : Bhaghat Singh and B.K.Dutt, two revolutionaries threw a bomb into the Central Legislative Assembly. Along with them a number of revolutionaries of Hindustan Republican Socialist Association were also arrested. Bhaghat Singh, Rajguru and Sukh Dev were sentenced to death for having killed the Superintendent of Police of Lahore. Many were sentenced to long imprisonment. This is known as the Lahore Conspiracy Case.

Poorna Swaraj Day (1930) : On the midnight of 31st December 1929, under the Presidentship of Jawaharlal Nehru, the Indian National Congress adopted a resolution to achieve complete independence. It was decided to celebrate 26th January 1930 as the Independence day. This day marked the beginning of a new spirit. To commemorate this day, India's Republic day is celebrated on 26th January since 1950.

Civil Disobedience (1930) : On 12th March 1930, Gandhiji undertook Dandi March from Sabarmati Ashram (Ahmedabad) to break salt law. He reached Dandi, a small village on Gujarat coast on 6th April 1930 after traversing 385 kms. with 78 followers. He broke the salt law by picking up a lump of natural salt. Mahatma was imprisoned. This movement gathered strength and within a month about one lakh people were sent to jail. This violation of salt law was the second great step in India's Freedom Movement.

First Round Table Conference (1930) : Dissatisfaction of Indian people over the Simon Commission Report was understood by the British. Hence the British Government called a Round Table Conference in London in November, 1930 to draw up a Constitution for India. Representatives from British India and Indian States participated. No one participated from the Congress, as the Civil Disobedience Movement was in full swing. The recommendations of the Conference were not found satisfactory.

Gandhi-Irwin Pact (1931) : Gandhi and Lord Irwin entered into a Pact known as Gandhi-Irwin Pact or Delhi Pact on 5th March 1931 in New Delhi to withdraw the Civil Disobedience Movement. Irwin released all the political prisoners and the salt laws were so amended that the people could collect salt from the seacoast for personal use. Gandhiji agreed to take part in the Second Round Table Conference.

Second Round Table Conference (1931) : Second Round Table Conference took place in September 1931 and lasted for three months. Gandhiji was the sole representative of the Congress party. The Conference promised partly responsible Government at the centre. No answer was found for communal problems. It was left to the discretion of Mr.Ramsay McDonald, the then Prime Minister of England.

Arrest of Mahatma Gandhi (1932) : Dissatisfied at the result of the Second Round Table Conference, Gandhiji on return to India in 1932, found British government on repressive ladder. Hence he started his Civil Disobedience Movement. Over a lakh of people were arrested and sent to jail. The Congress was declared illegal. However, this campaign came to an end in 1934 when the Congress decided to consider the new reforms proposed by the Government.

Communal Award (1932) : Mr.Ramsay McDonald came out with his 'Communal Award' on 6th August 1932 to fix seats for the various communities in the provincial legislatures. Separate electorates were decided and depressed classes were given separate representation. The Muslims received more than they demanded. The Hindus and the Sikhs were dissatisfied. The Award tried to weaken the national unity.

Poona Pact (1932) : The Communal Award gave separate representation for the depressed class. Mahatma Gandhi, who was in Yeravada Jail in Poona saw the motive to divide the Hindus by this Award. Hence he went on a fast unto death on 20th September 1931. The leaders of the depressed classes came to an understanding and a partially joint electorate was accepted. Gandhiji broke his fast on 26th September. The British also accepted to amend the Communal Award accordingly. Gandhiji came out of the jail and devoted himself towards the upliftment of Harijans.

Third Round Table Conference (1932) : The Third Round Table Conference was held in November 1932 and lasted for five weeks. Deliberations were held on the Indian Constitution. It was proposed among other things that there should be All India Federation comprising British India and Indian States. The proposals of this conference were published in a white paper.

The Government of India Act of 1935: The British Parliament passed a new Act which was to come into force from 1st April 1937. The Act proposed an (a) All India Federation consisting of British India and Indian states; (b) Dyarchy at centre; and (c) Autonomy in provinces. But the special provisions given to the Governor-General and the provincial Governors under this Act deflated its very purpose.

Congress and Government of India Act-1935: When the Act came into force on 1st April 1937, the provincial autonomy was established but the federation never came. Elections were held under this Act. Congress came to power in eight out of eleven provinces. The Congress declined to include Non-Congress Muslims in their Ministries. This enraged Mr. Jinnah. The work done by the Congress Ministries was commendable. But after a little over two years, the year 1939 saw the outbreak of Second World War. The Viceroy without consulting the Central Legislature involved India in the war with Germany. All the Congress Ministries resigned as a protest in October 1939 and the governors assumed the administration of those provinces. This led to a deadlock until 1947.

The Day of Deliverance or Thanks-giving Day (1939) : Mr.Jinnah declared that the Indian Muslims could not expect any justice at the hands of Congress Ministries. He charged the ministries with atrocities committed on the Muslims. Thus the Muslims celebrated 'The Day of Deliverance' or 'Thanksgiving Day' on Friday, 22nd December 1939, when the Congress Ministry resigned.

Demand for Pakistan (1940) : In his Presidential address at the Lahore session of the Muslim League, Mr.Jinnah stressed that the Muslims could no longer tolerate the Hindu rule and thus he gave rise to the 'Two Nation Theory' on 22nd March 1940. A resolution was passed demanding that provinces with Muslim majority should be created as a separate Sovereign State called Pakistan.

Cripps Mission (1942) : On 7th December, Japan declared war on Britain and America. Her initial victories baffled political pandits in Britain. Hence, in order to get the support of the Indian people, Sir Stafford Cripps, a distinguished member of the British Cabinet visited India to have consultations with the Congress and Muslim League. He promised the Indians the right to draw up the Constitution and Dominion Status. There was no proposal for immediate transfer of power. Gandhiji called this offer a 'post dated cheque on a crashing bank'. Both Congress and Muslim League were dissatisfied though on different grounds.

Quit India Resolution (1942) : On 8th August 1942, the Congress Committee passed the Quit India Resolution. Immediately Gandhiji and Congress Working Committee members were arrested. The Congress was banned and the Police took possession of all the offices of the Congress. There were violent riots. Official machinery broke down. Mr. Jinnah took this Quit India Movement differently. He viewed that this movement was not only to drive away the British but to subjugate the Muslims as well. The Muslim League started raising the slogan of division of India.

Indian National Army (1942) : The two inseparable names in the history of Indian Independence struggle are Netaji Subash Chandra Bose and Indian National Army. For his patriotic activities, Netaji was interned in his house at Calcutta. Towards the end of January 1941, he mysteriously disappeared from the house. In 1942, he managed to reach Burma which had been occupied by Japan by that time. The Japanese had captured a large number of Indian soldiers as prisoners of war. Out of these men, he formed the INA (Azad Hind Fauj) in 1943 in Singapore and gave the slogan **'Jai Hind'**. After the British recaptured Burma, many INA soldiers were brought as prisoners to India. Some of them were prosecuted. The Congress supported the cause of the INA officers. Netaji is believed to have died in an air accident. Of late Khosla Commission was appointed to enquire into the last days of Netaji. The commission was much alive until 1972. But no concrete results emerged.

C.R. Formula (1944): C. Rajagopalachari, realizing the necessity of a settlement between Congress and Muslim League for the attainment of

Independence by India evolved this formula. The contents were the Muslim League should co-operate with Congress in the formation by Provisional Interim Government. After the end of war, a Commission shall be appointed to demarcate boundaries of Muslims dominated north-west and east parts of India. In the event of separation, mutual agreement should be signed between two Government's for jointly safeguarding defence, commerce, communication etc.

End of Second World War (1945) : In May 1945, the war came to an end. The Congress leaders were released and a political amnesty was declared. But no concrete move was made or declaration announced towards transfer of power.

Wavell Plan (1945): After the failure of Gandhi-Jinnah talks based on C.R. Formula, Lord Wavell offered new plans to end the Constitutional deadlock. His plans proposed to leave the Executive Council completely incharge of the Indians, excepting commander-in-chief and to give equal representation to Muslims and Hindus in the Council. This was to be an interim arrangement till a new Constitution was drafted for India.

Parliamentary Delegation (1946) : The Labour Party came to power in England with Mr. Clement Attlee as the Prime Minister. It raised hopes of Indian Independence. A Parliament Delegation consisting of leaders of various parties of England arrived in India in January 1946 to interview leaders of various parties and to make recommendations on the framing of the Constitution of India. The Delegation toured India returned to England in February 1946 and favoured Independence to India at the earliest.

Cabinet Mission (1946) : A Cabinet Mission consisting of three Cabinet Ministers - Lord Pethic Lawrence, the then Secretary of State for India, Sir Stafford Cripps and Mr. A.V.Alexander, arrived in India in March 1946 to help India achieve its Independence and prepare the Constitution for India. In May 1946, the mission convened a conference at Simla consisting of our representatives of Congress and Muslim League. The conference lasted for a week but unanimity was absent.

Elections to Constituent Assembly (1946) : In the elections to Constituent Assembly in July, 1946, Congress won most of the seats. Muslim League got enraged at this and decided to achieve Pakistan by direct action.

Direct Action Day (1946) : The Muslim League observed 16th August 1946 as direct action day at Calcutta. The Muslim League ministry of Bengal declared this day a public holiday. Calcutta went through a blood bath that day.

Interim Government (1946) : On 2nd September 1946, an Interim Government was set up at the Centre with Pt. Jawaharlal Nehru as the Vice-President (Prime Minister). At the first instance, the Muslim League refused to join the ministry. Later five of its representatives joined. However, both the Congress and the Muslim League could not get along.

Meeting of the Constituent Assembly (1946) : The Constituent Assembly first met on 9th December 1946 to draw up the Constitution for India.

Dr.Rajendra Prasad was its president and Dr.Ambedkar was chairman of the Drafting committee. However, the Muslim League kept aloof.

Declaration of 20th February, 1947: Mr.Clement Attlee made a declaration on 20th February 1947 that the power would be transferred to the Indians by June 1948, and Lord Mountbatten would succeed Lord Wavell to accomplish this task. There was a hint that demand for Pakistan would be conceded if made. Mountbatten arrived at Delhi in March 1947.

Indian Independence Act, 1947: As there were disturbances in Punjab and Bengal for Partition, there was no other alternative than conceding the demand. Thus India was partitioned into Indian dominion and Pakistan dominion on 15th August 1947. The princely states were left free either to join with India or with Pakistan or to remain independent taking into account the geographical location and religion. Thus India became independent on 15th August 1947.

WORLD WARS

WORLD WAR I (1914-1918)

After the dismissal of Bismarck, the young, Kaiser William II of Germany wanted to dominate the Atlantic nations and expand to the East. His policy was known as Drang nach Osten. He had to face his rivals–the Triple Etente, formed by Britain, France and Russia. The ambition of Germany was to have her 'Place in the Sun'. To achieve this purpose, Germany acquired a dominating influence in Turkey and supported the Balkan policy of Austria.

The Arch Duke Ferdinand, the Austrian heir apparent to the throne was murdered in the street of Sarajevo, the capital of Bosnia which was under the control of Austria. Austria made Serbia responsible for this crime and denounced Serbians as the 'Nation of Assassins'. After one month of this incident, Austria served an ultimatum and was ready for war. This brought Russia into the field as it felt kinship with Slavic people. Russia's entry brought Germany to the side of Austria. One by one France and England entered the war. Thus one was Central powers comprising Germany, Austria, Hungary, Turkey and Bulgaria and the other was the Allied powers consisting of England, France, Belgium, Serbia, Russia and Japan. Italy and U.S.A. joined the allied powers latter in 1915 and 1916 respectively.

The Central powers were completely defeated and an Armistice was signed on 11th November 1918, followed by a peace conference at Paris and the Treaty of Versailles in 1919, the principal Treaty, curbing the power of the German Empire.

According to this Treaty, boundaries of European countries were rearranged and many new states Czechoslovakia, Yugoslavia, Poland etc. were formed. The League of Nations came into existence on 10th January 1920 to prevent future wars.

WORLD WAR II (1939 - 1945)

The Treaty of Versailles itself was the reason for World War II. It was an unjust Treaty. The Allied powers sought territorial and economic benefits. The discontented Germany, during the recession brought a determined man to the power to free it from the shackles of the Versailles Treaty.

Adolf Hitler became the Chancellor of Germany in 1933. He joined with Mussolini, the Fascist leader of Italy to tear away the Treaty of Versailles. Hitler's first step towards the breaking of the Treaty of Versailles was occupation of Sarr, Alsace-Loraine, Sudetenland and Czechoslovakia. Mussolini attacked Abyssinia and Japan attacked China. These acts alarmed Britain and France. The more shocking event was the formation of an Axis providing for mutual aid in the international sphere.

Hitler demanded from Poland a corridor to establish a direct link with East Prussia. Britain and France guaranteed aid to Poland in the event of any aggression and they started friendly negotiations with Russia. Britain's negotiations with Russia failed. Taking advantage of this, Hitler signed a Non-Aggression Pact with Russia. With the hope that Britain would not help Poland, Hitler attacked Poland on 1st September, 1939 and this started the World War II. Britain and France under treaty obligations declared war against Germany on 3rd September 1939.

Germany, Italy and Japan - the Axis powers were on one side and Britain, France, Russia, U.S.A., Poland and others - the allies were on the other side. The World War II came to an end after two nuclear bombs were dropped on Japan. The war actually ended on 14th August 1945.

The damage caused by the World War II was widespread and so complex that no formal Peace Conference could be held immediately after the war. The conferences that took place at Cairo, Teheran, Yalta and Potsdam saw only disagreements among the victorious powers. Germany was divided into four zones each under the occupation of one great power. Ultimately Germany was divided into two states - East Germany and West Germany - the former under the control of Soviet Union and the latter under the Allies. In the post war period the emergence of U.S.S.R. as one of the biggest powers is noteworthy.

In order to avoid future wars on global scale, United Nations Organisation was established in 1945.

IMPORTANT INTERNATIONAL EVENTS AND MOVEMENTS

Bill of Rights: Passed by the British Parliament in 1689, it gave the rights and the liberties of the British subjects. It settled the question of succession to the British crown. It brought the British monarchy on Constitutional basis. The Bill of Rights was a stepping stone in the British Constitutional system.

French Revolution 1789: It proved 'Pen is mightier than the Sword'. The revolutionary teachings by Rousseau, Voltaire, Montesquieu about Liberty, Equality and Fraternity brought down the despotic rule of Louis XVII who was executed in 1793. The French monarch enjoyed luxuries at the expense of the poor people. The revolution put an end to this. Napoleon emerged as the Emperor of France.

Glorious Revolution in England: It was a bloodless revolution and it had far-reaching consequences. This revolution ended the despotic rule of the Stuarts in England and reduced the Monarchy into nothing but a crowned Presidency.

Industrial Revolution in England: Mechanisation of British industry in the second half of the eighteenth century is known as Industrial Revolution. Steam Engine was invented.

Magna Carta - 1215 A.D.: Signed by King John II in 1215 A.D., it gave way for transfer of the powers thereto held by the King of England to the Parliament. It warranted definite laws for Englishmen and not by whims and fancies of Kings and Queens. It laid a foundation stone for the liberty of the English people.

Russian Revolution of 1917: A full-scale nation-wide revolt took place against the oppressive rule of Czar Nicholas. The Army and the Police refused to obey the orders of Czar. The participation of agricultural workers led by Industrial workers resulted in the government of Bolsheviks. Lenin was the Revolutionary figure.

UPPER ECHELON OF INDIAN GOVERNMENT

PRESIDENTS OF INDIA

1950-1962	-	Rajendra Prasad
1962-1967	-	S. Radhakrishnan
1967-1969	-	Zakir Hussain
1969-1974	-	V.V. Giri
1974-1977	-	Fakhruddin Ali Ahmed
1977-1982	-	N. Sanjiva Reddy
1982-1987	-	Gyani Zail Singh
1987-1992	-	R. Venkataraman
1992-1997	-	Dr. Shanker Dayal Sharma
1997-2002	-	K.R. Narayanan
2002-2007	-	Dr. A.P.J. Abdul Kalam
2007	-	Mrs. Prathiba Patil

VICE-PRESIDENTS OF INDIA

1952-1962	-	S. Radhakrishnan
1962-1967	-	Zakir Hussain
1967-1969	-	V.V. Giri
1969-1974	-	G.S. Pathak
1974-1979	-	B.D. Jatti
1979-1984	-	Md. Hidayatullah
1984-1987	-	R. Venkataraman
1987-1992	-	Dr. S.D. Sharma
1992-1997	-	K.R. Narayanan
1997-2002	-	Krishan Kanth

2002-2007	-	Bhairon Singh Shekawath
2007	-	Mohammad Hamid Anzari

PRIME MINISTERS OF INDIA

August 15, 1947	- May 27, 1964	- Jawaharlal Nehru
May 27, 1964	- June 9, 1964	- Gulzari Lal Nanda (Acting)
June 9, 1964	- January 11, 1966	- Lal Bahadur Shastri
January 11, 1966	- January 24, 1966	- Gulzari Lal Nanda (Acting)
January 24, 1966	- March 24, 1977	- Indira Gandhi
March 24, 1977	- July 28, 1979	- Morarji Desai
July 28, 1979	- January 14, 1980	- Charan Singh
January 14, 1980	- October 31, 1984	- Indira Gandhi
October 31, 1984	- December 1, 1989	- Rajiv Gandhi
December 2, 1989	- November 10, 1990	- V.P. Singh
November 11, 1990	- June 21, 1991	- Chandra Shekhar
June 21, 1991	- May 16, 1996	- P.V. Narasimha Rao
May 16, 1996	- June 1, 1996	- Atal Behari Vajpayee
June 1, 1996	- April 21, 1997	- H.D. Deve Gowda
April 21, 1997	- March 18, 1998	- I.K. Gujral
March 19, 1998	- Oct. 12, 1999	- Atal Behari Vajpayee
Oct. 13, 1999	- May 21, 2004	- Atal Behari Vajpayee
May 22, 2004	-	- Dr. Manmohan Singh

HISTORICAL DATES AND EVENTS

B.C.

6000	- Neolithic settlements at Mehrgarh, Baluchistan and in the Indus Valley
5000	- First Pharaoh's rules in Egypt
	- Development of farming in the Indus Valley
3102 or 2449	- Epoch of the Kaliyuga Era and of the Bharata War
3000	- Building of the Great Pyramid
2500	- Early Chinese civilisation
2000	- The rule of Abraham and Isaac
	- Aryan settlements in India
	- Vedic civilization takes shape
	- The composition of the Rig Veda
1900	- Aryans invade India
3000-1500	- Indus Valley Civilization
1000	- Egypt ceases to be a power; Epic civilization in India
776	- First Olympiad in Greece
599	- Birth of Mahavira
590	- Jews captive in Babylon
563	- Birth of Buddha

544	- Buddha's Nirvana
527	- Mahavira's Nirvana
509	- Foundation of the Roman Republic
487	- Death of Buddha in India
480	- Battle at Thermopylae; Persians defeated Greeks
	- Battle at Salamis; Greeks defeated Persians
461	- Pericles comes to power in Athens
430	- War between Athens and Sparta
404	- Beginning of Spartan supremacy in Greece
399	- Execution of Socrates
360	- The time of Plato and Aristotle
356	- Birth of Alexander the Great
347	- Death of Plato
338	- Philip II of Macedon defeats the Greek city states and becomes supreme in Greece
336	- Alexander becomes the King of Macedonia
334	- Battle of Granicus
	- Alexander's first victory over the Persians
333	- Battle of Issus
	- Alexander's second victory over Darius of Persia
332	- Alexander captures Tyre and occupies Egypt
331	- Alexander finally defeats Persians
326	- Alexander defeats Porus of India and conquers the Punjab
323	- Death of Alexander at Babylon (near Baghdad)
	- Ptolemy I founds dynasty in Egypt
	- Alexandria (in Egypt) becomes the intellectual centre of the world
321	- Chandragupta Maurya establishes the Mauryan Dynasty in India
	- Death of Aristotle
312	- Seleucus I founds dynasty in Asia
275	- Battle of Beneventum
274	- Asoka becomes Emperor of India
261	- Asoka's conquest of Kalinga
214	- The construction of the Great Wall of China
212	- Archimedes killed
185	- Pushyamitra defeated pragathirtha of mauryan king
145	- Chola King Elara conquered Ceylon
	- Kharavela builds Kalinga Empire
80	- Romans conquer Gaul (France)
63	- Romans conquer Jerusalem
58	- Caesar begins conquest of Gaul
	- Beginning of Vikrama Era
55	- Caesar's conquest of Britain
48	- Caesar defeats Pompey

46	– Caesar reforms the calendar, later known as the Julian Calendar
44	– Murder of Julius Caesar
27	– Roman Senate confers the title of Augustus on Octavian
	– Octavian becomes Caesar Augustus
26 - 20	– Indian Ambassador sent to Augustus
4	– Birth of Jesus Christ
A.D	
15	– Beginning of Kushan Dynasty under Kadphises I
29	– Crucifixion of Jesus Christ
34	– Roman Conquest of Britain
78	– Accession of Kanishka, Beginning of Saka Era (our Indian Government uses Saka Calendar)
80	– Completion of the Roman Colosseum
360	– A Ceylonese embassy comes to the court of Samudragupta
375	– Invasion of Europe by Huns
380	– Accession of Vikramaditya
399 - 411	– Fahien's Travel
410	– Alaric the Goth captures and destroys Rome. This is taken to be the end of the Roman Empire
415	– Accession of Kumara Gupta-I
454	– First Hun invasion
455	– Accession of Skanda Gupta
570	– Birth of Prophet Mohammed
600	– The decline of Roman Empire
609	– Coronation of Pulakesin-II
612	– Mohammed proclaims the religion Islam
622	– Hijira or flight of Mohammed from Mecca to Medina
	– Beginning of the Mohammedan era
629 - 646	– Hiuen Tsang's Travel
630 - 644	– Reign of Harsha
632	– Death of Mohammed
	– Accession of Abu Baker
641	– Harsha's embassy to China
643	– Harsha's meeting with Hiuen Tsang
712	– Arab Mohd.Bin Qasim conquest Sind from Dahir
715	– Arab empire at the height
735	– First Parsi settlement
750	– Arab empire ends
	– Beginning of Abbasid Caliphate
760-1142	– Palas of Bengal and Bihar
786	– Accession of Haroun-al-Rashid in Baghdad
820	– Death of Sankaracharya
836	– Accession of King Bhoja of Kanauj
960 - 1200	– Chandellas of Bundelkhand
985	– Accession of Raja Raja Chola, the Great

1000 - 1026	- Mohd. Ghazni's attack
1012 - 24	- Reign of Rajendra Chola
1025 - 26	- Destruction of Somnath Temple by Mohd. Ghazni
1066	- Norman Conquest of England - Battle of Hastings
	- William-I, Duke of Normandy, conquers England
1191	- First Battle of Terrain
1192	- Second Battle of Terrain
1206	- Accession of Qutub-ud-din Aibak to the throne of Delhi
	- Chengiz Khan becomes King of the Mongols and overruns Central Asia
1210	- Death of Qutub-ud-din Aibak
1215	- Signing of Magna Carta by King John II
1221	- First Mongol Chengiz Khan invade in India during the period of Iltumish
1231 - 32	- Qutub Minar built
1236 - 40	- Reign of Razia Sultana in Delhi
1260	- Kublai Khan rules in China
1320 - 1414	- Reign of Tughlak Sultans of Delhi
1336	- Vijayanagar Empire was founded by Harihara and Bukkha
1338	- Beginning of the Hundred Years' War between England and France
1347	- Bahmani Kingdom was founded
1351	- Accession of Firoz Shah
1363	- Timur (Tamerlane) begins his career of conquest in Asia
1381	- Peasants' Revolt in England
1398	- Invasion of Timur Lang in India during the period of Mohd. Shah
1451-1526	- Reign of Lodi Sultans of Delhi
1453	- End of the Hundred years' war
1469	- Birth of Guru Nanak
1488	- Bartholomeo Diaz rounds Cape of Good Hope
1492	- Christopher Columbus discovers West Indies
1494	- Foundation of Agra by Sikandar Lodi
	- Accession of Babur in Fargana
1497	- John Cabot discovers Newfoundland
1498	- Vasco da Gama reached Calicut via Cape of Good Hope
1499	- Amerigo Vespucci charts part of the South American Coast
1509	- Accession of Krishnadeva Raya
1509-27	- Reign of Rana Sanga in Mewar
1510	- Portuguese Viceroy Albuquerque captured Goa from Bijapur dynasty
1517	- Martin Luther begins the Reformation
1522	- First voyage round the world by Magellan of Spain
1526	- First Battle of Panipat
	- Babur founds Moghul Empire in India
1527	- Battle of Khanua (Babar defeated Rana Sanga)

1534	- Act of Supremacy
1539-45	- Reign of Sher Shah
1540	- Battle of Kannoj (Shershah Suri defeated Humayun)
1542	- Birth of Akbar at Amarkot
1556	- Second Battle of Panipat
	- Akbar becomes Moghul Emperor
1557	- Macao becomes a permanent Portuguese port in China
1558	- Elizabeth I becomes Queen of England
1556-1605	- Reign of Akbar
1562	- Akbar marries a Rajput princess Amba
1564	- Abolition of Jizya tax
1565	- Battle of Talikota
1571	- Foundation of Fatehpur Sikri
1576	- Battle of Haldighat
	- Akbar defeats Rana Pratap
1582	- Pope Gregory XIII introduces (New style) Gregorian Calendar
1591	- Death of Rana Pratap
1600	- Foundation of East India Company
1602	- Dutch East India Company founded
1605	- Death of Akbar
1605-1627	- Reign of Jahangir
1606	- Execution of Guru Arjan Dev
1611	- Jahangir marries Nur Jahan
	- Publication of the authorised version of the English Bible
1612	- First English Factory at Surat
1616	- Sir Thomas Roe visits Jahangir
1620	- Pilgrim Fathers settle in New England
1627	- Birth of Shivaji
1628	- Shah Jahan becomes Emperor
1631	- Death of Mumtaz
1648	- Taj Mahal completed by Shah Jahan
1649	- King Charles I of England executed
	- Cromwell becomes Protector of England
1657	- War of succession among sons of Shah Jahan
1658	- Battle of Dhasmat
1659	- Battle of Samugarh, Aurangzeb's accession to the throne
1659-1707	- Reign of Aurangzeb
1660	- The restoration of British Monarchy
	- Charles II founds the Royal Society
1664	- Shivaji crowns himself
1666	- Shivaji's visit to the Mughal Court at Agra
1668	- Death of Shah Jahan
	- 1st French factory set up at Surat
1674	- Assumption of Royal title by Shivaji

1675	- Execution of Tej Behadur
1680	- Death of Shivaji
1686-87	- Fall of the Kingdoms of Bijapur and Golconda
1688	- Bloodless or Glorious Revolution in England
	- James II abdicates the British throne
1689	- Establishment of British Constitutional Monarchy
1694	- Founding of the Bank of England
1696	- Peter the Great becomes Czar of Russia
1707	- Death of Aurangzeb
1708	- Death of Guru Gobind Singh
1717	- Battle of Kirkee
1721	- Robert Walpole becomes the first Prime Minister of England
1739	- Nadir Shah of Persia sacks Delhi
1740	- Frederick the Great becomes King of Prussia
1751	- Clive takes and holds Arcot in India and checks French advance
	- Chinese conquest of Tibet
1757	- Battle of Plassey (June 23)
	- Dawn of British rule in India
	- Clive conquers Bengal
1760	- Battle of Wandiwash
	- The English defeat the French in India
1761	- Third Battle of Panipat
1764	- Battle of Buxar
1765	- Grant of Diwani of Bengal, Bihar and Orissa by Mughal Emperor Shah Alam to the East India Company
1770	- Famine in Bengal
1772	- Warren Hastings was appointed First Governor General of British India
	- Boston Tea Party
1773	- The Regulating Act
1774	- Birth of Raja Ram Mohan Roy
1776	- Treaty of Purandar
	- Declaration of American Independence (July 4)
1780	- Birth of Maharaja Ranjit Singh
1781	- First Newspaper published by James Hickey (Bengal Gazette) on January 29
1784	- Pitt's India Act passed
1785	- Resignation of Warren Hastings
1789	- French Revolution begins
	- Storming of the Bastille (July 14)
	- George Washington becomes the first President of USA
1790	- Third Mysore War
1793	- Permanent Settlement of Bengal by Lord Cornwallis
1799	- Fourth Mysore war, Death of Tipu Sultan

1802	- Treaty of Bassein
1804	- Napoleon becomes Emperor in France
1805	- Battle of Trafalgar and Nelson's death
1807	- Napoleon controls all Europe
1809	- Treaty of Amritsar
1815	- Battle of Waterloo
	- The Vienna Settlement
	- Napoleon sent to St. Helena
1818	- Third Maratha War
	- Peshwa was defeated
1823	- U.S. President announces "Monroe Doctrine"
1828	- Brahmo Samaj was founded by Raja Ram Mohan Roy
1829	- Prohibition of Sati
1830	- Raja Ram Mohan Roy visited England
1832	- First Reform Bill in England
1833	- Death of Raja Ram Mohan Roy
1835	- Introduction of English as medium of instruction by Lord Macaulay
1837	- Queen Victoria succeeded to the throne
1839	- Death of Maharaja Ranjit Singh
1851	- Submarine telegraph cable between Dover and Calais
1852	- First postage stamp released (Oct. 1)
1853	- Opening of first railway line in India between Bombay and Thana (April 16)
	- The first telegraphic communication during the period of Lord Dalhousie
1856	- Birth of Bal Gangadhar Tilak (July 26)
	- Introduction of Hindu widow marriage
1857	- First war of Indian Independence (May 10)
1858	- British Crown assumes power in India
	- East Indian Company rule ended
1861	- Indian Councils Act
	- Birth of Rabindranath Tagore
	- Abraham Lincoln becomes President of the United States
	- American Civil War
1863	- Slavery abolished in the U.S. by Lincoln's Proclamation
	- Birth of Swami Vivekananda
1864	- Establishment of Red Cross Society in Geneva
1865	- Assassination of Lincoln
1869	- Birth of Mahatma Gandhi (2nd Oct.)
	- Suez Canal opened for traffic
1874	- Great Famine of Bengal
1875	- Arya Samaj founded by Dayananda Saraswathi
1876-77	- Delhi Darbar

1878	- Treaty of Berlin
1879	- C.Rajagopalachari born (7th Dec.)
1884	- Birth of Dr.Rajendra Prasad (3rd Dec.)
1885	- Indian National Congress was founded (29th Dec.) in Bombay
1889	- Birth of Jawaharlal Nehru (14th Nov.)
1892	- Indian Councils Act
1895	- Discovery of X-Ray
1896	- Invention of Wireless
1899 - 1901	- Boer War
1900	- Australian Commonwealth proclaimed
1901	- Queen Victoria dies (Jan. 22)
	- Russia and Britain agree on the partition of China
1902	- Death of Swami Vivekananda (July 4)
1905	- First partition of Bengal under Lord Curzon
1906	- Foundation of Muslim League
1909	- Minto-Morley Reforms
1910	- Mother Teresa born in Albania as Agnes Ganxha Bojaxhiu
1911	- Partition of Bengal revoked
	- Delhi becomes the capital
	- King George V crowned "King of the United Kingdom and Emperor of India"
	- King George V and Queen Mary the first ever British King and Queen land in Bombay
1912	- Establishment of Chinese Republic
	- Titanic, world's biggest ship, sinks in North Atlantic, killing 1513 people
	- The 5th Olympic Games open in Stockholm
1913	- Mohandas K. Gandhi arrested in Johannesburg
	- Nobel Prize awarded to Rabindranath Tagore for "Gitanjali" - first Asian
1914	- World War I declared (28th July)
1915	- Death of Gopala Krishna Gokhale
1918	- End of the World War I (11th Nov.)
	- Women vote for first time in UK election
1919	- Montague-Chelmsford Reforms
	- Jallianwala Bagh massacre (13th April)
	- Satyagraha Movement (16th April)
	- Treaty of Versailles
1920	- Non-cooperation Movement in India
	- Khilafat Movement
	- Foundation of League of Nations by Woodro Wilson
	- The seventh modern Olympic Games inaugurated at Antwerp
1921	- Congress Party to boycott foreign cloth and visit of the Prince of Wales to India

1922	- Chauri-Chaura incident un U.P. on Feb. 5
	- Gandhi arrested for the first time in India
1923	- Republic proclaimed in Turkey
	- Indian National Congress agrees to launch a civil disobedience campaign
	- Swarajya party was formed by C.R. Das and Motilal Nehru
1924	- Death of Lenin
1925	- Death of C.R.Das
1926	- Women are allowed to stand for election to public office in India
1927	- Broadcasting starts in India
	- Simon Commission set up
1928	- Death of Lala Lajpat Rai
	- Olympics open in St.Moritz, Switzerland
	- India wins an Olympic gold medal in hockey
1929	- Resolution of complete Independence passed at Lahore Congress
	- Communal riot in India
1930	- Salt Satyagraha, Gandhiji and others marched from Sabarmati Ashram to Dandi (March 12 - April 6)
1931	- Second Round Table Conference
	- Gandhi-Irwin pact
1932	- Election of Roosevelt as President of America
	- McDonald's communal award
1933	- Hitler became the Chancellor of Germany
1935	- Government of India Act 1935 passed
1937	- Inauguration of Provincial Autonomy
1939	- World War II Declared (1st Sept.)
1941	- Death of Rabindranath Tagore
	- Hitler invaded Russia
	- U.S.A. entered World War II
	- Subhash Chandra Bose escaped from India
	- Pearl Harbour bombed
1942	- Quit India Movement (8 August)
	- Indian National Army (INA) was formed by S.C. Bose at Singapore
	- Battle of El Alamein
1943	- Bengal Famine
1944	- Franklin D.Roosevelt re-elected, first American President to serve a fourth four-year term
1945	- INA trial at Red Fort
	- Shimla Conference
	- Failure of Wavell Plan
	- Death of President Roosevelt of U.S.A.
	- First Atom bomb dropped (6th August) on Hiroshima (Japan)

	- Second Atom bomb dropped (9th August) on Nagasaki (Japan)
	- United Nations comes into existence
	- End of World War II (14th August)
1946	- Cabinet Mission's Plan
	- Interim Government with Nehru as Prime Minister
	- To set up constituent assembly
1947	- Partition of India - India achieved Independence (15th August)
1948	- Kashmir accedes to India
	- Integration of princely states
	- Burma achieves Independence (14th January)
	- Assassination of Mahatma Gandhi (30th January)
	- Ceylon achieves Independence (16th February)
	- Jewish State of Israel formed (14th May)
	- Rajaji appointed Governor General of India
	- Enactment of Indian Constitution (26th Nov.)
	- GATT enters into force
1949	- Indonesia declared Republic
	- Ceasefire in Kashmir
	- Enactment of Indian Constitution (Nov. 26th)
1950	- India becomes Republic (Jan. 26th)
	- Dr. Rajendra Prasad sworn as President
	- Nehru and Liaquat Ali khan sign the Indo-Pakistani pact
1950 - 53	- War in Korea
1951	- First Five Year Plan launched
	- First Asian Games held at Delhi
	- First General Elections in India
	- Enumeration work of Free India's first census
1952	- General Eisenhower elected as American President
	- India's First International Film Festival opened in Mumbai
	- World's first official family planning programme launched in India
1953	- Death of Stalin (6th March)
	- University Grants Commission (UGC) constituted.
1954	- Panchshila agreement held between India and China
	- Visit of Chou En-lai to India
1955	- Bandung Conference
1956	- Suez Canal nationalised by Gamal Abdul Nassar (20th July)
	- Transfer of Pondicherry and other French Settlements to India
	- States Reorganisation Act came into force (Nov. 1)
	- Second Five Year Plan launched
1957	- Second General Elections in India
	- First artificial satellite launched by Soviet Union (Oct. 4)
	- First Sputnik by U.S.S.R
1958	- Mihir Sen, first Indian, crossed English channel

1959	- De Gaulle became the President of France
	- Explosion of Atom-bomb by France in the Sahara desert
	- Partition of Bombay into Maharashtra and Gujarat
	- Dalai Lama escaped to India
	- China-India relations strain as China demanded Ladakh and NEFA
1960	- John F. Kennedy elected President of U.S.A.
	- Mrs. Sirimavo Bandaranaike sworn in as the world's first woman Prime Minister in Sri Lanka
1961	- India's first aircraft carrier INS Vikrant commissioned.
	- The U.S. and Britain call for a ban on nuclear tests in the atmosphere
	- U. Thant elected as Secretary General of United Nation Organisation (UNO)
1962	- Third General Elections
	- China attacked India (20th Oct.)
	- Man's first entry into Space
	- Nuclear Test Ban Treaty (5th May)
	- U Thant became Secretary-General of UN
1963	- Assassination of U.S. President John F.Kennedy
1964	- Death of Jawaharlal Nehru (27th May)
	- Lal Bahadur Shastri became the Prime Minister
	- Lyndon B.Johnson elected President of U.S.A.
1965	- Death of Sir Winston Churchill
	- Singapore became Sovereign Independent nation
	- Indo-Pak war
1966	- Death of Lal Bahadur Shastri (Jan. 11)
	- Tashkent Declaration
	- Indira Gandhi became the Prime Minister
	- Punjab divided into Punjab and Haryana
	- First India-made Computer commissioned in Jadavpur University campus
	- Indian medical student Reita Faria elected Miss World
1967	- Fourth General Elections
	- Suez Canal closed
1968	- Martin Luther King assassinated
	- Robert Kennedy assassinated
	- Dara Singh became World Wrestling Champion
	- Hargobind Khorana shared Nobel Prize for Medicine and Physiology
	- Maldives became a republic
1969	- Split in Congress Party
	- Death of President Zakir Hussain
	- Richard Nixon elected as 37th President of U.S.A.
	- US astronauts Neil Armstrong and Edwin Aldrin set foot on the Moon

1970	- Creation of Meghalaya State
	- Third Non-aligned Summit Conference at Lusaka
	- Mrs. Sirimavo Bandaranaike elected Prime Minister of Ceylon (Sri Lanka)
	- Death of Dr. C.V. Raman
1971	- Elections to the Fifth Lok Sabha
	- Indo-Pak war.
	- Birth of Bangladesh
	- Creation of Himachal Pradesh
	- Indian PM Indira Gandhi receives Bharat Ratna, the highest award
1972	- Simla Conference.
	- Indo-Pak Peace Treaty between Indira Gandhi & Z.A.Bhutto
	- C. Rajagopalachari, the only Indian Governor General died
	- Sheikh Mujibur Rahman released from Pakistan jail and became Prime Minister of Bangladesh
1973	- Fakhruddin Ali Ahmed became President of India
1974	- India's first Nuclear Test Bomb blasted at Pokharan
	- Emergency declared in India
	- Sikkim became 22nd state
1975	- Communists take over in Vietnam, Cambodia and Laos
	- Suez Canal reopened
1976	- Vietnam unified (June 24)
	- Indira Gandhi and Brezhnev signed Moscow declaration of friendship and cooperation
1977	- Elections to the Sixth Lok Sabha (Mar. 16-20)
	- Janata Party formed and came to power
	- Indira Gandhi defeated & Morarji Desai became Prime Minister
	- Split in Congress (I) again
	- Death of President Mr.Fakhruddin Ali Ahmed.
	- Mr. N.Sanjiva Reddy became sixth President (July 25)
1978	- Rs.1,000, Rs.5,000 and Rs.10,000 were demonetized
	- Second split in Congress under Mrs.Indira Gandhi on Nov.5th.
1979	- Charan Singh became the Prime Minister
	- Lok Sabha dissolved
	- Jayaprakash Narayan passed away (Oct.8)
1980	- Lok Sabha Election
	- Congress I regained power
	- Birth of Bharatiya Janata Party (April 6th)
	- Rohini launched from Sriharikota
	- Syria and Libya proclaim merger of their countries
	- Ronald Reagan, Republican leader, wins election for American Presidency
1981	- APPLE launched
	- Third split in Congress under Jagjivan Ram

1982	- Mr. Zail Singh became 7th President of India
	- Death of Acharya Vinoba Bhave
	- 9th Asiad held in New Delhi
	- Second Indian team landed in Antarctica (Dec.28)
	- Halley's comet sighted for the first time since 1910
1983	- Seventh Non-Aligned Summit held in New Delhi.
	- Kalpakkam Atomic station commissioned (July 23)
	- INSAT-1B multi purpose satellite launched by Challenger from Cape Canaveral USA (Aug. 30)
1984	- Indira Gandhi assassinated (Oct. 31)
	- Sqn.Ldr. Rakesh Sharma was the first Indian cosmonaut in space (April 3)
1984	- Bachendri Pal became the first Indian woman to reach Mount Everest (May 23)
	- Bhopal Gas tragedy killed over 2200.
1984	- Rajiv Gandhi became the Prime Minister of India
	- P.T. Usha becomes the first Indian woman to appear in an Olympic final
1985	- Michael Gorbachev elected General Secretary of Soviet Communist Party
	- Indian National Congress celebrated its centenary (May 6)
	- Government declared 5 days-a-week work for Government staff
1986	- 10th Asian Games at Seoul
	- India's first test tube baby born (June 14)
	- Second SAARC summit held at Bangalore (Nov. 16)
	- US Space Shuttle 'Challenger' exploded in space
1987	- Goa became 25th State of India (May 31)
	- Mr. R.Venkataraman became the President of India (July 25)
	- Tamil Nadu Chief Minister Mr.M.G.Ramachandran died (Dec. 24)
1988	- 'Operation Black Thunder' commanded by K.P.Gill made 151 terrorists surrender in the Golden Temple Complex in Amritsar
	- Indian Constitution amended to reduce the voting age from 21 to 18 years (Dec. 15)
1989	- Satwant Singh and Kehar Singh involved in the assassination of Mrs.Indira Gandhi, executed (Jan. 1)
	- Bhopal gas tragedy case settled in Supreme Court for 470 million dollars
	- ISRO launched first stage giant booster motor of the four stage PSLV (Nov. 29)
	- V.P.Singh sworn in as the seventh Prime Minister of India
1990	- Nag, Akash' missiles test fired successfully
1991	- India's second remote sensing satellite IRS-1B was launched successfully from Baikanour Cosmodrome (Aug. 29)

1992	- Golden Jubilee of 'Quit India Movement'
	- Ms. Santosh Yadav of Indo-Tibetan Border police was the first woman who climbed Mt.Everest twice
1993	- The Supreme Court upheld the Union Govt's decision to reserve 27% Government jobs for Backward classes
1994	- Successful launch of Prithvi, surface-to-surface missile, at Chandipur -on-sea (Orrisa).
	- Aishwarya Rai was crowned Miss World 1994
	- (Nov. 19) Shoemaker Levy 9, a comet crashes into Jupiter
1995	- Myanmar's leader Ms. Aung San Suu Kyi was awarded Jawaharlal Nehru Award for International Understanding for 1993
1996	- Bombay and Madras renamed as Mumbai and Chennai respectively
1997	- Princess Diana of England killed in a car crash in Paris.
	- Mother Teresa, 87, died.
1998	- India exploded 5 nuclear devices at Pokhran - 3 were blasted on 11th May and 2 on 13th May.
1999	- Agni-II test fired successfully from Wheeler Island in Balassore District of Orissa.
	- Oct. 13: A.B. Vajpayee sworn-in as Prime Minister and other Cabinet Ministers also took oath of office.
	- Nov. 16: 2nd National Labour Commission constituted.
	- Dec.2: Ministerial Conference of the World Trade Organisation held in Seattle.
	- Dec. 15: Panama Canal control handed over to Panama President, (Built in 1977 by America)
2000	- Nov. 1: India's 26th State, Chattisgarh formed. ◆ Nov. 9: Uttaranchal, the India's 27th State formed. ◆ Nov. 15: Jharkhand, the India's 28th State carved.
2001	- Jan. 20: George W. Bush takes oath as the 43rd President of the United States. ◆ Sep 11: International Terrorists' massive plane attack on America's busiest World Trade Centre and Pentagon buildings. Thousands of people died. ● Dec. 13: Terrorists squad storms Indian Parliament.
2002	- Jan. 1: New currency, Euro becomes legal tender for 300 million people of European Commonwealth. ◆ Sept. 19: India's first exclusive meteorological satellite 'METSAT' successfully switched on Very High Resolution Radiometer (VHRR).
2003	- Feb. 12: 'Brahmos', the supersonic anti-ship cruise missile successfully test-fired from Balasore. ◆ Apr. 11: 'Janani Suraksha Yojana', a scheme for mother-child welfare launched. ◆ May 9: 'ASTRA': air-to-air missile test fired in Balassore of Orissa. ◆ Oct. 8: Chinese official website shows, for the first time, Sikkim as part of India. ◆ Oct. 17: The PSLV-C5, with India's most sophisticated remote sensing satellite Resourcesat-1, blasts off from Satish Dhawan Space Centre in Sriharikota.

2004 - **Jan. 10:** Inauguration of New District of Krishnagiri in Tamil Nadu
◆ **April 25:** 'INS Tarangini' becomes the 1st Indian Naval ship to complete a voyage around the world. ◆ **May 1:** European Union strength goes to 25 as 10 new countries joined. ◆ **Aug. 3:** NASA launches *Messenger* to Mercury from Cape Canaveral (USA). ◆ **Aug. 4:** NASA dedicates its new Altix supercomputer 'KC' to the memory of India born astronaut Kalpana Chawla.
- **Oct. 18:** The elusive forest brigand Veerappan shot dead by the Tamil Nadu special Task Force. ● **Dec. 26:** 'Tsunami', the undersea earthquake of huge waves off Sumatra in Indonesia lash Tamil Nadu, Kerala, W. Bengal, Andamans and many southern coastal regions of India.

2005 - **April 2:** Pope John Paul II, aged 84 died at Vatican after a long illness. ◆ **July 11:** The Archaeological Survey of India (ASI) unearths remains of the 1200-year-old Subrahmanya temple belonging to the Pallava period (circa 8th century AD) in Mamallapuram, Tamil Nadu. ◆ **Oct. 1:** An annular eclipse of the sun was seen between 4.25 p.m. and 6 p.m. ◆ **Oct.8:** 40,000 people were feared killed and several thousand injured as a powerful earthquake measuring 7.6 on the Richter scale hit large parts of Pakistan, Pak-occupied Kashmir (PoK) and Jammu Kashmir.
- **Oct. 20:** The Union Cabinet decides to rename the Varanasi Airport (Uttar Pradesh) as Lal Bahadur Shastri Airport, as a tribute to the late Prime Minister, Lal Bahadur Shastri. ◆ **Nov. 14:** 14th International Children's Film Festival gets off to a colourful start in Hyderabad. ◆ **Dec. 1:** The second prototype of the *Tejas* combat aircraft (PV2), India's indigenously built Light Combat Aircraft, makes its maiden flight in Bangalore (Karnataka).

2006 - **Jan. 3:** The 93rd session of the Indian Science Congress is inaugurated by Dr. Manmohan Singh in Hyderabad (Andhra Pradesh). ◆ **Feb 5 :** A moderate earthquake, measuring 5.0 on the Richter scale, rocks parts of Andaman Islands. ◆ **Mar 1 :** The US President, Mr. George W. Bush arrives in New Delhi along with his wife Ms. Laura Bush and a high power delegation on a State visit. ◆ **Mar 15 :** The 18th Commonwealth Games are inaugurated in Melbourne (Australia) by the British Queen Elizabeth II. ◆ **Mar 29 :** A total solar eclipse is observed in many parts of the world including Eastern Brazil, West and North Africa, Turkey, Central Asia and Mongolia.
- **Apr 1 :** The five Bharatiya Janata Party (BJP) ruled States - Chhattisgarh, Gujarat, Jharkhand, Madya Pradesh and Rajasthan - switch over to the Value Added Tax (VAT) regime from the sales tax system. ◆ **Apr 11 :** *'The Venus Express'*, spacecraft of the European Space Agency approaches Venus

approximately five months after it was launched and starts its main engine burn to slow itself down and allow itself to be captured into orbit around Venus.

2006
- **May 8:** State Assembly elections polled in four states are Assam, West Bengal, Kerala & Tamilnadu. ◆ **May 30 :** The European Union (EU) imposes a ban on the Liberation Tigers of Tamil Eelam (LTTE), clearing the way for the 25- nation bloc to freeze the group's assets within the EU. ◆ **June 16 :** Mr. Girija Prasad Koirala, Prime Minister of Nepal and Mr. Prachanda, Maoist supremo, reach a 'historical' eight-point agreement on Nepal, in their first meeting in Kathmandu (Nepal). ◆ **June 20 :** Sri Lanka win the second ODI against England by 46 runs. ◆ **June 21 :** Oxford University grants a status of Recognised Independent Centre to the Oxford Centre for Hindu Studies, the only academic institution in Europe dedicated to studying Hindu philosophy and culture. ◆ **June 26 :** Deputy Chief of the Sri Lankan Army, Parami Kulatunga, is assassinated by a suspected member of the LTTE in Pannipitiya (Sri Lanka). ● Justice Mr. K. Narayana Kurup is nominated as the 'Global Ambassador of Peace' by the New York-based World Trade Centres Association.

- **July 1 :** Prime Minister Dr. Manmohan Singh announces a Rs. 3,750 crore package of relief measures for Vidarbha (Maharashtra) as part of the UPA Government's bid to solve the problem of rural indebtedness. ◆ **July 3 :** Li Na becomes the first Chinese to make it to a Grand Slam quarter-final after defeating Nicole Vaidisova of the Czech Republic. ◆ **July 6 :** 4,310 metres high Nathu La Pass bordering between India and China, before the opening of the pass for Sino Indian trade after a gap of 44 years. ◆ **July 7 :** Mr. L.N. Mittal, Chairman of Mittal Steel announced his plan to set up a Rs. 40,000 crore 12 million tonnes capacity steel plant in Orissa. ◆ **July 16 :** Prime Minister Dr. Manmohan Singh reaches St. Petersburg (Russia) to attend the G-8 Summit. ◆ **July 17 :** The Space Shuttle *Discovery* carrying a 6-member crew, led by the mission STS - 121 Commander Steve Lindsey lands safely at Kennedy Space Centre's shuttle landing facility in Cape Canaveral (Florida) after a 13-day, five million-mile journey in space.

- **July 20 :** The Union Government setting up the Sixth Pay Commission to submit its recommendations on wage revision and retirement benefits for Central Government employees. ● Bollywood superstar Amitabh Bachchan is conferred an honorary degree of Doctor of Arts by De Montfort University at Leicester (England). ◆ **July 22 :** The Union Cabinet rejects Hon'ble President Dr. APJ. Abdul Kalam's call for reconsideration of the Office-of-Profit Bill.

2006

- **July 26** : Jamaican sprinter Asafa Powell, who shares the world mark with American Olympic Champion Justin Gatlin in 100 metres at 9.77 seconds, romps home in 9.86 seconds at the Stockholm Super Grand Prix held in Stockholm (Sweden).
  ◆ **July 29** : Sri Lanka President Mr. Mahinda Rajapakse inducts a fifth rebel member of the main Opposition, United National Party (UNP) into the Government. ◆ **July 31** : Mr. Aravind Kejriwal, head of a *Parivartan citizen's movement*, selected for Magsaysay award for "activating India's Right to Information movement.

- **August 2** : Israel sends as many as 8,000 troops into Lebanon to crush Hezbollah even as the Lebanon-based Shia militia fires 190 rockets. ◆ **August 5** : Pepsi and Cocacola soft drinks are disclosed many States in India, the ingredients in these products. ◆ **August 8** : Iraqi Prime Minister Mr. Nouri Al Maliki criticises a US-Iraqi attack on a Shia militia stronghold in Baghdad (Iraq), exposing a rift with his American partners on security tactics.

- **August 9** : Heavy rain continues to lash Maharashtra bringing the death toll beyond 110; the situation goes from bad to worse in parts of Gujarat, particularly Surat, forcing the State Government to seek Rs. 200 crore Central assistance.
  ◆ **August 11** : Narender Kumar (50 Kg) and Apoorva Tyagi (40 Kg) clinch Gold medals at the Asian Cadet Wrestling Championships in Bangkok (Thailand). ● The strongest typhoon to hit China in half a century, called Saomai, kills over 100 people in Cangnan country in the eastern province of Zhejiang.

- **August 14** : PepsiCo, the global soft drink major that has been in the eye of storm appoints Ms. Indra Nooyi, the company's CFO of Indian origin, as its worldwide Chief Executive Officer. ◆ **August 17** : Solar system count now set to swell to 12 planets. They will be Mercury, Venus, Earth, Mars, Ceres, Jupiter, Saturn, Uranus, Neptune, Pluto, Charon and provisionally, '2003 UB313'. ◆ **August 18** : Hon'ble President Dr. APJ. Abdul Kalam gives assent to the amended Parliament (Prevention of Disqualification) Act, 1959, popularly known as the office-of-Profit Bill. ● The South Asian Games (SAF) are opened in a colourful ceremony in Colombo (Sri Lanka). ◆ **August 20** : 10,000 Refugees from Sri Lanka arrived at Arichamunai in Ramanathapuram district, Tamilnadu. ◆ **August 26** : Quota Bill in Lok Sabha to provide 27 per cent reservation for Other Backward Classes (OBCs) in Central Educational Institutions.

2006   - **September 4** : Indian President APJ. Abdul Kalam inaugurates the 150th year foundation day celebrations of University of Madras. ● Militants kill more than 60 persons in Baghdad, dealing a severe blow to Iraq's fledling hopes for peace only a day after the launch of national reconciliation talks by the Government. ● Due to heavy rain-induced flood, the Kashmir valley remains cut off from the rest of the country for the fourth consecutive day. ● Popular Australian "crocodile hunter" and television environmentalist Steve Irwin loses his life following a stingray blow while filming a documentary on the Great Barrier Reef off northwestern Australia. ◆ **Sep 6** : India is ranked fourth among 100 top travel destinations, according to travel and tourism magazine *Conde Nast Traveller UK* while it is ranked 134 among 175 countries in the case of doing business in *Doing Business 2007: How to Reform,* a report released by International Finance Corporation, an arm of the world Bank.

- **Sep 9** : Film actress Ms. Shabana Azmi is named the recipient of the prestigious Gandhi International Peace Prize for the year 2006, given away by the London based Gandhi Foundation. ● England beat Pakistan by 8 wickets in the fourth ODI criket match in Nottingham (England). ◆ **Sep 10** : Roger Federer of Switzerland beats Andy Roddick of USA to win the men's singles final of the US Open tennis tournament in New York (USA). ◆ **Sep 12** : The BSNL announced a 40 per cent reduction in the ISD rates to Sri Lanka and a 20 per cent cut to West Asian countries from next month.

- **Sep 13** : Bollywood scriptwriter and lyricist Javed Akhtar is chosen for the Indira Gandhi Award for National Integration for the year 2005. ◆ **Sep 14** : The Arjun Munda led-NDA (National Democratic Alliance) Government in Jharkhand falls, thereby paving the way for the formation of a UPA (United Progressive Alliance) Government under the leadership of Independent MLA Mr. Madhu Koda. ◆ **Sep 15** : The 14th NAM (Non-Aligned Movement) Summit opens in Havana (Cuba). ● Indian writer Ms.Kiran Desai is shortlisted for the Man Booker Prize for the year 2006 for her novel. *'The Inheritance of Loss'.* ● Australia beat South Korea, 4-2, in the first semi-final to enter the final of the World Cup Hockey tournament in Germany. ◆ **Sep 23** : Mr. Anand Satyanand is sworn in as New Zealand's Governor-General. ◆ **Sep 25**: Pope Benedict XVI with ambassadors of 22 Islamic nations at his summer residence in Castel Gandalfo, outside Rome. ◆ **Oct 4**: Railway Minister Lalu Prasad flagged off the poor man's AC train "Garib

Rath" here with almost 50 per cent cut in fares. It was bound for Amritsar. ◆ **Oct 5:** The Sri Lanka Government announced that fresh talks with the Liberation Tigers of Tamil Eelam in Switzerland. ● The Employees State Insurance Corporation has raised the wage limit for coverage of employees under the ESI Act from Rs.7,500 a month to Rs.10,000 a month. ◆ **Oct 7:** Film director Jahnu Barua has won the Kodak Vision Award for his film Maine Gandhi Ko Nahin Mara at the just-concluded Fukuoka International Film Festival in Japan. ◆ **Oct 10:** Britain's leading Indian industrialist and Labour peer Swraj Paul was installed as the first-ever Chancellor of the University of westminster.

2006 - **Oct 12:** Novelist Orhan Pamuk, whose prosecution for "insulting Turkishness" raised concerns about suppression of free speech in Turkey, won the Nobel prize for literature. ◆ **Oct 13:** Bangladesh's Muham mad Yunus, dubbed the "Banker to the poor," and his Grameen Bank won the Nobel Peace Prize. ● The first phase of local body elections held in Tamil Nadu. ◆ **Oct 14:** Ban Ki-moon, the newly appointed Secretary-General of the United Nations. ◆ **Oct 15:** The second phase of local body elections held in Chennai's suburbs. ◆ **Oct 17:** Union Health and Family Welfare Minister Anbumani Ramadoss said the Goverment had cleared Rs.1.156 crore for the Revised National Tuberculosis Control Programme (RNTCP) for the next five years. ◆ **Oct 18:** In most of local body posts won by DMK collision parties. ◆ **Oct 26:** Six corporations Mayors, Deputy Mayors are elected by local body councilors in Tamil Nadu. ◆ **Oct 27:** Heavy rain fall occurred in Chennai and Tamil Nadu due to low atmospheric pressure. ◆ **Oct 31:** Reserve Bank of India announced the new monitary policy for next financial year. ◆ **Nov 1:** Dr. Manmohan singh inaugurates the 50-day golden jubilee celebrations to mark the formation of Kerala in Thiruvananthapuram. ◆ **Nov 20 :** Chinese president Hu Jintao arrives in New Delhi on four day state visit as part of expanding leadership level contacts between the two countries. ◆ **Nov 29 :** Inaugurated a two day India Disaster Management Congress in New Delhi by Dr. Manmohan Singh. ◆ **Dec 7 :** The Government decided against splitting OBCs into creamy and non-creamy layers for reservation to the Central Government aided educational institutions. ◆ **Dec 22 :** Space shuttle Discovery and its seven astronauts safely returned to the earth. ◆ **Dec 30 :** The former Iraqi President Saddam Hussein was hanged.

2007

- **Jan 1** : Mr. Ban-Ki-Moon of South Korea has been appointed as the New Secretary-General of the UN (United Nations) w.e.f. January 2007. ◆ **Jan 2** : The Union Cabinet decided to rename 'Uttaranchal' as the 'Uttarakhand'. ◆ **Jan 3** : The 94th edition of the Indian Science Congress was inaugurated by the Prime Minister Manmohan Singh in Chidambaram (Tamil Nadu). ◆ **Jan 4** : Defence Minister A.K. Antony dedicated INS Shardul, a landing warship to the nation at the Karwar Naval Base, INS Kadamba, in Karwar. ◆ **Jan 11** : In a significant judgement, a nine-judge Bench of the Supreme Court held that there could not be any blanket immunity from judicial review of laws inserted in the Ninth Schedule of the Constitution. ◆ **Jan 13** : The 12th ASEAN (Association of South East Asian Nations) Summit officialy opened in Cebu (The Philippines) on January 13, 2007 ◆ **Jan 22** : With the successful return to the Earth of the Indian Space Research Organisation's 550kg SRE-1 (Space capsule Recovery Experiment), India became only the fourth country after the US, Russia and China, to have expertise in re-entry technology. ◆ **Jan 25** : 79th Annual Academy Oscar Awards were presented in Hollywood, California (U.S.A.) for the Best Picture: The Departed, Best Actor: Forest Whitaker; Best Actress: Helen Mirren. ◆ **Jan 29**: The Planning Commission agreed in principal to a proposal made by the Labour Ministry on adopting a more inclusive approach to end the problem of child labour. ◆ **Feb 2** : Jammu and Kashmir Chief Minister Ghulam Nabi Azad announced that eight new districts would be demarcated in six months. New districts are Kishtwar, Samba, Reasi, Ramban, Bandipore, Kulgam, Ganderbal and Shopian. ◆ **Feb 7** : Supersonic cruise missile BrahMos, with an advanced capability of sharp manoeuvring, was successfully test-fired. From the Integrated Test Range at Chandipur-on-sea near Balasore (Orissa) ◆ **Feb 9** : 33rd National Games were held in Guwahati from 9th to 18th February. 11,000 athletes from 33 team participated in the event. Karate has been included as a discipline in this games. ◆ **Feb 27** : The Congress Party lost power in Punjab & Uttarakhand, but managed to stay in office in Manipur with support from its allies. Results of the assembly elections to the three states were declared ◆ **Mar 13** : The 2007 (9th) edition of the ICC Cricket World Cup is being held in West Indies from March 13 to April 28, 2007. ◆ **Mar 31** : Air Marshal Fali H. Major, Air Officer-Commanding-in-Chief, Eastern Air Command became the first Helicopter pilot to be named as the Chief of Indian Air Force. Fali H. Major, the seniormost Air Marshal in the IAF, was succeeded Air Chief Marshal S.P. Tyagi.

2007   – **Apr 3** : The 14th summit of the South Asian Association for Regional Cooperation (SAARC) was taken place in the Indian capital New Delhi. ◆ **Apr 23** : PSLV-C8, satellite was successfully launched from Satish Dawan Space Centre, Sriharikota. ◆ **Apr 28** : Australia won the 2007 World Cup Cricket Championship in the final match against Sri Lanka at Barbados Stadium, West Indies. This is the Australia's Hat-trick record. ◆ **May 6** : The world's largest passenger aircraft Air bus A 380 lands for the first time in India at the Indira Gandhi International Airport in New Delhi. ◆ Mr. Nicolas Sarkozy a conservative Party leader is elected president of France with 53 percent of the vote, beating his socialist rival, Mr. Segolene Royal. ◆ **May 9** : The medium range, surface-to-surface missile Prithvi is test-fired from the Integrated Test Range at Chandipur-on-sea near Balasore in Orissa. ◆ **May 11** : Bahujan Samaj Party supremo Ms. Mayawati wins the UP Assembly elections with majority and is set to become the Chief Minister of Uttar Pradesh for the fourth time. ◆ Singapore will lost a formula one race during night in 2008, the first in the world. ◆ **May 13** : Union Minister of communications and Information Technology, Mr. Dayanidhi Maran resigned. ◆ **May 15** : Rajasthan Chief Minister Ms. Vasundhara Raje receives the prestigious "Women Together Award" at the United Nations Headquarters in New York (USA). ◆ Indira clinches the one-day series against Bangladesh. India claimed the honours 2-0 with M.S. Dhoni being declared the "Man of the Serids". ◆ **May 17** : India is re-elected to the Geneva based UN Human Rights Council for the three-year term getting 185 votes, the maximum obtained by any contestant in the 192 member General Assembly. ◆ Prime Minister Dr. Manmohan Singh is declared elected unopposed to Rajya Sabha for the fourth consecutive term from Assam. ◆ **May 19** : Prime Minister Dr. Manmohan Singh lays foundation stone for 1200 MW power project in Hissar (Haryana). ◆ **May 21** : The Chief of the Army Staff General J.J. Singh makes his first official round of meetings in Beijing (China). He is on a five-day trip to China, the first such visit by the Chairman of the Chiefs of Staff Committee of the Indian Armed Forces. ◆ **May 23** : President Dr. A.P.J. Abdul Kalam presents the National Communal Harmony Award to octogenarian social activist Mr. Rabindra Nath Upadhyay from Assam and Delhi-based Institute for Socialist Education; social activist Mr. Rambabu Singh Chauhan from Uttar Pradesh is conferred the Kabir Puraskar for his outstanding contribution to promoting communal harmony.

2007   - **May 24** : The Chief Justices of High Courts and Chief Ministers of various States agree to introduce a shift system in the subordinate courts to dispose off appropriate cases, including those relating to petty offences. ◆ The ITTF (International Table Tennis Federation) Chief Mr. Adham Sharara says that the use of solvent-based speed glue, which increases speed and spin but is hazardous to health, will be banned from September 1, 2007. ◆ **May 25** : Iraqi Oil Minister Mr. Hussain al-Shahristani calls on Prime Minister Dr. Manmohan Singh and discusses with him issues like India's cooperation in rebuilding his country, investment and joint ventures. ◆ Dera Sacha Sauda moves to the Supreme Court for a direction to various State Governments to protect the life, liberty and the property of the Deras and followers. ◆ **May 26** : China's Guo Yue defeats Li Xiaoxia in the women's singles final at the World Table Tennis Championship in Zagreb. ◆ **May 27** : Reliance Industries Ltd. Chairman Mr. Mukesh Ambani becomes the first trillionaire in the country with over Rs. 1,00,000 crore of networth through his shareholdings. ◆ In Ireland's general elections, Prime Minister Mr. Bertie Ahern's party Fianna Fail wins 78 seats and is seeking coalition partners to give Mr. Ahern a record third term. ◆ Spain's two-time Formula One world champion Fernando Alonso wins his successive Monaco Grand Prix in Monte Carlo. ◆ **May 28** : Mr. A.R. Lakshmanan, retired judge of the Supreme Court, assumes charge as the Chairman of the 18th Law Commission. ◆ In the first US-Iran bilateral talks in 27 years, Iran proposes establishment of a 'trilateral security mechanism' to defuse violence in Iraq and slams the political pressures being exerted by Washington and Europe on UN nuclear watchdog Chief Mohamed ElBaradei over Tehran's undisputed atomic programme. ◆ **May 29** : Prime Minister Dr. Manmohan Singh announces at the 53rd Meeting of the NDC (National Development Council) on Farming & Allied Sectors, a Rs.25000-crore plan plan for new farm sector projects by States, besides launching a food security mission to enhance the output of wheat, rice and pulses. ◆ Mr. Umaru Yar'Adua is sworn in as the President of Nigeria, Africa's most populous oil-rich country, succeeding Mr. Olusegun Obasanjo. ◆ The 17th Commonwealth Table Tennis Championships begins at the Sawai Mansingh Indoor Stadium in Jaipur (Rajasthan). ◆ **May 30** : Thailand's Constitutional Court bans the deposed Prime Minister Mr. Thaksin Shivawatra from politics for five years. ◆ **May 31** : The Union Cabinet approves a scholarship scheme for higher education for students of the Scheduled Castes and Scheduled Tribes to be implemented from current financial year and covering students whose family income does not exceed Rs. 2 lakh a year. ◆ Sepp Blatter is re-elected unopposed as FIFA President for another four-year term in Zurich (Switzerland).

2007 - **June 1** : The US Under Secretary of State for Political Affairs Mr. Nicholas Burns and India's Foreign Secretary Mr. Shiv Shankar Menon hold talks on the proposed civil nuclear cooperation agreement. ◆ **June 2** : The Sixth Asian Security Conference is held in Singapore where India and China reiterate that their current status as rising powers, independent of each other, will help in establishing the global political order. ◆ Singapore win 3-0 over India in the men's final of the 17th Commonwealth Table Tennis Championships at the Sawai Man Singh Indoor Stadium in Jaipur; Singapore also win the women's final defeating Malaysia 3-1 thereby winning the title. ◆ **June 4** : Brazilian President Mr. Luiz Inacio Lula da Silva receives the Jawaharlal Nehru Award for International Understanding 2006 in recognition of his steadfast commitment to the eradication of poverty and hunger. ◆ The Union Commerce and Industry Mr. Kamal Nath says that Brazil has emerged as India's largest trading partner in Latin America with bilateral trade crossing the record $2 billion mark in 2006. ◆ China releases its first national strategy to combat global warming promising to make strong efforts to curb green house emissions. ◆ **June 6** : The 33rd Summit of leaders of G8, the grouping of world's eight most industrialised nations (USA, UK, Japan, France, Germany, Italy, Canada and Russia) and five 'outreach nations' (India, China, Brazil, Mexico and South Africa) begins in Heilingendamm (Germany). ◆ **June 7** : Seven-time Grand Slam singles champion tennis legend John McEnroe is honoured with the International Tennis Federation's highest accolade, the Philippe Chatrier Award. ◆ **June 8** : In the Joint statement issued at the end of the G8 Summit at Heilingendamm, the leaders of the world's most industrialised nations agree on halving global CO_2 emissions by 2050 and pledge more aid for Africa. ◆ The Golden Green Golf and Country Club in Gurgaon are slated to host the Rs. 25 lakh Color Plus Open, the 10th leg of the Professional Golfer's Tour of India (PGTI) 2006-07. ◆ **June 9** : The Rajasthan Government gives administrative and financial clearance to the proposed Rs. 4,600-crore 1000 MW Kali Sindh super thermal power project in Jhalawar with equity participation of Rs. 920 crore from the State Government. ◆ Three of Indian cinema's biggest icons—Mr. Amitabh Bachchan, Ms. Shabana Azmi and Mr. Yash Chopra—are conferred with honorary Doctorate by the Leeds Metropolitan University of the United Kingdom for their contribution to cinema. ◆ Justine Henin of Belgium claims her third consecutive French Open women's singles title defeating Serbia's Ana Ivanovic 6-1, 6-2 at Roland Garros.

2007 **- June 10 :** As a sign of Moscow's shifting priorities from the West to the East, Russian President Mr. Vladimir Putin calls for creating a Eurapian alternative to the WTO (World Trade Organisation) and promises to step up energy supplies to Asian consumers. ◆ Rafael Nadal of Spain wins the French Open men's singles title for the successive third time by defeating Roger Federer of Switzerland 6-3, 4-6, 6-3, 6-4. ◆ **June 11 :** The Government proposes to expand the National Child Labour Project to all endemic districts during the 11th Five-Year Plan period; the scheme started operation in 1998 and is presently operational in 250 districts in 20 states, where 7,328 special schools are functioning for children withdrawn from work. ◆ The Centre decides to revise the norms of central assistance for calamity relief from the national Calamity Relief Fund (CRF) after a high-level committee chaired by Agriculture Minister Mr. Sharad Pawar approves the proposal to raise the relief from National Calamity Contingency Fund (NCCF) and CRF by 35 percent. ◆ **June 12 :** Kenya will be the host for the third and final Afro-Asia Cup series in June 2008. ◆ **June 13 :** Renowned Nigerian novelist Chinua Achebe wins the 2007 Man Booker International Prize for fiction. ◆ **June 15 :** The United Nations declares Gandhi Jayanti, celebrated every year on October 2, as International Day for Non-Violence; the UN General Assembly voted for the move with 114 countries as co-sponsors. ◆ **June 16 :** Mr. Srinivasan Padmanaban, a senior energy advisor with the US Agency for International Development (USAID), is presented the 'World Clean Energy Award' for his contributions to the Green Business Centre and the Water-Energy Nexus Activity in India. ◆ Noted novelist Mr. Salman Rushdie is conferred 'Knighthood' by Queen Elizabeth II of Great Britain in London, for his 'services' to literature; he is the first writer from the Indian subcontinent in the post-colonial era to be given Britain's highest honour. ◆ The United States praises Pakistan for its contribution in the "war against terrorism" and announces a $750 million package for the development of the country's frontier tribal areas. ◆ Asia's No. 1 Jeev Milkha Singh times his birdie on the 17th hole in the second round to make the cut at the 107th US Open golf tournament at Oakmount Country Club.

2007 - **June 17** : Twelve firms including Tata Motors, Larsen and Toubro, Tata Power Company, Mahendra and Mehendra, Godrej and Boyce, Infosys Technologies, Bharat Forge, Wipro Technologies and Tata Consultancy Services are cleared for Raksha Udyog Ratna (RUR) status by a Ministry of Defence committee. ◆ Bollywood actress Shilpa Shetty is presented the 'Silver Star Award' for her outstanding contribution to international humanitarian causes, particularly for increasing AIDS awareness. ◆ United States' Andy Roddick clinches his fourth Queen's Club trophy in five years with a dramatic 4-6, 7-6(7), 7-6(2) win over France's Nicolas Mahut. ◆ **June 18** : Two US astronauts commence the fourth and final spacewalk of the Atlantis mission after the shuttle got the green signal to return to Earth bringing back Indian-American Ms. Sunita Williams, who has set a record for the longest uninterrupted stay in space by a woman. ◆ Golfer Angel Cabrera of Argentina wins the US Open Championship defeating United States' Tiger Woods with a 1-under-par 69 at Oakmont (USA). This is the first Argentine win in a major championship event in 40 years. ◆ Lewis Hamilton of the UK wins his second straight Formula One victory in the US Grand Prix, becoming the first black driver in F1's 60-year history to finish all seven races in this season in the top three. ◆ **June 19** : The India International Friendship Society (IIFS) selects ernior faculty members of the Punjab University, Prof. T.R. Bhardwaj and Dr. Bhupinder Singh Bhoop, from the Institute of Pharmaceutical Sciences (IPS) for the 'Shiksha Ratna Puraskar'. ◆ Indonesian President Mr. Susilo Bambang Yudhoyono calls for the "intensification of cooperation" with India in the defence domain, as the two countries agree upon a "plan of action" to translate their "new strategic partnership" into a reality. ◆ The French Government presents the 'Chevalier de l'Ordre National du Merite' (Knight of theOrder of Merit) award to Kolkata Book Fair Director, Mr. Kalyan Shah for his contribution to the development of Indo-French relations, particularly in publishing. ◆ **June 20** : Indian wrestlers return to the international arena from a forced liberation to strike a rich haul of 11 Gold, 14 Silver and 3 Bronze medals at the Commonwealth wrestling championship in Ontario, Canada. ◆ **June 22** : The space shuttle Atlantis carrying Ms. Sunita Williams and six other astronauts lands safely at Edwards Air Force Base in California. Earlier, NASA gave the space shuttle the green signal to leave orbit for a planned landing in California after rain blocked attempts to land in Florida.

2007

- **June 23** : Defending champion Justine Henin of Belgium wins the Eastbourne International women's singles title 2007 defeating Amelie Mauresmo of France with a 7-5, 6-7(4), 7-6(2). ◆ **June 24** : Armaan Ebrahim of India wins the Formula Renault V6 Grand Race at the F-1 Sepang Circuit in Kuala Lumpur, Malaysia. ◆ **June 26** : The Hangzhou Bay Bridge, a 36-km-long bridge near Cixi in China's Zhejiang Province, regarded as the world's longest sea crossing structure, takes final shape. The bridge connects Haiyan of Jiaxing city to Cixi of Ningbo city in Zhejiang Province. ◆ **June 27** : In one of the largest support packages, the World Bank approves a $600-million loan and credit to India aimed at transforming farmers' access to financial services. ◆ Mr. Gordon Brown takes over as the new Prime Minister of Britain succeeding Mr. Tony Blair. Mr. Brown is the 52nd Prime Minister. ◆ **June 28** : The majestic 17th century architecture, Red Fort, built by the Mughal ruler Shah Jahan, is included in the UNESCO's World Heritage List. ◆ Indian wrestler Kripa Shankar Patel wins Gold in the Greco-Roman championship. ◆ India's Koneru Humpy wins the HSG Open International chess tournament in Hilversum (the Netherlands) with 7.5 points from nine rounds defeating Grand Master Erik Van Den Deol of the Netherlands. ◆ **July 1** : The Union Panchayati Raj Minister, Mr. Mani Shankar Aiyar with 57-member delegation, arrives at Lahore in Pakistan for a three-day visit. The visit marks the attending of a symposium on local self-governance. ◆ Honda Siel Cars India Ltd. (HSCI) lays the foundation for its second plant in the Tapukara industrial area in Rajasthan. ◆ Ferrari's Kimi Raikkonen wins the French Grand Prix at Magny Cours (France) while Ferrari's Felipe Massa and McLaren's Lewis Hamilton stand second and third, respectively. ◆ **July 2** : The United States aircraft carrier, USS Nimitz, one of the largest warships in the world, reaches India and drops anchor two miles off the Chennai port. ◆ Iranian President Mr. Mahmoud Ahmadinejad and his Venezuelan counterpart Mr. Hugo Chavez seal their anti-American alliance by laying the foundation stone for a joint petrochemical plant at Asaluyeh in Iran. ◆ **July 5** : Sochi, the Russian Black Sea resort, wins the right to host the 2014 Winter Olympic Games at the International Olympic Committee meeting in Guatemala City. ◆ **July 6** : Visiting Vietnamese Prime Minister Mr. Nguyen Tan Dung favours a Free Trade Agreement (FTA) between Vietnam and India in New Delhi besides promising to create a favourable investment environment for Indian companies in Vietnam. ◆ **July 7** : In a glittering ceremony in Lisbon, a private Swiss foundation chooses seven "new" wonders of the world which include the Great Wall of China, the Taj Mahal in India, the Colosseum in Rome, centuries-old pink ruins of Petra in Jordan, the Statue of Christ the Redeemer in Rio de Janeiro, the Incan ruins of Machu Picchu in Peru and the ancient Mayan city of Chichen Itza in Mexico. ◆ Venus Williams of USA defeats Marion Bartoli of France, 6-4, 6-1 in the Wimbledon women's singles in London.

2007

- **July 8** : Roger Federer of Switzerland defeats Spaniard Rafael Nadal 7-6 (7), 4-6, 7-6 (3), 2-6, 6-2 in the men's singles final at Wimbledon in London. ◆ World No. 1 Viswanathan Anand of India defeats Bulgarian Grand Master Veselin Topalov in the final to win the Magistral Ciudad de Leon chess tournament for a record seventh time. ◆ **July 10** : Abdul Rashid Ghazi, the Islamic cleric who gave a spark to Lal Masjid's confrontation with the Pakistan Government and 50 other suspected militants are killed in bloody fighting during an all-out strike on the mosque by the security forces under "Operation Silence". ◆ **July 11** : Hon'ble President Dr. A.P.J. Abdul Kalam confers the 'Silver Elephant Award', the highest prestigious award of scouting and guiding in India on Mr. M. Ramachandran, Secretary, Union Ministry of Urban Development in New Delhi. ◆ The Royal Society, UK's National Academy of Science in London confers the King Charles II Medal on Hon'ble President Dr. A.P.J. Abdul Kalam in recognition of his extraordinary contribution to promotion of science in India. ◆ Wu Jingjun, Chief Engineer for the Beijing 2008 Olympics project, announces the completion of two of 12 new Beijing Olympics venues. ◆ **July 12** : The United Progressive Alliance Chairperson Ms. Sonia Gandhi inaugurates the Lifeline Express in New Delhi, a hospital train that will provide medical service to the poor in remote rural areas. ◆ The Neyyar Wildlife Sanctuary in Kerala draws international attention with the opening of a Crocodile Rehabilitation and Research Centre in memory of Australian crocodile hunter and environmentalist, Steve Irwin. ◆ **July 13** : Mr. Ratan Tata, the famous industrialist, has been given the honorary fellowship of the London School of Economics and Political Science for his contribution to global industry. ◆ **July 14** : Karan Rastogi of India wins the singles title in the $10,000 ITF men's Future tennins tournament on clay at Khemisset, Morocco. ◆ **July 15** : Koneru Humpy of India beats German International Master Sebast Siebrecht in the final round to win the Kaupthing Open chess title in Luxembourg. ◆ **July 25** : Mrs. Pratibha Patil became the first woman President of India.

●●●

GEOGRAPHY OF INDIA

India derives its name from the river Sindhu (Indus). It has a total area of 32,87,263 sq.km. with a land frontier of 15,200 kms. It measures 3,214 km from north to south and 2,933 km, from east to west. India is the seventh largest country in the world. India stands apart from the rest of Asia, marked off as it is by mountains and the sea, which give the country a distinct geographical entity.

India is bordered with Pakistan on the west and Bangladesh and Myanmar on the east, China, Tibet, Nepal and Bhutan are on the northern border. Bounded by the Great Himalayas in the north, it stretches southwards and at the Tropic of Cancer tapers off into the Indian Ocean between the Bay of Bengal on the east and the Arabian Sea on the west. India lies to the north of equator between 8° 4' and 37°6' north latitude, and 68°7' and 97° 25' east longitude.

GEOLOGICALLY INDIA IS MADE UP OF FOUR WELL-DEFINED REGIONS

1. *Peninsular Region*
2. *Himalayan Ranges*
3. *Indo-Gangetic plains formed by the rivers - Indus and Ganges.*
4. *The Desert Region.*

The Peninsular India is flanked on one side by the Eastern Ghats where the average elevation is about 610 metres and on the other side by the Western Ghats whose elevation is generally from 915 to 1,220 metres rising in some places to over 2,400 metres. The southern point of the Deccan Plateau is Nilgiri Hills where the Eastern and Western Ghats meet.

The Himalayas comprise three almost parallel ranges interspersed with large plateaus and valleys some of which - like Kashmir and Kulu valleys are fertile. The high altitudes limit travel only to a few passes notably the Jelep La and Natu La through Chumbi Valley on the Indo-Tibetan border. In the east, between India and Myanmar and India and Bangladesh, the ranges are much lower.

The Indo-Gangetic plain is 2,400 km long and 240 to 320 km broad. These plains are one of the world's greatest stretches of flat alluvial soil and also one of the most densely populated areas on the earth. There is hardly any variation in relief. Between the Yamuna at Delhi and the Bay of Bengal, nearly 1,600 km away there is a drop of only 200 metres in elevation.

The desert region can be divided into two parts - the great desert and the little desert. The great desert extends from the edge of Rann of Kachch beyond the Luni river northward. The whole of Rajasthan and Sind frontier runs through this. The little desert extends from the Luni between Jaisalmer and Jodhpur upto the north-west. Between the great and little deserts lie rocky landscape of limestone ridges with no surface water which makes this region sterile.

India has Seven Principal Mountain Ranges:

1. The Himalayas	2. The Patkai
3. The Vindhyas	4. The Satpura
5. The Aravalli	6. The Western Ghats
7. The Eastern Ghats	

The river system in India can be divided into four:

1. *The Himalayan rivers* **2.** *Peninsular rivers* **3.** *Coastal rivers* **4.** *Rivers of the inland drainage basin*

Rivers of India carry 16,83,000 million cubic metres of water per year. All rivers are east-flowing except the Narmada and the Tapti which are west-flowing.

The Himalayan rivers are perennial. During the monsoon, the Himalayas receive very heavy rainfall and the rivers often cause floods. During summer the rivers are snowfed. The peninsular rivers are generally rain-fed. The coastal streams especially of the west coast, are short in length and have limited catchment areas. The streams of the inland drainage basin of Western Rajasthan are a few and far between. Most of them are of an ephemeral character having no outlet to the sea. The Ganga basin carries water to one quarter of the total area of the country. The Ganga is joined by a number of Himalayan rivers including the Yamuna, Ghaghra, Gomti, Gandak and Kosi. The Godavari in the southern peninsula has the second largest river basin in the country covering 10% of the area of India. The Krishna and the Mahanadi basins are the second and third largest in the peninsula respectively. The basins of the Narmada and of the Kaveri are of about the same size.

FLORA AND FAUNA

India possesses rich and varied vegetation in its eight botanical regions namely Deccan, Malabar, Indus plain, Gangetic plain, Assam, Eastern Himalayas, Western Himalayas and the Andamans. India is rich in flora. Currently available data place India in the tenth position in the world and fourth in Asia in plant diversity. From about 70 per cent geographical area surveyed so far, 49,000 species of plants have been described by the Botanical Survey of India. The vascular flora, which forms the conspicuous vegetation cover comprises 15,000 species. The flora of the country is being studied by the Botanical Survey of India. The total plant wealth of the country includes not only the flowering plants but non-flowering plants like ferns, liverworts, algae and fungi. Owing to the destruction of forests, many Indian plants face extinction.

Collections of dried samples of these plants are preserved in the Central National Herbarium. The faunal resource of our country is surveyed by the Zoological Survey of India (ZSI), with its headquarters at Calcutta in 1916 and 16 regional stations located in different parts of the country. Possessing a tremendous diversity of climate and physical conditions, India has great variety of fauna numbering 81,251 species. Of these, insects constitute about 60,000, molluscs a little over 5,000, mammals 372, birds 1,228, reptiles 446, amphibians 204, and fishes 2,546. The mammals include the Asiatic lion, a rare species, is found in the Gir forest in Gujarat. The great Indian one-horned rhinoceros is found in Assam. *The Indian peocock with blue plumage has been declared the National Bird.* The tiger which is the National Animal numbers about 4,230. The Wildlife (Protection) Act, 1972 governs the Wild Life Conservation and protection of endangered species. There are presently 84 national parks and 447 wildlife sanctuaries covering about 1.50 lakhs sq.km. area which is nearly 4.5 percent of the total geographical area of the country.

Climate and Rainfall: India has varied temperatures. While Darjeeling and Simla have the lowest temperatures between 15.7°C and 16.9°C, Nagpur registers 35.5°C. Rainfall is erratic. Areas like West Coast, Bengal, Assam, etc. get the heaviest rain of above 200 cm annually. Mumbai, Madhya Pradesh, Bihar, etc. receive 100 to 200 cm and Chennai, North Western Deccan and upper Gangetic Plain have 50 to 100 cm. The Thar Desert receives only 10 cm of rainfall. While the rainy season in most parts of the country is from June to September, in Tamilnadu & Andhra Pradesh, it is during North East Monsoon.

The Monsoons: India gets rains by South West Monsoon and North East Monsoon. The South West Monsoon brings more rain. North East Monsoon is shorter in duration and comes after South West Monsoon. Tamilnadu & Andhra Pradesh receives heavy rain during North East Monsoon or Retreating Monsoon.

The South West Monsoon starts in May/June and North East Monsoon starts in November/October.

VITAL STATISTICS OF THE PEOPLE

Population Census 2001 - India's 14th Census (Revised)

The much awaited Census 2001 was held from February 9 to 28. The census, which is the country's largest administrative exercise, was carried out all over the country barring Jammu and Kashmir, where it had already been held. In this massive exercise, over 20 lakh enumerators and supervisors collected information on demographic, social and economic aspects.

Every sixth person in the world is an Indian. According to the provisional population figures of the 14th Census, India has 102.8 crore on March 1, 2001, India's population comprises of 53.2 crore men and 49.6 crore women. The figures take into account the data accumulated from all 35 States (including Union Territories) and are tentative and show only broad trends.

According to the Census data, there has been an addition of 181 million persons (more than the population of Brazil) in the last decade. India has now become the second country in the world after China to cross the one billion mark. Decadal growth marginally declined from 24.80% in 1971 to 24.66% in 1981, 23.85% in 1991 and 21.34% in 2001. Bihari (28.62%) has higher decadal growth than all other states and UP, Nagaland (64.41%) had highest growth rate and Kerala

(9.43%) the lowest growth rate. Uttar Pradesh continued to be most populous state of the country with a net share of 16.17 percent of the national population.

The number of literate people, however, has gone up significantly. Three-fourth of the male population and more than half of the female population above the age of seven are now classified as literate. Literacy in net terms has recorded impressive hike of 13.17 per cent, from 52.21 per cent in 1991 to 64.8 per cent in 2001. Three/fourths of the male population and more than half of the female population across the country was literate as per the latest census estimates.

Kerala, expectantly, had the highest literacy rate (90.92 per cent), followed by Mizoram (88.8 per cent), Bihar recorded a low of 47.53 percent literacy. Uttar Pradesh continued to be the most populous State in country with 16.17 percent of the national population followed by Maharashtra (9.42 percent) and Bihar (8.07 percent). West Bengal is the most densely populated State with 903 persons living per sq.km. followed by Bihar with 881 persons per sq. km. The sex ratio (number of women per 1,000 men) is 933, which is an improvement of six point over 927 recorded in the 1991 Census. The highest sex ratio (1,058 women per thousand men) has been recorded in Kerala and Haryana has the lowest (861 women per thousand men). Possibly the largest enumeration exercise of its kind in the world, the Census concluded on February 28, with a revision rounds upto March 5, 2001.

CENSUS OF INDIA - 2001

	Population	Decadal Growth	(%)	Literates	(%)
Persons	1028 million	181.0 million	21.34%	566,714,995	64.8%
Males	532 million	92.0 million	20.93%	339,969,048	75.2%
Females	496 million	89.0 million	21.79%	226,745,947	53.6%

Density (per sq.km.)	:	325
Sex Ratio (females per 1000 males)	:	933

NATIONAL SYMBOLS

The Constitution has ordained Hindi in the Devanagiri script as the common language throughout India and Arabic numerals as the common numerals. English was to be retained as an Official language until 1965, when it was to be replaced by Hindi completely.

National Flag: The National Flag of India is a tricolour with three equal horizontal stripes - saffron on top, white in the middle and dark green at the bottom in equal proportion. Safron stands for courage, sacrifice and renunciation. White stands for truth and purity. Truth in words and actions, and purity in thoughts. Green is symbol of life, abundance and prosperity. A Chakra, dark blue in colour and having 24 spokes is superimposed on the middle white strip. Chakra is the symbol of progress and of movement. This emblem in the flag is an exact reproduction of the Dharma Chakra on the Capitol of Ashoka's Pillar at Saranath.

The ratio of the width to length of the flag is two to three. The national flag of India was adopted by the Constituent Assembly on 22nd July 1947 and it was presented to the Nation on behalf of the **Women of India**, at the midnight session of the Assembly on **14th August 1947**.

The dipping of the flag by any person or thing is prohibited. No other flag or emblem is to be placed above or to the right of the flag. When flown or raised with other flags, the national flag must be the highest. The saffron strip should always be at the top when the flag is displayed.

National Emblem: The National Emblem and seal of the Government is a replica (duplicate) of the Capitol (top part) of Ashoka's Pillar at Saranath. In the Original, there are four lions standing back to back with their mouths wide open. In the emblem however, only three lions are visible. The Capitol is mounted on an abacus (a flat slab). There is a Dharma Chakra in the centre of the base plate on the right of which stands the figure of the bull and on the left, that of a horse. Thus there are six animals in our national emblem.

The words 'Satyameva Jayate' inscribed below the base plate of the emblem are in the Devanagari script. The words 'Satyameva Jayate' are taken from **'Mundaka Upanishad'** meaning 'Truth alone triumphs'. This was adopted as the national emblem on 26th January, 1950 by the Government of India.

National Anthem: The song 'Jana Gana Mana' was first sung on 27th December 1911 at the Kolkata Session of the Indian National Congress. It was adopted as the National Anthem of India on **24th January, 1950**. 'Jana Gana Mana' was composed by Rabindranath Tagore and it was published in January, 1912 under the title 'Bharat Vidhata' in the 'Tatva Bodhini Patrika' edited by Tagore himself. The song was translated into English by Tagore in 1919 under the title *'Morning Song of India'*. The playing time of the full version of the National Anthem is about 52 seconds.

National Song: The song 'Vande Matharam' composed by Bankhim Chandra Chatterjee in his novel, 'Anand Math' published in 1882 was a source of inspiration to the people in their struggle for freedom. It has an equal status with 'Jana Gana Mana'. It was first sung at the 1896 Calcutta session of the Indian National Congress.

National Calendar: The National Calendar of India is based on the **Saka Era** which began with vernal equinor of 78 A.D with Chaitra as its first month and Phalguna as the last month of a normal year of 365 days. The days of this calendar permanently correspond with the Gregorian calendar and Chaitra falls on March 22nd in a common year and March 21st in a leap year. It was introduced on March 22, 1957 because Kanishka came to the throne on March 22.

National Animal: The majestic tiger - *panthera tigris* (Linnaeus) is the National Animal of India, for its rich colour, illusive design and formidable power. Out of eight races of the species, known the world over, the Indian race is the Royal Bengal tiger. The Royal Bengal Tiger is seen thoughout the country.

National Bird: The Indian Peacock - *pavo cristatus* - is the National Bird of India. From time immemorial, the Peacock has found its profound place in Indian literature, folklore and legends. The bird is found throughout India. It is fully protected under the Indian Wildlife Act.

National Tree: Banyan Tree; **National Game:** Hockey; **National Flower:** Lotus; **National Fruit:** Mango. .

PLANNING

Though planned economy was in operation even before independence, it was only in March, 1950, the Government of India set up a 'Planning Commission', to prepare plan for the most effective and balanced utilisation of the country's resources. Planning in India derives its objectives and social promises from Directive Principles of State Policy enshrined in the Constitution.

While documenting the schedules of the planning so many uncertainties may have to be dealt with, hence, delay in finalising a plan document, is inevitable. The Planning Commission members are generally, experts in different aspects of the economy without any political affiliation, and as such, are to plan on the basis of the resources in sight for achieving the socio-economic objectives defined by the party in power. The Prime Minister is the Chairman of the Planning Commission.

First Plan (1951-1956): It had a two fold objective to correct the disequilibrium in the economy caused by Second World War and partition of the country and to initiate simultaneously a process of all-round balanced development, which would ensure a rising national income and a steady improvement in the living standards over a period of time.

Since the country had to import foodgrains on a large scale in 1951 and there were inflationary pressures in the economy, the plan accorded the highest priority to agriculture, including irrigation and power projects. About 44.6 per cent of the total outlay of Rs.2,069 crore in the public sector (later raised to Rs.2,378 crore) was allotted for its development. The plan also aimed at increasing the rate of investment from five per cent to about seven per cent of the national income.

In 1954, the Parliament declared that the broad objectives of economic policy should be to achieve a 'socialistic pattern of society' under which the basic criteria for determining the lines of advance would be social gain and greater equality in income and wealth and not private profit.

Second Plan (1956-1961): It therefore sought to promote a pattern of development which would ultimately lead to the establishment of a socialistic pattern of society in India. In particular, it stressed that the benefits of economic development should accrue more to the relatively less privileged sections of society and there should be progressive reduction in the concentration of income, wealth and economic power.

The main aims of the Second Plan were (i) an increase of 25 per cent in the national income (ii) rapid industrialisation with particular emphasis on the development of basic and heavy industries (iii) large expansion of employment opportunities, and (iv) reduction of inequalities in income and wealth and a more even distribution of economic power. The Plan also aimed at increasing the rate of investment from about seven per cent of the national income to 11 per cent by 1960-61. The Plan laid special stress on industrialisation, increased production of iron and steel, heavy chemicals including nitrogenous fertilizers and development of heavy engineering and machine building industry.

Third Plan (1961-1966): It aimed at securing a marked advance towards self-sustaining growth. Its immediate objectives were to (i) secure an increase in the national income of over five per cent per annum and at the same time ensure a pattern of investment which could sustain this rate of growth during subsequent plan periods; (ii) achieve self-sufficiency in foodgrains and increase agricultural production to meet the requirement of industry and exports; (iii) basic industries like steel, chemicals, fuel and to establish machine-building capacity, so that the requirements of further industrialisation could be met within a period of 10 years or so, mainly from the country's own resources; (iv) utilise fully the manpower resources of the country and ensure a substantial expansion in employment opportunity and (v) establish progressively greater equality of opportunity and bring about reduction in disparities of income and wealth and a more even distribution of economic power. The Plan aimed at increasing the national income by about 30 per cent from Rs.14,500 crore in 1960-61 to about Rs.19,000 crore by 1965-66 (at 1960-61 prices) and per capita income by about 17 per cent from Rs.330 to Rs.385 during the same period.

Annual Plans (1966-1969): The situation created by the Indo-Pakistan conflict in 1965, two successive years of severe drought, introduction of green revolution, devaluation of the currency, general rise in prices and erosion of resources available for plan purpose, delayed finalisation of the Fourth Five Year Plan. Instead, between 1966 and 1969, three Annual Plans were formulated within the framework of the Draft Outline of the Fourth Plan. They took into account the conditions prevailing at that time. The state of the economy and the non-availability of financial resources for plan purposes kept down the size of development outlay during this period.

Fourth Plan (1969-1974): It aimed at accelerating the tempo of development and reducing fluctuations in agricultural production as well as the impact of uncertainties of foreign aid. It aimed at raising the standard of living of the people through programmes which were designed to promote equality and social justice.

The Plan laid particular emphasis on improving the condition of the less privileged and weaker sections of the society especially through the provision of employment and education. Efforts were also directed towards reduction of concentration and a wider diffusion of wealth, income and economic power. The Plan aimed at increasing the net domestic product (at 1968-69 factor cost) from Rs.29,071 crore in 1969-70 to Rs.38,306 crore in 1973-74. The average annual compound rate of growth envisaged was 5.7 per cent.

Fifth Plan (1974-1979): It was formulated at a time when the economy was facing severe inflationary pressures. The major objectives of the Plan were to achieve self-reliance and to adopt measures for raising the consumption standards of the people living below the poverty line. The Plan also gave high priority of bringing inflation under control and to achieve stability in the economic situation. It was subsequently decided to end the Fifth Plan with the close of the Annual Plan, 1978-79 and to initiate work for a new plan for the next five years with new priorities and programmes.

Sixth Plan (1980-1985): It had been formulated after taking into account the achievements and shortcomings of the past three decades of planning. Eradication of poverty has been the foremost objective of the Plan even though it was recognised that the task of such magnitude could not be accomplished in a short period of five years.

The Sixth Plan actual expenditure stood at Rs.1,09,291.7 crore (current prices) as against the envisaged total public sector outlay of Rs.97,500 crore (1979-80 prices) accounting for a 12 per cent increase in nominal terms. The average annual growth rate for the Sixth Plan was 5.26 per cent.

Seventh Plan (1985-1990): The total expenditure during the entire Seventh Plan stood at Rs.2,18,729.62 crore (current prices) as against the envisaged total public sector outlay of Rs.180,000 ended with an average rate of growth of the Gross Domestic Product (GDP) at 5.8 per cent per annum, which was well above the targeted rate of 5 per cent. To reduce unemployment and the incidence of poverty **Jawahar Rozgar Yojana** scheme launched.

Annual Plans (1990-91, 1991-92):

The new Government assumed power at the Centre by June 1991, decided that the 8th Five Year Plan would commence on April 1, 1992 and that 1990-91 and 91-92 should be treated as separate Annual Plans.

Eighth Plan (1992-97): It was launched after the initiation of structural adjustment policies and macro stabilisation policies which were necessitated by the inflation position and the worsening Balance of Payments position during 1990-91. The Plan aimed at an average annual growth rate of 5.6 percent and an average industrial growth rate of about 7.5 percent.

The total expenditure during the entire Plan stood at Rs.4,95,669 crore at current prices as against envisaged total public sector outlay of Rs.4,34,100 crore (1991-92 prices) resulting in a 14.2 percent in nominal terms. During the Plan, the GDP grew at an average rate of 6.8 percent exceeding the targeted growth rate of 5.6 percent.

Ninth Plan (1997-2002): It was launched in the fiftieth year of India's Independence. The Approach Paper was approved unanimously by the National Development Council. The salient features of the Approach Paper were (i) a targeted GDP growth rate of 7 per cent per annum for the Ninth Plan period; (ii) Emphasis on the seven identified Basic Minimum Services (BMS) with additional Central Assistance earmarked for the basic amenities of the people with a view to obtaining a complete coverage of the population in a time bound manner. The specific objectives of the Ninth Plan as endorsed by the National Development Council in its 48th Meeting are: (i) priority to agriculture and rural development; (ii) accelerating the growth rate of the economy with stable prices; (iii) ensuring food and nutritional security for all; (iv) providing the basic minimum services; (v) containing the growth rate of population;

(vi) ensuring environmental sustainability of the development process; (vii) empowerment of women and socially disadvantaged groups; (viii) promoting and developing people's participatory institutions like *Panchayati Raj* institutions, cooperatives and self-help groups; and (ix) strengthening efforts to build self-reliance.

The Ninth Plan envisaged an average target growth rate of 6.5 per cent per annum in GDP as against the growth rate of 7 per cent approved earlier in the Approach Paper. During 1997-98, the first year of the Ninth Five Year Plan there was a slow down in the growth rate of Indian economy to 4.8 per cent. In the second year and third year of the Plan, the economy grew by about 6.6 and 6.4 per cent respectively.

The Plan proposes an investment of Rs. 2,171 thousand crore during the period 1997-2002 at 1996-97 prices, most of which (92.6 per cent amounting to Rs. 2,011 thousand crore) could be financed from domestic resources. Investment in the public sector would be Rs. 726 thousand crore constituting about 33 per cent of the total investment. The public sector outlay is proposed at Rs. 8,59,200 crore, out of which the Central Plan outlay would be Rs. 4,89,361 crore, which includes provision to implement the additional requirements of Special Action Plans. The Central Budgetary Support to the Plan was targeted at Rs. 3,74,000 crore at 1996-97 prices.

Achievements under Five Year Plans

In the last 52 years (1950-51 to 2002-03), since India became a Republic, the National Income - Net National Product (NNP) has increased 8.7 times from Rs. 1,32,367 crore to Rs. 11,56,714 crore (at 1993-94 prices) implying a compound growth rate of 4.3 per cent per annum. The per capita income has increased 3 times from Rs. 3,687 to Rs. 10,964 (at 1993-94 prices) registering a compound growth rate of 2.1 per cent - all the aggregates measured at factor-cost at 1993-94 prices.

Despite the successive drought conditions that prevailed during the first three years of the Seventh Plan (1985-90), the economy fared exceptionally well during the Plan period with a growth rate of GDP at six per cent per annum as against the target of five per cent. Important policy reforms have been made since June 1991. For the year 2000-01, the growth rate has been estimated at six per cent as per the Advanced Estimates of National Income, 2000-01.

The average inflation rate measured by changes in the Wholesale Price Index (WPI) (1993-94 series) was 4.4 per cent, 5.9 per cent, 3.3 per cent during the years 1997-98, 1998-99, 1999-2000 respectively. During the financial year 2000-01, the average inflation rate has been estimated at about 7.2 per cent.

Growth Trends and Crop Production: Foodgrains production was to reach 234 million tonnes target by the terminal year of the Ninth Plan (2001-02) as envisaged earlier. But considering less than the expected performance, the production target has been revised downward to 218 million tonnes. The estimated foodgrains production of only 196.13 million tonnes during 2000-01 implied a fall of 12.74 million tonnes over the previous years.

Horticulture and Plantation Crop: Horticulture is being carried out on eight per cent of the cultivated area in the country, whereas it contributes 24.5 per cent towards agriculture GDP (1998-99): The estimated production of fruits was 46 million tonnes and that of vegetables 91 million tonnes during 1999-2000.

Tenth Five Year Plan

The Tenth Five Year Plan (2002-07) was approved by the National Development Council on 21 December 2002. The Plan has further developed the NDC Mandated objectives of doubling per capita income in ten years and achieving a growth rate of eight per cent of GDP per annum. Reduction in poverty ratio from 26 per cent to 21 per cent, by 2007; Decadal Population Growth to reduce from 21.3 per cent in 1991-2001 to 16.2 per cent in 2001-11; Growth in gainful employment to, at least, keep pace with addition to the labour force; All children to be in school by 2003 and all children to complete 5 years of schooling by 2007; Reducing gender gaps in literacy and wage rates by 50 per cent; Literacy Rate to increase from 65 per cent in 1999-2000, to 75 per cent in 2007; Providing potable drinking water in all villages; Infant Mortality Rate to be reduced from 72 in 1999-2000, to 45 in 2007; Maternal Mortality Ratio be reduced from four in 1999-2000, to two in 2007; Increase in Forest/Tree Cover from 19 per cent in 1999-2000, to 25 per cent in 2007; and Cleaning of major polluted river stretches are the major objectives.

The Tenth Plan has a number of new features, that include, among others, the following:

Firstly, the Plan recognises the rapid growth in the labour force over the next decade. Secondly, the Plan addresses the issue of Poverty and the unacceptably low levels of social indicators. Thirdly, since national targets do not necessarily translate into balanced regional development and the potential and constraints of each State differ vastly, the Tenth Plan has adopted a differential development strategy. It is also for the first time that statewise growth and other monitorable targets have been worked out in consultation with the States. This will enable the States to better focus their own development plans. Another feauture of this Plan is the recognition that Governance is perhaps one of the most important factors for ensuring that the Plan is realised, as envisaged.

Finally, considering the present market-oriented economy, the Tenth Plan has dwelt at length about the policies that would be necessary and the design of key institutions. The Tenth Plan not only includes a carefully crafted medium term macro-economic policy stance, both for the Centre and the States, but also lays out the policy and institutional reforms that are required for each sector.

Target for 11th Five Year Plan (2007-12)

Seeking to emulate tiger economies such as China and Korea, the Planning Commission has set an ambitious 8.5 per cent growth target for the 11th Five Year Plan, commencing in 2007-08. The Plan aims to reach 9.5 per cent growth in the final year, according to the approach paper. The paper, in a break with tradition, has been circulated to Chief Ministers and Union Ministers well in advance of a formal meeting of the National Development Council (NDC).

The Commission is believed to have described the high growth path as "feasible but not inevitable," while flagging a number of hard decisions essential to achieve this objective. It has placed the focus of the next plan on agriculture, social sector and manufacturing.

BANKING IN INDIA

The Reserve Bank of India Act, 1934 regularised the central banking system in India for the first time. Until then the Imperial Bank of India, which is now known as 'State Bank of India' functioned as a Central Bank for all purposes. The Reserve Bank of India came into existence on 1st April 1935 and was nationalised on 1st January 1949. The Reserve Bank is divided into two departments, the Issue Department and the Banking Department.

The primary functions of the Reserve Bank are issue of paper currency, acting as bankers to Government, controlling the activities of commercial banks, acting as bank of accommodation and lender in the last resort, maintenance of foreign exchange, provision of agricultural credit and collection and publication of monetary and financial information.

The Reserve Bank of India Act classified the banks into Scheduled and Non-Scheduled. The Scheduled banks are those with a minimum capital and reserves of over Rs.5 lakhs, and the banks which having satisfied the Reserve Bank that their activities are not detrimental to the interests of the depositors, are included in the second Schedule of the Reserve Bank of India Act, 1934.

The role of Reserve Bank of India is two fold - *promotional* and *regulatory*. It helps the Government in its developmental projects by raising loans at low interests and providing funds for deficit financing. The credit control and other monetary directives announced by Reserve Bank of India from time to time have had a salutary effect on the Indian Economy.

The affiliates of the Reserve Bank of India are:

1. *Agricultural Refinancing Corporation* 2. *Deposit Insurance Corporation* 3. *Unit Trust of India*

Commercial Banking System in India can be traced to European Agency Houses in Calcutta and Mumbai. The Presidency Bank of Mumbai was established in 1804 and was liquidated in 1868 owing to heavy losses in speculation. It was then replaced by a second Bank of Mumbai in 1868 itself. The two other Presidency Banks were Bank of Bengal (1806) and the Bank of Madras (1843). These Banks were mainly bankers to the East India Company. All these three banks were amalgamated into the Imperial Bank of India in 1920. In the modern banking line, the first bank established was the Bank of Upper India in 1863 and the Allahabad Bank in 1865.

The Punjab National Bank purely an Indian venture, was established in 1894. Many other banks, the Bank of India, established in 1906, the Bank of Baroda in 1908, the Central Bank of India 1911 followed suit. Many other banks were established and soon died of one or other reasons.

Nationalisation of Banks

The Presidential Ordinance of 19th July 1969 nationalised 14 major banks each with a deposit of Rs.50 crore or more. In 1980, 6 more banks with deposits of Rs.200 crore and more were nationalised. The public sector banks comprising the State Bank of India and its 7 subsidiaries and the 20 major banks nationalised, go to make a total of 28 banks. The objectives of the public sector banking system were outlined by the then Prime Minister in Parliament on 21 July 1969.

Commercial Banking System in India consisted of 286 Scheduled Banks (including foreign banks) at the end of 31st March 2006. In the public sector there are 133 Regional Rural Banks and these account for about 77.5 per cent of the deposits of all scheduled commercial banks and these are specially set up to increase the flow of credit to small borrowers in the rural areas. The remaining 27 banks in the public sector (i.e., nationalised banks and SBI Group) are commercial banks.

Among the public sector banks, as on 31st March 2006, the State Bank of India (SBI) group (SBI and its seven associates) is the second largest unit with 33,868 offices and deposits aggregating Rs.10,13,664 crore and advances of Rs.7,21,066 crore. The SBI and its associate banks as a group account for around 32.7% of aggregate banking business (aggregate of deposits and advances) conducted by the public sector banks and around 23.3% of the aggregate business of all scheduled commercial banks.

Regional Rural Banks

RRBs were set up to take the banking services to the doorsteps of rural masses especially in remote rural areas. As much as Rs.62,143 crore were mobilised as deposits by RRBs at the end of March 2005 and the loans and advances stood at Rs.32,870 crore during the same period. Consequent upon the permission of the Reserve Bank to determine their own lending rate with effect from 22 March, 1997 most of the RRBs have been charging interest rate on loans varying between 14% and 18% per annum.

Small Industries Development Bank of India (SIDBI)

SIDBI was established as a wholly-owned subsidiary of the Industrial Development Bank of India (IDBI) under the Small Industries Development Bank of India Act, 1989 as the principal finance institution for promotion, financing and development of industries in the small scale sector. It started its operation from 2 April 1990 to provide assistance to the small scale industrial sector through the State Finance Corporation, Commercial Banks, etc. The financial assistance sanctioned and disbursed aggregated to Rs.11,975 crore and Rs.9,100 crore, respectively during 2005-2006.

Deposit Mobilisation and Deployment

There has been a substantial increase in the deposits of scheduled commercial banks in the post-nationalisation period. At the end of March 2006, deposits of these banks increased to Rs.20,93,042 crore and deposits with public sector banks were Rs.15,74,664 crore. Deposits mobilised by the banks are utilised for: **(i)** loans and advances to borrowers; **(ii)** investments in government securities and other approved securities in fulfilment of the liquidity stipulations; and **(iii)** investment in Commercial paper, shares, debentures, etc., upto a stipulated ceiling.

There has been a significant increase in the investment of banks in government and other approved securities were Rs.7,17,454 crores as at the end of March 2006. The advances of scheduled commercial banks have grown to Rs.15,07,077 crore during the same period. The share of priority sectors has shown significant improvement over the years.

Credit flow to Weaker Sections

To augment credit facilities to rural sector, Commercial Banks were advised by the Reserve Bank of India to provide atleast 10% of their net bank credit or 25% of their priority sector advances to weaker sections comprising of small and marginal farmers, landless labourers, tenant farmers and share-croppers, artisans, village and cottage industries, where individual credit limits do not exceed Rs. 50,000 beneficiaries of Schemes of Swarnajayanti Shahari Rozgar Yojana (SSRY) and beneficiaries of Swarnajayanthi Gram Swarojgar Yojana (SGSY) and Scheme for Liberation and Rehabilitation of Scavengers (SLRS), Scheduled Castes and Scheduled Tribes and beneficiaries of Differential Rate of Interest (DRI) Scheme.

At the end of March 2006, the amount of outstanding advances to weaker sections amounted to Rs.78,374 crore and accounted for 7.7% of their net bank credit.

Differential Rate of Interest Scheme

Under this scheme, which was introduced in 1972, public sector banks are required to fulfil the target of lending atleast one percent of the total advances as at the end of the preceding year to the weakest of the weak sections of the society at the interest of four percent per annum. This scheme covers poor borrowers having an annual income of not more than Rs. 6,400 in rural and Rs. 7,200 in other areas and not having more than 2.5 acres of unirrigated or one acre of irrigated land Rs. 6,500 is being given as term loan and working capital for productive ventures. At the end of March 2006, the public sector banks had an outstanding of DRI Credit amounting to Rs. 490 crores.

Credit Flow to Agriculture

Banks were initially given a target of extending 15% of the total advances as direct finance to the agriculture sector to be achieved by March 1985. This target was subsequently raised to 18% to be achieved by March 1990. In terms of the guidelines issued by the RBI (in October 1993), both direct and indirect loans for agriculture together are assessed at 18% provided lending for indirect credit should not exceed one fourth of the total lending of the net bank credit. As at the end of March 2006, public sector banks had extended Rs.1,54,900 crore constituting 15.22% of the net bank credit to the agriculture sector. Private sector banks extended Rs.36,185 crore constituting 13.5% of net bank credit.

Advances to SC/ST Borrowers

Banks took special efforts to help the vulnerable section (SC/ST) to undertake self-employment ventures which would enable them to acquire income generating capital assets and thereby raise their standards of living. The total outstanding amount of loan extended to SC/ST by public sector banks was Rs.22,666 crore in 84.38 lakh borrowal accounts as at the end of March, 2006.

Swarna Jayanthi Gram Swarozgar Yojana

Swarnajayanthi Gram Swarozgar Yojana (SGSY) has replaced IRDP and its allied sechemes,viz, TRYSEM, DWCRA, SITRA, GKY and MWS with effect from April 1999. SGSY is a holistic programme covering all aspects of self-employment such as organisation of poor into self help groups, training, credit, technology infrastructure and marketing. The scheme will be funded on 75:25 basis by the Centre and the States and, will be implemented by DRDAs, through Panchayat Samitis. The year 2005-06 was the sixth year of implementation of the scheme. Up to March 2006 the total number of *Swarojgaris* assisted were 12,07,078. Bank credit to the tune of Rs. 1125.42 crore and Government subsidy amounting to Rs. 375.09 crore were disbursed. Out of total *Swarojgaris* assisted, 4,26,000 (35.29%) were SC and ST, 6,08,756 (50.43%) were women and 20,788 (1.72%) were physically handicapped.

Progress of Commercial Banking in India

S. No.	Item	March 2004	March 2005
1.	Deposits of scheduled Commercial Banks (Rs. crore)	15,42,284*	17,32,858*
2.	Credit of Scheduled Commercial Banks (Rs. crore)	8,65,594	11,24,300
3.	Per Capita Deposits of Scheduled Commercial Banks (Rs. crore)	14,550	16,091

* Including India Millennium Deposits (Rs. 25,662 crore).

Prime Minister's Rozgar Yojana (PMRY)

PMRY for educated unemployed youth was launched on 2nd October, 1993. This scheme was implemented in urban areas during 1993-94 and from 1st April 1994, to provide employment to 10 lakh educated unemployed urban youth in micro-enterprises during the Eighth Five Year Plan. Self-employment Scheme for Educated Umemployed Youth (SEEUY) has been included under PMRY. During 2005-06, total sanctions by commercial banks amounted to Rs.1,923 crore in 2.98 lakh accounts, while disbursements amounted to Rs.1521 crore in 2.49 lakh accounts. (data provisional)

Swarnajayanthi Shahari Rozgar Yojana

This scheme (SJSRY) is in operation from 1st December 1997 in all urban and semi-urban towns of India. This scheme has two sub-schemes; namely, Urban Self-Employment Programme (USEP) and Development of Women and Children in Urban Areas (DWCUA). Under this scheme, women are to be assisted to the extent of not less than 30 per cent, disabled at 3 per cent and SC/STs according to the proportion of their strength. This scheme is funded 75:25 basis between the Central and State Govts. Under USEP, projects costing upto Rs. 50,000 are to be financed by banks. Subsidy is 15% of the project cost subject to maximum of Rs. 7,500. Under DWCUA, women groups should consist of atleast 10 urban poor women. The group is entitled to a subsidy of Rs. 1,25,000 or 50 per cent of the project cost whichever is less. During the end of March 2006 of the total 68,579 applications sanctioned under the scheme 55,023 cases were disbursed amounting to Rs. 49.68 crore by the scheduled commercial banks.

Industrial Development Bank of India (IDBI)

IDBI established under Industrial Development Bank of India Act, 1964. IDBI is the principal financial institution for providing credit and other facilities for development of industry, co-ordinating working of institutions engaged in financing, promoting or developing industries and assisting the development of such institutions. Aggregate assistance (provisional) sanctioned during 2004-05 amounted to Rs.6,314 crore registering a of 120.8% over the preceding year. Disbursements amounted to Rs.2,085 crore in 2005-06.

Industrial Finance Corporation of India (IFCI)

Established in July 1948 with an authorised capital of Rs.50 crore, IFCI's role now extends to the entire industrial spectrum in the country. As on 31st December, 1992, the net cumulative financial assistance sanctioned by IFCI aggregated to Rs.14,608.65 crore to 4,211 industrial projects. IFCI was restructured from a statutory corporation of a company from 1st July 1993.

Industrial Credit and Investment Corporation of India (ICICI)

ICICI was established in 1955, as a public limited company to encourage and assist industrial units in the country. It provides term loans in Indian and Foreign currencies, underwrites issues of shares and debentures, makes direct subscription to these issues. The assistance sanctioned and disbursed by ICICI during 2005-06 aggregated to Rs.35,589 crore and Rs.25,050 crore, respectively (provisional), registering a growth of 36.2% and 20.9%, respectively, over the previous year. The ICICI was merged with ICICI Bank Ltd. through the reverse merger process effective from March 31, 2005.

Export-Import bank (EXIM Bank)

EXIM Bank was established on 1st January 1982 for financing, facilitating and promoting foreign trade in India. It co-ordinates with export-import institutions. During the year ended 31st March 2006, EXIM Bank sanctioned loans of Rs.20,489 crore while disbursements amounted to Rs.15,039 crore. Net Profit (after tax) of the Bank for the period 2005-06 on account of General Fund amounted to Rs.271 crore.

National Housing Bank

National Housing Bank (NHB) the apex institution of housing finance in India was set-up as wholly-owned subsidiary of the Reserve Bank of India (RBI) under the National Housing Bank Act, 1987. It started its operation from July 1988. As on 30th June 2005, the paid-up capital stood at Rs. 450 crore and the reserves and surplus were Rs. 1,201.32 crore. Authorised share capital is Rs. 500 crore. A major activity of NHB includes extending financial assistance to various eligible institutions by way of (a) refinance and (b) direct finance. The cumulative refinance assistance provided stood at Rs. 7,500 crore upto 30th June 2005. Total number of Housing Finance Companies stood at 29 upto 31st March 2006.

Under the Direct Financing Window, NHB so far sanctioned 282 projects under its various project finance schemes both direct as well as through the refinance window. During the year 2001-02, 2.5 lakhs dwelling units were successfully completed. The target for 2005-06 is to finance 2.5 lakh dwelling units and 2.58 lakh units had been financed upto December 2003. During the 58th year of Independence, NHB had launched the **Golden Jubilee Rural Housing Finance Scheme.**

NABARD

The National Bank for Agriculture and Rural Development (NABARD) was established on 12th July 1982 by recommendation of **B. Sivaraman** Committee. NABARD as the apex institution, is concerned with all policy planning and operations in the field of credit for agriculture and other economic activities in the rural areas.

NABARD provides refinance to the state land development banks, state co-operative banks, scheduled commercial banks and regional rural banks. The short-term (ST) credit limits for 2000-01 sanctioned by NABARD to State Co-operative Banks of Seasonal Agricultural Operations (SAO) up to the end of March 2003 aggregated to Rs.7,452.63 crore. Outstandings against these limits stood at Rs.4,966.39 crore as at the end of March 2003. The credit limits sanctioned for 2001-02 included Rs.261.48 crore for Development of Tribal Population (DTP), Rs.988.53 crore for Oilseeds Production Programme (OPP) and Rs.55.43 crore for National Pulses Development Programme (NPDP). The outstanding there under amounted to Rs.2000 crore under all ST credit limits as on 31st March 2006.

Life Insurance Corporation of India (LIC)

When India attained Independence there were 245 Indian and non-Indian insurance companies. The life insurance business was nationalised on 1st September 1956 and on that day came into existence LIC of India. LIC is associated with joint ventures abroad in the field of insurance. During the year 1994-95 LIC's total income was over Rs.18,102.32 crore. The income consists of premium, investment and miscellaneous incomes, etc. LIC with its central office in Mumbai and seven zonal offices at Mumbai, Kolkata, Delhi, Chennai, Hyderabad, Kanpur and Bhopal, operates through 101 divisional offices in important cities and 2,048 branch offices. It has 10,52,283 lakh agents.

The total new business of the Corporation during 2005-06 was Rs.2,78,530.24 crore of sum assured under 315.73 lakh policies. LIC's group insurance business during the year was Rs.3,919.01 crore (provisional) providing cover to 51.27 lakh people. The Life Fund of LIC on 31st March 2006 amounts to Rs. 4,63,147.62 crore. During 2005-06, it made payments of Rs. 3,769.04 crore under death claims and Rs. 24,743.42 crore under Maturity Claims and Rs. 1,977.54 crore under annuities.

Janashree Bima Yojana

The **Janashree Bima Yojana** was launched on 10 August 2000. The scheme has replaced Social Security Group Insurance Scheme (SSGIS) and Rural Group Life Insurance Scheme (RGLIS). The Scheme provides for an insurance cover of Rs. 20,000 on natural death. The premium for the scheme is Rs.200 per member.

The Central Government will bear 50 per cent which will be met out of Social Security Fund. As on 31st March 2006, about 39.87 lakh people have been covered. Social Security Group Scheme, *Bima Yojana* (10.08.2000) and *Krishi Shramik Samajik Suraksha Yojana* (01.07.2001), *Siksha Sahayog Yojana* (31.12.2001) have also been introduced.

General Insurance Corporation

The general insurance industry in India was nationalised and a government company known as General Insurance Corporation of India (GIC) was formed by the Central Government in November 1972. Following nationalisation with effect from 1 January 1973, these 107 units were grouped and merged into four operating companies formed as subsidiaries of the General Insurance Corporation of India. The General Insurance Corporation was set up as the Holding Company.

The four subsidiary companies are:

1. *National Insurance Company Limited, Kolkata*

2. *The New India Assurance Company Limited, Mumbai*

3. *The Oriental Insurance Company Limited, New Delhi*

4. *United India Insurance Company Limited, Chennai*

General Insurance covers spectrum of economy, ranging from manufacture of shoes to aircraft, from agricultural wells to oil wells, from launching of satellites to manufacture of chemicals, its investments totalling to Rs.26,424.03 crore by the end of March 2006. As compared to 799 offices in 1973, the network consisted of 4,151 offices as on 31st March, 2006.

The IRDA was constituted on 19th April, 2000 has already notified 50 regulations. So far certificate of registration has been issued to 12 new private companies.

The Mediclaim Insurance Policy (MIP) provides for reimbursement of medical expenses. *Jan Arogya Bima Policy (JABP)* is primarily meant for the larger segment of the population who cannot afford the high cost of medical treatment. *Videsh Yatra Mitra Policy (VYMP)* covering supplementary benefits besides providing indemnity for medical expenses during the period of travel has been introduced by the four nationalised general insurance companies with effect from 1st January 1998. *Baghyashree Child Welfare Bima Yojana* was introduced with effect from 19th October, 1998. *Raj Rajeshwari Mahila Kalyan Yojna* offers Security to women in the age-group of 10 to 75 years was introduced from 19th October, 1998. *National Agricultureal Insurance Scheme (NAIS)* was introduced from Rabi 1999-2000 season replacing the Comprehensive Crop Insurance Scheme. Since the inception of *Lok Adalat* in 1985 till 31st March 2000, it has participated in over 12,000 'Lok Adalats'; settled 4,74,000 claims involving disbursement of over Rs. 1,946 crore by way of compensation. *Jald Rahat Yojana* was introduced to expedite payment of compensation to road accident victims.

The gross direct premium income of the general insurance industry within India during 2002-03 amounted to Rs.12,629 crore. Similarly the net premium income of the general insurance industry in India during 2002-03 was Rs.9,637 crore. The gross profit of the industry was Rs.842 crore in 2002-03 and the net profit of the industry during 2002-03 amounted to Rs. 626 crore.

Unit Trust of India (UTI)

The Unit Trust of India (Transfer of Undertaking and Repeal) Act, 2002 enacted in December 2002 provides, inter-alia, that erstwhile Unit Trust of India shall be bifurcated, and the "specified undertaking", viz., UTI-I, comprising of US-64, Assured Return Schemes and Development Reverse Fund (appearing in the Schedule-I to the Act) will be transferred and vest in a government appointed Administrator, and the "undertaking", viz., UTI-II comprising of Net Asset Value (NAV) based schemes (appearing in the Schedule-II to the Act), will vest in a specified company from an Appointed Day, which is 1 February 2003.

UTI-I has been named as "Administrator of the Specified Undertaking of the Unit Trust of India. For the UTI-II, the State Bank of India, Punjab National Bank, Bank of Baroda and the Life Insurance Corporation of India have set up a mutual fund, named, UTI Mutual Fund, UTI Trustee Company and the UTI Asset Management Company as per SEBI (Mutual Fund) Regulations. UTI Trustee Company has been notified as the specified company. Employees have been transferred to the UTI Asset Management Company keeping in view practice in the mutual fund industry. The Government signed an agreement on 15 January 2003 with above banks and financial institutions for transfer of undertaking which has come into effect from 1 February 2003, the Appointed Day.

Guidelines on avoiding conflict of interest: The JPC suggested that the government may issue guidelines for avoiding conflict of interest as the sponsors of the UTI-II have their own mutual fund outfits. Based on inputs received from SEBI and sponsors, SEBI has since issued guidelines.

US-64: On 31 May 2003, US-64 has come to an end. Investors of US-64 were given option of 6.75 per cent per annum tax-free, interest payable half-yearly, Government guaranteed tradable bonds in lieu of cash payment as on 31 May 2003. The bonds have received overwhelming response. Till 24 July 2003 approximately 28.87 lakh bond certificates were issued to investors covered under 17.93 lakh Investor Identification Numbers.

Assured Return Schemes: Seven Assured Return Schemes, viz., MIP 99, MIP 98 (V), CGGF 86, RUP-II CGGF 99, RUP 99 and BGVMIP are being foreclosed as the returns assured under these schemes are out of alignment with returns in the market and, hence, are not sustainable.

Foreign Direct Investment Policy: This policy provides for investment in Indian companies/setting up of wholly-owned subsidiary in most of the areas.

Foreign capital mobilisation through Euro issues (ADRs/GDRs/FCCBs)

A scheme has been initiated during 1992 to allow the Indian Corporate Sector to have access to the Global Capital markets through issue of Foreign Currency Convertible Bonds (FCCBs)/Equity Shares under the Global Depository Mechanism.

Under this scheme, companies with consistent track record of good performance (financial or otherwise) for minimum period of three years can have access to international capital market. The three year track record requirement has been relaxed for companies making Euro issues for financing projects in the infrastructure sector like power generation, telecommunication, petroleum exploration and refining, ports, airports and roads.

Cases involving funding of activities outside Annexure III and also where foreign equity holding after the Euro issue is likely to exceed 51 per cent would require FIPB approval after an in principle approval by the Department of Economic Affairs. Comprehensive guidelines for GDR issues were announced in a phased manner from time to time.

Taxes

Indian taxing system is of two types – Direct and Indirect. Direct taxes play a significant role not only as a source of income but as an instrument for India's socio-economic policies. Direct taxes include Income-Tax, Wealth-Tax, Gift-Tax, Estate Duty, Companies', Profit, etc.The tempo of search and survey operations is being maintained to combat tax evasion.

For 2003-04, the revenue from Customs duties was Rs.48,613 (provisional) crore and from Union Excise duties Rs.90,907 crore (provisional).

Implementation of VAT

At the meeting of the Empowered Committee of State Finance Ministers held on 18 June 2004, it was resolved to introduce VAT at the State level from 1st April 2005. VAT being a State subject, the Central Government has been acting as a facilitator for its successful launching and implementation. A Technical Expert Committee that will work closely with State Governments for smooth implementation of VAT with effect from April 2005 has since been set up with the following terms of references: (i) Steps to ensure that VAT is revenue enhancing. (ii) Principles and levels of compensation to be paid to states for revenue loss, if any, because of the implementation of VAT. (iii) Strategy required for education, training and publicity for implementation of VAT. (iv) Transitional issues which will emerge in the context of switchover to VAT (administrative and legal issues). (v) Modalities of phasing out Central Sales Tax.

Anti-Smuggling Drive

Drive against smuggling, tax evasion and other economic offences strengthening the intelligence network. Narcotic Control Bureau, a separate authority was also created during 1986 for co-ordinating efforts in preventing and combating trafficking in narcotic drugs and psychotropic substances.

As a result of these efforts, contraband goods valued at Rs.288.24 crore were seized during 2005-06. Cases of customs duty evasion amounting to Rs.468.65 crore were also detected.

Corporate Sector-Companies at work

6,41,512 companies limited by shares were at work in the country as on 31st March 2006. These comprised of 1,309 Government companies and 6,40,203 non-Government companies.

DEFENCE

India's defence policy aims at promoting and sustaining durable peace in the sub-continent and equipping the defence forces adequately to safe-guard against aggression. The Supreme Command of the Armed Forces is vested in the President of India. The Defence Minister is responsible to Parliament for all matters concerning defence. There are three divisions each functioning under their respective Chief of Staff. Administrative and operational control of the armed forces is exercised by the Ministry of Defence and the three services headquarters. Today India has the 4th largest army, 5th largest airforce and the 7th largest navy in the world.

ORGANISATION

The three services function under their respective Chiefs of Staff

Chief of the Army Staff	:	*General Joginder Jaswant Singh*
		General Deepak Kapoor
		(2007, Sep. 30 onwards)
Chief of the Naval Staff	:	*Admiral Sureesh Metha*
Chief of the Air Staff	:	*Air Chief Marshal Fauli H. Major*

ARMY

At the Army Headquarters in New Delhi, the Chief of the Army Staff is assisted by the Vice-Chief of the Army Staff and seven other Principal Staff officers namely, the two Deputy Chiefs of the Army Staff, Adjutant General, Quarter-master General, Master-General of Ordnance and the Military Secretary, besides a Head of Branch, namely the Engineer-in-Chief.

The Army is organized into five commands, viz., Southern, Eastern, Western, Central and Northern. Each command is under a General Officer Commanding-in-Chief who holds the rank of Lieutenant General. General Officer Commanding-in-Chief is the Commander of a demarcated geographical area and has both field and static formations under his command. The major field formations are Corps, Division and Brigade commanded by a General Officer Commanding of the rank of Lieutenant General, a General Officer Commanding of the rank of Major General, and a Brigadier, respectively. The major static formations are Areas, Independent Sub-Areas and Sub-Areas. An Area is commanded by a General Officer Commanding of the rank of Major General and an Independent Sub-Area and Sub-Area by a Brigadier.

The Army consists of a number of arms and services. These are: Armoured Corps, Regiment of Artillery, Corps of Air Defence, Artillery, Army Aviation Corps, Corps of Engineers, Corps of Signals, Infantry, Mechanised Infantry, Army Service Corps, Military Nursing Service, Army Medical Corps, Army Dental Corps, Army Ordnance Corps, Corps of Electrical and Mechanical Engineers, Remount and Veterinary Corps, Military Farms Service, Army Education Corps, Intelligence Corps, Corps of Military Police, Judge Advocate General Department, Army Physical Training Corps, Pioneer Corps, Army Postal Service, Territorial Army, Defence Security Corps. In addition, the Army has its own Recruiting Organization, Record Offices, Colleges, Schools, Depots, Boys Establishments, Training Institutions and Selection Centres.

According to the changing times, induction of women is approved and several women officers have joined in various departments. More than 72 women officers have been commissioned in various Arms/Services.

Integrated Guided Missiles Development Programme (IGMDP)

This programme comprises four missiles system: **Prithvi** surface-to-surface tactical battle field missile; **Akash** medium range surface-to-air missile;

Trishul short range surface-to-air missile; and **Nag** third generation anti-tank missile and **Prithvi** (army and air force version) is also getting ready for flight trials.

India's advanced medium range surface-to-air missile **'Akash'** was successfully test-fired from the Interim Test Range at Chandipur in Orissa in 1990. India's first indigenous third generation anti-tank missile **'Nag'** was test-fired on November 29, 1990. 'Nag' which has a fire and target attack capability can be launched both from land-based missile carriers as well as helicopters.

'Akash' and 'Nag' belong to a family of five missiles. The other three are **Agni, Prithvi** and **Trishul**. In 1989, India became the 5th Nation in the world capable of making Intermediate Range Ballistic Missiles (IRBM) when the 19 metre long and 14 tonne two stage missile 'Agni' was lifted off successfully from the Interim Test Range at Chandipur on May 22, which splashed down, 1,000 km away in the Bay of Bengal. **'Trishul'**, the short range surface-to-air missile, successfully test-fired earlier has a wheeled version for multiple-launch capability. The country's first Air-borne Early Warning Aircraft (AEW) made its maiden flight at Bangalore on 9th November, 1990. This aircraft developed at Air-craft Safety and Test Establishment, (ASTE) Bangalore, is a fitting match to Pakistan's acquired P3E Orion airborne warning aircraft equipped with Harpoon missiles.

'Samyukta' presented to the Army

'Samyukta', an indigenous, state-of-the-art Integrated Electronic Warfare (IEW) system was presented by the President, A.P.J. Abdul Kalam, to the Chief of the Army Staff, Gen. N.C. Vij, on 19th January, 2004.

It is capable of handling both ground-based and airborne threats. It has the capability to intercept, detect, search, identify and locate complex communication and radar signals. It monitors and analyses communication and radar activity across Forward Edge of the Battle Area (FEBA) and many other sophisticated features. Once deployed, the system has operational frontal coverage of 150/70 km.

BrahMos

BrahMos is a cruise missile jointly developed by India and Russia under an agreement signed in 1998. The name BrahMos has been derived from Brahmaputra, river of India and Moskva, river of Russia. It has a range of 300 kms and can deliver payload of 300 kg over three times the speed of sound. The 13th flight of BrahMos was conducted in Feb. 2007 at Chandipur (Orissa). The anti-ship missile, flies at 2.8 times the speed of sound and can take out targets upto 300 km. It stands eight metres tall, weighs three tonnes, and carries a conventional 200 kg war head. It was inducted to Navy on June 28, 2006.

NAVY

The Navy is responsible for the defence and security of India's maritime interests and assets, both in times of war and peace.

The Chief of the Naval Staff at Naval Headquarters in New Delhi, exercises control on the Indian Navy through a chain of three Commands: Western, Eastern and Southern, each under a Flag Officer Commanding-in-Chief, in the rank of Vice-Admiral, having their Headquarters at Mumbai, Vishakhapatnam and Kochi, respectively. At Naval Headquarters, he is assisted by four Principal Staff Officers, namely the Vice Chief of Naval Staff, Chief of Personnel, Chief of Material and Deputy Chief of Naval Staff.

The Navy has two fleets - Western Fleet and Eastern Fleet which consist of two aircraft carriers, destroyers, frigates, including some of the latest type of anti-submarine and anti-aircraft frigates, submarine depot ship, a squadron of anti-submarine patrol vessels and other special vessels. In addition, there are survey ships, training ships, fleet tankers, landing crafts and a number of auxiliary craft. India has acquired two aircraft carriers namely **INS-Mysore, INS-Viraat.** India launched its first missile boat-**INS Vibhuti** on 26th April 1991. '**INS Savithri'**, the first warship built by the Government controlled Hindustan Shipyard was delivered to the Navy in 1990. A project of Very Low Frequency Communication facility was set up on 20th October 1990, at south Vijayanarayanam in Tirunelveli District of Tamil Nadu. India is the fifth maritime power to have the Technology of VLF system.

INS Shalki was the first indigenously built submarine which was commissioned in 1992. India also joins the group of nations possessing Nuclear Powered submarines with **INS Chakra** having been acquired on lease from the USSR in February 1988. The only unified command in the country headed by a Naval Officer, the Fortress Commander of, Andaman and Nicobar ensures the security of our island territories in the Bay of Bengal and the exclusive economic zone around them. The recently commissioned naval aircraft carrier, stationed at Port Blair, **INS Utkrosh**, not only carries out the air surveillance of these far flung islands but also renders timely and effective assistance to the civil administration and the islands in remote areas. **INS-Mysore,** the country's second indigenously built guided missile destroyer, was commissioned on 2nd June 1999. **INS Aditya**, the 24,000 tons fleet replenishment tanker of the Indian Navy was commissioned on April 3, 2000. It is the fastest tanker in Indian Navy, the other two being **INS Shakti** and **INS Jyoti**. **INS Brahmaputra,** called the Razing Rhino, the Navy's latest and finest guided-missile frigate has been commissioned.

INS Satpura—second indigenously-built stealth ship the second indigenously built stealth ship, INS Satpura, was launched on June 4, 2004 at the Mazgaon Docks, Mumbai. The vessel, 143 metres long and 16.9 metres wide, cost an estimated Rs 1,000 crore. It will have advanced surface-to-surface and surface-to-air missiles and hi-tech radar and communications equipment on board. Powered by gas turbines and diesel engines, the warship can move at speeds of up to 30 knots and operate two helicopters for surveillance and anti-submarine operations. **INS Kadamba** commissioned in Karwar, Karnataka on May 31, 2005. **INS Beas** commissioned in Kolkata on July 11, 2005. **INS Shardul** commissioned in Karwar, Karnataka on January 4, 2007. It was built by the Garden Reach Ship Builders and Engineers. The naval forces at present, has two major naval bases at Mumbai and Vishakhapatnam. **INS Jalashwa:** Commissioned on June 22, 2007 at Landing Platform Dock (LPD). The ship is the first of its class to be inducted into the Navy and was acquired from the US, in the process marking a milestone in the bilateral relationship.

COAST GUARD

The Coast Guard came into being on 1 February 1977 and was constituted as an Independent Armed Force of the Union of India with the enactment of Coast Guard Act 1978 on 18 August 1978. It forms a part of the Defence Ministry. Its headquarters is in New Delhi and it is headed by a Director General. It has three regional headquarters at Mumbai (Western Region), Chennai (Southern Region) and Port Blair (Andaman and Nicobar Islands).

The main duties of the Coast Guard are protection of coastal and offshore installations and terminals, protection of fisheries, patrol of the exclusive economic zone (2.8 million sq.kms) to prevent poaching, anti-smuggling work and search and rescue missions. The Coast Guard fleet comprises ships such as KUTHAR (ex-navy), VIKRAM, VIJAY, VEERA (indigenously built), a number of offshore patrol vessels and a number of inshore patrol vessels. Coast Guard Ships regularly assist the customs authorities in anti-smuggling operations and have been responsible for apprehending contraband worth several crores of rupees. The development of the Coast Guard in accordance with a long term perspective plan has been approved by the Government. Besides, the force is available for search and rescue operations, anti-pollution and other duties in the maritime zones of the country.

AIR FORCE

The Indian Air Force is organised on both functional as well as geographical basis. There are five Operational Commands. They are Western Air Command, South-Western Air Command, Central Air Command, Eastern Air Command and Southern Air Command. In addition, the Maintenance Command and the Training Command are two functional commands. At the Air Headquarters in New Delhi, the Chief of the Air Staff is assisted by the Vice-Chief of the Air Staff, Deputy Chief of the Air Staff, Air Officer Incharge Administration, Air Officer Incharge Maintenance, Air Officer Incharge Personnel and Training, and Inspector General of Flight Safety and Inspection. These six principal Staff Officers are assisted each by an Assistant Chief of Air Staff. Today, the Air Force consists of an array of modern aircraft. The teeth of the Air Force is in MIG-29 aircraft, Mirage-2000, SU-30, Jaguar, MIG-21, MIG-23, MIG-25 and MIG-27. The IAF has attack helicopters like MI-25 and MI-35. The transport fleet consists of IL-76s, AN-32s, Boeing-737 and indigenously produced HS-748. Dornier-228 has replaced the Otter aircraft and is manufactured under licence by the HAL. The helicopter fleet consists of Chetak, Cheetah MI-8, MI-7 and heavy lift MI-26 helicopters.

HPT-32 manufactured by HAL is used as the basic trainer aircraft. HJT-16 (Kiran) and Polish Iskara aircraft are used as trainers in the applied stage of training. HS-748 is used as transport aircraft trainer. The Air Force MI-8 helicopters are specially modified to undertake tasks in Antarctica. M-17 and Chetak are used for high altitude operations. They provide logistic support to ground forces. The Indian Air Force, which began humbly with four Westland Wapiti Aircraft in Karachi in 1932 celebrated its golden jubilee in 1982. In the recent past, modern weapon systems have been acquired to strengthen the combat force. Modern avionics have been fitted in transport and combat aircraft to enhance flight safety and optimise flight operations. Air Defence Ground Environment is being modernised by deploying advanced technology radars and automatic data handling systems.

The first batch of women pilots were commissioned on 17th December 1994. Since then women pilots are serving in frontline transport and helicopter squadrons. Women officers are also serving in Technical, Administrative, Logistics, Education and Medical branches. The first batch of women Air Traffic Controller and Fighter Controller/D ATS was commissioned in May 1996. The Air Force has carried out a major air to ground exercise termed Vayushakti in February 1999 where it displayed its awesome fire power to the public.

Commissioned Ranks: The following are the commissioned ranks in the three services; each rank is shown opposite to its equivalent in the other services:

Army	Navy	Air Force
General	Admiral	Air Chief Marshal
Lieutenant General	Vice-Admiral	Air Marshal
Major General	Rear Admiral	Air Vice-Marshal
Brigadier	Commodore	Air Commodore
Colonel	Captain	Group Captain
Lieutenant Colonel	Commander	Wing Commander
Major	Lieutenant Commander	Squadron Leader
Captain	Lieutenant	Flight Lieutenant
Lieutenant	Sub-Lieutenant	Flying Officer
Second Lieutenant	Acting Sub-Lieutenant	Pilot Officer

A jawan enters service at the age of 16. The upper age limit varies for various categories. Under the modified system of recruitment since 1981, a candidate has to undergo literary as well as physical tests. The selection should be made within two days. Recruitment is made by 58 branch recruiting offices and 12 zonal recruiting offices, besides an Independent Recruiting office at Delhi. Recruitment is done twice or thrice a year. The minimum qualification for entry into Air Force is matriculation or its equivalent. Screening test is done in more than 66 centres all over the country.

Sainik Schools: 20 Sainik Schools in our country one each in all major states prepare boys academically and physically for entry into National Defence Academy. The schools are affiliated to CBSE and follow the 10+2 pattern of education. Admission is made to Class VI & IX on the basis of an all-India entrance examination.

Rashtriya Indian Military College (RIMC): It prepares students for the entrance examinations for entry into National Defence Academy. The college is run on the lines of Public Schools.

National Defence Academy (NDA) : Situated at Khadakvasla near Pune, the Academy conducts a three-year combined basic military training course for potential officers of the three services. The cadets are also trained in academics to the degree level. Admission to this Academy is made on the basis of a qualifying bi-annual examination conducted by UPSC, the entry qualification being matric or equivalent. The present strength of Army, Navy and Air force cadets at the academy is 1960 including 69 cadets from Bhutan, 9 from Palestine and 8 from Maldives.

Indian Military Academy (IMA): IMA, Dehradun is the premier institution for training officers for the Army. It offers training to NDA cadet graduates, for one year. After completion of the training in IMA which offers one and a half year training to higher age group graduates also, the personnel are granted commission in the army. Started in 1932, at present its strength is 1298.

Officers' Training Academy (OTA): Located at Chennai, it trains candidates for Short Service Commission in the Army, Navy and Air Force for holding staff appointments in their own services. About 500 officers receive training every year. So far more than 581 lady cadets have been granted short service commission.

National Defence College (NDC) : It is a premier institution at New Delhi dedicated to promoting understanding between military and civil authorities and for preparing them for higher responsibilities in national and international affairs.

Armed Forces Medical College (AFMC): It was established on 1st May 1948 as an institution for Post-graduate medical education and to conduct research. A graduate wing to train students for the M.B.B.S. degree of Poona University was started in August 1962. College of Nursing was added in 1964 to train for B.Sc., (Nursing) degree.

OTHER ARMY INSTITUTIONS

Institution	Place
College of Combat	Mhow
College of Military Engineering	Kirkee (Pune)
Military College of Telecommunication Engg.	Mhow
Armoured Corps Centre and School	Ahmednagar
School of Artillery	Deolali
The Infantry Schools	Mhow & Belgaum
College of Material Management	Jabalpur

NAVAL ESTABLISHMENTS

Naval Academy	Kochi	New Naval Academy	Ezhimala (Kerala)
INS Shivaji	Lonavala	INS Kunjali	Mumbai
INS Hamla	Marve Malad (Mumbai)	INS Agrani	Coimbatore
		INS Aswini	Mumbai
INS Satpura	Magaon Docks (Mumbai)	INS Beas	Kolkata
INS Valsura	Jamnagar	INS Chilka	Bhubaneshwar
INS Hansa	Goa	INS Satavahana	Vishakapatnam
		INS Kadamba	Karwar, Karnataka
		INS Shardul	Karwar, Karnataka
		INS Jalashwa	Landing Platform Dock
College of Naval Warfare	Mumbai	Navy Shipwright School	Vishakapatnam

AIR FORCE TRAINING INSTITUTES

Air Force Academy	Hyderabad
Helicopter Training School	Hakimpet
Flying Instructors' School	Tambaram (Chennai)
The College of Air Warfare	Secunderabad
Air Force Administrative College	Coimbatore
The Air Force Technical College	Jalahalli

Ordnance Factories: There are 39 Ordnance factories with a manpower of 1.48 lakh. There are eight public sector enterprises under the Department of Defence Production and Supplies. They are 1. Hindustan Aeronautics Ltd., 2. Bharath Electronics Ltd., 3. Bharath Earth Movers Ltd., 4. Mazagon Dock Ltd., 5. Garden Reach Ship Builders & Engineers Ltd., 6. Goa Shipyard Limited, 7. Bharath Dynamics Limited, and 8. Mishra Dhatu Nigam Limited.

Territorial Army: The Territorial Army is a citizens' volunteer force established in 1949 and designed to give the citizens an opportunity to receive military training in their spare time. The territorials serve the country in times of emergency and aid the civil power in dealing with natural calamities. There are at present 27 departmental and 25 non-departmental TA units. All able-bodied nationals of India in the age group of 18 to 35 years are eligible to join. Presently, its size is 40,000.

National Cadet Corps (NCC): Established in 1948, on 15th July, it is open to the students of Universities, Colleges and Schools on voluntary basis. It has a strength of 13 lakh cadets. During 1998-99, 21 centrally organised camps were held in which 39,818 cadets participated from Army, Navy and Air wings. It aims at development of qualities such as leadership, character, comradeship and the ideal of service among the youth. The cadets and NCC Commissioned Officers have no liability of military service. The NCC consists of three divisions namely Senior Division for college boys, Junior Division for school boys and the Girls Division. The training programme of the cadets has a defence bias.

For resettlement and welfare of ex-servicemen, various schemes are introduced by The Directorate General of Resettlement (DGR) under the Ministry of Defence (MoD).

SCIENTIFIC RESEARCH

The Indian Space Programme

1962: Indian National Committee for Space Research (INCOSPAR) formed by the Department of Atomic Energy, Government of India to aid and advise in starting the space programme.

1963: Thumba Equatorial Rocket Launching Station (TERLS) established in response to the long felt need of scientists to make in situ measurements of upper atmospheric parameters, particularly of equatorial trajectory.

1965: The Space Science and Technology Centre (SSTC) established in Thumba as a research and development laboratory in space technology for achieving self-reliance in this field.

1967: An earth station for satellite telecommunication was set up at Ahmedabad to provide facilities for training and research in this technology. Engineers trained here helped to set up India's first commercial satellite telecommunication earth station at Arvi, near Poona.

1968: TERLS dedicated to the United Nations.

1969: ISRO formed under Department of Atomic Energy.

1972: Space Commission and Department of Space set up.

1972-1974: A number of air-borne remote sensing experiments conducted for surveying earth's resources.

1975: The first Indian Satellite, Aryabhatta launched (April 19) from the Soviet Union.

1975-76: The first major space application programme. Satellite Instructional Television Experiments (SITE) conducted during August 1975 - July 1976 using the American Satellite, ATS-6.

1977: Satellite Telecommunication Experiments Project (STEP) carried out from the middle of 1977 to 1979 using the Franco-German Satellite, Symphonie.

1979: The second Indian Satellite, a Satellite for Earth observations, Bhaskara-I, launched (7June) from the Soviet Union.

1980: SLV-3, India's first Satellite Launch Vehicle, puts Rohini Satellite, into a near-earth elliptical orbit from Sriharikota (18 July).

1981: India's first experimental geostationary communication satellite, APPLE, successfully launched by ESA's Ariane Launch Vehicle from Kourou, French Guyana, (19 June). India's second satellite for Earth observation, Bhaskara-II, launched from the Soviet Union (20 November).

1983: Second developmental launch of SLV-3 successfully conducted from Sriharikota (17 April) and RS-D2 satellite orbited INSAT-1B India's multipurpose domestic satellite, launched on board USA's space shuttle 'Challenger' (30 August).

1984: The first joint Indo-Soviet manned space mission launched (3 April). Sqn.Ldr. Rakesh Sharma became the first Indian cosmonaut.

1985: Two Indians selected for Indo-US joint shuttle flight.

1987: ASLV with SROSS-1 satellite on board launched.

1988: First Indian Remote Sensing Satellite, IRS-1A·launched from Baikanour, USSR (March 17). INSAT-1C launched from Kourou, French Guyana (July 2). Later, abandoned as non-usable.

1990: INSAT-1D launched from Cape Canaveral, USA (June 12).

1992: Augmented Satellite Launch Vehicle (ASLV-D3) launched with stretched Rohini Satellite System SROSS-C on board (May 20). First indigenously built satellite, INSAT-2A launched from Kourou, French Guyana (July 10).

1993: INSAT-2B launched (July 23).

1994: ASLV-D4 launched with SROSS-C2 as payload (May 4). PSLV with IRS-P2 launched (October).

1995: INSAT-2C launched from Kourou, French Guyana (December 7).

1996: PSLV-D3 with IRS-P3 launched (March).

1997: INSAT-2D launched (June 4), became inoperational in October. ARABSAT (later renamed INSAT-2DT) acquired in November. First operational launch of PSLV with IRS-1D (September).

1999: INSAT-2E launched (May). IRS-P4 launched by indigenously built PSLV-C2 vehicles.

2000: INSAT-3B launched (22-3-2000).

2001: GSLV-D1 lifted off on (18-04-2001); PSLV-C3 launched (22-10-2001)

2002: INSAT-3C launched (24-01-2002)

2002: METSAT PSLV-C4 launched (13-9-2002) (KALPANA-1)

2003: GSAT-2 launched (08-05-2003)

2003: INSAT-3E launched (28-09-2003)

2003: PSLV-C5 launched (17-10-2003)

2004: EDUSAT launched (20-09-2004) from Sriharikota

2005: PSLV-C6 (Cartosat-1 & Hamsat) launched (05-05-2005) from Sriharikota

2005: INSAT-4A launched on 22-12-2005 from French Guyana.

2006: INSAT-4C (GSLV-F02) unsuccessfully launched on 10-07-2006 from Satish Dhawan Space Centre, Sriharikota (Andhra Pradesh).

2007: PSLV-C7 (Cartosat-2, SRE-1, Lapan Tubsat, Penuensat-1) launched on 10-1-2007 from Sriharikota

2007: On March 12, INSAT-4B was successfully launched from Kourou island in French Guiana.

2007: On April 23, PSLV-C8 was successfully launched from Satish Dhawan Space Centre, Sriharikota

The Indian Space programme was formally organised in 1972 to promote development and application of space technology in the areas of telecommunication, television broadcasting, meteorology, resources survey and management. Development of satellites, launch vehicles and associated ground systems is integrated in the space programme objective. The space programme is executed through Indian Space Research Organisation (ISRO), National Remote Sensing Agency and Physical Research Laboratory.

Indian Space Research Organisation (ISRO) comprises - (1) Vikram Sarabhai Space Centre (VSSC) Thiruvananthapuram (2) Satish Dhawan Space Centre, Sriharikota (3) ISRO Satellite Centre (ISAC), Bangalore (4) Auxiliary Propulsion System Unit (APSU), Bangalore (5) Space Applications Centre (SAC), Ahmedabad (6) Development and Educational Communication Unit (DECU), Ahmedabad and (7) ISRO Telemetry, Tracking and Command Network (ISTRAC) with its headquarters at Bangalore.

The Indian National Satellite System (INSAT) is a multi-purpose satellite system for telecommunications, meteorological observations and data relay, television broadcasting and radio and television programme distribution.

INSAT system was established in 1983 with the commissioning of INSAT-1B. Today, the system is served by the first generation satellite INSAT-1D, three ISRO-built second generation satellites, INSAT-2B, INSAT-2C and INSAT-2E, and INSAT-2DT procured from ARABSAT. INSAT has enabled a vast expansion in the television service with over 900 TV transmitters linked through INSAT, providing access to over 85 percent of the population.

The Indian Remote Sensing (IRS) satellite system was operationalised with the commissioning of IRS-1A in 1988. The IRS system has been further enhanced by IRS-1B, IRS-1C, IRS-P3 and IRS-1D. IRS-1C and IRS-1D have enhanced capabilities in terms of spatial resolution, additional spectral bands, stereoscopic imaging, wide field coverage and a more frequent revisit capability than their predecessors. Another satellite IRS-P4 (OCEANSAT) was launched on 26.5.1999 from SHAR Centre, Sriharikota as the main payload and Korean KITSAT-3 and German DLR-TUBSAT as the auxiliary payloads. Remote Sensing applications in the country cover diverse fields such as crop acreage and yield estimation, drought warning and assessment, flood control and damage assessment, wasteland management, under-ground water exploration, etc.

ANTRIX: The commercial arm of ISRO is a single window agency for marketing Indian space capabilities.

Today, India has realised the operational launch vehicle, PSLV, capable of launching 1,200 kg IRS satellites into polar sunsynchronous orbit. The Geosynchronous Satellite Launch Vehicle (GSLV), which will be capable of placing 2,500 kg INSAT class of satellites in geosynchronous transfer orbit, lifted off on 18th April, 2001 from Sri Harikota Range. PSLV-C3 was launched on 22.10.2001 carrying an Indian Technology Experiments Satellite (TES), the German space agency, DLR's satellite, BIRD (Bispectral Infrared Detection Satellite) and a Belgian firm's satellite PROBA (Project for On Board Autonomy).

INSAT-3C was launched on 24th January, 2002 from the French Guyanese Spaceport, Kourou. METSAT on 13th September, 2002 and GSAT-2 on 8th May 2003 were launched from Sriharikota range. Communication satellite INSAT-3E was launched from French Guyana on 28th September 2003. PSLV-C5 and EDUSAT satellites were launched on 17-10-2003 and 20-9-2004 respectively from Sriharikota. PSLV-C6 (Cartosat-1 & Hamsat) was launched from Sriharikota on 5th May, 2005. ISRO launches the 4th generation communication satellite INSAT-4A on Ariane-5G rocket from Kourou in French Guyana on 22.12.2005. INSAT-4C (GSLV-F02) unsuccessfully launched on 10-07-2006 from Satish Dhawan Space Centre, Sriharikota (Andhra Pradesh). PSLV-C7 (Cartosat-2, SRE-1, Lapan Tubsat, Penuensat-1) successfully launched on 10.1.2007 from Sriharikota. INSAT-4B was successfully launched by Ariane Space's Ariane-5 Vehicle from Kourou island in French Guiana on March 12, 2007. The satellite is intended to augment the Direct To Home (DTH) television and communication services. The vehicle lifted off with INSAT-4B and co-passengers Skynet-5A, a military communication satellite of UK. PSLV-C8 was successfully launched on April 23, 2007. The launch vehicle also carried an Italian astronomical satellite AGILE from Satish Dhawan Space Centre, Sriharikota. It was the first commercial launch of a foreign satellite.

The space science research is carried out at Physical Research Laboratory, Ahmedabad, Space Physics Laboratory, Thiruvananthapuram, Space Applications Centre, Ahmedabad, ISRO Satellite Centre, Bangalore. A National Mesosphere-Stratosphere Radar Facility (NMRF) at Gadanki (near Tirupati) studies atmospheric dynamics, atmospheric turbulence, cloud physics, etc.

The concept of GRAMSAT is (GRAMEEN Satellite) to spread literacy in the rural areas and to update the knowledge of workers on the shop floor. This (GRAMSATS) would be a dedicated system incorporating the talk-back facility by which workers can put questions to the telecaster and get answers at once. It is also used for spreading national integration as two such satellites can cover all areas and languages throughout the country. For instance Kanadians living in Tamilnadu can listen programmes in their languages as well. Each of such GRAMSAT will cost Rs.60 crores.

COMMUNICATIONS

The origin of modern postal system in India can be traced back to 1837 when postal service was opened to the public. The first postage stamp was issued in Karachi in 1852, though it was valid only in Sind. When a separate postal department was set up in 1854, seven hundred post offices were already functioning in the country.

The money order system was introduced in 1880; The Post Office Savings Bank started in 1882, the Postal Life Insurance in 1884, the Railway Mail Service in 1907, the Airmail Service in 1911, the Posts and Department of Telecommunications on 31st December 1984, VPP and Parcel service in 1877, post card in 1879, and Indian postal order was introduced in 1935. The system of Postal Index Number (PIN) was introduced throughout the country in 1972. In 1985 the postal and telecom department were separated. In 2004 the e-post system was introduced. The Indian Postal network is the largest postal network in the world. As on March 2005 the country has 1,55,516 post offices. Out of these, 16,396 are in urban and 1,39,120 in rural areas. On an average each post office serves 6,609 persons and covers an area of

21.10 sq.km. In terms of the mail volume handled, India ranks just after UK, Germany, Japan, France and Russia. Around 9.93 crore pieces were handled in 2003-04, in which Money orders valued Rs.8,650 crore.

Quick Mail Service (QMS)

It was introduced in 1975. This service now covers all state capitals, headquarters of all Union Territories and important commercial towns.

For efficient handling of the growing volume of mail, a numerical postal address code known as Postal Index Number (PIN) was introduced in 1972. The code has six digits which help identify and locate every departmental delivery post office excluding branch post offices. The first digit indicates the region, the second the sub-region and the third the sorting district whereas the last three digits indicate a particular delivery post office in the areas served by the sorting district. In order to have a dedicated mail transmission system, following 6 channels have been introduced: (1) Rajdhani Channel, (2) Metro Channel, (3) Green Channel, (4) Business Channel, (5) Periodical (Patrika) Channel, (6) Bulk Mail Channel. Automatic Mail Processing Centres have been set up.

Speed Post Service

Introduced in 1986, it offers guaranteed time bound delivery. It now connects 163 National and 953 State Speed Post Centres and also 97 foreign countries on the network in addition to point to point centres. In International level, commercial documents, computer data like disks, magnetic tapes can be sent.

Post office Computerisation

More than 839 Head Post Offices have been fully computerised. 6861 Departmental Sub-Post Offices have been provided with Multi-purpose Computerised Counter Machines (MPCMs).

Telecommunications

Telecommunication services were introduced between Kolkata and Diamond Harbour in 1851. By March 1854, telegraphic message could be sent between Agra and Kolkata. Indian Railways used telegraphic and telephone services in 1900. Telephone services were first introduced in Kolkata in 1881-82, six years after telephone was invented. The first automatic exchange was commissioned in 1913-14 at Simla with 700 lines. As in March 2006, India was the 10th largest telecom networks in the world comprising about 37,903 telephone exchanges, with a total equipped capacity of 142.09 million lines and 2.34 million public call offices. Satellite based Remote Area Business Management Network, a new technology is under operation for exchange of data facsimile, telex message etc. There are over 69.20 million cellular subscribers in the country.

Value Added Services are enhanced services which add value to the existing basic tele and bearer service. The following services have been identified as Value Added Service. (i) Radio Paging Service (ii) Cellular Mobile Telephone Service (iii) Mobile Radio Trunking Service (iv) Electronic Mail Service (v) Voice Mail Service (vi) Audiotex Service (vii) 64 kbps Domestic Data Service using VSAT (using Satellite) (viii) Videotex Service (ix) Video Conferencing and Credit Card Authorisation.

Mahanagar Telephone Nigam Limited (MTNL)

It was formed in April 1986 to serve Mumbai and Delhi telephone districts. Reasons for formation of MTNL is to mobilise resources by public borrowings and serve better. Started with a share capital of Rs.800 crore. The government the paid capital is Rs.630 crore has already disinvested 56.25% of its shares.

Videsh Sanchar Nigam Limited (VSNL)

It was formed on 1st April 1986 after the conversion of the Overseas Communication Service. It looks after international telecommunication services. The services are provided by submarine underline cable between Chennai and Penang (Malaysia) and by the INTELSAT position over Indian Ocean. It has been privatised from 13.1.2002 with 25% of Govt. equity. VSNL provides live relay of international TV broadcast programmes via satellite. VSNL handles over 8,00,000 international telephone calls and 45,000 telex calls every day.

Bharat Sanchar Nigam Limited (BSNL)

It was formed on 1st October 2000 by corporatisation of the erstwhile Department of Telecom Services. It is a 100 per cent Government of India-owned PSU with an authorized capital of Rs. 17,500 crore, a paid-up capital of Rs. 12,500 crore, a net worth of Rs. 80,099 crore, a skilled work force of approximately 3.39 lakh and an annual revenue of approximately Rs. 26,897 crore, making it the largest PSU in the country.

Unified Messaging Service

UMS is a system by which voice mails, fax and e-mails can be received from one mail box using telephone, fax machine, mobile phones, internet browsers etc. Tele-medicine, Tele-education, Tele-banking, call centre are covered under other service providers.

MASS COMMUNICATION

Radio broadcasting started in India in 1927 with two privately owned transmitters at Mumbai and Calcutta. The Government took over them in 1930 and started operating them under the name of Indian Broadcasting Service. It was changed to All India Radio (AIR) in 1936 and since 1957, AIR is known as Akashvani. All India Radio's network consisted of six radio stations in 1947. With a network of 208 radio stations, AIR covers 98.8% of the population. Stereo FM service is available at Mumbai, Delhi, Kolkata, Chennai, Panaji and Cuttack. FM RDS paying service is being introduced from 91 centres in the country. Sky radio service with 327 channels has been launched. Some of the music events held in our country are covered by AIR. Two major festival excerpts which are broadcast on the national as well as zonal hook-up level are the Thyagaraja and Tansen festivals. About 40% of the total broadcast time of AIR now caters to music programmes.

Popular entertainment programme, known as Vividh Bharathi, is broadcast from 39 centres, including three short wave transmitters at Mumbai, Delhi and Chennai. Film music, humorous skits, short plays and features are presented in these programmes.

Commercial broadcasting on the radio introduced on 1st November 1967 from Mumbai-Nagpur-Pune, on an experimental basis, is at present carried by 39 centres. Advertisements are accepted in any language as tape-recorded slots. Sponsored programmes were introduced in a limited experimental scale on the Primary Channel with advertisements being allowed for a minute. The commercial service on the Primary Channel (Phase 2) has also been introduced from 26th January 1986. At present, commercials are broadcast from 60 stations. The revenue earned by radio during 1998-99 was Rs.92.96 crore. Sports/sponsorships are being accepted in rural programmes, women's programmes, film/light music (Indian and Western) including listeners' choice, plays and other popular programmes. AIR is also now hooked to 'INTERNET' for on-line information service. Six super power short wave transmitters of 500 KW each have been commissioned at Bangalore to strenghten the external services of All India Radio for covering Latin American and European countries. This has made Bangalore one of the biggest transmitting complexes in the world.

Doordarshan: Television was started in India on an experimental service on 15th September, 1959. Regular service began in 1965 but only in 1976 it was delinked from AIR and Doordarshan has emerged as an extensive national network, expanding its reach and area of activities in the sphere of information, education and entertainment after 1982. The Parliament in 1990 passed the Prasar Bharathi (Broadcasting Corporation of India) bill to give autonomy to Doordarshan and Akashvani. The Corporation came into existence on 23 November 1997. A Board consisting of a Chairman, an executive member and a number of part-time, full-time, ex-officio and elected members manages the affairs of Prasar Bharathi.

INSAT multiple service project has been made use by Doordarshan for direct telecast of the programmes and for national networking of the existing terrestrial transmitters through the use of microwave system. Telecasts of higher education programmes which commenced on August 16, 1984, via INSAT-IB continue successfully. As on 31 March 2000, Doordarshan network had 1,042 transmitters. TV covers 87 per cent of population. The number of TV programme producing centres is being increased to 49. The country's highest TV Tower (235 meters) three times taller than the Qut-ub-Minar was commissioned at Peetambara, New Delhi on 7th November 1988. A Central Production Centre was opened in Asiad Village, New Delhi on 6th February 1989. As on 1998-99 Doordarshan reached 360 million viewers in their homes and it earned Rs.4 billion from the commercial advertisements.

The country's second television centre came up in Mumbai in 1972. It was followed by Srinagar, Amritsar, Kolkata, Chennai and Lucknow. Following one year's rich experience of SITE in 1975-76, India has introduced its own multipurpose satellite - INSAT which is being used for the telecommunication, meteorology and radio besides television. From 15th August 1982, Doordarshan started its national programme (relayed simultaneously from all centres). From the same day, it also introduced a regular INSAT service in Andhra Pradesh, Orissa, Maharashtra, Gujarat, Bihar and Uttar Pradesh. The entire service is telecast via satellite and at the receiving end a combination of

Direct Receiver Sets (DRS) and Very High Frequency (VHF) sets have been installed in these states. Conversion of black and white to Colour TV Transmission commenced from that day.

Doordarshan introduced its first School Television (ETV) in October 1961. At present, educational programmes, both of enrichment type and syllabus oriented, are put out by serveral Doordarshan Kendras as well as CIET and SIET centres. Teletext Service Known as INTEXT was introduced at Delhi Doordarshan Kendra in November 1985.

With the approval of General Committee of both Houses of Parliament, Doordarshan commenced the experimental telecasts of proceedings of Sabha and Rajya Sabha, telecast of address by the President, and presentation of Union and Railway Budgets with effect from 3 December 1991.

Delhi, Mumbai, Kolkata and Chennai have second channel. Now Doordarshan has started its third channel (Doordarshan-India) reaching about 50 countries in Asia, Africa and Europe. The third channel can be seen by the Metropolitan citizens whereas the cable connection provides the same facility to the rural areas. The fifth channel telecasts entertainments and movies mostly. In order to face the challenges of Satellite TV's, Doordarshan has started telecasting its regional services from 11 states via INSAT I-D and INSAT II-A can now be received throughout the country with the help of dish antenna systems. Doordarshan has begun Digital Terrestrial Transmission (DTT) on experimental basis. Under DTT, one digital transmitter can carry 4 to 6 channels.

DTH: Direct to Home broadcasting is a mode of delivery of satellite channels, which will help the cable operators to deliver directly to the end user as on 16th Dec. 2004.

TRANSPORT

Railways

The Indian Railway system is the largest in Asia and the second largest in the world. It is also the biggest public sector enterprise in India, with an investment of over Rs.7,000 crore and a gross annual revenue of over Rs.2000 crore.

Evolution of the Indian Railways

The first railways in India, also first in Asia, was opened by the Great Indian Peninsular Railway Company (now the Central Railway) formed in England. The company took up the survey in 1850. In about 3 years the work was completed and the first train steamed out of Bombay on April 16, 1853, and reached Thane covering a modest distance of about 34 kms.

Indian railways have grown into a vast network of more than 7,133 stations spread over 63,465 km with a fleet of 7,910 locomotives, 42,447 coaches, 5,822 electric multiple units and 2,22,379 wagons as on 31st March 2005. The growth of Indian railways in the 154 years of its existence is thus phenomenal. It has played a vital role in the economic, industrial and social development of our country. The network runs multigauge operations extending over 63,465 route kilometre. The gauge-wise route and track lengths of the system as on 31st March 2005 were as under:

Gauge	Route/length km	Running track km	Total track km
Broad Gauge (1,676 mm)	47,749	67,932	89,771
Metre Gauge (1,000 mm)	12,662	13,271	15,684
Narrow Gauge (762 mm & 610 mm)	3,054	3,057	3,350
Total	**63,465**	**84,260**	**1,08,805**

About 28% of the route kilometre, 39% of running track kilometre and 40% of total track kilometre is electrified. Indian Railway is the second biggest electrified system in the world, after Russia.

Administration

The Indian Railways network is owned and managed by the Central Government. The operations are controlled and directed by the Railway Board under the overall supervision of the Minister for Railways. The Board has a Chairman and 6 members including the Financial Commissioner. The Chairman is the Ex-Officio Principal Secretary to the Government of India. The Board thus performs the dual functions of a secretariat to the Ministry of Railways and that of an executive body responsible for railway operations. The Railways' annual budget is approved by the Parliament and accounts are audited by the Comptroller and Auditor General of India.

Administrative Divisions: The Indian Railways network is divided into 16 Zones each headed by a General Manager. Zonal Divisions in Railways are given below:

ZONAL DIVISIONS

Railways	Headquarters	Date of Inauguration
Southern	Chennai	Apr. 14, 1951
Central	Mumbai CST	Nov. 5, 1951
Western	Mumbai Churchgate	Nov. 5, 1951
Northern	New Delhi	Apr. 14, 1952
North Eastern	Gorakhpur	Apr. 14, 1952
Eastern	Kolkata	Aug. 1, 1955
South Eastern	Kolkata Garden Reach	Aug. 1, 1955
Northeast Frontier	Maligaon (Guwahati)	Jan. 15, 1958
South Central	Secunderabad	Oct. 2, 1966
East-Coast (ECR)	Bhubaneswar	Aug. 8, 1996
North Western (NWR)	Jaipur	Oct. 10, 1996
South-East Central(SEC)	Bilaspur (M.P.)	Sep. 9, 1998
East Central (ECR)	Hajipur	Oct. 1, 2002
North Central (NCR)	Allahabad	Apr. 1, 2003
South Western (SWR)	Hubli	Apr. 1, 2003
West Central (WCR)	Jabalpur	Apr. 1, 2003

Every year, new trains on long distance as well as trains with high speed are introduced. Gauge conversion is a continuous process. The conversion of metre and narrow gauges into broad gauge (Uni-gauge) is on full swing.

Railway Production Units

Locomotives are built in Chittaranjan Locomotive Works, Chittaranjan, Diesel Locomotive Works, Varanasi and BHEL, Bhopal. Chittaranjan has built an indigenous 3-phase state-of-art 6000 HP freight electric locomotive 'Navyug'. Passenger coaches are manufactured in Integral Coach Factory, Perambur, Chennai and Rail Coach Factory, Kapurtala. In addition, two more units in public sector, M/s Jessops, Kolkata and Bharat Earth Movers Limited, Bangalore, also manufacture coaches and electrical multiple units. Diesel Component Works at Patiala manufactures components of diesel locomotives. Wheel and Axle Plant, Yelahanka (Bangalore), went into production in 1983. A wheel and Axle Plant, Chapra in Bihar will be setup. New Integral Coach Factory will be set up at Alapuzha, Kerala (in 2007-08 Railway Budget).

Public Undertakings

The Ministry of Railways has five undertakings under its administrative control. They are **(i)** Rail India Technical and Economic Services Limited; **(ii)** Indian Railway Construction Company Limited; **(iii)** Indian Railway Finance Corporation Limited; **(iv)** Container Corporation of India Limited; and **(v)** Konkan Railway Corporation Limited. Centre for Railway Information System was set up as a registered society to design and implement various railway computerisation projects.

There is also a **Research, Design and Standards Organisation** at Lucknow which is an attached office of the Railway Board and is headed by a Director General.

Freight Traffic

Rapid progress in industrial and agricultural sectors has generated higher level of demand for rail transport, particularly in the core sectors like coal, iron and steel ores, petroleum products and essential commodities such as foodgrains, fertilizers, cement, sugar, salt, edible oils, etc. Revenue freight traffic increased from 73.2 million tonnes in 1950-51 to 602.1 million tonnes in 2004-05. Transport effort measured in terms of Net Tonne Kilometres (NTkm) increased from 38 billion in 1950-51 to 407.4 billion in 2004-05. Freight trains carry over 12 lakh tonnes of originating goods traffic.

Container Service: A new marketing strategy of container services was introduced in the year 1989 with 7 container depots. In 1996 it was expanded to 32 locations.

Passenger Traffic

There has been an impressive increase in volume of passenger traffic both in terms of number of passengers and passenger kilometres, which is a product of passengers carried and average distance traversed. Passengers originating had risen from 1,284 million in 1950-51 to 5,378 million in 2004-05 and passenger kilometre from 66.52 billion in 1950-51 to 576 billion in 2004-05. During 2007-08, Indian Railways introduced 40 new trains including 8 new Garib raths, extended the run of 23 trains. Each day, more than 7,575 passenger trains carry more than 136 lakh passengers.

Handicaps to Railway Revenues

The Railways suffer from serious handicaps which erode the revenue on three counts. *(1) Ticketless travel (2) Uneconomic lines (3) Social burdens and (4) Separate Coaches.*

PROGRESS OF RAILWAYS' TRAFFIC AND INPUTS

Year	Route length (kilometre)			Running track total (km)	Passengers originating (lakh)	Goods originating (lakh tonne)
	Electrified	Non-Electrified	Total km			
1997-98	13,490	49,005	62,495	80,908	43,480	4,455
1998-99	13,765	49,044	62,809	81,511	44,110	4,416
1999-00	14,261	48,498	62,759	81,252	45,849	4,782
2000-01	14,856	48,172	63,028	81,865	48,327	5,042
2001-02	15,994	47,146	63,140	82,354	50,927	5,222
2002-03	16,272	46,850	63,122	82,492	49,708	5,187
2003-04	17,503	45,718	63,221	83,859	51,123	5,573

For long-term requirements, the railways have also prepared a 'corporate plan' covering 15 years period, 1985-2000. It seeks to provide 370-400 billion net tonne km freight traffic, 310-330 billion non-suburban passenger kilometre and 105-110 billion suburban passenger kilometre by the turn of the century.

Gauges

Broad Gauge	-	5'6"	or	1.68 metres
Metre Gauge	-	3'3" 3/8	or	1 metre
Narrow Gauge	-	2'6"	or	0.762 metre

Longest railway tunnel in India is Torsi Tunnel 3/4th of a mile long. Longest railway platform is at Kharagpur station (2733 feet / 833 m) in West Bengal. Longest railway bridge is Sone Bridge. The railways are the largest employers in the country (more than 1,723,125 people).

Konkan Railway

The 760-km Konkan Railway has become fully operational on Roha to Mangalore section from January 26th, 1998. Konkan Railway is jointly owned by Indian Railways and four states - Maharashtra, Karnataka, Goa and Kerala.

Konkan Railway Corporation has invested Rs.3,500 crore, now it generates a revenue of around Rs.90 lakhs a day from passenger fares and freight charges. It is the longest rail line laid in the country, which has 179 major bridges, 1,819 minor bridges, 92 tunnels (83.4 km added length and 88.77 million cubic metres of earthwork in cuttings and embankments.

RAKSHA KAVACH

World's first Networked Anti-Collision Devices (ACDs)

Raksha Kavach, invented by Konkan Railway, is an intelligent microprocessor based system comprising of a central processing unit, a Global Position System (GPS) Receiver and a digital radio modem for communication between the ACDs. When fitted to a guard-van, it becomes a Guard ACD. When fitted at stations, it becomes a Station ACD and when fitted at level crossing gates, it becomes a Gate ACD. They all network among themselves, exchange information and take decision to prevent collision type of dangerous situations well in time, automatically, without manual inputs, forming Raksha Kavach against collisions. Survey for implementation of ACDs has already been completed for over 3,300 route km on Indian Railways and 760 route km on Konkan Railway. In the first Phase, 1736 Route km on North-east Frontier Railway has been covered at a cost of Rs. 50 crore. It was launched on 20-1-04 at Kishanganj Rly. Station.

SOME OTHER IMPORTANT LONG DISTANCE TRAINS

1007/1008	Mumbai CST-Pune (Deccan Express)
1077/1078	Pune-Jammu Tawi (Jhelum Express)
1097/1098	Pune-Ernakulam (Poorna Express)
2001/2002	Bhopal-New Delhi (Sadapti Express)
2105/2106	Mumbai-Nagpur (Vidarba Express)
2123/2124	Mumbai-Pune (Deccan Queen Express)
2279/2280	Jancy-Nizamuddin (Taj Express)
2303/2304	Howrah-New Delhi (Poorva Express)
2333/2334	Howrah-Varanasi (Vibudi Express)
2419/2420	Lucknow-New Delhi (Gomati Express)
2473/2474	Ahamadabad-Jammu Tawi (Sarvodaya Express)
2605/2606	Chennai Egmore-Trichirapalli (Pallavan Express)
2607/2608	Chennai-Bangalore (Lalbagh Express)
2611/2612	Chennai-Nizamuddin (Garib Rath)
2621/2622	Chennai-New Delhi (Tamilnadu Express)
2641/2642	Kanyakumari-Nizamuddin (Thirukural Express)
2655/2656	Ahmadabad-Chennai (Navajeevan Express)
2661/2662	Chennai Egmore-Tenkasi (Podigai Express)
2669/2670	Chennai-Chhapra (Ganga Kaveri Express)
2719/2720	Tenali-Secundrabad (Nagarjuna Express)
2763/2764	Tirupati-Secundrabad (Padmavathi Express)
2841/2842	Howrah-Chennai (Coramandal Express)
2859/2860	Mumbai-Howrah (Geetanjali Express)
2915/2916	Ahamadabad-New Delhi (Ashram Express)
2961/2962	Mumbai-Indore (Avandika Express)
3301/3302	Dhanpad-Tata Nagar (Swarna Rekha Express)
4005/4006	Samastipur-New Delhi (Lichchavi Express)
4095/4096	Nizamuddin-Kalka (Himalayan Queen)
4163/4164	Allahabad-Meerut City (Sangam Express)
5311/5312	Madura-Lalkuan (Kumaun Express)
5321/5322	Gorakhpur-Gonda (Kabilavashtu Express)
6057/6058	Chennai-Tirupathi (Saptagiri Express)
6089/6090	Chennai-Tirupathur (Yelagiri Express)
6123/6124	Chennai Egmore-Thiruvananthapuram (Ananthapuri Express)

Introduction of 40 New trains including 8 new Garib Raths and Extension of 23 trains have been proposed in 2007-08 Railway Budget.

The year 2007 was declared by Government of India as "Cleanliness Year".

Modernisation of railways, replacement and renewal of assets, particularly track renewal, safety of passengers, cleanliness, improvement in passenger amenities, control over expenditure and prevention of leakage of revenue would be the thrust areas. Over 1,280 unmanned level crossings would be maned over a period of time. Train protection and warning system and provision of anti-collision device were other measures planned. An institute of rescue and medical relief would be set up in Bangalore with training modules on disaster management.

A nation-wide cleanliness drive had been launched by infusing a spirit of competition. Disposable mud cups would be made available and use of plastic cups discouraged. Development of an environment-friendly coach toilet discharge system had been taken up and upholstery and linen used on railways would henceforth be of handloom and khadi variety.

A target of completion of 1,000 kms of gauge conversion had been fixed for the current year along with 381 kms of doubling. The target for new electrification had been kept at 375 kms this year.

Setting-up of a Wheel and Axle plant at Chapra also planned in 2005-06 budget.

CIVIL AVIATION

The Ministry of Civil Aviation looks after the department of Civil Aviation. There are two corporations in India namely 'Indian Airlines' (recently named Indian) and 'Air India' which came into existence on 15th June, 1953.

Indian Civil Aviation celebrated its golden jubilee in October 1982. To commemorate the occasion, Mr. J.R.D. Tata repeated the historic first flight from Karachi to Mumbai (Bombay), in his 'Leopard Moth' on October 15, 1982. The Indian Airlines Corporation provides services within India and also to the neighbouring 14 countries.

There are about 11 international, 87 domestic aerodromes and 25 civil enclaves at defence air fields controlled and operated by the Airports Authority of India. Five aerodromes at Mumbai (Sahar), Delhi (Indira Gandhi), Kolkatta (Dum Dum), Chennai (Anna) and Amritsar (Raja Sansi) are International Airports to which aids and services are provided by International Airports Authority of India Limited. The aerodromes at Ahmedabad, Amritsar, Mumbai, Kolkatta, Delhi, Chennai, Port Blair, Tiruchirapalli and Thiruvananthapuram have been declared as customs aerodromes.

There are 18 flying clubs and seven gliding clubs. Indira Gandhi Rashtriya Uran Academy was set up on 7th November, 1985 at Fursatganj (Uttar Pradesh) to standardise and improve training facilities for commercial pilots. On 18th February 1911, the first official airmail was flown from Uttar Pradesh Exhibition grounds, Allahabad to Naini.

Air India has fleets of Boeing 747-200, Airbus A300-B4, Air Bus 310-300, Boeing 747-300 (Combi), HS- 78, F-27, 18B-737. Indian Airlines owns fleets of A-300, A-320, B-737, Dornier-228 and one of the biggest Aeroplane Airbus - A380 will be built up in 2011 in India.

Airports Authority of India (AAI): AAI was formed on 1 April 1995 by the merger of the International Airports Authority of India and the National Airports Authority.

Pawan Hans Helicopters Limited has been providing helicopter support services to the petroleum sector, certain State governments and public sector undertakings and in the north-eastern States. Sahara Airlines, Jet Airways, Gujarat Airways, and UP Airways are the private air taxi operators.

SOME PRINCIPAL AIRLINES OF THE WORLD

Aeroflot (Russia)	Air India (India)
Air Lanka (Sri Lanka)	Air France (France)
Alitalia (Italy)	Ariana Afghan Airlines (Afghanistan)
British Airways (England)	Cathay Pacific (Hongkong)
Finnair (Finland)	Garuda Airways (Indonesia)
Japan Airlines Limited (Japan)	K.L.M.Royal Dutch (Netherlands)
Lufthansa (Germany)	Pan American Airways (USA)
Qantas Empire Airways (Australia)	Royal Nepal Airlines (Nepal)
Sabena (Belgium)	Scandinavian Airlines System (Sweden)
Swissair (Switzerland)	Thai Airways International (Thailand)
Trans-World Airlines (USA)	Olympic Airways (Greece)

ROADS

Little attention was paid to road development in India till the 1920s. After the First World War, however, motor transport increased considerably and with a total road length of 3.32 million km as on 31 March 2005 excluding those under Jawahar Rozgar Yojana, India has the third largest road network in the world.

The Tenth Plan outlay proposed for Central Sector Roads is Rs. 59,490. Under the Ninth Plan, the allocation was Rs.17,748.82 crore for the central sector road programme.

Types of Roads

Roads under the Nagpur Plan, were classified as: **(1)** *National Highways,* **(2)** *State Highways,* **(3)** *Major District Roads,* **(4)** *Minor District Roads,* and *Village Roads.*

National Highways: With the framework of the road system, predominant role is played by the National Highways, which are the main arteries running through the country connecting state capitals, major ports, industrial complexes, etc. Total length of National Highways is 65,600 km. National Highway No.1 runs between Delhi and Pakistan Border (near Amritsar). Roads of strategic importance for defence are also included in National Highways. Though the national highways constitute only two percent of the total road length, they carry nearly 40 percent of road traffic.

State Highways: These are trunk roads interlinking State capitals with important areas in the district and intersect National and State Highways or railways passing through the district.

Minor District Roads and Village Roads: These connect different villages to one another and to the nearest district road and inland water-way.

National Permit Scheme: The Government of India introduced in 1975 a 'National Permit Scheme' to facilitate inter-state movement of vehicles. Permits under the scheme are granted.

An Express Highway 'Golden Quadrilateral' (GQ) with six lanes running 13,000 kilometres from Kashmir to Kanyakumari and from Porbundar to Silchar covering mostly all States has been proposed to be completed by December 2007.

SHIPPING

India ranks 19th in the world in shipping tonnage and has the largest merchant shipping fleet among developing countries. Shipping plays an important role in India with a vast coastline of about 7,516 km and over 2 million sq.km. of Exclusive Economic Zone. As on 31st Dec. 2005 the net operative tonnage consisted of 707 ships totalling to 8.29 million GRT (gross registered tonnage) and 13.72 million DWT.

There are 140 shipping companies in the country in operation as on 31st Dec. 2005 including the Shipping Corporation of India, a public sector undertaking and ten other Government agencies. Of these, 107 are engaged exclusively in coastal trade, 32 in overseas trade and 10 in both coastal and overseas trade. Shipping Corporation of India, which is the biggest shipping line of the country had a merchant fleet of 88 vessels of 2.66 million GRT and operated on almost all maritime routes. Its tonnage accounts are about 42% of the total Indian tonnage. There are three training establishments for Navy Officers. The Hindustan Shipyard at Visakhapatnam has built 107 ships. The Cochin Shipyard set up with Japanese collaboration has so far built and delivered the largest nine ships (five bulk carriers and four crude oil tankers). There are 12 major ports in the country, apart from 184 minor working ports along the coastline of about 5,600 km. The Dredging Corporation of India renders maintenance and capital dredging services in major Ports, Shipyards, Shipping Harbour, Navy, State governments etc. The Tenth Plan outlay for the Ports sector is Rs. 5,418 crore for schemes/projects.

TOURISM

Tourism in India has grown substantially over the last three decades. During 2005 foreign tourist recorded an increase of 13.2%. Foreign exchange earnings from tourism during 2005 were provisionally estimated at Rs.25,172 crore. Tourism thus has become the second largest net foreign exchange earner of the country. The department of tourism has undertaken many steps to promote tourism. It has constructed many forest lodges and hotels at tourist resorts. Indian Railway pass facilities are available for foreign tourists and non-resident Indians against payment in convertible currencies. Besides these, Indian Airlines have introduced two concessional fares. Indian Railways and Rajasthan State Tourism Development Corporation have jointly organised the 'Palace on Wheels' train in order to promote places of tourist interest in Rajasthan. Another special tourist train by name *'Orient Express'* has been introduced in the Gujarat sector and a few more in the private sector are likely to be introduced.

India Tourism Development Corporation (ITDC) was established on 1st October 1966. It operates Ashoka Group of Hotels (the largest hotel chain), Beach Resort Accommodation, Tourism Transport Services, Duty Free Shops, a travel agency and other services. ITDC continues to organise food-cum-cultural festivals in India and abroad. There are 21 field offices of the Ministry of Tourism in India and 18 of them in the overseas markets to undertake both developmental and promotional activities. 18 hotels have so far been disinvested.

PRESS

The office of the Registrar of Newspapers for India commonly known as Press Registrar came into being on 1st July, 1956. The duties and functions of the Press Registrar are defined in the Press and Registration of Books Act, 1867 as amended from time to time. Apart from these duties, the Registrar also allots newsprint and recommends import of printing machinery for newspapers.

As on 31st March, 2006, the total number of newspapers and periodicals was 62,550 as compared to 49,145 in 2000. There were 6,800 dailies, 369 tri/bi weeklies, 21,453 weeklies, 18,545 monthlies, 8,227 fortnightlies, 4,340 quarterlies, 584 annuals and 2,032 publications with periodicities like bi-monthlies, half yearlies etc. Newspapers were published in as many as 123 languages and dialects during 2001. Apart from English and 22 principal languages enumerated in the Eighth Schedule of the Constitution, newspapers were published in 81 other languages, mostly Indian languages or dialects and a few foreign languages. The highest number (24,017) of newspapers were published in Hindi language. Daily newspapers were brought out in 22 principal languages and Kashmiri was the only principal language that did not have a daily newspaper.

Newspapers were published from all states and union territories. Uttar Pradesh with 9,757 newspapers retained the prestigious position of publishing the largest number of newspapers in India. In the case of dailies also, Uttar Pradesh held the top position with 841 dailies.

Bombay Samachar, a Gujarati daily published from Mumbai since 1822, is the oldest existing newspaper in Asia.

In 2003, the total circulation of Indian Press was 14,20,05,543 copies. *As per Audit Bureau of Circulation/Jan-June 2003 (Preliminary)* **Hindustan Times**, an English Daily from Delhi with a circulation of 11,12,160 copies occupied the 1st position. **The Hindu** English daily published from Chennai occupied the 2nd position with a circulation of 9,22,407 copies. **Times of India,** an English daily from Delhi with a circulation of 8,20,289 copies was in third position.

The largest circulated multi-edition Daily: Dainik Bhaskar, (18 editions), Hindi (17,17,294 copies). **The second largest circulated multi-edition Daily:** The Times of India (Eight editions), English, (13,94,646 copies). **The largest circulated periodical:** Saras Salil, (Fortnightly) Hindi, Delhi (10,49,362). The total circulation of newspapers showed an increase of 23.21 per cent from 11,52,53,948 copies in 2001 to 14,20,05,543 copies in 2003-04.

Among periodicals, **Saras Salil,** Hindi monthly from Delhi was the largest circulated periodicals with 10,49,362 copies. **The Hindu Weekly Magazine** was second with 9,95,469 copies, **The Sunday Times of India,** weekly from Delhi stood in third with 7,59,942 copies and **Malayala Manorama,** a Malayalam weekly published from Kottayam with a circulation of 6,35,701 copies occupied the fourth position. The first newspaper (weekly) published in India - **Bengal Gazette** (also called Hicky's Gazette) was in English, in 1780 in Calcutta. The editor was an Englishman - James Hicky; **Dig Darshan** (Bengali) was the first language newspaper also from Kolkata (1818).

Press Information Bureau (PIB): It is the nodal agency of the Government of India for disseminating the information on its policies, programmes and activities to the print and electronic media. PIB distributes its press material to over 8,400 newspapers and media organisations. PIB arranges photocoverage of Government activities.

The Bureau has a Home Page on Internet. It is accessible at website **www.pib.nic.in**. The Bureau has granted professional facilities to 155 technicians and 71 editors/media critics.

The PIB is linked with 43 of its Regional and Branch Offices over computer to facilitate speedy feeding of information. It also has a link with the INTERNET system which makes materials available for international consumption. PIB has started photo transmission by computer to some of its offices. A Bulletin Board Service (BBS) has been introduced on computer which contains releases, features, photos and graphics.

The Bureau also arranges press conferences and briefings to enable media representatives to get the news and clarification at first hand.

The Headquarters of the Bureau is in Delhi. It has a network of 8 regional offices (Mumbai, Chennai, Chandigarh, Kolkata, Lucknow, Guwahati, Bhopal and Hyderabad) and 35 Branch Offices and Information Centres. The Bureau is the implementing agency for exchange of delegations of journalists between India and foreign countries.

News Agencies: India has 4 news agencies - *Press Trust of India (PTI), United News of India (UNI), Samachar Bharati* and *Hindustan Samachar.* The four news agencies were merged in 1976 to form **Samachar.** Two years later, Samachar was dismantled and the news agencies regained their separate identity from 14th April 1978.

PTI, India's largest news agency, was set up on 27th August 1947. It took over from the Associated Press of India (API) and Reuters. PTI has computerised its news operations in four metropolitan cities and has embarked

Number of Newspapers in 2004-05 (Language and Periodicity)

S. No.	Languages	Dailies	Tri/Bi-weeklies	Weeklies	Fort-nightlies	Monthlies	Quarterlies	Bi-monthlies Half yearlies, etc.	Annuals	Total
1.	English	437	37	1,086	789	3,255	1,401	925	211	8,141
2.	Hindi	2,645	127	10,802	3,300	4,122	775	251	45	22,067
3.	Assamese	20	3	80	39	69	13	10	1	235
4.	Bengali	107	15	657	593	754	513	205	25	2,869
5.	Gujarati	170	14	1,197	241	658	72	54	15	2,421
6.	Kannada	396	6	444	315	793	57	27	4	2,042
7.	Kashmiri	0	0	1	0	0	0	0	0	1
8.	Konkani	1	0	3	1	5	2	0	0	12
9.	Malayalam	231	6	190	169	866	67	40	9	1,578
10.	Manipuri	16	0	7	5	11	7	5	0	51
11.	Marathi	433	21	1,473	249	647	134	54	127	3,138
12.	Nepali	4	2	26	6	13	18	7	0	76
13.	Oriya	80	3	179	100	317	94	23	4	800
14.	Punjabi	107	15	379	105	294	36	19	1	956
15.	Sanskrit	4	0	9	5	18	18	6	0	60
16.	Sindhi	13	0	40	11	39	10	2	0	115
17.	Tamil	373	43	422	262	1129	40	27	8	2,304
18.	Telugu	210	4	293	244	671	34	18	2	1,476
19.	Urdu	550	21	1,370	387	554	79	19	3	2,983
20.	Bilingual	92	21	758	426	1,491	423	180	46	3,437
21.	Multilingual	20	5	130	77	272	72	38	14	628
22.	Others	57	15	85	32	131	54	15	1	390
	Total	6,530	364	20,831	7,959	17,813	4,227	1,925	556	60,205

on electronification, of its remaining 136 news bureaux in the country and all its services. It started in early 1986, a Hindi language news service, PTI BHASHA, a precursor to services in other languages in the near future. PTI has completed 50 years of its operations and brought out a 15-rupee multi-colour postage stamp to mark its golden jubilee on 5th March 1999.

PTI has full-fledged news bureaux in London and New York and has news exchange arrangements with about 100 countries. It is an active participant in the Non-Aligned News Agencies Pool and the Organisation of Asia-Pacific News Agencies (OANA). PTIs website is **www.ptinews.com**

United News of India (UNI): was registered as a company in 1959 and started news operations from 21 March 1961. In May 1982, UNI launched its news service in Hindi under the credit line of UNIVARTA. It operates a news service to the media in four Gulf countries as well as Mauritius and Bhutan. It started its own TV news wing in July 1986 and has been making regular contribution of news clips and news features to Doordarshan and other Organisations. A national photo service (started in 1987) is a pioneering venture.

Hindustan Samachar is the only multi-lingual News Agency which is run by its workers under the Co-operative Society Act. It is the first News Agency which started the use of Nagari Teleprinter and ushered a new era in language journalism in India.

Non-Aligned News Agencies Pool was set up on 13th July 1976. It is a system of news exchange among the pool partners. The Press Trust of India operates India News Pool Desk of Non-Aligned News Agencies Pool. The Pool news is exchanged in four languages — English, French, Spanish and Arabic.

Under the Press Council Act, 1978, the first **Press Council of India** was constituted in 1979, the second in 1982 and the third in 1985 and the fourth in September 28, 1988. The term of the council is three years. The Press Council safeguards freedom of the press. It is comprised mainly of representatives. The Council is a body corporate having perpetual succession. It consists of a Chairman and 28 other members. During 2005-2006, the council received 829 complaints. It adjudicated 169 cases.

IMPORTANT FOREIGN NEWS AGENCIES

Reuters	- UK
Associated Press (AP),	
International News Service,	
United Press International (UPI),	
United Press of America (UPA),	
Near and Far East News Agency	- USA
Agence France Presse (AFP)	- France
Potka Agencia Prasova	- Poland
Ceteka	- Czech Republic
Xinhua New China News Agency	- China
Antara	- Indonesia
Arab News Agency	- Africa
TASS	- Russia
UNB	- Bangladesh
GNA	- Bahrain
KUNA	- Kuwait

Some foreign news agencies supply news to Indian papers and send Indian news to their clients abroad.

SOME IMPORTANT FOREIGN NEWSPAPERS

The Times	- United Kingdom
Manchester Guardian	- United Kingdom
The Daily Mirror	- United Kingdom
New York Times, Washington Post	- USA
People's Daily	- China
Izvestia	- Russia
Le Monde	- France
Al-Ahram	- Egypt

IMPORTANT NEWSPAPERS IN INDIA

Name of the Newspaper	Place of Publications
The Times of India	Mumbai, Delhi, Ahmedabad, Bangalore, Patna
The Statesman	New Delhi, Kolkata
The Indian Express	New Delhi, Mumbai, Ahmedabad, Vijayawada, Bangalore, Chennai, Madurai, Cochin, Chandigarh, Hyderabad and Vizianagaram
The Hindu	Chennai, Bangalore, Coimbatore, Madurai, Hyderabad, Delhi, Visakhapatnam, Kochi, Vijayawada, Mangalore, Trichy, Thiruvananthapuram
Amrita Bazar Patrika	Kolkata, New Delhi
The Hindustan Times	New Delhi
The Hindustan Standard	Kolkata
The Telegraph	Kolkata
Tribune	Chandigarh
The Assam Tribune	Guwahati
The Free Press Journal	Mumbai
The Searchlight	Patna
The Indian Nation	Patna
The Hitavada	Nagpur
The Nagpur Times	Nagpur
The Pioneer	Lucknow
The National Herald	Lucknow and Delhi
The Daily Post	Bangalore
Deccan Herald	Bangalore
The Eastern Times	Cuttack
The Daily News	Bangalore and Secunderabad
The Patriot	New Delhi
The Deccan Chronicle	Secunderabad & Chennai

LEADING PERIODICALS

English

Blitz (Weekly)	Mumbai
Frontline (Fortnightly)	Chennai
Femina (Fortnightly)	Mumbai
Filmfare (Fortnightly)	Mumbai
Reader's Digest (Monthly)	Mumbai
Sunday Times of India (Weekly)	Kolkata
India Today (Weekly)	New Delhi
The Week	Kottayam
Sportstar (Weekly)	Chennai

Hindi

Chandamama (Monthly)	Chennai
Dharmayug (Weekly)	Mumbai
Kalyan (Monthly)	Gorakhpur
Nandan (Monthly)	Delhi
Parag (Monthly)	Mumbai
Saras Salil (Fortnightly)	Delhi
Sapthahik Hindustan (Weekly)	Delhi

Malayalam

Mathrubhoomi (Weekly)	Kozhikode
Malayala Manorama (Weekly)	Kottayam
Mangalam	Kottayam
Kerala Kaumudi	Thiruvananthapuram
Vanita	Kozhikode

Tamil

Ananda Vikatan (Weekly)	Chennai
Kumudam (Weekly)	Chennai
Kalki (Weekly)	Chennai
Kungumam (Weekly)	Chennai

Telugu

Andhra Prabha (Weekly)	Chennai
Swati (Weekly)	Visakhapatnam

LEADING NEWSPAPERS IN OTHER LANGUAGES

Anand Bazar Patrika	Bengali
Gujarat Samachar	Gujarati
Sandesh	Gujarati
Dinakaran	Tamil
Dinathanthi	Tamil
Dinamalar	Tamil
Dinamani	Tamil
Kannada Prabha	Kannada
Malayala Manorama	Malayalam

Mathrubhoomi	Malayalam
Akale Patrika	Punjabi
Andhra Prabha, Vaartha	Telugu
Eenadu	Telugu
Loksatta	Marathi
Sakal	Marathi
Inquilab	Urdu
Nav Bharat Times	Hindi
Punjab Kesari	Hindi
Dainik Baskar, Dainik Jagran	Hindi

THE LARGEST CIRCULATED DAILIES IN INDIA

Newspaper/Editions	Language	Circulation
Dainik Bhaskar (17 editions)	Hindi	17,17,294
The Times of India (8 editions)	English	13,94,646
Dainik Jagran (11)	Hindi	13,78,386
Malayala Manorama (8)	Malayalam	12,43,434
Hindustan Times (8 centres)	English	11,12,160
Gujarat Samachar (5)	Gujarati	10,09,972
The Hindu (12 centres)	English	9,22,407
Mathrubhumi (6)	Malayalam	8,90,984
Anand Bazar Patrika (1)	Bengali	8,88,855
Aj (10)	Hindi	8,78,516
Punjab Kesari (3)	Hindi	8,69,220
Eenadu (10)	Telugu	8,41,890
Sandesh (5)	Gujarati	7,06,577
Hindustan	Hindi	6,59,141
Amar Ujala	Hindi	6,39,014
Daily Thanthi (12)	Tamil	6,01,809
Nav Bharat (7)	Hindi	5,91,831
Rajasthan Patrika	Hindi	5,72,026
Sakal (4)	Marathi	5,23,813
Navbharat Times (3)	Hindi	5,01,496
Dinamalar (8)	Tamil	4,91,090
Bartaman (1)	Bengali	3,69,807
Loksatta (3)	Marathi	3,67,711
The Economic Times (7)	English	3,41,911
The New Indian Express (13)	English	3,24,161

CULTURAL ACTIVITIES

Between 1952 and 1958, a number of steps were taken at the national level which were of far reaching consequences both for the capital and the rest of the country, in the field of Art.

Sangeet Natak Academy: In 1953, the Sangeet Natak Academy (National Academy of Music, Dance and Drama) was set up by the Government of India with the task of promoting research, organising training institutions, holding seminars and festivals.

It also maintains libraries of records, taped music, books, films and photographs. Reorganised and registered in 1961, the Academy has since set up two galleries of musical instruments, masks and costumes. The Academy presents awards to outstanding artistes in the field of music, dance and drama for hall-mark of distinction and classical maturity. Occasionally prizes for books are also given. In order to encourage play-writing in Indian languages a prize of Rs.50,000 is given annually for plays in various Indian languages. Out of the funds placed at its disposal by Government, the academy assists a number of non-governmental institutions in different parts of the country. Generally, this assistance is for training, cost of new productions, purchase of technical equipments and survey and research.

The Academy has been responsible for the establishment and maintenance of two national institutions each of which had made a distinct contribution to the promotion of the art with which it has been concerned. These are the Kathak Kendra, New Delhi and the Jawaharlal Nehru Manipuri Dance Academy, Imphal.

National School of Drama (NSD): NSD is one of the foremost theatre training institutions in the world. It was set up by Sangeet Natak Akademi in 1959. Later in 1975, it became autonomous. The systematic study and practical performing experience give the students a solid grounding in the art of theatre. The school has its performing wing, a Repertory Company, and Theatre-in-Education Company. Its Regional Resource-cum-Research Centre is in Bangalore.

Sahitya Academy: The Sahitya Academy was founded in March 1954 and registered as a Society in 1956. The Sahitya Academy has undertaken a major programme of publishing translations of major works of literary value from various regional languages. A selection from Tagore's writing has been published in eight volumes. The Academy's publications up to the end of 2000 totalled 3,200. The Bibliography of Indian Literature (20th century) covering all books of literary merit in all the major Indian languages as well as books in English published in India or written by Indian authors is a major contribution of the Academy. A comprehensive Who's Who of Indian writers was published by the Academy in 1961.

A series under the title 'Makers of Indian Literature' has also been sponsored by the Academy. Each volume gives the life and contribution of an important Indian writer.

The Academy publishes three journals, a bi-monthly in English called 'Indian Literature' Samakaleena Bharatiya Sahitya (bi-monthly) in Hindi and a half-yearly in Sanskrit called 'Samskrita Pratibha'. It arranges occasional seminars, weekly discussions and lectures in New Delhi.

The Academy gives annual awards to authors of outstanding books published in Indian languages. Several award winning books have been translated into other languages.

Lalit Kala Academy: Lalit Kala Academy (National Akademi of Fine Arts) was established at New Delhi in 1954 with the object of promoting fine arts and undertaking programmes for the growth and nourishment of painting, sculpture and other graphic arts. The Academy co-ordinates the activities of regional state Academies, encourages exchange of ideas among various schools of art, publishes literature and posters, promotes inter-regional and international contacts through exhibitions and exchange of personnel and art objects.

The Academy organises national exhibitions of contemporary Indian art with 15 national awards, each of Rs.50,000. Every year the Academy holds a National Art Exhibition. Once in every three years the Academy holds an international exhibition called **Triennale India abroad** to propagate Indian art outside.

The Academy brings out two bi-annual art journals *Lalit Kala Contemporary* and *Lalit Kala Ancient* in English and *Samkaleen Kala* in Hindi. The same year as the Lalit Kala Academy was established, Government of India set up the National Gallery of Modern Art with a collection of 17,858 works of art, representing various styles for over hundred years.

Another institution deserving mention is the Indian Council of Cultural Relations established by the Government of India in order to interpret aspects of Indian culture to foreign countries and to give facilities to those who wish to know more about it or to do serious studies and research. It is also concerned with the sending of Indian teams of performances, etc., to other countries.

ARTS IN STATES

Tamil Nadu: The Kalakshetra established by Mrs. Rukmini Devi Arundale in Chennai has been for long the upholder of pure classicalism in Bharatha Natyam. As a training centre it remains unique. It has been a second home for stalwarts who give Carnatic Music. Grants from the Sangeet Natak Academy have stimulated its programmes. Even older than Kalakshetra the other conservative organisation of Tamil Nadu is the Chennai Music Academy. Mrs. Subbulakshmi, Dr. M. Balamurali Krishna, Mandolin Srinivas and others have been exponents of Carnatic Music from Tamil Nadu.

Kerala: Kathakali style of dance, originated from Kerala has its origin in the courts of the Kings of Kerala. It is more than 300 years old. It is considered to be a highly synthetic art form, combining in itself the rudiments of its earlier forms like Krishnanattam and Ramanattam plus a highly scientific dance drama form. It is not folk, but highly classical though not very old.

Poet Vallathol can be said to be the fountain head of all inspirations in regard to today's Kathakali. He authored many scripts. Kerala Kalamandalam at Cheruthuruthy on the bank of Bharathapuzha is the premier institution in this regard.

Karnataka: Though no particular style of dance originated from Karnataka, some of the plays written by authors like B.V.Karanth & Girish Karnad have been noteworthy. K.S.Karanth has dedicated himself to the rehabilitation of the famous 'Yakshagana' of Karnataka. But he tries to present Yakshagana without dialogue. But recent experience has shown that the Yakshagana in its original Udipi style commands greater respect.

Andhra Pradesh: In Andhra Pradesh the appearance of Kuchipudi on the all-India stage has been a notable event. Kuchipudi, a style of dance-drama, goes back to the 15th century. But for a long time it was regarded only as a simplified version of Bharatha Natyam.

Actually its grammar is in one sense more complex having to maintain balance between prose, dialogue, classical songs and intricate tala system. Vedantam Satyanarayana, the Academy award winner, an exponent of Kuchipudi, can hold an audience in spell, anywhere in the world.

Orissa: Odissi style of dance as classical form has brought a much needed and richly deserved sense of self-confidence to Orissa. Odissi is a carefully structured blend of the classical and the devotional temple dance. Kelucharan Mohapatra is the eminent Guru of Odissi.

Maharashtra: Though the Maharashtrians in Mumbai are keen in keeping pace with the Metropolitan cultures of modern cities of the world, they have significantly contributed to the revival of traditional Marathi culture. It is no exaggeration to say that the culture of Maharashtra has always sought heights of splendour through the path of austerity. During the last twenty-five years, Marathi genius has found expression in two different styles of theatre, one is respresented by the modern critical and the other outrageously frank drama of Vijay Tendulkar, as well as the bold and symbolical theatre productions of Satyadeva Dube. In classical music, Maharashtra has continued to give the lead. Even in popular film music none has held the field for so long and with such distinction as Lata Mangeshkar.

Gujarat: The foundations of the plastic and the performing art of Gujarat and Saurashtra are primarily folk. By 1947 the popular plays of Jayasukhlal Sundri had already given place to the modernised versions of Bhavani presented by Deena Gandhi and others. The Baroda College of arts has played a role in this revival. Mrinalini Sarabhai founded Darpana. She is a highly talented dancer.

Madhya Pradesh: Tribal dances, folk plays and folk songs are the characteristics of Madhya Pradesh. The romantic folk drama of Malwa, has received country-wide attention. Kumar Gandharva, Habib Tanwir and Puna Ram are notable persons in the field of dance and music.

Rajasthan: The art received royal patronage from princes in the pre-independence era itself. This patronage is being continually offered by Rajasthan's Sangeet Natak Academy. The puppet shows given by the Bharatiya Lok Kala Mandal have won acclaim in Europe and Asia in several international festivals by the hard efforts of Samar, a pupil of Uday Shankar. Through the Kuchaman, Chirawa and other styles of Kyall, the folk drama of Rajasthan has come to be well-known.

Jammu and Kashmir: Jammu and Kashmir was once the home of the cream of ancient India's arts and letters. Now the Bhan Jashn, a traditional folk play of the Kashmir Valley too is in danger of extinction. The sofiana music of Kashmir has now been brought to the notice of tourists.

Himachal Pradesh: Though a musical link can be established between Jammu and Himachal Pradesh, there is nothing comparable to Himachal Pradesh's satirical folk play, Kariala. Both Jammu and Himachal Pradesh could emerge as excellent centres of painting. Their 18th and 19th century Kangra Pahari Schools of painting are at present the subject of eulogistic scholarly studies.

Punjab and Haryana: These two states have the true Indian character of accommodating the other forms of art and music. Pankra is a style of dance originate from Punjab. Punjab is perhaps the state which has contributed the largest number of stage actors and actresses to the Hindi theatre. Even Prithiviraj Kapoor who recently died was a pupil of the late Mrs. Norach Richards. Haryana's Academy has been very active in refining the folk play Haryanvi Swang without losing its character.

Uttar Pradesh: Uttar Pradesh's progress after independence has been more marked in the Kathak dance. Though Uttar Pradesh's Academy was started very late, one of its major tasks was to ensure that the famous Ramila of Ramnagar (Kashi) which has a unique style, is not allowed to die down.

Bihar: Bihar was the first state to have its Academy soon after independence. The Bihar Nritya Kala Mandir, Patna is a training institute imparting training in the Kathakali style and also Bharatha Natyam.

Assam and Manipur: The Sangeet Natak Academy of Assam started enthusiastically by Rani Sabita Devi has concerned itself with, promoting modern Assamese theatre as also the Satirya dance of the Ankiya Naat and the Bihu festival. For the preservation of the traditional Manipuri style of dancing, the Sangeet Natak Academy established Jawaharlal Nehru Manipuri Dance Academy. It maintains a high standard.

West Bengal: Bengali Cinema Directors like Satyajit Ray have produced films which have won international awards. The significance of the Bengal theatre lies in the strong formative influence, it has on the Hindi theatre. Calcutta seems to provide the ideal situation in which commercial Hindi theatre has risen.

The department of culture has been actively pursuing a policy of cultural co-operation with many countries in the world. At present, India has cultural agreements with 74 countries and 2-3 year cultural exchange programmes with forty eight countries.

India in World Heritage: World Heritage committee constituted by the UNESCO under the provision of the International convention for production of World Cultural and Natural Heritage, has recommended the inscription of 23 cultural monuments and 6 natural sites from India in World Heritage list. These are:

(a) Cultural Monuments: Ajanta caves, Ellora caves, Agra Fort, Taj Mahal, Sun Temple at Konark, Churches and Convents of Goa, Group of Monuments at Khajuraho, Mahabalipuram, Hampi, Fatehpur Sikri, Pattadakal Elephanta caves and Brahadeeswara temple at Tanjore, Qutub Minar, Humayun's Tomb, Airavatesvara Temple, Champaner - Pavagadh, Victoria Terminus, Nilgiri Mountain Railway, Darjeeling Himalayan Railway, Mahabodhi Temple, Bhimbetaka. UNESCO announced the Red Fort as one of Heritage site in India in 2007.

(b) Natural sites: Kaziranga National Park, Manas Wildlife Sanctuary, Keoladeo National Park, Sunderbans National Park and Nanda Devi National Park and Valley of Flowers, Uttarakhand.

World Heritage Day and Week: The World Heritage Day on 18th April 1992 and World Heritage Week from 19 to 25 November 1992 were celebrated.

Festivals of India: The Government of India has organised nine festivals of India in the United Kingdom, USA, France, Soviet-Union, Sweden, Germany, China, Japan and Thailand. Reciprocally, festivals of USSR, France, Sweden, Japan, China and Thailand have been held in India. The Festival of India in Italy was held in October 1998. The first festival of India was held in U.K. in 1982. The main thrust of the Festival of India (FOI) has been to project its multi-faceted cultural life, highlighting scientific and technological programme and advancement through series of exhibitions, performing acts, workshops, youth meetings, sport festivals, etc.

The Festival of India in Germany held in 1992, exposed German audiences to all the Indian classical dance forms and a careful selection of Hindustani and Carnatic vocal and instrumental music. Folk and traditional arts were also presented.

CINEMA

Over the years, about 29,000 feature films have been produced in India which now leads the world in the annual output of feature films. Feature films are being produced in India since 1912-13. While R.G.Torney along with N.G.Chitre made Pundalik in 1912, Dhundiraj Govind Phalke (1870-1944) produced Raja Harishchandra in 1913. Even though Ardeshir Irani (1886-1969) had produced the first talkie 'Alam Ara' in 1931, silent movies continued to be produced till 1934.

Films can be exhibited in India only after they are certified by Central Board of Film Certification. The Board functions with headquarters at Mumbai and nine regional offices at Bangalore, Mumbai, Kolkata, Hyderabad, Chennai, Thiruvananthapuram, New Delhi, Cuttack and Guwahati. The Censor Board consists of a Chairman and a minimum of 12 and a maximum of 25, non-official members.

During 2000, as many as 693 Indian and 432 foreign feature films were certified by the Central Board of Film Certification for public exhibition. Mumbai, Kolkata and Chennai are the most important production centres.

The Films Division is the largest national agency devoted to the production and distribution of documentaries and news magazines. In 1948, the Films Division was set up to revive the production of news reels and documentary films. Its role has been one of interpreting India to Indian and foreign audience. During 2004-05, the Division produced 34 news magazines, 84 documentaries and short feature films and earned a total revenue of Rs.13.77crores. 16 mm films are produced for exhibition in rural areas. It is estimated that four crore rural audience is exposed to 'Film Division' films every year. The Division has emerged as a powerful force behind the documentary film movement in the world.

Dada Saheb Phalke Award: Instituted in 1969, It is a film award given to an outstanding contributor to Indian Cinema in a notable way. The award comprises a Swarna Kamal (Golden Lotus), a shawl and a cash prize of Rs.3lakh.

The recipients of this award are:

Devika Rani Roerich (1969), Birendra Nata Sircar (1970), Prithviraj Kapoor (1971), Pankaj Mullick (1972 Posthumously), Ruby Mayers (Sulochana) (1973), B.N.Reddy (1974), Dhiren Ganguly (1975), Kanan Devi (1976), Nitin Bose (1977), Rai Chand Boral (1978), Sohrab Modi (1979), Naushad Ali (1980), P. Jairaj (1981), L.V.Prasad (1982), Durga Khote (1983), Satyajit Ray (1984), V.Shantaram (1985), B.Nagi Reddy (1986), Raj Kapoor (1987), Ashok Kumar (1988), Lata Mangeshkar (1989), A.Nageswara Rao (1990), Bhalji Pendharkar (1991), Dr.Bhupen Hazarika (1992), Majrooh Sultanpuri (1993), Dilip Kumar (1994), Dr.Raj Kumar (1995), Sivaji Ganesan (1996), Kavi Pradeep (1997), B.R. Chopra (1998), Hrishikesh Mukherji (1999), Asha Bhonsle (2000), Yash Chopra (2001), Dev Anand (2002), Mrinal Sen (2003), Adoor Gopalakrishnan (2004), Hrishikesh Mukherjee (2005).

Bharat Award: It is a film award given to the best actor of the year. In 1988, it was awarded to Premji, *Piravi - Malayalam. In 1989*, Mammooty was awarded for his role in Malayalam films *Mathilugal*, and *Oru Vadakkan Veerakatha'*. In 1990, it was awarded to Amitabh Bachchan for his role in *Agneepath*. In 1991, it was awarded to Mohanlal for his role in *Bharatham* and in 1992 to Mithun Chakraborthy for his role in *Tahader Katha*. In 1993, it was awarded to Mammooty for his role in *Ponthan Mada and Vidheyan*. In 1994, it was awarded to Nana Patekar for his role in the Hindi film *Krantiveer* In 1995 it was awarded to Rajit Kapoor for his role in the English film *The Making of the Mahatma* and in 1996 it was awarded to Kamalahasan for his role in the Tamil film *Indian*. For 1997, the award was shared by Suresh Gopi *(Kaliyattam)* and Balachandra Menon *(Samantharangal)*, Malayalam. For 1998, it was shared by, Mammootti (Dr. Baba Saheb Ambedkar - English) and Ajay Devgan (Jakhm - Hindi). For 1999, Mohanlal for his role in Malayalam film *'Vaanaprastham'*. For 2000, Anil Kapoor for his role in *'Pukar' (Hindi)*. For 2001, Murali for his role in *'Neythukaran' (Malayalam)*, For 2002, Ajay Devgan for his role in *'The Legend of Bhagat Singh' (Hindi)*. For 2003, Vikram for his role in *'Pithamagan'*. For 2004, Saif Ali Khan for his role in 'Page-3' (Hindi).

Urvashi Award: It is a film award given to the best actress of the year. In 1972, it was given to Ms.Sharada, Malayalam actress. She has been awarded thrice. In 1980, it was given to late Ms.Shoba, *Pasi-Tamil*. In 1983 and 1984, it was awarded to Ms.Shabana Azmi. In 1985, it was awarded to Ms.Suhasini, *Sindu Bairavi-Tamil*. In 1986, it was given to late Ms.Monisha, *Nakakshathangal-Malayalam*. In 1987 and 1988, it was given to Ms.Archana, *Veedu-Tamil* and *Daasi-Telugu* respectively. In 1989, it went to Sreelekha Mukherji, *Parashuramer Kuttar*. In 1990, it was awarded to Ms.Vijaya Shanthi for her role in the Telugu film *'Karthavyam.'* In 1992, it was awarded to Ms.Dimple Kapadia, *Rudali-Hindi*. In 1993, it was awarded to Ms.Shobhana for her role in the Malayalam film *'Manichithrathazhu'*. In 1994, it was awarded to Ms.Debasree Roy for her role in the Bengali film *'Unishe April'*. In 1995 it was awarded to Ms.Seema Biswas for her role in the Hindi film *'Bandit Queen'* and in 1996 it was awarded to Ms.Tabu for her role in *'Maachis'*. For 1997, the award was shared by Indrani Haldar and Rituparno Sengupta for their roles in the Bengali film *'Dahan'*. For 1998, it was awarded to Shabana Asmi for her role in the Hindi film *'God Mother'*. In 1999, Kiren Kher was awarded for her role in the Bengali film

'Baariwali'. In 2000, Raveena Tanden won the award for her role in 'Daman' (Hindi). For 2001, jointly to Tabu for her role in 'Chandini Bar' (Hindi) and Shobana for her role in 'Mitr - My Friend' (English), For 2002, given to Konkana Sen for her role in 'Mr. & Mrs. Iyer'. For 2003, Meera Jasmine for her role in 'Paatam Onnu Oru Vilaapam'. For 2004, Tara for her role in Kannada film 'Haseena.'

The Golden Lotus Award (Swarna Kamal): The Golden Lotus Award (Swarna Kamal), the Silver Lotus (Rajat Kamal) and cash prizes are given under the National Film Awards Scheme starting from 1982. The Children's Film Society of India (CFSI) also known as National Centre of Films for children and Young People (NCYP) was established in 1955 as an autonomous body with the objectives of promoting and encouraging the children's film movement in the country. In 1989, Swarna Kamal was awarded to Hindi film *Bagh Bahadur* directed by B.Das Gupta. In 1990, the award went to the Tamil Feature Film *Marupakkam* directed by K.S.Sethumadhavan, produced by NFDC & Doordarshan. In 1992, Swarna Kamal was given to the Sanskrit film *Bhagavad Gita* directed by G.V.Iyer. In 1993, this award was given to the Bengali film *Charachar*. In 1994, again to the Bengali film *Unishe April*. In 1995, Swarna Kamal was given to the Malayalam film *Kathapurushan* directed by Adoor Gopalakrishnan. For 1997, it was given to the Kannada film *Thai Saheb* directed by Girish Kasaravalli. For 1998, the award was given to the Hindi film *Samar* directed by Shyam Benegal. For 1999, 'Vaanaprastham', Malayalam film directed by Shaji N. Karun has been selected for this award, 'Shantham' (Malayalam) directed by Jayaraj won the award for the year 2000. For 2001, 'Dweepa', Kannada film directed by Girish Kasaravalli, For 2002, 'Monde Meyer Upakhyan', Bengali film directed by Buddadeb Dasgupta. For 2003, 'Shwaas', Mahrati film directed by Sandeep Sawant. For 2004, 'Page-3' Hindi film by Madhu Bhandarkar. For 2005, 'Kaalpurush', Bengali film.

The Film Industry has been greatly disturbed by the ever increasing incidence of video piracy. A number of steps have been taken to end this menace. Cinematography Act, 1952, and Copyright Act, 1957 both amended in 1984 provide for enhanced punishment. In recent times, cinema industry has been threatened by another piracy, the cable T.V. Hence agitations and demonstrations were held by members of the Film Industry against this, who demanded it to be banned.

NFDC: The National Film Development Corporation (NFDC) Limited established in 1975, aims at improving the quality of cinema in India and increasing its access. The erstwhile Film Finance Corporation and Indian Motion Picture Export Corporation were merged to form NFDC. Its activities include production of films, export of Indian Films, import of foreign films, distribution of films, financing of cinema theatres, etc. The Corporation launched its programme of foreign co-productions with 'Gandhi' and recently co-produced 'The Making of Mahatma', 'Jaya Ganga', 'Sanshodhan', and 'The Show goes on'.

The Cine Artistes Welfare Fund of India (CAWFI) set up by the NFDC with a corpus of Rs.3 crore (which has now grown to Rs.3.88 crore), provides pensionary and other benefits to more than 475 cine artistes.

Film Festivals: The Directorate of Film Festivals (DFF) was set up in 1973 to promote good cinema. The Directorate holds Film Festival every year. Every alternate year the festival is held in New Delhi and the following year it is held in state capitals. The 37th International Film Festival of India (IFFI) was held in Goa in November 2006.

NATIONAL AWARDS

Bharat Ratna: This is the highest award in India. It is given to those who have made exceptional service for the advancement of art, literature, science and public service of the highest order. It was discontinued in 1977 by Janata Party but in 1980 it was decided to revive the National awards. But for the year 1993, 1994, 1995 the awards were not announced as the government decided to await the verdict of the court on the constitutionality of these awards which were challenged in two High Courts.

RECIPIENTS OF BHARAT RATNA

	Awarded in
Dr. Sarvepalli Radhakrishnan (1888-1975)	1954
Chakravarthi Rajagopalachari (1878-1972)	1954
Dr. Chandrasekhar Venkatraman (1888-1970)	1954
Dr. Bhagwan Das (1869-1958)	1955
Dr. Mokshagundam Viswesvaraya (1861-1962)	1955
Jawaharlal Nehru (1889-1964)	1955
Govind Ballabh Pant (1887-1961)	1957
Dr. Dhondo Keshav Karve (1858-1962)	1958
Dr. Bidhan Chandra Roy (1882-1962)	1961
Purushotham Das Tandon (1882-1962)	1961
Dr. Rajendra Prasad (1884-1963)	1962
Dr. Zakir Hussain (1897-1969)	1963
Dr. Pandurang Vaman Kane (1880-1972)	1963
Lal Bahadur Shastri (Posthumous)(1904-1966)	1966
Indira Gandhi (1917-1984)	1971
Varaha Giri Venkata Giri (1884-1980)	1975
Kumaraswami Kamaraj (Posthumous) (1903-1975)	1976
Mary Teresa Bojaxhiu (Mother Teresa) (1910-1997)	1980
Acharya Vinoba Bhave (Posthumous)(1895-1982)	1983
Khan Abdul Ghaffar Khan (1890-1988)	1987
M.G.Ramachandran (Posthumous) (1917-1987)	1988
Dr. B.R.Ambedkar (Posthumous) (1891-1956)	1990
Dr.Nelson Mandela (1918-)	1990
Morarji Desai (1896-1995)	1991
Rajiv Gandhi (Posthumous) (1944-1991)	1991
Sardar Vallabh Bhai Patel (Posthumous) (1875-1950)	1991
J.R.D. Tata (1904-1993)	1992
Satyajit Ray (Posthumous) (1922-1992)	1992
Subhash Chandra Bose (Posthumous) (1897-1945)	1992
Moulana Abul Kalam Azad (Posthumous) (1888-1958)	1992
Aruna Asaf Ali (Posthumous) (1909-1996)	1997
Gulzarilal Nanda (Posthumous) (1898-1997)	1997
A.P.J. Abdul Kalam (1931-)	1997
M.S.Subbulakshmi (1916-2004)	1998
C. Subramaniam (1910-2000)	1998
Jayaprakash Narayan (Posthumous) (1902-1979)	1999

Prof. Amartya Sen (1933-)	1999
Pandit Ravi Shankar (1920-)	1999
Gopinath Bordoloi (Posthumous) (1890-1950)	1999
Latha Mangeshkar (1929-) and Ustad Bismilla Khan (1916-2006)	2001

Padma Awards' 2007

On the eve of 58th Republic Day held on 26th January 2007, the following is the list of recipients of Padma Awards:

Padma Vibhushan (10): Prof. Balu Sankaran, Medicine; Fali Sam Nariman, Public Affairs; Khushwant Singh, Literature and Education; N.N. Vohra, Civil Service; Naresh Chandra, Civil Service; Justice (Retd.) Prafullachandra Natwarlal Bhagwati, Public Affairs; Raja Rao (Posthumous), Literature and Education; Dr. Raja Jesudoss Chelliah, Public Affairs; Sudarshan Erinackal Chandy George, Science and Engineering; Dr. Venkataraman Krishnamurthy, Civil Service.

Padma Bhushan (32): Prof. Bhikhu Parekh, Literature and Education; Chandra Prasad Saikia (Posthumous), Literature and Education; Ela Gandhi, Public Affairs; Rev Father Gabriel, Literature and Education; Gopaldas Neeraj, Literature and Education; Dr. Gurcharan Singh Kalkat, Science and Engineering; Ms. Indra Nooyi, Trade and Industry; Jamshed J. Irani, Trade and Industry; Javed Jan Nisaar Akhtar, Literature and Education; Prof. Jeffrey D. Sachs, Literature and Education; Justice K.T. Thomas, Public Affairs; Kavalam Narayan Panikkar, Art; Captain L.Z. Sailo, Literature and Education; Dr. Manju Sharma, Science and Engineering; Dr. N. Mahalingam, Trade and Industry; O. Suzuki, Trade and Industry; Dr. Prithipal Singh Maini, Medicine; Pandit Rajan Misra, Art; Ramankutty Nair, Art; Pandit Sajan Misra, Art; Dr. Saroj Ghose, Science and Engineering; Dr. Shiv Kumar Sarin, Medicine; Prof. (Vaidya) Shriram Sharma, Medicine; Somnath Hore (Posthumous), Art; Sunil Bharti Mittal, Trade and Industry; Syed Haider Raza, Art; Hakim Syed Mohammad Sharfuddin Quadri, Medicine; Prof. T.N. Srinivasan, Literature and Education; Prof. Tapan Ray Chaudhuri, Literature and Education; Tyeb Mehta, Art Dr. V. Mohini Giri, Social Work; Dr. Vilayanur Ramachandaran, Science and Engineering.

Padma Shri (79): A. Sivasailam, Trade and Industry; Prof. Adya Prasad Mishra, Literature and Education; Amitav Ghosh, Literature and Education; Prof. Ananda M. Chakrabarty, Science and Engineering; Dr. Ananda Shankar Jayant, Art; Prof. Anoop Misra, Medicine; Dr. Ashok Kumar Hemal, Medicine; Astad Aderbad Deboo, Art; Dr. Atul Kumar, Medicine; Dr. B. Paul Thaliath, Medicine; Dr. Bakul Harshadrai Dholakia, Literature and Education; Dr. Balbir Singh, Medicine; Dr. Baldev Raj, Science and Engineering; Shri Bharath Balachandra Menon, Art; Prof. Devindra Rahinwal (Posthumous), Social Work; Prof. Dilip K. Biswas, Science and Engineering; Gajendra Narayan Singh, Art; Geeta Chandran, Art; Giriraj Kishore, Literature and Education; Rajmata Goverdan Kumarri, Art; Prof. Harpinder Singh Chawla, Medicine;Jeev Milkha Singh, Sports; Dr. K.R. Palani Swamy, Medicine; Khalid Zaheer, Social Work; Prof. Kharak Singh Valdiya, Science and Engineering; Kiran Karnik, Science and Engineering; Ms. Koneru Humpy, Sports; Dr. Lalit Pande, Environment Protection; Louis Remo Fernandes, Art; Dr. M. Mohan Babu, Art; Dr. Mahadev Prasad Pandey, Literature and Education; Dr. Mahipal S. Sachdev, Medicine; Dr. Manjunath Cholenahally Nanjappa, Medicine; Dr. Mayilvahanan Natarajan, Medicine; Ms. Meenakshi Gopinath, Literature and Education; Ms. Miriam L'vovna Salganik, Literature and Education; Dr. Mohsin Wali, Medicine; Mujtaba

Hussain, Literature and Education; Prof. Mushirul Hassan, Literature and Education; Ms. Naina Lal Kidwai, Trade and Industry; Prof. Narmada Prasad Gupta, Medicine; Neelamani Devi, Art; P. Gopinathan, Art; P.R. Thilagam, Art; Pannuru Sripathy, Art; Prof. P. Namperumalsamy, Medicine; Prof. Pratibha Ray, Literature and Education; Pushpa Hans, Art; Rabinder Gokaldas Ahuja, Sea Cadet Corps Management; Rajinder Gupta, Trade and Industry; Dr. Ravi Narayan Bastia, Science and Engineering; Ravindra Dayal, Literature & Education; Prof. Rostislav Borisovich Rybakov, Literature and Education; Ms. Runa Banerjee, Social Work; S. Dhakshinamurthy Pillai, Art; Sister S.M. Cyril, Social Work; Shanti Hiranand, Art; Shashikala Jawalkar, Art; Prof. Shekhar Pathak, Literature and Education; Dr. Sheo Bhagwan Tibrewal, Medicine; Sonam Skalzang, Art; Sonam Tshering Lepcha, Art; Prof. Sudhir Kumar Sopory, Science and Engineering; Dr. Sukumar Azhikode, Literature and Education; Sushil Gupta, Social Work; Dr. Syeda Saiyidain Hameed, Public Affairs; T.S. Rangarajan @ Kavingar Vaali, Literature and Education; Ms. Tarla Dalal, Cookery; Ms. Teesta Setalvad, Public Affairs; Dr. Temsula Ao, Literature and Education; Dr. Thanu Padmanabhan, Science and Engineering; Dr. Thekkethil Kochandy Alex, Science and Engineering; Thingbaijam Babu Singh, Art; Lama Thupten Phuntsok, Social Work; Valayapatti A.R. Subramaniam, Art; Vijaydan Detha, Literature and Education; Vikram Seth, Literature and Education; Waman Thakre, Art; Dr. Yusufkhan Mohamadkhan Pathan, Literature and Education.

Gallantry Awards' 2007

The following persons were awarded the country's second highest peacetime award for gallantry, Kirti and Shaurya Chakra Awards on January 26, 2007.

Kirti Chakra: Col. Gulbir Singh Sarna (29 RR); Maj. Manish Hiraji Pitambare (Parachute Regiment); Capt. Vishal Bhandral (Garhwal Rifles); Lt. Natarajan Parthiban (Jammu & Kashmir); Light Havildar Manjit Singh (Sikh Regiment); Sub-inspector Dhirendra Nath Pratap Singh (CISF).

Shaurya Chakra: Of the 31 Shaurya Chakras, 12 were awarded posthumously. This included two Border Roads Organisation personnel killed while undertaking road clearance operations in hazardous conditions. Lt. Col. Raj Kumar (Kumaon Regiment); Lt. Col. Vinay R. Chauhan (1 Gorkha Rifles, posthumous); Maj. Jung Bahadur Singh (SM Army Service Cops); Maj. Naveen Bindal (Army Air Defence); Maj. Shineesh Mukundan (Grenadiers); Maj. Virinder Sidhu; Maj. Krishnan Nishant Nair (Bihar Regiment); Maj. Manvendra Singh (20 Jammu and Kashmir Rifles); Capt. Nayanjyoti Buragohain (1 Naga Regiment); Capt. Shashi B. Singh (SM Corps of Engineers, posthumous); Capt. Ajit Anthony (Rajputana Rifles, posthumous); Lt. Thiyam Ibungochouba Luwang (21 Parachute Regiment); Subedar Samde Khan (14 Grenadiers); Naib Subedar M.A. Cruz (201 Engineer Regiment, posthumous); Havildar Santosh Kumar (14 Grenadiers); Havildar Bhag Singh (16 Sikh Regiment); Lance Havildar Sishpal Singh (Dogra Regiment); Sepoy Satnam Singh (Mahar Regiment); Subedar Sant Kumar (SM Grenadiers).

Besides the Kirti Chakras, anti-terrorist operations have won 73 Sena Medals and one Vayu Sena Medal for the armed forces personnel. The President awarded 393 medals to the uniformed personnel on the occasion of Republic Day.

Param Vishisht Seva medals

The President's honours list also includes 19 senior Army officers who have been decorated with Param Vishisht Seva Medals. This includes the new Vice-Chief of Army Staff Lt. Gen. Deepak Kapoor, Western Army Commander

Lt. Gen. Daljit Singh and Director - General of Military Operations Mohan Pandey.

President APJ Abdul Kalam has also approved four Bar to Sena Medals (Gallantry), one Bar to Ati Vishisht Seva Medal, 52 Ati Vishisht Seva Medals, one Youth Seva Medal, four Bar to Vishist Seva Medals, 123 Vishist Seva Medals, two Bar to Sena Medals, 41 Sena Medals, 12 Nao Sena Medals and Vayu Sena Medals (15).

President's Medal for Delhi Police Officers

Sixteen Delhi Police officers and personnel have been conferred the President's Police Medals for 2007. Joint Commissioner of Police (Rashtrapati Bhavan) K.K. Maheshwari, Joint Commissioner of Police (Traffic) Qamar Ahmad, Assistant Commissioner of Police Hanuman Singh and Inspector Data Ram have been awarded President's Police Medal for Distinguished Services.

Additional Commissioner of Police (Crime Against Women Cell) T.S. Luthra, Additional Commissioner of Police N. Dilip Kumar, Deputy Commissioner of Police (Economic Offences Wing) Prabhakar, Assistant Commissioner of Police Sriram Meena, Assistant Commissioner of Police Yashwant Singh, Inspectors Achala Rani, Ramesh Kumar and Chander Das Sub-Inspector Rajinder Singh, Assistant Sub-Inspector Girdhari Singh, Head Constables Kesar Chand and Chura Mani have been awarded Police Medal for Meritorious Services.

LIST OF JNANPITH AWARDEES

1965	-	Mahakavi Shankar Kurup (Malayalam)
1966	-	Tara Shankar Bandopadyaya (Bengali)
1967	-	Uma Shankar Joshi & Dr. K.V.Puttappa (Gujarathi & Kannada)
1968	-	Sumithranandan Pant (Hindi)
1969	-	Firaq Ghorakhpuri (Urdu)
1970	-	Dr. V.Satyanarayana (Telugu)
1971	-	Bishnu Dey (Bengali)
1972	-	Ramadhari Singh Dinakar (Hindi)
1973	-	D.R.Bendre (Kannada), Gopinath Mohanty (Oriya)
1974	-	V.S.Khandekar (Marathi)
1975	-	P.V. Akilandam (Tamil)
1976	-	Ashapurna Devi (Bengali)
1977	-	Dr. K.Shivarama Karanth (Kannada)
1978	-	S.H.Vatsyayan (Hindi)
1979	-	B.K.Bhattacharya (Assamese)
1980	-	S.K.Pottekkat (Malayalam)
1981	-	Amrita Pritam (Punjabi)
1982	-	Mahadevi Verma (Hindi)
1983	-	Dr.Masti Venkatesh Iyengar (Kannada)
1984	-	Thakazhi Sivasankaran Pillai (Malayalam)
1985	-	Pannalal Patel (Gujarathi)
1986	-	Satchidanand Routray (Oriya)
1987	-	V.V.Shirwadkar (Marathi)
1988	-	C.Narayana Reddy (Telugu)
1989	-	M.S.Qurratul-ain-Haider (Urdu)
1990	-	Prof. Vinayak Krishna Gokak (Kannada)
1991	-	Subash Mukhopadyaya (Bengali)

1992	-	Naresh Mehta (Hindi)
1993	-	Dr. Sitakant Mohapatra (Oriya)
1994	-	Prof. U.R.Anantha Murthy (Kannada)
1995	-	M.T. Vasudevan Nair (Malayalam)
1996	-	Mrs. Mahasveta Devi (Bengali)
1997	-	Ali Sardar Zafri (Urdu)
1998	-	Girish Karnad (Kannada)
1999	-	Nirmal Verma (Hindi), Guru Dayal Singh (Punjabi)
2000	-	Dr. Indira Goswami (Assamese)
2001	-	Rajendra Keshavlal Shah (Gujarathi)
2002	-	Jayakanthan (Tamil)
2003	-	Vinda Karandeekar (Marathi)
2004	-	**Rahman Rahi (Kashmiri) (2007)**

SPORTS AWARDS

Rajiv Gandhi Khel Ratna award- 2007

Pankaj Advani (Billiards & Snooker) has been given the country's highest sports award. This award comprising cash award of Rs.5 lakh, a scroll of honour and a medal. Manavajit Singh (Shooter) won Rajiv Gandhi Khel Ratna award in 2007.

Arjuna Awards-2007

It was awarded to the following persons : Jayanth Taluktar (Archery), K.M. Pinu (Athletics), Chetan Anand (Badminton), Vijayendar (Boxing), Harikrishna (Chess), Anju Chopra (Cricket), Jothi Kullu (Hockey), Navaneeth Gautam (Kabaddi), Vijaykumar (Shooting), Saurav Koshal (Squash), Subajith Shaga (Table Tennis), Geetha Rani (Weight Lifting), Keethika Jhagar (Wrestling), Rohit Bahar (Physically Handicapped). This awards comprising a cash award of Rs.3 lakh, a statute and a scroll of honour.

Dronacharya Awards-2007

It was awarded to R.D. Singh (Athletics), Damodar Chanderlal (Boxing), Koneru Ashok (Chess). This awards comprising cash award of Rs.3 lakh, a plaque and a scroll of honour.

Dhyan Chand Awards-2007

It was awarded to Virender Singh (Hockey), Rajinder Singh (Wrestling), Samsher Singh (Kabaddi). This awards for lifetime achievement in sports and games comprising a cash award of Rs,3 lakh, plaque and a scroll of honour.

Tenzing Norgay National Adventure Awards-2006

It was awarded to Nawang Gombu (Lifetime Achievement), Chhering Norbu bodh (Land Adventure), Shital Kamalakar Mahajan (Air Adventure), Comdr. Mukul Asthana (Water Adventure).

Moulana Abul Kalam Azad Trophy-2006

It was awarded for the best performance by an University. For 2005 it goes to Punjab University.

INTERNATIONAL AWARDS

Nobel Prize: Alfred Bernard Nobel who invented dynamite, died on December, 10, 1896 bequeathing 9,000,000 dollars, the interest of which is to be distributed yearly to those who had rendered service to mankind during the preceding year in different spheres.

Awards for Physics and Chemistry are made by the Swedish Academy of Science, Medicine or Physiology by the Stockholm Faculty of Medicine; Literature by the Swedish Academy of Literature and Peace by five persons elected by the Norwegian Parliament (Storting). The fund is managed by a board of directors, the head of which is appointed by the Swedish Government. Nobel Prize in Economics known as "Alfred Nobel Memorial Prize in Economic Science" was instituted by the Central Bank of Sweden, to mark its tercentenary in 1968. The Prize was first awarded in 1969.

Nehru Award for International Understanding: This award carries an amount of 15 lakh rupees in cash and a citation which is presented to the recipient at a special ceremony in India. It is awarded to those who have contributed for international peace and understanding.

THE RECIPIENTS OF NEHRU AWARD

U.Thant (Secretary General of the UNO)	1965
Dr. Martin Luther King (Posthumous)	1966
Khan Abdul Ghaffar Khan (Frontier Gandhi)	1967
Yehudi Menuhin (Violinist)	1968
Mother Teresa (Nun)	1969
Kenneth David Kaunda (President of Zambia)	1970
Marshal Tito (President of Yugoslavia)	1971
Andre Malraux (French Statesman)	1972
Julius Nyrere (President of Tanzania)	1973
Paul Prebisch	1974
Jonas Salk (Inventor-Vaccination)	1975
Giuseppe Tucci	1976
Tulsi Mehrji Shrestha	1977
Nichidatsu Fuji	1978
Nelson R.Mandela (ANC President)	1979
Mrs. Barbara Ward (Economist)	1980
Gunnar Myrdal and Alva Myrdal (Economists)	1981
Dr. Leopold Sedar Senghor (Ex-President, Senegal)	1982
Dr. Bruno Kreisky	1983
Mrs.Indira Gandhi (Posthumous)	1985
Olof Palme (Prime Minister of Sweden)	1986
Perez de Cuellar (Secretary General of the UNO)	1987
Yasser Arafat (PLO Leader)	1988
Robert Mugabe (President of Zimbabwe)	1989
Helmut Kohl (Chancellor of Germany)	1990
Aruna Asaf Ali (Social Worker, India)	1991
Maurice F.Strong (environmentalist, Canada)	1992
Ms. Daw Aung San Suu Kyi (Myanmar)	1993

Dr. Mahathir-bin-Mohammed (Prime Minister, Malaysia)	1994
Md.Hosni Mubarak (President, Egypt)	1995
Goh Chong Tong (Prime Minister, Singapore)	2003
Julius Namrai (Princess of Tanzania)	2004
Wangari M. Maathai (Environmentalist, Kenya)	**2005**
Luiz Nacio Lula Da Silva (President of Brazil)	**2006**

Magsaysay Awards: The award instituted in 1957 to honour the memory of Ramon Magsaysay, the late President of the Philippines, honours 6 Asians each year who exemplify Magsaysay's "greatness of spirit, integrity and devotion to liberty". The award consists of a gold medal, a certificate and 50,000 U.S. dollars.

The following were awarded for the year 2007: (1) **Government Service** - Jonito R. Salonga (Phillipines); (2) **Public Service** - Kin Sun-Tae (South Korea) (3) **Community Leadership** - Mahabir Pun (Nepal); (4) **Peace and International Understanding** - Tang Xiyang (China); (5) **Journalism** - P. Sainath (India); (6) **Emergent Leadership** - Chung To and Chen Guangcheng (China).

Kalinga Prize: The Kalinga Prize for the popularization of science is an international award presented each year by the United Nations Educational Scientific and Cultural Organisation (UNESCO) to a person with a distinguished career of service in the interpretation of science and research to the public.

The Kalinga Prize was instituted by Biju Patnaik, Former Chief Minister of Orissa, industrialist and politician, who is the Founder and Chairman of the Kalinga Foundation Trust in the State of Orissa. UNESCO awarded the prize for the first time in 1952.

Kalinga Prize commemorates the ancient name of Orissa which was known as Kalinga. The winner of the prize also receives the UNESCO Gold Medal and is invited to visit India as a guest of the Kalinga Foundation Trust.

International Gandhi Peace Prize: The Gandhi Peace Prize was instituted by the Govt. in 1995 and administered by the Ministry of Culture. It was awarded to Actress Sapna Azmi in 2006, for her outstanding contribution in promoting peace in Indian union. (1 crore rupees prize Award)

U Thant Peace Prize: The award originally established by U Thant and named after him since his death, is made to an outstanding personality who through his or her efforts has contributed to the enhancement of cultural understanding and development between nations.

Past recipients were:

1. Dr. S. Radhakrishnan, 2. Prof. Arnold Toynbee, 3. Mrs. Barbara Ward, 4. Mr. U Nu, 5. Mr. Lester Pearson, 6. Mr. Adlai Stevenson, 7. Ms. Nancy Wilson Ross, 8. Mrs. Indira Gandhi (1982), 9. Nepalese Prime Minister Mr. Krishna Prasad Bhattarai.

Man Booker Prize-2006

Indian author Ms. Kiran Desai won the Man Booker Prize 2006 for her second novel *The Inheritance of Loss* on October 10, 2006. Ms. Desai, became the youngest woman and the third Indian to win the coveted prize.

Man Booker International Prize for Fiction 2007 : Nigerian novelist Chinua Achebe won the 2007 Man Booker International prize for fiction. He received the prize on June 28, 2007 at a ceremony in Oxford. He is professor of Language and Literature at Bard College, New York.

UNITED NATIONS ORGANISATION

The UNO formally came into existence on 24th October,1945. October 24, is celebrated as the UN Day throughout the world.

The United Nations is an international organisation whose members are sovereign, independent countries. The UN is not a super state nor a world government. It does not make any laws. The UN makes it possible for member-states to cooperate in an organisation of sovereign states. Mr. Ban-Ki-Moon of South Korea who is presently the Secretary- General of UN succeeded, Kofi Annan of Ghana. Languages used by the UNO are: (1) Chinese (2) English, (3) French, (4) Russian, (5) Spanish, (6) Arabic.

The U.N.O. has at present 192 members (As per September 2006).

The aims:

1. To maintain international peace and security.
2. To develop friendly relations among nations based on respect for the principle of equal rights and self-determination.
3. To achieve cooperation in solving world problems like poverty, illiteracy, diseases, etc and to promote respect for human rights and fundamental freedom.
4. To harmonise the actions of nations in achieving these ends.

Major organs of the UNO:

General Assembly (GA): All member nations are represented in the General Assembly, which meets once in a year. Each nation can send upto five representatives, but has only one vote, and all matters are decided by a two-third majority. It discusses the world's views on the work of all the UN organs.

Security Council (SC): It consists of 15 members. Five of them are permanent members - USA, USSR, UK, France and China, while the other 10 are non-permanent members elected every two years by the General Assembly. The Security Council is the nerve centre of the UNO and takes all important decisions on policy matters of the UNO.

Veto in the SC: The five permanent members of the SC have veto power, i.e., no resolution can be passed if one of the permanent members casts a negative vote. This is known as the 'veto power'. All important resolutions must be voted 'yes' by five permanent members and at least two non-permanent members. In practice, if a permanent member abstains from voting it is not considered as veto. The Security Council remains in session throughout the year.

The Economic and Social Council (ECOSOC): It consists of 54 members and works for establishment of world peace by promoting better social, economic, educational and health conditions and respect for human rights and fundamental freedom for all people.

The Trusteeship Council: It oversaw the transition of Trust Territories to self-government. It was suspended at the end of 1994.

International Court of Justice (ICJ): The seat of the ICJ is at Hague. It consists of 15 judges elected by the General Assembly for a period of 9 years. The judges are eligible for re- election.

Its main functions are the settling of disputes between member nations regarding treaties and question of International law and giving advisory opinions at the request of the General Assembly, the SC or any other bodies of the UNO.

The Secretariat: It is the administrative unit of the UNO. It is composed of the Secretary-General who is the chief administrative officer and head of international staff (16,000 at the headquarters and 50,000 worldwide) who carry out the day-to-day operations of the UNO.

The Secretary-General of the UNO is appointed by the General Assembly for a five year term and may be reappointed.

AGENCIES OF THE UNO AND THEIR HEADQUARTERS

International Labour Organisation (ILO): Geneva

Food and Agriculture Organisation (FAO): Rome (Italy)

United Nations Educational Scientific and Cultural Organisation (UNESCO): Paris (France)

World Health Organisation (WHO): Geneva (Switzerland)

International Bank for Reconstruction and Development (IBRD)/World Bank: Washington (USA)

International Finance Corporation (IFC): Washington (USA)

International Monetary Fund (IMF): Washington (USA)

International Civil Aviation Organisation (ICAO): Montreal (Canada)

Universal Postal Union (UPU): Berne (Switzerland)

International Telecommunication Union (ITU): Geneva (Switzerland)

World Meteorological Organisation (WMO): Geneva (Switzerland)

International Atomic Energy Agency (IAEA) (Autonomous Organisation under the UNO): Vienna (Austria)

Inter-Governmental Maritime Consultative Organisation (IMCO): London (UK)

United Nations International Children's Emergency Fund (UNICEF): New York (USA)

Economic Commission for Asia and Far East (ECAFE): Bangkok (Thailand)

The General Agreement of Tariffs and Trade (GATT): Geneva (Switzerland)

International Development Association (IDA): Washington (USA)

International Fund for Agricultural Development (IFAD): Rome (Italy)

International Telecommunications Satellite Consortium (INTELSAT): Geneva (Switzerland)

United Nations Environment Programme (UNEP): Nairobi (Kenya)

United Nations Conference on Trade and Development (UNCTAD): Geneva (Switzerland)

United Nations Industrial Development Organisation (UNIDO): Vienna (Austria)

United Nations High Commission for Refugees (UNHCR): Geneva (Switzerland)

World Intellectual Property Organisation (WIPO): Geneva (Switzerland)

United Nations Development Programme (UNDP): New York (USA)

The International Air Transport Association (IATA): Montreal (Canada) and Geneva (Switzerland)

IMPORTANT YEARS DECLARED BY THE UNO

1968	International Human Rights
1970	International Education Year
1972	International Book Year
1973	Copernicus Year
1974	World Population Year
1975	International Women's Year
1979	International Year of Children
1980-89	International Water-Supply & Sanitation Decade
1981	International Year of the disabled

1983	World Communication Year
1985	International Youth Year
1986	International Year of Peace
1987	International Year of Shelter for the Homeless
1990	International Literacy Year
1992	International Space Year
1993	International Year for the Indigenous Populations
1994	International Year of the Family
1995	International Year of Tolerance
1998	International Year of Ocean
1999	International Year of Older Persons
1991-2000	Development Decade
2000	International Year of Universal Cultural Values
2001	International Year of Women's Empowerment
2002	International Year of of Ecotourism
2003	International Year of Fresh Water
2004	International Year of Rice
2005	International Year of Physics
2007	**International Polar Year**

SECRETARIES-GENERAL OF THE UNO

1. Trygve Lie (Norway 1946-53)
2. Dag HammarsKjoeld (Sweden1953-61)
3. U Thant (Myanmar 1962-71)
4. Kurt Waldheim (Austria 1971-81)
5. Javier Perez de Cuellar (Peru 1982-92)
6. Dr.Boutros Boutros Ghali (Egypt 1992-97)
7. Kofi Annan (Ghana 1997-2002)
8. Kofi Annan (Ghana 2002-2006)
9. Ban-Ki-Moon (South Korea, January 1, 2007-)

GEOGRAPHY

THE UNIVERSE:

Galaxies: Galaxies are huge congregations of stars that are held together by force of gravity. Our Earth and the Solar System are contained in the galaxy called 'Milky Way' which belongs to a cluster of galaxies called the 'local group' covering an area of about 3 million light years in diameter. The two nearest galaxies are the Megallanic Cloud and the Small Megallanic cloud.

Stars: Stars account for 98 per cent of the matter in a galaxy. The stars nearest to the earth are Proxima Centauri, Alpha Centauri, Barnard's Star, Sirius and so on. Of these, the Sirius is the brightest.

Solar System: The solar system is centred around the Sun. There are eight planets in the system. They are - Mercury, Venus, Earth, Mars, Jupiter, Saturn, Uranus, Neptune. There are 33 satellites and many asteroids and comets in the solar system.

The sun, which is one of the stars in the Milky Way, is composed mainly of hydrogen. The sun consists of the Photosphere, the Chromosphere and Corona. There are dark patches on the surface of the sun known as Sunspots occurring due to lower temperature of certain portions of the sun. The Auroras

(Aurora Borealis and Aurora Australias) occurring in the Poles are due to the sunspots. They are multi-coloured lights that sweep across the sky in waves seen in the Arctic and Antarctic regions. The age of the sun is about 5 billion years. Its diameter is 13,92,540 km. It is about 149.6 million km. away from the earth.

The Mercury is the smallest planet and the nearest to the sun. It is the only planet without a satellite. Jupiter is the largest planet. It has 16 satellites. Saturn is most remarkable due to a system of rings which surround it. It is now believed that it has 22 satellites. It is the only outer planet visible from the earth. Venus is the planet which is closest to the Earth. It is the brightest object in the sky, apart from the sun and the moon. It is called the evening or the morning Star. Pluto is the outermost planet, far away from the earth. (At present it losses the planet category).

The moon is the only satellite of the earth. It has a diameter of 2,169 miles and has 1/8th of the earth's area. Its gravitational pull is 1/6th of the earth's pull. The maximum distance of the moon from the earth (apogee) is 4,04,336 kms and minimum distance (perigee) is 3,54,342 kms. It revolves round the earth once in $27\frac{1}{3}$ days.

EARTH: The earth is a bit pear-shaped rather than a true sphere. It is the third nearest planet from the sun. It moves in an elliptical orbit around the sun known as revolutions. The earth completes one revolution around the sun in $365\frac{1}{4}$ days. (exactly 365 days 5 hrs. 48 min. 45.51 sec.) The earth revolves around itself from west to east once in 24 hours called the rotation of the earth (exact time 23 hrs. 56 min. 40.9 sec.). The earth is inclined at an angle of $66\frac{1}{2}$ degrees in its orbit/Equatorial. Its circumference is 40,067 kms and Polar circumference is 40,000 kms.

Composition of the Earth: Aluminium (0.4%), Sulphur (2.7%), Silicon (13%), Oxygen (28%), Calcium (<1%), Nickel (2.7%), Magnesium (17%), Iron (35%).

The age of the earth is estimated to be around 4.6 billion years. Its total area is 315,12,000 sq.kms. About 3/4 of it is covered by water.

(a) Earth's Surface: The outer surface of the earth is divided into four spheres. They are:

(i) *Atmosphere:* The mass of air surrounding the earth upto height of 64,000 kilometers. It is this envelope of air that hase made life possible on earth. The atmosphere close to earth because of the earth's gravitational force. The atmosphere of earth has definite structure and composition. Structure of atmosphere is more complex and layered arrangement.

Atmosphere divided into many layers based on temperature, composition, ionisation and chemical reactions, such as (1) Troposphere (2) Stratosphere (3) Mesosphere (4) Thermosphere (5) Exosphere.

Troposphere: Troposphere is lowest layer of atmosphere. It contains 75% of the total molecular (or) gaseous mass. Its thickness varies from about 8 km at poles to about 16 km at equator. Lapse rate occur in this layer. Lapse rate is 6.5° C temperature decrease for every one kilometer. Friction layer influences windspeed and circulation. It contains atmospheric pollutants. Troposphere is capped by temperature inversion zone. This layer is called as Tropopause. Tropopause layer occur in between Troposphere and Stratosphere.

Stratosphere: It extends from tropopause to about 50 kilometer. It contains ozone layer. Temperature rise in this layer because sun radiation obsorbed by ozone. Ozone layer protect human life because it absorb ultra violet radiation from sun (ultra violet radiation affect skin, eye of human being). Mother of pearls (or) nacreous clouds are found in this layer.

Mesosphere: This layer extends upto a height of about 80 km. Temperature decreases uniformly with height increases. Lowest temperature in the atmosphere record - 100° C at around 80 km. Noctilutent clouds are seen in the mesopause. Pressure is very low decreasing from 1 mb at 50 km to 0.01 mb at 90 km.

Thermosphere: Lower proportion is composed of N_2 and O in molecular and atomic forms. But above 200 km Oxygen predominates over nitrogen. Region of rapid temperature increase approaching 1200° C at 350 km. High temperature is due absorption of Ultra violet solar radiation with wavelength loss than 0.2 μ.

Exosphere: This layer extends above from thermosphere. It constitute atoms of oxygen, hydrogen and helium. Solar wind occur in this layer. The charged particles are concentrated in two bands at about 3000 km and 16000 km above the surface a result of trapping by earth magnetic field called Van Allen Radiation Belt. Auroras (Aurora Borealis in northern hemisphere, Aurora australis in Southern hemisphere) are produced in the region.

(ii) *Lithosphere:* The lithosphere forms about 3/10th of the earth's crust. It is the entire land surface of the earth and contains the continents.

(iii) *Hydrosphere:* It is the water surface of the earth including oceans, lakes and rivers. It occupies about 7/10th of the earth's crust.

(iv) *Biosphere:* It is the life which is found in all the other spheres.

(b) **Continents:** There are seven continents. Asia (29.5% of earth's area), Africa (20%), N.America (16.3%), S.America (11.8%), Europe (6.5%), Australia (5.2%) and Antarctica (9.6%).

(c) **Oceans:** It is a vast body of salt water which covers almost three-fourths of the earth's surface.

There are five oceans. They are: (i) The Atlantic Ocean (ii) The Pacific Ocean (iii) The Indian Ocean (iv) The Arctic Ocean and (v) The Antarctic Ocean.

(i) *The Atlantic Ocean:* The Atlantic Ocean is bounded by North America and South America in the Western Hemisphere and by Europe and Africa in the Eastern Hemisphere. Area is about 82,362,000 sq.km. with connecting seas about 41,000,000 sq.miles. The greatest known depth is 30,246 feet.

(ii) *The Pacific Ocean:* The Pacific Ocean is bordered by the western side of the American continents, Asia and Australia. It is the largest ocean in the world and divided by the equator into the North Pacific and the South Pacific. Area is about 165,242,000 sq.km. The greatest known depth is 35,610 feet.

(iii) *The Indian Ocean:* The Indian Ocean lies South of Asia, East of Africa and West of Australia. Area is about 75,556,000 sq.km.

(iv) *The Arctic Ocean:* The Arctic Ocean lies North of North America, Asia and the Actic Circle. Area is about 13,986,000 sq.km.

(v) *The Antarctic Ocean:* It is the ocean surrounding Antarctica, comprising the southernmost parts of the Pacific, Atlantic, and Indian oceans.

(d) Seasons: Seasons occur due to the revolution of the earth. The seasons include summer, autumn, winter and spring. However, in tropics and sub-tropics, like India there are only two seasons - summer and winter. Days and nights are caused by the rotation of the earth. The days and nights are of unequal lengths due to the inclination of the earth's axis to the plane of its orbit. However on two days of the year 21st March and 23rd September, days and nights are equal all over the world. These days are called equinoxes (summer and winter). When the sun's rays fall directly on the equator and the distance of the sun from the earth is minimum.

On June 21 (Summer solstices), Day is longer than night in northern hemisphere. Night is longer than day in Southern hemisphere. Because sun overhead above northern hemisphere. On December 22 (winter solstices) its opposite to summer solstices.

(e) Rocks: A rock can be defined as an aggregate of minerals. Rocks are divided into three groups such as (1) Igneous rocks (2) Sedimentary rocks (3) Metamorphic rocks. Igneous rocks are formed by cooling and solidification of molten magma. Solidification of molten magma cool very quick above the earth surface. Such a rock known as extrusive igneous rocks or volconic rocks. volconic rocks are small size of particle, low silica and high density, example: basalt. Solidification of molten magma cool very slow below the earth surface. Such a rock known as intrusive igneous rocks or plutonic rocks. Plutonic rocks are large size of particle, high silica and low density, example: granite. Sedimentary rocks: It is derived from accumulated sedimentary material that is transformed into rock by compartion and cementation, such as process known as Lithification. Sedimentary rocks are arranged in layer (strata). It contain fossils. 80% of rocks are sedimentary rocks in the earth. Metamorphic rocks: It is formed by change in existing igneous or sedimentary rocks under high pressure or temperature. Gneiss, marble, slate are some important metamorphic rocks.

(f) Weather and Climate: Weather is the atmospheric condition prevailing for a short period of time, i.e., a day and includes the temperature, rainfall, humidity, winds, sunshine of a particular place on a particular day. Climate is the average condition of weather in a country or a place for a considerable period of time. Climate of a place is constant while weather changes are according to seasons.

(g) Tides: Tides are caused due to the gravitational pull of the moon and to a lesser degree, the sun on the earth. Tides are the alternate rise and fall of waters of the ocean twice in the course of twenty-four hours. Tides are of two kinds - *spring tides* and *neap tides*. Spring tides are high tides which occur during full and new moon days when the sun, moon and earth are in a straight line and the gravitational pull is maximum. Neap tides are low tides occuring during first Quarter and third Quarter of moon when the sun and moon are at right angles to the earth and the gravitational pull is nullified.

(h) Eclipses: An eclipse is the obscuration of the light of the moon by the intervention of the earth between it and the sun - (Lunar Eclipse) or the obscuration of the light of the sun by the intervention of the moon between it and the earth - (Solar Eclipse). Solar Eclipse is the partial or complete obscuration of the sun and occurs when the moon comes in between the earth and the sun. When the moon completely obscures the sun it is termed as a total solar eclipse and alternately when only part of the sun is eclipsed, it is a partial eclipse.

Lunar eclipse is the partial or complete obscuration of the moon's surface when the earth comes in between the moon and the sun.

(i) Mountains: *Fold Mountains:* They are formed due to buckling of rocks during earthquakes over a long period of time and form into folds. Fold mountains are of two kinds - old fold mountains formed before the continental drifts and include the Applachians of America, Perrines of Europe and Aravallis of India. New fold mountains are the post continental drift mountain formations and include all the major mountain ranges like the Himalayas (India), the Rockies (N.America), the Andes (S.America) and the Alps (Europe).

Block Mountains: These were formed by vertical earth movements when a mass of land was pushed up between cracks.

(j) Rivers: Rivers are the main source of denudation, i.e., wearing away. They work in three stages - mountain stage, plain stage and delta stage. In the mountain stage, rivers are swift and carry down debris and earth, carving wide valleys. The plain stage is slow and gradual and the rivers deposit the silt and soil on the banks making the area fertile. The delta stage of the rivers is when they reach their mouth and fall into the seas. There are two kinds of delta stages, i.e., the estuary and the delta. Estuaries are formed when the seas at the mouth of rivers are rough and have tides, thus washing away all the silt deposited. Estuaries are formed when the coastland is low, e.g., St.Lawrence basin in Canada and the Narmada and Tapti in India. Deltas are fertile triangular pieces of land formed at the mouths of rivers by deposit of mud and silt. The fertile river basins have been the seats of civilization flourished around fertile deltas. The fertile delta of the Ganges called the 'Sunderbans' is the largest in the world and a major producer of jute and rice.

(k) Rainfall: Rainfall is of three kinds - convectional, relief and cyclonic. Convectional rainfall occurs when the waters of the rivers and seas evaporate due to heat and rise up to get cooled in the cool upper regions of the atmosphere.This type of rain occurs mostly in Equatorial regions. Relief rains occur when rain bearing winds get blocked by mountains. They hit against the mountains which receive rains is called the windward side. The other side of the mountains are dry because the winds reaching that side, lose the moisture. This side is called the leeward side. But in order to receive relief rains, the mountains should be obstructing the winds and not be parallel to them. The Aravallis in India lie parallel to the south west monsoon and hence do not cause relief rains thus making Rajasthan a dry desert. Cyclonic rains are experienced greatly in the coastal regions of India. These rains are caused by low pressure troughs created in the seas from which winds blow at great speeds towards land masses with high pressure and cause heavy rainfall. Cyclonic winds blow in anti-clockwise direction.

(l) Winds: Winds are streams of air moving horizontally from one region to another due to difference in atmospheric pressure and temperature. Air flows from high pressure regions to low pressure regions. Due to the rotation of the earth, the winds are deflected and move crosswise. Winds are deflected towards the right in the Northern hemisphere and towards the left in the Southern Hemisphere.

The important wind belts of the world are:

Trade Winds: The winds blow in the tropics towards the equator. Trade winds bring rains to the eastern side of land masses. Trade winds are regular and constant.

Polar Winds: They blow from the polar regions to the temperature zones and bring bitter cold with them.

(m) Natural regions of the world: There are nine regions.

1. *Equatorial Regions* extending on either side of the equator.They are regions of great heat and heavy rainfall. These regions are called the tropics.

2. *Hot Grassland Regions:* They are sub-tropical zones lying on either side of the equator. These regions also have great heat but scanty rainfall. Hence the vegetation is mainly grasslands, like the savannas of South America and Africa.

3. *Monsoon Regions:* They are mostly found in regions of S.E. Asia and northern Australia which receive rains from the monsoons.

4. *Hot Deserts:* They are found all over the world in the sub-tropical regions on the left side of land masses. Important hot deserts are Sahara (Egypt), Thar (India), Kalahari (S.Africa) and so on. The regions have no vegetation and have extreme climates, i.e., very hot during day time and very cold during night time, due to sandy soils and high cloudless skies.

5. *Mediterranean:* These regions are characterised by hot dry summers and cool wet winters. The mediterranean region in Europe is specially characteristic of this climate. The regions lie above the sub tropics. The mediterranean regions are the home of citrus fruits like oranges and lemons and also grapes and olives. In Australia, the mediterranean type regions have great deal of eucalyptus trees. The trees are generally short with thick waxy leaves.

6. *Steppes:* They are the temperate grasslands of the World - Prairie (N.America), Pampas (S.America), Steppes (Europe), Velds (Africa) and Downs (Australia). The grasslands are fertile pastures and homegrounds of sheep and cattle rearing. The downs are especially in the USSR and the USA.

7. *Warm Temperate Regions:* They are found in temperate zones and are the best and invigorating climate in the whole world, characterised by warm summers and cool winters with rains throughout the year. These regions are most developed regions of the World including Great Britain, France, USA, Japan, Germany, Argentina and Southern Australia.

8. *Cold Temperate Regions:* These lie in the temperate zone above the warm temperate regions and are more colder due to nearness to Poles. Canada, China, parts of Norway, Sweden, the USSR and New Zealand have this climate. These regions contain the soft-wooded coniferous forests which are ideal for wood pulp and matches. The regions also are the home ground of fur bearing animals and the hunting of animals is a major occupation of the people.

9. *Tundras or Cold Desert Regions:* They are found in the extreme north and south of the world near the Poles. They are bitterly cold and are snow covered most of the year. Population is very scarce, mainly made up of the

eskimos who live in the igloos made of ice. The South Pole which contains the huge land mass of Antarctica is uninhabited.

GEOGRAPHICAL TERMS

Abrasion: The wearing away of the earth's surface by natural agencies such as wind, water etc.

Accretion: The gradual building up of water-borne material such as mud and sand in an area that is regularly flooded.

Advection: The term used to refer to the movement of warm air from tropical to temperate latitudes or from sea to land.

Afforestation: Planting of trees on barren land or transforming an area into forest.

Agglomerate: A mass of broken rocks or lumps of lava thrown out by a volcano and cemented to form ash.

Alpines: The typical plants of high mountain slopes, called so because they grow in profusion on the upper slopes of the Alps.

Alps: The central, greatest mountain system of Europe, consisting of an arc of fold mountains running about 800 km. Its highest peak is Mont Blanc, 4810 m.

Altiplano: A high plain in the Andes mountains. Specially it refers to a barren plateau 3960 m above the sea level in Bolivia.

Altitude: (i) Height or elevation of a place measured above sea level (usually measured in feet or m). (ii) Angular distance measured vertically, e.g., heavenly body above the horizon. Since sea level is continuously changing with the tides, a standard sea level at Liverpool has been fixed as the mean sea level. This is the zero line from which the height of a place is measured (see Mean sea level).

Altocumulus: A cloud formation made up of small, round, white or grey clouds massed closely together at a height of 2500-6000 m.

Altostratus: A type of cloud that forms a thick, greyish blue sheet or veil at a height of about 2000-6000 m. Sometimes it produces heavy rain.

Andes: The mountain system which extends from north to south of South America along the Pacific coast measuring about 8000 km and forms the backbone of that continent. Its highest peak is Ojos del Salado, 7084 m. It is the highest mountain in the Southern Hemisphere and the second largest mountain range in the world.

Anemometer: An instrument by which the velocity (speed) and the direction of wind is measured, usually in km/h or m/s.

Anticline and Syncline: An anticline is a fold with strata sloping downwards on both sides from a common crest to form an arch. The top of the arch, being pressed upward, is the loosest and weakest part and as such is quickly eroded. A syncline is a low trough like area in bedrock with rocks inclined together from opposite sides. The rocks at the lowest part are under great pressure from all sides; they become compact and hard and erode slowly.

Antipodes: Place(s) that are diametrically opposite each other. People in Britain sometimes call Australia and New Zealand the 'Antipodes' because they are at the opposite end of the earth. At the antipodes, both the seasons and day and night are reversed. While one place experiences winter, the other faces summer. Change of season, however, does not apply to the antipodes of equatorial regions. The antipodes of any place on the equator is also on the equator, and so has exactly the same season. While it is noon at one place it is midnight at the other. The antipodes of any region, being at the opposite side of the world, differ from one another by 12 hours in time.

Antarctic: Southern-most part of the earth which surrounds the South Pole. It is the part where the Indian Ocean, Arabian Sea and Bay of Bengal meet.

Anticyclone: An anticyclone occurs when winds blow outward from high pressure region at the centre towards the low pressure region round it. The winds blow spirally outwards in a clockwise direction in the northern hemisphere and an anti-clociwise direction in the southern hemisphere.

Antipodes: The region or place on the opposite sides of the earth.

Arctic: Northern-most part of the earth which surrounds the North Pole. Due to severe cold, most of its part remains frozen throughout the year.

Atoll: A coral reef in the shape of a horse shoe or ring with a lagoon in the centre, e.g., Murora Atoll in the Pacific Ocean.

Alluvial soil and Black soil: Alluvial soil is that soil which is formed by deposition of silts brought down by the rivers.

Aphelion: The point in its orbit at which a heavenly body or planet is farthest from the sun. The earth at this point (July 4) is about 94 million miles (151 million km) from the sun (see Perihelion).

Appleton Layer: A layer in the ionosphere about 241 km high, that reflects radio waves back to the earth. It is named after Sir Edward Appleton, the physicist who discovered it (see Ionosphere).

Apogee: A heavenly body's point of greatest distance from the earth; the sun's greatest meridional altitude.

Arable Land: Land that is used for growing crops or is suitable for cultivation.

Archipelago: a group of islands in large expanse of water (Indonesia).

Artesian Basin: When a basin-shaped layer of porous rock on the earth's crust is trapped between layers of non-porous rock, water accumulates in the porous rock forming an artesian basin.

Artesian Well: Artesian well is made by boring down to saturated layers of rock in an artesian basin.

Asthenosphere: Soft semifluid layer of rock on which the earth's continents and ocean floors float. The asthenosphere is a part of the earth's mantle, the rest of which is solid both above and below.

Asteroids: Are minor planets. They are small bodies which revolve round the sun between the orbits of Mars and Jupiter.

Attrition: The constant wearing down of pieces of rock into even finer particles as they are carried of along by wind, water or ice.

Aurora Borealis: beams of many coloured light quivering in the sky in the northern hemisphere. Similar light seen in the southern hemisphere is called Aurora Australis.

Avalanche: Great mass of snow or ice. It splits off in summer and goes down on slope of the mountain at great speed. At times it causes severe damage.

Axis of the Earth: An imaginary line through the earth round which the earth spins (rotates) once in 24 hours. The earth's axis runs from the North to the South pole. It is inclined to the place at an angle of $23\frac{1}{2}°$. The equator is the circumference of the earth half-way between the poles.

Azimuth: (i) A horizontal bearing measured clockwise from a given direction; (ii) The horizontal angular distance from a fixed reference direction to a position, object or object referent, as to a great circle intersecting a celestial body, usually measured clockwise in degress along the horizon from a point due south.

Azoic: The term literally means 'without life'; and refers to the earliest part of the Pre-Cambrian Era, when there was no animal life on the earth (see Pre-Cambrian Era).

Backing: An anticlockwise change in the direction of the wind, e.g. from north to north-west (see Veering).

Basalt: A dark volcanic, fine-grained rock which often occurs in sheets of great thickness formed by the solidification of lava.

Bayou: A marshy creek found in flat country, e.g., along the lower reaches of the Mississippi river in the USA.

Bedrock: Solid, unweathered rock lying beneath the soil and subsoil.

Bill: A long narrow cape or headland jutting into the sea (see Cape, Headland, Peninsula, Point).

Biosphere: The organic life on earth both animate and inanimate.

Blizzard: A violent windstorm accompanied by intense cold and driving, powdery snow or ice crystals.

Bog: An area of water-logged, spongy ground with rotting vegetation lying on the surface. Eventually the layer turns into a layer of peat (see Peat, Marsh).

Bora: A cold and dry wind which blows along the eastern coast of the Adriatic Sea and northern Italy in winter.

Butte: A flat-topped hill found in relatively flat terrain.

Buys Ballot's Law (1857): This law states that in the northern hemisphere the winds move anticlockwise round centres of low pressure and clockwise round centres of high pressure; the reverse being true for the southern hemisphere.

Cascade: A series of small waterfalls flowing down a bed resembling stairs.

Cataract: It is a large waterfall or a series of waterfalls, as on the Nile.

Canyon: It is a gorge, formed by a river cutting through the soft rocks of a deep narrow valley with steep sides.

Cape: The point of ending of land which extends the sea, e.g., Cape Comorin.

Cirrus: A type of high cloud with wispy and fibrous-looking bands.

Cliff: A steep rock face. Cliffs on the sea coast are formed by the wearing away action of the waves and canyon cliffs are cut by deep rivers. Glaciers also grind out cliffs between mountain sides.

Cloud Burst: A phenomenon in which a huge mass of moisture-carrying cloud bursts into a heavy downpour on account of condensation of its entire volume of water vapour at the same time.

Constellation: Group of stars moving together such as the Great Bear and the Scorpion.

Coniferous forest: A forest of evergreen coniferous or conebearing trees carrying needle shaped leaves. Soft wood timber is obtained from these forests. They are found mostly in Canada and Europe.

Contours: Lines connecting places of equal heights above sea level in a map.

Coral: A small invertebrate animal found in high seas. They are united together to form coral reef.

Coral reef: A chain of rocks at or near the sea. Fragments of shells, coral, sand, etc., piled up by winds and waves from coral reef.

Confluence: The meeting of two or more rivers at a place.

Continental Climate: The climate occurring in the interior part of the continent.

Continental Shelf: A part of land submerged under the sea. The depth is about 100 fathoms. It is a rich ground for fishing.

Continental Slope: A continental shelf extends into the sea as a continental slope, descending to a depth of 2,000 fathoms (see Continental Shelf)

Comets: Luminous celestial bodies moving round the sun.

Crops Rotation: If the same crop is cultivated, the land may remain vacant for months and lose fertility. To offset both these, a variety of crops are cultivated on the same land. This is known as rotation of crops.

Cordillera: A name given specifically to the mountain range of the Andes in South America and the other great ranges in North America. The word 'cordillera' is derived from the Spanish word meaning 'chain'.

Coriolis Force: The force exerted on the atmosphere by earth's rotation.

Crater: Is the small mouth of a volcano. It is usually cup-shaped and serves as a vent for lava to flow out of the volcano.

Crater Lake: A lake formed in the crater of a volcano (see Crater, Lake, Volcano).

Creek: A small stream; a smaller inlet or tidal estuary of a river.

Cumulonimbus: A heavy dark thunderstorm cloud towering upwards with a depth of about 15,000 feet. It is spread out aloft in the form of an angle. It indicates the oncoming of rains.

Cyclones: The winds which blow from outward high pressure area towards the inward low pressure areas are cyclones.

Dateline or International Dateline: The line situated 180° meridian from Greenwich. A ship while crossing the line eastward goes forward by a day while towards westward it goes backwards by a day.

Deciduous Forests: It consists of trees having broad leaves. They shed leaves in autumn. The forests are found in temperate region.

Deccan Trap: It is the old name of the Deccan lavas, an extensive series of basaltic lava deposits several thousand feet thick which cover nearly an area of two lakh square miles in the north-west of Deccan.

Delta: A triangular shaped piece of land formed at the mouth of the river by deposition of mud and silt brought by the river.

Denudation: Wearing away of earth by natural agencies.

Depressed Seas: Large inland seas. These levels are low and inflow of water is less, e.g., Dead Sea.

Dew: Moisture deposited on exposed objects by condensation of water vapour. The formation of dew is more during clear cloudless nights.

Doldrums: The regions lying in between 5° N and 5° S of Equator where the air is rising and pressure is low. Calm prevails for weeks. It is suddenly broken by winds. It is the region of high humidity and uncomfortable temperature.

Dunes: Sand dunes generally found in deserts, are elliptical or crescent-shaped mounds of loose sand formed by wind action. A dune has a gentle slope on the wind-ward side and a steep slope on the leeward side.

Dust Devil: A dusty whirl wind. Low pressure at the centre and strong vertex winds cause dust and small debris to be carried upwards making the whirl appear as a vertical tube or funnel. It forms over strongly heated barren lands of deserts.

Earthquakes: Movements of the earth's crust. These may be caused by volcanic eruption, the sudden generation and expansion of steam, actual sinking of portion of the crust or by breaking of the strata under the strain of contraction caused by the cooling of earth's crust.

Echo-sounding: A method to calculate the depth of the ocean. It is calculated by sending sound waves into the sea water. The waves strike at the bottom and get reflected. By calculating the time taken, the depth of the ocean is calculated.

Escarpment: A steep inland cliff. An escarpment is found where layers of hard rock slope upwards to the surface over softer rocks below.

Estuary: A channel formed by mixing of sea and river water, e.g., Thames Estuary.

Epicentre: The point at which the earthquake breaks out.

Equator: An imaginary line encircling the earth at equal distance from the poles. The parts of the earth on the north and on the south are known as northern and southern hemispheres respectively.

Equigravisphere: The locus of a point where the gravity does not change. It is almost a spherical surface around the earth.

Equinox: The time or date twice in a year at which the sun crosses the celestial equator when day and night are equal length. When it occurs the sun is vertical over the Equator on these dates. On March 21 and on 22nd September the days and nights are equal. The equinox on March 21 is known as vernal or spring equinox and 22nd September is known as autumnal equinox.

Exosphere: The uppermost region of the ionosphere and also the fringe of the atmosphere. It lies about 480 km from the earth's surface and has almost no air molecules.

Fathom: A unit of length to measure the depth of water. One fathom is equal to 1.8 m.

Fault: An enormous crack or break in the rock strata of the earth's crust caused by horizontal or vertical movement. The slipping of strata is one of the causes of earthquakes.

Fohn: A warm dry wind which blows down the ice-ward slope of a mountain best known in the valleys of the northern Alps.

Fauna: The animal life of a region or of a geographical period.

Fjord or Fiord: It is a long, narrow rock-bound sea-inlet; as on the Coast of Norway.

Flora: The plant life of a region or of a geographical period.

Fossils: Remains of plants or animals buried in the rocks of the earth's crust. These help trace the evolutionary changes in animal and plant life.

Freezing point: That temperature at which a liquid becomes a solid.

Fog: It is formed by the presence of particles of condensed water vapour or smoke in the surface layers of the atmosphere. In the fog the objects are invisible at a certain distance.

Fumarole: A hole or vent in the ground in volcanic regions through which fumes or gases escape.

Gale: A strong wind that blows at a speed of 62-101 kmph.

Geosyncline: An enormous downward curve or inverted arch in the earth's crust.

Geysers: The fountain of hot water coming out of a hole which extends deep into the earth. The water is hurled high into the air by the force of steam formed low down in the hole. It contains minerals in solution and they get deposited around the hole from which the water gushes out.

Glaciers: A large mass of snow which comes down the slopes on the mountain. It gets melted when it crosses the snowline. There are 4 types of glaciers (1) valley glacier (2) piedmont (3) ice-cap; and (4) continental.

Gorge: A narrow opening between hills. It may be formed by erosion of rivers.

Great Bear: A constellation of seven stars.

Great Circle: A circle on a sphere passing through two opposite points (Poles). The equator is a great circle as its centre coincides with that of the earth. Every parallel other than the equator is small circle because its plane does not pass through the centre of the earth. A great circle bisects the earth into hemispheres.

Groynes: Short walls built into the sea to check erosion by the tides and especially to prevent a beach from being washed away.

Greenwich Mean Time: (G.M.T.) Local time of Greenwich observatory, London. It is presumed that the zero meridian passes through it.

Gulf Stream: A warm ocean current emerging from the gulf of Mexico. It finally washes the western shores of England, moderates the temperature and keeps the harbours open throughout the year.

Hachures: Lines drawn on maps to indicate the incline of slopes. Steep slopes are indicated by lines drawn close together and shallow slopes by lines drawn relatively far apart.

Haff: A lagoon usually kept open by a river flowing through it. The long spit of sand which separates the Haff from the open sea is called *Nehrung*, e.g. the southern Baltic coast (see Lagoon).

Haloes round the Moon: A ring of light witnessed around the moon. It is caused by the reflection of light by ice crystals on the surface of the moon.

Habitat: A natural environment of a plant or animal.

Harmattan: A strong, hot, dusty wind that blows over parts of Western Africa from the Sahara desert.

High Seas: The middle parts of the oceans. They are not under the jurisdiction of any particular country.

Hinterland: The region lying behind a sea port which supplies the bulk of exports and the import in the port is distributed in that region.

Horizon: The circular line of the sky which appears to meet the earth or sea.

Humus: The decomposed and partly decomposed organic matter of animal or vegetable origin in the soil. It contains three acids such as (1) Fulvic acid (2) Humic acid (3) Humine.

Hoarfrost: Needle shaped crystals of ice deposited on the ground. It is just like dew.

Hurricane: A gale of extreme violence characterised by changes of the wind and sometimes thunder and lightning.

Hydrosphere: The oceanic part of earth. It accounts for 71% of the earth's total surface. It consists of a number of oceans, bays, gulfs and lakes.

Ice Age: A period when Ice-sheets and glaciers covered large areas of the continent.

Icecap: A mass of ice covering the land in polar regions. Huge ice caps, such as those that cover Antarctica and much of Greenland, are sometimes called 'Ice-sheets'.

Ice Fall: The part of a glacier where the sudden change of slopes has caused crevasses and broken the ice surface into pillars of ice.

Iceberg: A mass of ice floating on the sea. It is formed by breaking off from the end of a glacier or from an ice-barrier.

Igloo: The name of Eskimo winter house.

Igneous rocks: Rocks formed by cooling of the molten matter which comes out of the earth from its interior parts.

Indian Standard Time: It is the local time of Allahabad which is 82-1/2° East longitude. It is exactly 5-1/2 hours in advance of the Greenwich Time.

Ionosphere: The region of the earth's atmosphere extending from 53 to 400 miles above the earth. In this region the gases are ionised. It reflects the electromagnetic radiations of radio frequencies.

Isobars: The lines on the map connecting places of same barometric pressure.

Isobaths: Lines on the map connecting parts of the ocean of the same depth.

Isogonic lines: Contour lines of magnetic declination.

Isohel: A line on a map marking an area having the same duration of sunshine.

Isohyte: A line drawn on a map joining places receiving equal amount of rainfall over a certain period.

Isohaline: Lines on map joining points in a sea or an ocean having equal salinity.

Isoneph: A line on a map joining places having equal average cloudiness over a certain period.

Isostasy: The state of balance or equilibrium that is said to exist between highlands and lowlands of the earth due to difference in the density of their respective rock material.

Isoseismic Lines: A line drawn on a map joining places experiencing equal intensity of shock in an earthquake.

Isotherm: Lines on a map joining those places which have the same mean temperature.

Isthmus: A narrow strip of land which joins two land areas- eg. Isthmus of Panama.

Japan Current: A warm Pacific current that flows northwards to Japan and eastwards to the coast of North America. The current resembles the Gulf Stream in its course and effect.

Kayak: The canoe of the Eskimo made by stretching animal skins on a framework of bones.

Khamsin: The hot, dry wind experienced in Egypt corresponding to the Sirocco of North America. 'Khamsin' is the Arabic word for 50; the wind is said to blow during the period of 50 days from April to June.

Kuro Siwo: Warm oceanic current of the Pacific Ocean which flows near the east coast of Japan and ultimately drifts along the west coast of Canada. It raises the temperature of Canada and Japan.

Laterite: A reddish porous rock produced by weathering. Found chiefly in humid tropical regions e.g., India, Malaysia, Indonesia, Sudan and parts of South America. Laterite is used in the manufacture of cement.

Lagoon: The stretch of shallow water at the mouth of a river or near sea but separated from it by sand.

Latitudes: The imaginary lines on the north and south of the equator. These are parallel to the equator.

Lava: It is an Italian word applied to the liquid products of volcanic activity. The term lava is applied to all matter of volcanic origin which is or has been in molten state.

Leap Year: It is the name given to a year containing 366 days. In early history a lunar calendar was used, but when man settled down into communities and cultivated crops, a solar calendar which coincided with the seasons was required. This raised many problems as the time taken by the earth to complete its orbit round the sun is not a whole number of days. The orbital period is 365.242 days to a first approximation of 365.25 days. To account, then for the odd quarter day an extra calendar day is added once every four years, as was first done in 46 B.C. under the direction of Julius Caesar.

Leeward: The side or direction which is sheltered from the wind, e.g., East side of western ghats.

Littoral: The land adjacent to the coast of a country. The littoral region of the ocean comprises the shallow waters adjacent to the sea coast and littoral countries are those that lie along the sea coast.

Light Year: It is an astronomical unit of distance, the distance travelled by light in one year being equivalent to about 9.46×10^{12} km.

Lignite: The brown coal in which the original wood texture can be still seen.

Limestone: Is a common and widely distributed sedimentary rock consisting essentially of calcium carbonate but varying greatly in composition, colour and texture.

Lithosphere: The solid rock-crust of the earth.

Loch: A Scottish lake or a long, narrow area of the sea, found along the coast of north-western Scotland.

Loam: Fertile soil consisting of sand, clay together with silt and humus.

Lode: A thick vein of mineral ore found in rocks or a number of closely parallel veins.

Llanos: The name given in the northern part of South America, particularly in Columbia and Venezuela, to vast plains almost entirely level and uninterrupted only at intervals by detached elevations called Spanish mesas.

Longitude: A measurement on the globe or map of location east or west of the Equator. Longitudes are vertical lines passing through the poles. Latitudes and Longitudes are measured in degrees.

Longitudinal Valley: The valley exactly parallel to a mountain range is known as longitudinal valley.

Magma: Rock which is in fluid condition due to heat and commonly said to be molten.

Magnetic Pole: Either of two spots on the earth's surface towards which a compass needle points from any direction throughout adjacent regions.

Magnetic Dip: The angle formed with the horizon by a magnetic needle free to move vertically in the plane of magnetic meridian. It is also called inclination or dip of the needle.

Magnetic Rocks: Those rocks of either igneous or sedimentary origin which have undergone sufficient heat and pressure to be altered into a different kind of rock. In this way limestone becomes marble.

Mean Sea Level (MSL): The average level of the sea, or the standard level used to calculate the height of a place.

Mesa: A flat-topped elevation with one or more cliff-like sides; common in south-west USA.

Meseta: The plateau of central Spain crossed by mountain ranges.

Mist: A mass of water drops present in the lower layers of the atmosphere caused by condensation of water.

Meteor: Refers to cosmic bodies which enter the earth's atmosphere from outside and survives its fiery passage to fall upon the earth's surface.

Midnight Sun: It is the appearance of the sun above the horizon at midnight. It may be witnessed at any point on the Arctic Circle on June 21 and on the Antarctic Circle on December 21.

Milky way or Galaxy: A nebulous band of faint stars extending entirely around the celestial sphere.

Mirage: An optical illusion produced in the atmosphere by an unusual refraction of the light rays. The illusion may result in the appearance of distant object floating mid-air or projected transparently against a ground or sea surface where the subject does not physically exist.

Nautical Mile: It refers to geographical miles. One minute (1/60) degree of longitude measured along equator 1854 metres (6082.66 feet) used by sailors in navigation.

Neap Tides: An especially small tidal range occurring twice monthly, produced by the tidal forces of the Sun and Moon acting in opposition. These tides rises just after the first and third quarters of the moon. The neap tides are lowest in the month as compared with their opposites - the spring tides.

Nebulae: Refers to luminous patches or areas of the sky. It can also refer to dark areas of matter which obscure what lies beyond them.

Oasis: Fertile place in a desert usually found where lack of vegetation is caused by lack of moisture.

Ocean Current: It refers to the large scale semipermanent horizontal water movements that occur in the oceans and seas.

Peat: A dark brown or black organic mass found in wet, marshy ground. It consists of partly rotted vegetation that has collected under waterlogged conditions over a long time. In some parts of the world it is used as fuel.

Perihelion: It refers to the position in the elliptical orbit of the Earth, planet or other object, the orbit of parabolic comets in which the object reaches its closest approach to the sun. The earth reaches this position about January 1 of each year.

Parasite: It is an organisms that lives on or into the body of other organism to get its food and shelter. Parasite are divided into saprophyte parasite and facultative parasite.

Peneplain: A plain resulting from the erosive activity of running water. A region worn by its rivers to the lowest possible level is said to be peneplained or base levelled.

Peninsula: A stretch of land almost surrounded by water.

Perigee: A heavenly body's point of lowest distance from the earth.

Piedmont Plateau: A plateau situated between a mountain range and a plain or sea, e.g. the Patagonian plateau of South America.

Plane of Ecliptic: A plane passing through the earth's orbit.

Planetary Presure Belts: There are pressure belts on the earth's surface which cause the planetary wind system.

♦   Equatorial low pressure belt due to excessive heat.

♦   Sub-tropical high pressure belt on both sides of the equator at about 30° north and 30° south.

♦   *High pressure belt* around 60° north and 60° south are temperate low pressure belts.

♦   Polar regions are regions of permanent high pressure.

Plutonic Rock: Solidification of molten magma cool very slowly below the earth surface. Such a rock known as intrusive igneous rocks or plutonic rocks. Plutonic rocks are large size of particle, high silica and low density. Granite is an example.

Plateau: Table or elevated land rising abruptly from the sea level.

Prairies: A treeless region in the Mississippi valley adjacent to the forest area, so called since the time of the early French explorers.

Planets: A massive spheroidal body of the solar system. They are of varying size and physical composition. They revolve round the sun in elliptical orbits in periods of time computable by Kepler's laws in order of distance from the Sun. They are Mercury, Venus, Earth, Mars, Jupiter, Saturn, Uranus, Neptune and Pluto.

Polar Easterlies: Polar winds that blow out from the polar high towards the temperate regions.

Polar regions: Arctic and Antarctic regions are known as Polar regions.

Polar Winds: Easterly Winds which blow from the cold Polar regions, warm regions.

Pole Star: The star visible in northern hemisphere only. It helps to determine the latitude of a place.

Pre-Cambrian Era: The time in the earth's history before the Cambrian period; the first of the four great geological Eras. During this forms of life appeared. The Era ended about 600 million years ago.

Prime Meridian: Zero degree longitude and is the Meridian from which the longitude of a place is measured.

Quicksand: A thick mass of wet, loose and unstable sand formed at the mouth of a river on the sea coast.

Rand: A familiar name for Wit Waters Rand, a ridge about 75 km long which lies south of Johannesburg 'the Gold-reef City'. On this ridge are the greatest gold mines of the world.

Relative Humidity: The ratio between the actual amount of water present in a given volume of air and the amount of water vapour which will be present if it is fully saturated at the same temperature.

Relief Rainfall or Orographic Rainfalls: Sometimes the winds of moisture rise to a very high level and strike big mountains that they rise up to reach colder layers of air where they condense and fall as rains. These rainfalls are known as orographic rainfalls.

Ria: A long narrow sea inlet, caused by flooding of a narrow valley, which unlike a fiord deepens towards the sea, and is typically found in southwest Ireland and northwest Spain. Also called 'river mouth'.

River Bar: A sandbank which forms across the mouth of a river that often makes navigation difficult.

Rift Valley: Valley formed by subsidence of a block of the Earth's crust between two or more parallel is the process known as fault. Rift valley steep side. Example: Great rift valley of East Africa.

Roaring Forties: A sailor's term for a region of the great southern ocean lying south of latitude 40° to 45° where strong and often stormy west, north west winds prevail.

Sand Dune: These are formed in the sea-beach or in deserts. Winds carrying sand coming against an obstacle; the sand piles up and dunes are formed. When the winds blow in the same direction, the dunes travel in the same direction. Sometimes the adjoining cities may be buried.

Sargasso Sea: part of the North Atlantic between 29° and 40° north latitude and 35° and 75° west longitude.

Satellites: The secondary bodies which revolve round a planet.

Savanna: A tropical grassland. It is the region bordering equator in each hemisphere. Savannas are found in South America and Africa.

Sea of Tranquillity: It is one of the maria on the moon, the place where astronauts Neil Armstrong and Edwin Aldrin and Colin's landed on July 21, 1969 and set foot on the lunar soil for the first time in the annals of man.

Sedimentary Rocks: It is derived from accumulated sedimentary material that is transformed into rock by compaction and cementation such a process known as Lithification. Sedimentary rocks are arranged in layer (strata) is known as stratification. It contain fossils. 80% of rocks are sedimentary rocks in the earth. Example: Shale, limestones, sandstones.

Selvas: The vast tropical forests of the Amazon and its tributaries.

Shott: A shott is also a shallow lake which turns dry in the hot season.

Sidereal Day: It is measured by the apparent diurnal motions of the stars due to the Earth's axial rotation. It is the time from the upper meridian passage of star until its next passage. Rigorously, it is from one such passage to the next of the vernal equinox point, the day by this becomes shorter by 1/120 of a second than that determined by stars.

Simos: The winds that blow from the desert over Arabia and North Africa accompanied by suffocating clouds of sand.

Smoke Screens: Smoke clouds formed by firing smoke shells, dropping smoke bombs, burning smoke pots or operating mechanical smoke generators in war to conceal their movements from enemies.

Snowline: The line of latitude above which there is perpetual snow. Its location which ranges from sea level in polar regions to about 16,000 feet, near the equator is affected by such factors, such as degree of slope, amount of rainfall and force of prevailing winds.

Solar Day: It is measured by the interval from one upper meridian passage to the sun to the next. Thus it depends upon the earth's axial rotation with respect to the sun.

Solar System: The sun, nine known planets and their satellites, the asteroids, comets and material between the planets that is under the gravitational pull of the sun are collectively known as the solar system.

Solstice: The instant at which the sun reaches its greatest angular distance north or south of the equator in the course of each year. For a few days it then changes very slowly in declination. The summer solstice occurs on or about June 21 and the winter solstice occurs on December 22.

Sirocco: A hot oppressive wind, experienced in spring and summer in the Mediterranean area. Originating in the Lybian desert is southerly in Italy, Sicily and adjacent lands; but since it also originates in the Syrian and Arabian deserts, it is easterly on the eastern border of the Mediterranean. As it flows over the sea, it becomes moist and enervating coming over the land. It becomes desiccating, dusty and irritating.

Stalactite and Stalagmite (Karst Landscape): Cave structures formed by the deposition of calcite dissolved in ground water. Stalactites grow downwards from the roofs or walls whereas stalagmites grow upwards from the cave floor.

Steppes: The area which is more or less level, unforested, not flooded by high water in the spring well-drained and covered throughout the entire vegetative season with grassy vegetation growing on black soils. Steppes are found in many parts of the world, in central plains of the U.S.A. and Australia. Steppes in Ukraine are well-known. The steppes have warm dry summers and cold winters.

Stars: Fixed, celestial, self-luminous, gaseous bodies all of great size of which sun is a specimen.

Strait: A narrow stretch of sea connecting two extensive areas of sea.

Stratus clouds: Clouds which are like a dark grey sheet extending from one side of horizon to the other and have uniform base.

Summit: Is the highest point of a mountain.

Sun Dogs: A mock sun or perihelion, a bright spot on the path of an astronomical body nearest to the sun.

Stratosphere: It is second layer after the troposphere from the earth surface. Height of this layer is upto 50 km. It contains ozone. Ozone layer help human health because, it absorb UV rays from solar radiation. (UV rays cause eye defect and skin cancer to human being).

Taiga: A belt of coniferous forests of the Northern Hemisphere, e.g. Siberia.

Terai: Region along the foothills of the Himalayas which receives much of the heavy rains that fall on the lower slopes.

Terrain: The physical characteristics and features of any stretch of country.

Tektites: Natural round shaped glassy objects found are the fall-out of the splash of meteoric matter on earth.

Time Determination: The difference in minutes between the Greenwich Time and the local time at a place can be derived by multiplying the longitude of a place by four.

Tornado: Extremely violent revolving storm with swirling, funnel shaped clouds, caused by a rising column of warm air propelled by strong wind. Tornado can rise to great height with diameter of few hundred metre or less. Tornadoes move with wind speeds of 160-480 kph, destroying everything in their path. They are common in central USA.

Trade Winds: Prevailing north easterly and south easterly winds of the sub-tropics deriving their name from their constant course. The trade winds occupy two belts between latitudes 5° and 25° north and south of equators.

Tributary: Small rivulet running into the main stream of water.

Tropical Cyclone: A small but intense depression which orginates in tropical regions.

Tropics: Imaginary circles over the earth about 23°28' North or South (Tropic of Cancer to Tropic of Capricorn respectively) of the Equator. These are the maximum limits to which sun reaches.

Tsunami: Tsunami (pronounced tsoo-nah-mee) is a Japanese word which means "harbour wave". 'Tsu' means 'harbour' and 'nami' stands for 'wave'. Tsunamis are large waves that are generated when the sea floor is deformed by seismic activity, vertically displacing the overlying water in the ocean. Throughout recorded history, tsunamis have caused significant damage to coastal communities all over the world.

The Tsunami which hit the Southern Coast of the Indian Peninsula on 26th December 2004 caused heavy damage both to life and property. An official estimate put the human death toll at more than 10,000 in India alone. Indonesia bore the brunt. Heavy devastation was reported in Srilanka and Andaman and Nicobar Islands of India. The waves caused by Tsunami travel at 600–1000 km speed under sea level. When the waves hit an obstruction like shores rise upto 60 metre high causing untold misery. Though India does not have a clear recorded history, Tsunami might have hit Indian coast about a lakh of years ago.

Tundras: Vast stretches of desert land in Antarctic and Arctic regions. The region is too cold. So there is no vegetation. The Reindeer is the only animal living there, to give milk to the poor inhabitants.

Twilight: The diffiused light seen before the sunrise and after the sunset.

Typhoons: Violent storms that occur between July and October along the eastern seaboard of Asia between Japan and Philippines.

Ursa Major: Constellation of seven stars clearly visible to the naked eye. It is known as Great Bear. It is a summer constellations.

Valley: A deep depression between hills or mountains; often carved out by a river or glacier.

Veering: A clock change in the direction of the wind, e.g. N to NE.

Wadi: It is a desert river which remains largely dry except when fed by rain water.

Water Parting: The elevated land separating the source of two different river systems; also called *watershed.*

Water-spout: Spout of water formed between the sea and cloud.

Water Table: The upper level of ground water (water collected underground in porous rocks). The water table rises and falls in response to rainfall and the rate at which water is extracted, for example for irrigation.

Zenithical Projection: Is adopted to construct equal area or equidistant maps. An equal area projection is frequently shown as a polar projection. Here concentric parallels are drawn with one of the poles at the centre and merdians as straight lines converging at the given pole.

IMPORTANT GEOGRAPHICAL DISCOVERIES

Amundson (*Norwegian*) - Discovered South Pole in 1911.

Armstrong, Neil A. (*U.S.A.*) - First person to set foot on the moon on July 21, 1969.

Byrd - American aviator and polar explorer. Flew over the North Pole in1926 and made the first flight over the South Pole in 1929. Discovered Edsel Ford Mountains.

Cabot (*Venetian*) - Discovered New Foundland in 1494.

Captain Cook (*English*) - Discovered Sandwich (now Hawaiian) Isles in 1770.

Columbus - Discovered West Indies in 1492 and South America in 1498.

Copernicus - Discovered *Heliocentric System* in 1540. Propounded the astronomical system which bears his name.

David Livingstone - Discovered course of the Zambezi, the Victoria Falls and Lake Nyasa in Africa.

Edmund Hillary - Joint conqueror of Mount Everest with Tenzing. He also led a Trans-Atlantic expedition and reached South Pole on January 3, 1958.

Ferdinand de Lesseps - Conceived the plan of the Suez Canal on which work was completed in 1869 through his efforts.

Francis Younghusband - Explored the frontier regions of India, China and Tibet.

Kepler - Discovered the Laws of Planetary Motion in 1609.

Lindbergh - Performed the first solo-flight across the Atlantic in 1927 from New York to Paris.

Magellan - Commanded the first expedition in1519 to sail round the world. Discovered passage to the Pacific from the Atlantic through Straits afterwards named after him.

Marco Polo - Venetian traveller who explored China, India, South eastern countries and published the record of his various explorations. He was the first European to visit China.

Nansen - Norwegian explorer who explored across Greenland and reached the highest altitude in the North Polar Region, till then not attained.

Peary, Robert - First to reach the North Pole in 1909.

Pedro Alvares Cabral (*Portuguese*) - Discovered Brazil in 1500.

Shackleton - Arctic explorer-reached within 160 km of the South Pole.

Sven Hedin - Swedish explorer. Made great contribution to the geographic and archaeological knowledge of large areas of Central Asia.

Tasman - Dutch navigator, discovered the Tasmania Island and New Zealand in 1642.

Tenzing - First to reach Mount Everest on 29th May, 1953 along with Edmund Hillary. The expedition was led by Col. Sir John Hunt.

Vasco da Gama (*Portuguese*) - Rounded the Cape of Good Hope and discovered the sea route to India in 1498.

IMPORTANT LINES OF DEMARCATION

Durand Line: The demarcation line drawn in 1896 by Sir Mortimer Durand. It defined the boundary between India (now Pakistan) and Afghanistan. Afghanistan refuses to recognise this line.

Hindenburg Line: The line to which the Germans retreated in 1917 during the First World War. This was the dividing line between Germany and Poland.

Hotline: Uninterrupted directed telephonic link between Kremlin (USSR) and the White House (USA) to avoid any accidental flare- up.

Maginot Line: A line of fortification constructed by France to protect her border from Germany's attack.

Mannerhiem Line: Line of fortification on Russo-Finnish border drawn up by Gen Mannerhiem.

McMohan Line: Demarcation Line between China and India.

Oder Neisse Line: The line defining the boundary between East Germany and Poland drawn after the Second World War. Russia and Poland are very particular that this line should be recognised as the final boundary line (between Germany and Poland) by the Western Powers and West Germany.

Radcliffe Line: The boundary line demarcated by Sir Cyril Radcliffe, Chairman of the Boundary Commission for India and Pakistan, at the time of Partition of India on August 15, 1947.

Siegfried Line: Line of fortification drawn up by Germany on her borders with France.

17th Parallel: Demarcation line between North and South Vietnams.

24th Parallel: It is the demarcation line in Kutch dispute claimed by Pakistan. It has been rejected by India.

38th Parallel: Demarcation line between North and South Koreas.

49th Parallel: Demarcation line between USA and Canada.

COUNTRIES, THEIR CAPITALS, CURRENCIES, PRINCIPAL LANGUAGES AND RELIGIONS

Country	Capital	Currency	Language	Religion
Afghanistan	Kabul	Afghani	Pakhto (Pusthu), Dari, Persian	Islam
Albania	Tirana	Lek	Albanian & Greek	Religion has been officially abolished
Algeria	Algiers	Dinar	Arabic & French	Islam
Andorra	Andorra la Vieille	Franc & French Spanish Peseta	Catalan, Spanish	Christianity
Angola	Luanda	Kwanza	Portuguese,	Tribal and Bantu Christianity
Antigua and Barbuda	St.John's	EC Dollar	English	Christianity
Argentina	Buenos Aires	Peso	Spanish	Christianity
Australia	Canberra	Australian Dollar	English	Christianity
Austria	Vienna	Euro	German	Christianity
Azerbaijan	Baku	Manat	Azeri, Turkish, Russian	Islam
Bahamas	Nassau	Bahamian Dollar	English	Christianity
The Bahrain	Manama	Dinar	Arabic & English	Islam
Bangladesh	Dacca	Taka	Bengali & Chakmamagh	Islam & Hindu
Barbados	Bridge Town	Barbados Dollar	English	Christianity
Belgium	Brussels	Euro	Dutch French & German	Christianity
Belarus	Minsk	Belarus Ruble (Zaichik)	Belorunian, Russian	Christianity
Belize	Belmopan	Belize Dollar	English, Spanish	Christianity
Benin	Porto Novo	Franc CFA	French & Tribal Dialects	Animism, Islam & Christianity
Bermuda	Hamilton	Bermuda Dollar	English	Christianity

Country	Capital	Currency	Language	Religion
Bhutan	Thimpu	Ngultrum	Dzongkha & Nepali	Buddhism & Hinduism
Bolivia	La Paz	Boliviano	Spanish & Aymara	Christianity
Botswana	Gaborone	Pula	English & Setswana	Christianity
Brazil	Brasilia	Real (BRC)	Portuguese & English	Christianity
Brunei	Bander Seri Begawan	Brunei Dollar	Malay, Chinese & English	Islam
Bulgaria	Sofia	Lev	Bulgarian, Turkish	Christianity & Atheism
Burundi	Bujumbura	Burundi Franc	French & Kirundi	Tribal & Christianity
Cambodia	Phnompenh	Riel	Khmer & French	Theravada & Buddhism
Cameroon	Yaounde	Franc CFA	French & English	Tribal, Islam & Christianity
Canada	Ottawa	Dollar	English & French	Christianity
Cape Verde	Praia	Escudo	Portuguese Criuolo	Christianity
Central African Republic	Bangui	Franc CFA	French & Sangho	Christianity and Tribal
Chad	N'djamena	Franc CFA	French & Arabic	Islam & Tribal
Chile	Santiago	Peso	Spanish	Christianity
China	Beijing	Yuan	Chinese (Mandarin) Mongol	Confucianism & Taoism, Buddhism
Colombia	Bogota	Peso	Spanish	Christianity
The Comoros	Moroni	Comorian Franc	Arabic & French, Shaafi Islam	Islam & Christianity
Congo (Belgium)	Brazzaville	Franc CFA	French & Lingala	Tribal & Christianity
Costa Rica	San Jose	Colon	Spanish	Christianity
Cote D'ivorie	Abidjan	Franc CFA	French Tribal	Islam & Christianity
Cuba	Havana	Peso	Spanish	Christianity
Cyprus	Nicosia	Cyprus Pound	Greek & Turkish	Christianity & Islam

Country	Capital	Currency	Language	Religion
Denmark	Copenhagen	Krone	Danish Krone	Lutheranism
Djibouti	Djibouti	Franc	Arabic & French	Islam
Dominica	Roseau	French Franc	English & French Patois	Christianity
Dominican Republic	Santo Domingo	Peso Oro	Spanish	Christianity
East Timor	Dili	Euro	English, Tetum, Bahasa	Christianity, Muslim, Hindu, Buddhist
Ecuador	Quito	Sucre	Spanish & Tribal dialects	Christianity
Egypt	Cairo	Pound	Arabic	Islam & Christianity
Elsalvador	San Salvador	Colon	Spanish	Christianity
Equatorial Guinea	Malabo (formerly Santa Isabel)	Franc CFA	Spanish & Fang	Christianity
Ethiopia	Addis Ababa	Birr	Amharic, Gallinga	Christianity and Islam
Fiji	Suva	Dollar	English & Figian	Christianity Islam & Hinduism
Finland	Helsinki	Euro	Finnish & Swedish	Lutheranism
France	Paris	Euro	French	Christianity
Gabon	Libreville	Franc	French & Bantu	Christianity and Tribal dialects
Gambia	Banjul	Dalasi	English & Mandinka	Islam & Christianity
Germany	Berlin	Euro	German	Christianity
Ghana	Accra	Cedi	English (Official Language) and eight Major national languages	Christianity
Greece	Athens	Drachma	Greek	Christianity

Country	Capital	Currency	Language	Religion
Grenada	St.Georges	E.C. Dollar	English & French-African Patois	Christianity
Guatemala	Guatemala City	Quetzal	Spanish, Indian dialects	Christianity
Guinea	Conakry	Guinean Franc	French & Tribal languages	Islam and 8 national
Guinea Bissau	Bissau	Peso	Portuguese Criolo, African languages	Islam Christianity and Tribal
Guyana	George Town	Guyana Dollar	English, Amerindian dialects	Christianity Islam & Hinduism
Haiti	Port-au-Prince	Gourde	French & Creole	Christianity
Honduras	Tegucigalpa	Lempira	Spanish	Christianity
Hungary	Budapest	Forint	Hungarian	Christianity
Iceland	Reykjavik	Krona	Icelandic	Christianity
India	New Delhi	Rupee	Hindi	Hinduism, Christianity, Islam etc.
Indonesia	Jakarta	Rupiah	Bahasa, Indonesian	Islam & Christianity
Iran	Tehran	Rial	Persian (Farsi)	Islam
Iraq	Baghdad	Iraqi Dinar	Arabic (Official) & Kurdish	Islam
Ireland	Dublin	Euro	Irish & English	Christianity
Israel	Jerusalem	New Sheker	Hebrew (Official) Arabic	Judaism & Islam
Italy	Rome	Euro	Italian	Christianity
Jamaica	Kingston	Jamaican Dollar	English Jamaican, Creole	Christianity

Country	Capital	Currency	Language	Religion
Japan*	Tokyo	Yen	Japanese	Shintoism & Buddhism
Jordan	Amman	Jordan Dinar	Arabic	Islam
Kazakhstan	Akmola	Ruble	Kazakh Russian German	Islam & Christianity
Kenya	Nairobi	Shilling	Swahili & Kikuio	Tribal, Islam & Christianity
Kiribati	Tarawa	Australian Dollar	Gilbertese and English	Christianity
Korea (N)	Pyongyong	Won	Korean	Buddhism & Confucianism
Korea (S)	Seoul	Won	Korean	Christianity & Confucianism
Kuwait	Kuwait City	Kuwait Dinar	Arabic & English	Islam
Kyrgyzstan	Bishkek	Som	Kirghiz, Russian	Islam, Christianity
Laos	Vientiane	Kip	Lao French & English	Buddhism & Tribal
Lebanon	Beirut	Lebanese Pound	Arabic	Islam & Christianity
Lesotho	Maseru	Loti	English & Sesotho	Christianity and Tribal
Liberia	Monrovia	Liberian Dollar	English & Tribal	Christianity & Islam
Libya	Tripoli	Libyan Dinar	Arabic	Islam
Liechtenstein	Vaduz	Swiss Franc	German	Christianity
Luxembourg	Luxembourg Ville (Lutzelburg)	Euro	French & German	Christianity
Madagascar	Antana-narivo	Franc	Malagasy & French	Islam, Tribal & Christianity
Malawi	Lilongwe	Kwacha	English & Chichewa	Christianity & Islam
Malaysia	Kuala Lumpur	Ringgit	Mala, Chinese & English	Islam & Buddhism
Maldives	Male	Rufiyaa	Divehi	Islam
Mali	Bamako	Franc CFA	French & Afirican language	Islam & Tribal

Country	Capital	Currency	Language	Religion
Malta	Valetta	Maltese Lira	Maltese & English	Christianity
Marshall Islands	Dalap-Uliga-Darrit	US Dollar	Marshallese English	Christianity
Mauritania	Nouakchott	Ouguiya	Arabic & French	Islam
Mauritius	Port Louis	Rupee	English, French & Creole, Hindi	Hinduism, Christianity & Islam
Mexico	Mexico City	Peso	Spanish Indian Language	Christianity
Micronesia	Palikir	US Dollar	English	Christianity
Monaco	Monaco-Ville	Franc	French & Monegasque	Christianity
Mongolia	Ulan Bato	Tugrik	Mongolian	Buddhism
Montserrat	Plymouth	E.C.Dollar	English	Christianity
Montenegro (192nd)	**Cetirrje**	**Euro**	**English, Italian & German**	**Christianity**
Morocco	Rabat	Dirham	Arabic, Bergar French	Islam
Mozambique	Maputo	Metical	Portuguese & Bantu	Islam Christianity
Myanmar	Yangoon	Kyat	Burmese	Buddhism
Namibia	Windhoek	Rand	English & Afrikaans, German	Christianity
Nauru	Yaren	Australian Dollar	English & Nauruan	Christianity
Nepal	Kathmandu	Nepalese Rupee	Nepali	Hinduism & Buddhism
Netherlands	Amsterdam	Euro	Dutch	Christianity
New Zealand	Wellington	Newzea-land Dollar	English & Maori	Christianity
Nicaragua	Managua	Cordoba	Spanish & English	Christianity
Niger	Niamey	Franc CFA	French	Islam and Tribal
Nigeria	Abuja	Naira	English Hausa, Ibo & Yoruba	Islam, Christianity & Tribal
Norway	Oslo	Kroner	Norwegian	Lutheranism
Oman	Muscat	Rial Omani	Arabic	Islam

Country	Capital	Currency	Language	Religion
Pakistan	Islamabad	Rupee	Urdu, Sindhi & Punjabi	Islam
Panama	Panama City	Balboa	Spanish & English	Christianity
Papua New Guinea	Port Morseby	Kina	Melanesian English	Christianity
Paraguay	Asuncion	Guarani	Spanish & Guarani	Christianity
Peru	Lima	Sol	Spanish & Quechua	Christianity
Philippines	Manila	Peso	Filipino	Christianity & Islam
Poland	Warsaw	Zloty	Polish	Christianity
Portugal	Lisbon	Euro	Portuguese	Christianity
Puerto Rico	San Juan	US Dollar	Spanish & English	Christianity
Qatar	Doha	Riyal	Arabic & English	Islam
Romania	Bucharest	Leu	Romanian	Christianity
Russia	Moscow	Rouble	Russian	Christianity & Islam
Rwanda	Kigali	Franc	French & Kinyarwanda	Tribal, Islam & Christianity
Samoa (Western)	Apia	Tala	Samoan & English	Christianity
San Marino	San Marino	Italian Lira	Italian	Christianity
Sao Tome and Principe	Sao Tome	Dobra	Portuguese	Christianity
Saudi Arabia	Riyadh (Royal) & Jeddah (Adminis-trative)	Saudi Rial	Arabic	Islam
Senegal	Dakar	CFA Franc	French	Islam,
Seychelles	Victoria	Rupee	Creole, French & English	Christianity
Sierra Leone	Freetown	Leone	English & Tribal	Islam & Christianity
Singapore	Singapore City	Singapore Dollar	Chinese, Malaya, Tamil	Multi Religions
Slovakia	Bratislava	Koruna	Slovak & Hungarian	Christianity & Jews

Country	Capital	Currency	Language	Religion
Slovenia	Ljubljana	Tolar	Slovenian & Serbo-Croatian	Christianity
Solomon	Honiara	Solomon Dollar	English & Pidgin	Christianity
Somalia	Mogadishu	Shilling	Somali & English	Islam
South Africa	Cape Town & Pretoria	Rand	Afrikaans & English	Christianity, Hinduism, & Islam
Spain	Madrid	Euro	Spanish	Christianity
Sri Lanka	Colombo	Sri Lanka Rupee	Sinhala, Tamil & English	Buddhism & Hinduism
St. Kitts Nevis	Basseterre	E.C.Dollar	English & Patois	Christianity
St.Lucia	Castries	E.C.Dollar	English & Patois	Christianity
St.Vincent and Grena Dines	Kingstown	E.C.Dollar	English & French Patois	Christianity
Sudan	Khartoum	Sudanese Pound	Arabic, English & Tribal dialects	Islam & Christianity
Suriname	Parmaribo	Suriname Guilder	Dutch, English & Surinamese	Islam & Hinduism Christianity
Swaziland	Mbabane	Lilangeni	English & Swazi	Christianity and Tribal
Sweden	Stockholm	Krona	Swedish	Lutheranism
Switzerland	Berne	Swiss Franc	German, French, Italian	Christianity
Syria	Damascus	Syrian Pound	Arabic	Islam
Taiwan	Taipei	New Taiwan Dollar	Mandarin Chinese	Buddhism, Taoism & Confucianism
Tanzania	Dodoma	Tanzanian Shilling	Swahili & English	Christianity & Islam
Thailand	Bangkok	Baht	Thai, Chinese & English	Buddhism

Country	Capital	Currency	Language	Religion
Togo	Lome	CFA Franc	French (official) & Tribal	Christianity, Tribal & Islam
Tonga	Nuku' alofa	Pa'anga	English & Tongon	Christianity
Trinidad & Tobago	Port-of-Spain	Trinidad Tobago Dollar	English	Christianity & Hinduism
Tunisia	Tunis	Tunisian Dinar	Arabic (official) & French	Islam
Turkey	Ankara	Turkish Lira	Turkish	Islam
Turkmenistan	Ashkhabad	Manat	Turkmen & Russian	Islam
Tuvalu	Funafuti	Australian Dollar	Tuvaluan& English	Christianity
U.A.E.	Abu Dhabi	Dirham	Arabic	Islam
Uganda	Kampala	Uganda Shilling	English & Luganda	Christianity & Islam
Ukraine	Kiev	Karbovanets	Ukrainian	Christianity & Islam
United Kingdom	London	Euro	English, Welsh & Scots	Christianity
United States of America	Washington (D.C.)	U.S. Dollar	English	Christianity
Volta	Ouagadougou	Franc	French & Native languages	Tribal & Islam
Uruguay	Montevideo	Uruguayan Peso	Spanish	Christianity
Uzbekistan	Tashkent	Ruble & Som	Uzbek & Russian	Islam
Vanuatu	Port Vila	Vatu	English & Pidgin	Christianity
Vatican City	Vatican City	Lira	Italian & Latin	Christianity
Venezuela	Caracas	Bolivar	Spanish	Christianity
Vietnam	Hanoi	Dong	Vietnamese	Buddhism & Taoism
Yemen (N)	Sana'a	Rial	Arabic	Islam
Yugoslavia	Belgrade	Dinar	Serbo-croatian	Christianity & Islam

Country	Capital	Currency	Language	Religion
Zaire	Kinshasa	Zaire	French, English & Swahili	Christianity
Zambia	Lusaka	Kwacha	Bantu & English	Christianity & Islam
Zimbabwe	Harare	Dollar	English & Shona	Tribal & Christianity

TERMINOLOGY - GENERAL

Abdication: Leaving the throne by a king in favour of somebody.

Accrual bond: A bond on which interest accrues, but is not paid to the investor during the time of accrual. The amount of accrued interest is added to the remaining principal of the bond and is paid at maturity.

Actuals: The physical commodity underlying a future contract.

Ad hoc Committee: A committee constituted for a special purpose.

Adult Franchise: Right of voting for all adults irrespective of education, sex, caste, creed, etc.

Ad-Valorem tax: An indirect tax which is expressed as a proportion of the price of a commodity. (e.g.) salex tax.

Affidavit: A written declaration of oath.

Aggression: If a country makes an actual attack or creates by its agencies internal trouble in another country, it is termed as aggression.

Agricultural Revolution: The transition from feudal to modern farming practices is referred to as agricultural revolution.

Air Pollution: It means fouling up of the atmosphere as a result of discharge into it, of noxious and even poisonous fumes, produced by automotive transportation, industries, nuclear explosions etc.

Alma mater: Is the university or school where one was or is educated. The phrase actually means 'foster mother'.

Allegiance: Remaining faithful to a king or a state.

Ambassador: The highest diplomatic representative of one country to another.

Amnesty: General pardon given to prisoners on some important days such as Republic day, Independence day and Gandhiji's Birthday.

Amortization: In finance, the term denotes repayment of a debt by monthly instalments which include part of the principal and interest due. In accounting, amortization means writing off an account pending over a number of years.

Anachronism: Assigning a thing or an event to an earlier period.

Anarchism: Prevalance of disorder in a country.

Antidilutive effect: Result of a transaction that increases earnings per common share (for example, by decreasing the number of shares outstanding).

Anti-Semitism: Opposition of Jews.

Antyodaya: It is a socio-economic scheme to banish poverty.

Apartheid: In African language apartheid denotes racial segregation of black people. It is rather a discrimination practised by the white people in some African countries especially in South Africa.

Appeasement: The policy of constantly trying to placate the neighbour country and keep at bay the forces of belligerency.

Appropriation request: Formal request for funds for capital investment project.

Armistice: Cessation of hostilities between two countries and establishment of peace.

ARMs *(Adjustable rate mortgage):* A mortgage that features predetermined adjustments of the loan interest rate at regular intervals based on an established index. The interest rate is adjusted at each interval to a rate equivalent to the index value plus a predetermined spread, or margin, over the index, usually subject to par-interval and to life-of-loan interest rate and/or payment rate.

Asian Currency Units (ACUs): Dollar deposits held in Singapore or other Asian centers.

Ask: This is the quoted ask, or the lowest price an investor will accept to sell a stock. Practically speaking, this is the quoted offer at which an investor can buy shares of stock; also called the offer price.

Ask price: A dealer's price to sell a security; also called the offer price.

Asset for asset swap: Creditors exchange the debt of one defaulting borrower for the debt of another defaulting borrower.

Asylum: A place of refuge or protection.

Autonomy: Right of self-government.

Automation: Energising machines in industry so that they run automatically.

Back-to-back financing: An inter-company loan channeled through a bank.

Back-to-back loan: A loan in which two companies in separate countries borrow each other's currency for a specific time period and repay the other's currency at an agreed time upon maturity.

Baker Plan: A plan by U.S. Treasury Secretary James Baker under which 15 principal middle-income debtor countries (the Baker 15) would undertake growth-oriented structural reforms, to be supported by increased financing from the World Bank and continued lending from commercial banks.

Bank line: Line of credit granted by a bank to a customer.

Bandh: Closure of all business activities and paralysing normal life in order to express the popular depth of feeling and grievance.

Balance of Power: Maintaining two countries with equal power in order to avoid war.

Balance of Trade: The difference between visible exports and imports of a country. If the difference is positive, it is known as favourable balance of trade and if it is negative, it is known as unfavourable balance of trade.

Ballot: Secret voting.

Balloon maturity: Any large principal payment due at maturity for a bond or loan with or without a sinking fund requirement.

Bamboo Curtain: No free exit and free accessibility. The Chinese practise it.

Bank Rate: It is the rate of interest charged by the Reserve Bank of India for lending money to commercial banks.

Bar: Slang for one million dollars.

Barter: Direct exchange of commodities, as opposed to exchange of goods or money.

Basic Education: Besides studying, teaching of handicrafts such as weaving, stitching, etc.

Bear market: Any market in which prices are in a declining trend.

Bear raid: A situation in which large traders sell positions with the intention of driving prices down.

Begger-thy-neighbour: An international trade policy of competitive devaluations and increased protective barriers where one country seeks to gain at the expense of its trading partners.

Begger-thy-neighbour devaluation: A devaluation that is designed to cheapen a nation's currency and thereby increase its exports at other countries' expense and reduce imports. Such devaluations often lead to trade wars.

Bhoodan (Bhoo-land, dan-donation): Free and voluntary land gift movement started by Vinoba Bhave on April 18, 1951. The movement started first in Andhra Pradesh.

Big Four: France, Britain, U.S.A. and U.S.S.R.

Bilateral: Something which involves two; e.g., bilateral treaties.

Bill of Rights: English charter of freedom, signed in 1688 by William II after the Glorious Revolution.

Blackmail: Extraction of money or some favour by threat of defamation or physical violence.

Black Money: Money earned and hoarded unscrupulously in order to avoid tax.

Black Market: Selling the goods at a higher price by creating artificial scarcity.

Blockade: Encircling of a harbour of an enemy country by ship so that, the country cannot have any external communication through sea.

Blue Chip: This is the common stock of a large, reputed corporation which has a stable and least risky growth path.

Blue-Print: Preliminary sketch of a plan.

Blue-stocking: This term refers to the educated women in England.

Blood Bank: It is a storing place of reserve blood kept for emergency transfusion.

Bolshevism: A form of communism.

Bond: It is a certificate issued by a government or a business company promising to pay back with interest, the money it has borrowed.

Book Value: The cash of the physical assets of a company, minus the liabilities payable to the debenture holders, represents the book value of the assets.

Boom: It is a period of rapid economic growth, when production, consumption, and employment are high and growing. A boom is also called a period of prosperity.

Bootlegging: Dealing in prohibited goods, especially wine and liquors.

Borstal School: Penal reformatory, where juvenile delinquents or young offenders are given education and industrial training to wean them from crime.

Bourgeois: The term which originally referred to middle class as applied to rich people.

Braille: System of reading and writing for the blind.

Brain drain: Talented men leaving one country for lack of opportunities and facilities and going away to foreign countries which provide better conditions. This kind of one way traffic of intellectuals is known as brain drain.

Brain-trust: A small group of specialists and intelligent people who advise the government on important policies and other matters.

Budget: Annual financial statement of revenues and expenditure.

Brain-washing: Making a person change his views by physical violence or mental torture.

Buffer state: It is a small neutral independent state existing between two enemy countries which prevents any accidental flare up.

Buffer stock: It is the stock of foodgrains or other commodities hoarded to meet any emergency.

Bureaucracy: A term which refers to official domination at government level.

Buyer's market: If a buyer gets the goods in the market at the prices he choose, it is said that the buyer's market is existing.

Cabinet: Small group of ministers holding important portfolios, responsible to the legislature for good government.

Carrot and Stick Policy: It is a policy of motivating the people on distant objects by the promise of reward for obedience and punishment for refusal.

Camcorder: It is a portable video camera with a built-in videotape recording.

Capital: It refers to factories, equipment, and property, other than land, that can be used to produce wealth. It also means money used to buy these things.

Capital Goods: These are goods that can be used to produce more goods in the future.

Capitalism: It is a system under which the private enterprise has complete freedom over control, production for their own profit.

Cartel: One method of monopoly formation is "cartelisation", decide on a common price policy, marketing control of output etc.

Casting Vote: The vote of the chairman in case of a tie.

CD-ROM: Stands for Compact Disk-Read Only Memory. (Also see Compact Disc).

Cellular Telephone: It is a movable telephone unit. It allows people to communicate over a wide area by using a combination of radio, telephone, and computer technology.

Census: Official enumeration of the population of a country and statistics related to them under various calculations.

Censure Motion: No confidence motion on a minister or ministers.

Central Planning: It is an economic model that calls for government control of all important economic activities.

Certiorari: It is a writ petition by which cases are removed from inferior courts to a High Court of Justice.

Charge d'affairs: A diplomatic representative lower to the rank of Ambassador.

Chauvinism: Aggressive regional patriotism, e.g., Linguistic Chauvinism.

Civil Disobedience: Violating Civil laws in a peaceful manner.

Citizens Band Radio: It is a method of short-distance communication used by private citizens.

Chilblain: In cold weather, persons with poor circulation generally suffer from chilblain which causes swelling in the toes and fingers, nose and ears.

Clearing House: Organisation of banks in city where cheques against one another are adjusted and balances are settled.

Coalition: Two or more parties joining together to form government.

Co-existence: Maintaining cordial relations with one another.

Cold war: It is an undeclared war with hostile preparations, short of physical confrontation.

Cod war: It was an issue between England and Iceland over fishing in the sea water between the two countries.

Collectivism: Theory of State Ownership, it is a creed of socialism and communism.

Compact Disc: CD is to store recorded stereophonic sound.

Confederation: Combination of States for a particular purpose. Units of a confederation enjoy more freedom than of a federation.

Confrontation: To come face to face. The word is also used to describe the situation where armies of two countries on the brink of war stand facing each other.

Consensus: Trend of opinion or sense of the House. Sometimes, in order to avoid an open split, the Chairman of a meeting studies the trend of the House to decide a point.

Conspicuous Consumption: Spending many lavishly on luxuries in order to project an image of prosperity and to show off in society.

Consumer Goods and Services: Goods and services produced for current use by the individuals and families, such as food, clothing, medical care and education.

Consumption Tax: It is a levy on consumer goods. The objective of such a tax is not only to raise revenue but, sometimes, it is also designed to regulate consumption and even production. Sales tax, excise duties etc. are illustrations.

Containment: It means to hold in check. For example, the U.S.A. followed for many years a policy of containment of China in South-East Asia. Following that policy, it has tried to prevent Communist China from establishing a dominant position in South-East Asia.

Convention: Conference of representative persons delegated to discuss or decide certain important questions.

Condominium: Joint sovereignty exercised over a country by other countries, e.g., Sudan was under Anglo-Egyptian condominium until 1956.

Constitution: Supreme law of a country.

Copyright: Right of an author to his work rendering its infringement actionable.

Contraband: Goods banned by international law for sale by neutrals to belligerents.

Constituency: Electoral district.

Corporation: It is a business organization formed and owned by a number of people. These people are known as stockholders.

Cost of living Index: A figure showing the prevailing cost of living as compared with that in a particular year which is taken as the base year to which the number 100 is assigned.

Coup-de-etat: Sudden change of government generally by violent means. Coup actually means stroke; but it is usually applied to an attempt to seize the government by force.

Crossed Cheque: As distinguished from "bearer" or "order" cheques, crossed cheques are not paid at the counter, but have to be passed through accounts of the payee or of the person to whom the payee endorses such a cheque.

Curfew: A martial law measure forbidding any movement during a period especially of riots.

Cybernetics: Science of the analysis of the brain, its structure and functions and applying the principles for the production of mechanical brains such as computers.

Cyberspace: A computer generated landscape which is actually not there. When you connect your computer to cyberspace, it opens up and you can do a wide variety of things.

Cryogenics: A branch of physics dealing with the production of low temperatures and their effect.

Customs Duty: The tax levied on imported and exported goods.

Dakhma: Tower of Silence where the Parsis place the dead bodies for vultures to eat. The Parsis do not bury or cremate the dead bodies.

Death Duty or Estate Duty: Tax payable on property by the inheritor when the owner dies.

Defection: Changing from one party to another.

Deficit Financing: When the expenditure exceeds the revenue and the gap left unfulfilled, it is called deficit financing.

Deflation: When there is a scarcity of money supply, deflation occurs and consequently the prices of commodities fall down.

Democratic State: Government through representatives elected by the people.

Demonetisation: Divesting money of its value by withdrawing from circulation.

Detente: The end of strained relations between two countries.

Devaluation: Reducing the value of home currency in relation to foreign currency. So, export of goods to other countries is also increased.

Dharna: A form of protest by an aggrieved person or a group of persons occupying a vantage point.

Dictatorship: One man rule.

Dialectic Materialism: A communist doctrine that progress involves 3 factors, thesis, antithesis and synthesis and ultimately communism will prevail.

Decree: Decision or judgement having the force of law.

Dividend: Share of the profits allotted to each share in a joint stock company.

Dumping: An economic measure to stifle competitions by selling below cost to get control of the market.

Dollar Diplomacy: It is a U S policy of winning friends by the lure of dollars, e.g., giving aids and loans.

Domino Theory: It is a theory which states that, when a country falls a prey to communism, the neighbouring countries will also follow suit.

Earthlock: Means orientation towards the earth; it is essential for uninterrupted transmission by a geo-synchronous satellite. Earthlock is ensured by the satellite sensors which "feel" the Earth's radiation.

Eco Mark: The ministry of environment in 1990 decided to launch a national scheme to grant "eco mark" on the lines of ISI (for quality) to different products on the basis of their environment friendliness. Similar schemes exist in Germany (Blue Angel), Sweden (White Swan), Canada (Eco Logo) and Japan.

E-Mail: Electronically transmitted messages.

Embargo: Ban on arrival and departure of foreign ships.

Encryption: A method of securing privacy on computer networks through use of complex algorithmic codes.

Enrichment: Make richer in quality, flavour, nutritive value, etc.

Envoy: A diplomatic correspondent ranking below the Ambassador.

Equity Capital: Ordinary share capital.

Equity Shares: Equity shares or ordinary shares are those shares the holders who take the maximum risk as there is no guarantee of dividend in their case; that is why equity capital is also called risk capital.

Espionage: Spying-practised by countries to get information on military, scientific and political developments in unfriendly or enemy countries.

Estate Duty: Same as Death Duty.

Extradition: Act of returning political and communal characters living in foreign countries, to their home country in fulfilment of a treaty obligation.

Euthanasia: Mercy-killing. When a person is suffering from fever disease beyond cure, he is put to death to relieve the pain.

Fascism: An Italian political creed developed by Mussolini in which the state represented by one person is supreme and an individual practically has no rights.

Federalism: System of government in which several autonomous states join together and surrender some important powers such as defence, foreign relation, etc. to the central authority for common good.

Fifth Column: It is a term of abuse denoting to the actions of those who carry on some advantage to the enemy country.

Floor-Crossing: Means changing from one party to another in the legislature.

Four-freedoms: Freedom of speech, freedom of worship, freedom from want and freedom from fear, propagated first by US President Roosevelt.

Fourth Estate: The press is known as the fourth estate, the other three estates being the King, the Church and the Parliament.

Free-port: It is a port where there are no duties payable on commercial goods to encourage transport. Kandla is a free port.

Fundamental Rights: Basic human rights of individual in a civilised country. In India these rights are justiciable.

Gallup Poll: It is one of the leading public opinion surveying system whose organizations in the United States are located in Princeton, New Jersey. It is named after 69-year-old Dr.George H.Gallup, who had founded the American Institute of Public Opinion in 1935.

Genocide: Deliberate mass killing of a racial, religious, social or political group in order to root it out.

Gentleman's Agreement: It is an informal agreement based on good faith.

Gherao: The illegal confinement of persons in authority by the agitators.

Gift-Tax: It is a tax on gifts to prevent tax evasion.

Gold Bonds: They were issued in 1962 to bring out hoarded gold. It entitles the holder to surrender gold to the government without having to account for it and receive the same quantity of gold after 15 years. It is exempted from gift and wealth tax upto 5 kilograms.

Golden Handshake: Retrenchment compensation given to workers is popularly known as "golden handshake".

Good Offices: It is mediation efforts by a third country between two belligerents.

Green-revolution: It refers to the spectacular increase in the yield of crop plants. It has been possible through the use of improved techniques of agriculture. The adoption of modern technical know-how such as chemical fertilisers, tractors, pesticides, etc., in agriculture to maximise the production.

Green Room: The place of accommodation for actors and actresses when off-stage.

Guerilla-war: It is an irregular war waged by independent groups.

Habeas corpus: It is a writ petition by which the prisoner gets the right to appear in person and to be tried in a court.

Hansard: Parliamentary reports of U.K.

Hard currency: It is foreign exchange which is very difficult to get.

Hartal: It is a symbol of protest, closing all local business and sometimes transport to express grievances usually voluntarily.

Harakiri: It means committing suicide by disembowelment of bowels practised in Japan.

Hashish: It is an intoxicating drug made of the leaves, shoots or resin of hemp or bhang.

Hawk: The term used to describe persons who favour war-like national policies.

Hijacking: Illegal diversion of vehicle by threatening the crew at gunpoint. Skyjacking means illegal diversion of an aeroplane at gunpoint.

High Commissioner: Ambassadors of Commonwealth countries are known as High Commissioners.

Home Guards: (India) Voluntary force for home defence in India.

Hot Line: Direct communication between two powers of nations such as Russia and USA. Instrument of international diplomacy.

Hot Money: Money or currency which everybody is anxious to drop for fear of a fall in its exchange rate.

Hydrosphere: It is area occupied by the ocean of the earth.

Impeachment: Prosecution of high officials such as the President, Chief Justice and other Judges of Supreme Court for serious offences against the Constitution.

I.M.F.: Means "International Monetary Fund". It is an organisation of the United Nations established with the object of stabilising the currency of member Nations by promoting exchange arrangements and eliminating unnecessary foreign exchange restrictions.

Inflation: Excess money in circulation and deficiency in goods leading to high prices and distress conditions.

Injunction: The judicial restraint order to prevent a wrongful act.

International Law: Rules governing the relations between civilised countries administered by the International Court of Justice. It deals with some important matters such as POWs and those wounded in war, contraband goods, blockade, etc.

Interpol: International Police Criminal Investigation Centre in which more than 90 countries are members. The HO is Lyons in Paris. It tracks and apprehends criminals operating internationally and evading arrests.

Iron Curtain: Russian policy of secrecy, preventing free contact with the external world. The term was used first by Winston Churchill.

Interpellation: Raising a question in the Legislature from a Minister on a matter of public importance.

Jettisoning: Throwing cargo away from a ship or an aircraft in times of danger to reduce the load.

Joint Council: A small body consisting of members from managements and representatives of labour to discuss some labour problems.

Kuomintang: It is Nationalist China, other name is Formosa under Chiang-Kai-Shek.

Khedda: Trapping and taming operations against wild elephants in forests.

Leftist: A term applied to Communists and Socialists. They advocate liberal and progressive ideas in politics.

Legal Tender: Money in accepted form which a creditor cannot refuse to accept in payment of a debt.

Legation: A diplomatic mission lower in status than embassy.

Liberalism: It is a political policy advocating free trade, religious liberty, etc.

Limited Company: Registered trading body in which liability of the members is limited to their shares.

Lobbying: Influencing by persuasion and pressure other legislators for their support in an important legislative matter usually conducted in lobby.

Lock-out: Voluntary closure of a business or factory by the employers where there is a labour dispute and fear of damage to machinery and property by the employees.

Mandamus: It is a superior court's order to a lower court.

Manifesto: Declaration of policies and intentions issued by a political party.

Marshall Plan: A programme of economic aid to war-torn Europe, also called the European Recovery Programme, sponsored by George C.Marshall, U.S. Secretary of State in 1947.

May Day: First of May of every year celebrated as the worker's day with slogan, "Workers of the world unite"

Mediation: It is a friendly intervention of third party to settle disputes between two parties in an amicable manner.

Mendelian Law: The principle of hybridisation discovered by Gregory Mendel, an Austrian monk. According to the law, if two different species are sexually united and if a hybrid is born, it will show the characteristics of the parent.

Micro-economics: It is a branch of economics concerned with the activities of individual consumers and producers.

Mid-term Poll: A mid-term poll is an election held out of schedule as a result of the dissolution of a State legislature before it has been in existence for its normal span of life.

Modem: The device that allows a computer to transmit information over a phone line.

Money Market: Field for the investment of money is termed as money market.

Monopoly: It exists when there is only one seller of a product in a market.

Mixed Economy: Economic policy of giving equal opportunity to private and public sectors for full development in their respective spheres.

Money Bill: It is a finance bill introduced in legislative assembly, e.g., Budget, etc.

Munro Doctrine: U.S. policy of mutual non-intervention between European countries and American countries.

Most Favoured Nations: Friendly nations which give mutual grant of tariff concession among them to promote trade expansion.

Motel: It is a large hotel for touring motorists providing all hotel facilities and garage accommodation for vehicles.

National Debt: It is the money borrowed by the country when it is unable to meet its own expenditure from its own resources.

Nationalisation: When the private ownership is taken over by the Government it is said to be nationalised. In capitalist countries, nationalisation is not a policy of the Government. But it is a general policy in socialist countries.

National Income: According to Marshall, national income is defined as "the labour and capital of a country acting on its natural resources, produce annually a certain net aggregate commodities material and immaterial, including services of all kind".

Naturalisation: Granting to a foreigner the privileges of its own citizens by the country. After naturalisation the foreigner becomes the citizen of the country.

Nautical mile: It is a unit of distance measurement in navigation. A nautical mile is approximately equal to 6080 ft. or 1854 metres.

Naxalites: The radical Communists who believe in brute force and in the type of revolution reached by Mao, are given the name Naxalites. They tried to launch a revolution nation-wide by exploiting the feelings of discontentment and poverty of the people. The first attempt of such a kind of revolution was made in Naxalbari, a place in West Bengal in 1967. The word Naxalites, is derived, from Naxalbari.

Nazism: The expansion of Nazism is National Socialism. Nazi was the name of the party led by Adolf Hitler in the thirties of the present century. Nazis persecuted the Jews. They believed in the supremacy of the Aryan race.

Need based Wages: The wages determined to cover the basic needs of the wage earners. The wages are not determined on the basis of the pure availability of labour productivity and profitability.

Neo-Colonialism: The neo-colonialism namely economic colonialism which still exists even after the disappearance of political colonialism by countries which try to control the affairs of under-developed countries by giving economic assistance.

Nippon: It is Japanese name for Japan. The term simply signifies Japan.

Node: Any device that is connected to a computer network.

Non-aggression Pact: It is an agreement reached between two countries not to wage war on each other. This pact may include a clause that they should take collective action when a third country attacks on either of them.

Nuclear Umbrella: It refers to the protection offered by a country against nuclear attack. America guaranteed nuclear umbrella to India in 1962 when the Chinese made aggression.

Nyaya Panchayat: These are the judicial bodies in the Panchayat Raj system. These Nyaya Panchayats have only limited power of punishment. Some disputes are decided by these bodies. They do not have judicial value.

Octroi: It is a form of tax levied on goods entering a municipal town. The tax thus collected is generally used for the maintenance of the town.

Oligarchy: Means government by a small exclusive class.

Open University: University wherein students are free to join, leave and rejoin at any stage in their education which is organized as a continuing process. One such University has been functioning in the U.K. for some time now.

Old Glory: This name refers to the flag of the U.S.A.

Open Door Policy: It is a trade policy according to which a country should be open on equal terms to all nations.

Ordinance: It is a measure having the force of law promulgated by the head of a state in his own authority to meet an emergency.

Ostopolitik: This German word was brought into use by West Germany to describe its new approach to the Communist countries of Eastern Europe. For this policy of ostopolitik Mr.Willy Brandt, the then Chancellor of West Germany was awarded Nobel peace prize in 1972.

Output: It is the quantity produced by a labourer or turned out by a machine.

Party Whip: It refers to the member in the Legislature. He issues directives to his party members specifying how they must vote or act in a certain contingency.

Pentagon: It refers to the building in Washington. It houses all war offices of the U.S.A. The building is neither square nor rectangle shaped, but it is pentagonal (five cornered).

Personality Cult: When a leader is idolised by the people, the personality cult results in. Though it helps the leader so idolised run the administration as he would like by the sheer effectiveness of his personality, sometimes it devises a way for dictatorship of some degree.

Persona Non Grata: It denotes a diplomat who is not acceptable to the country to which he is sent. Sometimes diplomats are declared persona non grata and asked to leave the country.

Planetarium: It is a device to show the motions and orbits of the planetary bodies.

Plebiscite or Referendum: It refers to the direct vote by the people on a controversial question.

Point of Order: It is a term used in legislative business. When a question is raised to get the decision on whether the proceedings are according to the rules, the point of order is said to have been raised.

Polaris: It is nuclear weapon.

Plutocracy: It denotes the Governments by the wealthy people.

Plenipotentiary: It refers to diplomatic official with full powers for assignment.

Oligarchy: It is Government by a few influential people.

Ombudsman: Is a vigilance officer with very wide powers to hold and protect the common men against official oppression. It is an institution created in Sweden. On this line, the Administrative Reforms Commission has recommended the appointments of Lokpal at the centre and Lok Ayukts in the states.

Polarisation: In science, polarisation means the separation of positive and negative charges of a molecule. In politics, when the like-minded parties join together, it is said that the parties have polarised.

Police State: When there is no individual freedom in a state, it is known as police state.

Political Sabotage: It means wiping out political opponent by any means.

Politburo: It is the name given to the central organ of the Communist party. It is the abbreviation of political bureau.

Population Explosion: When there is sudden increase of population it is referred as population explosion.

Power Politics: In politics when the sole aim becomes the capture of power neglecting the welfare of the people it is known as power politics.

Preamble: It is the introductory part especially of the constitution. It explains the aims and sometimes the ways to achieve them.

Preference Share: Shares or stocks whose entitlement to dividend takes priority over that of the ordinary shares.

Price Index: It is a figure which discloses the relative change in prices between one period and the other period of time selected as the base year. The base year is assigned to the index number of 100.

If a comparison is made between the cost of living between one period and the other it is known as cost of living index.

Privy Purses: These were the certain privileges and annual payments granted to the Rulers of Princely States which were in existence before independence. These practices continued even after independence. Now these privy purses and annual payments have been discontinued (see the 26th Amendment of our Constitution).

Primary Gold: Gold of the highest purity i.e., 24 carats.

Prohibition: It is a measure banning the sale and consumption of alcoholic drinks. Now in India, in all states except Gujarat, the prohibition has been scrapped.

Prize Court: It is a court set up by a country at war to settle disputes regarding enemy ships seized on the high seas during war.

Proportional Representation: This system is in operation in the election of the President of India. The President of India is elected by an electoral college consisting of the elected members of the Lok Sabha and Rajya Sabha and those of the Legislative Assemblies of States. Each member of the college represents the wider base of the electorate. Each member commands a number of votes in proportion to the number of electors he represents.

Prorogation: The prorogation of legislature means the discontinuance of its meetings for a time without being dissolved. The prorogation is ordered by the Governor as far as the state legislature is concerned and by the President so far as the Parliament is concerned.

Protocol: It refers to the first draft of a diplomatic or international agreements or treaties.

Proxy: Means one who acts for another or the agency of one acting as such.

Psephology: Sociological and statistical study of election results and trends.

Public Debt: It is the money borrowed by the government from the public in the shape of different funds.

Public Provident Fund: According to this scheme introduced on July 1, 1968, an individual contributes to the fund a sum between Rs.10/- and Rs.15,000/- per year. It is exempted from income tax. It will not be subjected to attachment even if the person goes bankrupt.

Public Sector: It denotes the sector financed, managed and completely controlled by the Government.

Quarantine: It refers to the compulsory isolation or detention to prevent spread of disease of an infectious or contagious nature.

Quorum: It denotes the minimum number of persons necessary to transact a business.

Quo Warranto: It is one of the five writs. It is a direction to the proper authorities to enquire into the circumstances under which any office or franchise was held.

Red Dollar: It is the name of the common currency proposed to be introduced, among the members of 'COMECON' to achieve full convertibility of all currencies within the area covered by the organisation.

Red Guards: It is the name assumed in China by the youngsters who had spearheaded the cultural revolution. They wear khaki uniforms with red armbands and enforce the ideas of Mao.

Red Tape: It is the official formality which results in unncessary delay.

Reds: The Communist countries are known as Reds.

Repatriation: It refers to the return to the native lands. It was much in use regarding the repatriation of prisoners of war from India to Pakistan and vice versa.

Republics: It is a political term which refers to the state which is not governed by any Regent or King but by the elected representatives of the people.

Revanchism: It means desire to seek revenge. This was a charge brought by all Communist countries on West Germany. West Germany was accused of making preparations with a view to engage in war against those who had defeated Germany in the Second World war.

Reverse Preferences: These are the preferences in trade given by the members of the E.C.M. to some African countries.

Rotel: It means a Rolling Hotel. It is a three decker bus. The first deck provides sitting accommodation and second and third decks provide sleeping accommodation.

Sanctions: It is a penalty or reward attached to non-observance or observance of law or a treaty. Economic sanctions were announced on South Africa by the U.N.O.

Sarvodaya: It means uplift towards welfare of all. The movement was started by Vinoba Bhave. It aims at non-violent socio-economic revolution.

Secular State: It is the state which recognises no particular religion. It debars discrimination on the grounds of race, religion, creed, sex, etc. India is a secular state while Pakistan is a theocratic state.

Self-generating Economy: If the economy of a country moves without any external assistance, it is known as self-generating economy.

Sit-down Strike: It is a form of strike in which employees do not carry on any work though they come to offices. It is also called pen down strike.

Snap Poll: Snap poll means a sudden election to a legislature held at short notice before the expiry of its full term.

Socialistic Pattern of Society: It is a society where equal distribution of economic power and reduction of inequalities are ensured. The Congress at its Avadi Session in 1955 passed the resolution of a 'Socialistic Pattern of Society'.

Soft Loan: A loan advanced on easy terms with regard to interest, repayment etc.

Stagflation: A state of inflation without a corresponding increase of demand and employment.

Sterling Area: It refers to the countries which keep their exchange in sterling instead of gold. Most of them are Commonwealth countries.

Stop Press: It is a special space left in a newspaper which is going to be just printed, for last minute insertion of any important news.

Summit Conference: It is the meeting of heads of two or more countries to deal with certain important matters.

Super Tax: It is a special tax levied on income. It is levied in addition to income tax.

Surrender Value: It means the value acquired by an insurance policy when it is surrendered to the insurer.

Take off Stage: It is a stage of economic development and rapid economic uplift.

Tariff Board: It is a board of members constituted by the Government to look after the industries and make recommendation for their sound functioning.

Tax Evasion: Failing to report income or improperly claiming deductions that are not authorised.

Tax Incidence: It denotes who actually pay taxes. If land lords or businesses have the ability to pass on taxes in the form of price and rent hikes, the tax incidence falls on someone else.

Territorial Waters (12 Nauticle miles): It refers to the limit of the water in the sea immediately adjacent to the shore of a state. The jurisdiction of that state over this limit is absolute.

Three Ms: These stands for men, material and money.

Time Capsule: Describes metallic cylinders filled with memorabilia and buried deep in the earth so that after a few thousand years, if somebody discovers such a capsule, he should be reminded of what life and times were like when the 'time capsule' had been initially buried.

Trade Mark: It is the name, sign or mark given to a particular product by the company. Trade marks should not be copied. Infringement of this is punishable.

Turnover: It denotes the total amount of money changing the hands in a business.

Ultimatum: It is the final term before a certain course of action is taken.

Universal Suffrage: It is right of voting given to all those who have attained the minimum prescribed age. It involves no discrimination on grounds of race, religion, caste, sex, etc.

Value-Added Tax (VAT): A tax on the value added is termed VAT. The principle governing this tax is that the person paying for goods or services pays a tax thereon and also collects tax on his sales. The net effect of this tax is that the tax paid is credited against tax collected and only the balance is payable to the taxing authority.

Veto: Right of executive head to refuse to approve any legislation.

Viet Cong: Otherwise called National Liberation Front are South Vietnamese communists who fought against U.S. intervention in their country.

Visa: A visa is evidence of permission to enter the issuing State under specified conditions and for a specified time.

Wealth-tax: Tax levied on wealth possessed by an individual.

Whip: (in the legislature) An M.P. responsible to his party for the organisation of the members to carry the vote through.

White Flag: It is a sign of surrender in battle by any of the opposing armies.

Write off: While book-keeping it is to cancel an unrealizable credit as a bad debt.

Yellow Peril: The fear that Oriental yellow races, particularly the Chinese will one day overwhelm the white races and dominate the world.

Yoga: Literally means "union" (or in unison with the divine spirit).

Young Turks: The term is generally used to describe youthful dissidents or hardliners in a party.

Zionism: Literally pertaining to the Jews.

SCIENCE
SCIENTIFIC GLOSSARY

Absolute Zero: On the temperature scale is the lowest temperature theoretically possible. The theoretical point is equivalent to 459.6°F or -273.16°C or 0°K at which all molecular motion stops.

Acceleration (LT^{-2}): It is defined as the rate of change of velocity of a body. It is a vector unit.

Acupuncture: It is an ancient technique of deademicy pain. The principle is that there are about 500 places in the body at which if needles are struck a numbing effect is produced.

Air Pollution: It means fouling up of the atmosphere as a result of discharge into it of noxious and even poisonous fumes produced by automotive transportation, industrial wastes, nuclear explosion, etc.

Alchemy: It is a branch of chemistry seeking to turn baser metals into gold and silver.

Algae: Lower plants in which there is no distinction of stem, root and leaf. They differ from Fungi in that they have chlorophyll and are habitually aquatic.

Allotropy: Existence of a chemical element in two or more forms differing in physical properties but giving rise to identical chemical compounds. Example: Graphite & Diamond.

Amoeba: It is the minutest animal consisting of a single gelatinous cell. Mostly it occurs in soil, yet some species also occur in fresh and stagnant water.

Anabiosis: It is a state of living organism in which as a result of freezing, the biological activity level of tissues and organs is reduced to a stage between life and death. Hibernation among bears, marmots, bats, etc. are examples of anabiosis in nature. In such a state, life does not discontinue, only the rhythm of Cardiac contraction is lessened, and respiration and metabolic processes slow down.

Angiosperm: Are those plants whose seeds are contained in an ovary. These are the true flowering plants.

Anti-Helium Nuclear: Russian scientists have succeeded in obtaining antinucleous of an isotope of Helium-3. The discovery is said to be of particular importance because it confirms the anti-matter theory.

Anti-Matter: It is made of atom consisting of nuclear of anti-protons and anti-neutrons with anti protons orbiting round these nuclear. Stable in itself anti-matter undergoes complete annihilation as soon as it comes into contact with matter. It is said that a collusion between matter and anti-matter would annihilate both in a flash.

Artificial Fertilizer: To enrich the soil for better production natural manures of animals or vegetable matter were used earlier. Now-a-days artificial fertilizer of various chemicals such as sodium nitrate, calcium nitrate, ammonium sulphate, nitroline potassium sulphate, super phosphate, basic slag etc, are used.

Atom : Its picture was first taken by Japanese Professor H.Hashimoto in 1971 with one of the world's biggest electronic microscope.

Atom Bomb: It is the artificial disintegration of Uranium 235. When it is bombarded by neutrons, uranium atoms split up and unfold energy in the form of X-rays, γ-rays, heat rays etc. Energy liberated in these forms plays havoc with animal life and property.

Atomic Energy: Can be produced by disintegration of atoms of certain radio-active elements which can be used for both useful purpose and destructive purpose.

Atomic Fusion: A new technique used by the Russian and USA scientists by heating the hydrogen to millions of degrees at which the atoms will fuse together releasing nuclear energy. This is done by blasting into a bottle of hydrogen gas, an intense beam of electrons carrying a large quantity of energy travelling at a speed close to that of light. In this way the energy in the electrons can be transferred to the hydrogen gas called plasma which, in turn, will become ignited to fusion temperature.

Atomic Pile: It is the original name for a nuclear reactor.

Allergy: It is a condition of altered reactivity in man and other animals to antigenic substances in the environment. Antigenic substances are substances that stimulate the production of antibodies in the body. A common synonym for allergy is hyper-sensitivity.

Analgesic: A drug that relieves pain by raising the pain in the place without disturbing consciousness. Many Analgesics reduce fever. Analgesics are usually divided into two classes: narcotic analgesics and non-narcotic analgesics.

Anaemia: It is a deficiency of red blood cells or haemoglobin or both. When the number of red cells or the amount of haemoglobin within them falls below certain levels, a person is said to be anaemic. Iron is important component in red blood cells.

Anesthesia and Anesthetics: Anesthesia is loss or absence of sensation and anesthetics are agents capable of producing anesthesia. It is induced to spare the patient from pain of surgical operations and it also occurs as a symptom of certain diseases of the brain or spinal cord. Anesthesia must be distinguished from analgesia, which is the loss only of the sense and not pain.

Anopheles: A female mosquitoes, species of which are the only known varieties transmitting malaria. A few anopheles also transmit filariasis and encephalitis.

Antacid: A drug that, on indigestion, neutralizes the hydrochloric acid present in the stomach fluids. The most common antacid is sodium bicarbonate which is used for simple indigestion and heart-burns.

Antibodies and Antigens: Antibodies are complex molecules manufactured in the body of an organism as a reaction to the presence of other complex molecules called antigens. The role of antibodies is primarily defensive; they combine with antigens that enter an organism and they may neutralize possible harmful effects of the antigens.

Antiseptics: Are substances used for the destruction of disease causing and other organisms on the surface of the body or in body cavities accessible from the outside. Antiseptics are in contrast to such agents are the sulfonamides and antibiotics which exert their bacteria killing action within the human and animal organism.

Artificial Respiration: It is the technique of forcing air into and out of the lungs when natural breathing ceases or seriously weakens. It is also used when breathing fails to begin in new born infants. Its aim is not only to supply needed oxygen, but also to get the natural breathing mechanism working normally.

Aorta: The largest artery of the body. The primary function of the aorta is to carry oxygenated blood from the heart to the cells of the body.

Aspirin (Acetyl Salicilic acid): Is one of the drugs most widely used to reduce fevers and to relieve pain. It reduces fever by increasing the blood flow to the surface of the body, thereby promoting sweating and heat loss.

Asthma: A disorder of the lung resulting in difficult breathing characterised by attacks of coughing and shortness of breath and accompanied by an audible wheeze or whistling sound during breathing. In severe attacks there may be varied degree of anosia (oxygen) deficiency.

Astigmatism: A condition of the eye in which part of an object being viewed appears blurred while another part is clear. It is corrected by use of cylindrical lens.

Arthritis: Is a general term used to denote an affliction which may be inflammatory of one or more joints. The symptoms of arthritis vary with the cause but they usually include pain on motion, tenderness, swelling, warmth and stiffness of the involved joints.

Autopsy: Post-mortem. The examination of the body after death. In autopsy, an attempt to ascertain the cause of the death is made.

Alternating Current: An electric current that changes direction at regular intervals. Most modern electricity supply systems provide A.C. currents that change between 50 and 60 times a second.

Ampere: A unit for measuring the amount of electricity flowing through a circuit.

Anticline: An arch-shaped fold in rock formation under which petroleum or natural gas may be lying trapped.

Atom: The smallest part of an element that can take part in a chemical reaction.

Atomic Weight: Weight of an atom of an element expressed on a scale in which the weight of the oxygen atom is exactly 16.

Atomic Number: The number of protons contained within the nucleus of an atom, equal to the number of electrons surrounding the nucleus.

Bacteria: Are one-celled plants that sometimes so small that they can be viewed by an electron microscope only. Some bacteria are free-living; they manufacture their own food. Others live on dead or decaying matter or as parasites on other living organism. Still others cause disease.

Bacillus: A genus of rod-shaped, spore-forming aerobic bacteria of the family. Bacillacese 66, the 25 or more species differentiated relatively few are disease producing. For example, Bacillus anthracis is the causative agent of anthrax.

B.C.G.: Bacillus Calmette Guerin. It is an anti-tuberculosis vaccine. The continuous treatment with this medicine will eradicate the disease.

Bile: A liquid secreted in liver. It emulsifies fat, prevents food from decomposing and forming gas. It helps the digested food to pass along the digestive canal smoothly. It is finally absorbed by the intestines, gets into the blood and helps to keep the body temperature.

Biological Clock: US Ornithologist, Stephen T. Emlen study on varying amounts of day-light and seasonal changes secrete in the bodies of birds, groups of hormones which govern their movements. The researcher is trying to identify these hormones to unravel the mystery of the biological clock carried by all living beings including homo sapiens.

Biometry: It means the application of statistical and mathematical methods to the study of biology.

Bionics (Biology & Electronics): It is the science which investigates the sensory perception of animals and makes use of the information in electronics.

Biopoesis: It is the creation of something that some people might wish to call living from non-living material according to N.W.Pire, who coined the word.

Blue Ice: It is natural ice exported from Greenland. The ice is virtually germ free and is said to be 2,000 to 3,000 years old mainly used by the whisky manufacturers to publicise their product. Recently Greenland is swamped with orders for Blue Ice from 19 countries including USA and Japan.

Burette: It is used in the volumetric analysis to measure the volume of liquid run out of the glass tube from the tap at the bottom.

Bladder: The membranous and muscular sac in animals that receives the urine from kidneys. The word is also used for any similar sac such as the gall bladder, the swim bladder in fishes or the small vesicle in various sea weeds.

Blood Bank: The blood bank, a key organisation in medical care collects, processes and transfuses blood. The first blood bank was established in 1937 at Cook country hospital, Chicago by Bernard Fants.

Blood Group: Blood Groups are biological categories found in man and many other animals. Members of a particular group have in common certain specific substances (antigens) on the red blood cells. The name was applied originally to the four categories of human blood discovered first those with antigen A, those with antigen B, those with both A and B and those with neither. These are four classical blood groups - A, B, AB and O - discovered by Karl Landsteiner in 1903 and found to be of great importance in blood transfusion.

Blood Pressure: Is the pressure exerted by blood against the walls of the arteries. The pressure is created by contractions of the heart and it is this that propels the blood through the blood vessels.

Blood Poisoning: Is a popular term usually referring to septicemia, a condition in which disease producing micro-organisms invade the blood stream. The organisms may gain entry into the blood from a wound even a scratch or during the course of acute infections such as pneumonia or typhoid fever. The micro-organisms and their poisonous products may cause high fever, chills, excessive sweating and weakness.

Battery: A device for producing electricity through chemical action. There are two kinds: (1) Dry battery (flashlight battery) which uses up its chemicals, become exhausted and has to be replaced; (2) The storage battery - this has a chemical action that can be reversed by passing a current through it in the opposite direction of that in which it discharges. Thus the battery can be alternately charged and discharged.

Bronchitis: Is a general term applied to any group of disorders of the tubular air passages that lead to the air sacs of the lung. Although these disorders are produced by several different causes, they have features in common - inflammation of the bronchi.

Calorie: The amount of heat required to raise the temperature of 1 gram of water through 1°C. The large number of calories is used (1000 calories) in describing the energy value of the food (1 Calorie is equal to 4.184 Joules).

Calorific Value: The amount of heat produced by the complete combustion, of a given weight of a flammable substance such as wood, coal, gas or oil. Calorific value of fuel = Heat produced / Mass of fuel burnt.

Camouflage: To conceal the troops or their movements by use of smoke screens, colour, tree branches etc., to hoodwink the enemy.

Carat: It is a measure of weight used for precious stones. 24 carat gold is the purest gold and thus 22 carat gold means a piece of gold in which 22 parts are pure gold and 2 parts of an alloy. 20 carat gold means 20 parts pure gold and 4 parts alloy.

Catalyst: It is the substance which alters (acceleration or retards) the rate of a chemical reaction without undergoing any change in itself during the whole reaction.

Coriolis Force: It is the horizontal force exerted by the earth's rotation on the atmosphere. It is in fact an accelerated motion in space as a result of the earth's rotation.

Cryogenics: It is the control and application of very low temperatures. This science is applicable in rocketry, for space exploration, electronics, refrigeration, biology and medicine.

Cumulonimbus: It is a heavy dark typical thunderstorm cloud of great vertical depth, towering upwards in huge, voluminous masses, the top being 15,000 ft or more above the base. It usually showers as rain, snow or hail.

Cyclotron: Cyclotron was discovered by E.O. Lawrence. It is an important instrument in nuclear research. It devices the accelerating particles protons, deuterons and heavier ions to energy - levels high enough to produce nuclear transformations.

Coal: The fossilised remains of vegetable growth produced mainly during the carboniferous era - about 275 million years ago. The decomposition of these remains in the absence of air and often under pressure of overlying rock has resulted in a material that is a mixture of carbon and hydrocarbons.

Coal Gas: A mixture of methane, hydrogen and carbon monoxide obtained by heating coal in the absence of air commonly used as a domestic fuel.

Coke: Greenish, porous fuel obtained as a residue in the manufacture of coal gas, almost pure carbon.

Conductor: Substance that permits heat or electricity current to flow through it. A good conductor of electricity is also a good conductor of heat, for instance, copper. A very bad conductor is called an insulator.

Control Rod: Rod made of a substance capable of absorbing neutrons in a nuclear reactor and used to control the speed of a nuclear chain reaction. Example : Boron, Cadmium rod.

Cracking: In oil technology the conversion of mineral oils of high boiling point into oils more suitable for gasoline engines by breaking down the large hydrocarbon molecules into smaller ones. This is done either by intense heat (thermal cracking or by catalytic cracking).

Gasoline: A product of the refining of petroleum used for fueling automobiles, aeroplanes, cigarette lighters etc.

Caesarian Operation (or Section): Is the surgical removal of a foetus on or before full term, from the uterus through an abdominal incision.

Carbohydrates: These are organic compounds which are composed of carbon, hydrogen and oxygen. These substances with proteins and fats form the major components of living matter, maintaining the functioning activity of the cells and serving as structural and reserve materials. Honey, cane, starch, etc. are rich in carbohydrates. It is divided into monsaccharides, Disaccharides and Polysaccharides. Monosaccharides are Glucose, fructose, galactose. Disaccharides are Sucrose, Maltose. Polysaccharides are starch, cellulose.

Cataract: A disease of the eye. Any clouding of opacity of the crystalline lens of the eye. The crystalline lens is small, normally transparent body that lies directly behind the pupil and the coloured portion of the eye.

Chicken Pox: A contagious disease characterised by an eruption of vesicles in the skin. The disease usually occurs in epidemics and the patients are generally between two and six years old.

Chilblains: Are red or purplish patches that itch and burn. These usually occur on the hands, feet and legs and are commonest in children and young women. Chilblains result from exposure to alternate extremes of heat and cold.

Cholera (Vibrio Cholerae): Is a term that has been applied to a wide variety of acute diarrhoeal diseases of short duration.

Colour Blindness: Is somewhat an inaccurate term referred to a great variety of defects of colour vision. A great deal is still unknown about colour blindness. Red and green blindness is the major type of defective of red and green vision. The other is yellow and blue blindness.

Common Cold (Virus): The term cold is applied in the most general way to various maladies of respiratory tract.

Chemotherapy: Is the treatment of disease by administering drugs that injure or kill the disease producing organisms without damaging the host. The term is also used more loosely to mean any use of drugs in the treatment of disease and particularly cancer.

Chlorophyll: Is the green pigment that plants use to carry out the process of photosynthesis. Its functions are to absorb the light energy and for the reduction of carbon-di-oxide to sugar and other plant material. The chlorophyll of the plant cells is contained within the organelles called the chloroplates.

Chromosomes: Chromosomes are microscopic bodies found in the nucleus of cells of most plants and animals. They carry hereditary material units which are called genes and which determine the growth, development and characteristics of an organism. The name chromosome was derived from the Greek words Chroma (colour) and Some (body), since chromosomes are deeply coloured by certain stains.

Compost: A mixture of various components used to fertilize and improve the structure of soils. The principal ingredient of compost also called artificial manure is decomposed organic matter. Composts are prepared in pits by alternating layers of plant residues 15 to 30 cm. thick, with layers of soil about 25 cm. thick. Each layer is dampened as it is laid down. In addition, nitrogen and phosphorus are usually added to the plant residue in the form of commercial fertilizer.

Computers: Are devices that perform calculations and process data. Modern computers are the culmination of a long line of devices used as an aid in calculation including fingers; tallying peffler, the abacus and the adding machines.

Cosmic Rays: Consist mainly of charged particles. Some particles are protons. These rays are dangerous to living beings. They are a powerful source of radiation. Some rays appear to be coming from the Sun.

Cryptogam: A plant with no flower and which reproduce by spores (hidden reproductive parts).

Cybernetics: A word coined by Norbert Wiener to describe the complex sciences with communications and control in the living organism and in the machine.

Congenital: Diseases acquired at birth or at infancy.

Contagious: Disease that can be spread from one person to another. Thus influenza is said to be a contagious disease but diseases like bubonic plague which can be transmitted only by bite of a flea are not contagious.

Corpuscles: Micro-cells present in the blood (white and red corpuscles).

Cortisone: A hormone produced by the adrenal cortex, is essential for the proper functioning of the body. The adrenal cortex produces a variety of related steroids including cortisone, cortisol, corticosterone and aldosterone.

Deuterium: An isotope of hydrogen prepared from heavy water D_2O.

Diesel Engine: An internal combustion engine in which the compression stroke raises the air temperature so high that the fuel is burnt without the aid of a spark.

Direct Current: An electric current or a stream of electrons that flow through a conductor in one direction only.

Dielectric: An insulator, substance in which an electric field gives rise to displacement of electric charge rather than to a net flow, a substance capable of supporting an electric stress, a non-conductor of electricity.

Dirty ice: It is the super cold grains of solid matter suspended in the thin gases in the space between the stars. The scientists state that it consist mainly of frozen methane and ammonia and a small admixture of heavy elements such as iron. It has a major role in the formation of stars and planets.

Dredger: It is a machine for dredging i.e. excavation under water or on land, or for scooping mineral deposits from depths.

Dynamo: A device for generating electric current by rotating a coil of wire in a magnetic field. A dynamo generates either direct or alternating current.

Deliquescence: Property of certain substances which when exposed to air, will absorb moisture and become liquid, e.g., calcium chloride.

Dry Docks: A concave structure in which a ship is supported out of water on blocks so that maintenance and repair work can be done on its underside.

Dry Ice: Is a common term for solid carbon dioxide. Its name arises from the fact that at normal pressure the substance sublimes (goes quickly from a solid to a gas), instead of melting, and leaves no liquid residue. Dry ice should be handled with great care because it is extremely cold and can cause severe burns. Dry ice is a good refrigerant and is widely used for shipping perishable goods over long distances. It can produce much lower temperatures than ordinary ice and occupies less space because it is more dense.

Dust Devil: A whirling funnel of sand and dust that occurs in the heat of the day as a result of strong convection in hot and dusty regions such as tropical deserts.

Diathermy: Is a form of heat therapy in which microwaves are transmitted to various body tissues below the skin.

Diphtheria: It is an infectious disease in which a false membrane is formed on the mucous surface usually on the throat.

Disinfectant: A chemical that kills micro-organisms, bacteria, viruses, protozoa, or fungi. Disinfectants are also called germicides. Strictly speaking disinfectants are used to kill pathogenic or disease causing organisms, white germicides kill all organisms.

Distilled Water: Pure water free from salts and other impurities. It is obtained by boiling water in specially made boilers.

Duct: A tube for the passage of excretion or secretion.

Dysentery: Is an infectious disease characterised by frequent loose stools and intestinal ulcer. There are two kinds of dysentery, caused by two different types of organism - bacteria and amoeba.

Echo Sounding: A method of measuring the depth of the ocean. According to this method, sound waves are sent into the sea to hear echo. The depth is calculated by taking into account the time taken.

Ecliptic: The apparent path that traces on the celestial sphere. This path is actually the projection of the earth orbital plane into the celestial sphere.

Ecology: Ecology is the word, was coined by Haeckel. Ecology is the study of the relationships among organisms and between organisms and their environments.

Efflorescence: In chemistry, is the process by which certain crystalline compounds lose water on exposure to air. The loss of water results in the formation of a powder on the surface of the crystals. The most familiar example of efflorescence is found in common washing soda. The glassy crystals of the washing soda (sodium carbonate) become white and powder in air.

Electricity: A form of energy believed to be due to the movement of electrons. It can heat substances, produce magnetic effects and cause chemical changes. There are two kinds of electricity (1) Dynamic electricity which is electricity moving through a conductor (2) Static electrical charge that can be built upon a metal conductor by friction.

Electric Motors: Devices for transforming or converting electrical energy into mechanical energy. The electric motor performs the reverse functions of the generator and several types of motors may also be used as generators. There are many millions of electric motors in use providing power for operating industrial plants, ships, railroads, buses and million more for operating home appliances such as washers, fans, cleaners and refrigerators.

Electrolysis: An electrochemical process by which a substance is separated into its constituent chemical elements by the passage of an electric current through the solution or substance.

Electrons: The basic negatively charged particle in the structure of the atom, which forms in turn the smallest material unit of any substance in nature (Mass 9.11×10^{-28} gram). Electron is most important particle in current because current is movement of electron in circuit.

Electric Transformer: A device used to increase or decrease the voltage of alternating current.

Elephantiasis: Also called pachyderma, elephant leg or Barbadoes leg is a progressive histopathologic state characterised by chronic inflammatory overgrowth of dermal connective tissues, preceded by and connected with lymphatic gland and vein stasis. This stasis produces mechanical interference with return of lymphatic and venous currents.

Endemic: A disease which becomes common due to surrounding conditions.

Energy: Capacity for action, movement or work. The principal forms of energy are heat and light; potential energy, kinetic energy, electrical energy and nuclear energy.

Enzyme: May be defined as an organic catalyst of high molecular weight and produced by living cells.

Equigravisphere: It is the locus of a point in space at which the gravity is constant. It is almost a spherical surface around the earth.

Escape Velocity: Is the minimum speed which a spacecraft must have to escape the earth's "Gravitational pull". It is 7 miles / sec. (11.2 km/sec.) from the earth.

Eugenics: Is the study of genetic control of population with a view to bringing about desired changes in the race of men to be procreated.

Euthanasia: Means mercy-killing or the deliberate ending of life to relieve incurable pain or disease. (Recently, the British House of Lords turned down a bill seeking to make euthanasia legal).

Exobiology: Science dealing with life or possibilities of life existing beyond the earth i.e., on other planets.

Fauna: The animal life of a region or of a geological period.

Flora: The plant life of a region or of a geological period corresponding to the term Fauna in animal life.

Flyash: It is a waste product from thermal power stations using coal. Germanium can be extracted from flyash with cement or lime. Flyash can be used for making bricks.

Fossils: The remains or the forms of a plant or animal which have been buried and preserved for a long period in the rocks of the earth's crust are called 'fossils'.

Fungus: A plant of the lowest order, having no chlorophyll in it, e.g., toadstools, mushrooms etc.

Fluidized Coal: Powdered coal that behaves like a liquid and can be pumped through pipes in a stream of compressed air.

Fumigations: An attempt at disinfection by gaseous or vaporous means. The term is also used to describe the application of fumes of medicinal substances to the respiratory tracts.

Fungi: A large group of primitive organisms which, with the bacteria, algae, and lichens, comprises the division of the plant kingdom known as Thallophyta. Unlike algae and higher plants, the fungi lack chlorophyll, the green colouring matter of plants, and therefore, are unable to make their own food.

Fermentation: It is the process where by organisms like bacteria and yeast degrade organic compounds in the absence of oxygen in order to release energy. It is form of anaerobic respiration.

$$C_6H_{12}O_6 \xrightarrow{\text{yeast}} 2C_6H_5OH + 2CO_2 + \text{energy}$$

Filariasis: It is parasitic disease. It is caused by nematode and transmitted by female Culex mosquitoes. It is characterised by high fever. Lymphagitis and swelling of lymph nodes. It is commonly termed as Elephantiasis.

Graham's law: It states, "velocity of diffusion gas inversely proportional to square root of its density $D \alpha \frac{1}{\sqrt{d}}$.

Graphite: A form of carbon in the shape of flat crystals. It is one of the softest minerals and is used in pencils and for lubrication. It is also a good conductor of electricity. It is used as a lubricant.

Gastric Juice: Liquid secreted by gastric glands situated in the walls of the stomach.

Geiger Counter: Instrument used to indicate the presence and intensity of radiation given off by radioactive substances.

Gene: Is an elementary unit of heredity. It occurs along the length of the chromosomes which the nuclei carry. Hundreds and even thousands of genes can be found arranged along the chromosome. These are made up of DNA (deoxyribonucleic acid) and have a constant effect on the development of the individual.

Gelatine: One of the commoner proteins, used for making jellies, is most familiar as a food.

Germanium: This is a metal with a marked crystalline form. It was extensively used in transistors, tiny amplifiers which control the release of current from a battery.

Goldmaster: It is an ultrasonic device which can detect precious metal and other objects lying up to six feet under the ground.

Grain silos: These are tall, hollow and cylindrical vessels built usually of reinforced concrete. These serve as wide containers for storing of loose grains etc. These are of great help in keeping the grains safe from moisture and insects.

Guided Missiles: The rocket-propelled missiles which are controlled during the flight either by self-activating or internal noming devices or by radio signal from the ground.

Gymnosperms: They are naked seed plants (Gymno means naked and sperms means seed).

Hard Water: Hard water does not form lather with soap easily. Hardness of water is mainly due to the Carbonate and Sulphate compounds of calcium and magnesium, particularly the soluble bicarbonates formed by the action of rain water and carbon dioxide from air on limestone. Hardness removed by boiling and addition of Sodium Aluminium Silicate.

Heat Energy: The energy or capacity for doing work that a substance possesses due to the movement of its molecules. The hotter the substance, the more molecular movement it has. Some, but not all of this energy can be converted into mechanical energy as in a steam engine.

Heavy Water: It is also called Deuterium Oxide (D_2O). It is a liquid similar chemically to ordinary water and occurring in it, in small quantities. It is used as a moderator in nuclear fission.

Hibernation: Dormancy during winter. The condition occurs in many mammals, most reptiles and amphibia, insects, plants etc. of temperate and arctic regions. The rate of Metabolism is greatly slowed down, and in mammals temperature drops to that of surroundings.

Holography: Discovered several years ago, is an improvement on photography. Instead of the two-dimensional picture obtained by the ordinary photographic process, holography, with the help of laser beams, reconstructs a three-dimensional image of an object. The 3-D image thus obtained is called a 'hologram'.

Homo-erectus: Name given to a group of fossilized remains of a primitive man, the skull cap and thigh bone which were discovered in 1891 in river deposits in Java by a Dutch Geologist, Eugene Dubois.

Horology: It is the science of measuring time or of constructing time pieces.

Horse Latitude: Region noted for its lack of winds, and lies across the Atlantic Ocean near the Tropic of Cancer between the belts of Trade and Westerly Winds.

Hovercraft: Cockrell invented Hovercraft. The craft ride over both on water surface and land.

Horse Power: A unit of rate of work evolved by James Watt, who found that a strong horse could raise a 1000 pound weight through 33 ft. in one minute. One horse power is thus work done at a rate of 33,000 foot-pounds per minute or more conveniently 550 foot-pounds per second (1 Hp = 746 watts).

Hybrid: It is an animal or plant produced by the union of two distinct species.

Hydrolysis: Whenever there is an addition of water molecule to a chemical compound, the reaction during the process is termed 'as Hydrolysis'.

Hydrophytes: Are plants whose roots naturally grow in water-saturated soils and absorb water readily from such soils, such as water lily and lotus.

Hydroponics: Is the practice and science of growing plants without using soil by feeding them on nutrient solutions. India has a Hydroponic Investigation Unit near Calcutta.

Hydrocarbons: A large group of chemical compounds made up entirely of hydrogen and carbon.

Haemoglobin: An organic compound with a molecular weight of 68,000 made of heme and globin. Hence it is a metal complex containing iron and imparts the red colour to the haemoglobin. Globin is a colourless protein containing many amino acids.

Hormones: Internal secretion of ductless glands. They are vital for regular growth. The failure of glands to secrete or when they over secrete, will result in abnormal growth of the body.

Implosion: It is a technique for detonating underground nuclear devices.

Infra-red Rays: Sunlight is composed of Ultraviolet, VIBGYOR, and Infra-red Rays; Infra-red Ray is invisible, having a wave length just greater than the red end of the visible light spectrum but less than that of radio waves.

Incandescence: The state of glowing of substance to give out heat and high temperature. The filament of an electric light bulb produces light by becoming incandescent when an electric current is passed through it.

Ion: An atom or group of atoms that, by loss or gain of one or more electrons, have acquired an electric charge positively charged.

Insulin: Is a hormone that is essential for the proper use and storage of undigested sugar in the body. The hormone is secreted by certain cells of the islets of Langerhans in the pancreas.

Iron Lung: A type of closed artificial respirator that has been used primarily for victims of respiratory paralysis particularly for people with poliomyelitis.

Immunity: It is ability of animals and plants to withstand harmfull infection agents and toxins.

Injection: The direct introduction of a drug or other fluid into the blood stream or body tissues.

Inverter: It is device that converts a DC into AC.

Inoculation: A weak strain of the germ or dead germ infected into the body to produce its immunity against the disease.

Ionisation: The process by which an electron is removed from an atom, molecule or ion. Ionisation takes place spontaneously when certain compounds are dissolved in water, e.g., sodium chloride becomes an electrolyte. Gases can also be ionised by passing high voltage current through them.

Isotopes (Soddy & Ramsay): Atoms of the same elements having the same atomic number but different atomic weights. The nuclei of isotopes contain identical numbers of protons but different numbers of neutrons and this accounts for the different atomic weights. All the isotopes of an element have the same chemical properties but their physical behaviour may differ. For instance, Uranium 235 is unstable and breaks up. Uranium 238 is physically inactive.

Jaundice: Is a condition in which skin and eyes become yellowish in colour. Jaundice also known as 'licterun' is not a disease but is usually a harmless symptom of an underlying disorder.

Jet Engine (Frank whittle): It's a type of aircraft. It is worked with a cheap fuel and is more economical for long distance air travels.

Kilocycle: A "cycle" is one complete oscillation of an electromagnetic wave. A kilo-cycle represents 1000 such oscillations.

Kinetic Energy: The capacity for doing work that a body possesses by virtue of its motion. For example, a bullet approaching a target at high speed possesses kinetic energy as is shown by its ability to penetrate a wood block or a steel plate.

Laser Beam: 'Laser' is the abbreviated form of "Light Amplification by Stimulated Emission of Radiation". A device which produces monochromatic and coherent beam of light used in medicine, the science of warfare etc.

Laser Listener: A device which picks up the vibrations and can later be turned back into speech.

Latent Heat: Specifically, the quantity of heat required to change the state of one gram of a substance from solid to liquid or liquid to vapour without changing its temperature.

Laughing Gas: Nitrous oxide, a compound of nitrogen and oxygen possessing mild anaesthetic power. It is used in dentistry and for minor operations.

Leukemia: A disease of unknown cause and fatal course encountered at all ages and in both sexes. The frequency, of the disease has substantially increased in the 20th century. Two main varieties are nyelogenous and the lymphatic.

Light Year: Astronomical measure of distance; the distance travelled by light in one year - approximately 6×10^{12} miles (6 million million miles). Light emitted by Sun reaches earth in about 8 minutes and 20 seconds.

Magnetic Storm: It is an abnormal disturbance of the magnetic field of the earth. Magnetic storms are associated with sunspots and occur almost simultaneously with the latter. They interfere a lot with radio and telegraphic communications.

Magnetic Field: An invisible zone of force that surrounds - (1) a wire carrying an electric current; or (2) a permanent magnet. If an electric conductor is moved via magnetic field, a current is induced in the conductor.

Magnetic Hydrodynamics: A new and experimental method of generating electricity by heating a gas to a very high temperature so that it becomes a conductor of electricity and then blowing it at high speed between the poles of a strong magnet.

Mesons: A particle which holds the protons and neutrons of the atomic nucleus.

Meningitis: Inflammation of the membranes of the brain and spinal cord. Inflammation of the dura mater is known as 'pachymeningitis'.

Metabolism: The term is used to designate the sum total of chemical processes by which living organisms maintain themselves and carry out the activities characteristic of the living state.

Moderator: A substance such as graphite or heavy water that slows down the neutrons that fly away from the nucleus of radioactive material in nuclear fission. This increases the chances of a further breakdown of atoms.

Mirage: When the traveller in the desert sees the image of the tree upside down, he takes it to be due to reflection in water, but he finds nothing there. The phenomenon of illusion is known as the 'mirage'.

Napalm Bomb: Means an incendiary bomb containing a highly inflammable jellied petrol and causes fires which are difficult to extinguish.

Natural Gas: Flammable gas occurring underground, with or near accumulation of crude oil. It is a mixture of gases, e.g., methane, ethane, propane and all hydrocarbons.

Neon: An inert gas which produces crimson glow when an electric discharge passes through it; familiar in advertising signs.

Nicotine: A poisonous alkaloid found in tobacco leaves.

Neutron: It is neutral particle of elements. It is high penetrating power than other particle. The mass of neuton is almost same mass of proton. Mass of neutron is equal to 1.675×10^{-24} g.

Nuclear Fission: The breaking up of a heavy atom, e.g., uranium, into two or more lighter atoms accompanied by an enormous release of energy. When such an atom breaks up particles called neutrons are liberated, and if one of those hits another uranium nucleus, it causes it to break up releasing more neutrons and so on. This is called a chain reaction. When it goes slowly under control, as in a nuclear reactor it can produce heat for conversion into electrical energy. Uncontrolled reaction becomes an atomic explosion.

Nuclear Fusion: The process of forcing the nuclei of light atoms (e.g., deuterium) to combine and form a heavier atom with an attendant release of energy. Temperatures of many millions of degrees are required to successfully break the hydrogen bomb where a small nuclear fission bomb is used to produce temperature. To achieve controlled fusion is much more difficult and is still the subject of experiment.

Nuclear Reactor: An arrangement of fissile material such as Uranium 235 together with a moderator (e.g., graphite or heavy water) so that energy is continuously released in a controlled manner as a result of nuclear fission. The rate of fission is regulated by control rods.

Nucleus, Atomic: This is the positively charged central core of an atom consisting of positively charged protons and neutral neutrons. Around the nucleus, rotate one or more negatively charged electrons. In radioactive material such as Uranium 235 it is the neutrons that fly away from the nucleus and if they hit another nucleus, it too breaks up.

Nuclear Fuel: A substance which undergoes nuclear fission in a nuclear reactor.

Ohm: A unit of electrical resistance. The amount of resistance in a circuit that will allow a source of electricity with an electromotive force or pressure of one Volt to pass a current of one Ampere. $R = V/I$.

Open Cut Mining: Direct excavation of minerals that lie near the earth's surface often removing any overburden of soil or rock. Also called 'open cast or strip mining'. Example : Coal mines.

Parasite: An animal or plant living in or upon another.

Partons: It is the particles tinier than protons or neutrons, further sub-divided into partons.

Pasteurization (Louis pasteur): A process of stopping liquid food from being spoiled. This is done by the application of mild heat under particular conditions to destroy any harmful micro-organism present and thus to enhance its keeping properties. The heat treatment kills the vegetative cells of most bacteria. The treatment was originally due to Louis Pasteur in the case of wine and beer which could be prevented from going bad by heating these beverages to about 135°F.

Penicillin: A new drug derived from mould of the genus penicillium; a powerful antibacterial and non-toxic agent. It works against pneumonia, meningitis, gonorrhoea, boils, impetigo and burns.

Photon: It is a quantum of light or electro-magnetic radiation. When a particle possessing an electrical charge changes its momentum, photons are generated.

Pipette: It is a glass tube with the aid of which a definite volume of liquid may be transferred.

Plasma-Cutter: It is a thin net of nitric plasma having a temperature varying from three to four times that of the "sun's surface", and can thus make any kind of material evaporate instantaneously. It can cut metal ingots up to a thickness of 25 cm.

Plowshare: Plowshare programme is a term used to refer to projects involving peaceful uses of atomic energy, e.g., excavation of mines, building of dams, extraction of oil from shore etc.

Plasma: The fluid portion of blood composed of serum and a soluble protein which in suitable conditions forms blood clots.

Plastic Surgery: The surgical speciality that deals with, the reconstruction and repair of certain congenital deformities, burns, injuries, surgical defects and wounds resulting from serious accidents of war.

Pneumonia: Any type of inflammatory disease of lung regardless of its extent, the germ causing inflammatory process or the duration of the inflammation of the lung.

Poliomyelitis: (Infantile Paralysis or Polio): An infectious disease which in temperate climates, often appears in the form of summer epidemics. It is known for its unfortunate capacity to give rise to crippling types of paralysis.

Prophylactic: Is a method by which disease is warded off by disinfectant or sterilization.

Proteins: Are nitrogen containing organic compounds that along with carbohydrates and fats form the bulk of air, food stuffs. Proteins are contained in every cell of plant and animal tissues, they are the very basis of protoplasm itself. Proteins are so universally distributed that it is not possible to eat naturally occurring food without eating some protein; for example - egg, cereals, fruits, vegetables.

Protoplasm: Is the living substance found in all plants and animals.

Pyorrhoea: A discharge of pus, specifically, pyorrhea (Pyorrhea alveolares) and inflammation and degeneration of the alveoli (Bony sockets of the teeth) and surrounding tissues of the gum, accompanied frequently by a pussy discharge and loosening of the teeth. The condition is recognised by the darkened colour bleeding and thickening of the gums which become loose and recede. It may be brought in by neglect of oral hygiene, faulty dental work or untreated tooth decay.

Psychedelic Drugs: Are drugs, which produce a mental state of great calm, intensely pleasureful perception of the senses etc.

Pollination: A botanical term for the transference of pollen, the dustlike powder produced by the stamen of seed plants, to the stigma (the receptive surface) of the ovules in the ovary and their subsequent development into seeds.

Polymerisation: Union of two or more molecules of the same compound chemically, to form a new compound of a higher molecular weight (but same empirical formula). Example: Polyvinyl Chloride, Neoprine.

Positron: Electrons having positive charges revolving around the nucleus of an atom.

Psychiatry: A branch of medicine concerned with the study, treatment and prevention of emotional, social and spiritual maladjustments.

Protoplasm: The characteristic organic substance on which all activities of living matter are based. The cell is the smallest structural unit of protoplasm that has all the properties essential for its maintenance (irritability, motility and basic metabolism) and propagation, growth and reproduction.

Pulsars: In radio astronomy, a kind of radio source first discovered in August 1967. After sometime the spinning neutron star start to emit radio waves. This star starts to glow due to emit radio waves. This glowing neutron star is called as pulsar.

Persistence of Vision: Is the creation of an impression as the actual phenomenon is and occurring by continuous and rapid impression on the screen, e.g., cinema.

Petroleum: Crude oil - consists of complex mixture of compounds mostly hydrocarbons. Believed to have been formed by the decomposition of microscopic marine organism in the absence of air.

Plutonium: A radioactive element that does not occur in nature but can be made from Uranium-235 by reaction with neutrons in a nuclear reactor. It can be used both in atomic bombs and as a fuel similar to Uranium 235.

Potential Energy: The energy possessed by body by virtue of its position. For instance, a pound of water in a reservoir 1000 feet above a hydroelectric station has a potential energy. PE = mgh

Power: The rate of doing work.

Pressure: The force acting upon a surface measured as weight per unit area, e.g., 50 lb. per square inch.

Proton: A positively charged particle that forms part of the nucleus of an atom. It has the same electric charges as the negatively charged electron, but its mass is approximately 1836 times greater. Hydrogen the simplest atom has one proton. Uranium the most complicated atom has 92 protons.

Pterodactyl: A fossil of flying reptile with large and bird-like skull, long jaws, and a flying-membrane attached to the long fifth finger.

Quasars: Abbreviation of Quasi-Stellar Radio Sources. They are immensely luminous celestial objects that have only recently been discovered. Their true physical nature is almost completely unknown. Superficially, they look like ordinary stars, but closer examination has shown them to have many properties common with galaxies.

Raduga Laser: Otherwise called rainbow laser used in organic dyestuffs as generating elements to produce light of any colour singly or various colours simultaneously.

Rabies: Is an acute, infectious disease of the brain invariably fatal in man. It may also be transmitted to any warm blooded animal generally with fatal results. The virus by which it is spread grows in dogs and related wild animals such as the wolf, fox and coyote. Infection is transferred in the saliva of rabid animals by bite. Rabies is common in Asia, Africa and Southern Europe.

Red Blood Corpuscles: Are pale yellow circular discs. These discs are so small that ten million of them do not occupy more than one square inch of space. They contain a red pigment known as haemoglobin which has great attraction for oxygen.

Respiratory Quotient: Is the ratio between the quantity of oxygen inhaled and of carbon dioxide exhaled. $RQ = \dfrac{\text{Volume of } CO_2 \text{ evolved}}{\text{Volume of } O_2 \text{ consumed}}$

Rickets: A deficiency disease of infants and yearly childhood marked by disordered ossification, the main disturbance being in calcium and phosphorus metabolism. The most important primary factor is the absence of vitamin D and sunlight.

Radiation: The term 'Radiation' is applicable to many types of energy emission from either the nucleus of an atom or from it as surrounding electron 'shells'.

Radioactivity: The emission of radiation and particles from the nuclei of unstable elements such as radium or Uranium 235.

Radio Stars: Heavenly bodies emitting electromagnetic radiation outside the solar system.

Reflex Action: A non-voluntary action affecting a muscular apparatus in reponse to some kind of sensory stimulus.

Refractive Index: The ratio between the sine of the angle of incidence and that of reflection is known as 'refractive index'.

Rockets: Comprise the large and fast-growing family of projectiles, missiles, instrument carriers and auxiliary aviation devices which move by reaction against their own exhaust blasts.

Saliva and Salivary Glands: Salivary glands secrete saliva in the mouth. The salivary glands in man and carnivores are helpful, in general cleansing of the mouth.

Smallpox: Once a plague of great impact and importance, smallpox (vasiola) is now rare in Europe and North America and in some other areas of the world. The conquest of this disease is one of the major accomplishments of preventive medicine.

Solid Oxygen: The spacemen visiting the moon have to carry frozen pellets of super-coiled oxygen. A two inch cube of solid oxygen can sustain an astronaut for nearly three hours.

Sonar: Is an apparatus for detecting the presence of enemy U- boats beneath the surface of the ocean with the help of ultrasonic echoes.

Space: The region beyond the earth's atmosphere lying between and beyond planets and stars.

Sterilisation: Is a process of rendering the hands, instruments, cloth or any others surgically clean, that is completely free from 'germs'.

Specific Gravity: Is the ratio of density of a substance to the density of water at 4°C.

Specific Heat: Is the quantity of heat required to raise the temperature of one gram of the substance through one degree centigrade. It is expressed in calories.

Spectrum: Is a multicolour image. When sun rays are allowed to pass through a prism, they are split into seven colours (VIBGYOR).

Stalactites and Stalagmites: Stalactites are elongated pendant forms of various minerals deposited from solutions where very slow drip may enter a void. Stalagmites are complementary forms of thicker proportions which grow up on the bottom of a cavity from the same drip water source but whose minerals are deposited after free fall across the open space in the rock. An inclusive name for both forms is dripstone.

Submarine: A naval vessel capable of sustained operation under water. They played major roles in World Wars I & II.

Sulphate Therapy: Is to treat the diseases with sulphur drugs.

Superheterodyne: Is a technique or radio reception in which the frequency of the carrier waves is changed in the receiver to a supersonic intermediate frequency by a heterodyne process.

Surface Tension: The property of liquids in virtue of which they tend to take such a form as to have the smallest surface possible. The name "Surface tension" has reference to the fact that liquids, when freed from the action of gravity and other comparatively powerful forces, behave as though their surface were elastic in membranes which are everywhere in a state of uniform tensions.

Supersonic: Speed greater than that of sound. When an aircraft exceeds the speed of sound (passes the sound barrier) shock waves are built up round the aircraft giving rise to a sonic boom, often heard at ground-level.

Solar Battery: An arrangement of metals that converts the light energy in the sun's rays into electric energy.

Tetanus: An infectious disease of central nervous system caused by Closetridium tetani which enters the body through an open and usually a punctured, penetrating wound.

Trachoma: Trachoma is a chronic type of infectious cornea conjuctival disease characterized by papillary hypertrophy of the conjuctiva and formation of conjuctival follicles, but recognised mainly by a definite style of cornal vascularization known as pannus.

Telex: Teleprinter Exchange. It is a method of exchanging the views in writing by typing the letters on both the sides.

Thermal Capacity: Is the quantity of heat required to raise the temperature of a body through 1°C.

T.N.T. (Tri Nitro Toluene): A chemical compound used as an explosive. TNT is made by the reaction of toluene and nitric acid in the presence of sulphuric acid. TNT has been employed extensively as an explosive in bombs, mines, grenades and torpedoes.

Torricellian Vacuum: Is the vacuum space left in the barometer which was invented by Torricelli.

Transuranium Elements: The chemical elements that follow uranium in the periodic system. These elements have an atomic number greater than 92.

Trench Foot: Frost-bite of the lower extremities from chronic exposure to cold. The name derives from the tendency of soldiers in water trench warfare to experience this effect.

Trench Mouth: An infection of the mucous membranes of the mouths caused by hymbiotic micro-organisms 'Bacillus fusiformies' and 'Borrelia vincentil'. The disease produces painful swelling of the gums especially at the tooth margins, bleeding and small irregular, very painful ulcers.

Trench Warfare: Warfare in which the opposite armies attack and counter attack from relatively permanent trench systems constructed in close proximity to each other.

Transistor: A device used to amplify current and perform other functions usually performed by the valve (thermionic tube). Transistor makes use of the semi-conductor germanium; and their advantages over valves are that they are forced to rotate by a stream of liquid or gas. Thus the turbine converts energy directly in rotatory motion.

Ultraviolet Radiation: Is electromagnetic radiation in the part of the spectrum between X-rays and visible light. Its wavelengths are too short to be visible to the human eye.

Vaccination: It is simply the process of administering a vaccine in such a way as to produce an effective immune response almost always by an injection into the tissues.

Vasectomy: Means severing a nerve in the male reproductive system to prevent spermatozoa from reaching the ovum to obviate conception.

Virus: Are the smallest of all known organisms. They range in virulence from viruses capable of causing some of the most severe diseases known to man such as small pox, yellow fever, etc., to certain other viruses which may remain silent within the cells of animals, plants, etc., revealing no sign of their presence.

Virology: The study of viruses.

Van Allen Radiation Belts: Are two natural zones of particles and intense radiation surrounding the earth at distances of thousands of miles above its surface.

Velocity: Is defined as the rate of displacement expressed in cm/sec^2.

Ventricle: Is a cavity in the brain or in the chamber of heart.

Vitamin: Organic compounds required in small amounts in the diet of one or more species of animals for proper biological functioning and maintenance of health. It has been shown that vitamins are required as metabolic essentials for all species, although they are not diet essential for all.

Water Gas: A manufactured gas mixture of hydrogen and carbon monoxide. Produced by passing steam over white coke at 1200°C. It is now used chiefly in the production of ammonia, methanol and liquid fuels and is known as synthesis gas.

Watt: When P.D. is one volt and one ampere of electric current is passing through an electric circuit, the power in the circuit is equivalent to one watt (Watt=1 Joule/sec. or 10^7 ergs/sec.)

Xerography: An electrostatic reproduction process invented in 1947 by Chester E.Carison and developed by the Battle Memorial Institute and the Haloid Company. A xerographic plate consists of an electrically conductive back with a photo conductive surface. This Plate-electrostatically charged - will when exposed to an image, discharge more in the bright areas and retain a latest electrostatic image. Such an image can be made visible by depositing electrically charged particles of appropriate colour by other means.

Xerophyte: Are numerous plants which can endure recurrent drought by means of special structural and functional adaptations notably by a remarkable resistance to wilting.

SCIENTIFIC PHENOMENA

1. Why does the same side of the moon face the earth?

The moon rotates on its axis once $27\frac{1}{3}$ days, during which it revolves around the earth. Due to this fact, only one side of the moon will face the earth.

2. Why does a needle sink in water whereas an iron ship floats?

The specific gravity of the needle which is a solid piece of iron is greater than that of water and so it sinks. But the ship is so designed that the weight of the ship is less than water displaced by it. The ship therefore floats while a needle sinks.

3. Why does an object weigh a little less at the Equator than at the Poles?

The value of acceleration due to gravity is different at various places on the earth's surface. It has the maximum value at the poles and decreases towards the equator. There are two causes for this variation of gravity namely - (a) rotation of the earth; and (b) the bulge at the equator. Hence the weight of an object is maximum at poles and minimum at the equator.

4. Why are we advised to empty the ink from our fountain pen before going up an aeroplane?

When we go up, the atmospheric pressure becomes lesser and lesser. So the outside atmosphere as we fly in an aeroplane is definitely lesser than that inside the fountain pen. Due to this variation of pressure the ink will come out of the pen and spoil the shirts. That is why we are advised to empty the ink from our fountain pen.

5. Why does the sky appear blue?

The sky appears blue because of the scattering of light by dust particles or air molecules in the atmosphere. This scattering is inversely proportional to the fourth power of wavelength. As a result of this, the shorter wavelengths are profusely scattered. As blue has the shortest wavelength of all colours, when we look at sky, it appears blue.

6. *Why cannot the petrol fire be extinguished by throwing water on it?*

As the density of petrol is less than that of water, the petrol floats on the water. So the petrol fire cannot be extinguished. Moreover the heat of the petrol fire is so intense that the water molecules will get decomposed, in the fire.

7. *Why is the rainbow seen after rains?*

The rainbow is formed only by the reflection of the sunlight at the back of the rain drops which act as prisms and which are quivering in the atmosphere immediately after the rain stops. So the dispersed rays of sunlight having suffered deviation give rise to concentrated beam of light indicating all the colours of the light.

8. *Why does hard water not readily form lather with soap?*

Soap is sodium salt of an organic acid. When soap is mixed with water they react chemically to form sodium hydroxide and organic acid is eliminated. The sodium hydroxide thus produced causes the lather. When soap solution is added to hard water, the soap reacts with the salts such as chlorides and bicarbonates present in hard water. Only after these salts are removed as organic salts, soap reacts with water and gives sodium hydroxide which causes the lather.

9. *A flash of lightning is seen before the sound of thunder is heard. Why?*

As light travels (1,86,000 miles/sec) at a much faster speed than sound which travels at a rate of 1100 ft/sec, we see the flash of lightning before the sound of thunder is heard.

10. *Exhaled air when bubbled through lime water turns milky. Why?*

Exhaled air contains carbon dioxide. So when this carbon dioxide reacts with lime water which is nothing but calcium hydroxide, calcium carbonate is formed which is milky.

11. *How does a soda straw work?*

When we suck out air from the straw, vacuum is created inside the straw. So soda rushes through the straw to our mouth.

12. *It is advisable to work electric appliances only when they are properly earthed. Why?*

In case of short-circuit, the current will pass into the earth without causing any damage to the electric appliances, when it is properly earthed.

13. *A certain amount of calcium should be a necessary compound of our food. Why?*

Calcium is an essential compound of bones and teeth. So calcium must be an essential compound of our food to replenish the wear-and-tear of our bones and teeth.

14. *Glass when heated cracks while metal does not. Why?*

As glass is a bad conductor of heat, when heated, outer layers of the glass only expand while the inner one remains unaffected. Due to this, the glass cracks. On the other hand, the metal, is a good conductor of heat, conducts heat uniformly. So the metal does not crack.

15. Why does one lean forward while climbing a hill?

While leaning forward, the centre of gravity of the body also shifts forward and this helps climbing.

16. Why does an electric bulb bang when it is broken?

Inside the bulb is the partial vacuum. When it is broken, the air outside rushes in to fill the vacuum and hence the noise is produced.

17. Why does ice wrapped in a blanket not melt away quickly?

As the blanket is a bad conductor of heat it cuts off all heat rays. So the ice wrapped in a blanket does not melt quickly.

18. Why is copper wire not used as heating element in electric heaters?

Copper melts at about 1000°C and reacts with air to form a black powder.

19. Why is rain water soft but river water hard?

River water in its course dissolves the calcareous matter and becomes hard. Rain water is pure because it does not mix with any other matter which makes it hard.

20. Why is water from a hand pump warm in winter and cold in summer?

The temperature underground does not appreciably alter or does not alter at all, while the outside temperature gets cooler in winter and hotter in summer than the temperature underground. That is why the pump water is warm in winter and cool in summer.

21. It takes less time to cook in pressure cooker than in an ordinary vessel. Why?

The increased pressure in the cooker raises the heat in it and so the food stuffs are cooked in a lesser time.

22. An iron nail floats on mercury but sinks in water. Why?

The densities of mercury and iron are 13.6/cc and 7.6/cc respectively. So, the mercury is displaced by the iron nail and hence the upward thrust is more. But this is not the case with water. Its density is 1 gm/cc.

23. Why is sea water saline?

The river water in its course brings all mineral salts which make the sea water saline.

24. Why are lightning conductors fixed to tall buildings?

The taller buildings are easily struck by lightning as the charged clouds are nearer to them. If the lightning conductors are fixed to tall buildings, even the enormous electric charges flow down to earth causing no damage to the buildings.

25. Why are fuse wires always used in electrical installations?

Fuse wire is an alloy which has high resistance and low melting point. So when there comes excess and strong currents, the fuse wire melts away avoiding damage to the installations.

26. Why does cooking take more time on mountain tops?

Remember, the boiling point is always proportional to pressure. As the pressure is low on mountain tops, the water boils at the lowest temperature. So the cooking takes more time.

27. How does the blotting paper absorb ink?

The blotting paper has a number of pores. The ink is sucked up into these pores by virtue of surface tension.

28. Why are the mornings and evenings comparatively cooler than noon?

The sun's rays at noon are vertical and slanting in the mornings and evenings.

29. Why does grass gather more dew at night?

During nights, the grass expels some amount of excess water which appear as dew drops on the leaves.

30. Why are white clothes more comfortable in summer than dark coloured ones?

White clothes absorb less heat than dark coloured ones. This is the very reason for blackening the bottoms of cooking vessels. They will absorb more heat and hence cooking will be easier.

31. Steam produces burns more easily than water at the same temperature. Why?

Steam contains 537 cal/gm heat more than water at the same temperature. So it causes more severe burns.

32. A ship rises as it enters the sea from a river. Why?

As the density of river water is less than that of the sea water, the water displaced by the ship in the river is more than that displaced in the sea. So it rises as it enters sea from river.

33. Why is sodium kept under kerosene?

Sodium dissolves in water and reacts to form sodium hydroxide. But it does not dissolve in kerosene. Hence it is kept in kerosene.

34. Why is phosphorus kept under water?

Phosphorus rapidly catches fire reacting with oxygen. Being insoluble in water, it does not react. So it is kept under water.

35. How do bats fly in dark?

Bats (1000 - 1,50,000 hertz) produce ultrasonic waves while flying. These waves are reflected back from any obstacle and thus help the bats find their way.

36. Why is it easier to roll a barrel than to pull it along the road?

As the rolling force of friction is less than the dynamic force of friction, it is easier to roll than to pull the barrel.

37. What is the distance between the moon and earth?

It is about 2,38,860 miles.

38. What is the diameter of the moon?

The diameter of the moon is about 2,100 miles. It is roughly one-fourth of that of the earth. The mass of the moon is nearly one-eighth of the latter's.

39. What is the shape of the moon?

The shape of the moon is spherical. The side facing the earth is thrusting out an extra bulge.

40. What is the ratio of the mass of the moon to that of earth?

It is 1 : 6.

41. Why is there no life on the moon?

There is no atmosphere. So the temperatures are extreme. The maximum temperature goes up as high as 120°C during lunar day and comes down as low as −172°C at night. Moreover the night and the day last about 14 days. So there is no life.

42. At what temperature are the readings in both centigrade and fahrenheit thermometers exactly the same?

At − 40°.

43. Why is a plane approaching at a speed of 1,000 m.p.h. not heard?

If the speed of any object exceeds 760 m.p.h. it cannot be heard. The speed of the sound is 760 m.p.h. This speed is known as 'ultrasonic'.

44. Why has moon no atmosphere?

It is because the gases released by the crust of the moon rapidly escape into the interplanetary system.

45. Why has moon extremes of temperature?

The surface of the moon is rocky and sandy. There is no air, no water and no agents which can mitigate extremes of temperature.

46. Why do day and night on the moon last for about 14 days?

The moon revolves around its axis once in 27⅓ days. Thus the lunar day and night each is equal to about 14 days.

47. Why is the weight of an object on the moon only one sixth of what is on the earth?

As the gravity of the moon is only one sixth of the earth, the weight of an object is also one sixth of what it is on the earth.

48. A highly corked glass bottle full of water left outside on a frosty night bursts. Why?

In a frosty night the water inside the glass bottle gets frozen and hence its volume is increased. As the bottle is tightly corked, it breaks.

49. How are the green plants active in modifying the composition of air?

In the presence of sunlight during the process of photosynthesis, they liberate oxygen equal to the amount of the carbon dioxide taken in. This balances the proportion of oxygen and carbon-dioxide in the air. Thus this process helps in modifying the composition of air to a great extent.

50. It is dangerous to touch the live electric wire with bare feet and hands. Why?

By touching the live electric wire, with bare feet and hands the current may pass through the body into the earth giving a severe shock which can be fatal.

51. Why are the places near the sea cooler in summer and warmer in winter than places farther inland?

Water has high specific heat. So it does not get cool much in summer or hot in winter. So the sea breeze keeps the nearby places cooler in summer and warmer in winter.

52. How do you convert centigrade reading to fahrenheit?

The formula is $\dfrac{C}{100} = \dfrac{F-32}{180}$

53. How does a parachute enable a person to descend safely from an aircraft?

The gravitational force of the earth attracts the man towards it. But the parachute is subjected to considerable resistance by the air and thus slows down the speed of descending man.

54. Why is a small drop of water or mercury on a clean glass plate circular in shape?

A force is developed on the surface of a liquid drop and so the molecules in the surface are bound together to form something like a stretched membrance tending to compress the molecules below to the smallest possible volume. That is why the drop of mercury or water assumes a spherical shape.

55. Why does a dead body float in water for some time?

The weight of the water displaced by the body is more than that of the body. Hence the body floats.

56. Why does a person tend to fall forward when the train slows down?

The lower part of the body is in contact with the train. So when the train slows down, the lower part of the body also slows down while the upper part of the body is in motion sharing the velocity of the train. So he falls forward.

57. Why do the water pipes burst in severe cold?

In severe cold, when the water gets frozen, its volume is increased. As a result of this, a great force is exerted on the walls of pipes. Hence they burst.

58. Water kept in earthen pots is cool in summer. Why?

Water oozes out of the earthen pots through pores. When they get evaporated, they take heat necessary for evaporation from the pot and consequently the water becomes cool.

59. Ice floats on water. Why?

The specific gravity of ice (920 gm/cc) is lower than that of water (1000 gm/cc). So ice floats.

60. A small gap is left between each set of two rails of a railway line. Why?

The small gap left between each set of two rails can accommodate the expansion of rails made up of iron, during summer. Otherwise the rails may collide and bulge upwards.

61. It is necessary to add manure or fertiliser to the field to get a good crop. Why?

As the plants absorb all energy of the soil, the soil is left with no ingredients necessary for better growth of plants. So in order to re-activate or energise the soil, it is necessary to add manure or fertilizer.

62. A lighted candle gets extinguished when covered with a tumbler. Why?

A candle needs oxygen for continuous burning. When the candle is closed with a tumbler, the necessary oxygen is not available for the candle to burn. So it gets extinguished.

63. A red tie appears black when seen under a blue mercury lamp?

The red tie absorbs the blue (colour) lights of the mercury lamp and no light is reflected. So the red tie appears black.

64. Why does the proportion of oxygen in air remain constant despite its utilisation in respiration?

Carbon dioxide is released while oxygen is taken in during respiration. But the use of oxygen is offset by the release of oxygen by the plants in photosynthesis.

65. Sunshine is the hottest at Equator. Why?

The sun's rays fall vertically on the Equator while the sun's rays fall at a slanting position at other places. So sunshine is hottest at the Equator.

66. A Clinical Thermometer has a constriction near the bulb. Why?

The constriction in the clinical thermometer prevents the mercury raised to show the temperature from coming down quickly so that the reading may be clearly noted.

67. By putting on a shirt, a person feels warm. Why?

An air layer is formed between the body and the shirt by putting on a shirt. As the layer does not move and no fresh air comes into contact with the body, a person feels warm.

68. Why does the green leaf appear dark in red light?

The red light is completely absorbed by the green leaf and does not reflect any colour. So it looks dark.

69. Why a convex mirror is used by motorists?

A convex mirror projects a large field of view so that the motorists can see all the objects behind the vehicle. Moreover sunlight is diverged and scattered by the mirror.

70. How can you estimate the height of a bridge by dropping a stone from it?

Note the time taken by the stone to reach the bottom. Use the formula.

$$s = ut + at^2 \quad a \qquad = 33 \text{ ft/sec}^2$$
$$t \qquad = \text{time}$$
$$u \qquad = 0$$
$$s \qquad = \text{height}$$

71. How does a refrigerator keep food fresh?

At the low temperature in the refrigerator, the fermentation does not take place. So the food is kept fresh.

72. Why is the curved track of a train banked outside?

It provides centripetal force so that the train can move round the curve, leaning inward.

73. How energies can be obtained by smashing the atom?

When uranium atom is bombarded with slow neutrons, it brakes up into medium sized atoms. The mass of the atoms thus formed is much less than the original atom and the difference in the mass reappears as energy, according to the Einstein's theory $E = mc^2$, where E is the energy, m, the mass effect and C, the velocity of light. This nuclear disintegration is known as "Nuclear Fission". This nuclear fission provides secondary neutrons, which at suitable velocities produce further divisions in uranium atom. Thus there is set up, self-propagating chain reactions in which neutrons produce in one fission process additional fission. This chain reaction will continue till all the atoms are used up. Thus an enormous store of energy in the atom as building energies of the nucleus will be released in a short time.

74. What is the use of fuse?

Compound of fuse wire is Lead and Tin, which has low melting point. Fuse prevent undulating current in circuit due to melting of wire. Fuse are always connected live wire.

75. From what are plastics made? Mention four main uses of Plastics?

Plastics are polymerised organic compounds. Plastics are manufactured by adjusting the chain lengths and compositions of high molecular weight compounds. Household appliances, packing materials, furniture, electric appliances etc., are some of the uses of plastic.

76. How is writing paper made?

Normally paper consists of cellulose free from lignin and other non-cellulose materials. Special wood choppings are made into a fine pulp. It is added with sodium sulphite for the extractions of cellulose from wood cells. These wood pulps are made into thin sheets and dried to make writing paper.

77. What are the explanations of scientists on milk absorbing status?

Scientists put the logical and scientific reasoning for two elementary principles in physics accounted for the illusion of deities drinking milk. These are the theory of surface tension and siphon action. In surface tension, the force that acts on the surface of the liquid tending to minimise its areas by which a liquid in contact with a solid surface rises or falls due to the relative attraction between the liquid molecules and solid surface. Some scientists however, suggested that the phenomenon being witnessed in temples was not a capillary action as claimed by some what could possibly be happening is siphon action where liquid milk flow from upper level to the lower. Therefore, there is nothing supernatural in it and it is purely a surface phenomenon.

78. How does a "Solar Cooker" work?

The cooker consists of an insulated box, the inside of which is painted black, to retain heat. It has a double-walled glass cover to trap the heat inside. A mirror is so placed that it reflects the sun's rays to the insulated box. The cooking containers are generally made of aluminium or steel and are provided with covers. These are painted black on the outside, to absorb radiation. The temperature of the box can reach up to 125°C which is adequate for cooking. The ingredients are put in the containers which are placed in the cooker. The glass cover is closed and the cooker is placed in direct sunlight. The sun's rays enter the box through the double glass cover and are also reflected by the mirrors so that they fall on it. The box absorbs the radiation and gradually heats up, cooking the food.

79. How do bubbles get into fizzy drinks?

When a fizzy drink is opened bubbles form inside the drink. These are bubbles of a gas called carbon dioxide that help the drink taste sharp. The gas is dissolved in the drink when it is made at the factory, where the carbon dioxide gas is forced into the drink under pressure so that it dissolves in the liquid. The drink remains under pressure in the bottle or can so that the gas stays dissolved in the drink. However, when the bottle or can is opened, the pressure is released. This is why the drink tries to get out as it is opened. The carbon dioxide escapes and form bubbles.

80. What is the difference between 'rayon' and 'nylon'?

Rayon is a regenerated textile filament made from cellulose, cotton linters or chips of hemlock, pine or spruce, by passing an appropriate solution of any of these through spinnerets. When rayon was first produced, it was called artificial silk. It was the first of the synthetics developed in the 1800s.

'Nylon' the widely used synthetic material is made from chemicals extracted chiefly from petroleum. It is a class of thermoplastic polymides capable of extrusion when molten into fibres, sheets etc., of extreme toughner strength and electricity synthetised by the interaction of a dicarboxylic acid with a diamine. It was commercially introduced in 1939, and when first appeared it was used for making women's stockings.

81. What are DNA Tests?

DNA (Deoxyribonucleic Acid) tests form, a sophisticated new method for criminal identification. This test developed by Dr. Alec Jefferys in 1985 in England was accepted by the legal system as an evidence in cases of rape, armed robbery, murder and even in paternity suits. In India, it was introduced by Dr. V.K.Kashyap at Hyderabad Central Forensic Laboratory in 1988. The coded genetic information hidden in the DNA is unique for every individual. All the billions of cells in the human body come from the multiplication of a single one that is formed by the fusion of the male sperm and female ovum. Each cell has an equal number of chromosomes from the father and mother. The chromosomes in turn contain DNA, which encodes the person's unique genetic make-up. Hence a body can be identified by a body sample or even hair, sperm, muscle, nerve or tissue sample.

82. What are teeth made of?

Teeth are made of enamel, denties and pulp. Enamel is mainly made of calcium and phosphorus. Enamel is hardest material in our body. This enamel is found as a coating on the part of the teeth that protrude from the gums. It is a substance that is harder than all but seven known substances including diamonds. When the teeth begins to deteriorate due to lack of proper care or any other reason, corrosive acids are formed that are actually able to break through the enamel and the bacteria, which aggravates the condition, reaches the dentin which is the bone like structure under the enamel. If it remains unchecked the rot goes even deeper, right into the centre of the tooth - the pulpy area where the blood vessel endings are found.

83. How is the distance between stars measured in light years and how long is a light year?

According to the scientists, the stars are spaced so far apart that any measurement of the distance between them in familiar units would be unwieldy. So scientists created a more manageable astronomical unit called the 'light year', which is the distance light takes to travel in one year, at a speed of about 186,200 miles a second. One light year is about 6,000,000,000,000 miles.

84. Why does the tail of a comet get shorter as it recedes from the sun?

As the comet recedes from the Sun, its tail gets shorter due to the decrease in the repulsive force of Sun's radiations. Because of the falling temperature with increasing distance from the Sun.

85. What causes wrinkles in the skin?

Wrinkles are caused mainly by ultraviolet radiation from the Sun. Over the years the ultraviolet rays break down the middle layer of skin, the dermis, coming it to loosen and allowing wrinkles to form. With extreme age, the dermis worsens on its own accord. To decrease the extent of wrinkles in the skin, one should limit exposure to direct sunlight, such as by using suncreams. Wrinkles are more likely to occur among people with lighter skin.

86. Why does paper tear easily?

Paper may look smooth and solid but it is not. If you could see if magnified, you would see that it is made up of many tiny fibres pushed together. If you pull on the paper, the fibres easily come apart and the paper tears.

87. Why do the stars twinkle?

The light from the stars travels though different layers of space of varying densities. Therefore, the light rays deviate from the original path. Further, these layers are not stationary but keep on moving. This leads to the twinkling of the stars.

88. If lime water is kept in air, what will happen?

It turns milky due to carbon dioxide in the air.

$$Ca(OH)_2 + CO_2 \rightarrow CaCO_3 + H_2O$$

89. Why does oil rise in a cloth tape of an oil lamp?

The pores in the cloth tape suck oil due to the capillary action of the oil.

90. Why is it dangerous to sleep under trees at night?

Plants respire at night and give out carbon dioxide which reduces the oxygen content of air required for breathing.

91. Sugar gets charred on heating. Why?

When sugar is heated above 200°C, it decomposes into carbon and water and therefore get charred.

$$C_6H_{12}O_6 \xrightarrow{200°C} 6C + 6H_2O$$

92. A man with a load on his head jumps from a high building. What will be the load experienced by him?

The load experienced by him will be zero, because the acceleration of his fall is equal to the acceleration due to gravity of the earth.

93. Which is more elastic, rubber or steel?

Steel is more elastic for the same stress produced in rubber is more than that in steel, the elasticity is α 1/strain.

94. Why does an ordinary glass tumbler crack when very hot tea or milk is poured in it?

When the inner layer of the tumbler gets heated, it expands before the outer layer and an unequal expansion of both layers causes the tumbler to crack.

95. Why is it difficult to breathe at higher altitudes?

Due to low air pressure at higher altitudes the quantity of air is less and so also that of oxygen.

96. How much blood does a normal person have in his body?

An adult human body contains about 4 to 5 litres of blood moving through the blood vessels in an endless circuit.

97. Why does an individual's nose run when he cries?

When a person cries, some tears gather in the eyes and there is a watery discharge from the nose, when tears are carried from the eyes to the nasal cavity.

98. Why do we place a wet cloth on the forehead of a patient suffering from high temperature?

Due to body's temperature water evaporating from the wet cloth produces cooling and brings the temperature down.

99. Why does milk turn sour?

The microbes react with milk and grow. They turn lactose into lactic acid which is sour in taste.

100. Why does moisture gather outside a tumbler containing cold water?

The water vapour of the air condenses on cooling and appears as droplets of water.

101. Why do not receive proper image from dark area to bright area?

Because Iris unable to dilate immediately.

102. How do classify the plastics?

The plastics are classified into two categories such as 1) Thermoset plastics (Melamine, Bakelite) 2) Thermoplastics (PVC).

INVENTIONS AND DISCOVERIES

Archimedean Screw (3rd Cen.BC)	Archimedes (Greece)
Atom Bomb (1945)	J.Robert Oppenheimer (U.S.)
Atomic Theory (1809)	Dalton (England)
Automatic rifle (1918)	John Browning (U.S.)
Avogadro's Hypothesis (1811)	Avogadro (Italy)
Ballistic missile (1944)	Wernher von Braun (Germany)
Balloon (1783)	Jacques & Joseph Montgolfier (France)
Ball-Point Pen (1888)	John J. Loud (U.S.)

Barometer (1644)	Evangelista Torricelli (Italy)
Battery (Electric) (1800)	Alessandro Volta (Italy)
Bifocal Lens (1780)	Benjamin Franklin (U.S.)
Boson (c.1950)	S.N. Bose (India)
Boyle's law (1662)	Boyle (Ireland)
Braille (1829)	Louis Braille (France)
Bunsen Burner (1855)	R. Willhelm von Bunsen (Germany)
Carburettor (1876)	Gottlieb Daimler (Germany)
Cellophane (1908)	Dr. J. Brandenberger (Switzerland)
Celluloid (1861)	Alexander Parkes (England)
Chronometer (1735)	John Harrison (England)
Cinema (1895)	Nicolas & Jean Lumiere (England)
Computer (1824)	Dr. Alan M. Turing (England)
Dynamite (19th Cen.)	Alfred Nobel (Germany)
Electric Flat Iron (1882)	H.W. Seeley (U.S.)
Electric Furnace (1861)	William Siemens (England
Electric Lamp (1879)	Thomas Alva Edison (U.S.)
Electro-Magnet (1824)	William Sturgeon (Britain)
Film (Movie) (1885)	Louis Prince (France)
Film (Talkie) (1922)	J.Engl, J.Mussolle & H.Vogt (Germany)
Fountain Pen (1884)	Waterman (U.S.)
Frequency Modulation (FM) (1933)	E.H. Armstrong (U.S.)
Galvanometer (1834)	Andre-Marie Ampere (France)
Glider (1853)	Sir George Cayley (Britain)
Gyro-compass (1911)	Elmer A. Sperry (U.S.)
Holography (1947)	Denis Gason (England)
Hydrogen bomb (1952)	Edward Teller (U.S.)
Isolation of metals by electricity (c.1800)	Davy (England)
Laser (1960)	T.H. Maimah (U.S.)
Launderette (1934)	J.F. Cantrell (U.S.)
Lightning Conductor (1752)	Benjamin Franklin (U.S.)
Linoleum (1860)	Frederick Walton (England)
Loudspeaker (1900)	Horace Short (England)
Magnetic Recording Tape (1928)	Fritz Pfleumer (Germany)
Microphone (1876)	Alexander Graham Bell (U.S.)
Micro-processor (1971)	Robert Noyce & Gordon Moore (U.S.)
Microscope (1590)	Z. Janssen (Netherlands)
Microwave Oven (1947)	Percy I. Spencer (U.S.)
Neon Lamp (1910)	Georges Claude (France)
Neutron bomb (1958)	Samuel Cohen (U.S.)
North Pole (1909)	Robert Peary (Cresson springs)
Nylon (1937)	Dr. Wallace H. Carothers (U.S.)
Optical Fibre (1955)	Narinder Kapany (Germany)
Photoelectric cell (1893)	Julius Elster, Hans F. Geitel (Germany)
Photography (on film) (1888)	John Carbutt (U.S.)

Rayon (1883)	Sir Joseph Swan (Britain)
Refrigeration (1850)	James Harrison, Alexander Catlin (U.S.)
Rubik Cube (1975)	Prof. Emo Rubik (Hungary)
Safety Match (1826)	John Walker (Britain)
Safety Pin (1849)	Walter Hunt (U.S.)
Solar System (1540)	Copernicus (Poland)
South Pole (1912)	Amundsen (Norway)
Stainless Stell (1913)	Harry Brearley (Britain)
Steam Engine (condenser) (1765)	James Watt (Britain)
Telegraph (1787)	M. Lammond (France)
Telegraph Code (1837)	Samuel F.B. Morse (U.S.)
Telescope (1608)	Hans Lippershey (Netherlands)
Television (1927)	P.T. Farnsworth (U.S.)
Transformer (1831)	Michael Faraday (England)
Transistor (1948)	Bardeen, Shockley & Brattain (U.S.)
Video tape (1956)	Charles Ginsberg (U.S.)
Watch (1462)	Bartholomew Manfredi (Italy)
West Indies (1492)	Coloumbus (Italy)
Xerography (c.1930)	Chester F. Carlson (U.S.)
Zip Fastener (1891)	W.I. Judson (U.S.)

MECHANICAL INVENTIONS AND DISCOVERIES

Aeroplane (1903)	Wright Brothers (U.S.)
Air Brake (1863)	George Westinghouse (U.S.)
Art of Printing (15th cen.)	Gutenberg (Germany)
Bicycle (1839)	Macmillan (England)
Calculating Machine (1647)	Pascal (France)
Disc Brake (1902)	Lanchester (England)
Dynamo (1832)	Michael Faraday (England)
Gas Engine (1885)	Daimler (Germany)
Globe (celestial and terrestial (c.1569)	Mercator (Belgium)
Gramophone (1888)	Emile Berliner (U.S.)
Helicopter (1930)	Ascanio (Italy)
Hovercraft (1955)	Cockerell (England)
Internal Combustion (Diesel) Engine (1897)	Diesel (Germany)
Jet Propulsion (1937)	Sir Frank Whittle (England)
Lift (1852)	Otis (U.S.)
Lynotype (1883)	Margenthaler (U.S.)
Machine Gun (1718)	James Puckle (England)
Military Tank (1914)	Sir Ernest D. Swington (England)
Miner's Safety Lamp (1820)	Davy Sir Humphry (England)
Motor Cycle (1885)	G. Daimler of Cannstatt (Germany)
Parachute (1797)	Garnerin (France)

Pendulum clock (1657)	Christian Huygens (Netherlands)
Petrol Car (1888)	Carl Benz (Germany)
Pneumatic Tyre (1845)	Boyd Dunlop (Scotland)
Printing Press (c.1455)	Johann Guterberg (Germany)
Radar (1922)	A.H. Taylor & Leo C. Young (U.S.)
Revolver (1835)	Samuel Colt (U.S.)
Rotary Printing Press (1846)	Richard Hoe (U.S.)
Safety Razor (1895)	Gillette (U.S.)
Sewing Machine (1755)	Weisenthal (U.S.)
Ship Propeller (1837)	Francis Smith (England)
Spinning Frame (1769)	Arkwright (England)
Steam Boat (c.1800)	Fulton (U.S.)
Steam Car (c.1769)	Cugnot (France)
Steam Engine (1698)	Thomas Savery (England)
Steam Engine (piston) (1712)	Thomas Newcomen (Britain)
Steam Ship (1775)	J.C. Perier (France)
Submarine (1776)	David Bushnell
Telephone (1876)	Bell Graham (U.S.)
Turbine Ship (1894)	Sir C. Parsons (England)
Typewriter (1864)	Mitterhofer (Austria)

MEDICAL INVENTIONS AND DISCOVERIES

Antiseptic treatment (1865)	Lister (England)
Bacteria (1683)	Leeuwenhock (Netherlands)
Biochemistry (1648)	Jan Baptista, Van Helmont (Belgium)
Cause of beriberi (19th cen.)	Eijkman (Netherlands)
Chloroform (1847)	Simpson (England)
Cholera bacillus (1883)	Koch (Germany)
Circulation of blood (17th cen.)	Harvey (England)
Hypodermic Syringe (1853)	Wood (England)
Insulin (c.1923)	Banting (Canada)
Leprosy bacillus (1873)	Hansen (Norway)
Morphine (1805)	Sertumer (Germany)
Penicillin (1928)	Fleming (Scotland)
Stethoscope (1819)	Rene Laennec (France)
Sulpha drugs as bactericides (c.1939)	Domagk (Germany)
Transfusion of blood (1625)	Denys (France)
Treatment of rabies; cure for hydrophobia (c.1881)	Pasteur, Louis (France)
Tuberculosis bacillus (1882)	Koch (Germany)
Vaccination (1796)	Jenner (England)
X-rays (1895)	Rontgen (Germany)

SUBJECTS

Acoustics	Science or study of sound
Anatomy	Internal structure of living organism
Anthropology	Mental and Physical states of mankind
Archaeology	Study of antiquities
Astrology	Predicting future of human beings
Astronautics	The science of space travel
Astronomy	Study of heavenly bodies
Astrophysics	A branch of astronomy dealing with physical nature of heavenly bodies
Bacteriology	Dealing with bacteria
Biology	Study of living bodies
Bionics	Study of mechanical system that function like living organisms
Botany	The study of Plant life
Ceramics	Art or technology of making objects from clay
Chemistry	Properties and composition of various elements
Chemotherapy	Treatment of a Disease by certain chemical compounds
Chronology	Computing of period of time and assignment of dates with events
Conchology	Study of shells
Cosmology	The science of universe as a whole
Cyrogenics	Production and application of very low temperatures
Cryptography	Study of secret writing
Cytology	Dealing with cells
Cytogenetics	Study of hereditory from the point of view cytology and genetics
Ecology	Study of Relations of animals and plants to their environments
Economics	Study of production, consumption and distribution of wealth
Entomology	Study of Insects
Epidemiology	Study of Epidemics
Epigraphy	Study of Inscriptions
Ergonomics	The study of work and working conditions
Ethics	Psychological Study of moral conduct and duty
Ethnology	Study of mental and physical differences of mankind
Etymology	Study of the origin and history of words

Exobiology	Science dealing with life existing beyond Earth
Genetics	Science of Heredity
Geology	Study of condition and structure of the Earth
Gerontology	Science of old age
Haematology	Science dealing with the formation, composition, functions and diseases of the blood
Horticulture	Garden cultivation
Hydrography	Treatment of diseases with water
Hydrophonics	Culture of plants without soil, only in solutions
Hydroponics	Culture of plants without soil
Hydrostatics	The relation of pressure to equilibrium of fluids
Hyetology	Study of rainfall
Hygiene	Study of Health
Jurisprudence	The science of knowledge of law
Iconography	Teaching by pictures and models
Lexicography	Compiling of dictionary
Mammography	A technique of quicker diagnosis of breast cancer among women
Metallurgy	Study of Science and Technology of metals
Meteorology	Atmospheric phenomena
Morphology	Position, structure and form of different plants and animals
Morphotogeny	Origin and growth of any living organism
Mycology	The study of fungi
Numismatics	Study of coins
Odontography	Study of teeth
Optics	Nature and properties of light
Ornithology	Study of birds
Osteology	The study of bones
Palaeontology	Study of fossils
Pathology	Nature, causes and remedies of diseases
Pedagogy	Art or method of teaching
Pedology	The study of soil
Perinatology	The study of disorders of the newborn that occur in the perinatal period
Phrenology	Skull and brain
Philately	Stamp collection
Philology	Study of written records and authenticity
Phonetics	Study of speech sounds and the production, transmission, reception, etc.
Physics	Material bodies
Physiology	Structure and function of animal and plant life

Physiography	Study of natural geography
Pomology	Fruits
Psychology	Study of human behaviour
Radiology	Radiant energy
Seismology	Science of earthquakes
Sericulture	Silkworm rearing
Sociology	Social problems and human progress
Telepathy	Communication between minds by some means other than sensory perception
Therapeutics	Science or Art of healing
Tribology	The study of interacting surfaces in relative motion
Virology	Study of Viruses
Zoology	The study of Animal life

SCIENTIFIC INSTRUMENTS

Altimeter: An instrument for measuring altitudes and heights.

Ammeter: Is used for measuring electric currents in Amperes.

Anemometer: An instrument to measure velocity of wind.

Audiometer: An instrument to measure intensity of sound.

Audiophone: An instrument to aid and improve the faculty of hearing.

Barograph: An instrument to record atmospheric pressure continuously.

Barometer: An instrument to measure atmospheric pressure.

Binocular: An instrument to view the distant objects clearly. In binoculars, two right angled prisms are used through which the rays are twice reflected.

Callipers: An instrument used to measure the inside or outside diameters of bodies.

Calorimeter: An instrument to measure the quantities of heat.

Carburettor: An arrangement in internal combustion engines to mix air with petroleum vapours.

Cardiogram: The record obtained from the Cardiograph.

Cardiography: A medical instrument used for tracing the movement of the heart.

Chronometer: An instrument used in ships to calculate accurate time.

Cinematograph: It is used to focus the films on the screen. It consists of a number of lenses arranged to throw on a screen an enlarged image of photographs.

Colorimeter: An instrument for comparing intensities of colour.

Commutator: It is a part in D.C. Dynamo. (split ring)

Crescograph: An instrument used in recording growth of plants. It was invented by Dr. J.C.Bose.

Cyclotron: An apparatus for electromagnetic acceleration of charged atoms.

Dictaphone: A machine which first records what is spoken into it and then reproduces it in type.

Dip circle: An instrument to determine the angle between the directions of the earth's magnetic field and the horizontal at a place. This particular angle is known as dip of that place.

Drinker's Apparatus: Is used to help breathing in infantile paralysis.

Dynamo: An electrical instrument in which the mechanical energy is converted into electrical energy. The principle of electromagnetic induction is involved in it.

Dynamometer: An instrument for measuring the electrical power.

Electrocardiograph (ECG): An instrument used for detection of electric impulses of the heart. Gives graphic picture of heart beats.

Electroencephalograph: Used to record and interpret the electrical activity of the brain.

Electrometer: An instrument for measuring electricity.

Electrophorus: An instrument for generating statical electricity by induction

Electroscope: An instrument for detecting the presence of electric charge.

Epidiascope: Used to project films and images of opaque articles on a screen.

Eudiometer: A glass tube for measuring volume changes in chemical reactions between gases.

Fathometer: An instrument for measuring the depth of the ocean.

Galvanometer: An instrument for measuring current of small magnitude.

G.M.Counter: A device used to detect the presence of radiation.

Gramophone: An instrument for reproducing sound stored in grooves on a disc.

Gravimeter: An instrument to record oil deposits under water.

Gyroscope: An instrument to illustrate the dynamics of rotating bodies.

Hydrometer: An instrument to measure specific gravity of liquids.

Hydrophone: An instrument used for recording sound under water.

Hydroscope: An optical instrument used for seeing objects below the surface of water.

Hygrometer: An instrument to measure the humidity in air.

Hygroscope: An instrument to show the changes in atmospheric humidity.

Hypsometer: An instrument to measure the height above sea level.

Kymegraph: An instrument to record graphically various physiological movement i.e., blood pressure, heart beating, study of lungs etc, in living beings.

Lactometer: An instrument used to measure density of milk.

Magnetometer: An instrument used to compare the magnetic moments and fields.

Mariner's Compass: An apparatus to guide sailors. The needle always points north-south.

Megaphone: An instrument for carrying sound to long distances.

Manometer: An instrument to determine the pressure of gases.

Microphone: An instrument used for converting sound waves into electrical signals.

Micrometer: An instrument to calculate the fraction of the lowest division of a given scale.

Microscope: An optical instrument for producing enlarged images of minute objects.

Microtome: An instrument used to cut an object into thin parts for microscopic inspection.

Odometer: An instrument used to determine the distance covered by wheeled vehicles.

Parachute: Umbrella shaped safety device used for landing from aircraft in an emergency.

Periscope: An instrument used by the crew of a submarine to survey the ships etc., on the surface of the sea. It is used in pits dug in war field.

Phonograph: An instrument for recording and reproducing sound stored as grooves cut in cylinders.

Photometer: An instrument to compare the illuminating power of two sources of light.

Photographic Camera: An apparatus to take the real photograph of a person.

Pipette: A glass tube with the aid of which a definite volume of liquid may be transferred.

Potentiometer: Is used to compare the E.M.Fs. of cells, to measure the thermal E.M.Fs. to determine the large potential difference currents and to measure the low resistances.

Pyknometer: An instrument used to measure the density and co-efficient of expansion of liquid.

Pyrheliometer: An instrument for measuring solar radiations.

Pyrometer: An instrument to record the high temperature of a distant object, e.g., the Sun.

Radar: Radio, Angle, Detection and Range. It is used to detect the direction and range of a flying aircraft by means of radiowaves.

Radiator of Car: An apparatus attached in the car engine to serve as a cooling agent.

Rain Gauge: An instrument for recording the rainfall at a particular place.

Radiometer: An instrument for measuring the emission of radiant energy.

Refractometer: An instrument to measure refractive indexes.

Resistance Thermometer: Used for determining the electrical resistance of conductor.

Salinometer: Used to determine the concentration of salt solutions by measuring their densities.

Saccharometer: An instrument to determine the amount of sugar content in a solution.

Seismometer or Seismograph: An instrument used to record the intensity of an earthquake.

Sextant: An instrument with a graduated arc used in navigation and surveying for measuring the angular distance of objects like the Sun or stars.

Spectroscope: An instrument used for spectrum analysis.

Spectrometer: An instrument used for the measurement of observed spectra.

Spherometer: An instrument used for accurately measuring the curvature of spherical objects.

Speedometer: An instrument which indicates speed at which a vehicle is moving.

Sphygmanometer: An instrument used to measure arterial blood-pressure.

Sphygmophone: An instrument with the help of which a pulse beat can be heard.

Sphygmoscope: An instrument by virtue of which arterial pulsations become visible.

Stereoscope: An instrument by which a double photograph snapped from two different angles by a two-lensed camera can be viewed.

Stethoscope: An instrument to hear and analyse the movements of heart and lungs.

Stop Watch: An instrument to record small intervals of time in laboratory, in races, etc.

Stroboscope: An instrument to bring the fast moving objects into view as if they were at rest.

Tachometer: An instrument to determine speeds of aeroplanes, motor boats, etc.

Tangent Galvanometer: An instrument for measuring the strength of direct current.

Telephone: An instrument by virtue of which two persons at different places can communicate.

Teleprinter: An instrument which prints automatically the messages sent from various places.

Telescope: An instrument to observe astronomical objects.

Television: An instrument to receive the images of moving objects transmitted by radio waves and convert into real sound and sight.

Telstar: It is a space satellite by which overseas communications are made possible.

Theodolite: An instrument for measuring horizontal and vertical angles with a rotating telescope.

Thermograph: An instrument, self-registering the record made by a Thermometer.

Thermostat: An apparatus to measure temperature to a particular degree. It is used in refrigeration.

Thermocouple: An instrument based on thermo-electricity used for measuring temperatures.

Thermometer: An apparatus used for measuring temperature.

Viscometer: An instrument to measure viscosity.

Voltmeter: An instrument to measure potential difference between two points.

ANSWER FOLLOWING QUESTION WITH AN 'YES' or 'NO'

1. Soap lathers well with hard water.
2. Heat from the Sun reaches us by radiation.
3. Moon is surrounded by a thick blanket of atmosphere.
4. Gravity of Moon is more than that of the Earth.
5. Echo in a furnished room is more than in an empty room.
6. The Sun is visible before it actually comes into the horizon.
7. We feel easy breathing at higher altitudes.
8. The rainbow is seen on the same side of the Sun.
9. 35°F is warmer than 25°C.
10. Hypo is used in photography.
11. Sir C.V.Raman is a great biologist of India.
12. Pineapple is a dry dehiscent fruit.
13. The simple electric cell was invented by Volta.
14. Harvey discovered circulation of blood.
15. Vermiform appendix is an important part of the human body.
16. Wright brothers invented diesel engine.
17. Alexander Fleming discovered Insulin.
18. The chemical name for blue vitriol is copper sulphate.
19. Newton discovered the laws of motion.
20. Animal which has a backbone is called vertebrate.
21. Haemoglobin is the carrier of oxygen in the human body.
22. Jenner discovered the laws of electrolysis.
23. The metal of salts which are sensitive to sunlight is lead.
24. The silvered walls in the thermos flask prevent the loss of heat by radiation.
25. Scurvy is a disease caused by the deficiency of Vitamin C.
26. Starch is digested by insulin.
27. When iron rusts, its weight increases.
28. The mineral fibre that does not burn is asbestos.
29. Bile is formed in liver.
30. The hottest planet of the solar system is Venus.
31. When acidified water is electrolysed, hydrogen is evolved at the anode.
32. Insulin is used in the treatment of diabetes.
33. Mica is non-conductor of heat and electricity.
34. Dry ice is solid carbon-di-oxide.
35. Sandalwood oil is manufactured in Karnataka state.
36. Electric current is measured in amperes.

37. Graphite is an allotropic form of carbon.
38. Air is mainly composed of oxygen and nitrogen.
39. Copper is a bad conductor of electricity.
40. Density of water is maximum at 4°C.
41. Gold is found in Karnataka.
42. Helium is heavier than hydrogen.
43. Protein builds bones.
44. Eskimos eat more fat than people in the tropics. It will maintain higher heat in their bodies.
45. A man who loses his way in a desert will die for lack of food. But by lack of water.
46. Bat is a bird which can see in the dark.
47. Goitre disease is caused by the deficiency of iodine.
48. Carbon is an inert gas.
49. Einstein is the formulator of special Theory of Relativity.
50. Atomic Mass of the Hydrogen atom is one.

ANSWERS:

NO: 1, 3, 4, 7, 8, 9, 11, 15, 17, 22, 23, 26, 39, 43, 45, 46, 48

YES: For other questions

IMPORTANT EVENTS

BIOLOGY AND MEDICINE

1902	-	Landsteiner discovers blood grouping.
1922	-	Banting and Best treat diabetic patients with insulin.
1928	-	Fleming discovers Penicillin.
1932	-	Domagk discovers first sulpha drug.
1950	-	Anti-depression drugs and Beta Blockers for heart developed.
1950	-	Sir Peter Medawar gives theory of tissue transplant.
1953	-	Crick and Watson discover the double helix.
1954	-	Polio vaccine developed by Salk.
1963	-	Gajdusek describes first slow human virus.
1970	-	Har Gobind Khorana synthesises a gene for the first time.
1972	-	The CAT scan introduced by Hounsfield.
1975	-	Milstein produces first monoclonal antibodies.
1980	-	Pruisner gives out his theory of prion i.e., neuro-degenerative diseases caused by a slow virus.
1983	-	AIDS virus isolated.
1984	-	Alec Jeffreys devices genetic finger printing
1984	-	First vaccine against Leprosy.
1989	-	Grafts of fetal brain tissue used to treat Parkinson's disease.
1993	-	Identification of genes causing colon cancer.
2000	-	First draft of human genome completed.

UNITS OF MEASUREMENT

Ampere	-	Electric current
Angstrom	-	Wave-length and also lengths of atomic dimensions (10^{-10}m)
Bar	-	Atmospheric pressure (760 mm height of mercury)
Becquerel	-	Radioactivity
Bel	-	Intensity of Sound
Calorie	-	Quantity of Heat (1 Calorie = 4.184 Joules)
Candela	-	Luminous intensity
Candle power	-	Illuminating power of source of light
Celsius (Centigrade)	-	Temperature
Coulomb	-	Electric Charge
Decibel	-	Intensity of sound ($\frac{1}{10}$th of Bel)
Dyne	-	Force
Electron-volt	-	Energy
Erg	-	Work or Energy (1 erg = 10^{-7} Joule)
Fahrenheit	-	Temperature
Farad	-	Electric Capacitance
Faraday	-	Electric Charge
Fathom	-	Depth of water
Foot Candle	-	Brightness
Gauss	-	Magnetic Induction
Henry	-	Inductance
Hertz	-	Frequency
Horse-power	-	Power
Joule	-	Work or Energy
Kelvin	-	Thermodynamic temperature
Kilogram	-	Mass
Knot	-	Speed of Ship (1 Knot - 1854 meters)
Lambert	-	Brightness
Light year	-	Stellar Distance
Lumen	-	Luminous flux
Maxwell	-	Magnetic flux
Metre	-	Length
Mole	-	Amount of Substance
Nautical Mile	-	Distance in Navigation
Newton	-	Force (metric)
Newton metre	-	Work
Oersted	-	Magnetic Intensity
Ohm	-	Electrical Resistance
Pascal	-	Stress
Poise	-	Viscosity
Quintal	-	Weight (metric)

Radian	-	Plane Angle
Second	-	Time
Tesla	-	Magnetic Flux Density
Volt	-	Electric Potential
Watt	-	Power
Weber	-	Magnetic Flux

BIOLOGY
EIGHT SYSTEMS OF HUMAN BODY

1. The Digestive System: The 'Alimentary Canal' - tube of about 33 ft. length with varying dimensions has certain glands which drop their juices into it. The food pipe known as 'Gullet' comes from the neck and drops into the stomach through chest. Its first part is narrower and 10 inches long. The 'Stomach' is a bag shaped organ. The stomach has two openings - the end of the food pipe and the beginning of the intestines. The gastric juice secreted by the glands converts proteins into peptones and coagulates milk. The alimentary tube narrows again and transfers it into small intestines which is about 22 ft. long. The first 10 inches of the small intestines cover the Duodenum and it forms a C-shaped loop in which lies an important gland 'Pancreas' which secretes 'insulin'. The 'large intestine' is coil-shaped which is 6 ft. long. At the junction of these two intestines, there is a blind pouch, 'Caecum'. A narrow tube known as the 'Vermiform appendix' - about four to six inches long hangs down from the Caecum. The part of large intestine above Caecum is known as 'Colon'. It then joins into a tube 'Rectum' which opens to the outside by the 'Anus'.

2. The Circulatory System: The heart - the main organ of this system is a hollow muscular organ which lies between lungs and in the middle of the chest cavity. The four chambers have been explained under the heading 'Heart'. Each auricle and ventricle is joined by an opening called 'auriculo-ventricular'. Each opening is guarded by a valve. On the right, the valve consists of three flaps known as tricuspid valve while there is a bicuspid valve on the left with two flaps. The impure blood from the upper and lower parts is brought to the heart by the Superior Vena Cava and Inferior Vena Cava respectively. The blood purified and oxygenated from the lungs is brought by two pulmonary veins. The pure blood is forced out into the aorta, the branches of which carry blood to all parts of the body.

3. The Respiratory System: The inhaled air enters into the lungs through nose or mouth via Pharynx into Larynx. The Larynx lies at the top of trachea, the opening of which is guarded by a cartilaginous lid known as epiglottis. The trachea or the wind pipe is 5 inches long made up of incomplete rings of cartilage. The trachea is divided into two branches known as the right and the left bronchi which enter the respective lung.

4. The Nervous System: It consists of brain, spinal cord and nerves. This system controls the working of the various organs of the body. The brain controls intellect, will, thought, memory, action, etc., while the spinal cord acts as sub-conscious brain and controls reflex action. The failure of this system will result in Paralysis, Coma, etc. There are 12 pairs of Cranial Nerves and 31 pairs of Spinal Nerves in our body.

5. The Muscular System: There are two types of muscles - Voluntary and Involuntary. The voluntary muscles act according to our will and are generally fixed to the bones. Involuntary muscles produce the movement of internal organs. (eg) Stomach, Heart etc.

6. The Reproductive System: Human beings are divided into males and females, without which the reproduction would have been impossible. The reproductive organs and glands are evident during the process of growth. The glands in the male body produce sperms and those of female body produce eggs. The mating of both, leads to fertilization. After ten months, a child is born.

7. The Skeleton System: There are 206 bones in our body forming various joints. It gives not only shape to the body but also protects the organs. The Skeleton system is divided into four parts, namely the skull, the vertebral column or the backbone, the bones enclosing the cavity of thorax and the bones of the upper and the lower limbs or extremities.

8. The Excretory System: The two main organs of this system are skin and kidneys. They expel waste products in the form of sweat and urine. The skin covers the whole body and protects the muscles and organs. The skin consists of two layers - the outer layer (epidermis) and the inner layer (dermis). The skin regulates the temperature, acts as organ of sense or touch, throws out nitrogenous waste in the form of sweat and gives shape to the body. Kidneys are two in number. They filter blood and the filtered products - nitrogenous waste is thrown out in the form of urine.

HUMAN ORGANS AND THEIR FUNCTIONS

Aorta: The largest artery of the body. The primary function of the aorta is to carry oxygenated blood from the heart to the cells of the body.

Bile: It is a liquid secretion of the liver. It emulsifies fat, prevents food from decomposing and forming gas. It helps the digested food to pass along the digestive canal smoothly. It is finally absorbed by the intestines, gets into the blood and helps to maintain the body temperature.

Bladder: The membranous and muscular sac that receives the urine from kidneys.

Blood: The food substances are absorbed by the blood in minute vessels in the intestines; hence it is a medium by which nutrient is taken to all parts of body. The plasma of the blood contains red blood corpuscles and white blood corpuscles. The red blood corpuscles play an important part in taking oxygen from air into the lungs and carrying it to various parts of the body. The white blood corpuscles are like soldiers, offering resistance to disease. There are other substances in the blood which assist in resisting diseases and among these are anti-toxins which neutralize poisons or toxins. There are four classical blood groups A, B, AB and O discovered by *Karl Landsteiner* in 1903 and found to be of great importance in blood transfusion.

Chromosome: Chromosomes are microscopic bodies found in the nucleus of cells. They carry hereditary materials, units of which have been called genes and which determine the growth, development and characteristics of an organism.

Ductless Glands: These are the glands which manufacture internal secretions which are passed directly into the blood inside vessels within the gland itself and not via duct or ducts as in the case of bile manufactured by the liver and passed into the intestine. They are namely thyroid gland, pituitary gland and supra renal gland, etc.

Heart: Lying between the lungs, it pumps the blood into blood vessels by the action of contraction. It is divided into four chambers - 2 auricles (Upper chambers) and 2 ventricles (Lower chambers). Right auricle is connected to right ventricle and left to left through valves. It pumps blood into aorta to be carried to all parts of the body. The impure blood is brought to heart through pulmonary veins of the respective lungs.

Kidneys: There are two kidneys situated one on each side of the spinal column. The blood is filtered through kidneys and the waste is passed as urine through ureters into bladder.

Liver: It is the largest gland in the body. It is dark red in colour and weighs about 50 ounces. It stores up glucogen and turns glucogen into sugar. Then sugar is sent to different parts of the body. It serves to destroy the wornout blood corpuscles and excrete the bile which is poured into the intestines.

Lungs: The organs of respiration. They purify blood. The minute blood vessels in the cell walls are constantly taking in the oxygen contained in the inhaled air and discharging impurities in the form of carbon dioxide and other waste matter.

Pancreas: Its function is to produce ferments which are passed into stomach to help the digestion of proteins. It secretes insulin. Its failure to secrete insulin will result in diabetes.

Pituitary: Lying at the base of the brain, a hormone secreted by it exerts powerful influence on the skeleton structure of the body. The excess secretion will result in abnormal growth.

Plasma: Plasma contains 92-95% of water and aqueous solution of ions of sodium, potassium and calcium. During the process of clotting, the blood becomes insoluble and forms a network of threads in which blood cells get entangled and bleeding stops.

Skin: It covers the whole body and protects the muscles lying under it. It consists of two layers - (i) the outer layer or the Epidermis; and (ii) the innermost layer or the Dermis. It regulates the temperature. It controls the sensation of touch and temperature of the body. It throws out the waste products via perspiration.

Spinal Cord: It is actually an extension of the brain in the form of a long cord through the back-bone or vertebral column and in it are situated centres of nerve tissues connected with reflex actions.

Spleen: It is about 5" x 3" size. Situated near the diaphragm on the left side of the body, one of its known functions is maintaining the proper condition of the blood cells. Spleen in person was affected by malaria.

Thyroid Gland: It acts as accelerator to the body. Situated at the base of the neck, it controls the speed at which the processes in the body are being carried out. When it overacts, a person feels-tension, nervous, blushed and his heart beats faster. The enlargement of the thyroid gland causes 'goitre' and when it underacts, it causes Myxoedema.

DISEASES - CAUSES AND CURES

AIDS: It is the abbreviated form of the disease 'Acquired Immune Deficiency Syndrome'. It is caused by virus called Human Immunodeficiency Virus (HIV). The virus in the blood multiplies many times faster than any other virus and progressively destroys T-cells which fight infections. Thus the defence mechanism is totally paralysed. As there is no certain cure, it can be prevented by avoiding sexual intercourse with different females, homo-sexual practices, screening of blood before transfusion, avoiding pregnancy in HIV infected females, etc.

Appendicitis: A disease of the large intestine which is symptomatised by pain over the stomach and vomiting. It is usually cured by surgery.

Beri-Beri: It is caused by lack of Vitamin B1 found in most grains principally in the embryo and the outer covering.

Cancer: Multiplicatiion or extra growth of cells. Though there is no certain cure, if detected in the early stages, radiotherapy and chemotherapy can cure to a large extent. The onset of cancer can be detected by symptoms like - a sore that does not heal, unusual and repeated bleeding especially in women after menopause, a lump in any part of the body, persistent hoarseness or cough, persistent indigestion, difficulty in swallowing, change in size and colour of a mole or wart in the body.

Cholera: Caused by swallowing Koch's 'Coma Bacillus' through infected water, food, etc. Medicine for curing it is Tomb's 'Cholera mixture'.

Diabetes: The cause though not definitely known, is the failure of pancreas to secrete insulin to absorb sugar. The symptoms are increasing appetite, thirst, frequent passing of urine, presence of sugar in the urine, increasing loss of weight, appearance of boils, itching skin, etc.

Filaria (Elephant foot): An infection of the body with tiny worm which block the lymph vessels. Spread by blood sucking flies and mosquitoes.

Gout: Caused due to excess of uric acid in the body. It can be cured by Sincophers.

Hepatitis B: Hepatitis is a debilitating liver disease. This disease is even more serious worldwide. The hepatitis vaccine is produced by collecting blood samples from persons who have been infected by the disease. It is transmitted through infected blood and parenteral infection. Using a technique to isolate the antigen, or surface protein, that identifies the disease-causing agent. This protein, called hepatitis B surface antigen, stimulates antibody production by the human immune system. Most other vaccines have been made by a process of attenuation.

Influenza: Caused by Pfeiffer's bacillus which is present in the respiratory tract. It is believed by others that it is caused by another organism called 'Bacterium Pneumocentes'.

Leprosy: Caused by Mycobacterium leprae, it affects skin and nervous system. It can be cured by sulpha drugs.

Malaria: Caused by the bite of female anopheles mosquito. A kind of cell organism enters into the blood and destroys red blood corpuscles. The newly entered parasites take up their abode in the blood after destroying considerable red blood corpuscles. The symptoms are high fever and trembling of the body. Medicines - Chloroquinine, atebrine, etc., are used to cure malaria. The prevention can be effected by destroying mosquitoes by spraying D.D.T., kerosene oil, etc.

Measles: A contagious disease marked by fever, redness of the eyes, appearance of rashes on the skin and mild bronchitis. It is a viral disease. Complete rest and light diet will cure the disease. The serious danger is complications in severely infected eyes, nose or throat.

Pellagra: A deadly disease caused by deficiency of nicotinic acid, characterized by cracking of the skin and often resulting in insanity.

Plague: Not much known nowadays, once it was a devastating disease. It is caused by the bite of infected rat flea. Anti-Plague inoculation can be given. Dead rats should be burned in the vicinity. It can be cured by sulpha drugs and streptomycin.

Polio: An acute infectious disease, it affects central nervous system and by destroying motor neutrons in the spinal cord causes flaccid paralysis. It is caused by a kind of virus found in throat and the stools. Entering through the mouth, the virus multiplies in the throat and the intestines. It can be avoided by preventing human contact and inter-family contact.

Pyorrhoea: Infection of the gums causing the edges of the tooth sockets. It can be cured by Penicillin dosages or Vitamin C tablets but the treatment depends on the cause and can best be carried out by a dentist.

Rabies: It is caused by the bite or even licking by a mad animal, generally a dog or a jackal. The bitten part should be cleaned with hot water and prophylactic vaccination (founded by the Pasteur Institute) should be given.

Rickets: This is a bone disease usually affecting artificially fed infants between the age of six to fifteen months. It is caused by the deficiency of vitamins A and D. The bones of the legs become crooked. The abdomen is usually enlarged. The child is weak and undersized. It is often due to lack of exposure to sunlight.

Scarlet Fever: It is caused by the infection of the germ known as streptococcus against which anti-toxin has been discovered. Sulphonamide drugs are applied for the treatment.

The symptoms are shivering attacks, later followed by fever, sometimes results in vomiting and sore throat. On the second day of illness, a rash or bright red spots appears which usually begins to fade on the third or fourth day.

Schizophrenia: Mental diseases are of two types - organic and functional. Schizophrenia is a functional disease known to be occurring in early adult life. The symptoms are fanatic and eccentric behaviour of the patient. These are delusions and hallucinations. Sometimes the patient is wildly excited. Although the disease is described as functional, recent discoveries seem to suggest some arrangement of blood chemistry. Tranquilising drugs are becoming helpful in treating the patients.

Scurvy: Caused by deficiency of vitamin-C. It can be prevented and cured by dietic treatment.

Typhoid: Caused by typhoid bacillus present in infected water, milk, ice-creams, shell-fish etc. It can be cured by inoculation or by prophylactic vaccination and chloromycetin.

Tuberculosis: An infectious disease which takes various forms. Pulmonary type of tuberculosis can be detected by symptoms such as loss of weight, general debility and night sweats. Tuberculosis of lungs and of lymphatic glands of the neck is spread by a person suffering from the disease during the act of coughing. The germs may enter through inhalation. The patient must be isolated. B.C.G. vaccine can be given.

VITAMINS

Vitamins are organic substances required for regulating the body processes and preventing certain diseases. Various vitamins are – Vitamin A, B, C, D, E etc. Vitamins are abundantly found in our daily food. The deficiency of vitamins will lead to diseases.

Vitamin A:	(Retinol) It is a derivative of β-Carotene. It is a fat soluble vitamin.
Function	Important for healthy skin, body growth and aids night vision. It is anti-infective
Deficiency	Night blindness, Rough and dry skin xerophthalmia, growth deformities
Sources	Milk, butter, animals' fats, eggs, carrots, mangoes, oranges, papayas, tomatoes
Vitamin B:	It is a mixture of number of water soluble vitamins like Vitamin B_1, B_2, B_6 and B_{12}.
Vitamin B_1	(Thiamine):
Function	Nerve cell, antineuritic, anti-beri-beri, carbohydrate metabolism
Deficiency	Neuritis, Beri-Beri, loss of appetite, pellagra, diarrhoea, adrenals, affects thyroid
Sources	Yeast, Milk, Eggs, Cereals, Rice polishings, meat, liver, pulses
Vitamin B_2	(Riboflavin):
Function	Protein metabolism
Deficiency	Skin disorders, sore tongue, fissures at the corners of the mouth
Sources	Milk, Green vegetables and Rice polishings

Vitamin B$_6$	(Pyridoxin): It is a mixture of three different derivatives - pyridoxal, pyridoxine and pyridoxamine.
Function	Cellular function
Deficiency	Nervous disorders
Sources	Cereal grains, vegetables, honey, egg yolk, peanuts
Vitamin B$_{12}$	(Cyano cobalamin): It contains a cobalt atom co-ordinated to four nitrogen atoms.
Function	Maturation of RBC, DNA synthesis
Deficiency	Incomplete maturation, some form of macrocytic anaemia
Sources	Milk and milk products, eggs, liver, pulses, cereals.
Vitamin C	(Ascorbic Acid): It is a water soluble vitamin.
Function	Formation of collagen, cold preventive, vascular function
Deficiency	Scurvy, gums and teeth bleeding
Sources	Tomatoes, lemon, oranges, leafy vegetables, cow's milk.
Vitamin D	(Ergo-calciferol): It is a complex mixture of D$_1$, D$_2$, D$_3$, D$_4$ etc. Ultraviolet rays from the Sun, change ergosterol present in human skin to vitamin D$_2$, and hence it is called sunshine vitamin.
Function	Bone formation, Calcium and phosphorus absorption
Deficiency	Rickets, poor formation of teeth
Sources	Oily fish, egg yolk, butter, milk, liver.
Vitamin E	(α-Tocopherol): It is a group of closely related compounds called tocopherols. They are known as α, β, γ - tocopherols a fat soluble vitamin.
Function	Assists cell respiration, helps in reproduction, intracellular antioxidant.
Deficiency	Liver damage, causes abortion, menstruation irregularities, sterility
Sources	Whole wheat, milk, eggs, meat, animal and vegetable oils.
Vitamin K	(Phylloquinone): It is a mixture of two compounds - K and K$_2$.
Function	Coagulation of blood, bile absorption
Deficiency	Poor coagulation of blood, liver damage
Sources	Leafy vegetables, oats, fish, peas, rye.

WELL-KNOWN INDIAN SCIENTISTS

Aryabhatta: He lived between 476 and 520 A.D. He was a great mathematician and an astronomer. His contributions include about the movement of earth around the Sun, determination of various physical parameters of various celestial bodies, such as diameter of Earth and Moon. He laid foundations of algebra and pointed out the importance of zero. The first Indian satellite was named after him.

Bhagavantam: His contribution to radio astronomy and cosmic rays is noteworthy. An associate of Sir C.V.Raman, Dr.S.Bhagavantam was scientific adviser in the Ministry of Defence and Director General of Defence Research Development Organisation.

Bhaskaracharya: Born in 1114 A.D., Bhaskaracharya was a great Hindu mathematician and Astronomer. His work 'Sidhanta Siromani' consists of two parts of mathematics and two parts of astronomy. He had a foresight on the modern theory of conventions.

S.S. Bhatnagar: A great Indian Scientist who lived between 1895 and 1955. He was the first Director General of Council of Scientific and Industrial Research. Under his directorship, many research laboratories were established throughout India.

J.C.Bose: He was an eminent Physicist and Botanist. He founded Bose Research Institute, Calcutta. He invented Crescograph and lived between 1858 and 1937.

S.N. Bose: He became well-known when he expounded the Bose Einstein theory which deals with the detection of a group of nuclear particles - named after him 'Boson'. His contribution to Planck's Law is laudable. He died in 1974.

Dr. S.Chandrasekhar: An Indian-born American, who won Nobel Prize for Physics in 1983. He is an Astrophysicist. His theory of Stellar Evolution - the birth and death of stars is 35 years old. His first discovery was laughed at. After three decades, it was recognised and today he is a Nobel Laureate. According to his theory, the old stars just collapse and disappear in the light of denser stars of low light popularly called Chandrasekhar Limit.

Charaka: He lived between 80 and 180 A.D. He was a court physician of King Kanishka. His writings on Hindu Medicine are invaluable.

Dhanvantri: He was a great physician during the period of Chandragupta Vikramaditya. His period was between 375 and 413 A.D.

Hargobind Khorana: He created an artificial gene and deciphered genetic code. He was awarded Nobel Prize for Medicine in 1968.

Homi J.Bhaba: He largely contributed to the development of Atomic Physics and he was primarily responsible for setting up of Nuclear reactors in India. He published important papers on Quantum Theory, Cosmic Rays, Structure of atom, etc. He was the first Chairman of Atomic Energy Commission. He died in a plane crash in 1966 over Alps.

Joshi: Prof. S.S.Joshi's works on physical and chemical reaction under electrical discharge on active nitrogen, colloids, hydrogen peroxide are noteworthy.

Nagarjuna: A great Buddhist Philosopher and Chemist. He mentioned about crucibles, sublimation, colouring process etc. His works are still available in China and Tibet. His theory on extraction of copper and metallic oxides are mention-worthy.

Nag Chowdhury B.D.: An eminent Indian Nuclear Physicist known all over the world.

Narlikar: J.V.Narlikar was the co-author of Hoyle-Narlikar theory of continuous creation which supplies missing links in Einstein's theory of Relativity. Hoyle and Narlikar have shown that the gravitation is always attractive and there is no gravitational repulsions.

Raja Ramanna: A great nuclear scientist, who was instrumental to stage India's first Nuclear explosion at Pokharan range in 1974.

Sir C.V.Raman: First Indian Scientist to receive Nobel prize for physics in 1930 for his invention 'Raman Effect'. His study of crystal structure is of unique importance. He founded Raman Research Institute at Bangalore. **Raman Effect** : Scattering of Light when monochromatic light passes through single transferable medium.

Sir C.P.Roy : Author of 'Hindu Chemistry'. He founded Indian Chemical Society and Bengal Chemical and Pharmaceuticals Ltd. He has done good work on nitrous acid and its salts. He lived between 1861-1944 AD.

Prof. V.Ramachandra Rao: Director of Indian Scientific Satellite Project (ISSP) at Peenya near Bangalore.

Saha Dr. Maghnad: Late Palit Prof.of Physics, University College of Scientific and Technology, Calcutta University well-known for his researches in nuclear physics, cosmic rays, spectrum analysis and other branches of theoretical physics. He lived from 1893-to 1956.

Srinivas Ramanujam: A mathematical wizard, contributed much to number theory, theory of partitions and theory of continuous fractions. He lived between 1887 to 1920 AD. His birth centenary was celebrated in 1987.

Satish Dhavan: He was chairman of Indian Space Research Organisation. He was instrumental to take India into space age by launching Aryabhatta in 1975.

Susruta: A fourth century Hindu Surgeon and Physician. He had written an important book on medicine and on medical properties of garlic.

Varahamihira: An Indian astronomer and astrologer of 6th Century A.D. He was a mathematician and philosopher. He was one of the nine gems of Vikramaditya.

WORLD'S PROMINENT SCIENTISTS

Alvares, Luis W.: An American won the Nobel Prize for elementary physics in 1960 when he discovered a new resonance particle - a discovery that shattered the then prevailing notions as to how matter was built.

Anfinsen, Dr. Christian B.: U.S.A.'s one of the three co-winners of the Nobel Prize in Chemistry, 1972.

Archimedes: Greek mathematician who lived about 250 B.C. discovery of the *Archimedes' principle Archimedean Screw*, a cylindrical device for raising water.

Arrow, Kenneth, J.: Harvard University, U.S.A. is co-winner of the Nobel Prize for Economics, 1972 with Sir John Richard Hicks of Oxford University. The two men are known for their pioneering contributions to general economic equilibrium and welfare theories.

Aryabhatta: (476-520 A.D.) after whom India's first scientific satellite has been named, was a great Indian astronomer and mathematician. Among his important contributions are the recognition of the importance of the movement of the earth round the Sun, determination of the physical parameters of various celestial bodies, such as diameter of the earth and the moon. He laid the foundations of algebra and was responsible for pointing out importance of "zero".

Avogadro, Amedeo : Italian physicist, founder of Avogadro's hypothesis. Equal volume of all gases under same temperature and pressure contain equal number of molecules.

Bardeen, Prof. John: U.S.A.'s co-winner of the Nobel Prize for Physics, 1972 (with Prof. Leon N.Cooper and Prof. John Robert Schrieffer) for researches into the "theory of super-conductivity" called BCS theory.

Barnard, Christian: South African surgeon who did the first heart transplant operation on Louis Washkansky in 1967.

Beadle, Dr. G.: American scientist awarded Nobel Prize for medicine in 1958 for the actual basis of heredity.

Becquerel, Henri: French physicist discovered in 1896 of *Becquerel rays*, the first indications of radio-activity; later named gamma rays. He shared Nobel Prize for Physics with the Curies in 1903. He lived between 1852 and 1908.

Berzelius, J.J: Swedish Chemist. Equal volume of all gases under same temperature and pressure contain equal number of atoms.

Bessemer, Sir Henry: English engineer invented the process for the manufacture of steel. He lived between 1813 and 1898.

Bhabha, Dr. H.J.: (1909-66) Indian scientist. He published important papers on Cosmic Rays and Quantum Theory. He was professor at the Indian Science Institute, Bangalore; Chairman, Atomic Energy Commission; Director, Tata Institute of Fundamental Research; President, Indian Science Congress in 1951 and presided at the Atoms for Peace Conference held at Geneva in 1956. He had many significant researches in structure of atom and contributed largely to the setting up of atomic reactors at Trombay (Mumbai).

Bohr, Neils: (born 1885) Danish Physicist awarded Nobel Prize for Physics in 1922. He extended the theory of atomic structure of devising an atomic model in 1913.

Boyle, Robert: Irish natural philosopher; one of the founders of modern chemistry and Boyle's law. He lived between 1627 and 1691.

Bragg, Sir William: British physicist researched on the behaviour of crystals with regard to X-rays incident upon them. He lived between 1862 and 1942.

Cavendish, Henry: English physicist and chemist; discovered properties of hydrogen in 1766. He lived between 1731 and 1810.

Chadwick, Sir James: British physicist discovered the particle in an atomic nucleus known as the neutron, because it has no electric charge. He lived between 1891 and 1974.

Charles, Jacques Alexander Cesar: A French scientist first to make a balloon ascension with hydrogen. He has worked on the effect of temperature on the volume of gases. He lived between 1746 and 1823.

Clark Maxwell, James: British physicist worked wireless telegraphy and telephony. His principal works include: *Perception of Colour, Colour Blindness, Theory of Heat, Electricity and Magnetism, Matter and Motion*. He lived between 1831 and 1879.

Claude, Albert: A Biologist shared the 1974 Nobel Prize in Medicine. His field of research relates to causes and treatment of cancer.

Columbus, Christopher: Italian navigator discovered West Indies Islands, Cuba, Bahamas, South America in 1498. He lived between 1446 to 1506.

Cooper, Leon N.: Of U.S.A. one of the three co-winners of the Nobel Prize in Physics, 1972 for theory of super-conductivity.

Copernicus: Astronomer of Poland who discovered the "Heliocentric System". He lived between 1413 and 1543.

Curie, Madame Marie: Polish physicist and chemist; discovered radium awarded Nobel Prize in chemistry in 1911 and Prize in physics in 1903, lived between 1867 and 1934.

Dalton, John: British scientist, founder of the Atomic Theory and law of Multiple Proportions. He lived between 1766 and 1844.

Darwin, Charles: British scientist who discovered the principle of natural selection. He lived between 1809 and 1882.

Davy, Sir Humphrey: British chemist. First to apply electric current for the isolation of metals. He lived between 1771 and 1829.

Debreu, Gerard: 1983 Nobel memorial prize in economics, is known for his research on market equilibrium incorporated "new analytical methods into economic theory".

Delbrueck, Dr. Max: American doctor, was one of the three American co-winners of the Nobel Prize for Medicine, 1969 for discoveries in molecular genetics.

Edelman, Dr. Gerald Maurice: Of U.S.A. is co-winner of the Nobel Prize for Medicine, 1972 found out "the chemical structure of blood-proteins or antibodies which shield the human body against infection".

Edison, Thomas Alva: American inventor of phonograph, the incandescent lamp, a new type of storage battery, an early form of cinematography etc. He lived between 1847 and 1931.

Einstein, Prof. Albert: German-Swiss, famous scientist known for his theory of relativity. He lived between 1879 and 1955.

Faraday, Michael: English scientist; prominent in the field of electro-magnetism; discovered the laws of electrolysis. He lived between 1791 and 1867.

Fleming, Alexander: British bacteriologist discovered Iysozyme (1922), followed by penicillin (1929) - and antibiotic drug. He lived between 1881 and 1955.

Fleming, Sir John Ambrose: British physicist and engineer pioneer in the development of the telephone, electric light and radio. He lived between 1849 and 1945.

Fraunhofer: German physicist researched on 'Light' while performing spectrum-analysis of Sunlight; discovered 'Fraunhofer Lines'.

Freud, Sigmund: Psycho-analysist. Works: *The Interpretation of Dreams; The Psychopathology of Every-day Life; The Ego and the Id; Civilization and Its Discontents.* He lived between 1856 and 1939.

Gabor, Dr Dennis: 1971 Nobel Prize award for Physics for his "invention in development of the holographic method" - three dimensional photography.

Galileo: Italian scientist viewed that all falling bodies, great or small, descend with equal velocity, invented telescope and became the first man to see the satellites of Jupiter. He lived between 1564 and 1642.

Gell-Mann, Prof. Murray: Recipient of the 1969 Nobel Prize in Physics, for his "classification of elementary particles and their interactions".

Goddard, Robert H.: An American pioneer of space research who mentioned the possibility of shooting a rocket to the moon in a paper entitled "A Method of Reaching Extreme Altitudes" published by him in 1919.

Graham, Thomas: Scottish chemist called the "father of colloidal chemistry". He worked on diffusion of substances in solution. He lived between 1805 and 1914.

Hahn, Otto: German pioneer of nuclear research, won the Nobel Prize for Chemistry in 1944, proved in 1938 that atomic fission can be achieved by bombarding uranium with neutrons.

Hall, Charles Martin: American chemist discovered the modern method of extraction of aluminium by electrolysis of bauxite in 1886. He lived between 1863 and 1914.

Harvey, William: English physician who discovered the circulation of blood. He lived between 1578 and 1675.

Herzberg, Dr. Gehard: The 1971 Nobel Prize winner in Chemistry, for his researches in atomic and molecular structures, particularly free radicals.

Holley, Robert: Nobel Prize winner for Medicine, 1968, the genetic code and its function in building protein led to the discovery of "the complete structure of a transfer of RNA molecule".

Hopkins, Sir Frederick Gowland: English biochemist worked on proteins and vitamins. He received the Nobel Prize in medicine in 1929 for the discovery of Vitamin D.

Hoyle, Fred: A British scientist and science-fiction writer who won the £ 1,000 Kalinga Prize in 1968. He was contribution to create the steady state theory.

Jenner, Edward: English physician discovered the vaccination system of alleviating small pox. He lived between 1749 and 1823.

Josephson, Dr. Brian: British scientist who co-shared the 1973 Nobel Prize for physics for his "theoretical predictions of the properties of a super-current through a tunnel barrier, known as Josephson effects".

Joule, James Prescott: English physicist who first demonstrated the mechanical energy can be converted into heat. He lived between 1874 and 1937.

Kepler, Johannes: German astronomer discovered 3 laws of planetary motion (1) The orbit of each planet is an ellipse with the Sun at one of the foci;

(2) the Radius vector of each planet describes equal areas in equal times; (3) The squares of the periods of the planets are proportional to the cubes of their mean distances from the Sun. He lived between 1571 and 1630.

Khorana, Hargobind: Who shared with two others the 1968 Nobel Prize for Medicine is an Indian by birth and an American by domicile. He deciphered the genetic code and later created an artificial gene.

Krishnan, Dr. K.S.: (born 1898) collaborated with Sir C.V.Raman in the discovery of "Raman Effect". President, Indian Science Congress, 1949; delegate to several international scientific conferences; Director, National Physical Laboratory, New Delhi.

Lavoisier, A.L.: French chemist; established "law of Indestructibility of Matter, Composition of Water and Air". He lived between 1743 and 1794.

Lister, Joseph: British surgeon who used antiseptic treatment for wounds; introduced antiseptic surgery. He lived between 1827 and 1912.

Lodge, Sir Oliver Joseph: British physicist, known for his researches on radiation, and the relation between matter and ether. He lived between 1851 and 1940.

Lysenko: Soviet geneticist declared the "Mendelian theory obsolete and erroneous" in 1948.

Marconi: Italian scientist pioneer in wireless telegraphy and radio. He lived between 1873 and 1937.

McClintock, Barbara: 1983 Nobel Prize winner in Medicine for her discovery of Jumbing gene.

Max Planck: German theoretical physicist who formulated the quantum theory. He was awarded the Nobel Prize in 1918.

Mendel, Johann Gregory: Austrian monk and naturalist discovered certain principles of inheritance of heredity. He lived between 1822 and 1884.

Mendeleef, D.I.: Russian chemist, founder of periodic table based on atomic weight of elements and the development of petroleum and other industries in Russia. He lived between 1834 and 1901.

Meyer, Victor: Discovered a method to determine the molecular weights of volatile substances. He lived between 1848 and 1897.

Morley, Edward William: American chemist and physicist known for his work in determining the composition of water by weight. He lived in 1818 and 1923.

Moseley, Henry G.: British physicist worked on atomic structure, and in 1913, devised the series of atomic numbers. He lived between 1887 and 1915.

Newton, Sir Isaac: British natural philosopher discovered "binomial theorem; the differential and integral calculus and the universal law of gravitation". He lived between 1642 and 1727.

Nirenberg, Dr. Marshall: U.S.molecular biologist 1968 Nobel Prize winner for Medicine with Dr. Robert Holley and Dr. Hargobind Khorana.

Ohm, George Simon: Physicist and mathematician; discovered the law known as Ohm's Law. He lived between 1787 and 1854.

Onsager, Lars: U.S. Professor who became a Nobel laureate of 1968 for Chemistry the discovery of "the reciprocal relations bearing his name which are fundamental for the thermo-dynamics of irreversible processes".

Paraceisus: Swiss mystic and chemist, he was the first to employ laudanum and antimony in Pharmacy. He lived between 1493 and 1541.

Pasteur, Louis: French chemist discovered the causes of fermentation in alcohol and milk and founded the Pasteur Institute in 1888. He lived between 1822 and 1895.

Pauling, Linus: American bio-chemist applied the quantum theory to chemistry received Nobel Prize (1954) for his contribution to the electrochemical theory of valency.

Porter, Dr. Rodney Robert: Biochemist known for his discoveries relating to the chemical structure of antibodies.

Prelog, Vladimir: Yugoslavian stereo-chemistry - research of organic molecules and reactions. He received (1975) Nobel Prize in Chemistry.

Priestley, Joseph: British Chemist; discovered oxygen and methods of collecting gases. He lived between 1733 and 1804.

Rao, Prof. U.Ramachandra: Is the Director of Indian Scientific Satellite Project (ISSP) at Peenya near Bangalore.

Rainwater, James: U.S.A. (1975) Nobel Prize winner in Physics for the development of the theory that atomic nucleus is not always spherical but can also be egg-shaped which has no immediate practical meaning but is extremely essential to scientists.

Richards, T.W.: He worked for the accurate determination of atomic weights and was awarded Nobel Prize in 1916.

Roger Bacon: Inventor of Gun Powder and founder of experimental science. He lived between 1214 and 1294.

Rontgen, W.Konrad: German physicist, discovered X-rays, or Rontgen rays for which he was awarded the first Nobel Prize for Physics in 1901. He lived between 1845 and 1923.

Ross, Ronald: British physician discovered the cause of Malaria; awarded Nobel Prize for medicine in 1902. He lived between 1857 and 1932.

Rutherford, Daniel: Scottish scientist discovered nitrogen. He lived between 1749 and 1819.

Rutherford, Lord: Won a Nobel Prize for his work on structure of atom and radio-activity. He lived between 1871 and 1937.

Ryle, Sir Martin: U.K. (1974) Nobel Prize winner in Physics for the development of "aperture synthesis" technique designed to identify stellar objects through radio signals.

Sarabhai, Dr. Vikram A.: Former Chairman of India's Atomic Energy Commission and the Indian Space Research Organization (ISRO) died on December 30, 1971. Dr. Sarabhai was an eminent physicist mainly interested in the astro-physical implications of Cosmic Ray Time Variations.

Sanger, Dr. Frederick (b.1918): First Scientist to receive two Nobel Prizes for Chemistry in 1958 (structure of insulin molecule) and in 1980 (molecular structures for nucleic acids)

Sen, P.K. (Dr.): is the Indian surgeon who performed Asia's first heart transplant operation in Mumbai.

Simpson, Sir James Young (1811-1870): British physicist to introduce chloroform as an anaesthetic in 1847.

Soddy, Frederick (1877-1956): British radio chemist pioneer to research in the atomic disintegration, discovered "isotopes"; for which he received the Nobel Prize for Chemistry in 1921.

Solvay, Earnest (1838-1922): Belgian chemist devised a process for manufacture of sodium carbonate.

Sutherland, Dr. Earl W.: Recipient of the Nobel Prize for Medicine, 1971, credited with the discovery, "that the hormones in the human body produce another substance known as cyclic A.M.P., can influence its disease-resisting capacity in the body".

Teller, Edward (Dr.): U.S. nuclear scientist developed the hydrogen bomb.

Thomson, Sir J.J. (1856-1940): British physicist discovered the electron which inaugurated the electrical theory of the atom.

Tsiolkovsky (1857-1935): Russian pioneer who developed the basic theory of rocketry.

Verne, Jules (1828-1905): French science-fiction writer; author of the book "From the Earth to the Moon". The book carried a more or less accurate prediction of the launching and flight of Apollo-8.

Volta, A. (1745-1827): Italian physicist and pioneer of electrical science; invented voltaic cell, the electrophorus and electroscope.

Voronoff, S.: Russian scientist known for grafting healthy animal glands, into the human body.

Watson and Crick: Known for DNA double helix.

Watson-Watt, Sir Robert: British physicist. He developed radar.

Watt, James (1736-1819): Scottish engineer who invented steam engine.

Yukawa, Dr. H.: (born 1907) Predicted a new particle meson which holds the protons and neutrons of the atomic nucleus, first Japanese to win the Nobel Prize in Physics (1949).

IMPORTANT PERSONALITIES (Past)

Abdullah, Sheikh Mohammad: (1906-1982) Founder of National Conference and Chief Minister of Jammu and Kashmir, Popularly known as Sher-e-Kashmir (Lion of Kashmir).

Abiden, Zain-ul: (15th Cen.AD) A benevolent and enlightened ruler of Kashmir; preceded Akbar in abolishing Jiziya, granting absolute religious freedom to all sects in his kingdom.

Abraham Lincoln: (1809-65) Was the 16th President of the U.S.A; abolished slavery; re-elected President-1864; assassinated in 1865 by John Wilkes Booth. Lincoln great advocate of democracy, believed in the equality of human race.

Abul Fazal: Was a famous Mughal Court Poet. He was counsellor of Akbar. His works are Akbar Nama and Aini-i-Akbari.

Acharya, Nirmalya: (1936-1995) Bengali writer-editor of the works of Nati Binodini, Manik Bandopadhyay, Krishna Bhattacharya and Satinath Bhaduri. Founder of Satyajit Ray Memorial at Nandan.

Acharya Vinoba Bhave: The architect of Sarvodaya and Bhoodhan movement started in 1951 and spiritual heir of Gandhiji. He lived an austere life at Paunar Ashram near Wardha. Awarded Bharat Ratna posthumously (1983).

Adiseshiah, Malcolm: (1910-1994) Indian educationist and economist. Vice-Chancellor of Madras University. Deputy Director General of UNESCO. Recipient of Padma Bhushan, 1976.

Adler, Alfred: (1870-1937) Viennese psychologist, famous for the theories on inferiority complex.

Aeschylus: (525-456 BC) Greek playwright, and Father of Greek Tragic Drama. Among his famous works are Prometheus Bound, The Seven against Thebes, Oresteia (comprises Agamemnon), and Suppliants.

Aesop: (620-544 BC) A Greek slave, became a writer. Wrote many fables like 'The Fox and the Grapes'. The Tortoise and the Hare, etc., each with a moral.

Agarwal, Om: (d.1994) The first Asian and the only Indian to win the World amateur snooker championship. Recipient of Padma Shri in 1985, and also of Arjuna award the same year.

Ahmed, Fakruddin Ali: (1905-1977) Indian freedom fighter, Union Minister in the Congress government, 1966. Fifth President of the Indian Republic, 1974-77.

Akbar: (1556-1605) The Mughal Emperor who established cordial relations between the Hindus and the Muslims. He founded a new religion known as Din-i-Ilahi. He is well-known for his revenue administration and military system.

Albuquerque: Was the real founder of the Portuguese Empire in India. He conquered Goa from ruler of Bijapur in 1510 and made it his capital.

Alexander, the Great: (356-323 B.C.) He was the king of Macedonia and son of Philips. Being a great conqueror he wanted to capture India. He invaded India in 326 B.C. He reached Beas but retreated as home sick army personnel wanted to return, and died on 323 B.C. at Babylon.

Ali, Aruna Asaf: (1888-1953) Indian nationalist leader and freedom fighter. General Secretary of Congress (1927). Secretary of INA Defence Committee (1945). A minister in the Interim Government (1946). India's first ambassador to U.S.A.

Ali, Maulana Muhammad: (1878-1931) Indian nationalist leader. Editor of Comrade (English), and Hamdard (Urdu), Led the Khilafat Movement. Organised anti-Simon Commission demonstrations.

Ali, Maulana Shaukat: (1873-1938) Indian nationalist leader. A leader of Khilafat Movement. Founder of Anjuman-e- Kaabaa.

Ali, Salim: (1896-1987) Indian ornithologist, known as "The Birdman of India". Contributed a lot to the study of Indian birds. Winner of several international and national honours, including Padma Vibhushan in 1976.

Amis, Kingsley: (1922-1995) British novelist, poet and story writer. A literary rebel, his first novel, Lucky Jim, won him reputation as an "angry young man". Recipient of 1986 Booker Prize for The Old Devils.

Ampere, Andre Marie: (1775-1836) French physicist and propounder of the theory that magnetism is the result of molecular electric currents (electrodynamic theory). The unit of electric current, ampere, is named after him.

Amrohi, Kamal: (d.1993) Indian writer, producer and director. Brought a Mughal touch to Indian films. Spent over 50 years in the industry. Husband of actress (Late) Meena Kumari.

Aryabhatta: (474-520 AD) The greatest Astronomer and Mathematician lived during the reign of Chandra Gupta Vikramaditya. Credited with the invention of algebra.

Ashoka: (264-228 B.C.) The famous Mauryan King. He denounced war after his victory over Kalinga, embraced and preached Buddhism.

Adolf Hitler: He rose from the rank of a corporal to become the dictator of Germany. He started a Fascist movement and under his leadership, the Nationalist Party (Nazi Party) came to power. He became Fuehrer in 1934. He launched the Second World War and was defeated in 1945. He committed suicide when the Russians closed in on Berlin.

Alan Octavian Hume: An Englishman who founded Indian National Congress in 1885.

Alberuni: (Born 973 A.D.) Arab Scholar in the court of Mahmud Ghaznavi, he accompanied Mahmud to India during his expeditions and wrote an account of India.

Alfred the Great: (849-99 A.D.) A great king of England, defeated the Danes, introduced reforms in the country, wrote and translated books, organised army; built strong and swift ships.

Ambedkar, Dr B.R.: Father of Indian Constitution. Leader of Scheduled Castes founded (1) Samaj Samata Sangh (2) All-India Scheduled Castes Federation and (3) The Independent Labour Party. Died in 1956.

Andrews, C.F. (Dheena Bandhu): British missionary came to India in 1904, devoted heart and soul to India's freedom struggle.

Annadurai, C.N.: (1909-1969) Founder of Dravida Munnetra Kazhagam. Former Chief Minister of Tamil Nadu.

Antony, Mark: (83-30 B.C) A Roman general, he was a supporter of Julius Caesar and fought Brutus after Caesar's death. Fell in love with Cleopatra. Committed suicide.

Amundsen, Captain Ronald: (1872-1928) Norwegian explorer; first to reach the South Pole in 1911; flew over the North Pole in 1926, was lost in the Arctic in 1928.

Annie Besant, Mrs.: (1846-1933) Irish lady, who admired India; actively participated in the Irish Home Rule Movement; a staunch supporter of India's freedom; Founder President of Theosophical society; was elected President of Indian National Congress. She published Common Wheel and New India. She formed Central Hindu School at Varanasi.

Archimedes: (287-212 B.C.) Greek mathematician, inventor and scientist, discovered the principle of the lever and of specific gravity; invented Archimedean screw.

Aristotle: (384-322 B.C.) Famous Greek Philosopher; disciple of Plato at Athens; tutor of Alexander the Great; founded a celebrated school of philosophy; wrote many treatises on various subjects; the Ethics and Poetics are among the best known of his surviving works.

Arkwright, Sir Richard: (1732-1792) In early life a barber and a travelling hair-dresser, became interested in mechanical problems; invented and manufactured the first spinning mill which worked by water power.

Arnold Mathew: (1822-1888) English poet and critic; some of his chief works are Sohrab and Rustum, Scholar Gypsy, etc.

Arnold, Thomas: (1795-1842) British educationist Headmaster of Rugby. Creator of Modern Public School system.

Ashapurna Devi: (1909-1995) Grand old lady of Bengali literature. First woman Jnanpith award winner (1976). Works include the trilogy Prathama Pratishruti, Subarnalata, Bakuler Katha.

Ashe, Arthur: (1944-1993) The Davis Cup legend, first Black to win Wimbledon in 1975. Succumbed to AIDS.

Asvaghosh: (2nd Cen.AD) Buddhist philosopher. Spiritual advisor of King Kanishka. Participated in the 4th Buddhist Council. Author of Sariputra Prakarma.

Attlee, Lord (Clemant Richerd Attlee): (1883-1967) Served as an army officer throughout World War I. Parliamentary leader of the Labour Party 1935-55; Deputy Prime Minister 1939-45, became Britain's Prime Minister in 1945. India achieved independence during his prime ministership.

Austen, Jane: (1775-1817) Famous woman novelist of England; wrote Emma, Persuasion, Pride and Prejudice, Sense and Sensibility.

Augustus, C.O.: (63 B.C.-14 A.D.) First Roman Emperor. Patronised art and literature. Writers like Horace and Virgil flourished during his time. Hence the period is named after him as "Augustan Age" in literature.

Aurangzeb: (1618-1707) Mughal emperor of India. Was the son of Shah Jahan. Ascended the throne by revolting against his father and brothers. After his death, the Mughal empire disintegrated.

Azad, Chandra Sekhar: (1906-1931) Indian revolutionary leader. Was involved in the Non-Cooperation Movement, Assembly bomb incident, Delhi conspiracy, Lahore conspiracy, Kakori conspiracy, etc.

Azad, Maulana Abul Kalam: (1888-1958) A nationalist Muslim scholar. President of Indian National Congress. Founded Al Hilal and Al Balagh, Urdu weeklies. Free India's first Union Education Minister, Established UGC, IIT (Kharagpur), posthumously conferred Bharat Ratna, 1992. Author of 'India Wins Freedom'.

Babur: (1483-1530) He was the founder of the Mughal Empire in India by defeating Ibrahim Lodi in the Battle of Panipat in 1526. He ruled for four years. His son was Humayun.

Bach, Johann S.: (1685-1750) German composer, Brandenburg Concertos, wrote concertos, suites, and many choral works, like Mass in B Minor and St.Matthew Passion.

Bacon, Francis: (1561-1625) British essayist and philosopher. Rejected Aristotelian deductive logic for inductive method. Author of Novum, Organum and Essays.

Bajaj, Jamnalal: (1889-1942) A close associate of Mahatma Gandhi. He gave Segaon village to Mahatma Gandhi, who renamed it as "Sevagram".

Balboa, Vasco Nunez de: (1475-1517) Spanish explorer. Discovered the Pacific Ocean in 1513 AD.

Bannerjee, Surendranath: (1848-1925) Indian patriot from Bengal, passed the ICS examination.

Barnado, Thomas: (1845-1905) A Philanthropist. Founder of homes for homeless children.

Baruah, Dev Kanta: (d.1996) The former Congress (I) President, who gave the slogan "Indira is India and India is Indira" died of cardiac arrest in New Delhi on January 28, 1996 at the age of 82.

Basheer, Vaikom Mohammed: (1908-1994) Legendary Malayalam writer. He was nicknamed "Sultan of Beypore". His works include Pathummayude Adu, Balyakalasakhi, etc. Winner of Padma Shri award.

Batuta, Ibn: (14th Cen. AD) South African scholar and traveller. Visited India in 1333, spent eight years in India and wrote about the reign of Muhammed Tughlaq (1325-1361 of which he was an eye witness .

Benz, Karl: (1844-1929) German engineer. His motor car, produced in 1885, was one of the first to be driven by an internal combustion engine.

Bahadur Shah II: He was the last Mughal Emperor in India. He took active part in Sepoy Mutiny in 1857. He was executed in Rangoon in 1862.

Bankim Chandra Chatterjee: He was popularly known as the literary king of Bengal. He has written many works such as Mrinalini, Durgesh Nandini Kapala Kundela. Raj Singh, Anand Math, etc. Our national song 'Vande Mataram' has been taken from his work. 'Anand Math'.

Bairam Khan: (16th Cen. AD) The Regent of Akbar, the Great. He was mainly responsible for Akbar's accession to the throne.

Baden-Powell: (1857-1941) Brilliant Cavalry soldier; founded the Boy Scout Movement (1907) and Girl Guides (1910) to promote good citizenship; Scout of the World, 1921-1941, His birth centenary was celebrated throughout the world in 1957.

Baird, J.L.: (1888-1948) Scottish, television inventor.

262 Sura's Latest G.K.

Balzac, H.: (1799-1850) A great French novelist; wrote more than eighty novels, to which he gave the covering title of La Comedie Humaine.

Banting, Sir Frederick Grant: (1891-1941) Canadian physician who discovered insulin; awarded Nobel prize in 1923 for medicine.

Beethoven, Ludwig Von: (1770-1827) Born of a poor family at Bonn, greatest musician and composer, player very skilful on violin and other instruments. Composed some of the greatest works between the years 1805 and 1809 and enjoyed the greatest musical fame; composed Fidelio and the Pastcrale.

Behring, Emil Von: (1854-1917) German Scientist, discovered antitoxin for diphtheria.

Bell, Alexander Graham: (1847-1922): British Scientist, invented telephone and photosphere; took great interest in the education of deaf-mutes.

Bhatnagar, Shanti Swarup: (1894-1955) Great Indian Scientist and administrator. Developed many CSIR labs. First Director General of CSIR. Bhatnagar award was instituted in his name.

Bessemer, Sir Henry F.R.S.: (1813-1898) Invented the process of converting cast iron into steel, popularly known as steel melting process.

Beveridge, Lord: (1879-1963) British economist, Director of London School of Economics, 1919-37, founder of the social security scheme in Britain.

Bhabha, Homi J.: (1909-1966) Indian physicist.

Bharati, Subramania: (1882-1921) Indian poet, journalist, patriot and philosopher, title 'Bharati' was conferred on him by the Raja of Ettayapuram.

Bhaskara I: (7th C. AD) Indian astronomer. A contemporary of Brahmagupta, another Indian astronomer.

Bhaskaracharya II: (12 C. AD) Indian mathematician and astronomer. First to state that anything divided by zero is equal to infinity. Invented calculus long before Newton and Leibnitz. Author of Sidhanta Shiromani.

Bhutto, Z.A. (1928-1979) Former Prime Minister of Pakistan. He was executed under the military dictatorship of General Zia-ul-Haq.

Bismarck, Prince Otto Von: (1815-1898) Most prominent German statesman of the 19th century; popularly known as The Man of Blood and Iron, directed the destiny of his country up to 1888; founded the German Empire.

Bismil, Ramprasad: (1897-1927) Indian revolutionist. Leader of Militant Hindustan Republican Association, involved in Kakori train dacoity case (1925). Executed.

Boris Pasternak: (1890-1960) Russian novelist and poet, who was awarded Nobel Prize for Literature in 1958 for his great work Dr.Zhivago.

Booth, "General" William: (1829-1912) He had a religious bent of mind; became a methodist local preacher, founded the Salvation Army in 1878.

Boccaccio, Giovanni: (1313-1375) Italian writer and humanist, considered as 'Father of the Novel'. His well-known works are Decameron and Life of Dante.

Bonaparte, Napoleon: (1769-1821) French military leader. Nicknamed "Little Corporal". Emperor of France from 1804 to 1815, was finally defeated at Waterloo in 1815. Exiled to St. Helena.

Bose, Khudiram: (1889-1908) Indian revolutionist. Took part in looting of mailbags at Hatgachha and in bomb attack on Bengal Governor's special train in 1907 Muzaffarpur. He was hanged to death.

Bose J.C.: He was an eminent Indian Physicist and Botanist. He founded Bose Research Institute, Calcutta. He invented Crescograph.

Bose, Rashbehari: (1886-1945) Indian revolutionary leader. Charged in Lahore Conspiracy Case for his plan to cut telegraph communications in North India. Married Tosiko Some and became a Japanese citizen. Founder-President of Indian Independence League at Bangkok in 1942.

Bose, Satyendra Nath: (1894-1974) Indian physicist, was Vice-Chancellor of Vishwabharati University, and President of National Institute of Sciences of India. Boson, an elementary particle, is named after him.

Bose, Subhash Chandra: (1897-1945) Did not believe in peaceful means to win freedom. Founded Forward Bloc. During World War II, formed Indian National Army.

Boyle, Robert: (1627-1691) Irish chemist, propounded that all substances are made up of atoms. Formulated Boyle's Law $\left(p \alpha \dfrac{1}{v} \right)$.

Braille, Louis: (1809-1852) French teacher of the blind; perfected his system of reading and writing for the blind, called Braille system.

Brahmachari, Dhirendra: (1924-1994) A hiflying Swami, dubbed as 'Resputin'.

Brahmagupta: (598-680 AD) Indian mathematician. First to treat zero as a number. Author of Brahma Siddhanta.

Brandt, Willy: (1913-1992) Social Democrat, Chancellor of West Germany. Won in 1971, Nobel Peace Prize for his policy of "Ostpolitik", which helped East-West relations thaw during War.

Brutus, Marcus Junius: (85-42 B.C.) Roman Governor and one of the framers of Roman Civil Law; principal assassin of Julius Caesar.

Buck, Pearl.S: (1892-1972): American novelist, won Nobel Prize for literature in 1938 and also Pulitzer Prize for her GOOD EARTH, visited India in 1962.

Buddha, Gautama: (563-483 BC) Founder of Buddhism. Attained enlightenment under a Bodhi tree at Bodh Gaya in Bihar.

Bunyan, John: (1628-1688) Religious thinker; fought on the Parliamentary side in the civil war, imprisoned after the Restoration; wrote 'Pilgrim's Progress' in Jail'.

Burke, Edmund: (1729-97) One of the greatest orators; entered Parliament, where he quickly made a name; an able debator; in 1790 his Reflections appeared on the French Revolution; he held very liberal views; took active part in the impeachment of Warren Hastings.

Beckett, Samuel: (1835-1902) English novelist, musician and scholar. Works: Erehwon, the Fair Haven, Life and Habit, The Way of All Flesh, etc.

Byron Lord: (1788-1824) English romantic poet; was born lame; exercised great influence upon European thought; among his chief works are Childe Harold's Pilgrimage, The Prisoner of Chillan, Don Juan.

Byrd, Richard Evelyn: (1888-1957) American explorer and aviator. Was the first to fly over both North and South Poles. Led five expeditions to the Antarctic.

Calvin, John: (1509-1565) Religious preacher who preached in Paris and then at Geneva; one of the leading reformers of the 16th Century; insisted on purity of life; his religious system is known as Calvinism.

Cama, Bhikaji: (1861-1936) First to unfurl the flag of Indian freedom at Stuttgart during Socialist Congress Session (1907). Founded Free India Society in U.K. Started a journal Bande Mataram.

Camus, Albert: (1913-1960) French writer and existentialist philosopher. Works include Caligula, The Outsider, The Plague, etc. Won in 1957, Nobel Prize for Literature.

Canning, Lord: (19th Cen.AD) A representative of the British power, was the last Governor General of East India Company, 1856-58, and the first Viceroy of India (1858-1862).

Cariappa, K.M.: (1899-1993) Grand old man of Indian Army and first Commander-in-Chief of free India. Was Indian High Commissioner to Australia and New Zealand. Was known as "Kipper".

Cave, Edward: (1691-1754) British publisher. Founder of the first modern magazine, The Gentleman's Magazine.

Carlyle, Thomas: (1795-1881) English essayist and historian of Victorian era; some of his works: - French Revolution, Past and Present, Heroes and Hero Worship, Sartor Resartus.

Cartwright, Edmund: (1743-1823) Invented the power-loom and also a Wool-Combing machine.

Cavendish, Henry: (1731-1810) English chemist and physicist, made researches into the nature of gases, discovered hydrogen and chemical composition of water.

Caxton, William: (1422-1491) Set up the first printing press at Westminster.

Cavour: He was a distinguished Italian statesman who endeavoured much to unify Italy.

Chaitanya: (1445-1533) Pioneer of Bhakti movement, greatest among the Vaishnava saints. Preached the doctrine of love and devotion to Lord Krishna.

Chand Bibi: She was the daughter of the king of Ahmednagar. She valiantly defended the fort of Ahmednagar against the Mughals during the period of Akbar. Ultimately she committed suicide.

Cervantes, Saavedra Miguel De: (1547-1616) Spanish novelist and dramatist; took part in many military expeditions, won world-wide reputation as author of Don Quixote.

Cezanne, Paul: (1839-1906) French painter, who deeply influenced the cause of modern art, had a decisive impact on future Fauvists and Cubists.

Chamberlain, Neville: (1869-1940) Prime Minister of England 1936 - 40. Known for his policy of appeasement, in 1938, he flew to Munich to sign the Four-Power Pact by which the border areas of Czechoslovakia were ceded to Germany. He was earlier Health Minister under Baldwin.

Chaplin, Sir Charles Spencer: (1887-1977) Born in London; enjoyed world-wide fame as a film star comedian; settled in Switzerland, refused permission to return to America in 1952 as he was suspected to be a communist; won the Lenin Peace Prize in 1954. He was knighted in 1975.

Charles De Gaulle, General: (1890-1970) Greatest French patriot; Commander-in-Chief of the free French forces for some time during World War II; strongly opposed to communism; provisional President when France was liberated, formed the Gaullist Party in the French Parliament; was appointed Prime Minister of France in June 1958, gave France a new constitution; he was elected the first President of the Fifth Republic of France, suppressed the Algerian revolt of 1961, thus he emerged as the strongest man of France since Napoleon. He granted independence to African Colonies, and also resolved the Algerian problem.

Chatham Earl of England (William Pitt the Elder): (1708-1778) English statesman, became Secretary of State and leader of the House of Commons in 1756; War Minister 1757-1761; defeated the French in seven years' War 1756-1761.

Chaucer, Geoffrey: (1340-1400) Father of English Poetry, his most famous work is Canterbury Tales.

Charle Magne (Charles the Great): (742-814) Emperor of the Romans, wise and powerful ruler, general and statesman, ruled vast territories; he laid the basis for the Holy Roman Empire.

Chanakya: (4th BC) Also known by the name Kautilya. Prime Minister of Chandragupta Maurya. Author of Artha Shastra, an authentic book on statecraft. He is considered as Indian Machiavelli.

Chand, Dhyan: (1905-1979) Indian hockey wizard. Won Olympic golds in 1928, 1932 and 1936. Awarded Padma Bhushan in 1956.

Chandragupta II (Vikramaditya): (400 AD) Emperor of Gupta dynasty. Fahien, the first Chinese pilgrim, visited India during his reign.

Chandrasekhar, Subramanyan: (1910-1995) Indian scientist, but a citizen of America. Won 1983 Nobel Prize in Physics. First to calculate the limits of the mass of star (1.4 times the Sun's mass), known as Chandrasekhar Limit.

Charaka: (2nd Cen. AD) Indian physician. Adorned the court of Kanishka. Author of Charakasamhita.

Chattopadhyay, Kamladevi: (1903-1988) Indian social worker and patron of art and culture. Magsaysay award for community leadership (1966).

Chauhan, Prithviraj: (12th Cen. AD) Rajput king of Delhi. He was defeated in the battle of Tarain 1192 by Muhammed Ghori which paved the way for Muslim rule in India.

Chenna Reddy, Dr.M.: C.M. of A.P and Governor of Tamil Nadu passed away following a massive heart attack on December 2, 1996 at the age of 78.

Cheshire, Leonard: (1918-1992) A World War II hero, commanded the legendary "Dambuster" squadron, witnessed the bombing of Nagasaki, then set up a global network of homes for the disabled known as "Cheshire Homes".

Chichester, Francis: (1901-1972) British aviator and yachtman. Sailed around the world singlehanded in Gipsy Moth IV in 1966-67.

Chinmayananda, Swami: (1916-1993) Real name Balakrishna Menon. Exponent of Bhagvat Gita and Vedanta Philosophy. Founder of Chinmaya Mission.

Chishti, Salim Shah: (16th Cen. AD) Sufi saint, blessed Akbar with a son. Buried at Fatehpur Sikri.

Chola, Rajaraja: (985-1014 AD) One of the mighty Chola rulers, built the Shiva temple in Thanjavur.

Chola, Rajendra: (1018-1042 AD) A king of the Chola dynasty. With an efficient naval fleet added Ceylon, Andaman, Nicobar, etc. to the Chola empire.

Christ, Jesus: (4 BC-33 AD) Praised as 'The son of God'. Spread the message of brotherhood of man. Crucified by the Jews for blasphemy.

Churchill, Sir Winston: (1877-1965) Politician, a soldier and writer; the greatest Englishman of all time; was a member of Parliament from 1900-1965; member of several cabinets, Prime Minister and Minister of Defence 1940-45; the success of the Allies in World War II was largely due to his efforts; led the opposition in 1945-51; became Prime Minister and Minister of Defence in the Conservative Government in 1951-55; won Nobel Prize for Literature in 1953. Famous works: The Gathering Storm, War Memoirs, The History of English Speaking People.

Chiang Kai Shek, Generalissimo: (1887-1975) Chinese general and statesman; commanded the forces against the Japanese invasion during the Civil War when he was defeated, and the Kuomintang regime collapsed; after the victory of the Communists he moved to Formosa (now Taiwan).

Cleopatra: (69-30 B.C) Egyptian Queen whose beauty fascinated Julius Caesar and with whom she went to Rome; she bore Caesar a son; after Caesar's death she married Antony, after whose death she committed suicide.

Coleridge, Samuel Taylor: (1772-1834) English poet and Philosopher; his poetic fame rests on the 'Rime of the Ancient Mariner', Christabel and Kubla Khan.

Colt, Samuel: (1814-1882) American inventor of revolver.

Columbus, Christopher: (1446-1506) Italian navigator; set out on his Voyage in 1492; he first discovered the Bahamas, Cuba and other West Indies Islands, it was in 1498 that he landed on the Low Lands of South America.

Comte, Auguste: (1798-1857) French philosopher and founder of Positivism. Was a disciple of Saint Simon.

Confucius: (551-479 B.C.) Chinese philosopher and sage, founder of the great religion of Confucianism, or the worship of superiors and ancestors, translated Chinese scriptures.

Cook, Captain James: (1728-1779) English navigator, made many voyages round the world and made many discoveries, discovered the Sandwich Islands (Hawaiian Islands).

Cook, Thomas: (1908-1982) An English priest-turned-tour operator, better known as Father of Modern Tourism.

Copernicus (or Kappernick) Nicolaus: (1473-1543) Polish astronomer, discovered the Solar System. Quintcentenary of his birth was celebrated in 1973.

Cripps, Sir Stafford: (1889-1952) British Labour statesman, came on a mission to India in 1942 and 1946; Chancellor of the Exchequer 1947-1950.

Cromwell, Oliver: (1599-1658) Took a leading part in the Civil War of England 1642-49; defeated the Royalists; became Lord Protector of England 1653-1658.

Corbusier, Le: (1887-1965) Swiss architect. Real name Charles Edward Jeanneret. Planned the city Chandigarh.

Cornwallis, Lord: (1738-1805) Governor General of India (1786-1793). Introduced permanent settlement for the zamindars and the Ryots in Bengal in 1793. He was the Commander of British forces in the American war of Independence.

Curie, Marie: (1867-1934) Polish physicist and chemist. Discovered radium, along with her husband, Prof. Pierre (1859-1906). Shared with her husband Nobel Prize in Physics (1903). Nobel Prize in Chemistry also (1911).

Curzon, Lord: (1859-1925) British administrator and statesman. Viceroy of India (1899-1905). First partition of Bengal took place during his tenure. He represented many world conferences after the First World War.

Curie, Prof. Pierrie (1859-1906) Jointly discovered radium, shared the Nobel Prize for Physics, 1903.

Curie, Joliot and Madame Irene Curie: Daughter of Prof. Pierre Curie, she made researches on artificial radioactivity, and shared the Chemistry Nobel Prize with her husband Joliot Curie in 1935.

Dahir: (7th-8th Cen. AD) Hindu Raja of Sind, repulsed the first attack of the Arabs on the Indian soil (712 AD).

Dalhousie, Lord: (19th C) Governor-General of India (1848-1856). Introduced Doctrine of Lapse led to the outbreak of Sepoy Mutiny. Introduced railways and telegraphs in India.

Damien, Joseph: (1840-1889) Belgian missionary. Worked for the leprosy-afflicted in Honolulu.

Dandekar, V.M.: (1920-1995) Director of Gokhale Institute of Politics and Economics. First to define poverty line in specific terms. Contributed to the cause of rural credit and land reforms. Author of Poverty in India and The Indian Economy-Agriculture.

Das, Jatindra Nath: (1904-1929) Indian revolutionist. He was arrested in Lahore Conspiracy case. Went on a prolonged, hunger strike in Lahore jail demanding better treatment for prisoners. Died in prison.

Das, Chittaranjan: (1870-1925) As defence lawyer defended and freed Aurobindo in Alipore Bomb case. Founded Swaraj Party in 1923. Investigated into Jallianwala Bagh tragedy with Jawaharlal Nehru as Secretary. Known as "Deshbandhu".

Desai, Mahadev: (1892-1942) Personal secretary of Mahatma Gandhi. Editor of Independent India and Navjivan.

Descartes, Rene: (1596-1650) French philosopher and mathematician. Invented analytic geometry.

Dayanand Saraswati: He was a great Hindu reformer of the 19th century. He founded Arya Samaj.

Daimler, Gottlieb: (1834-1890) German Inventor; He invented Carburettor. Carburettor is used to mixture of petrol and air in petrol engine.

Dalton, John: (1776-1844) English chemist and mathematician. His New System of Chemical Philosophy was published in 1810, founder of Atomic Theory.

Dante: (1265-1321) Italian poet; wrote Divine Comedy.

Darwin, Charles Robert: (1809-1882) English naturalist; well-known for his "Theory of Evolution" or "The Law of Natural Selection". His chief works are Origin of Species; Descent of Man.

Davy, Sir Humphry: (1778-1829) English Chemist; inventer of Davy's Lamp.

Demosthenes: (385-322 B.C.) Greek, orator, statesman and writer; roused the Athenians to resist the growing power of Philip II of Macedon.

Dev, Acharya Narendra: (1889-1956)) A great Indian educationist, Principal of Kasi Vidya Peeth. Vice Chancellor of Lucknow and Banaras Universities, Founder Chairman Socialist Party (1948); which finally emerged as Praja Socialist Party after merging with Kisan Majdoor Praja Party; wrote Budha Dharma Darshan.

Dhanvantri: He was the court physician of Chandra Gupta Vikramaditya.

Disraeli: He was a well-known English statesman and novelist. He became the Prime Minister of England in 1868.

Dickens, Charles: (1812-70) Eminent English novelist. His best- known works include Pickwick Papers, Oliver Twist, and David Copperfield.

Diesel, Rudolf: (1858-1913) German Engineer; invented internal coumbustion engine which he patented in 1893.

Disney, Walter Elias ("WALT"): (1901-1966) American film cartoonist; producer of Micky Mouse, Silly Symphonies, and Donald Duck; created a fairyland atmosphere at Disneyland, California. Disneyland is a great amusement park. Winner of 35 Oscar awards.

Dostoevsky. F.M: (1821-1881) Russian novelist, author of Crime and Punishment, The Idiot, The Possessed, and many others.

Doyle, Sir Arthur Conan: (1859-1930) English writer of detective stories. 'Adventures of Sherlock Holmes' is best known.

Drake, Sir Francis: (1540-1596) Admiral in the time of Queen Elizabeth I; played a great part in the destruction of the Spanish Armada in 1588.

Dumas, Alexander: (1802-1870) French novelist and dramatist. Author of The Count of Monte Cristo and The Three Musketeers.

Dupleix: He was appointed Governor of French possessions in India in 1742. After Clive's victory at Plassey, he returned to France and fell into disgrace and poverty.

Dweight, F.Davis: (1879-1945) American leader. Donated the trophy of International Lawn Tennis Championship for men, which is named after him as "Davis Cup".

Edison, Thomas Alva: (1847-1931) American who invented and improved printing and telegraph system; made over 1,000 inventions including telephone transmitter, megaphone, phonograph, incandescent bulb, cinematograph, etc.

Ehrlich, Paul: German Scientist, made researches in connection with cancer, discovered 'salvarson' for the treatment of syphilis. He shared the Nobel Prize for Medicine in 1908.

Eiffel, Alexandre Gustave: (1832-1923) French Engineer, bridge and viaduct builder; authority on Aerodynamics; Eiffel Tower in Paris and Panama Canal locks are among his notable works.

Einstein, Albert: (1879-1955) Mathematician and Physicist, enjoys world fame for his "Theory of Relativity", revised his 'Field Theory'; considered as the foremost scientist of the 20th Century.

Eisenhower, General Dwight: (1890-1970) President of U.S.A. 1952-60; a great military General, Commander-in-Chief of Allied Forces in North Africa, 1942-43 and in Europe in 1943-45; became the Supreme Commander of Atlantic forces in Europe in December 1950; a strong advocate of collective military alliances; re-elected President of U.S.A. in 1956; propounded a Doctrine for the Middle East to ward off communism popularly known as Eisenhower Doctrine. He was the first American President to visit India.

Eliot, George: (1819-1880) The pen name of Marian Evans, famous English woman novelist; her most memorable novels are Adam Bede, Middle March, Daniel Deronda, The Mill on the Floss, Silas Marner.

Eliot, T.S.: (1888-1965) One of the foremost lyric poets of the 20th century. Born in U.S.A. Became a naturalised British citizen in 1927; Works: Murder in the Cathedral, The Cocktail Party, Confidential Clerk, etc. Wasteland won him the Nobel Prize for literature in 1948.

Elizabeth I: (1533-1603) Ascended the throne of England in 1558 after the death of her sister Mary Tudor and ruled for 45 years; an enlightened ruler; England became a great power in her time. Shakespeare lived during her reign.

Elizabeth II: (b.1926) Ascended the throne of England in February 1952 at the age of twenty-five on the death of her father George VI; married the

Duke of Edinburgh, son of the Prince Andrew of Greece. They have three sons and a daughter. Prince Charles is the heir apparent.

Erikson, Erik: (1903-1994) Psychoanalyst. Applied Freudian theory to adolescence and adulthood. Coined the phrase "Identity crisis".

Euclid: (330-269 B.C.) Greek mathematician.

Euripides: (480-406 B.C.) Was the greatest of the Greek dramatists. He wrote eight plays. His best known play is the Trojan Woman. It is an antiwar play.

Epicurus: (342-270 BC) A famous Greek Philosopher. He founded Epicurean philosophy.

Fahien: (5th C. AD) Earliest Buddhist pilgrim from China who visited India during the time of Chandragupta II to collect Buddhist relics and sacred literature; he stayed in India from 401 to 410 A.D.

Faraday, Michael: (1791-1867) English scientist in the field of electricity and magnetism; discovered the Laws of Electrolysis.

Fidel Castro: He is the President of Cuba. He is a well-known Communist leader.

Firdausi: (930-1020) Epic poet of Persia; wrote Shahnama in verse which describes the history of Persia.

Fleming, Sir Alexander: (1881-1955) Bacteriologist and discoverer of penicillin. Received Nobel Prize for medicine jointly with Florey and Dr. E.B. Chain, 1945.

Ford, Henry: (1863-1947) Founder of Ford Motor Co., became the world's leading industrialist, and its second richest man; a great philanthropist.

Franco, General Francisco: (1892-1975) Spanish director, started as a soldier; Chief of the General staff 1935-36; Commander-in-Chief of Nationalist forces during the Spanish Civil War (1936- 39); He was succeeded by King Juan Carlos who visited India in January 1982 as Chief Guest at the Republic Day parade; democracy was restored by him in Spain.

Franklin, Benjamin : (1706-1790) A great statesman and scientist of America. He invented Lightning conductor and Bifocal lens

Frederick II (The Great): (1712-1786) King of Prussia from 1740 till his death, greatly increased the power of his country by his able rule; he was also a great scholar.

Freud, Sigmund: (1856-1939) Psychiatrist and founder of psychoanalysis; Professor Neurology, Vienna University, 1902-1928; was elected a member of the Royal Society, London in 1936. His works: Interpretation of Dreams, the Egorth Id.

Froebel, F.W.August: (1782-1852) German educational reformer who founded the kindergarten system of education.

Gagarin, Yuri: (1934-68) First Russian Cosmonaut who orbited the earth on 12th April, 1961 in Vostok-7; killed in an aircrash on 25th March, 1968.

Galileo: (1564-1642) Italian scientist and astronomer. He was a professor of mathematics. He improved the telescope. He was the first man to see the satellites of Jupiter.

Galsworthy, John: (1867-1933) English novelist and dramatist; awarded Nobel Prize for Literature in 1932 for Forsyte Saga.

Gama, Vasco da: (1460-1524) Was a native of Portugal, discovered sea route to India in 1498 via the Cape of Good Hope. Reached Calicut in 1492.

Garbo, Greta: (1905-90) Swedish film actress; the most charming and poetical actress on the screen. Her films include Anna Karenina, Ninotchka.

Garibaldi: (1807-1882) A famous Italian soldier and patriot who was condemned to death in 1834. But he escaped to South America. Later, after his return to Italy, he strengthened his movement to liberate Italy.

Ghosh, Aurobindo: (1872-1950) Founded Jugantar, Karma Yogin and Dhama. First editor of Bande Mataram. Became a yogi and philosopher later. He set up an Ashram in Pondicherry.

Ghosh, Tushar Kanti: (1898-1994) Indian journalist. Was editor of Amrit Bazar Patrika since 1928. India's longest served editor.

Gibbon, Edward: (1737-94) English historian; wrote Decline and Fall of the Roman Empire.

Giri, V.V.: (1894-1980) Third Vice-President and fourth President of India. Awarded Bharat Ratna in 1975.

Gladstone, William: (1809-98) Was a renowned liberal statesman of Britain; became four times Prime Minister, his financial policy was accurate and successful; popularly known as the grand old man.

Godrej, Naoroji P.: (1927-1990) Indian Industrialist. Manufactured first indigenous machine tools and typewriters.

Gokhale, Gopal Krishna: (1866-1915) Indian statesman. Political guru of Mahatma Gandhi. Founded Servants of India Society (1905).

Gopi Krishna: Kathak exponent, choreographed over 800 films over a period of four-and-a-half decades. His Janak-Janak-Payal-Paje was a hit.

Goering, Field Marshal Hermann: (1893-1946) One of the ablest generals of Nazi Germany; was right hand man of Hitler; was a Minister of Police and Aviation and President of Reichstag. After the Fall of Germany, he was to be executed as a war criminal but he committed suicide.

Goethe, J.W.: (1749-1832) German poet and dramatist. His famous works are Faust and Wilhelm Meister.

Goldsmith, Oliver: (1728-74) Irish poet, dramatist and novelist of the 18th century; author of the Vicar of Wakefield, The Deserted Village and She Stoops to Conquer. Died in debt and poverty.

Good year, Charles: (1800-1860) American inventor; invented the art of Vulcanising rubber.

Gordon, Charles George: (1833-85) British soldier and administrator, served in Crimea, China and India. When he was facing Mehdi revolt in Sudan, he was captured and killed.

Gray, Thomas: (1716-1771) English poet, famous for Elegy written in a Country Churchyard.

Guru Gobind Singh: He was the tenth and the last Guru of the Sikhs. He spent his life in fighting against Mughals.

Guru Nanak: He was born in 1469 at Talwandi which is now in Pakistan. He was the founder of the Sikh faith. He died in 1538.

Guru, Shri Narayana: (19th-20th Cen AD.) Indian social reformer, saint and philosopher from Kerala. Worked for the eradication of untouchability.

Gutenberg, Johann: (1400-1468) German printer. First European to make a printing press (1430).

Harsha Vardhana: He was the last Hindu king of northern India. He ruled in the 7th century A.D. During his time Yuan Chwang visited India. Harsha was a Buddhist.

Hardayal, Lala: (1884-1939) Indian nationalist in San Francisco. Published a magazine, Vande Mataram.

Harishchandra, Bharatendu: (1850-1883) Indian playwright. First to make Khariboli medium of prose and plays.

Hafiz: (1320-1389) Persian lyrical poet. Diwan-i-Hafiz is his principal work.

Haile Selassie: (1891-1975) Emperor of Ethiopia 1930-36 and 1941-1974 when Ethiopia was liberated by the Allies. In March 1974, Haile Selassie was dethroned. He died in a military camp in 1975.

Hammarskjoeld, Dag: (1895-1961) Swedish diplomat, Secretary-General of the United Nations 1953-61. He played a very prominent part in easing the tension between East and West. His careful handling of the Middle East crisis prevented the Third World War in August 1958. He worked with the singleness of purpose to bring peace to the world; played a prominent part in easing the Congo situation, died in an air crash over Katanga (Congo) in September 1961; awarded Nobel Peace Prize posthumously in 1961.

Hardy, Thomas: (1840-1928) A great English novelist, dramatist and poet; his famous works are; Return of the Native, Under the Greenwood Tree, Tess, A Pair of Blue Eyes and Mayor of Casterbridge and Dynasts.

Harvey, William: (1578-1657) English doctor and scientist, became Physician Extraordinary to James I; discovered the circulation of blood in 1616.

Hastings, Warren: (1732-1818) First Governor-General for East India Company from 1773 to 1783. On his return to England, he was impeached on charges of excessive cruelty and corruption, but acquitted; the trial lasted for seven years and cost him 76,000 pounds.

Hegel, George Wilhelm Friedrich: (1770-1831) German Philosopher; a contemporary of Karl Marx and Engels. Among his important works are: The Phenomenology of the Spirit, The Science of Logic, Philosophy of Right. His name is associated with the dialectic method of reasoning.

Hemingway, Ernest: (1898-1961) An eminent American novelist, wrote For Whom the Bell Tolls, The Sun Also Rises and Farewell to Arms; awarded Nobel Prize for his Old Man and the Sea.

Hertz, Heinrich: (1857-1895) German physicist who demonstrated similarity between electro-magnetic light and heat waves; transformed sound waves into radio waves.

Herodotus: (485-425 B.C.) Greek historian. Was called "Father of History" by Cicero.

Hecadeus: Greek geographer, was called "Father of Geography".

Hill, Sir Rowland: (1795-1879) Introduced penny postal system.

Hitler, Adolf: (1889-1945) Austrian by birth, adopted German nationality; leader of the Nazi Party; a man of iron will and ruthless determination; started the World War II; Dictator of Germany 1938-45. Author of Mein Kampf.

Hirohito: He was the emperor of Japan. After Japan's defeat in 1945, he accepted the 1946 constitution greatly curtailing his powers and rejecting the prevalent belief in the divinity of the emperor.

Hippocrates: (460-370 B.C.) Greek physician, "Father of Medicine". Rules of conduct for doctors are based on Hippocratic Oath.

Hitchcock, Alfred: (1899-1980) British-American film director, often called "Master of Suspense".

Hobbes, Thomas: (1588-1679) English philosopher and political thinker; author of Leviathan; he favoured strong government and supported the supremacy of the state even in religion.

Ho Chi Min: (1892-1969) Organised the Viet Min or League of Independence, the revolutionary nationalist party of Indo-China against French rule; led the struggle for Vietnam's independence during World War II; As President of North Vietnam he defied the U.S.A. and fought for the unification of Vietnams; one of the greatest communist leaders; North Vietnam and South Vietnam were united in 1975. Saigon, which was the capital of South Vietnam, has been re-named Ho Chi Min City.

Homer: (700 B.C.) The most famous Greek epic poet who wrote two of the world's best epics, Iliad and Odyssey.

Howe, Elias: (1819-1867) American who invented sewing machine.

Hieun Tsang (or Yuan Chwang): Famous Chinese Buddhist pilgrim who came to India in the time of Harsha Vardhana and wrote about his reign; he stayed in India from 629 to 644 A.D.

Hugo, Victor: (1802-85) French novelist, dramatist and poet; author of World famous novels, Les Miserables and Hunchback of Notre Dame.

Hume, Allan Octavian: Founder of the Indian National Congress in 1885, which later developed into a powerful political party.

Huxley, Aldous: (1894-1963) Noted English author. His famous work was End and Means.

Ichiro, Kato: (1925-1994) Japanese scientist, known as "Dr. Robot". Invented 2-legged walking automation that read music.

Jayadeva: (12th Cen. AD) Sanskrit poet from West Bengal. Pioneer of Bhakti poetry.

Jeans, Sir James: (1877-1946) British mathematician and astronomer; author of many popular works on astronomy such as The Mysterious Universe and the Universe Around Us.

Jenghiz Khan or Chengiz Khan: (1162-1227) Ferocious Mongol ruler, notoriously known as 'Scourge of God'; he overran the greater part of Asia bringing devastation wherever he went. He came to India during the reign of Iltutmish.

Jenner, Edward: (1749-1823) English physician; discovered vaccination against small pox. The world was declared small pox-free in 1979. His discovery helped to lay the foundation fo Modern Immunology.

Jefferson, Thomas: (1743-1826) American spokesman for human liberty. Third President of U.S. (1801-1809).

Jinnah, Mohammad Ali: (1876-1948) Founder of Pakistan. Was president of Muslim League. First Governor-General of Pakistan (1947).

Joan of Arc: (1412-1431) "Maid of Orleans", peasant girl whose heroism inspired the French to drive the English out of Orleans, and enabled Charles to become king; she was burnt alive as a heretic.

Johnson, Dr. Samuel: (1709-1784) Writer, conversationalist and a literacy figure of England in the 18th century; Rambler, the Idler, Lives of the Poets are his chief works; Boswell made him immortal by writing his Biography.

Joule, James Prescott: (1818-1889) One of the greatest of English physicists; made important researches in electro-magnetism and determined the mechanical equipment of heat.

Joyce, James: (1882-1941) Irish author; Portrait of the Artist as A Young Man and Ulysses are among his main works.

Julius Caesar: A well-known Roman General who invaded Britain in the first century B.C. He defeated Pompeii. He was assassinated by his trusted friend Brutus at the age of 58.

Kabir: He was one of the greatest exponents of Bhakti Movement which aimed at the reconciliation of the Hindus and Muslims. He believed in the oneness of God and equality of all religions.

Kalidasa: A famous Sanskrit scholar and dramatist. His works include Shakuntala, Raguvamsa, Kumara Sambhava, Meghdoota and Rithusamhara.

Kanishka: Third and the greatest king of Kushana dynasty. A patron of Buddhism. The only ruler of India to extend his empire beyond the Pamirs in Central Asia. He spread Mahayana form of Buddhism.

Kemal, Ataturk: (1881-1938) First President of the Turkish Republic (1923-28) which he established in 1922. He defended the Dardenelles against the British in 1921 and drove the Greeks out of Turkey and deposing the Sultan; a fine soldier and statesman; maker of modern Turkey. He reduced the influence of the religious leaders and secularised Turkey.

Kant, Immanuel: (1724-1804) German Philosopher, founder of the so called critical philosophy; wrote Critique of Pure Reason.

Kapur, Rippan: (1954-1994) Founder of Child Relief and You (CRY), 1979. Its aim is to restore to Indian children their basic right to food, shelter, health and education.

Karve, D.K.: (1858-1962) Indian social worker. Established several institutions for the welfare of women. Awarded Bharat Ratna, in 1958.

Keats, John: (1795-1821) English poet; one of the youngest poets of the Romantic Revival; famous for his richness of imagination and beauty of thought;

famous poems, Isabella, The Eve of St.Agnes, Ode to a Nightingale, Ode to a Grecian Urn, Hyperion, etc.

Kennedy, John. F: (1917-1963) The most popular and youngest President (1961-63) of USA; the first Roman Catholic to be elected President; signed the Partial Nuclear Test Ban Treaty, established better relations with Russia; sponsored the Civil Rights Bill; his intervention in Congo brought about its unification, a man of vision and courage, was assassinated on 22nd November 1963.

Kepler, Johannes: (1571-1630) German astronomer, who discovered the laws of planetary motion.

Khruschev, N.S.: (1894-1971) First Secretary of the Communist Party and also Prime Minister of U.S.S.R. from March 1958 to October 1964. Denounced Stalin for his ruthlessness; he was responsible for the withdrawal of offensive missile equipment from Cuba and thus saved the world from a nuclear war; Author of Khruschev Remembers. He died in 1971.

Kipling, Rudyard: (1865-1936) Born in India in 1865 of English parents; famous short story writer, novelist, and poet. The Jungle Book, Soldiers Three, Kim are among his famous works. Fifth English author to be awarded Nobel Prize for literature.

Kitchner of Khartoum: (1850-1916) Commander-in-Chief in India 1902-1909; was made Secretary for war during World War I; brilliant English soldier who won great victories, defeated the Sudanese darvishes in the Battle of Omdurman; was drowned on June 5, 1916 by the torpedoeing of The Hamphire, while on his way to Russia. Popularly called K.

Koch, Robert: (1843-1910) Bacteriologist, made important discoveries connected with tuberculosis, cholera and bubonic plague.

Khan Abdul Gaffar Khan: Popularly known as 'Frontier Gandhi', he was a prominent Congress leader of the North West Frontier Province. Nehru Award for International Understanding (1967). Bharat Ratna (1987).

Khan, Liaquat Ali: (1895-1951) First Premier of Pakistan (1947). Was leader of Muslim League (1946). Assassinated.

Khusru, Amir: (1253-1325) Persian scholar, courtier, saint and master of music. Father of Sahatara (Sitar).

Kripalani, Sucheta: (1908-1974) Indian nationalist leader and freedom fighter. Was the first woman Chief Minister (U.P.) of independent India, 1963-67. Wife of Acharya Kripalani.

Krishna Devaraya: A prominent king of Vijayanagara Kingdom, the last famous Hindu ruler of South India. He was a great educationist as well as a great warrior. He often defeated the Muslims. He brought many reforms in social, economic and other fields.

Kubla Khan: (1216-1294) Mongol emperor and grandson of Jenghiz Khan. He extended greatly the Mongol Empire by conquest, and lived in unparalled splendour.

Kumar, Nanda: (d.1775) A Bengali patriot, was sentenced to death by Warren Hastings on charges for forgery.

Lao Tsze: (B.C. 604 to 518) Chinese Philosopher; founded Taoism, one of the oldest religions of China, The Path of Virtue is his best work.

Laplace, Pierre Simon, Marquis De: (1749-1827) French astronomer and mathematician known as the Newton of France.

Lawrence, David Herbert: (1885-1930) English novelist and poet; wrote White Peacock, The Rainbow, Sons and Levers, Lady Chatterley's Lover, etc.

Lawrence, T.E.: (1888-1935) British soldier, archaeologist and explorer; organised and led the Arabs to revolt against Turkey in the war of 1914-18 better known as Lawrence of Arabia, author of Seven Pillars of Wisdom.

Larwood, Harold: (1905-1995) England's fast bowler. Known for bodyline bowling.

Lesseps, Ferdinand: (1805-1904) French engineer. Builder of Suez Canal (1869).

Lord William Bentinck: He was the Governor of Madras Presidency during Vellore Mutiny (1806) and he became the Governor General of India (1828-1835). He is well-known for his reforms such as suppression of Thuggees (dacoits), prohibition of Sati, female infanticide, and human sacrifices.

Lord Clive: (1725-1774) He came to India as a clerk in the East India Company and then he became the Commander-in-Chief. He defeated Siraj-ud-Daula who was supported by the French in the Battle of Plassey in 1757. He became the governor of Bengal in 1765. After returning to England in 1790 he committed suicide.

Lala Lajpat Rai: He was an able writer and eloquent orator. A congress leader of United Punjab popularly known as Sher-e- Punjab. Dayanand Anglo-Vedic College in Lahore was founded by him. He was the leader of the Nationalist Party in the Assembly. While lecturing against Simon Commission in Lahore, he was beaten by the police and died of fatal lathi blows.

Lenin Vladimir Ilyich: (1870-1924) He was the founder of modern Communist Russia. He was responsible for the successful Soviet revolution of October-November 1917. Lenin was of the opinion that only force could bring drastic social changes. He was distinguished by his simplicity and devotion to the cause of workers' revolution in which he had abundant faith. Head of the Soviet Government from 1917 to 1924.

Leonardo-da-Vinci: (1452-1519) He was a famous Italian painter who latter settled in France. He painted the Last Supper and Monalisa and other great works. He was also a great musician, sculptor and engineer.

Lister, Lord Joseph: (1827-1912) English surgeon; introduced antiseptic surgery (1867); President of the Royal Society.

Livingstone, Dr. David: (1813-79) Scottish explorer and missionary; his discoveries in Africa included Zambezi, the Victoria Falls and Lake Nyasa; preached against slave trade.

Lloyd George: (1863-1945) Prime Minister of England 1916-1922; Chancellor of the Exchequer 1908-1915; success of the Allies in World War I was largely due to his efforts.

Lord Nelson: English General. He was the commander of the British Fleet in the War of Trafalgar against Napoleon.

Lord Tennyson: English poet. He was the poet laureate for 42 years till his death in 1892. He was the author of 'In Memorium'.

Louis XVI: (1754-93) King of France, married Marie Antoinette. His extravagant policies were responsible for the French Revolution; he and his queen were guillotined by the French Revolutionists. (1793) It is apt to remark that the history of Louis XVI is the history of French Revolution.

Lutyens, Sir Edwin: (1869-1944) Architect; designer of New Delhi, Rashtrapati Bhavan; British Embassy at Washington; President of Royal Academy, 1938-43.

Luther, Martin: ((1483-1546) German religious reformer; founder of Reformation movement and protestantism in Europe.

Macadam, John Loudon: (1756-1836) Scottish engineer; invented the process of modern road making (Macadamising), which greatly improved road travel.

Macaulay, Lord: (1800-59) English essayist, historian and politician; member of the Supreme Council, Calcutta, for five years, famous for his Minutes on Education when in 1883 he recommended the introduction of English as the medium of instruction in India; his best works are: (a) History of England, (b) Essays, (c) Land of Ancient Rome.

Machiavelli, Niccolo: (1439-1527) Italian diplomat and historian; The Prince is one of his chief works, it explains in a masterly way the art and science of government; he believed that end will justify the means.

Megasthenes: Greek envoy at the court of Chandragupta Maurya. He has given a reliable account of the civil and military administration of the country under Chandragupta Maurya's rule.

Magellan, Ferdinand: (1480-1521) Portuguese navigator and commander of the first expedition (1519) to sail round the world.

Malthus, Thomas Robert: (1766-1834) English Clergyman and political economist; in his famous Essay On The Principle Of Population he suggests that marriage should be discouraged to limit the increase of population; Mallthusian Theory of Population is that population increases faster than the means of support and, unless checked by sexual restraint, is restricted only by famine, pestilence, war, etc.

Mannerheim, Field Marshal: (1867-1951) Finnish soldier and statesman; established an independent Finnish State at the end of the World War I; fought against Russia (1939-40), to preserve that independence.

Martin Luther King: (1929-1968) U.S. negro civil rights leader who believed in Mahatma Gandhi's philosophy of Satyagraha; it was due to his efforts that the U.S. Civil Rights Act was passed in 1964. He was shot dead on 4th April 1968 at 'Memphis'; awarded posthumously Nehru Peace Prize for International Understanding, also won the Nobel Peace Prize in 1964 at the age of 35.

Mao Tse-Tung: (1893-1976) Chairman of the Chinese Communist Party 1936-59; first Chairman of the Central Government of the Peoples Republic of China, 1949-59. The country made tremendous progress under his regime; His experiment of 'Communes' and his Great Leap forward met with little success. In 1966-67, he organised the Red Guards to start the Cultural Revolution to propagate his own ideas and to maintain his leadership.

Marx, Karl: (1818-83) German economist and Socialist; took up the cause of the labour classes; founded modern communism theory; author of Communist Manifesto (written in collaboration with his lifelong friend Fredrick Engels) and Das Kapital. He was born in Germany, but worked for a major portion of his life in England.

Mazzini, Guiseppe: (1805-1972) An Italian patriot; driven out of Italy, went to England, came back and was appointed dictator of the Italian Republic in 1848; driven to England again; lived to see a unified Italy.

Mahatma Gandhi: (1869-1948) The father of the India nation. He was mainly responsible for India to get freedom. He launched Non-Cooperation Movement in 1942. He was assassinated by a Hindu fanatic on 30th January 1948. October 2 is his birthday.

Madam Montessori: (1869-1952) Founded the Montessori system of child education. She hailed from Italy. This system provides the child to learn naturally and easily.

Mahavira Vardhamana: (559-528 BC) An apostle of non-violence, he preached observance of chastity. Strengthened Jainism.

Man Singh: He was the Governor of Kabul under Akbar. He fought against Rana Pratap.

Marconi, Guglielmo: (1874-1937) Italian electrical engineer. Invented wireless telegraphy and radio.

Mendel, Gregory Johann: (1822-84) Austrian botanist; known for his laws of heredity.

Menuhin, Yehudi: (b.1916) Born of Jewish parents in New York; great composer and musician; visited India in 1952 and again in 1964. He was awarded Nehru Peace Prize in 1970.

Mehta, Pheroze shah: (1845-1915) Indian leader of moderate school. Founder of Bombay Chronicle (1913).

Michelangelo: (1475-1564) Italian painter, sculptor, architect and poet who did much to beautify the churches of Rome and Florence by his genius.

Mira Ben: (b.1892) Real name Madeline Slade. British disciple of Mahatma Gandhi who gave her the name Mira Ben.

Miss, J.S.: (1806-73) English philosopher and political thinker; propounded the theory of utilitarianism which ensures greatest good for the greatest number.

Millikan, Robert Andrews: (1868-1954) American physicist; made important researches about electrons and discovered cosmic rays; awarded Nobel Prize for Physics, 1923.

Milton, John: (1608-74) English poet whose Paradise Lost is one of the most beautiful epics in English literature. He also wrote Paradise Regained, Comus 'Ill, Pensero' Lycidas.

Mohammed (Prophet): (570-632) Founder of Islam - born in Mecca, fled from Mecca to Medina in 622, for the people of Mecca did not like his teachings and reforms; the year 622 is known as Hijri and denotes the commencement of Muslim era; conquered Mecca in 630.

Moliere: (1622-73) French writer of comedies Tartuffe and Le Misanthrope are among his important works.

Monroe, James: (1758-1831) Fifth President of U.S; famous for Monroe Doctrine propounded in 1823, which debarred Europeans from colonising the American Continent.

Montgolfier, Joseph Michael: (1745-1799) Two French brothers who made several balloon experiments, and thus made flying possible, they are known as the fathers of modern flying.

Morse, S.F.B. (1791-1872) American inventor who invented the telegraphic code known as Morse Code in which various combinations of dots and dashes represent letters of the alphabet and numbers.

Mountbatten, Lord: (1900-79) Allied Supreme Commander, South East Asia Command, 1956; Viceroy of India, March, 1947 to 15th August, 1947; the first Governor General of free India, August 1947 - June 1948. He was killed by the IRA terrorists in August 1979.

Mozart, W.A: (1756-91) Austrian composer; showed musical talent while very young; musical composer at the Imperial court of Vienna.

Motilal Nehru: A leading Lawyer, father of Jawaharlal Nehru. He belonged to Swaraj Party and then joined Congress.

M.S.Golwalkar: He was the chief organiser of the R.S.S. He was one of the direct disciples of Ramakrishna Paramahamsa. His organisation tries to uphold Hinduism.

Mussolini, Benito: (1883-1945) Fascist dictator of Italy 1922-43; entered the Second World War in 1940 on the side of Hitler; was shot dead by partisans while trying to escape to Switzerland.

Mueller, Max: (1823-1900) German. Sanskrit scholar and philosopher.

Nansen, Fridtjof: (1861-1930) Norwegian explorer who reached the highest altitude in North Pole expedition; "Farthest North" contains an account of his expedition. Won Nobel Peace Prize in 1922.

Napier, John: (1550-1617) Scottish mathematician and astronomer; invented logarithms (published in 1614)

Napoleon I (Bonaparte): (1769-1821) Born in Corsica; one of the three greatest generals of the world: Commander-in-Chief of the French Army he secured brilliant victories over Austrians and Russians, which made him practically the master of Europe; was defeated at the Battle of Waterloo in 1815; died in exile at St.Helena.

Nasser, Col.: (1918-70) One of the leaders of coup d'etat in Egypt, was virtually the dictator of Egypt up to 1970, believed in the policy of non-alignment, a great leader of the Arab World, and a staunch nationalist; nationalised the Suez Canel in July, 1956, visited India and joined the tripartite summit beginning in 1966. He had lost much of his popular fame when he suffered a crushing defeat at the hands of Israel in 1967. He was responsible for bringing an end to the civil war in Jordan, died suddenly in September 1970, succeeded by Anwar Sadat.

Nagarjuna: (2nd C. AD) Indian philosopher and scientist (chemist). Adorned the court of King Kanishka.

Naina Devi: (1920-1993) Dadra and thumri singer.

Nelson, Horatio: (1758-1805) A daring sea commander of England; lost his right eye at the siege of Calvi in 1794 and his right arm at the siege of Santa Cruz in 1797; defeated the French at Nile in 1798, and at Trafalgar in 1805; he destroyed the French fleet, but lost his life.

Newton, Sir Isaac: (1642-1727) English scientist; well-known for his work on the composition of white light, the calculus, and laws of gravitation; Mathematical Principles of Natural Philosophy is his most important work; President of Royal Society (1703-27).

Narayan, Jaya Prakash: (1902-1979) Indian freedom fighter, Socialist and Sarvodaya leader. Responsible for the Congress defeat in 1977. His works: Why Socialist from Socialist into Sarvodaya etc.

Nero: Notorious Roman Emperor. He is said to have been fiddling while Rome was burning.

Nicholas, St.: (4th C. AD) Russian patron saint. Associated with Christmas as 'Santa Claus', a person said to fill children's stockings with presents on Christmas eve.

Nicholas II: (1868-1918) Last emperor and Czar of Russia. Japan defeated Russia (1904-5) during his time. Russia fared very badly in the 1914-18 war; Nicholas was ineffective and he lacked ability. Revolution broke out in 1917. He and his family were shot dead in July 1918.

Nietzsche, Friedrich Wilhelm: (1844-1900) German philosopher. His teaching that only the strong should survive, and his doctrine of superman are expressed in his Thus Spake Zarathustra, Beyond Good and Evil and The Will to Power. His philosophy is popularly known as Nietzscheism.

Nightingale, Florence: (1820-1910) British nurse and pioneer of hospital reform, who enthusiastically served the British wounded soldiers in Crimean War (1854-56) with a band of nurses; visited sick wards at night with lamp in hand, so known as The Lady with the Lamp.

Nobel, Dr. Alfred Bernard: (1833-96) Swedish inventor of dynamite, engineer and chemist, amassed huge wealth from the manufacture of explosives; he left a large fortune; out of these funds five prizes are given annually for outstanding work in Physics, Chemistry, Physiology or Medicine, Literature and Peace; a sixth prize was instituted in 1969 for economic science.

Nu, U: (1907-1995) First Prime Minister of Independent Myanmar (Burma). Father of Myanmar Independence.

Ohm, Georg Simon: (1787-1854) Physicist and mathematician of Bavania; discovered the laws of electric resistance known as Ohm's Law.

Omar Khayam: (1050-1123) Poet of Persia; he was also a great astronomer; his Rubaiyat has won universal fame; Edward Fitzgerald translated it into English in 1859.

Oppenheimer, J.Robert: (1902-67) The U.S. atomic scientist - he was later suspected to be a Communist, so he was relieved of his post; received the Fermi Award in 1965; died in February, 1967.

Otto Hahn: German Scientist, who invented the atom bomb.

Oliver Cromwell: He was a soldier-statesman of England. He established Commonwealth in Britain.

Pasteur, Louis: (1822-95) French chemist and scientist; made researches in connection with hydrophobia, bacteriology, cholera, etc, founded Pasteur Institute in Paris.

Pal, Bipin Chandra: (1858-1932) Indian national leader. A radical, led the Swadeshi movement. With Tilak and Lajpat Rai, formed the extremist group in Congress known as 'Garam Dal'.

Pande, Mangal: (d.1857) First martyr of India's Freedom Movement.

Panini: (5th C. BC) Sanskrit grammarian. His Ashtadhyayi contains rules of syntax, moods, word derivation, etc.

Pericles: He was the General of Athens. Under his rule, Athens reached the pinnacle of its glory.

Peary, Robert Edwin: (1856-1920) American explorer who visited Arctic regions several times; finally succeeded in reaching the North Pole in 1909.

Petain, Marshal: (1856-1951) French general; successfully defended Verdun in 1916 and became Commander-in-Chief of all French forces; During the second World War, when French resistance collapsed, he collaborated with the Germans and headed the government of Vichy. He was sentenced to life imprisonment after the war.

Peter, The Great: (1672-1725) Russian Emperor; won many victories; reorganised administration of Russia and introduced many beneficial reforms.

Phule, J.G.: (1827-1980) Indian social reformer and Guru of B.R.Ambedkar.

Picasso, Pabilo Ruiz: (1881-1973) Spanish painter and sculptor; his work is found in public galleries and private collections all over the world; he founded the Cubist school of Painting. Spain celebrated Picasso's 100th birth anniversary in 1891. His civil war painting "Guernica" was brought from the U.S.A. to Spain and shown publicly for the first time in his own country during the celebrations.

Pitman, Sir Isaac: (1813-97) Founder of Pitman system of phonographic shorthand.

Planck, Max: (1858-1947) German physicist, his researches about radiation of energy culminated in 1901 in his law of radiation which laid the foundation of Quantum Theory, in 1918, he got Nobel Prize for Physics.

Plato: (427-347 B.C.) Greek philosopher; disciple of Socrates; wrote several works; the most important of his works are The Republic and Dialogues of Socrates.

Plimsoll, Samuel: (1824-98) British Social reformer who as M.P procured the passing of the Merchant Shipping Act of 1878; it prescribed a line above which no ship must sink in water when loaded, thus overloading became illegal; it is known as Plimsoll Line.

Polo, Marco: (1256-1323) Venetian traveller and explorer; travelled through many eastern countries and published the record of his journey.

Pope, Alexander: (1688-1744) Notable English poet; author of several books such as Rape of the Lock and Essay on Man.

Ptolemy: (90-168) Greek astronomer and mathematician; founded the Ptolemic system which taught that the earth was stationary, and the other bodies revolved around it.

Pulakesin II: Famous king of Chalukya dynasty. He was defeated by the Pallava ruler Narasimha Varman in a conflict.

Pushyamitra Sunga: First king of Sunga dynasty. He was the Commander-in-Chief of Mauryan Army. Brahminism flourished under his reign.

Pythagoras: (6th Century B.C.) Greek philosopher and mathematician; took keen interest in astronomy and geometry.

Quisling, Vidkun: (1887-1945) Norwegian military officer, who deserted the Norwegian army and joined the Nazis; was appointed Premier by Hitler in 1942, but he was shot dead due to his unpopularity.

Raleigh, Sir Walter: (1552-1618) English courtier, sailor and statesman during the period of Queen Elizabeth and James I; wrote History of the World, introduced potato plant and tobacco in England; was imprisoned and beheaded on a charge of conspiracy against James I.

Raphael, Santi: (1483-1520) Italian painter; his works are renowned for beauty and colour.

Rasputin, G.Y.: (1871-1916) Russian fanatic; an enigmatic personality, to some he represented the devil and to others a saint; later he pretended to possess miraculous powers; wielded great influence over the Czar Nicholas II of Russia, he was murdered by Russian revolutionaries.

C.V.Raman: Second Indian to receive Nobel Prize for the discovery of 'Raman Effect'.

Ramakrishna Paramahamsa: Great religious sage. Teacher of Swami Vivekananda. Reformer of present Hinduism in West Bengal.

Rama Rao, N.T.: (d.1996) The Chairman of the National Front and former Chief Minister of Andhra Pradesh died on January 18, 1996. He was an eminent flim actor.

Ramanuja, Acharya: (11th C. AD) Indian religious teacher and founder of Rama Bhakti movement.

Ramanujam, Srinivasa: (1887-1920) Indian mathematician. Contributed to the theory of numbers.

Rana Pratap: Great Rajput leader who opposed Akbar.

Rana Sanga of Mewar: Great Rajput leader who fought against Babur. But Babur defeated Rana in the Battle of 'Khanwa'.

Ranjit Singh: Founder of Sikh rule in Punjab.

Ray, Satyajit: (1922-1992) Indian film maker. Winner of Bharat Ratna, Special Oscar and many other awards.

Razia Sultana: (13th C.) Daughter of Sultan Iltutmish, she was the first and only Muslim lady ever to rule from the throne of Delhi.

Raja Ram Mohan Roy: A great social reformer. He was mainly responsible for the suppression of 'Sati'. Founded Brahma Samaj.

Reuter, Paul Julius Von: (1821-1899) German pioneer of telegraphic press service; organised Reuter's International News Agency.

Rolland, Romain: (1886-1944) French author; awarded Nobel Prize for Literature in 1915 for writing Jean Christopher in 10 volumes. Also wrote books on Mahatma Gandhi and Sri Ramakrishna.

Rommel, Field Marshal: (1891-1944) German general who played a very significant part in North African and Western Europe in the Second World War; he committed suicide.

Roentgen, W.K.: (1845-1923) German scientist who discovered the Roentgen rays in 1895; awarded Nobel Prize for Physics in 1901.

Roosevelt, Franklin Delano: (1882-1945) American statesman; entered politics 1910; Governor of New York 1929-33; President of USA 1932-36 and 1939-40; he met the economic crisis of 1933 with a policy for a "New Deal"; elected President third time 1944; died 1945. (The first American to be elected President for more than two terms).

Ross, Ronald: (1857-1932) British physician born in India; discovered the cause of malaria; got Nobel Prize for Medicine in 1912.

Rousseau, Jean Jacques: (1712-78) French Philosopher and Writer; his writings particularly confessions and the 'Social Contract' gave the French people a new field of thought; his writings were to a certain extent responsible for the French revolution.

Robespierre: Was leader of Jacobian Party; participated in the French Revolution.

Roger Bacon: Inventor of Gun-Powder.

Roy, Bidhan Chandra: (1882-1962) First Indian to obtain MRCP and FRCS in one calendar year. Mayor of Calcutta (1931). Chief Minister of West Bengal (1948-1962). Awarded Bharat Ratna, 1961.

Ruskin, John: (1819-1900) English social reformer and art critic; acknowledged to be one of the greatest thinkers of his time; his works gave inspiration to many great men, especially Mahatma Gandhi. Unto The Last is his great work.

Russell, Bertrand: (1872-1970) Philosopher, pacifist and mathematician; visited many countries; received Nobel Prize for Literature in 1950; works: Principia Mathematica, Marriage and Morals, History of Western Philosophy, Commonsense and Nuclear Warfare, etc;

Rutherford, Lord: (1871-1937) British physicist announced his nuclear theory of the atom and succeeded in splitting the atom; got Nobel Prize for Chemistry in 1908.

Saadi: (1184-1292) Persian poet; Gulistan, Bostan are his famous works.

Saha, Meghnad: (1893-1956) Indian scientist research in astrophysics of thermal ionisation.

Sadat, Anwar: President of Arab Republic of Egypt. He was responsible for the expulsion of the Russian technicians in 1972, on 6th October 1973, he sprang a major surprise on Israel, when he launched a major offensive in order to recover the area lost in the 1967 conflict. He visited Jerusalem, Israel in November 1977 in order to initiate a dialogue with Israel for restoring peace in the war-torn West Asia. He signed the Camp David agreement in September 1978. His policy of friendship with Israel isolated Egypt from the Arabs; he was assassinated in 1981.

Sankaracharya: (b.788 A.D.) Indian philosopher and scholar. Revived Hindu religion. Founder of Advaita School of Philosophy.

Samudra Gupta: Well-known as Indian Napoleon, Samudra Gupta lived in the 4th century A.D. He was son and successor of Chandragupta I of Gupta Dynasty. He was a great scholar, musician, poet and military genius.

Sardar Patel: Known as the 'Iron Man of India' was Home Minister of Free India. He was instrumental in merging 600 princely states with the Indian Union after Independence.

Saraswati, Anandbodh: (1903-1994) Was president of International Arya League.

Savarkar, V.D. : (1883-1966) Indian Revolutionary and staunch Hindu started Free India Society in London. Authored Indian war of Independence. Founder of Abhinav Bharat.

Sarla Ben: (1900-1932) Real name Katherine Mary Heilani. European disciple of Mahatma Gandhi.

Satyamurti, S.: (1887-1943) Known as Fire-brand of South India. Made plans for Poondi Dam Project.

Scott, Sir Walter: (1771-1832) Scottish poet and novelist; his popular writings are: The Talisman, Kenilworth, Ivanhoe, The Lady of the Lake.

Shakespeare, William: (1564-1616) Greatest dramatist and poet of England; was born at Stratford on Avon; author of 30 plays such as Hamlet, Julius Caesar, Merchant of Venice, Romeo and Juliet, Macbeth, Othello, As You Like It, Cymbeline. His 400th birth anniversary was celebrated throughout the world in 1964.

Shaftesbury, 7th Earl of: (1801-1885) British social reformer. Responsible for Factory Acts forbidding children and women to work in mines.

Shankar: (1902-1989) Indian cartoonist, and founder of International Dolls Museum.

Shastri, Lal Bahadur: (1904-1966) Prime Minister of India, 1964. Signed Tashkent Agreement and died in Tashkent itself.

Shelley, P.B.: (1792-1822) English poet; renowned for his daring and outspoken views; his works include Ode to the West Wind, The Skylark, Prometheus Unbound, etc.

Sheridan, R.D.: (1751-1816) English playwright; author of the most distinguished comedies, The School for Scandal and The Rivals.

Shah Jahan: Son of Jahangir and father of Aurangzeb. His period (1625-58) in Indian History is well-known as the golden age of the Mughals. He built Taj Mahal in memory of his wife Mumtaz. Art and Architecture flourished in his period.

Sher Shah Suri: The period of Sher Shah and of his successors known as Suri Interregnum in Indian history is notable for revenue reorganisation and administration. He drove Humayun out of India. Grand Trunk Road was built during his time.

Shivaji: (1627-1680) Hindu king of Maharashtra who offered challenge to the Mughals. His period is well known for military reforms and revenue administration.

Simuka: Founder of Satavahana dynasty. He destroyed the power of Kanvas and Sungas.

Siemens, Sir William: (1823-83) German born scientist and inventor settled in England, made researches in heat and electricity.

Singh, Bhagat: (1907-1931) Known as Shahi-e-Azam. Founded Naujawan Bharat Sabha.

Singh, Brijendra: (1918-1995) Last king of the former princely state of Bharatpur.

Singh, Charan: (1902-1987) Lok Dal leader, was Prime Minister for a brief period in 1979-80.

Singh, Giani Zail: (1916-1994) President of India, 1982-87.

Singh, Gurcharan: (1898-1995) Grand old man of Indian pottery. Pioneer of "art pottery", founder-member of All-India Fine Arts and Crafts Society.

Singh, Nagendra: (d.1988) First Indian President of International Court of Justice (1970).

Singh, Udham: (1898-1940) Shot Michael O'Dwyer, Governor of Punjab, responsible for Jallianwala Bagh Massacre.

Simpson, Sir James Young: (1811-70) Scottish surgeon, discovered the utility of chloroform as an anaesthetic.

Sitaramaiah, Pattabhi: (1880-1959) Responsible for reorganisation of states on linguistic basis (1956), and also for setting up of cooperative banks.

Slovo, Joe: (1927-1995) Leader of Black Liberation Movement. Chief of Communist Party of South Africa.

Smuts, Field Marshal: (1870-1950) South African soldier and statesman. Prime Minister 1912-24, and Prime Minister, Foreign Minister and Minister of Defence from 1939 to 1945; defeated by the Nationalist Party of Dr. Malan at the general elections of 1946.

Smith, Adam: (1723-90) Scottish economist; author of Theory of Moral Sentiments and Wealth of Nations.

Socrates: (470-390 B.C.) Greek Philosopher; he had Plato and Xenophon as his pupils; he was sentenced to death for "Corrupting youth of the country". Died as nobly as he lived.

Sophocles: (495-406) Dramatist of Athens; author of many plays, Oedipus, Electia and Antigone.

Spencer, Edmund: (1552-90) English poet of Elizabeth's reign; his best work; Faerie Queene.

Solomon: King of Jews, known for his wisdom. He lived in the 10th and 11th century B.C. He wrote 'Song of Solomon'.

Stalin, Joseph: (1879-1953) Soviet dictator, played an important part in the Russian Revolution of 1917, became the outstanding leader of Russia after the death of Lenin in 1924; introduced in 1929 the famous Five Year Plan to build new Russia; General Secretary of the Central Executive Committee of the U.S.S.R., 1924-1941; died on March 5, 1953; succeeded by George Malenkov; personality cult of Stalin has been denounced by the present Russian leaders.

Stephenson, George: (1781-1848) English Engineer; inventor of locomotive engine; improved Watt's steam engine.

Stevenson, Robert Louis: (1850-94) Scottish novelist and essayist, author of Treasure Island, Kidnapped, Dr. Jekyll and Mr.Hyde.

Sir Syed Ahmed: A great educationist of the Muslim community. He established the M.A.O. college at Aligarh in 1874 which later emerged as Aligarh Muslim University.

Sherpa Tenzing: Indian mountaineer who conquered Mt. Everest as the first man on 29th May 1953. He died recently.

Sun Yat Sen, Dr.: (1867-1925) First President of the Chinese Republic of which he was the founder, unified the whole of China, played a significant part in the revolution of 1911; founder of Kuomintang (Chinese Nationalist Party)

Surdas: (12th C.) A blind poet. Worshipped Krishna and spread Krishna Bhakti cult.

Susruta: (4th C. AD) Indian surgeon. Father of Modern Plastic Surgery. Devised an artificial nose, diagnosed cataract and described hernia and medicinal value of garlic.

Swift, Jonathan: (1667-1745) Irish writer of powerful satire, poems and discourses; his best known works are: A Tale of a Tub, The Battle of the Books and Gulliver's Travels.

Schweitzer, Albert: (1875-1965) German medical missionary, philosopher, musician, humanitarian and pacifist, who dedicated his life to the service of the Africans in Lambarene (Gabon Republic) and worked there for over fifty years; awarded Nobel Peace Prize in 1952.

Tagore, Rabindranath: (1861-1941) Famous Bengali poet, playwright, educationist, actor, humanist and philosopher, awarded Nobel Prize (First Asian - Indian) for Literature in 1913 for his great work Gitanjali; founded the

Shanti Niketan University at Bolepur; famous works: Gitanjali, Gora, Wreck, Post Office, Chitra. His birth centenary celebrations were held all over the world in 1961.

Tamerlane or Timur: (1336-1405) Also called Tamerling i.e., Timur the Lame. A great warrior of Central Asia, conquered Turkistan, Persia and Syria; very cruel and blood thirsty, was called the Scourge of the East in his days.

Tasman, Abel Janszoon: (1602-59) A noted Dutch navigator who discovered the Island of Tasmania in 1652 and also New Zealand.

Thyagaraja (18th Century): A great saint and musician. Exponent of carnatic music. Thyagaraja Aradhanas are held every year in India.

Thackeray, W.M.: (1811-83) English novelist; author of Vanity Fair, The Newcomes, Henry Esmond, etc.

Thant, U.: A devout Buddhist from Burma, who was elected Secretary General of the U.N. after the death of M.Dag Hammerskjoeld in 1961; he tackled various international issues like the West Irian, Cuba; he won the Nehru Peace Award for 1966.

Tito, Marshal: (1892-1980) Yugoslav leader, visited India in 1954; approved the Panch Shila. He called the Neutral Nations Conference at Belgrade in September 1961, a firm believer in non alignment, visited India to join the tripartite summit of October 21-24, 1966. He represented his country at the non-aligned summits of 1964, 1970 and 1973, 1976 and 1979. He was awarded the Nehru Prize for Peace and International Understanding, visited India in January 1974. He visited China in 1977, the visit resulted in restoring friendship between Yugoslavia and China, which was disrupted in the 1950's. He played a very important role during the Havana summit of the non-aligned nations in 1979.

Tolstoy, Count Leo: (1828-1910) Russian writer and philosopher; author of Childhood, Tales from Sebartopol, War and Peace, Anna Karenina, The Cossacks.

Tombaugh, Clyde: The astronomer who discovered the planet Pluto before he even had a college degree died on January 19, 1997 at the age of 90.

Tope, Tantia: (1814-1859) Real name Ramachandra Panduranga. Maratha patriot. Took part in First War of Indian Independence in 1857 with Nana Sahib and Rani Lakshmibai of Jhansi.

Toynbee, Arnold: (1889-1975) World famous British historian. A pioneer in the field of comparative study of independent civilisations.

Trotsky, Leon: (1879-1940) A prominent leader of Bolshevik Revolution in Russia; War Minister in the Bolshevik Government, differed with Stalin in policy, so he was dismissed from office, was assassinated in a hotel at Mexico in 1940.

Tarabai: Valiant heroine in Indian history. She resisted the attempts of Lord Edinborough to annex, Gwalior. She became a widow at the age of 13.

Timur Lane: Turkish invader. He ransacked Delhi in 1738 A.D.

Todar Mal: One of the Nau Rattans or nine gems and Revenue Minister of Akbar.

Tsze, Lao: (604-518 B.C.) Chinese philosopher, founder of Taoism. Authored The Path to Virtue.

Tulsi Das: Great Hindu religious preacher. He wrote Ram Charit Manas.

Tunku, Abdul Rehman: (1903-1990) Malaysia's first Prime Minister. Had Malaysia to independence from British rule in 1957.

Tyabji, Badruddin: (1844-1906) Indian national leader. First Indian Barrister of Bombay High Court.

Uday Shankar: (d.1977) Indian classical dancer. First dancer to perform abroad.

Urey, H.C.: (1893) American chemist who made a special study of the structure of atom and molecule; discovered heavy water; got Nobel Prize for Chemistry in 1934.

Valmiki: (800 BC) Sanskrit poet. Author of Ramayana.

Van Gogh, Vincent: (1853-90) Distinguished Dutch Painter.

V.V.Giri: The former President of India was once a well-known labour leader. He made history by appearing in person before the Supreme Court in connection with the case on his Presidential elections. He died in 1980.

Varahamihira: Hindu astronomer and mathematician in the court of Vikramaditya in the 6th century A.D.

Vespucci, Amerigo: (1454-1512) Explored Venezuela and Gulf of Mexico (1507). United States is named after him as 'America'.

Visvesvarayya: (1861-1962) Eminent architect. Builder of Modern Mysore. Built the dam across Cauveri in Mysore. Recipient of Bharat Ratna, 1955. His works include, 'Reconstructing India' and 'Planned Economy for India'.

Vivekananda: (1862-1902) Hindu religious leader. His speech at Chicago was memorable. He led the Vedanta Movement.

Victoria: (1819-1901) Queen of Great Britain and Ireland; she was the daughter of the Duke of Kent and ascended the throne in 1837 on the death of her uncle William VI; the Golden Jubilee of her ascendency was celebrated in 1887, and the Diamond Jubilee in 1897. Hers was the most glorious period of British History.

Vidyasagar, Ishwar Chandra: (1820-1898) Indian social reformer and educationist from Bengal. Did pioneering work in the field of primary education and widow remarriage.

Virgil: (70-19 B.C.) Roman poet; his most famous work in Aenid.

Volta, A: (1745-1827) Professor of Natural Philosophy at Pavia University (Italy), discovered the Voltaic Cell, discovered the electrical unit, the Volt.

Voltaire, F.M.: (1694-1778) French philosopher and writer; author of philosophical letters, Discourse on Man, Essay on the Morals and Spirit of Nations, etc.

Vyas, Ved: (800 BC) Sanskrit scholar. Wrote Mahabharat. Bhagawad Gita, the great religious and moral code for Hindus, forms a part of it.

Walpole, Robert: (1676-1745) First Prime Minister of Britain. A Whig M.P., became the Chancellor Exchequer in 1715. Was appointed head of the government by George I, because of his dexterous handling of South Sea Bubble Crisis in 1720.

Walton, Ernest: (1904-1995) Ireland's nuclear scientist.

Wellesley, Lord: (1760-1842) Irish administrator, Governor General of India, 1797.

Washington, George: (1732-99) Commander-in-Chief of the American army during the American War of Independence (1775-83) first President of the American Republic in 1770; re-elected President in 1793; refused election for a third time; it is said of him, "First in peace, first in war and first in the hearts of his countrymen".

Watt, James: (1736-1819) Scottish engineer and inventor; discovered the principle of steam engine.

Watson Watt, Sir Robert: (1892-1973) Scottish physicist who played a major part in the development of radar.

Weizmann, Chaim: (1874-1952) The veteran Zionist leader, became provisional president of Israel in May, 1948, and was elected first President in 1949, a famous scientist.

Wellington, Duke of (Arthur, Wellesley): (1769-1852) Was the most famous British General of the 19th century; distinguished himself in India and in the Peninsular War; was British Ambassador at Paris in 1814; defeated Napoleon at Waterloo; Prime Minister of England (1828-30).

Wells, Herbert George: (1866-1946) A distinguished English novelist; treated social, political and educational problems with breadth of vision; Works: A Short History of Mankind, Wealth and Happiness of Mankind, The Shape of Things to Cense, Time Machine, Kipps.

Wheatstone, Sir Charles: (1802-75) English electrician, scientist and inventor; his name is intimately associated with electric telegraph and the invention of the stereoscope.

Whittle, Sir Frank: (b.1907) Pioneer in the field of jet propulsion.

Wilberforce, William: (1759-1833) British M.P. took a prominent part in the movement for abolishing slave trade in Britain; abolished in 1807.

Wilde, Oscar: (1856-1900) Irish poet and dramatist, best known for his brilliant witty comedies. Author of A Woman of No Importance, The Ideal Husband, De Profundis, The Importance of Being Earnest, etc.

Wilson, Woodrow: (1856-1294) President of the United States (1913-21); brought America into the First World War on the side of the Allies; played an important part in the formation of the League of Nations but could not persuade his country to join the League; was awarded Nobel Prize for Peace.

Wordsworth, William: (1770-1850) English poet; is unrivalled as an interpreter of nature in her various moods; made poet Laureate in 1843; some of his most famous poetical works are Lyrical Ballads, Lucy, The Prelude, To the Cuckoo, The Green Linnet Recuse, Solitary Reaper etc..

Womesh Chandra Bannerji: He was the first President of the Indian National Congress in 1885. The first session of the Congress was held in Mumbai.

Warren Hastings: First Governor-General of the British India during the period 1774 to 1785. Regulating Act and Pitt's India Act were passed during his times.

Walt Whitman: American Poet, aimed at forming a New American outlook.

Xenophon: (434-355 B.C.) Greek historian and general. Studied philosophy under Socrates.

Xerxes (Circa 519-465 B.C.): King of Persia and a great Commander; son of the first Darius. He defeated the Spartans at Thermopylae, but his fleet was overcome at Salamis; he was assassinated.

Yukawa: He was awarded the 1949 Nobel prize for Nuclear Physics.

Yasser Arafat: Chairman of Palestine Liberation Organisation. He gained fame because he recognised Israel's right to exist in peace and security.

Yat-Sen, Sun: (1867-1925) Founder-President of Chinese Republic (1921-1925). Founder of Chinese Nationalist Party (Kuomintang). Played a prominent part in 1911 Revolution of China which brought an end to Manchu empire.

Yun, Chen: (1905-1995) Architect of China's economic policies.

Zafar, Bahadur Shah: (1807-1862) Last ruler of Mughal dynasty. Fought against the British in the first War of Indian Independence in 1857.

Zia-ul-Haq: (1924-88) He was killed by a bomb blast in air when he was the President of Pakistan.

Zeppelin, Count Von Ferdinand: (1838-1917) German inventor; invented the huge diligible airship bearing his name. It was used in the first World War.

Zola, Emile: (1840-1902) French novelist; author of L'assommoir and Nana.

Zoroaster: Also known as Zarathustra, Persian founder of the Parsee religion; lived about the 6th century; his teachings are to be found in Zend Avesta.

BOOKS AND AUTHORS

A

BOOKS	AUTHORS
A Bend in the River	V.S. Naipaul
A Brush with Life	Satish Gujral
A Call of Honour : In Service of Emergent India	Jaswanth Singh
A Conceptual Encyclopaedia of Guru Granth Sahib	S.S. Kohli
A Foreign Policy for India	I.K. Gujral
A Fortune Teller Told Me	Tiziano Terzani
A Gender Lens on Social Psychology	Judith A Howard and Jocelyn A.Hollander
A General and His Army	Georgy Vladimov
A Himalayan Love Story	Namita Gokhale
A Last Leap South	Vladimir Zhirinovsky
A National Flawed—Lession from India History	P.N. Chopra

BOOKS	AUTHORS
A Peep into the Past	Vasant Navrekar
A Possible India	Partha Chatterjee
A Psychoanalysis of the Prophets	Abdulla Kamal
A Revolutionary Life	Laxmi Sehgal
A Secular Agenda	Arun Shourie
A Simple Path	Lucinda Vardey
A Suitable Boy	Vikram Seth
A Tale of Two Gardens	Octavio Paz
A Tribute to People's Princess: Diana	Peter Donelli
A Tryst With Destiny	Stanley Wolfer
A Variety of Absence	Dom Moraes
Abbot	Walter Scott
Absalom, Absalom	William Faulkner
Absalom and Achitophel	John Dryden
Accession to Extinction	D.R. Mankekar
Across Borders, Fifty-years of India's Foreign Policy	J.N. Dixit
Adam Bede	George Eliot
Adhe Adhure	Mohan Rakesh
Adonis	P.B. Shelley
Adrain Mole—The Wilderness Years	Sue Townsend
Adventures of Huckleberry Finn, The	Mark Twain
Adventures of Robinson Crusoe	Daniel Defoe
Adventures of Sally	P.G. Wodehouse
Adventures of Sherlock Holmes	Sir Arthur Conan Doyle
Adventures of Tom Sawyer, The	Mark Twain
Adversary in the House	Irving Stone
Advice and Consent	Allen Drury
An Ordinary Person's Guide to Empire	Arundhati Roy
As I See	Ms. Kiran Bedi
Athenian Constitution	Aristotle
Atoms of Hope	Mohan Sundara Rajan
August 1914	Alexander Solzhenitsyn
August Coup, The	Mikhali S. Gorbachev
Author's Farce	Henry Fielding
Autobiography of an Unknown Indian	Nirad C. Chaudhuri
Avanti Sundari	Dandin
Ayodhya : 6 December, 1992	P.V. Narashimha Rao

B

Baburnama	Babur
Baby and Child	Penelope Leach
Back to Methuselah	G.B.Shaw
Backward Place, A	Ruth Prawer Jhabwala
Bandicoot Run	Manohar Malgonkar

BOOKS	AUTHORS
Bang-i-Dara	Mohammad Iqbal
Bangla Desh—The Unfinished Revolution	Lawrence Lifschultz
Banyan Tree, The	Hugh Tinker
Beach Boy	Ardesher Vakil
Beast and Man	Murry Midgley
Beating the Street	Peter Lynch
Beginning of the Beginning	Acharya Rajneesh
Being Indian	Pawan Verma
Beloved	Toni Morrison
Ben Hur	Lewis Wallace
Bend in the Ganges, A	Manohar Malgonkar
Bermuda Triangle	Charles Berlitz
Berry Patches	Yevgeny Yevtushenko
Best and the Brightest, The	David Halberstan
Betrayal of Pearl Harbour	James Rusbridger and Eric Nave
Between Hope and History	Bill Clinton
Between the Lines	Kuldip Nayar
Bewildered India–Identity, Pluralism, Discord	Rasheedud-din Khan
Beyond Boundaries: A Memoire	Swaraj Paul
Beyond the Horizon	Eugene O'Neill
Beyond Modernisation, Beyond Self	Sisir Kumar Ghose
Beyond Peace	Richard Nixon
Brideless in Wembley	Sanjay Suri
By Love Possessed	James Gould Cozzens
Byzantium	W.B. Yeats

C

Caesar and Cleopatra	G.B.Shaw
Call the Briefing	Martin Fitzwater
Cancer Ward	Aleksandr Solzhenitsyn
Candida	George Bernard Shaw
Candide	Voltaire
Candle in the Wind	Aleksandr Solzhenitsyn
Canterbury Tales, The	Geoffrey Chaucer
Canvass of Life	Sheila Gujral
Caravans	James A. Michener
Castle, The	Franz Kafka
Catch-22	Joseph Heller
Catcher in the Rye	J.D. Salinger
Cell	Stephen King
Complete Taj Mahal, The	Ebba Koch
Courts and Their Judgements	Arun Shourie
Corporate Governance Economic Reforms and Development	Darryl Reed and Sanjay Mukherjee
Chance	Joseph Conrad

BOOKS	AUTHORS
Chandalika	Rabindranath Tagore
Childhood Regained	Kalpana Shankar, Kalyani Rajaraman
Chemmeen	Thakazhi Sivasankara Pillai
Corruption in India	N. Vittal
Crabwalk	Gunther Grass
Curtain Raisers	K. Natwar Singh

D

BOOKS	AUTHORS
Damsel in Distress	P.G. Wodehouse
Dancing with the Devil	Rod Barker
Dangerous Place, A	Daniel Patrick Moynihan
Dangerous Summer, The	Ernest Hemingway
Dangling Man	Saul Bellow
Daniel Deronda	George Eliot
Dark Room, The	R.K. Narayan
Dark Home Coming	Eric Lustbader
Dark Side of Camelot	Seymour Hersh
Darkness at Noon	Arthur Koestler
Das Kapital	Karl Marx
Dashkumar Charitam	Dandi
Da Vinci Code, The	Martin Lunn
Daughter of the East	Benazir Bhutto
David Copperfield	Charles Dickens
Day in Shadow, The	Nayantara Sehgal
Day of the Jackal	Frederick Forsyth
Days of Grace	Arthur Ashe & Arnold Rampersad
Days of His Grace	Eyvind Johnson
De Profundis	Oscar Wilde
Dean's December	Saul Bellow
Death and After	Annie Besant
Death Be Not Proud	John Gunther
Death By Fire	Mala Sen
Death in the Castle	Pearl S. Buck
Death in Venice	Thomas Mann
Death of a City	Amrita Pritam
Death of a Patriot	R.E.Harrington
Death on the Nile	Agatha Christie
Death of a President	William Manchester
Deathof a Salesman	Arthur Miller
Death—The Supreme Friend	Kakasaheb Kalelkar
Death Under Sail	C.P. Snow
Deception point	Dan Brown
Dragon's Seed	Pearl S. Buck
Dragon's Teeth	U.B.Sinclair

BOOKS	AUTHORS
Dream of Fair to Middling Women	Samuel Beckett
Dreams, Roses and Fire	Eyvind Johnson
Drunkard	Emile Zola
Dude, Where's My Country?	Michael Moore
Durgesh Nandini	Bankim Chandra Chatterjee
Dynamics of Social Change	Chandra Shekhar

E

Earth	Emile Zola
Earth in the Balance: Forging a New Common Purpose	Al Gore
Earth Mother, The	Pupul Jayakar
East of Eden	B.N.Mullick
East West	Salman Rushdie
East Wind	Pearl S. Buck
Economic Planning of India	Ashok Mehta
Economics of corruption	Ajit Mishra
Economics of Peace and Laughter	John K. Galbraith
Economics of Public Purpose	John K. Galbraith
Economics of the Third World	S.K. Ray
Education of Public Man, The	Hubert Humphrey
Edwina and Nehru	Catherine Clement
Egmont	J.W. Von Goethe
Envisioning Empowered Nation	A.P.J. Abdul Kalam & A. Sivathanu Pillai

F

Faces to Everest	Maj. H.P.S. Ahluwalia
Facts are Facts	Khan Abdul Wali Khan
Fairie Queene	Edmund Spencer
Faith & Fire: A Way Within	Madhu Tandon
Fall of a Sparrow, The	Salim Ali
Family Moskat	Issac Bashevis Singer
Family Reunion, The	T.S.Eliot
Far From the Madding Crowd	Thomas Hardy
Far Pavilions, The	M.M. Kaye
Faraway Music, The	Svetlana Allilueva
Farewell to the Trumpets	James Morris
Farewell to a Ghost	Manoj Das
Farewell to Arms, A	Ernest Hemingway
Farm House	George Orwell
Faster than the Speed of the Light	Joao Magueijo
Fathers and Sons	Ivan Turgenev
Faust	J.W. Von Goethe
Fidelio	L. Beethoven

BOOKS	AUTHORS
Fiesta	Ernest Hemingway
Firefly: A Fairytale	Ritu Beri
From Surprise to Victory	Gen. V.P. Malik
Fury	Sulman Rushdie

G

Gambler, The	Fyodor Dostoevsky
Ganadevata	Tara Shankar Bandopadhyaya
Gandhi and Stalin	Louis Fisher
Gandhi vs Jinnah	Allen Hayes Merriam
Gardener	Rabindranath Tagore
Gathering Storm	Winston Churchill
Ghasiram Kotwal	Vijay Tendulkar
Ghosts in the Machine	Arthur Koestler
Girl in Blue, Girl On the Boat	P.G. Wodehouse
Gita Rahasya	Bal Gangadhar Tilak
Gitanjali, Gora	Rabindranath Tagore
Gladiators	Arthur Koestler
Glimpses of Indian Ocean	Z.A. Quasim
Glimpses of Some Great Indians	M.L. Ahuja
Glimpses of World History	Jawaharlal Nehru
Go Down Moses	William Faulkner
Goa	Asif Currimbhoy
God and the Bible	Matthew Arnold
Godfather, The	Mario Puzo
God of Small Things, The	Arundhati Roy
God's Little Soldier	Kiran Nagarkar
Godrej: A Hundred Years	B.K. Karanjia
Gold Bat, The	P.G. Wodehouse
Golden Borough	James Frazer
Golden Gate, The	Vikram Seth
Golden Threshold	Sarojini Naidu
Gone Away	Dom Moraes
Gone with the Wind	Margaret Mitchell
Good Earth	Pearl S.Buck
Goodbye, Mr. Chips	James Hilton
Guiding Souls: Dialogues on The Purpose of Life	Dr. A.P.J. Abdul Kalam & Arun K. Tiwari

H

Half A Life	V.S. Naipaul
Hamlet	William Shakespeare
Hard Times	Charles Dickens
Harsha Charita	Bana Bhatt
Handful of Dust, A	Evelyn Waugh
Happy Death	Albert Camus

BOOKS	AUTHORS
Harlot High and Low	Honore de Balzac
Harry Potter and the Deathly Hallows	J.K. Rowling
Harvest	Manjula Padmanabhan
Heart of Darkness	Joseph Conrad
Heaven Has No Favourites	Eric Maria Remarque
Heart to Heart	K. Natwar Singh
Heat and Dust	Ruth Prawer Jhabwala
Heavy Weather	P.G. Wodehouse
Heir Apparent	Dr.Karan Singh
Heritage	Anthony West
Hero of Our Times	Richard Hough

I

I am not an Island	K.A. Abbas
I follow the Mahatma	K.M.Munshi
Idylls of the King	Tennyson
I Muse; Therefore I am	V.N. Narayanan
Idiot, The	Fyodor Dostoevsky
Idols	Sunil Gavaskar
If I am Assassinated	Z.A. Bhuto
Imperial Woman	Pearl S. Buck
India 2020	Dr. A.P.J. Abdul Kalam
India's Foreign Policy	V.P. Dutt
Indian Power Sector: Challenge and Response	R.V. Shabi
India Remembered	Pamela Mountbatten
India Towards Economic Super Power	Ajit Kumar Sinha
India and China in the Asian country	P. Jegadish Gandhi
India's Water Resources - Comtemporary	A. Vaidhyanathan
Infinite Justice	Arundhati Roy
Issues on Irrigation	
India's Globalization - Evaluating the Economic Consequences	Baldev Raj Nayyar

J

Jack and Jackie—Portrait of an American Marriage	Christopher Anderson
Jai Somnath	K.M.Munshi
Jaguar Smile	Salman Rushdie
Jajar, Churashir Maa	Mahashweta Devi
Jane Eyre	Charlotte Bronte
Jawaharlal Nehru—A Communicator & Democratic Leader	A.K. Damodran
Jawaharlal Nehru, Rebel and Statesman	B.R. Nanda
Jazz	Toni Morrison
Jean Christopher	Romain Rolland
Jesus Rediscovered	Malcolm Muggeridge

BOOKS	AUTHORS
Jewel	Danielle Steel
Jhoota Sach	Yashpal
Jobs for Millions	V.V. Giri
Joke, The	Milan Kundra
Judge's Miscellany, A	M. Hidayatullah
Julius Caesar	William Shakespeare
Jungle Book	Rudyard Kipling
Junglee Girl	Ginu Kamani
Jurassic Park	Michael Crichton

K

Kadambari	Bana Bhatt
Kagaz Te Kanwas	Amrita Pritam
Kaleidoscope of India	Tomoji Muto
Kali Aandhi	Kamleshwar
Kamadhenu	Kubernath Ray
Kamasutra	S.H. Vatsyayan
Kamayani	Jai Shankar Pralad
Kanthapura	Raja Rao
Kanyadaan	Vijay Tendulkar
Kapal Kundala	Bankim Chandra Chatterjee
Kashmir—A Tale of Shame	Hari Jaisingh
Kashmir—A Tragedy of Errors	Tavleen Singh
Kashmir—Behind the Vale	M.J. Akbar
Kashmir Diary—Psychology of Militancy	Gen. Arjun Ray
Kashmir—The Wounded Valley	Ajit Bhattacharjee
Kashmir in the Crossfire	Victoria Shaffield
Katghare Main	Ram Sharan Joshi
Kayakalp	Munshi Prem Chand
Kayar	Thakazhi Sivasankara Pillai
Keepers of the Keys, The	Milan Kundra
Kenilworth	Sir Walter Scott
Khak-i-Dil	Jan Nissar Akhtar
Kidnapped	R.L.Stevenson
King Lear	Shakespeare

L

L'Allegro	John Milton
La Divine Comedia	A. Dante
La Peste	Albert Camus
Lady Chatterley's Lover	D.H.Lawrence
Lady of the Lake	Sir Walter Scott
Lady with the Lapdog	Anton Chekhov
Lajja	Taslima Nasreen

BOOKS	AUTHORS
Lal Bahadur Shastri	C.P. Srivastava
Last Analysis	Saul Bellow
Last Burden	Upamanyu Chatterjee
Last Days of Pompeii	Edward George Lytton
Last Maharaja, The	Jean Louis Nou & Jacques Pouchepadass
Last Orders	Graham Swift
Last Phase, The	Pyare Lal
Last Testament, The	San Bourne
Last Things	C.P.Snow
Law, Lawyers & Judges	H.R. Bhardwaj
Laws Versus Justice	V.R. Krishna Iyer
Le Contract Social (The Social Contract)	J.J. Rousseau
Leaders	Richard Nixon
Leaves of Grass	Walt Whiteman
Lead Kindly Light	Cardinal Newman
Legacy of a Divided Nation	Prof. Mushirul Hasan
Living with Honour	Shiv Kera

M

Macbeth	William Shakespeare
Madame Secretary	Madeleine Albright
Magic Fishbone, The	Charles Dickens
Mahabharata	Vyasa
Malati Madhav	Bhavabhuti
Magnificent Maharaja, The	K. Natwar Singh
Mahatma Gandhi	Romain Rolland
Main Street	Sinclair Lewis
Main Waqt Ke Hoon Samane	Girija Kumar Mathur
Major Barbara	George Bernard Shaw
Making of a Midsummer Night's Dream, The	David Selbourne
Making of Indian Atom Bomb, The	Itty Abraham
Malavikagnimitra	Kalidas
Malgudi Days	R.K. Narayan
Man, The Unknown	Lewis Carroll
Man and Superman	G.B.Shaw
Man for Moscow	G. Wynne
Man of Property	John Galsworthy
Maneaters of Kumaon	Jim Corbett
Managing of the Future	Peter F. Drucker
Mama	Terry McMillan
Man for All Seasons, A	Robert Bolt
Man of Destiny	George Bernard Shaw
Man Who Changed China	Pearl S. Buck
Mandarin, The	Simon de Beauvoir
Mangal Pandey: The True Story of Indian Revolutionary	Amaresh Misra

BOOKS	AUTHORS
Mankind and Mother Earth	Arnold Toynbee
Mansfield Park	Jane Austen
Many Worlds	K.P.S. Menon
Marriage and Morals	Bertrand Russell
Masters, The	C.P. Snow
Mati Matal	Gopinath Mohanty
Maurice	E.M. Forster
Mayor of Casterbridge, The	Thomas Hardy
Meghdoot	Kalidas
Mein Kampf	Adolf Hitler
Memoirs of the Second World War	Churchill
Merchant of Venice	Shakespeare
Memoirs of a Bystander: Life in Diplomacy	Iqbal Akhund
Memories of Hope	Charles de Gaulle
Men Who Kept the Secrets	Thomas Powers
Men Who Killed Gandhi, The	Manohar Malgonkar
My Life	Bill Clinton

N

Naari	Humayun Azad
Nana	Emile Zola
Nagananda	Harsha Vardhana
Nehru: The Invention of India	Shashi Taroor
Nai Duniya Ko Salam & Pathor Ki Dewar	Ali Sardar Jafri
Naivedyam (The Offering)	N. Balamani Amma
Naked Came the Stranger	Penelope Ashe
Naked Face, The	Sydney Sheldon
Naked Triangle, The	Balwant Gargi
Napoleon of Notting Hill, The	G.K. Chesterton
Nature of Mass Poverty, The	J.K. Galbraith
Natya Shastra	Bharat Muni
Nehru and the Language Politics of India	Robert D. King
Nehru Family and Sikhs	Harbans Singh

O

O'Jerusalem	Larry Collins and Dominique Lapierre
Occasion for Loving	Nadine Gordimer
Oddakkuzal	G.Shankara Kurup
Odessa File, The	Frederick Forsyth
Odyssey	Homer
Of Human Bondage	W. Somerset Maugham
Oh, Le Beaux Jours	Samuell Beckett
Old Curiosity Shop	Charles Dickens

BOOKS	AUTHORS
Old Goriot	Honore de Balzac
Old Man and the Sea	Ernest Hemingway
Old Path: White Clouds	Thick Nht Hanh
Oliver's Story	Erich Segal
Oliver Twist	Charles Dickens
Omeros	Derek Walcott
On History	Eric Hobswan
On the Threshold of Hope	Pope John Paul
One Day in the Life of Ivan Denisovich	Aleksandr Solzhenitsyn
One-eyed Uncle	Laxmikant Mahapatra
One Hundred Years of Solitude	Gabriel Garcia Marquez
One Upmanship	Stephen Potter
One World and India	Arnold Toynbee
Out of My Comfort Zone	Steve Waugh

P

Paddy Clarke Ha, Ha, Ha	Roddy Doyle
Padmavati	Malik Mohammed Jayasi
Painted Veil	W. Somerset Maugham
Painter of Signs	R.K.Narayan
Pair of Blue Eyes, A	Thomas Hardy
Pakistan in the 20th Century—A Political History	Lawrence Ziring
Pakistan Crisis	David Loshak
Pakistan Cut to Size	D.R.Mankekar
Pakistan Papers	Mani Shankar Aiyer
Pakistan-The Gathering Storm	Benazir Bhutto
Panchagram	Tarashankar Bandopadhyaya
Panchayats, Democracy and Development	Vinod Vyasulu
Panchtantra	Vishnu Sharma
Paradise Lost	John Milton
Paradise Regained	John Milton
Partition - Can it be undone	Lal Khan
Passage to England, A	Nirad C. Chaudhuri
Passage to India, A	E.M. Forster
Past and Present	Thomas Carlyle
Past Forward	G.R. Narayanan
Pather Panchali	Bibhuti Bhusan Bandyopadhyaya
Path to Power	Margaret Thatcher

Q

Quarantene	Jim Crass
Quest for Conscience	Madhu Dandvate

BOOKS	AUTHORS

R

R Documents, The	Irving Wallace
Rabbit, Run	John Updika
Radharani	Bankim Chandra Chatterjee
Rage of Angels	Sydney Sheldon
Raghuvamsa	Kalidas
Ragtime	E.L. Doctorow
Rain King, The	Saul Bellow
Rainbow, The	Pearl S. Buck
Rains Came	Louis Bromefield
Raj of the Rani	Tapti Roy
Raj—The Making & Unmaking of British India	Lawrence James
Rajtarangini	Kalhana
Ram Charit Manas	Tulsidas
Ramayana	Maharishi Valmiki (in Sanskrit)
Ramayana Dharshanam	K.V. Puttappa
Rangbhoomi	Prem Chand
Rang-e-Shairi	Raghupati Sahai 'Firaq' Gorakhpuri
Rape of the Lock, The	Alexander Pope
Rape of Nanking (Nanjing): An Undeniable History of Photographs	Shi Young
Rare Glimpses of the Raj	Pran Nevile
Rationality and Freedom	Dr. Amartya Sen
Ratnavali	Harsha Vardhana
Ravi Paar (Across the Ravi)	Gulzar
Razor's Edge	Somerset Maugham
Riot After Riot	M.J. Akbar

S

Sadar-i-Riyasat	Karan Singh
Sardar Patel and Indian Muslims	Rafiq Zakaria
Saket	Maithli Saran Gupta
Sakharam Binder	Vijay Tendulkar
Samler's Planet	Saul Bellow
Sanctuary	William Faulkner
Sands of Time	Sidney Sheldon
Santa Evita	Tomas Eloymartinez
Satanic Verses	Salman Rushdie
Satyartha Prakash	Swami Dayanand
Savitri	Aurobindo Ghosh
Scam, The—Who Won, Who Lost, Who Got Away	Debashis Basu and Sucheta Dalal
Scarlet Letter, The	Nathaniel Hawthorne

BOOKS	AUTHORS
Scarlet Pimpernel, The	Baroness Orczy
Scenes from a Writer's Life	Ruskin Bond
Sceptred Flute	Sarojini Naidu
Schindler's List	Thomas Keneally
Sunday Sentiments	Karan Thapar

T

BOOKS	AUTHORS
Tale of a Tub, A	Jonathan Swift
Tale of Two Cities, A	Charles Dickens
Tales from Shakespeare	Charles Lamb
Tales of Sherlock Holmes	Sir Arthur Conan Doyle
Tales of the Open Road	Ruskin Bond
Talisman	Sir Walter Scott
Tamas	Bhisham Sahni
Tar Baby	Toni Morrison
Tarkash	Javed Akhtar
Tarzan of the Apes	Edgar Rice Burroughs
Tehriq-e-Mujahideen	Dr. Sadiq Hussain
Temple Tiger	Jim Corbett
Tess of D'Urbervilles	Thomas Hardy
Thank You, Jeeves	P.G. Wodehouse
3001: The Final Odyssey	Arthur C. Clarke
The Age of Extremes	Eric Holsbawm
The Ageny and Ecstasy	Irving Stone
The Argumentative Indian	Amartya Sen
The Assassination	K. Mohandas
The Best and the Brightest	David Malberstam
The Beach Tree	Pearl S. Buck
The Betrayal of East Pakistan	Lt. Gen. A.A.K. Niazi
The Butcher of Amritsar	Nigel Collett
The Calcutta Chromosome	Amitav Ghosh
The Cancer Ward	Alexander Solzhenitsyn
The Career & Legend of Vasco da Gama	Sanjay Subramanyam
The Changing Global Order: World Leaders Reflect	Nathan Gardels
The Changing World of Executive	Peter Drucker
The Chinese Betrayal	B.N.Mullick
The Collector's wife	Mitra Phukan
The Commitments	Roddy Doyle
The Cardinal	Henry Morton Robinson
The Clinton Wars	Sidney Blumenthal
The Congress Splits	R.P.Rao
The Dark Side of Camelot	Seymore Hersh
The Defeat or Distant Drumbeats	Bhaskar Roy
The Diplomatic Bag	John Ure
The Distorted Mirror	R.K. Laxman

BOOKS	AUTHORS
The Divine Discovery	V.N. Narayanan
The Economic Policy, Preparing the 21st Century	Bimal Jalan
The Empowerment of Women in Islam	Zeenat Shaukat Ali
The End of India	Khushwant Singh
The Essence of the Thing	Madeline St. Joan
The Future of India	Bimal Jalan
The Future of War	George G. Meredith
The Google Story	David A. Vise
The Inheritance of loss	Kiran Desai
The Moonlit Cage	Linda Holeman
The Making of Modern India	K.R. Narayanan
The Muslims of India	A.G. Noorani
The Name Sake	Jhumpa Lahiri
The Sea	John Banville
The Shadow of Kamakhya	Indira Goswami
Tremors of Violence	Rowena Robinson
Too Many with Little - The Challenges for India's Development Paradigm	George B. Asaf
Touchplay	Dev Sukumar
Tsunami - 7 Hours That Shook the World	Satinder Bindra

U

Ugly Duckling, The	H.C. Anderson
Ulysses	James Joyce
Uncle Tom's Cabin	H.B. Stowe
Under Western Eye	Joseph Conrad
Universe Around Us, The	James Jeans
Unto This Last	John Ruskin
Untold Story	Gen.B.M.Kaul

V

Valley of Dolls	Jacqueline Susanne
Vanity Fair	William Thackeray
Vedant and Modern Physics	U. Chandra Sekharayyaa
Vendor of Sweets, The	R.K.Narayan
Venisamhara	Narayana Bhatt
Vernon God Little	D.B.C. Pierre
Very Old Bones	William Kennedy
Victim, The	Saul Bellow
Victory	Joseph Conrad
View from Delhi, A	Chester Bowles
View from the UN	U Thant
Vikram and the Vampire	Sir Richard Burton
Vikram Sarabhai - A Life	Amrita Shah
Village by the Sea, A	Anita Desai

BOOKS	AUTHORS

W

Waiting for Godot	Thomas Becket
Waiting for the Mahatma	R.K. Narayan
Waiting to Exhale	Terry McMillan
Wake Up India	Annie Besant
Walls of Glass, The	K.A. Abbas
War and Peace	Tolstoy
War and No Peace Over Kashmir	Maroof Raza
War Minus the Shooting	Mike Marquesee
War of Indian Independence	Vir Savarkar
War of the Worlds, The	H.G. Wells
Waste Land, The	T.S.Eliot
Water	Bapsi Sidhwa
Way of the World, The	William Congreve
Way of All Flesh	Samuel Butler
We, Indians	Khushwant Singh
Weight Loss	Upamanyu Chatterjee
We Need to Talk About Kevin	Lionel Shriver
Wings of Fire	Dr. A.P.J. Abdul Kalam

Y

Yajnaseni	Pratibha Roy
Yama	Mahadevi Varma
Yashodhara	Maithili Sharan Gupt
Yayati	V.S.Khandekar
Year of the Upheaval	Henry Kissinger
Year of the Vulture, The	Amita Malik
Years of Pilgrimage	Dr.Raja Ramanna
Yesterday and Today	K.P.S.Menon
Yugant	Mahesh Elkunchwar

Z

Zhivago, Dr.	Boris Pasternak
Zlata's Diary-A Child's Life in Sarajevo	Zlata Filipovic
Zulfi, My friend	Piloo Mody
Zulfikar Ali Bhutto & Pakistan	Rafi Raza

CHARACTERS, WORKS AND AUTHORS

Character	Work	Author
Adam	Paradise Lost	Milton
Alice	Alice in Wonderland	Lewis Carroll
Ancient Mariner	Ancient Mariner	S.T.Coleridge
Anna Karenina	War & Peace	Leo Tolstoy
Antonio	Merchant of Venice	Shakespeare
Ariel	Tempest	Shakespeare
Bassanio	Merchant of Venice	Shakespeare
Beatrice	Much Ado About Nothing	Shakespeare
Beatrix	Henry Esmond	Thackeray

Character	Work	Author
Brutus	Julius Caeser	Shakespeare
Christian	Pilgrim's Progress	John Bunyan
Clare	Tess of the D'Urbervilles	Thomas Hardy
Claudius	Hamlet	Shakespeare
Cordelia	A Midsummer Nights Dream	Shakespeare
Cleopatra	Antony and Cleopatra	Shakespeare
David Copperfield	David Copperfield	Charles Dickens
Desdemona	Othello	Shakespeare
Don Quixote	Don Quixote	Cervantes
Don Juan	Don Juan	Lord Byron
Eustacia	The Return of the Native	Thomas Hardy
Faust	Faust	Goethe
Frankenstein	Frankenstein	Mrs.Shelly
Gora	Gora	Rabindranath Tagore
Hamlet	Hamlet	Shakespeare
Hawkins	Treasure Island	R.L. Stevenson
Hyde	Dr.Jekyll and Mr.Hyde	R.L. Stevenson
Iago	Othello	Shakespeare
Ivanhoe	Ivanhoe	Sir Walter Scott
Jeeves	Thank You Jeeves	P.G.Wodehouse
Juliet	Romeo and Juliet	Shakespeare
Kim	Kim	Rudyard Kipling
Macbeth	Macbeth	Shakespeare
Micawber	David Copperfield	Charles Dickens
Mephistopheles	Faust	Goethe
Miranda	Tempest	Shakespeare
Oliver Twist	Oliver Twist	Charles Dickens
Peggotty	David Copperfield	Charles Dickens
Pickwick	Pickwick Papers	Charles Dickens
Perry Mason	Perry Mason	E.S.Gardner
Portia	Merchant of Venice	Shakespeare
Rip Ván Winkle	Three Men in a Boat	W.Irwing
Sancho Panza	Don Quixote	Cervantes
Sherlock Holmes	Adventures of Sherlock Holmes	A.Conan Doyle
Shylock	Merchant of Venice	Shakespeare
Silas Marner	Silas Marner	George Eliot
Tess	Tess of the D'Urbervilles	Thomas Hardy
Tom Sawyer	Adventures of Tom Sawyer	Mark Twain
Dr.Watson	Sherlock Holmes	A.Conan Doyle
Dr.Zhivago	Dr.Zhivago	Boris Pasternak

IMPORTANT PLACES IN INDIA

Abu, Mount (Rajasthan): Hill station in Rajasthan; contains famous Dilwara Jain Temple, and Training college for the Central Reserve Police.

Adam's Bridge: Very nearly joined to India between two points *viz.* Mannar Peninsula and Dhanushkodi by a line of sand banks and rocks called *Adam's Bridge.*

Adyar (Tamil Nadu): A suburb of Chennai, headquarters of the Theosophical Society.

Afghan Church (Mumbai): It is built in 1847 known as St.John's Church. It is dedicated to the British soldiers who died in the Sind and Afghan campaign of 1838 and 1843.

Aga Khan Palace: In Pune where Mahatma Gandhi was kept interned with his wife Kasturba Gandhi. Kasturba died in this palace.

Agra (Uttar Pradesh): Famous for Taj Mahal, Fort and Pearl mosque. Sikandra, the tomb of Akbar, is situated here. It is also a centre of leather industry.

Ahmednagar (Maharashtra): It was founded by Ahmed Nizam Shahi. It is the district headquarters of Ahmednagar district. It is an industrial town well known for its handloom and small scale industries.

Ahmedabad (Gujarat): Once capital of Gujarat. A great cotton textile centre of India. Anti-reservation riots rocked the city in April 1985.

Ajmer (Rajasthan): It has Mayo college and the tomb of Khwaja Moin-ud-din Chishti, which is a pilgrim centre for Muslims; Pushkar Lake, a place of Hindu pilgrimage, is about two miles from here.

Aliabet: Is the site of India's first off-shore oil well—nearly 45 km from Bhavnagar in Gujarat State. On March 19, 1970, the Prime Minister of India set a 500-tonne rig in motion to inaugurate "Operation Leap Frog" at Aliabet.

Aligarh (Uttar Pradesh): Seat of Muslim University; manufacture locks, scissors, knives and dairy products.

Allahabad (Uttar Pradesh): A famous and important place of pilgrimage for Hindus, confluence of three rivers – Ganges, Yamuna and the invisible Saraswati. It is the seat of a University and trading centre.

Alandi (Maharashtra): Popularly called 'Devachi Alandi' is hallowed by the association of saint Dhyaneshwar the author of 'Dhyaneshwari' who lived and attained Samadhi here at the age of twentyone. Two fairs are held annually one on Ashadha Ekadasi and the other Karthikai Ekadasi.

Amber Palace: Deserted capital near Jaipur (Rajasthan) containing the finest specimens of Rajput architecture.

Almora (Uttaranchal): This city is on the Kashaya hill. The clean and majestic view of the Himalayan Peak is breath catching. The woollen shawl of Almora is very famous in the region. It is a good hill resort.

Amarnath (Kashmir): 28 miles from Pahalgam, and is a famous pilgrim centre of Hindus.

Amboli (Maharashtra): Nestling in the ranges of Sahyadri, Amboli is a beautiful mountain resort in Ratnagiri district. The climate is cool and refreshing; an ideal place for holiday.

Amritsar (Punjab): A border town in the Punjab, sacred place for Sikhs (Golden Temple), scene of Jallianwala Bagh tragedy in April 1919. The 400th anniversary of Amritsar was celebrated with great gusto in October 1977. The city was founded by Guru Ram Dass.

Arikkamedu (Puducherry): It is one of the archaeological place. It describe the relationship between Tamils and Romes (Yavanas) for trade purpose.

Arvi (Maharashtra): Near Pune, India's first satellite communication centre has been located here.

Ashoka Pillar (Madhya Pradesh): It was erected by Emperor Ashoka. It is now the official symbol of Modern India and the symbol is four back-to-back lions. In the lower portion of the column are representation of a lion, elephant, horse and bull. The pillar stands about 20 m high.

Aurangabad (Maharashtra) : It is one of the important towns in Maharashtra. Tomb of Emperor Aurangzeb and his wife attract many tourists. Ellora and Ajanta caves are reached from here.

Auroville (Puducherry) : It is an international township constructed near Pondicherry with the help of UNESCO.

Avadi: Situated at Chennai in Tamil Nadu, it is known for the government-owned Heavy Vehicles Factory. *Vijayanta* and *Ajit* tanks are manufactured here.

Ayodhya (Uttar Pradesh): Birth place of Rama is situated on the banks of the river Gogwa. The famous 'Babri Masjid' built on the birth place of Rama by the Mughal rulers in 15th century has been taken over by the Hindus after 400 years.

Badrinath (Uttarakhand): It is a place of pilgrimage noted for the temple of Lord Vishnu for the Hindus, near Gangotri Glacier in Himalayas.

Bahubali (Maharashtra): A pilgrim centre for jains, of both Svetambar and Digambar Jains; there is a giant idol of Shree Bahubali the son of Bhagwan Adinath, the first Tirthankar.

Bangalore (Karnataka) : It is the capital city of Karnataka State and an important industrial centre. The places worth-seeing are Vidhan Saudha, Lal Bagh gardens, etc. The BHEL, HAL, IIM are situated here.

Barauni (North Bihar): Famous for a big oil refinery.

Bardoli (Gujarat) : Bardoli in Gujarat State has occupied a permanent place in Indian History for no-tax payment campaign launched by Sardar Vallabhbhai Patel against the British rule.

Baroda (Gujarat) : Baroda, (Vadodara) the capital of former Baroda State is one of the main towns in Gujarat State. Laxmi Vilas Palace is a tourist attraction.

Belur (West Bengal): Near Calcutta, famous for a monastery founded by Swami Vivekananda; a beautiful temple dedicated to Shri Ramakrishna Paramahamsa. It is also known for paper industry. There is another place of the same name in Karnataka, it is a famous pilgrim centre known for Channa Keshava Temple.

Belgaum (Karnataka) : It is a border town in Karnataka State. It has remained a place of dispute between Maharashtra and Karnataka States.

Bhakra (Punjab) : It is a village in Punjab State where the Bhakra Dam has been constructed across the river Sutlej in a natural gorge just before the river enters the plains 80 km upstream ropar.

Bhilai (Chhattisgarh) : It is known for the gigantic steel plants set up with the help of Russian Engineers.

Bhimashankar (Maharashtra) : One of the five Jyothirlingas in Maharashtra is at Bhimashankar. The beautiful Shiva temple here was constructed by Nana Parnavis the ancient statesman of the Peshwas.

Bhopal (Madhya Pradesh): Capital of Madhya Pradesh. MIC gas leaked out from the Union Carbide factory in December 1984, and more than 3000 persons died. It was the worst industrial disaster in the world.

Bhubaneswar (Orissa) : It is the capital city of Orissa. Lingaraja Temple is worth-seeing.

Bijapur (Karnataka) : It was the capital of old Adil Shahi Sultan of Bijapur. Gol Gumbaz, the biggest tomb in India constructed here, is called the whispering gallery. The town is rich with the remains of palaces, mosques and tombs.

Bodh Gaya (Bihar) : It is situated six miles south of Gaya in Bihar State. Gautama Buddha attained enlightenment in a full moon light in the month of Baisakha under the peepal tree.

Bokaro (Jharkhand) : The fourth and the biggest steel plant is here.

Buland Darwaza (Uttar Pradesh) : It is the Gateway of Fatehpur-Sikri built by Akbar. This is the highest and the greatest gateway in India. It was erected to commemorate the victorious campaign of Akbar in the Deccan in 1602 A.D.

Bull Temple (Karnataka): It is situated near Bugle Hill, with a height of 6.2 m (20 ft) high stone monolith Nandi Bull. The Bull is carved out of a single stone.

Chandernagore (West Bengal) : Situated on the river Hooghly. It was previously a French settlement. Now it has been merged with the Indian Union.

Chennai (capital of TamilNadu): It is the third largest city in India. Known for Fort St George, Light-house, St Thomas Mount, Integral Coach Factory.

Chandigarh (Punjab & Haryana) : Chandigarh the joint capital of the States of Punjab and Haryana is a planned and beautiful city. It is situated at the foot of the Himalayas. It was designed by Mont Corbusier.

Cherrapunji (Meghalaya): It is the place of heaviest rainfall. It receives 426" of rain yearly.

Chidambaram (Tamil Nadu) : It is a town in South Arcot district of Tamil Nadu. It is famous for its great Hindu Siva Temple dedicated to Lord 'Nataraja', the cosmic dancer. It is the seat of 'Annamalai University' founded in 1929. The name of the town comes from Tamil 'Chit' plus 'Ambalam' - *the atmosphere of wisdom'*.

Chilka Lake (Orissa): It is the Queen of Natural Scenery in Orissa, though separated from the Bay of Bengal by a long strip of sandy ridge, exchanges water with the sea. It is an excellent place for fishing and duck shooting.

Chittaranjan (West Bengal) : It is famous for locomotive works. Railway engines are manufactured here.

Chittorgarh (Rajasthan) : It was once the capital of Udaipur. It is known for the Tower of Victory built by Rana Kumbha and Mira Bai Temple.

Chowpathy Beach (Mumbai): A popular beach with Lokmanya Tilak and Vallabhbhai Patel statues where the political meetings for freedom struggle took place, now the coconut day celebration and Ganesh Chaturthi immersion take place.

Chusul (Ladakh) : It is situated in Ladakh at a height of about 14,000 feet. Chusul is perhaps the highest aerodrome in India.

Coimbatore (Tamil Nadu) : It is famous for Textile Industry. Government of India Forest College is situated here.

Courtallam (Tamil Nadu): Adjoining Tenkasi and 3 miles south is a common man's health resort. Famous for its waterfall and a good summer resort.

Cuttack (Orissa): It is the oldest town and once upon a time the capital of Orissa during the medieval period to the end of the British rule. The city is noted for fine ornamental work of gold & silver.

Dakshineswar (Kolkata) : It is at a distance of about five miles from Calcutta where Swami Vivekananda was initiated into religious life by Swami Ramakrishna Paramahamsa.

Dalal Street: Stock exchange Market in Mumbai.

Dalmianagar (Jharkhand): Cement manufacturing.

Dandi (Gujarat) : It is famous for Salt Satyagraha (Dandi March) staged by Mahatma Gandhi in 1930.

Darjeeling (West Bengal): Famous for tea, orange and cinchona, fine hill station, famous for its scenic beauty.

Daulatabad (Maharashtra): The fort previously called Devagiri is believed to have constructed by the Yadava Kings in 1338. The fort is very impregnable.

Dayalbagh (Uttar Pradesh): Near Agra; known for Dayalbagh Industrial Institute, shoe manufacture. Religious and cultural seat of a section of the Hindus.

Dehu (Maharashtra): Dehu, a town on the banks of the river Indrayani is the birth place of the famous saint-poet Tukaram whose 'Abhangas' have a pride of place in Marathi literature.

Dehradun (Uttarakhand): It is the gateway to the Garhwal Himachal such as Badrinath and Joshimath. The Forest Research Institute is situated here.

Delhi: India's capital. The Red Fort, the Jama Masjid, the Qutub Minar, the Rajghat (Mahatma Gandhi's Samadhi), the Humayun's tomb, Shanti Van (where Prime Minister Nehru was cremated), are located here. It established by Tomaras in 736 AD.

Dhanbad (Jharkhand): Famous for coal mines and the Indian School of Mines, National Fuel Research Institute.

Dhariwal (Punjab): It is famous for woollen goods.

Dibrugarh (Assam) : It is a town in Assam and the terminus of rail and river communications along the Brahmaputra from Calcutta.

Digboi (Assam): It is known for its oil-fields and oil refinery. It is one of the oldest oil refineries which is still operative in the world.

Dilwara Temples (Rajasthan) : It is near Mt. Abu. There are five Hindu Temples constructed here between 11th and 13th Century A.D.

Dindigul : (Tamil Nadu) It is famous for cigar, tobacco and locks.

Dum Dum (Kolkata) : It is a famous Air Port and Government Arsenal.

Durgapur: In West Bengal is known for a gigantic steel plant set up here with the help of British Engineers.

Dwaraka (Gujarat): It is one of the seven most important places of Hindu pilgrimage. Krishna the eighth incarnation of Lord Vishnu made Dwaraka as his centre to recapture Mathura.

Eagle's Nest: It is the name given to the historic fort at Ralgarh in the Kolaba district of Maharashtra where, 300 years ago, Chhatarpati Shivaji, the great warrior-statesman, was crowned.

Elephanta Caves (Maharashtra): Situated in an island 15 miles from Mumbai famous for the statues of Siva and Parvati. The most striking statue of Trimurti, Siva in three moods as the Creator, the Destroyer and the Preserver.

Ellora and Ajanta (Maharashtra) : It is in Aurangabad district of Maharashtra State. The Buddhist cave temples richly ornamented with sculpture and carved with paintings of exceptional skill attract many tourists.

Ernakulam (Kerala) : The back-waters in Ernakulam is a tourist attraction. The Central Institute of Fisheries Technology is situated here.

Faridabad (Haryana): It is an industrial township situated at about 18 miles from Delhi.

Fatehpur Sikri (Uttar Pradesh): It was once the capital of the Mughal Empire. This city was built by Emperor Akbar in 1569. It is now in a deserted condition.

Ferozabad (Uttar Pradesh): Noted for glass bangle industry.

Gateway of India (Mumbai) : It is in Mumbai harbour erected in 1911 on King George V's visit to India.

Gangotri (Uttarakhand): This is the source of the holy Ganges. The tiny village has the temple of the Goddess Ganga on the banks of the Bhagirathi river, which eventually becomes the holy Ganges.

Gaumuka (Uttarakhand): Gaumukh the actual source of the river, is at the base of the Bhagirathi peaks. The glaciers of Gangotri which is 24 km long, ends at Gaumukh where the Bhagirathi river finally appears.

Gazipur (U.P.): Known for the government opium factory.

Gaya (Bihar) : It is the place where Lord Buddha got enlightenment. It is a pilgrimage centre not only for the Buddhists but also for the Hindus. Hindus from all over the country come here to make offerings and pray for the salvation of their ancestors.

Gilgit (Kashmir) : It is now under the illegal occupation of Pakistan. It is of great strategic importance.

Golconda (Hyderabad) : It is an ancient city of India situated about 7 miles west of Hyderabad. Formerly there was a diamond mine.

Golconda Fort (Andhra Pradesh): The historical fort is well praised in the literature, prose and poetry. Golconda was the capital of Qutub Shahi Sultans who ruled Deccan from 1518 to 1687 AD.

Golden Temple (Punjab) : It is a sacred place of the Sikhs in Amritsar.

Gol Gumbaz (Karnataka) : It is the biggest dome in India.

Gomateswara (Karnataka) : This is a 2,000 year old and very high statue of a Jain sage, carved out of a single stone.

Gorakhpur (Uttar Pradesh) : The famous temple of Gorakhnath is here which specialises in publishing Hindu religious literature.

Guntur (Andhra Pradesh) : It is a centre of cotton and tobacco production in Andhra Pradesh.

Gulbarga (Karnataka): It was the capital of Bahmani Kingdom. Its fort is a remarkable building with 15 towers, within the fort is a large mosque built on the model of the famous mosque of Cordoba in Spain.

Gwalior (Madhya Pradesh) : Situated in M.P. is famous for Rani Lakshmi Bai's Chaatri and Tansen's tomb.

Haldighat (Uttar Pradesh) : A famous mountain pass where Rana Pratap fought Mughal forces led by Man Singh and Asaf Khan.

Hampi (Karnataka) : In Karnataka State, is the location of ruins of Vijayanagar. The capital of famous Vijayanagar Empire.

Haridwar (Uttarakhand): It is at the base of the Siwalik Hills, where the Ganges river coming down from the Himalayas passes and enters the plains. The Daksha Mahadev Temple, 4 km downstreams in Hardwar is the most important temple.

Hirakud (Orissa): Twenty six kilometres from one end to the other on the river Mahanadi is Hirakud the longest mainstream dam in the world.

Howrah Bridge (Kolkata) : A cantilever span bridge over river Hoogly connecting Howrah and Kolkata.

Hyderabad-Secunderabad : Twin city capital of Andhra Pradesh. It is on the banks of the river 'Musi' and famous for Salarjung museum - one of the best in Asia. It is also a famous communication centre in India as it is centrally situated. Charminar built in 1591 is located here.

Imphal (Manipur) : Situated in the north-east frontier, is the capital of Manipur state on the border of India and Myanmar (Burmah). Famous for handloom industry and the Manipuri dance.

Ita Nagar (Arunachal Pradesh): The capital of Arunachal Pradesh is a tropical forest region in the foothills surrounded with wild mountain stream and placid lakes with abundant opportunities for river rafting, boating and trekking.

India Gate (New Delhi) : A memorial in New Delhi facing the Rashtrapathi Bhavan.

Jabalpur (Madhya Pradesh) : Standing on the river Narmada, Jabalpur is a city in Madhya Pradesh famous for Marble Rocks and Dhunva Dhar waterfalls.

Jadugoda: In Bihar is famous for Uranium Ore Mill.

Jagdish Temple: It is a fine Indo-Aryan temple built by Maharana Jagat Singh in 1651. A blackstone image of Lord Vishnu as Lord Jagdish is found here.

Jaipur (Rajasthan) : A historically important place and is famous for its handicrafts. Maharaja Jai Singh Observatory and Hawa Mahal are situated here. It is the capital of Rajasthan or called rose-pink city, a huge historic fort (Amber) is situated here. The city was founded by astrologer Maharaja Sawai Jai Singh II.

Jaisalmer (Rajasthan) : The remote fortress city on the edge of Rajasthan's Thar Desert. It is 287 km from Jodhpur.

Jakrem (Tripura): It is 64 km from Shillong and is known for its hot spring which is said to possess curative qualities.

Jalandhar (Punjab) : Situated in Punjab is the centre for surgical and sports goods industry.

Jallianwala Bagh (Amritsar, Punjab): It was the scene of indiscriminal shooting by General Dyer on 13th April 1919, when a meeting was being held. A Martyr's memorial has been erected to commemorate those killed in the firing.

Jama Masjid (Hyderabad, AP): The Masjid lies near the North-east point of the building of Charminar, built by Sultan Mohammed Qutub Shah the fifth King of the Qutub Shahi dynasty in 1594.

Jamshedpur (Jharkhand): Centre of iron and steel industry. Tata Iron and Steel Factory is located here.

Jantar Mantar (Delhi): Site of the famous observatory constructed in 1724 by Maharaja Jai Singh II. Sawai Jai Singh built many fine observatories, Jantar Mantar being the last and largest.

Jaswant Thada (Rajasthan) : The dazzling white preamble of Maharaja Jaswant Singh built in 1899 is found in Rajasthan.

Jealgora: In Bihar is known for Central Fuel Research Institute.

Jhansi (Uttar Pradesh) : A key railway junction in Uttar Pradesh. It is noted for the part played by Queen Rani Lakshmi Bai of Jhansi in the War of Independence in 1857.

Jharia: In Bihar is famous for coal-mining.

Jog Falls (or) Gersoppa Falls (Karnataka) : Formed by river Sharavati, falls through a height of 830 ft.

Juma Masjid, Mandu: Is in Madhya Pradesh. It depicts a synthesis of Hindu and Muslim styles in architecture.

Junagadh (Gujarat) : Located below Girnar Hill in Gujarat State is an ancient city in India. Gir Forest, a wildlife sanctuary famous for its lions is located here.

Kailasha Temple (Maharashtra): A rock-cut temple in Ellora caves.

Kalpakkam: Near Chennai in Tamil Nadu is known for Madras Atomic Power Station (MAPS).

Kanchi or Conjeevaram (Tamil Nadu) : This was the famous capital of Pallavas and is situated near Chennai. Famous ancient temples here, are well-known for its architecture.

Kandala (Maharashtra): It a popular mountain resort in Maharashtra. Nestling in the western ghats it is an ideal resort for a peaceful holiday.

Kandla (Gujarat): The Kandla port is the main gateway for the trade of north-west India.

Kanheri (Mumbai) : Situated near Mumbai, the famous spot of the ancient Buddhist caves of 1st Century A.D.

Kanpur (Uttar Pradesh) : An industrial city of U.P. famous for its sugar, cotton, woollen, soap, iron, leather, tent and hosiery industries situated on the banks of the Ganga.

Kanyakumari (Tamil Nadu): The southernmost tip of India where the Arabian Sea, the Bay of Bengal and the Indian Ocean meet. The sun-rising and sun-setting are picturesque scenes. Vivekananda rock memorial has also been constructed now. On the rock called Sripadaparai, a mammoth 133 ft. statue of the unmatched Poet-Saint Thiruvalluvar was unveiled on 1 January 2000.

Kapilavastu (Bihar) : Ancient kingdom in north India connected with Lord Buddha.

Kasauli (Himachal Pradesh) : A hill station in Himachal Pradesh where the famous Pasteur Institute is located.

Kaveripumpattinam (Tamil Nadu): The place where the river Cauvery mingles with the ocean. Two great epics of Tamil literature Manimegalai and Silappadhikaram vividly portray life scenes of this place during Chola and Pandya period.

Kaziranga (Assam) : In Assam, is the sanctuary of the Indian one-horned rhinos.

Kedarnath (Uttarakhand): The temple of Lord Kedar (Shiva), surrounded by snow-capped peaks is one of the Hindu pilgrimage centres.

Khadakvasla (Pune) : Near Pune. National Defence Academy is situated here.

Khajuraho (Madhya Pradesh) : Famous for its temples and erotic sculpture.

Khindsey Talao (Mumbai): This beautiful lake is set like a gem in the green expanse at the foot of the Ramtek hill.

Kodaikanal (Tamil Nadu): A hill station in Tamil Nadu situated near Madurai.

Koderma (Bihar) : In Bihar famous for mica mines.

Kolar (Karnataka) : It is known for its gold fields.

Kolhapur (Maharashtra): Kolhapur possess historical as well as mythological importance. It is known as Dakshin Kashi on account of its deity Mahalakshmi or Ambabai built by Chalukya King Karnadev in 634 AD. Kolhapur was the capital of Chatrapati Shivaji in 1708.

Kolkata (West Bengal) : It is known as the commercial capital of India. It has a port of heavy traffic. Dum Dum airport, National Library, Diamond harbour, Victoria Memorial are well-known.

Konark (Orissa) : Town, north of Puri is famous for black pagodas and Sun Temple.

Koyna (Maharashtra) : Hydroelectric project in Maharashtra, supplies power to Mumbai and Pune. The place was hit by earthquake in December 1967.

Kundanpur (Bihar): The birth place of the 24th Jain Tirthankar Mahaveer is well-known as a pilgrim centre.

Kurukshetra (Haryana) : The town near Ambala. Here the great battle Mahabharatha took place between Kauravas and Pandavas.

Leh (Ladakh) : Capital of Ladakh; once a caravan centre of Central Asia.

Lothal (Gujarat): Ancient town 450 miles south to Mohenjodaro.

Lucknow (Uttar Pradesh) : Capital of Uttar Pradesh known for its goddess Imambara. Tomb of Wajid Ali Shah, Chattar Manzil, Alambagh, Havelock's Tomb are the places of historical importance situated here.

Lumbini (Nepal) : In Nepal, the birth place of Lord Buddha.

Lunej (Gujarat) : Oil wells in Cambay Basin.

Madurai (Tamil Nadu) : Famous Meenakshi Temple dedicated to Lord Siva is located here.

Mahabaleshwar (Maharashtra) : Hill station in Maharashtra is situated at a height of 4500 ft. in the Western Ghats.

Mahabalipuram (Tamil Nadu) : Famous for the monumental architecture of Pallavas. An atomic power station is located near at Kalpakkam.

Mahabodhi Temple (Bihar): It is a Buddha temple with the Jataka stories engraved on the walls. The famous Magadha University exists beside the temple.

Mahrangarh Fort (Rajasthan) : Five km away from the centre town of Jodhpur. Commissioned by Roa Jodh in 1959, this fortran eyrie is a master piece of medieval defence.

Mandore (Rajasthan) : The ancient capital of the Rathore Marwars, the Rajputs of Rajasthan.

Meerut (Uttar Pradesh) : This was the first place where the 1857 Mutiny first broke out. The Suraj Khund is the most interesting temple and there is a Moghul Mausoleum, near the old Shapir Gate.

Mirzapur (Uttar Pradesh) : Place of Ram Ganga, famous for cutlery, brassware and mangoes.

Mukteshwar (Uttar Pradesh) : Veterinary Research Institute is located here.

Murad (Maharashtra) : Seaside holiday resort of Maharashtra.

Mathura (Uttar Pradesh) : It is a holy city and birth place of Lord Krishna.

Meenakshi temple (Tamil Nadu) : Famous Hindu temple in Madurai, Tamilnadu. It is remarkable for its most picturesque 850 ft. high temple with its magnificent Gopurams. One of its principal structures is the hall of thousand pillars in which a group of figures are carved out of a single stone.

Mussoorie (Uttarakhand): A hilly resort has good rock climbing and mountaineering assets and has good fishing spots.

Mumbai (Maharashtra) : Called the gateway of India is the second biggest city and port in India. It is the capital of Maharashtra state. The Prince of Wales Museum, Aarey Milk Colony, film capital of the country, Centre of oil industry and Petrochemicals, etc. are noteworthy.

Nagpur (Maharashtra) : Former capital of Madhya Pradesh now in Maharashtra. Famous for textiles and oranges.

Nagercoil (Tamil Nadu) : There is a temple of snakes or Nagaraja-snake god. The temple is filled with images of snakes and the Dvarapalakas are the snakes guarding the temple.

Nagarjuna Konda-Sagar (Andhra Pradesh): The reservoir is named after Buddhist Philosopher Acharya Nagarjuna who propounded the Madhyamik school of Mahayana Buddhism.

Naharkhatia (Assam) : Place near Digboi in Assam where oil has been struck.

Nainital (Uttarakhand): This lake dotted area of the Kumaon Hills, was the summer capital of Uttar Pradesh. The legend believed is that Goddess Shakti lost her eyes when Lord Shiva was curling her and the spot where the eyes fell became a lake called 'naina' (eyes) Tal (lake) was thus given its name.

Nalanda (Bihar): Here was the famous University and Educational centre of ancient times. The Chinese traveller Hieun Tsang visited India in 7th century had mentioned about this University.

Narsobachiwadi (Maharashtra): It is a prominent pilgrimage of Lord Shree Dattatreya, situated near the confluence Krishna and the Panchaganga rivers.

Nasik (Maharashtra) : Site of Security Printing Press in Maharashtra.

Nilgiris (Tamil Nadu) : The Blue Mountains of Tamil Nadu. Famous for tea plantation.

Nilokheri (Haryana) : Place in Haryana, famous community development project of Dr. S.K. Dey.

Pataliputra (Bihar) : Ancient name of Patna. Capital of Bihar State. Famous for Ashoka edicts inscribed on rocks and pillars.

Palitana (Gujarat) : Famous for its holy hills.

Pali (Sudhagad, Maharashtra): One of the Ashta Vinayak, Shree Bullaleshwar "Swayambhu" idols of Shree Ganesh popularly known as "Ashta Vinayak".

Pandharpur (Maharashtra) : One of the most sacred places known for the temple of Vithoba, an incarnation of Lord Vishnu, it is also called Dhakshina Kashi, a pilgrim centre.

Panipat (Haryana) : Historical place in Haryana, famous for the three battles in 1526, 1556, and 1761.

Pawapuri (Bihar): It is one of the holiest of Jain pilgrim places. The Jal Mandir (water temple) in Kamal Sarovar (Lotus pool) is most sacred. The big lake filled with lotus is a charming place and the white marble temple stands in the middle.

Planetarium, Birla (Kolkata): It is a dome-shaped building where the exact panorama of the sky is depicted, and the position of various constellations is clearly shown. The second planetarium in India has been set up in Mumbai. The third planetarium was opened in New Delhi in 1984.

Plassey (West Bengal) : A village in West Bengal, famous for the Battle of Plassey where Clive beat Siraj-ud-Daulah.

Puducherry : A Union Territory - formerly under French possession. Famous for Aurobindo Ashram and 'Auroville' international township, built in the name of Aurobindo.

Ponpadirkootam (Tamil Nadu): A village in Chingleput where a unique four hand Rama in gold is a feast for our eyes.

Port Blair (Gujarat) : Capital of Andaman & Nicobar islands.

Porbandar (Gujarat) : The Birth Place of Mahatma Gandhi. It is identified with Sudamapuri of the epic times and we can still see the old temple of Sudama, a friend of Lord Krishna.

Pune (Maharashtra): Pune, capital of Maratha Empire during Shivaji's rule, had turned to be an educational and cultural centre.

Puri (Orissa) : Summer capital of Orissa famous for Jagannath Temple.

Pusa (West Bengal) : Famous for agricultural station.

Qutub Minar (Delhi) : The tallest minaret in the world (990 ft. high) completed by Sultan Iltutmish in 1232 A.D.

Rajghat (New Delhi) : Famous for the samadhi of Mahatma Gandhi on the banks of the river Yamuna.

Rajgir (Bihar): Rajgir was called Rajgriha or King's home in olden days. Ajatashatru named it Giribraja. It was Jarasandha's capital. Vardhaman Mahavir, who preached the Jain Religion had spent 14 years of his active life here. Mahaveer called his first Dharma Sabha or religious assembly on Bipul Parbat here.

Rashtrapati Bhavan (New Delhi) : The official residence of the President of India in Delhi, built by the British architect Edwin Lutyens.

Ratnagiri (Maharashtra): Birth place of Lokmanya Tilak. It has a minor port Bhagvati and a fort belonging to the 15th century.

Rameswaram (Tamil Nadu): A pilgrimage spot in South India as equal to that of Benaras. There is the temple of Lord Shiva.

Red Fort (Delhi) : It is a fort built of red stone by Shah Jahan in Delhi on the banks of the river Yamuna. It consists of Diwan-i-Am, Diwan-i-Khas and other wonderful creations. In 2007, UNESCO announced the Red Fort as one of the Heritage site in India.

Rishikesh (Uttarakhand) : It is a Hindu pilgrim centre. Rishikesh is the starting point for treks to Himalayan pilgrimage centres like Badrinath, Kedarnath and Gangotri.

Rourkela (Orissa): Rourkela is the first steel plant of India envisaged in the public sector and has been in operation since February 1959 which has set in a new era in the Steel Industry of India.

Salar Jung Museum (Andhra Pradesh): It is the personnel collection of Mir Yusuf Ali Khan, better known as Salar Jung who had devoted his wealth and leisure to gather out treasures from every walk of life.

Sambhar (Rajasthan) : It is a salt lake in Rajasthan. Only lake of its kind in India.

Sanganer (Rajasthan): It is the centre of hand block printing and hand made paper industry.

Sabarmati (Gujarat) : It is a place in Gujarat where Gandhiji established a Harijan Ashram. It is also the name of a river in Gujarat.

Sathanur Dam (Tamil Nadu): 22 miles from Tiruvannamalai a vast forest has been turned into a huge reservoir and a dam is a tourist spot.

Satara (Maharashtra): It is a glorious historical city, was capital of Shivaji's empire in 1699.

Sanchi (Madhya Pradesh) : Famous Buddhist stupa, the diameter of which is 108 ft. was built in ancient times. It is the largest stupa in India.

Sarnath (Madhya Pradesh) : It is a Buddhist pilgrim centre. In the Deer Park, Buddha delivered his first sermon. Famous Ashoka Pillar is located here.

Srirangapattanam (Karnataka) : It was the capital of Tipu Sultan during his time. The third Mysore war was fought here and Tipu died in the battle in 1799 AD.

Sevagram (Maharashtra) : It is near Wardha in Maharashtra State. It is well-known for Gandhiji's Ashram where Gandhi lived and worked for many years.

Shantiniketan (West Bengal): About 90 miles from Calcutta, seat of the famous Viswa Bharati University founded by poet Rabindranath Tagore. It is now a Central University.

Shanti Van or Shanti Ghat (Delhi) : The place where Pt.Jawaharlal Nehru was cremated on 28th May, 1964, on the banks of Yamuna about 300 yards from Rajghat, Shri Lal Bahadur Shastri has been cremated by the side of Shanti Van. Mrs.Indira Gandhi was cremated close to Shanti Van on November 3, 1984. This site is called 'Shakti Sthal'.

Shivneri (Maharashtra): It is the birth place of Chatrapati Shivaji. The hill has about 50 Buddhist caves bearing inscription of various donors.

Sholapur (Maharashtra): 'Sholapur Chaddan's are the very famous bedsheets. Handloom and powerloom industry is flourishing in this town. Near the city a fort built by Hasan Gangu who was the founder of the Bahaman dynasty stands erect.

Shree Kshetra Audumbar (Maharashtra): An important pilgrim place in Sangli district, Audumbar is famous for the temple of Shree Dattatreya. There is well-known "Brahmanand Swami Math".

Sasaram (Bihar) : It is known for Sher Shah's Tomb. Sher Shah was the famous Afghan king who drove away Humayun.

Shivapuri (Madhya Pradesh) : It is well-known for its national park in Madhya Pradesh.

Sibsagar (Assam): 56 km from Jorhat is most interesting historical city. It was the capital of Ahom Kings who ruled Assam for 600 years. The Shiva temple called the "Shivadol" is said to be the tallest Shiva Temple in India.

Sikandra (Uttar Pradesh) : Situated near Agra, Akbar's Tomb stands here. It was commenced by Akbar and completed by his son Jahangir, after 14 years at a cost of Rs.15 lakhs.

Singareni (Andhra Pradesh) : It is well-known for coal mines in Andhra Pradesh..

Sindri (Jharkhand): The largest fertiliser factory in India and the whole of Asia is in Sindri, 77 km from Maithan. It is built on ultra-modern lines and manufacturing ammonium sulphate fertiliser since 1956. The factory can be visited with prior permission.

Somnath (Gujarat) : It is historically famous for the temple which was destroyed by Mohammed of Ghazni in 1025 A.D.

Somnath Patan (Gujarat): It is also known as Prabhas Patan and Deva Patan which is the 'Somnath' of Marco Polo.

Sravanabelagola (Karnataka): Wedged in between the two hills of Chandragiri and Indragiri, which rise abruptly from a flat plains, Sravanabelagola 100 kms from Mysore, is famous for Jain Colossus (17m height) Gomateswara which is said to be the tallest and most graceful monolithic statues in the world, erected in 10th century AD.

Sriharikota (Andhra Pradesh) : India's Satellite launching station is located here. It is on the Andhra coast, in Nellore District.

Sriperumbudur (Tamil Nadu): Birth place of Sri Ramanuja, the propounder of Vishistadvaita. It was here Rajiv Gandhi, former Primer Minister of India was assassinated.

Srirangam (near Trichy, Tamil Nadu): The largest temple in South India dedicated to Lord Ranganath (Vishnu).

Sundarbans (West Bengal) : It is the largest delta in India, housing rich forests.

Surat (Gujarat): It is popularly known as "Gate of Mecca". The English got trading rights from the Mughal in 1612. Most of the population are engaged in diamond cutting and polishing gold and silver. Surat is equally known for its distinctive cuisine.

Taj Mahal (Uttar Pradesh) : Erected by Shah Jahan in memory of his wife Mumtaz. It has been estimated that the cost of it was about Rs.3 crores at that time. It is tear drop on the cheek of eternity. It was designed by Shiraz (Iranian Architect). Over 20,000 men were employed for its construction for over twenty years. The environmentalists fear that the beauty of the Taj would be marred, with the Mathura Oil Refinery going into full operation.

Tawang (Arunachal Pradesh): It has a monastery of the Mahayana sect of Buddhists built in 17th century. Still it is the centre of religious life and rituals in the region. It is a treasure home of old scriptures, priceless images and painted tapestries.

Thanjavur (Tamil Nadu) : Popularly known as granary of South India. It was once the capital of the Cholas. Famous for Brihadeeswara temple, a Hindu temple. It was built by Rajaraja, the great.

Thiruvananthapuram (Kerala) : The Capital City of Kerala State. Padmanabha Temple is here.

Thumba (Kerala) : India's first rocket launching station.

Thiru Alangadu (Tamil Nadu): Thirty seven miles from Chennai to the west and very near to Arakonam is the holy place of Thiru Alangadu connected with Karaikkal Ammayar and the cosmic dancer Lord Nataraja.

Thiruvalam (Tamil Nadu): Capital of 'Banars' during the early Pallava period is famous for Saivite temple with the Nandi not facing the deity but in the opposite direction.

Thekkady (Tamil Nadu): The central spot of the Periar wildlife sanctuary is in between Kerala and Tamil Nadu.

The Mysore Palace (Karnataka): Built in 1897, it was the residence of the Ex-ruler of Mysore state is an imposing structure. It is a good example for the Hoysala art and architectures.

Tiruchi (Tamil Nadu) : It is an Educational Centre in Tamil Nadu. Bharat Heavy Electricals Limited is established here.

Tiruparankundram (Tamil Nadu): A cave temple near Madurai is one of the famous shrines of Lord Muruga.

Tirunelveli (Tamil Nadu): It is an old town which once served as the capital of Pandya Kingdom for sometime.

Tiruvidandai (Tamil Nadu): A famous early Chola Vaishnavaite shrine housing a huge stucco image of Varaha holding Bhudevi near Mahabalipuram in Tamil Nadu.

Tipu's Fort (Karnataka): The fort is built of mud by Kempegowda in 1537; it was rebuilt in stone in 1761 by Hyder Ali. Inside the fort walls is Tipu Sultan's wooden palace with enough elaborate paint work surviving on the walls, niches, and railing columns to give an idea of its former glory.

Triveni (Uttar Pradesh) : Here meet the rivers Ganges, the Yamuna and the mythical Saraswathi. Kumba Mela is celebrated here once in 12 years when the Sun is in Aquarius facing Jupiter in the zodiac sign Leo.

Trithamukh (Tripura): It is a popular pilgrim centre for the Tribal people of Tripura. Thousands of people assemble here in January-February during the festival called *Uttarayana Sankranti* and have a holy bath in the river Gomati.

Tripolia Gate (Rajasthan) : A gate with eight carved marble crunches under which the ruler was weighed on his birth day against money of equal weight distributed to the poor. The city was found in 1567 by Maharana, Udai Singh.

Udaipur (Rajasthan) : Popularly known as city of lakes. Pichola Lake is a famous one.

Udipi (Karnataka): This is the seat of Dvaita system of Hindu Philosophy propounded by Sri Madhva Changa. The beautiful Sri Krishna temple is very famous Hindu pilgrimage centre.

Udayagiri-Khandagiri Caves (Orissa): These two hills are little far away from Bhubaneshwar. This was a seat of a Jain saint who lived 2000 years ago. 'Rani Gumpha' and 'Hathi Gumpha' are the most famous; consist of the rock cut inscription in India which records chronologically the deeds of King Kharavela.

Uttiramerur (Tamil Nadu): A city near Chingleput boasts of Sundara-varadaperumal temple of the period of Dandivarma Pallava is of complex design.

Ujjain (M.P.) : Mahakaleeswar Temple is sacred for the Hindus.

Vaishali (Bihar): Vaishali has witnessed the major parts of Gautama Buddha's life. He gave his last message to his disciples at Kolhua village in the suburbs of Vaishali. On the eve of Buddha's death centenary, the 2nd Buddhist council was held here. The 24th Jain Tirthankar Vardhaman Mahavir was born at Kundagram in the suburbs of Vaishali in 599 BC.

Varanasi (Uttar Pradesh) : 'The Eternal City' is an important pilgrimage of the Hindus. Lord Viswanatha's temple is here. It was a learning place for over 2000 years. *Kashi* and *Benaras* are the other two names of *Varanasi* which means the city between two rivers - *Varanama and Asi*. It is the seat of Banaras Hindu University. Aurangzeb's Mosque is here.

Vedanthangal (Tamil Nadu): A bird sanctuary in the swamps of Madurantakam Lake.

Visakhapatnam (Andhra Pradesh) : It is a natural and protected harbour on the eastern coast in Andhra Pradesh. A shipbuilding yard is located here.

Vivekananda Rock (Tamil Nadu) : Mandapam of Vivekananda is in Cape Comerin.

Victoria Memorial (Kolkata): Magnificent building having an art gallery depicting the history of the British rule in India, it was erected by voluntary collections in the memory of Queen Victoria. A well laid out garden adds to the beauty.

Wardha (Maharashtra) : It is a cotton producing centre in Maharashtra. It is on Chennai-Delhi rail route. Mahatma Gandhi was imprisoned here.

Warrangal (Andhra Pradesh): It has historical evidence about on the seat of the Kakatiya rulers. Its chief tourist attraction is the thousand pillared temple at Hanam-Konda built by King Rudra Deva in 12th century.

Yamunotri (Uttarakhand) : It is the source of the Yamuna River. It emerges from the frozen lake of ice and glaciers on the Kalinga Parvat. There is a temple of the goddess Yamunotri on the left banks of the river. Below the temple there are many hot springs where the water emerges at boiling point.

Yercaud (Tamil Nadu): It is a hill station 8 km away from Salem at an altitude of 5000 ft. It is a part of Servarayan hills.

Zojila (Jammu & Kashmir) : It is a pass on the way from Srinagar to Leh.

TOWNS AND INDUSTRIES

Town	State	Industries
Agra	Uttar Pradesh	Stoneware, marble, leather and carpets
Ahmedabad	Gujarat	Cotton Textiles
Aliabet	Gujarat	Oil Well
Alwaye	Kerala	Aluminium, Monazite, Rare Earths Factory
Aligarh	Uttar Pradesh	Locks

Town	State	Industries
Ambala	Haryana	Scientific goods
Ambernath	Maharashtra	Machine Tool Prototype Factory
Amritsar	Punjab	Shawls, acid, carpet, woollen goods, cloth printing, Baby Food
Ankleshwar	Gujarat	Oil
Avadi	Tamil Nadu	Heavy Vehicles Factory 'Vijayanta Tank'
Bangalore	Karnataka	Hindustan Aeronautics Ltd., Indian Telephone Industries Ltd. and Hindustan Machine Tools
Barauni	Jharkhand	Oil Refinery
Bareilly	Uttar Pradesh	Resin, industries, woodwork
Basti	Uttar Pradesh	Fruit Research
Bhadravati	Karnataka	Alloy Steel
Bhatinda	Punjab	Thermal Plant
Bhilai	Chattisgarh	Steel Plant
Bhopal	Madhya Pradesh	Heavy Electricals
Bailadila	Madhya Pradesh	Iron ore, Mechanised mine
Bokaro	Jharkhand	Steel Plant
Cambay	Gujarat	Petroleum
Chapra	Bihar	Wheel Axel Plant
Chindwara	Madhya Pradesh	Limestone, Coal
Chittaranjan	West Bengal	Locomotives
Dalmia Nagar	Jharkhand	Cement
Delhi	Delhi	DDT, Textiles and Housing Factory
Dhariwal	Punjab	Woollen goods
Digboi	Assam	Petroleum
Dum Dum	West Bengal	Aerodrome
Durgapur	West Bengal	Steel Plant, Dry Ice
Ennore	Tamil Nadu	Thermal Power
Ernakulam	Kerala	Cables
Firozabad	Uttarakhand	Glass
Guntur	Andhra Pradesh	Cotton Manufacture, Tobacco
Gwalior	Madhya Pradesh	Pottery, Textiles
Haldia	West Bengal	Oil Refinery
Haridwar	Uttarakhand	Heavy Electricals
Jalandhar	Punjab	Surgical goods and sports articles
Hissar	Haryana	Indo-Australian sheep farm
Hirzapur	Uttar Pradesh	Carpet, pottery, stoneware and bran industries
Hoshangabad	M.P.	Security Paper Mill
Howrah	West Bengal	Jute

Town	State	Industries
Jaduguda	Jharkhand	Uranium Ore Mill
Jalsindhi	Maharashtra	Hydro-electric
Jabalpur	Madhya Pradesh	Vehicles
Jaipur	Rajasthan	Embroidery
Jalahalli	Karnataka	Machine Tool Factory and Electronics
Jamshedpur (Tatanagar)	Jharkhand	Iron & steel goods
Jharia	Jharkhand	Coal
Jetsar	Rajasthan	Mechanised Farm (India's Second)
Jwalamukhi	Himachal Pradesh	Petroleum
Kakrapara	Gujarat	Atomic Power Plant
Kalol	Gujarat	Fertiliser
Kalpakkam	Tamilnadu	Atomic Power Plant
Kandla	Gujarat	Fertilizer
Kanpur	Uttar Pradesh	Leather, Shoes
Khetri	Rajasthan	Copper
Kirloskarvadi	Maharashtra	Agricultural Implements
Kochi	Kerala	Shipbuilding
Kolar	Karnataka	Gold mine
Kolkata	West Bengal	Jute manufacture, Electric bulb and Lamps
Korba	Madhya Pradesh	Coal mine, Aluminium
Koyali	Maharashtra	Power Generation
Koyna	Maharashtra	Aluminium
Kozhikode	Kerala	Calico, Rubber coir
Kurukunta	Karnataka	Cement Plant
Ludhiana	Punjab	Hosiery
Lucknow	Uttar Pradesh	Gold, Silver, Lac and embroidery work
Manali	Tamil Nadu	Fertiliser / Oil Refinery
Madurai	Tamil Nadu	Cotton and Silk weaving
Mettur	Tamil Nadu	Aluminium
Motipur	Uttar Pradesh	Mechanised Farming
Mohali SAS Nagar	Punjab	Colour picture Tube, LCVs Tractors, Micro-chips
Moradabad	Uttar Pradesh	Utensils
Mumbai	Maharashtra	Cotton Textile and other Industries
Mysore	Karnataka	Silk
Nangal	Punjab	Fertilizer, Heavy Water Plant
Narora	Uttar Pradesh	Atomic Power Plant

Town	State	Industries
Nagpur	Maharashtra	Cotton Mills, Oranges
Nepanagar	Madhya Pradesh	Newsprint
Neyveli	Tamil Nadu	Lignite
Ogalewadi	Maharashtra	Hurricane lanterns, Stoves
Ootacamund	Tamil Nadu	Photo-films
Pilani	Rajasthan	Thermal Power
Pattabhiram	Tamil Nadu	Micro Tools
Perambur	Tamil Nadu	Integral Coach Factory
Pimpri, Pune	Maharashtra	Antibiotics
Pipri	Uttar Pradesh	Power generation
Pinjore	Haryana	Machine Tools
Rana Pratap Sagar	Rajasthan	Atomic Power Plant
Ranchi	Jharkhand	Heavy Machine-buildings, Foundry Forge
Ranigunj	Jharkhand	Coal mining
Ranipur	Uttarakhand	Heavy Electricals
Renukoot	Uttar Pradesh	Aluminium
Rourkela	Orissa	Steel Plant
Rupanagar	West Bengal	Telephone Cables
Sindri	Jharkhand	Fertilizer
Sriharikota	Andhra Pradesh	Satellite Station
Srinagar	Kashmir	Woollen shawl, embroidery
Suratgarh	Rajasthan	Mechanized Farm (India's First)
Singareni	Andhra Pradesh	Coal
Singhbhum	Jharkhand	Copper
Surat	Gujarat	Textiles
Tarapur	Maharashtra	Nuclear Power
Tiruverumbur	Tamil Nadu	Pressure Boiler
Trombay	Maharashtra	Atomic Reactors, Plutonium, Fertilizer, Thorium Plant
Tiruchirapalli	Tamil Nadu	Cigar, B.H.E.L
Titagarh	West Bengal	Paper
Thiruvananthapuram	Kerala	Wood Carving, coir matting
Tuticorin	Tamil Nadu	Fertilizer, Thermal Power, Copper smelter plant
Udaipur	Rajasthan	Zinc Project
Varanasi or Benaras	Uttar Pradesh	Silk and brocade, brassware lac bangles, diesel locomotives
Visakhapatnam	Andhra Pradesh	Shipbuilding
Zaina Kot	Jammu and Kashmir	HMT Watch Factory

ABBREVIATIONS
A

A	:	Adult, Audit, First Class
A.A	:	Alchoholic Anonymous
A.A.F.I	:	Amateur Athletics Federation of India
A.A.P.S.O	:	Afro-Asian Peoples' Solidarity Organisation
A.B.C	:	Atomic Biological and Chemical (Warfare)
	:	Audit Bureau of Circulation
	:	Australian Broadcasting Corporation
A.B.V.P.	:	Akhila Bharatiya Vidyarthi Parishad
A.C	:	Alternating Current, Air-conditioned
	:	Ante Christum (Before Christ)
ACL	:	Access Control List
A.D.	:	Anno Domini (in the year of our Lord)
A.D.A.M.	:	Animated Dissection of Anatomy for Medicine
A.D.B	:	Asian Development Bank
A.D.C	:	Aide-de-Camp (helper or assistant)
A.D.I.	:	Archaeological Department of India
A.E.R.B	:	Atomic Emergy Regulatory Board
A.E.R.E.	:	Atomic Energy Research Establishment
A.F.P.	:	Agence France Presse
A.G.P.	:	Accelerated Graphics Port
A.H.	:	Anno Hegirae (Mohammed's flight from Mecca to Medina, 622 AD)
A.I.	:	Artificial Intelligence; Artifical Insemination
A.I.C.C.	:	All India Congress Committee
A.I.C.T.E.	:	All India Council of Technical Education
A.I.D.S.	:	Acquired Immune Deficiency Syndrome
A.I.F.F.	:	All India Football Federation
A.I.I.M.S	:	All India Institute of Medical Sciences
A.I.M.C.E.T.	:	All India Common Entrance Test (for Master of Computer Applications)
A.I.N.E.C.	:	All India Newspaper Editors Conference
A.I.T.U.C	:	All India Trade Union Congress
A.L.G.O.L.	:	Algebraic Oriented Language (ALGOrithmic Language)
A.M.I.E	:	Associate Member of Institute of Engineering
A.M.	:	Anti Meridiem / Amplitude Modulation
A.N.C	:	African National Congress
A.N.E.R.T.	:	Agency for Non-conventional Energy and Rural Technology
A.N.N.	:	Artificial Neural Network
A.P.C.T.T.	:	Asian and Pacific Centre for Transfer of Technology
A.P.E.C	:	Asia Pacific Economic Cooperation

A.P.M.C.	:	Agricultural Produce Marketing Committee
ARPANET	:	Advanced Research Project Agency Network
A.S.C.I.I.	:	American Standard Code for Information Interchange
A.S.E.A.N	:	Association of South East Asian Nations
A.S.E.M	:	Asia Europe Meeting
A.S.L.V	:	Augmented Satellite Launch Vehicle
A.S.S.O.CHAM.	:	Associated Chamber of Commerce and Industry
A.T. & T	:	American Telegraphic and Telephone Co.Ltd.
A.T.C	:	Air Traffic Control
A.T.M.	:	Automatic Teller Machine
A.T.P.	:	Adenosine Tri-Phosphate
A.T.R.	:	Action Taken Report
A.T.S	:	Anti Tetanus Serum
A.U.	:	Astronomical Units
A.V.A.	:	Audio Visual Aids
A.V.R.C.	:	Audio Visual Research Centre
A.V.S.M	:	Ati Vishisht Seva Medal
A.W.A.C.S	:	Airborne Warning and Control System
A.W.A.N.	:	Army Wide Area Network

B

B.A.R.C.	:	Bhaba Atomic Research Centre
B.B.C.	:	British Broadcasting Corporation
B.C.	:	Before Christ
B.C.C.I.	:	Board of Control for Cricket in India
B.C.G.	:	Becillus Calmettee Guerin
BENELUX	:	Belgium, Netherlands and Luxembourg
B.F.A.	:	Boao Forum for Asia
B.H.E.L.	:	Bharat Heavy Electricals Limited
bhp	:	brake horsepower
B.I.F.R.	:	Bureau of Industrial and Financial Reconstruction
B.I.O.S.	:	Basic Input Output System
B.I.S.	:	Bank of International Settlement
B.J.P.	:	Bharathiya Janata Party
B.L.O.	:	Binary Large Objects
B.L.T.F.	:	Bodo Liberation Tigers Force
B.O.L.T.	:	Bombay Stock Exchange On-Line Trading;
	:	Build-Operate-Lease-Transfer
bps	:	bytes per second
B.P.	:	Blood Pressure
B.P.R.	:	Business Process Re-engineering
B.R.O.	:	Border Roads Organisation
B.S.E.	:	Bombay Stock Exchange
B.S.F.	:	Border Security Force
B.S.I.	:	Botanical Survey of India
B.Sky.B.	:	British Sky Broadcasting
Bureaufax	:	International Public Facsimile Service

C

C.A.D.	:	Command Area Development
	:	Civil Aviation Department
	:	Computer-Aided Design
C.A.D.A.	:	Command Area Development Agency
C.A.G.	:	Comptroller and Auditor-General of India
C.A.N.	:	Calcium Ammonium Nitrate
Cantab	:	Cantabrigienis (of Cambridge University)
C.A.P.A.	:	Centre for Asia - Pacific Aviation
C.A.P.A.R.T.	:	Council for Advancement of People's Action and Rural Technology
C.A.P.E.S.	:	Computer-Aided Paperless Examination System
C.A.T.	:	Career Aptitude Test
	:	Computerized Axial Tomography
C.B.A.	:	Colliding Beam Accelerator
C.B.D.T.	:	Central Board of Direct Taxes
C.B.F.C.	:	Central Board of Film Certification
C.B.I.	:	Central Bureau of Investigation
C.C.I.	:	Cotton Corporation of India
C.C.W.	:	Convention of Conventional Weapons
C.D.	:	Compact disk / Certificate of Deposit
	:	Cash Deposit
C.D.A.C.	:	Centre for Development of Advanced Computing
C.D.M.	:	Cold Dark Matter
C.D.S.	:	Compulsory Deposit Scheme
C.E.	:	Civil Engineer
C.E.C.P.A.	:	Comprehensive Economic Co-operation and Partnership Agreement
C.E.C.R.I.	:	Central Electro-Chemical Research Institute
C.E.O.	:	Chief Executive Officer
cf	:	compare/refer (L.confer)
C.F.C.	:	Chloro Fluoro Carbon
C.F.L.	:	Compact Fluorescent Lamps
C.F.S.I.	:	Children's Film Society of India
C.F.S.L.	:	Central Forensic Science Laboratory
C.F.T.R.I.	:	Central Food Technology and Research Institute
C.G.I.	:	Common Gateway Interface
C.G.S.	:	Chief of General Staff
	:	Centimeter, Gram, Second
C.I.A.	:	Central Intelligence Agency
C.I.D.	:	Criminal Investigation Department
Cif	:	Cost, insurance and freight
C.G.I.A.R.	:	Consultative Group on International Agricultural Research
C.I.I.	:	Confederation of Indian Industry

C.I.S.	:	Commonwealth of Independent States
C.I.S.C.	:	Complex Instruction - Set Computing
C.I.T.U.	:	Centre of Indian Trade Unions
C.J.	:	Chief Justice
C.L.R.I.	:	Central Leather Research Institute
C.M.E.R.I.	:	Central Mechanical Engineering Research Institute
C.N.N.	:	Cable News Network
C.O.	:	Commanding Officer
C.O.A.I.	:	Cellular Mobile Operators Association of India
C.O.F.E.P.O.S.A.	:	Conservation of Foreign Exchange and Prevention of Smuggling Act
C.O.M.P.S.	:	Coastal Ocean Monitoring & Prediction System
COMSAT	:	Communications Satellite Corporation
C.O.N.C.O.R.D.	:	Council of North Indian States for Co-operation and Regional Development
C.O.P.R.A.	:	Consumer Protection Act
COSMEP	:	Consortium of Schools of Mathematics Experience Programme
Costford	:	Centre of Science & Technology for Rural Development
C.P.A.	:	Common Parliamentary Association
C.P.I./M	:	Communist Party of India/Marxist
C.R.I.D.A.	:	Central Research Institute for Dryland Agriculture
C.R.I.S.	:	Centre for Railway Information Systems
C.R.I.S.I.L.	:	Credit Rating Information Services of India Ltd.
C.R.R.	:	Cash Reserve Ratio
C.R.Y.	:	Child Rights and You
C.S.B.I.	:	Central Sheep Breeding Institute
C.S.I.R.	:	Council of Scientific and Industrial Research
C.S.I.R.O.	:	Commonwealth Scientific and Industrial Research Organization
C.S.M.	:	Company Sergeant - Major
C.S.M.C.R.I.	:	Central Salt & Marine Chemicals Research Institute
C.S.O.	:	Central Statistical Organisation
C.T.	:	Computerised Tomography
C.T.B.T.	:	Comprehensive Test Ban Treaty
ct	:	carat, cent
C.T.O.	:	Commercial Tax Officer
C.V.R.	:	Cockpit Voice Recorder
C.V.	:	Curriculum Vitae
C&W	:	Cable and Wireless
Cwt	:	Hundred weight (112 lbs.)
CMYK	:	Cyan, Magenta, Yellow, Kinda

D

D.D.T.	:	Dichloro Diphenyl Trichloroethane.
D.E.T.	:	Directory Entry Table

D.G.	:	Dei gratia (by the grace of God)
D.G.M.O.S.	:	Director General of Military Operations
D.H.S.D.	:	Duplex - High Speed Data Service
D.I.A.S.	:	DOT's Internet Access Service
D.I.N.	:	(Deutsche Industrie-Norm) German Standard
D.I.G.	:	Deputy Inspector General
D.N.A.	:	Deoxy-Ribo Nucleic Acid
D.Phil.	:	Doctor of Philosophy
D.P.B.S.	:	Developmental Press Bulletin Service
D.P.T.	:	Diphtheria, Pertussis and Tetanus (Vaccine)
	:	Diploma in Printing Technology
D.S.B.	:	Digital Satellite Broadcasting
D.S.P.	:	Digital Signal Processing
D.T.A.C.	:	Double Taxation Avoidance Convention
D.T.E.	:	Directorate of Technical Education
D.T.P.	:	Desk Top Publishing
D.T.S.	:	Digital Theatre System
D.V.	:	Deo Volente (God willing)
D.V.D.	:	Digital Versatile/Video Disc
D.V.I.	:	Digital Video Interactive
D.V.S.	:	Desktop Video-Conferencing Software
D.W.C.R.A.	:	Development of Women & Children in Rural Areas

E

E & O.E.	:	Errors and Omissions Excepted
E.C.A.	:	Essential Commodities Act
E.C.G.	:	Electrocardiogram
ECOSOC	:	Economic and Social Council (UN)
E.C.R.	:	Electron Cyclotron Resonance
		East Coast Roadways
E.D.M.S.	:	Electronic Document Management System
E.E.G.	:	Electro Encephalogram
E.E.Z.	:	Exclusive Economic Zone
E.F.A.	:	Essential Fatty Acid
E.F.T.A.	:	European Free Trade Association
eg	:	exempli gratia (for example)
E.G.P.	:	Exterior Gateway Protocol
E.I.S.	:	Executive Information System
E.L.	:	Electro-luminescent
ELINT	:	Electronic Intelligence
E.L.I.S.A.	:	Enzyme Linked Immuno-Sorbent Assay
E.L.T.	:	English Languages Teaching
E-Mail	:	Electronic Mailing
E.M.R.C.	:	Educational Media Research Centre
ENIAC	:	Electronic Numerical Integrator & Calculator

E.N.S.	:	Eastern Newspapers Society
E.O.U.	:	Export Oriented Units
E.P.A.B.X.	:	Electronic Private Automatic Branch Exchange
E.P.C.I.	:	Enhanced Proliferation Control Initiative
E.P.I.R.B.	:	Emergency Position Indicating Radio Beacon
E.P.S.	:	Encapsulated Postscript
E.P.Z.	:	Export Processing Zone
E.R.M.	:	Exchange Rate Mechanism
ERNET	:	Educational and Research Network
E.S.A.	:	European Space Agency
E.S.C.	:	Electronics and Computer Software Export Promotion Council
E.S.C.A.P.	:	Economic and Social Commission for Asia and the Pacific
E.S.M.A.	:	Essential Services Maintenance Act
E.S.P.	:	Extra Sensory Perception
E.S.R.	:	Electron Spin Resonance
et al	:	et alii (and others)
E.S.I.C.	:	Employees' State Insurance Corporation
et.seg	:	et sequentia (& what follows)
etc	:	et cetera (& others and so forth)
E.T.T.	:	Embryo Transfer Technology
EURATOM	:	European Atomic Community
EUTELSAT	:	European Telecommunications Satellite
E.V.R.	:	Electro Video Recording

F

F.A.O.	:	Food and Agiculture Organisation
F.A.Q.	:	Fair Average Quality
F.B.I.	:	Federal Bureau of Investigation
F.B.T.R.	:	Fast Breeder Test Reactor
F.B.W.	:	Fly By Wire
F.C.I.	:	Food Corporation of India
F.C.N.R.A.	:	Foreign Currency Non-Resident Accounts
F.C.R.A.	:	Foreign Contribution Regulation Act
F.E.M.A.	:	Foreign Exchange Management Act
F.E.R.A.	:	Foreign Exchange Regulation Act
F.I.C.C.I.	:	Federation of Indian Chambers of Commerce and Industry
F.I.D.E.	:	Federation International d'Echecs
F.I.F.A.	:	Federation of Internationale de Football Association
F.I.P.B.	:	Foreign Investment Promotion Board
F.I.R.E.	:	Fully Integrated Robotised Engine
F.L.A.G.	:	Fibre Optic Link Around the Globe

F.L.C.	:	Foreign Legal Consultant
F.L.Cs.	:	Foreign Legal Consultants
F.M.	:	Frequency Modulation
F.M.C.T.	:	Fissile Material Cut-off Treaty
F.P.D.	:	Flat Panel Display
F.P.O.	:	Fruit Product Order
F.R.A.S.	:	Fellow of the Royal Asiatic Society
F.R.C.P.	:	Fellow of the Royal College of Physicians
F.R.C.S.	:	Fellow of the Royal College of Surgeons
F.R.G.S.	:	Fellow of the Royal Geographical Society
F.R.S.	:	Fellow of the Royal Society
F.T.I.I.	:	Films and Television Institute of India

G

G.A.I.L.	:	Gas Authority of India Ltd.
G.A.R.C.	:	Global Automotive Research Centre
G.E.F.	:	Global Environment Facility
G.A.T.E.	:	Graduate Aptitude Test in Engineering
G.A.T.S.	:	General Agreement on Trade in Service
G.A.T.T.	:	General Agreement on Tariff and Trade
G.B.P.	:	Geosphere - Biosphere Programme
G.C.C.	:	Gulf Control Council
G.C.M.M.F.	:	Gujarat Cooperative Milk Marketing Federation
G.D.P.	:	Gross Domestic Product
G.E.D.I.S.	:	Gateway Electronic Data Interchange Services
G.E.F.	:	Global Environment Facility
G.E.M.S.	:	Gateway Electronic Mail Service
Ge.S.C.I.	:	Global e-School and Communities Initiative
G.I.	:	Government Issue (American soldiers)
G.I.A.S.	:	Gateway Internet Access Services
G.I.F.	:	Graphic Interchange Format
G.I.S.	:	Geographical Information System
G.I.S.T.	:	Graphics and Intelligence-based Script Technoogy
G.K.Y.	:	Ganga Kalyan Yojana
G.M.A.T.	:	Graduate Management Aptitude Test
G.M.O.	:	Genetically Modified Organisms
G.M.R.T.	:	Giant Metrowave Radio Telescope
G.M.T.	:	Greenwich Mean Time
G.M.U.NET	:	Global Mega University Net
G.N.P.	:	Gross National Product
G.O.C.	:	General Officer Commanding
G.P.F.	:	General Provident Fund
G.P.S.	:	Global Positioning System
G.P.S.S.	:	Gateway Packet Switching System
G.P.T.S.	:	Generation & Pronouncement Text System

G.R.A.C.E.	:	Ground Rules and Code of Ethics
G.R.A.M.	:	Geo Referenced Area Management
G.R.E.	:	Graduate Record Examination
G.R.S.	:	Gender Reassignment Surgery (sex change)
G.S.I.	:	Geological Survey of India
G.S.L.V.	:	Geo-Synchronous Satellite Launch Vehicle
G.S.M.	:	Global System for Mobile Communications
G.S.P.	:	Generalised System of Preference
G.U.I.	:	Graphical User Interface

H

H.A.L.	:	Hindustan Aeronautics Limited
H.B.V.	:	Hepatitis-B Virus
H.E.M.R.L.	:	High Energy Materials Research Laboratory
H.F.	:	High Frequency
H.F.D.	:	High Frequency Doppler
H.F.D.C.	:	Housing Finance Development Corporation
H.I.V.	:	Human Immunodeficiency Virus
H.M.T.	:	Hindustan Machine Tools, Head Micro Telephone
H.M.V.	:	His Master's Voice
	:	Heavy Motor Vehicle
H.P.	:	Horse Power, Hire Purchase
H.R.P.T.	:	High Resolution Picture Transmission
H.R. & D.	:	Human Resources and Development
H.R. & C.E.	:	Hindu Religious and Cultural Endowment
H.S.D.	:	High Speed Diesel
H.S.R.R.S.S.	:	High Spatial Resolution Remote Sensing Satellite
H.T.	:	Hypertension
H.T.M.L.	:	Hyper Text Markup Language
H.T.R.	:	High Temperature Reactor
http	:	Hypertext Transfer Protocol
HUDCO	:	Housing and Urban Development Corporation
HV	:	High Voltage
HVNET	:	High Speed VSAT Network

I

I.A & A.S.	:	Indian Audit and Accounts Service
I.A.A.I.	:	International Airport Authority of India
I.A.A.P.	:	Intensive Agricultural Area Programme
I.A.E.A.	:	International Atomic Energy Agency
I.A.M.R.	:	Institute of Applied Manpower Research
I.A.R.I.	:	Indian Agricultural Research Institute
I.A.S.	:	Indian Administrative Service
I.A.T.A.	:	International Air Transport Association
I.B.M.	:	International Business Machines
I.B.R.D.	:	International Bank for Reconstruction and Development

I.B.S.	:	Indian School of Business
I.C.A.N.N.	:	Internet Corporation for Assigned Names and Numbers
I.C.A.O.	:	International Civil Aviation Organisation
I.C.A.R.	:	Indian Council for Agricultural Research
I.C.A.L.	:	Institute of Chartered Accountants of India
I.C.B.L.	:	International Campaign to Ban Landmines
I.C.B.M.	:	Intercontinental Ballistic Missile
I.C.C.R.	:	Indian Council for Cultural Relations
I.C.D.S.	:	Integrated Child Development Services
I.C.E.	:	Institution of Civil Engineers
I.C.I.C.I.	:	Industrial Credit and Investment Corporation of India
I.C.J.	:	International Court of Justice
I.C.M.R.	:	Indian Council of Medical Research
I.C.R.A.	:	Investment Information and Credit Rating Agency of India
ICRISAT	:	International Crops Research Institute for the Semi-Arid Tropics
I.C.W.A.	:	Indian Council of World Affairs
I.C.W.A.I.	:	Institute of Cost and Works Accounts of India
I.C.S.R.	:	Indian Council for Scientific Research
I.D.A.	:	International Development Agency
I.D.B.I.	:	Industrial Development Bank of India
I.D.E.	:	Integrated Device Electronics
I.E.E.E.	:	Institute of Electronics & Electrical Engineers
I.E.L.T.S.	:	International English Language Testing System
I.F.D.C.	:	Intenational Financial Development Corporation
I.F.A.D.	:	International Fund for Agricultural Development
I.F.C.	:	Industrial Finance Corporation
	:	International Finance Corporation
I.F.R.I.	:	Indian Forest Research Institute
I.F.S.	:	Indian Foreign Service
	:	Indian Forest Service
I.F.G.	:	India Growth Fund
I.G.S.	:	Indian Government Science
I.G.I.D.R.	:	Indira Gandhi Institute of Development Research
I.G.N.O.U.	:	Indira Gandhi National Open University
I.I.P.A.	:	Indian Institute of Public Administration
I.I.S.Co.	:	Indian Iron and Steel Company
I.I.T.	:	Indian Institute of Technology
I.L.O.	:	International Labour Organisation
I.M.A.P.	:	Internet Mail Access Protocol
I.M.C.O.	:	Inter-government Maritime Consultations Organisation
I.M.E.W.S.	:	Integrated Missile Early Warning Satellites

I.M.F.	:	International Monetary Fund
in cog	:	in cognito (in disguise)
INPEX	:	Indian National Philatelic Exhibition
infra dig	:	infra dignitatum (below status)
I.N.S.	:	Indian Newspaper Society
INSAT	:	Indian National Satellite
INSDOC	:	Indian National Scientific Documentation Centre
INTACH	:	Indian National Trust for Art and Cultural Heritage
INTELSAT	:	International Telecommunication Satellite Consortium
INTERPOL	:	International Criminal Police Organisation
I.N.T.U.C.	:	Indian National Trade Union Congress
I.O.U.	:	I owe you
I.O.S.Co.	:	International Organisation of Securities Commission
I.P.E.C.L.	:	International Programme on the Elimination of Child Labour
I.P.C.	:	Indian Penal Code
I.P.C.D.	:	International Conference on Population Development
I.P.C.L.	:	Indian Petro-chemicals Corporation Ltd.
I.P.S.	:	Indian Police Service
	:	Inter Press Service
I.P.X.	:	Inter-network Packet Exchange
I.Q.	:	Intelligent Quotient
iq	:	idem quod (the same as)
I.R.A.	:	Irish Republican Army
I.R.A.S.	:	Infrared Austronomical Satellite
I.R.B.M.	:	Intermediate Range Ballistic Missile
I.R.C.	:	International Red Cross
	:	Indian Roads Congress
I.R.D.P.	:	Integrated Rural Development Programme
I.R.E.D.A.	:	Indian Renewable Energy Development Agency
I.R.R.I.	:	International Rice Research Institute
I.R.S.	:	Indian Revenue Service
I.S.B.N.	:	International Standard Book Number
I.S.D.N.	:	Integrated Services Digital Network
I.S.F.O.C.	:	Intelligence-based Script Font Code
I.S.I.	:	Indian Standards Institution
I.S.K.O.N.	:	International Society for Krishna Consciousness
I.S.R.O.	:	Indian Space Research Organisation
I.S.T.	:	Indian Standard Time
I.T.	:	Information & Technology
I.T.A.	:	Information Technology Agreement
I.T.B.P.	:	Indian-Tibetan Border Police
I.T.I.	:	Indian Telephone Industries
	:	Industrial Training Institute

I.T.U.	:	International Telecommunication Union
I.U.C.A.A.	:	International University Centre for Astronomy and Astrophysics
I.U.C.D.	:	Intra-Uterine Contraceptive Device
I.U.I.	:	Intra-Uterine Insemination
I.V.F.	:	In-Vitro Fertilisation
I.V.M.	:	In-Vitro Maturation
I.W.O.C.	:	Internet Way of Computing
I.W.R.S.	:	Isolated Word Recognition System
I.C.S.	:	Indian Civil Service
I.G.	:	Inspector General
I.M.S.	:	Indian Medical Service
I.O.B.	:	Indian Overseas Bank
IOCOM	:	Indian Ocean Commonwealth
I.O.C.	:	Indian Oil Corporation
I.O.J.	:	International Organisation of Journalists
I.P.U.	:	International Parliamentary Union
I.R.C.I.	:	International Reconstruction Corporation of India
I.S.B.A.	:	International Sea-Bed Authority
I.T.D.C.	:	India Tourism Development Corporation
I.T.O.	:	International Telecommunication Union
I.U.T.F.	:	International Union of Trade Fairs
I.Y.C.	:	Indian Youth Congress

J

J.C.O.	:	Junior Commissioned Officer
J.P.	:	Justice of Peace
JIPMER	:	Jawaharlal Nehru Institute of Post-graduate Medical Education and Research
J.L.P.	:	Janata Legislature Party
J.P.E.G.	:	Joint Photographic Expert Group
J.P.P.	:	Janata Parliamentary Party
J.S.C.	:	Joint Stock Company
J.V.M.	:	Janata Vidyarthi Morcha

K

K.A.L.	:	Korean Airlines
K.A.N.U.	:	Kenya African National Union
K.R.C.	:	Konkan Railway Corporation
K.G.	:	Kinder Garten
K.G.P.	:	Komitet Gosudarstvennoye Bizo Pasnosti (Russian Secret Police)
Kg.	:	Kilogram
KKK	:	Ku Klux Klan (U.S. Secret Society - Anti-Negro, Anti-Jewish)

km	:	kilometre
kmph	:	kilometre per hour
K.M.T.	:	Kuomintang (Chinese National Party)

L

LALGI	:	Landless Agricultural Labourers Group Insurance Scheme
LASER	:	Light Amplification by Stimulated Emission of Radiation
LASIK	:	Laser in situ Keratomileusis
lb; lbid	:	lbidem, in the same place (book or chapter)
L.C.A.	:	Light Combat Aircraft
L.D.C.	:	Lower Division Clerk
L.C.D.	:	Liquid Crystal Display
L.E.R.M.S.	:	Liberalised Exchange Rate Management Scheme
L.E.S.	:	Lunar Eclipse System
L.I.P.S.	:	Language Independent Programme Subtitles
L.I.S.	:	Land Information System
L.L.B.	:	Bachelor of Laws
L.P.G.	:	Liquefied Petroleum Gas
L.M.C.	:	Large Megallanic Cloud
Loc cit	:	Loco citato (at the place quoted)
L.S.D.	:	dextro-lysergic acid diethylamide
L.S.G.	:	Local Self Government
Lt.com.	:	Lieutenant Commander
Lt. Gen.	:	Lieutenant General
Lt.Col.	:	Lieutenant Colonel
L.T.T.E.	:	Liberation Tigers of Tamil Eelam

M

M 1	:	Money Supply with Public
M 3	:	Aggregate Monetary Resources
M.A.I.T.	:	Manufacturers Association for Information Technology
MASER	:	Micro-wave Amplification by Stimulated Emission of Radiation
M.B.A.	:	Master of Business Administration
M.B.B.S.	:	Bachelor of Medicine and Bachelor of Surgery
M.C.C.	:	Marylebone Cricket Club
M.C.I.	:	Medical Council of India
M.C.L.R.	:	Medium Capacity Long Range
M.E.N.A.	:	Middle East News Agency
M.E.P.	:	Malaria Eradication Programme
Misc.	:	Miscellaneous
M.K.S.	:	Metre Kilogram Second (System)
M.I.D.I.	:	Musical Instrument Digital Interface
M.I.S.A.	:	Maintenance of Internal Security Act
M.I.T.	:	Massachusetts Institute of Technology, US.
M.L.A.	:	Member of Legislative Assembly

M.L.C.	:	Member of Legislative Council
Mlle	:	Mademoiselle (Miss)
M.M.T.C.	:	Minerals and Metals Trading Corporation
MMX	:	Matrix Manipulation Extension
	:	Multimedia Extension
M.N.C.	:	Multinational Company
M.N.F.	:	Mizo National Front
Mo.DEM	:	Modulator Demodulator
MODVAT	:	Modified Value Added Tax
M.O.S.F.E.T.	:	Metal Oxide Semiconductor Field Effect Transistor
M.O.U.	:	Memorandum of Understanding
M.P.E.G.	:	Motion Picture Experts Group
M.P.L.A.D.	:	Member of Parliament Local Area Development
M.R.A.	:	Moral Re-armament
M.R.C.P.	:	Member of Royal College of Physicians
M.R.D.	:	Movement for Restoration of Democracy (Pakistan)
M.R.T.S.	:	Mass Rapid Transit System
M.T.C.R.	:	Missile Technology Control Regime
M.V.C.	:	Maha Vir Chakra
M.W.S.	:	Million Wells Scheme

N

N.A.A.I.	:	National Airports Authority of India
N.A.B.A.R.D.	:	National Bank for Agriculture and Rural Development
N.A.F.E.D.	:	National Agricultural Co-operative Marketing Federation
N.A.F.T.A.	:	North America Free Trade Agreement
N.A.G.	:	National Air Guard
N.A.I.P.	:	National Agricultural Innovation Program
N.A.S.A.	:	National Aeronautics and Space Administration
N.A.M.	:	Non-Aligned Movement
N.A.S.D.A.Q.	:	National Association of Securities Dealers Automated Quotation
N.A.S.S.C.O.M.	:	National Association of Software and Service Companies
N.A.T.O.	:	North Atlantic Treaty Organisation
N.A.T.P.A.C.	:	National Transportation Planning and Research Centre
N.B.R.I.	:	National Banana Research Institute
N.B.G.R.B.	:	National Bureaue of Genetic Resources and Biotechnology
N.C.A.	:	National Commission on Agriculture
N.C.A.E.R.	:	National Council for Applied Economic Research
N.C.E.P.C.	:	National Committee of Environmental Planning & Co-ordination
N.C.E.R.T.	:	National Council of Educational Research and Training
N.C.O.	:	Non-Commissioned Officer

N.C.S.A.	:	National Centre for Super Computing Applications
N.C.S.T.	:	National Committee of Science and Technology
	:	National Conference on Science & Technology
NCSC & ST	:	National Commission for Scheduled Castes & Scheduled Tribes
N.C.T.E.	:	National Council for Teacher Education
NEC.	:	North-Eastern Council
N.D.A.	:	National Defence Academy
N.D.C.	:	National Development Council
N.D.I.S.	:	Natural Disaster Information System
N.D.M.A.	:	National Disaster Management Authority
N.D.P.	:	National Domestic Product
N.E.E.R.I.	:	National Environmental Engineering Research Institute
N.E.F.A.	:	North-East Frontier Agency
N.E.I.A.	:	National Export Insurance Account
N.E.P.A.	:	National Environment Protection Act
NexGeRad	:	Next Generation Radar (Doppler Radar)
N.F.D.C.	:	National Film Development Corporation
N.G.R.I.	:	National Geophysical Research Institute
N.I.C.D.	:	National Institute of Communicable Diseases
N.I.D.	:	National Institute of Designs
N.E.O.	:	National Economic Order
N.I.M.H.A.N.S.	:	National Institute of Mental Health and Neuro Sciences
N.I.O.	:	National Institute of Oceanography
N.I.V.	:	National Institute of Virology
N.M.D.C.	:	National Mineral Development Corporation
N.M.R.	:	Nuclear Magnetic Resonance
N.M.I.T.L.I.	:	The New Millennium Indian Technology Leadership Initiative
N.N.N.	:	NAM News Network
N.N.P.	:	Net National Product
N.P.C.	:	National Productivity Council (India)
N.P.L.	:	National Physical Laboratory
N.P.T.	:	Nuclear Non-Proliferation Treaty
N.R.C.	:	Nuclear Regulatory Commission
N.R.E.G.A.	:	National Rural Employment Guarantee Act
N.R.E.G.S.	:	National Rural Employment Guarantee Scheme
N.R.F.	:	National Renewal Fund
N.R.I.	:	Non-Resident Indian
N.R.S.A.	:	National Remote Sensing Agency
N.S.C.	:	National Security Council
	:	National Service Corps
N.S.E.I.	:	National Stock Exchange of India
N.S.G.	:	Nuclear Suppliers' Group

N.S.S.	:	National Social Service
N.S.U.I.	:	National Students Union of India
N.T.C.	:	National Textile Corporation
N.T.P.C.	:	National Thermal Power Corporation
N.T.S.C.	:	National Television System Commission
N.U.T.P.	:	National Urban Transport Policy
N.W.D.A.	:	National Water Development Agency

O

O & M	:	Organisation and Methods
O.A.N.A.	:	Organisation of Asia-Pacific News Agency
O.A.P.E.C.	:	Organisation of Arab Petroleum Exporting Countries
O.A.S.	:	Organisation of American States
O.A.S.I.S.	:	Old Age Social and Income Security
O.A.U.	:	Organisation of African Unity
O.C.D.	:	Obsessive Compulsive Disorder
O.D.A.	:	Overseas Development Administration
O.D.I.	:	Open Data Link Interface
O.E.C.D.I.	:	Organisation for Economic Co-Operation and Development of India
O.I.C.	:	Organisation of Islamic Conference
O.L.E.	:	Object Linking and Embedding
O.N.G.C.	:	Oil and Natural Gas Commission
O.O.P.	:	Object Oriented Programme
Op.Cit.	:	Opero citato (in the work cited)
O.P.E.C.	:	Organisation of Petroleum Exporting Countries
O.P.V.	:	Oral Polio Vaccine
O.R.T.	:	Oral Rehydration Therapy
O.I.C.	:	Organisation of Islamic Conference
O.X.F.A.M.	:	Oxford Committee for Famine Relief
Oxon.O.U.	:	Oxoniensis (of Oxford University)

P

P.A.C.	:	Public Accounts Committee
	:	Political Affairs Committee
P.A.C.S.	:	Primary Agricultural Credit Society
P.B.X.	:	Private Branch Exchange (for Telephone)
PC	:	Personal Computer
P.C.A.	:	Professional Chess Association
P.C.T.A.	:	Percutaneous Transluminal Coronary Angioplasty
P.D.A.	:	Preventive Detention Act
	:	Personal Digital Assistant
P.D.P.	:	Plasma Display Panel
P.E.R.T.	:	Project Evaluation and Review Technique
P.E.S.O.	:	Petroleum and Explosives Safety Organisation
P.G.I.M.E.R.	:	Post Graduate Institute of Medical Education and Research

Ph.D.	:	Doctor of Philosophy
P.F.A.	:	Press Foundation of Asia
	:	Prevention of Food Adulteration
P.H.C.	:	Primary Health Centre
P.I.B.	:	Press Information Bureau
P.I.G.S.	:	Pre-implantation Genetic Screening
P.I.L.	:	Public Interest Litigation
P.I.N.	:	Postal Index Number
P.I.I.	:	Press Institute of India
P.L.A.B.	:	Professional and Linguistic Assessment Board
P.L.O.	:	Palestine Liberation Organisation
P.M.	:	Post Meridiem / Prime Minister
P.M.L.A.	:	Prevention of Money Laundering Act
P.M.U.P.E.P.	:	Prime Minister's Urban Poverty Eradication Programme
P.O.W.	:	Prisoner of War
P.P.P.	:	Purchasing Power Parity
	:	Pakistan People's Party
P.R.O.	:	Public Relations Officer
P.S.C.	:	Public Service Commission
P.S.P.	:	Praja Socialist Party
P.S.L.V.	:	Polar Satellite Launch Vehicle
P.T.A.	:	Parent-Teacher Association
P.T.I.	:	Press Trust of India
P.U.D.R.	:	People's Union for Democratic Rights
P.V.C.	:	Param Vir Chakra
	:	Poly Vinyl Chloride
P.V.S.M.	:	Param Vishisht Seva Medal
P.W.D.	:	Public Works Department
P.E.C.	:	Project and Equipment Corporation
P.K.I.	:	Partai Kommunis Indonesia
P.P.S.	:	Post Post Scriptum (additional Post Script)

Q

Q.M.G.	:	Quarter Master General
Q.E.D.	:	Quod Erat Demonstrandum (that which was to be proved)
Q.M.S.	:	Quick Mail Service
Q.V.	:	Quode Vide (which see)

R

R & D	:	Research and Development
R.A.B.M.N.	:	Remote Area Business Message Network
R.A.M.	:	Random Access Memory
RADAR	:	Radio Detecting and Ranging
R.A.P.D.	:	Random Amplified Polymorphic Dexoyribonucleie Acid

R.C.C.	:	Reinforced Cement Concrete
R.A.W.	:	Research and Analysis Wing
R.B.I.	:	Reserve Bank of India
R.C.D.	:	Regional Co-operation for Development
R.D.F.	:	Rapid Development Force
R.E.C.	:	Rural Electrification Corporation
R.D.X.	:	Research and Development Explosive (Cyclotrim-ethylin Trinitrate)
R.I.L.	:	Regional Institute of Labour
R.E.M.	:	Rapid Eye Movement
R.I.S.C.	:	Reduced Instruction - Set Computing
R.I.T.E.S.	:	Rail India Technical and Economic Services
R.L.D.A.	:	Railway Land Development Authority
R.L.E.G.S.	:	Rural Landless Employment Guarantee Scheme
R.L.O.	:	Returned Letter Office
R.L.M.	:	Rashtriya Loktantric Morcha
R & M	:	Renovation and Modernisation
R.M.S.	:	Railway Mail Service
R.N.	:	Royal Navy
R.N.A.	:	Ribo Nucleic Acid
R.O.N.W.	:	Return on Net Worth
R.P.M.	:	Revolutions Per Minute
R.R.B.	:	Railway Recruitment Board
	:	Regional Rural Bank
R.R.C.	:	Regional Reactor Centre

S

SACEUR	:	Supreme Allied Commander in Europe
SACLANT	:	Supreme Allied Commander in Atlantic
S.A.S.E.	:	Self-addressed Stamped Envelope
S.A.C.	:	Space Application Centre
S.A.F.I.R.	:	South Asia Forum for Infrastructure Regulation
S.A.F.T.A.	:	South Asian Free Trade Area
S.A.S.E.C.	:	South Asian Sub-regional Economic Co-operation
S.A.I.L.	:	Steel Authority of India Limited
S.A.L.T.	:	Strategic Arms Limitation Treaty
S.A.M.	:	Surface-to-Air Missile
S.A.R.F.	:	South Asia Regional Fund
S.A.P.T.A.	:	South Asian Preferential Trading Agreement
S.A.S.E.R.	:	Sound Amplification by Stimulated Emission of Radiation
S.A.V.E.	:	SAARC Audio-Visual Exchange
S.C.I.	:	Shipping Corporation of India
S.C.S.I.	:	Small Computer Systems Interface
SEANWFZ	:	South East Asian Nuclear Weapons Free Zone

SEA-ME-WE 3	:	South East Asia, Middle East, Western Europe
S.E.A.T.O.	:	South-East Asia Treaty Organisation
S.E.B.I.	:	Securities Exchange Board of India
S.E.C.A.M.	:	Sequence Electronique Couleur avec Memoire (Electronic Colour Sequence with Memory)
S.E.R.C.	:	Structural Engineering Research Centre
SENSEX	:	Sensitivity Index of Share Price
S.E.T.L.	:	Search for Extra Terrestrial Life
S.E.W.A.	:	Self - Employed Women's Association
S.F.C.I.	:	State Farm Corporation of India
S.H.C.I.L.	:	Stock Holding Corporation of India Ltd.
S.I.D.S.	:	Sudden Infant Death Syndrome (Crib Death)
S.I.M.I.	:	Students Islamic Movement of India
S.F.T.	:	System Fault Tolerance
S.G.P.C.	:	Siromani Gurudwara Prabandak Committee
S.H.A.P.E.	:	Supreme Headquarters Allied Powers, Europe
S.I.D.B.I.	:	Small Industries Development Bank of India
S.I.T.A.	:	Suppression of Immoral Traffic in Women and Girls Act
S.I.T.E.	:	Satellite Instructional Television Experiment
S.I.T.R.A.	:	Supply of Improved Tool-kids to Rural Artisans
S.I.F.T.	:	Sperm Intra-Fallopian Transfer
S.I.G.V.R.	:	Special Interest Group on Virtual Reality
S.L.E.	:	Systemic Lupus Erithematosis
S.L.F.P.	:	Sri Lanka Freedom Party
S.L.R.	:	Statutory Liquidity Ratio
	:	Single Lens Reflex
S.L.V.	:	Satellite Launch Vehicle
S.M.T.P.	:	Simple Mail Transfer Protocol
S.N.A.	:	System Network Architecture
SOLAS	:	Safety of Life at Sea
SOLAT	:	Style of Learning and Thinking
S.P.C.A.	:	Society for the Prevention of Cruelty to Animals
S.P.E.C.T.	:	Single Photon Emission Computed Tomography
S.P.T.M.	:	Self Printing Ticketing Machine
S.P.X.	:	Sequential Packet Exchange
S.S.C.	:	Staff Selection Commission
S.S.L.	:	Social Service League
S.S.P.	:	Single Superphosphate
STAR (TV)	:	Satellite Television Asian Region Ltd.
S.T.A.R.S.	:	Satellite Tracking and Ranging Station
S.T.A.R.T.	:	Strategic Arms Reduction Talks
S.T.C.	:	State Trading Corporation
S.T.D.	:	Subscribers Trunk Dialling
	:	Sexually Transmitted Disease

S.T.P.	:	Software Technology Park
S.T.Q.C.	:	Standardization Testing and Quality Control
S.U.N.F.E.D.	:	Special United Nations Fund for Economic Development
S.V.P.	:	Saturated Vapour Pressure
S.W.A.P.O.	:	South-West African People's Organisation

T

T&D	:	Transmission and Distribution
T.A.	:	Travelling Allowance / Territorial Army
TACAMO	:	take charge and move over
T.A.F.T.A.	:	Trans-Atlantic Free Trade Agreement
TADA	:	Terrorist and Disruptive Activities (Prevention) Act
T.A.P.S.	:	Tarapur Atomic Power Station
T.A.S.S.	:	Telegraph Agency of the Soviet Soyuza
T.A.X.	:	Trunk Automatic Exchange
T.B.	:	Tubercle bacillus (Tuberculosis)
T.B.S.E.	:	Technology Bureau for Small Enterprise
T.C.	:	Transfer Certificate
T.C.P.	:	Transfer Call Protocol
	:	Transmission Control Protocol
T.D.A.	:	Trade Development Authority
T.E.C.	:	Technical Evaluation Committee
	:	Technical Education Committee
TELCO	:	Tata Engineering and Locomotive Company
T.E.R.I.	:	Tata Energy Research Institute
T.E.R.L.S.	:	Thumba Equatorial Rocket Launching Station
T.H.I.	:	Temperature Humidity Index
T.F.T.	:	Thin-Film Transistor
T.I.F.A.C.	:	Technology Information, Forecasting and Assessment Council
T.I.F.R.	:	Tata Institute of Fundamental Research
T.I.P.S.	:	Technology Information Pilot System
T.N.F.	:	Tumour Necrosis Factor
T.N.T.	:	Trinitro-toluene
T.O.E.F.L.	:	Test of English as a Foreign Language
T.P.M.	:	Total Productivity Maintenance
T.Q.M.	:	Total Quality Management
T.R.A.C.T.	:	Transportable Remote Area Communications Terminal
TRIMs	:	Trade Related Investment Measures
T.R.I.P.R.	:	Trade Related Intellectual Property Rights
T.R.Y.S.E.M.	:	Training of Rural Youth for Self-employment
TTC	:	Telemetry, Tracking & Command
	:	**Teachers Training Course**

T.R.A.I.	:	Telecom Regulatory Authority of India
T.U.L.F.	:	Tamil United Liberation Fund
T.W.A.	:	Trans World Airlines

U

U.A.E.	:	United Arab Emirates
U.A.N.C.	:	United African National Council
U.A.R.	:	United Arab Republic
U.C.T.A.	:	United Chamber of Trade Association
U.C.I.L.	:	Uranium Corporation of India Ltd.
U.G.C.	:	University Grants Commission
U.H.F.	:	Ultra High Frequency
U.L.E.V.	:	Ultra Low Emission Vehicle
U.N.C.E.D.	:	United Nations Conference on Environment and Development
UNCIP	:	United Nations Commission for India and Pakistan
UNCITRAL	:	United Nations Conference on International Trade Law
UNCLOS	:	United Nations Convention on the Law of the Sea
U.N.F.P.A.	:	United Nations Fund for Population Activities
UNCNRSe	:	United Nations Conference for New & Renewable Sources
UNCSTD	:	United Nations Conference on Science and Technology Development
UNCTAD	:	United Nations Conference on Trade and Development
U.N.C.O.D.	:	United Nations Conference on Desertification
U.N.D.F.	:	United Nations Democracy Fund
U.N.D.O.F.	:	United Nations Disengagement Observer Force
U.N.D.C.	:	United Nations Disarmament Commission
U.N.D.P.	:	United Nations Development Programme
U.N.E.F.	:	United Nations Emergency Force
U.N.E.P.	:	United Nations Environment Programme
U.N.E.S.C.A.P.	:	United Nations Economic and Social Commission for Asia and the Pacific
U.N.G.A.	:	United Nations General Assembly
U.N.I.P.O.M.	:	United Nations India-Pakistan Observation Mission
U.N.I.C.E.F.	:	United Nations International Children's Emergency Fund (now, 'United Nations Children's Fund')
U.N.I.D.O.	:	United Nations Industrial Development Organisation
U.N.I.T.A.	:	Union for the Total Independence of Angola
U.N.I.F.I.L.	:	United Nations Interim Force in Lebanon
UNISPACE	:	United Nations Conference on Peaceful Uses of Space
U.N.I.T.A.R.	:	United Nations Institute for Training & Research
U.N.I.T.C.	:	United Nations International Trade Centre
U.N.L.A.	:	Uganda's National Liberation Army
UNMOGIP	:	United Nations Military Observer Group in India & Pakistan

U.N.O.P.S.	:	United Nations Office for Project Services
UNPROFOR	:	United Nations Protection Force
U.N.R.R.A.	:	United Nations Relief and Rehabilitation Administration
U.P.I.	:	United Press International
U.P.S.	:	Uninterrupted Power Supply
U.P.S.C.	:	Union Public Service Commission
U.D.C.	:	Upper Division Clerk
U.N.L.O.	:	United Nations Labour Organisation
U.N.E.S.C.O.	:	United Nations Educational, Scientific and Cultural Organisation
U.S.P.	:	Unique Selling Proposition
U.T.I.	:	Unit Trust of India
U.S.I.S.	:	United States Information Service

V

V.A.B.A.L.	:	Value Based Advanced Licensing
V.A.T.	:	Value Added Tax
V.A.T.I.S.	:	Value Added Technology Information Service
V.B.T.	:	Vainu Bappu Telescope
V.C.	:	Vice-Chancellor
V.D.I.S.	:	Voluntary Disclosure of Income Scheme
V.G.	:	Vicar-General
V.H.F.	:	Very High Frequency
V.H.M.	:	Village Head Man
V.H.R.R.	:	Very High Resolution Radiometer
V.H.S.	:	Videl Home System
	:	Voluntary Health Services
V.I.R.U.S.	:	Vital Information Resources Under Siege
V.P.P.	:	Value Payable Post
Vr.C	:	Vir Chakra
V.R.D.E.	:	Vehicles Research and Development Establishment
V.R.M.L.	:	Virtual Reality Modelling Language
V.S.A.T.	:	Very Small Aperture Terminal
V.S.N.L.	:	Videsh Sanchar Nigam Limited
V.S.S.C.	:	Vikram Sarabhai Space Centre
V.V.T.L.E.C.	:	Variable Valve Timing and Life Electronic Control
V.T.R.	:	Video Tape Recorder
V.C.	:	Vice Chancellor
Viz.	:	namely (Videlicet)
V.V.F.	:	Village Volunteer Force (in India)

W

WARDEC	:	Wargaming Development Centre
W.A.S.M.E.	:	World Assembly of Small and Medium Enterprises

W.C.A.I.	:	Women's Cricket Association of India
W.D.M.	:	World Debt Market
w.e.f.	:	with effect from
W.F.C.	:	World Food Council
W.F.P.	:	World Food Programme
W.F.T.U.	:	World Federation of Trade Unions
W.G.I.G.	:	Working Group on Internet Governance
W.H.O.	:	World Health Organisation
W.I.M.A.X.	:	Worldwide Interoperability for Microwave Access
W.I.M.P.	:	Weakly Interacting Massive Particle
	:	Windows, Icons, Menus, Pointers
W.M.O.	:	World Meteorological Organisation
W.P.I.	:	Wholesale Price Index
W.T.O.	:	World Trade Organisation
W.W.F.	:	World Wildlife Fund / (new) Worldwide Fund for Nature
W.W.W.	:	World Wide Web

X

X.B.T.	:	Expandable Bathy Thermographic
X-mas	:	Christmas
X.P.D.	:	X-Ray Photoelectron Diffraction

Y

Y.M.C.A.	:	Young Men's Christian Association
Y.M.I.A.	:	Young Men's Indian Association
Y.W.C.A.	:	Young Women's Christian Association

Z

Z.A.N.U.	:	Zimbabwe African National Union
Z.A.P.U.	:	Zimbabwe African People's Union
ZBB	:	Zero-based Budgeting
Z.I.F.T.	:	Zygote Intra Fallopian Transfer
Z.I.P.	:	Zone Improvement Plan
Z.O.P.F.A.N.	:	Zone of Peace Freedom and Neutrality
Z.E.T.A.A.	:	Zero Energy Thermonuclear Assembly
Z.S.I.	:	Zoological Survey of India
Z.U.P.O.	:	Zimbabwe United People's Organisation

FIRSTS IN THE WORLD

Field	Person
The first person to land on the moon	: Neil A. Amstrong (U.S.A.)
The first to launch search Satellite or "artificial moon"	: Sputnik (USSR), 1957
The first man to enter space	: Late Maj. Yuri Gagarin (USSR)
The first woman cosmonaut in the world	: Valentina Tereshkova
The first woman astronaut pilot	: Lt.Col. Eileen Marie Collins (US)
The first person to float in space	: Alexei Leonov (Russia)
The first American astronaut (2nd in world) to float in space	: Edward White
The first Russian cosmonaut to make two space flights	: Late Col. Vladimir Komarov
The first American astronaut to make two space flights	: Gordon Cooper (U.S.A)
The first manned spaceship longest stay in space for 11 days	: Apollo - 7 (U.S.A)
The first manned spaceship to space flight round the moon	: Apollo - 8 (U.S.A)
The first spacecraft to leave solar system	: Pioneer-II (U.S.A)
The first country to launch a cosmic space rocket towards moon	: U.S.S.R. (former)
First crew transfer between orbiting spaceships	: Soyuz-4 and Soyuz-5 (U.S.S.R.-former)
The first man to stay long in space	: Valery Ryumin
The first space shuttle	: Columbia (U.S.A)
The first woman to command a space shuttle mission (Columbia)	: Eileen Collins (U.S.A)
The first tourist to space	: Dennis Tito (U.S.A)

FIRSTS IN INDIA

Field	Person
WOMEN	
First Prime Minister	: Mrs. Indira Gandhi
First Chief Minister of State	: Mrs. Sucheta Kripalani
First Speaker of State Assembly	: Mrs. Shanno Devi
First Governor of a State	: Mrs. Sarojini Naidu
First President of UN General Assembly	: Mrs. Vijayalakshmi Pandit
First to sit on the throne of Delhi	: Razia Sultana
First to swim across the English Channel	: Mrs Arati Saha
First to climb Mount Everest	: Bachendri Pal

Field		Person
First IPS Officer	:	Kiran Bedi
First Judge of a High Court	:	Anna Chandi
First Judge of Supreme Court	:	Ms. M. Fathima Bevi
First Chief Justice of a High Court	:	Ms. Leila Seth
First Doctor	:	Kadambini Ganguli
First editor of English newspaper	:	Dina Vakil
First to climb Mount Everest two times	:	Santosh Yadav (ITBF Officer) - 1993
First Magistrate	:	Mrs. Omana Kunjamma
First to be crowned Miss World	:	Reita Faria
First to be crowned Miss Universe	:	Sushmita Sen
First Woman Secretary of a State	:	Lakshmi Pranesh (Tamil Nadu)
First Woman Astronaut	:	Kalpana Chawla
Second Woman Astronaut	:	Suneeta Williams
First Woman Vice-admiral in the Navy	:	Ms. Punita Arora
First City Police Commissioner in Chennai	:	Lathika Charan
The first woman D.G.P.	:	Kanchan Choudry Bhattacharya
First Woman President in India	:	Mrs. Pratibha Patil

MEN

Field		Person
First Indian to swim across the English Channel	:	Mihir Sen
First to Climb Mount Everest	:	Tenzing Norgay
First to climb Mount Everest without Oxygen	:	Phu Dorjee
First Indian to climb Mount Everest twice	:	Nwang Gombu
First Indian to get Nobel Prize	:	Rabindranath Tagore
First Indian to get nobel prize in science	:	Sir C.V. Raman
First Indian in Space (first Indian cosmonaut)	:	Sqn. Ldr. Rakesh Sharma
First Governor General of Free India	:	Lord Mountbatten
First and the last Governor General of free India	:	C. Rajagopalachari
First President of India	:	Dr. Rajendra Prasad
First Vice-President of India	:	Dr. S. Radhakrishnan
First Prime Minister	:	Pt. Jawahar Lal Nehru
First Speaker of Lok Sabha	:	G.V. Mavlankar
First Chief Justice of India	:	Justice H.J. Kania
First President of Indian National Congress	:	W.C. Bannerjee
First Indian to become member of Viceroy's Executive Council	:	Sir S.P. Sinha
First Field Marshal	:	S.H.F.J. Manekshaw
First Indian Commander-in-Chief of India	:	Gen K.M. Cariappa
First Chief of the Army Staff (Indian)	:	Sinhji
First Chief of the Naval Staff (Indian)	:	Vice Admiral R.D. Katari
First Chief of the Air Force Staff (India)	:	Subroto Mukherjee
First Indian to make a solo air flight	:	J.R.D. Tata
First Bar-at-Law	:	J.M. Tagore
First Indian Test Cricketer	:	K.S. Ranjit Singh
First Air Marshall	:	Arjun Singh

FIRST VISITORS, INVADERS ETC.

The first European invader on Indian soil	:	Alexander, the Great
The first European to visit China	:	Marco Polo
The first Chinese Pilgrim who came to India	:	Fahien
The first British Prime Minister to visit India	:	Harold Macmillan
The first U.S. President to visit India	:	D. Eisenhower
The first Soviet Prime Minister to visit India	:	V. Bulganin

SPORTS

Field		Person
The first Indian woman to swim across the English Channel	:	Miss. Arati Saha
The first Indian to win world Billiards Trophy	:	Wilson Jones
The first to cross the Dardanelles by swimming	:	Mihir Sen
The first to conquer Everest	:	Sherpa Tenzing (1953)
The first to sail round the world	:	Magellan
The first person to win Wimbledon title five times in a row	:	Bjorn Borg
The first woman who conquered Everest	:	Jungko Tabei (Japan)
The first person to reach North Pole	:	Robert Peary
First woman Olympic Medallist (Weight Lifting - Bronze)	:	Karnam Malleswari (2000)
The first person to reach South Pole	:	Amundsen
The first Indian to win All England Badminton Championship	:	Prakash Padukone
The first Indian woman to conquer Everest	:	Bachendri Pal
The first man to climb Everest twice	:	Nawang Gombu
The first person to complete solo walk to magnetic North pole	:	David Hempleman Adam (UK)
The first woman to reach North pole	:	Ann Bancroft
The first woman to sail non stop around the world alone	:	Kaycottee

Field	Person
The first deaf & dumb to cross the strait of Gibraltar	: Taranath Shenoy (India)
The first woman to climb Mt. Everest twice	: Santosh Yadav (India)
The youngest woman to climb Mt. Everest	: Dicky Dolma (India)
The first black player to win the Wimbledon men's singles title	: Arthur Ashe (US)
The first person to win the Palk Strait ocean swimming contest	: Baidyanatha Nath
The first person to win the silver medal for shooting in 2004 olympics	: Major Rajyawardhan Singh Rathore

PERSONS AND PLACES

Bardoli	: Sardar Patel
Belur	: Ramakrishna Paramahamsa
Chittor, Haldighat	: Rana Pratap
Corsica, Elba, Waterloo	: Napoleon Bonaparte
Fatehpur Sikri	: Akbar, the Great
Jerusalem	: Jesus Christ
Kapilavastu, Lumbini	: Buddha
Kanchipuram	: C.N.Annadurai
Macedonia	: Alexander, the Great
Maniachi	: Vanchinathan
Mecca	: Mohammed, the Prophet
Paunar	: Acharya Vinoba Bhave
Puducherry	: Aurobindo Ghosh
Porbundar, Rajghat, Sabarmathi	: Mahatma Gandhi
Srirangapattinam	: Tipu Sultan
Sriperumbudur	: Rajiv Gandhi, Ramanujar
Shakti Sthal	: Indira Gandhi
Shanti Van	: Jawaharlal Nehru
Trafalgar	: Nelson
Tuticorin	: V.O.Chidambaram Pillai
Ujjain	: Mahavira
Vedaranyam	: C.Rajagopalachari
Vrindaban (U.P.)	: Lord Krishna
Vijay Ghat	: Lal Bahadur Shastri

POPULARLY KNOWN AS

Andhra Kesari	: T.Prakasam
Anna	: C.N.Annadurai
Badshah, Frontier Gandhi, Khudaighitmatkar	: Khan Abdul Ghaffar Khan

Bangabandhu	:	Sheikh Mujibur Rahman
Bard of Avon	:	Shakespeare
Chacha	:	Jawaharlal Nehru
C.R.	:	C.Rajagopalachari
Deshbandhu	:	C.R.Das
Desert Fox	:	Gen. Erwin Rommel
Deenbandhu	:	C.F.Andrews
II Duce	:	Benito Mussolini
EL Caudillo	:	Francisco Franco
Enlightened one	:	Mahatma Buddha
Father of the Nation, Bapuji	:	Mahatma Gandhi
Fuehrer	:	Adolf Hitler
Father of English Poetry	:	Geoffery Chaucer
"G.B.S."	:	George Bernard Shah
Gold woman of India	:	P.T. Usha
Grand Oldman of India	:	Dadabhai Naoroji
Grand Oldman of Britain	:	William Ewart Gladstone
Great Commoner	:	Pitt, the Younger
Gurudev	:	R.N.Tagore
Ike	:	Dwight David Eisenhower
Kuvempu	:	K.V.Puttappa
King Maker	:	Earl of Warwickshire
Kipper	:	Field Marshal K.M. Cariappa
Lal, Bal, Pal	:	Lala Lajpat Rai, Bal Gangadhar Tilak & Bipin Chandra Pal
Lok Nayak	:	J.P.Narayan
Lady of the Lamp	:	Florence Nightingale
Lion of Punjab, Punjab Kesari	:	Lala Lajpat Rai
Little Corporal	:	Napoleon
Man of Destiny	:	Napoleon
Lokmanya	:	Bal Gangadhar Tilak
Maiden Queen	:	Elizabeth-I
Maid of Orleans	:	Joan of Arc
Mark Twain	:	Samuel Clemens
Man of Blood and Iron	:	Bismarck
Man of Iron, Strong man of India	:	Sardar Patel
Man of Peace	:	Lal Bahadur Shastri
Netaji	:	Subhas Chandra Bose
Nightingale of India	:	Sarojini Naidu
Sher-j-Kashmir	:	Sheikh Mohammad Abdullah
Saint of the Gutters	:	Mother Teresa
Tiger of Snows	:	Tenzing Norgay
Wizard of the North	:	Sir Walter Scott

SYMBOLS

Black arm band	:	Sign of mourning (protest)
Black flag	:	Protest
A blindfolded woman holding a balanced scale	:	Justice
Dove	:	Peace
Gopuram	:	Symbol of Tamil Nadu Government
Green Light	:	Line clear signal
Red Light	:	Stop, danger or emergency
Lotus	:	Culture and civilisation
Maharaja	:	Air India
Flag flown half-mast	:	National mourning
Flag flown upside down	:	Distress
Olive Branch	:	Peace
Red flag	:	Revolution, danger
Red Cross	:	Hospital
Inverted Red Triangle	:	Family Planning
Stars and stripes (old glory)	:	National Flag of the U.S.A.
Tricolor with chakra	:	National Flag of India
Two bones kept cross in upper quardrant of a skull	:	Danger
Union Jack	:	National Flag of the U.K.
Hammer and Sickle	:	National Flag of USSR
Yellow Flag	:	Sign of carrying infectious person, show on ships
White flag	:	Truce
Wheel	:	Progress

NAMES OF PARLIAMENTS OF SOME IMPORTANT COUNTRIES

Country		Name of Parliament
Afghanistan	:	Hal-o-Aqad (National Assembly)
Albania	:	People's Assembly
Algeria	:	National People's Assembly
Argentina	:	National Congress
Austria	:	Bundesversammlung
Bhutan	:	Tshogdu (National Assembly)
Brazil	:	National Congress
Britain	:	Parliament (House of Commons and House of Lords)
Bulgaria	:	Narodno Subranie (National Assembly)
Canada	:	Parliament (House of Commons and Senate)
China, Mainland	:	National People's Congress
China, National	:	Yuan (National Assembly)

Country	Name of Parliament
Cuba	: National Assembly of People's Power
Denmark	: Folketing
Egypt	: People's Assembly
France	: National Assembly
Germany	: Bundestag (Lower House) and Bundestrat (Upper House)
Hungary	: National Assembly
Iceland	: Althing
India	: Parliament (Lok Sabha and Rajya Sabha)
Iran	: Majis
Israel	: Knesset
Japan	: Diet
Kenya	: National Assembly
Kuwait	: National Assembly
Laos	: People's Supreme Assembly
Malaysia	: Parliament (Dewan Rakyat and Dewan Negara)
Maldives	: Majlis
Nepal	: National Panchayat
The Netherlands	: Staten Generaal
New Zealand	: Parliament (House of Representatives)
Norway	: Storting
Papua New Guinea	: National Parliament
Russia	: Supreme Soviet
Seychelles	: People's Assembly
South Africa	: House of Assembly
Spain	: Cortes
Surinam	: Staten
Sweden	: Riksdag
Turkey	: Grand National Assembly
U.S.A.	: Congress (House of Representatives and Senate)
Venezuela	: National Congress
Vietnam	: National Assembly
Zaire (Democratic Republic of Congo)	: National Legislative Council
Zambia	: National Assembly

INDEPENDENCE DAYS OF VARIOUS COUNTRIES

Country	Date
Afghanistan	: 19th August
Armenia	: 28th May
Australia	: 26th January
Bangladesh	: 16th December
Belgium	: 21st July

Country		Date
Brazil	:	7th September
Canada	:	1st July
China	:	1st October
Chile	:	18th September
Colombia	:	20th July
Finland	:	6th December
France	:	14th July
Greece	:	25th March
India	:	15th August
Indonesia	:	17th August
Israel	:	3rd April
Italy	:	26th March
Japan	:	29th April
Korea	:	15th August
Mexico	:	16th September
Myanmar	:	4th January
Maldives	:	26th July
Norway	:	17th May
Philippines	:	12th June
Peru	:	28th July
Poland	:	3rd May
Portugal	:	10th June
Pakistan	:	14th August
Rwanda	:	4th July
Sri Lanka	:	4th February
Switzerland	:	1st August
Spain	:	10th April
Thailand	:	24th June
Turkey	:	1st November
Uzbekistan	:	1st September
Ukraine	:	24th August
Uganda	:	9th October
U.S.A.	:	4th July
Zimbabwe	:	18th April

OFFICIAL BOOKS AND PAPERS

Blue Book	:	Official report of the Government of United Kingdom
Green Book	:	Official publication of Italy and Iran
Grey Book	:	Official reports of the Japanese and Belgian governments
Orange Book	:	Official publication of Netherlands
Red Book	:	Book banished in a country

White Book	:	Official publication of Germany, China and Portugal
White Paper	:	Short pamphlet giving authoritative recital of facts issued by the Indian government stating its views on a particular issue for the knowledge of general public
Yellow Book	:	Official publication of France

NATIONAL EMBLEMS

Australia	:	Kangaroo
Denmark	:	Beach
India	:	Lioned Capitol
Ivory Coast	:	Elephant
Hong Kong	:	Bauhinia (Orchid tree)
Luxembourg	:	Lion with Crown
Mongolia	:	The Soyombo
New Zealand	:	Southern Cross, Kiwi, Fern
Pakistan	:	Crescent
Spain	:	Eagle
Sri Lanka	:	Lion
Syria	:	Eagle
Turkey	:	Crescent and Star
U.S.A.	:	Golden Rod
Zimbabwe	:	Zimbabwe Bird

FLOWER EMBLEMS

Bangladesh	:	Water Lily	Canada	:	Maple
France	:	Lily	Germany	:	Corn Flower
India	:	Lotus	Ireland	:	Shamrock
Italy	:	White Lily	Japan	:	Chrysanthemum
Scotland	:	Thistle	Spain	:	Pomegranate
United Kingdom	:	Rose	UNO	:	Olive Branch

EPITHETS

Bengal's Sorrow	-	Damodar River
Blue Mountains	-	Nilgiri Hills
Britain of the South	-	New Zealand
City of the Golden Gate	-	San Francisco
City of the Golden Temple	-	Amritsar
City of Dreaming Spires	-	Oxford (UK)
City of Magnificent Distance	-	Washington, D.C.
City of Sky scrapers	-	New York
City of Seven Hills	-	Rome
City of Palaces	-	Kolkata
China's Sorrow	-	Huang-Ho

Cockpit of Europe	-	Belgium
Dark Continent	-	Africa
Eternal City	-	Rome
Emerald Island	-	Ireland
Empire City	-	New York
Forbidden City	-	Lhasa, Tibet
Garden of England	-	Kent, England
Gate of Tears	-	Bab-el-mandab, Jerusalem
Garden City	-	Chicago
Gateway of India	-	Mumbai
Gift of the Nile	-	Egypt
Granite City	-	Aberdeen, Scotland
Great Broad Way	-	New York
Granary of South India	-	Thanjavur
Herring Pond	-	Atlantic Ocean
Hermit Kingdom	-	Korea
Holy Land	-	Palestine
Island Continent	-	Australia
Island of Cloves	-	Zanzibar
Island of Pearls	-	Bahrain
Key of the Mediterannean	-	Gibraltar
Lady with the lamp	-	Florence Nightingale
Land of Cakes	-	Scotland
Land of the Golden Fleece	-	Australia
Land of the Golden Pagoda	-	Myanmar
Land of Kangaroo	-	Australia
Land of Lilies	-	Canada
Land of Morning Calm	-	Korea
Land of Thunderbolt	-	Bhutan
Land of Five Rivers	-	Punjab, India
Land of the Rising Sun	-	Japan
Land of the Midnight Sun	-	Norway
Land of Thousand Lakes	-	Finland
Land of Maples	-	Canada
Land of White Elephants	-	Thailand
Mysore Tiger	-	Tipu Sultan
Manchester of India	-	Mumbai
Manchester of Tamil Nadu	-	Coimbatore
Never Never Land	-	Prairies of N.Australia
Pearl of the Pacific	-	Guyayaquil Port of Ecuador
Playground of Europe	-	Switzerland
Playground of India	-	Kashmir
Pearl of the Antilles	-	Cuba
Pillars of Hercules	-	Gibraltar

Pink City	-	Jaipur
Quaker City	-	Philadelphia, U.S.A
Queen of the Adriatic	-	Venice, Italy
Queen of the Arabian Sea	-	Kochi
Roof of the World	-	Pamirs, Central Asia
Saint of the Gutters	-	Mother Teresa
Sickman of Europe	-	Turkey
Spice Garden of India	-	Kerala
Sugar Bowl of the World	-	Cuba
Venice of the East	-	Alappuzha, India
Venice of the North	-	Stockholm, Sweden
White City	-	Belgrade, Yugoslavia
Windy City	-	Chicago, U.S.A.
White Man's Grave	-	Guinea Coast
World's Bread Basket	-	Prairies of N.America
World's Loneliest Island	-	Tristan da Cunha
Yellow River	-	Huang-Ho

WELL-KNOWN PLACES IN THE WORLD

Place		City / Country
Abu Musa	-	United Arab Emirates
Aswan Dam	-	Egypt
Atlanta	-	USA
Al Aqsa Mosque	-	Jerusalem
Babylon	-	Baghdad
Bangkok	-	Thailand
Barcelona	-	Spain
Beijing	-	China
Berlin Wall	-	Germany
Bethlehem	-	Israel
Brandenburg Gate	-	Berlin
Broadway	-	New York (USA)
Buckingham Palace	-	London (UK)
Caracas	-	Venezuela
Cenotaph	-	London
Clask Air Base	-	Philippines
C.N. Tower	-	Canada
Colosseum	-	Rome
Davos	-	Switzerland
Diego Garcia	-	An Island in Indian Ocean
10, Downing Street	-	England
Eritrea	-	Africa
Eiffel Tower	-	Paris (France)
Empire State Building	-	New York (USA)

Place		City / Country
Fleet Street	-	London
Golan Heights	-	Israel
Genghiskhan Palace	-	Mongolia
Geneva	-	Switzerland
Harley Street	-	London (UK)
Hague	-	The Netherlands
Havana	-	Cuba
Hyde Park	-	London
India House	-	London
Independence Hall	-	Philadelphia (USA)
Jakarta	-	Indonesia
Jerusalem	-	Israel
Karakoram Highway	-	Links Pakistan occupied Kashmir with China
Kaaba	-	Mecca
Kimberley	-	South Africa
Kremlin	-	Moscow
Leh	-	Ladakh (J & K)
Lillehammar	-	Norway
Limassol	-	Cyprus
Lap Nor	-	China
Lords	-	London
Leaning Tower	-	Pisa
Louvre	-	Paris
Male	-	Maldives
Mina	-	Saudi Arabia
Mindona	-	Island, Philippines
Monte Carlo	-	France
Merdeka Palace	-	Jakarta
Nehru Square	-	Russia
Okinawa	-	Japan
Oval	-	London
Pearl Harbour	-	Hawaii
Pentagon	-	Washington
Pisa	-	Italy
Potala	-	Lhasa
Porcelain Tower	-	Nanking
Pyramid	-	Egypt
Red Square	-	Moscow
Scotland Yard	-	London
Shwe Dragon Pagoda	-	Rangoon
Sphynx	-	Egypt
Statue of Liberty	-	New York

Place		City / Country
St. Sophia	-	Constantinople
Vatican	-	Rome
Wailing Wall	-	Jerusalem
Wall Street	-	New York
Waterloo	-	Belgium
Wembley	-	London
Westminster Abbey	-	London
White Hall	-	London
White House	-	Washington
Wimbledon	-	London
Windhoek	-	Namibia
Victoria	-	Canada
Yellowstone	-	U.S.A.

IMPORTANT SITES IN INDIA

Place		City/State
Ajanta Caves	-	Aurangabad (Maharashtra)
Akbar's Tomb	-	Sikandra (Uttar Pradesh)
Ambernath Cave	-	Kashmir (Jammu & Kashmir)
Amber Palace	-	Jaipur (Rajasthan)
Anand Bhavan	-	Allahabad (Uttar Pradesh)
Bhakra Dam	-	Punjab (Punjab)
Birla Planetarium	-	Kolkata (West Bengal)
Black Pagoda	-	Konark (Orissa)
Bodhisattva (Ajanta Caves)	-	Aurangabad (Maharashtra)
Brihadeeswara Temple	-	Thanjavur (Tamil Nadu)
Brindavan Gardens	-	Mysore (Karnataka)
Buland Darwaza	-	Fatehpur Sikri (Uttar Pradesh)
Charminar	-	Hyderabad (Andhra Pradesh)
Chenna Kesava Temple	-	Belur (West Bengal)
Chilka Lake	-	Near Bhubaneswar (Orissa)
Dal Lake	-	Srinagar (Jammu & Kashmir)
Dilwara Temple	-	Mt. Abu (Rajasthan)
Elephanta Caves	-	Mumbai (Maharashtra)
Golden Temple	-	Amritsar (Punjab)
Gol Gumbaz	-	Bijapur (Karnataka)
Hanging Gardens	-	Mumbai (Maharashtra)
Hawa Mahal (Palace of winds)	-	Jaipur (Rajasthan)
Howrah Bridge	-	Kolkata (West Bengal)
Island Palace	-	Udaipur (Rajasthan)
Itmad-ud-Daulah's Tomb	-	Agra (Uttar Pradesh)
Jagannath Temple	-	Puri (Orissa)
Jumma Masjid	-	Delhi (Delhi)

Place		City / State
Jantar Mantar	-	New Delhi (Delhi)
Jog (Gersoppa) Falls	-	Mysore (Karnataka)
Kailasanath Temple	-	Ellora (Maharashtra)
Kanyakumari Temple	-	Kanyakumari (Tamil Nadu)
Khajuraho Temples	-	Bhopal (Madhya Pradesh)
Konarak Temple	-	Puri (Orissa)
Lal Bagh Gardens	-	Bangalore (Karnataka)
Mahakaleeswar Temple	-	Ujjain (Madhya Pradesh)
Mahesuramurthi (Trimurti)	-	Elephanta Caves (Maharashtra)
Malabar Hills	-	Mumbai (Maharashtra)
Manmandir Palace	-	Gwalior Fort (Madhya Pradesh)
Marble Rocks	-	Jabalpur (Madhya Pradesh)
Marina Beach	-	Chennai (Tamil Nadu)
Meenakshi Temple	-	Madurai (Tamil Nadu)
Padmanabha Temple	-	Thiruvananthapuram (Kerala)
Panch Mahal	-	Fatehpur Sikri (Uttar Pradesh)
Tower of Fame	-	Chittorgarh (Rajasthan)
Thiruvalluvar Statue	-	Kanyakumari (Tamil Nadu)
Vivekananda Memorial	-	Kanyakumari (Tamil Nadu)

SANCTUARIES AND PARKS IN INDIA

Name	Location	Reserve for
Achanakmar Sanctuary	Bilaspur, Chattisgarh	Tiger, bear, chital, sambar, bison
Bandipur Sanctuary	Border of Karnataka and Tamil Nadu	Elephant, tigers, panther, sambar, deer, birds
Bondla Wildlife Sanctuary & Salim Ali Birds Sanctuary	Goa	Elephant, gaur, deer, squirrel, chital, fowl, partridge etc.
Borivli National Park	Varanashi (Uttarakhand)	Panther, sambar, langur, wild boar, chinkara
Chandraprabha Sanctuary	Near Varanasi Uttar Pradesh	Famous for Gir lions, chital and sambar
Corbett National Park	Nainital, Uttarakhand	Tiger, leopards, elephants, sambar named in memory of Jim Corbett, famous sportsman
Dachigam Sanctuary	Dachigam, Kashmir	Kashmiri stag
Dudhwa National Park	Lakhimpurkheri U.P.	Tiger, panther, sambar, chital, nilgai, barking deer
Gandhi Sagar Sanctuary	Mandsaur, M.P.	Chital, sambar, chinkara, barking deer, wild birds

Name	Location	Reserve for
Ghana Bird Sanctuary	Bharatpur, Rajasthan	Water birds, black-buck, chital, sambar
Gir Forest	Junagarh, Gujarat	India's biggest wildlife sanctuary famous for Gir lions
Hazaribagh Sanctuary	Hazaribagh, Jharkhand	Tiger, leopard, chital, nilgai, sambar, wild cat
Jaldapara Sanctuary	West Bengal	Rhinoceros
Kangerghat National Park	Chhattisgarh	Tiger, barasingha, chital, sambar deer, nilgai.
Kaziranga National Park	Jorhat, Assam	Horned rhinoceros, gaur, elephant, leopard, wild buffalo
Nawegaon National Park	Bhandara, Maharashtra	Tiger, panther, sambar, chital, nilgai
Orang Sanctuary	Assam	Buffalow, elephant, gaur, sambar, python, pelican
Pachmarhi Sanctuary	Hoshangabad, M.P.	Tiger, panther, bear, sambar, nilgai, barking deer
Pakhal Sanctuary	Warangal, A.P.	Tiger, panther, sambar, chital, nilgai
Parambikulam Sanctuary	Palghat, Kerala	Tiger, leopard, gaur, elephant, nilgai, chital
Periyar Sanctuary	Idukki, Kerala	Elephant, tiger, panther, gaur, nilgai, sambar, wild bear
Ranganthittoo Bird Sanctuary	Mysore, Karnataka	Important bird sanctuary
Rohla National Park	Kulu, H.P.	Snow leopard, brown bear, musk deer, snow cock, snow pigeon
Sharaswathy Valley Sanctuary	Shimoga, Karnataka	Elephant, tiger, panther, sambar, gaur, chital, wild bear
Shikari Devi Sanctuary	Mandi, H.P.	Black bear, musk deer, panther, leopard, partridge
Shivpuri National Park	Shivpuri, M.P.	Tiger, panther, sambar, hyena, sloth bear, nilgai
Sunderban Tiger Reserve	South 24 parganas, West Bengal	Tiger, deer, wild boar, crocodile, Gangetic dolphin
Tadoba National Park	Chandrapur, Maharashtra	Tiger, panther, sambar, nilgai, chinkara, chital
Tungabhadra Sanctuary	Bellary, Karnataka	Panther, chital, sloth bear, four-horned antelope
Ushakothi Wildlife Sanctuary and Nandan Khanan Tiger Reserve	Orissa	White Tiger, chital, gaur, elephant, pelicans, flamingoes, deer.
Vedanthangal Bird Sanctuary	Tamil Nadu	Important bird sanctuary

Name	Location	Reserve for
Waynad Sanctuary	Cannanore and Kozhikode, Kerala	Elephant, gaur, sambar, chital, wild boar, deer
Wild Ass Sanctuary	Little Rann of Kutch, Gujarat	Wild ass, wolf, nilgai, chinkara

MAJOR PORTS IN INDIA

Major port is one which is capable of accommodating ocean going steamers of a tonnage of 4000 or more and those steamers carrying a minimum trade of 50,00,000 tonnes annually. The port must have sheltered nature, broadly laid-out channels, docking facilities, transit sheds, railway connections and ability to serve the needs of the hinterland. It must also have facility for satisfying defence requirements. It must be an all-weather port. India ranks 16th in the world in terms of shipping tonnage.

There are Twelve Major Ports in India

Western Coasts
Mumbai (Maharashtra)
Kandla (Gujarat)
New Mangalore (Karnataka)
Nhava Sheva (Maharashtra)
Kochi (Kerala)
Mormugao (Goa)

Eastern Coasts
Kolkata (West Bengal)
Paradeep (Orissa)
Visakhapatnam (Andhra Pradesh)
Tuticorin (Tamil Nadu)
Chennai (Tamil Nadu)
Ennore (Chennai)

Our Constitution says that the responsibility for major ports vests with the Central Government while all the other ports are in the executive jurisdiction of State Governments.

HILL STATIONS IN INDIA

Almora (Kumaon hills)	-	Uttarakhand
Cherrapunji (Shillong)	-	Meghalaya
Coonoor (Nilgiri hills)	-	Tamil Nadu
Dalhousie	-	Himachal Pradesh
Darjeeling	-	West Bengal
Gulmarg	-	Kashmir (Highest)
Kasauli (Shimla)	-	Himachal Pradesh
Kodaikanal	-	Tamil Nadu
Mahabaleshwar	-	Maharashtra
Mt. Abu	-	Rajasthan
Mussoorie	-	Uttarakhand
Nainital	-	Uttarakhand
Pachmarhi	-	Madhya Pradesh
Ranchi	-	Jharkhand
Shillong (Khasi hills)	-	Meghalaya
Shimla	-	Himachal Pradesh
Srinagar	-	Jammu & Kashmir
Udhagamandalam (Ooty)	-	Tamil Nadu
Yercaud	-	Tamil Nadu

WORLD'S HIGHEST MOUNTAIN PEAKS

Name	Height (in metres)
Asia	
Mt.Everest (Himalaya-Nepal/Tibet)	- 8,848
K2 (Mt.Godwin Austen) (Karakoram-India)	- 8,611
Kanchenjunga (Himalaya-India/Nepal)	- 8,597
Lhotse (Himalaya-Nepal-China)	- 8,501
Makalu I (Himalaya-Nepal)	- 8,470
Dhaulagiri (Himalaya-Nepal)	- 8,172
Nanga Parbat (Himalaya-Nepal)	- 8,126
Gasherbrum I (Karakoram-India)	- 8,068
Gosainthan (Himalaya-Tibet)	- 8,013
Nanda Devi (Himalaya-India)	- 7,817
South America	
Aconcagua (Andes-Argentina)	- 6,959
North America	
Mount McKinley (Alaska-USA)	- 6,194
Africa	
Kilimanjaro (Kenya-Tanzania)	- 5,895
Europe	
Mount Elbrus (Caucasus-Russia)	- 5,642
Mont Blanc (Alps-France)	- 4,807
Antartica	
Vinson Massif (Ellsworth Mountains)	- 5,140
Oceania	
Caestensz (Nassau Range-New Guinea)	- 5,000

HEIGHTS OF SOME IMPORTANT INDIAN PEAKS

	Peak		Height (in metres)
1.	K2	-	8,611 In Pak occupied territory
2.	Kanchenjunga	-	8,597
3.	Nanga Parbat	-	8,126 In Pak occupied territory
4.	Gasherbrum I	-	8,068 -do-
5.	Broad - highest	-	8,047 -do-
6.	Disteghil Sar	-	7,885
7.	Masherbrum E	-	7,821 -do-
8.	Nanda Devi	-	7,817
9.	MasherBrum W	-	7,806 In Pak occupied territory
10.	Rakaposhi	-	7,788 -do-
11.	Kamet	-	7,756
12.	Saser Kangri	-	7,672
13.	Skyang Kangri	-	7,544 In Pak occupied territory
14.	Sia Kangri	-	7,422 -do-
15.	Chaukhamba (Badrinath Peak)	-	7,138 -do-

Peak	Height (in metres)
16. Trisul West	- 7,138
17. Nunkun	- 7,135
18. Pauhunri	- 7,128
19. Kangto	- 7,090
20. Dunagiri	- 7,066

WORLD'S LONGEST RIVERS

River	Length (in km)
Nile (Egypt)	- 6,690
Amazon (Brazil)	- 6,570
Mississippi-Missouri (USA)	- 6,020
Chang Jiang (China)	- 5,980
Yenisey (Russia)	- 5,870
Amur (Russia)	- 5,780
Ob-Irtysh (Russia)	- 5,410
Plata (Argentina/Uruguay)	- 4,880
Huang Ho (Chinna)	- 4,840
Congo (Angola-Zaire)	- 4,630
Lena (Russia)	- 4,400
Mackenzie (Canada)	- 4,240
Mekong (Vietnam)	- 4,180
Niger (Nigeria)	- 4,100

LENGTHS OF SOME IMPORTANT INDIAN RIVERS

River	Length (in km)
1. Indus	- 3,000
2. Brahmaputra	- 2,900
3. Ganga	- 2,540
4. Godavari	- 1,450
5. Narmada	- 1,290
6. Krishna	- 1,290
7. Mahanadi	- 890
8. Cauvery	- 760

HIGHEST WATERFALLS

Name	Location	River	Height in metres
Angel	Venezuela	Tributary of Caroni	972
Tugela	Natal, South Africa	Tugela	914
Cuguenan	Venezuela	Cuguenan	610
Sutherland	New Zealand	Arthur	580
Takkakaw	British Columbia	Tributary of Yoho	503
Ribbon (Yosemite)	California	Yosemate Greek	491
Upper (Yosemite)	California	Tributary of Merced	436
Gavernic	France	Gavadepan	422
Vettisfoss	Norway	Morkedola	366
Widow's Tears (Yosemite)	California	Tributary of Merced	357

LARGEST ISLANDS

Island	Location and Status	Area in sq.km.
Greenland	North Atlantic (Danish)	2,131,600
New Guinea	Southwest Pacific (Irian Jaya, Indonesian, west part; Papua New Guinea, east part)	790,000
Borneo	West mid-Pacific (Indonesian, south part; British protectorate, and Malaysian, north part)	737,000
Madagascar	Indian Ocean (Malagasy Republic)	587,000
Baffin	North Atlantic (Canadian)	507,000
Sumatra	Northeast Indian Ocean (Indonesian)	473,600
Honshu	Sea of Japan—Pacific (Japanese)	228,000
Great Britain	Off coast North-west Europe (England, Scotland and Wales)	219,000
Vancouver I	North Atlantic (Canada)	217,300
Ellesmere	Arctic Ocean (Canadian)	196,000
Sulawesi (Celebes)	West mid-Pacific (Indonesian)	174,000
South Island	South Pacific (New Zealand)	151,000
Java	Indian Ocean (Indonesian)	129,000
North Island	South Pacific (New Zealand)	114,000
New Foundland	North Atlantic (Canadian)	109,000
Cuba	Caribbean Sea (Republic)	105,000
Luzon	West mid-Pacific (Phillippines)	105,000
Iceland	North Atlantic (Republic)	103,000
Mindanao	West mid-Pacific (Phillippines)	94,600
Novaya-Zemlya	Arctic Ocean (Russia)	90,600
Ireland	West of Great Britain (republic, south part; United Kingdom, north part)	84,100
Hokkaido	Sea of Japan—Pacific (Japanese)	78,500
Hispaniola	Caribbean Sea (Dominican Republic, east part; Haiti, west part)	77,200
Sakhalin (Karafuto)	North of Japan (Russia)	75,100
Tierra del Fuego	Southern tip of South America (Argentinian, east part; Chilean, west part)	71,200
Tasmania	South of Australia (Australian)	67,900
Sri Lanka (Ceylon)	Indian Ocean (Republic)	65,610
Kyushu	Sea of Japan—Pacific (Japanese)	42,084

LARGEST LAKES

Name	Location	Area in sq. km
Caspian Sea	Iran/Russia	3,71,000
Superior	USA/Canada	82,260
Victoria	East Africa	62,940
Aral Sea	Kazakhstan	62,000
Huron	USA/Canada	59,580

Name	Location	Area in sq. km
Michigan	USA	58,020
Tanganyika	East Africa	32,000
Baikal	Russia	31,500
Great Bear	Canada	31,330
Nyasa	Malavi, Mozambique and Tanzania	30,044
Great Slave	Canada	28,570
Erie	USA/Canada	25,710
Winnipeg	Canada	24,390
Malawi/Nyasa	East Africa	22,490
Balkhash	Kazakhstan	17,000-22,000
Ontario	Canada	19,270
Ladoga	Russia	18,130
Chad	West Africa	10,000-26,000
Maracaibo	Venezuela	13,010
Patos	Brazil	10,140
Onega	Russia	9,800
Rudolf	Kenya	9,100
Eyre	Australia	8,800
Titicaca	Peru/Bolivia	8,300

LARGEST DESERTS

Name	Approximate area in sq.km.	Territories
Sahara	8,600,000	Algeria, Chad Libya, Mali, Mauritiania, Niger, Sudan, Tunisia, Egypt, Morocco. Embraces the Libyan Desert (1,550,000 sq.km.) and the Nubian Desert (260,00 sq.km.)
Australian Desert	1,550,000	Australia, Embraces the Great Sandy (or) Warburton (420,000 sq.km.) Great Victoria (325,000 sq.km.) Simpson (310,000 sq.km.) Gibson (220,000 sq.km.) and sturt desert.
Arabian Desert	1,300,000	Southern Arabia, Saudi Arabia, Yemen, includes the Ar Rab'al Khale or Empty Quarter (647,500 sq.km.) Syrian (325,000 sq.km.) and An Nafud (129,000 sq.km.)
Gobi	1,166,000	Mongolia and China
Patagonian	673,000	Argentina
Kalahari	520,000	Botswana
Great Basin	492,000	SW USA
Chihnahuan	450,000	Maxico

Name	Approximate area in sq.km.	Territories
Great Sandy	450,000	NW Australia
Great Victoria	325,000	SW Australia
Takla Makam	320,000	Sinkiang, China
Sonoran	310,000	Arizona & California, USA and Mexico
Kyzl-Kum	300,000	Uzbekistan-Kazhakstan, Russia
Kara-Kum	260,000	Turkmenistan
Kavir	260,000	Iran
Syrian	260,000	Saudi Arabia/Jordan/Syria/Iraq
Nubian	260,000	Sudan
Thar Desert	200,000	North Western India and Pakistan

OCEANS OF THE WORLD

Name	Area (sq.km)	Greatest known depth in metres	Place of greatest known depth
Pacific	18,13,00,000	11,776	Marianas Trench
Atlantic	8,22,17,000	8,648	Puerto Rico Trench
Indian	7,34,26,000	7,725	Java Trench
Arctic	1,39,86,000	5,122	Eurasia Basin

LARGEST SEAS

Name	Area (in km)
Coral Sea	4,791,000
Arabian Sea	3,863,000
South China (Nan) Sea	3,685,000
Caribbean Sea	2,515,000
Mediterranean Sea	2,510,000
Bering Sea	2,304,000
Bay of Bengal	2,172,000
Sea of Okhotsk	1,590,000
Gulf of Mexico	1,543,000
Gulf of Guinea	1,533,000
Barents Sea	1,405,000
Norwegian Sea	1,383,000
Gulf of Alaska	1,327,000
Hudson Bay	1,232,000
Greenland Sea	1,205,000
Arafura Sea	1,037,000
Philippine Sea	1,036,000
Sea of Japan	978,000
East Siberian Sea	901,000
Kara Sea	883,000

Name	Area (in km)
East China Sea	664,000
Andaman Sea	565,000
North Sea	520,000
Black Sea	508,000
Red Sea	453,000
Baltic Sea	414,000
Celebes Sea	280,000
Persian Gulf	240,000
St.Lawrence Gulf	238,300

SEVEN CONTINENTS OF THE WORLD

Name	Area in sq.km	Approx. % of the world's land
Asia	44,493,000	29.6
Africa	30,293,000	20.2
N. America	24,454,000	16.3
S. America	17,838,000	11.9
Antarctica	13,975,000	9.3
Europe	10,245,000	6.7
Oceania	8,945,000	6.0

SEVEN WONDERS OF THE ANCIENT WORLD

The Pyramids of Egypt
The Temple of Diana at Ephesus
The Tomb of Mausolus at Halicarnassus
The Pharos of Alexandria.
The Hanging Gardens of Babylon
The Statue of Zeus at Olympia
The Colossus at Rhodes

SEVEN WONDERS OF THE MEDIEVAL WORLD

The Colosseum of Rome
The Great Wall of China
The Porcelain Tower of Nanking
The Mosque of St.Sophia (Constantinople)
The Stonehenge of England
The Catacombs of Alexandria
The Leaning Tower of Pisa

NEW SEVEN WONDERS OF THE WORLD

The Great Wall of China
The Pink Ruins of Petra in Jordan
The Statue of Christ the Redeemer
   in Rio de Janeiro
Incan Ruins of Machu Picchu
The Ancient Mayan City of
   Chicken Itza in Mexico
The Colosseum in Rome
The Taj Mahal in India

IMPORTANT DAYS

Pravasi Bharatiya Day .... January 9
World Laughter Day .... January 10
National Youth Day .... January 12

Army Day	January 15
Desh Prem Diwas / Patriotism Day	January 23
Indian Tourism Day / International Excise Day	January 25
Republic Day / International Customs Day	January 26
Republic Day & World Leprosy Day	January 26
Martyrs' Day	January 30
World Wetland Day	February 2
Valentine's Day	February 14
National Science Day	February 28
International Women's Day & Literacy Day	March 8
World Consumers Rights Day & World Disabled Day	March 15
International Day for the Elimination of Racial Discrimination	March 21
World Forestry Day	March 21
World Day for Water	March 22
World Meteorolcgical Day	March 23
World TB Day	March 24
Bangladesh Day	March 26
National Maritime Day & Samta Diwas	April 5
World Health Day	April 7
Water Resources Day	April 10
World Aviation and Cosmonautics Day	April 12
World Haemophilia Day	April 17
World Heritage Day	April 18
Earth Day	April 22
World Book & Copyright Day	April 23
Manav Ekta Divas	April 24
May Day (Workers' Day; International Labour Day)	May 1
World Press Freedom Day	May 3
World Red Cross Day & V-E Day	May 8
National Solidarity Day	May 13
International Day of Families	May 15
World Telecommunication Day	May 17
Anti-terrorism Day	May 21
Commonwealth Day	May 24
No-Tobacco Day	May 31
International Day of Innocent Children Victims of Aggression	June 4
World Environment Day	June 5
World Blood Donar Day	June 14
UN Charter Signing Day	June 25
International Day Against Drug Abuse and Illicit Trafficking	June 26
World Diabates Day	June 27
World Population Day	July 11
Breast Feeding Week	August 1-7
International Friendship Day	August 3
National Friendship Day	August 7
Hiroshima Day	August 6

Nagasaki Day & Quit India Day	August 9
Independence Day	August 15
Sadhbhavana Divas	August 20
National Sports Day	August 29
Teachers' Day	September 5
International Literacy Day	September 8
World Ozone Day	September 16
World Tourism Day	September 27
International Day for the Elderly	October 1
World Vegetarian Day & World Animal Day	October 2
World Habitat Day	October 3
World Animal Welfare Day	October 4
International Day for Natural Disaster Reduction	October 7
Air Force Day	October 8
World Post Office Day	October 9
World Standards Day	October 14
World Food Day	October 16
Police Commemoration Day	October 21
UN Day	October 24
World Literary Day	October 27
World Thrift Day	October 30
National Integration Day & Rededication Day	October 31
Children's Day	November 14
Sappers' Day	November 18
Citizens Day	November 19
World AIDS day	December 1
International Day of Disabled Persons	December 3
Navy Day	December 4
International Volunteer Day for Economic and Social Development	Dec. 5
Flag Day	December 7
Human Rights Day (UN)	December 10
Kisan's Day	December 23

INDIAN TOWNS ON RIVERS

Town	River	Town	River
Agra	- Yamuna	Ahmedabad	- Sabarmati
Allahabad	- Confluence of Ganges, Yamuna and the Mythical Saraswathi		
Ayodhya	- Sarayu	Badrinath	- Alakanda
Kolkata	- Hooghly	Cuttack	- Mahanadi
Delhi	- Yamuna	Dibrugarh	- Brahmaputra
Ferozepur	- Sutlej	Guwahati	- Brahmaputra

Town	River	Town	River
Haridwar	- Ganga	Hyderabad	- Musi
Jabalpur	- Narmada	Kanpur	- Ganga
Kotah	- Chambal	Kurnool	- Tungabhadra
Ludhiana	- Sutlej	Leh	- Indus
Madurai	- Vaigai	Lucknow	- Gomti
Patna	- Ganga/Sone	Nasik	- Godavari
Srirangapatnam	- Cauvery	Sambalpur	- Mahanadi
Surat	- Tapti	Srinagar	- Jhelum
Tiruchirapalli	- Cauvery	Thanjavur	- Cauvery
Varanasi	- Ganga	Tirunelveli	- Tamraparani
Vijayawada	- Krishna		

FOREIGN TOWNS ON RIVERS

Town	River	Town	River
Akyab	- Kaladan	Antwerp	- Scheldt
Baghdad	- Tigris	Bangkok	- Menam
Basra	- Shatt-al-arab	Belgrade	- Danube
Berlin	- Spree	Bonn	- Rhine
Bristol	- Avon	Brussels	- Seine
Budapest	- Danube	Buenos Aires	- La Plater
Cairo	- Nile	Canton	- Chaton
Chittagong	- Karnafuli	Chungking	- Yangtze-Kiang
Cologne	- Rhine	Dublin	- Liffey
Dresden	- Elbe	Dundee	- Tay
Gdansk	- Vistula	Glasgow	- Clyde
Hamburg	- Elbe	Hankow	- Yangtze
Hull	- Humber	Kabul	- Kabul
Karachi	- Sindh	Khartoum	- Nile
Lahore	- Ravi	Lisbon	- Tagus
Liverpool	- Mersey	London	- Thames
Madrid	- Manzaneres	Montreal	- St. Lawrence
Moscow	- Moskva	Moulmein	- Salween
Nanking	- Yangtze-Kiang	New Castle	- Tyne
New Orleans	- Mississippi	New York	- Hudson
Ottawa	- Ottawa	Philadelphia	- Delaware
Prague	- Vltava (Moldan)	Paris	- Siene
Quebec	- St. Lawrence	Rangoon	- Irrawaddy
Rome	- Tiber	Rotterdam	- New Maas
Shanghai	- Yangtze-Kiang	St. Louis	- Mississippi
Sydney	- Darling	Tokyo	- Arakawa
Vienna	- Danube	Warsaw	- Vistuala
Washington	- Potomac	Alexandria	- Nile

FOREIGN TOWNS AND INDUSTRIES

Town	Country	Industry
Abadan	Iran	Oil refineries
Aberdeen	Scotland (UK)	Granite mining
Baku	Azerbaijan	Petroleum
Bangkok	Thailand	Shipping
Belfast	N. Ireland (Ulster)	Ship-building, linen
Buenos Aires	Argentina	Dairy products
Cadiz	Spain	Cork
Chicago	USA	Gramophone, agricultural implements, meat products
Detroit	USA	Automobiles
Dhaka	Bangladesh	Jute
Dresden	Germany	Optical and photographic instruments
Dundee (World First Jute Industry)	Scotland (UK)	Jute, linen
Essex	England (UK)	Engineering works
Geneva	Switzerland	Watches
Glasgow	Scotland (UK)	Machinery, Textiles
Havana	Cuba	Cigars, Sugar
Hollywood	USA	Films
Johannesbourg	South Africa	Gold mines
Kansas	USA	Meat packing
Leeds	England (UK)	Woollen garments
Los Angeles	USA	Films, Oil mining
Lyons	France	Silk
Melbourne	Australia	Chocolate
Milan	Italy	Silk
New Orleans	USA	Cotton
Northampton	UK	Leather goods
Oporto	Portugal	Wine
Oslo	Norway	Paper
Ottawa	Canada	Paper
Pittsburgh	USA	Iron and Steel
Plymouth	England (UK)	Ship-building
Port Louis	Mauritius	Sugar
Rotterdam	Netherlands	Ship-building
Sheffield	England (UK)	Cutlery
Teheran	Iran	Carpets
Tokyo	Japan	Rayon and Textiles
Venice	Italy	Glass
Vienna	Austria	Glass
Wellington	New Zealand	Dairy products
Yenang Yaung	Myanmar	Oil fields

LARGEST PRODUCERS

Product	Country
Aluminium	Australia, Jamaica
Carpets	Afghanistan, Iran
Coal	Russia, U.S.A.
Copper	Chile, U.S.A.
Electric Bulbs	England, U.S.A.
Gold	South Africa, Australia
Ilmenite	India
Iron ore	U.S.A., Russia
Manganese	Ukraine, India
Petroleum	U.S.A., Venezuela
Plastic goods	U.K., U.S.A.
Rubber	Thailand, Indonesia
Silver	Mexico, Canada
Steel	U.S.A.
Tin	Malaysia, Brazil

MINERALS IN INDIA - STATE FIRSTS

Mineral	States	Mineral	States
Iron Ore	Jharkhand, Orissa	Bauxite	Jharkhand, M.P.
Copper	Jharkhand, MP, Rajasthan	Gold	Karnataka, A.P.
Lead	A.P., Orissa	Zinc	Rajasthan, Gujarat
Manganese	Orissa, Karnataka, M.P.	Mica	Jharkhand, Bihar, A.P.
Limestone	Madhyapradesh, Chhattisgarh	Marble	Rajasthan
Granite	Tamilnadu, Karnataka	Gypsum	Rajasthan, Tamilnadu
Nickel	Orissa, Jharkhand, Tamilnadu	Silver	Karnataka, Rajasthan,
Antimony	Punjab, Karnataka		Jharkhand, Tamilnadu
Asbestos	A.P., Jharkhand	Barytes	A.P., Maharashtra
Chromite	A.P., Jharkhand	Dolomite	M.P. Chhattisgarh
Graphite	Orissa, A.P., Tamilnadu	Sulphur	Tamilnadu
Tin	Bihar, Jharkhand	Thorium	Kerala, Tamilnadu, A.P.
Uranium	Jharkhand, M.P.	Beryllium	Rajasthan, Jharkhand, T.N.
Ilmenite	Tamilnadu, Kerala	Magnesite	Tamilnadu, H.P.
Rock Phosphate	M.P., Rajasthan, U.P.	Salt	Gujarat, Rajasthan
Coal	Jharkhand, West Bengal,	Lignite	Tamilnadu (Neyveli)
	M.P., A.P.		Jammu & Kashmir
Petroleum	Assam, Gujarat	Diamond	M.P., A.P., Karnataka

INDIA'S CURRENT SITUATION IN THE WORLD LEVEL ON VARIOUS ASPECTS

1. India has the largest mileage of canals in the world.
2. Possesses the world record in per hectare yield of wheat. Producing about 3000 kgs.
3. Ranks second in world's coconut production - the first being Philippines.
4. World's second biggest producer of silk - the first being China.

5. Ranks first in the production of milk and milk products.
6. World's second place in prawn (shrimp) fishing - the first being China.
7. India is in the second place in Tobacco production - the first being U.S.A.
8. India is in the first place in wheat production surpassing U.S.A.
9. More than half of the world's tea comes from India alone.
10. Third largest producer of castor in the world.
11. More than half of the groundnut area and production is from India alone.
12. Second largest producer of rice and cotton yarn.
13. More than one-third of the world sugarcane area is in India.
14. India is in the fourth place in cotton production.
15. India has one-sixth of the world population of sheep.
16. With regard to area, India is the 7th largest country in the world.
17. Represents 4th place in fish catching while Japan leads the world.
18. India ranks 17th among countries of the world in shipping tonnage.
19. India ranks second in population.
20. India ranks first in postal network.

CHIEF CROPS PRODUCING COUNTRIES

1. Rice	- China, India	2. Wheat	- China, India
3. Maize	- USA, China	4. Millets	- India, Nigeria
5. Barley	- Russia, Canada	6. Groundnut	- India
7. Soyabeans	- USA, China	8. Mustard &	
9. Coconut	- Phillipines, India	Castor	- India, Brazil
10. Linseed Oil	- Argentina, Canada	11. Tea	- India, China
12. Coffee	- Brazil, Columbia	13. Cocoa	- Ghana, Nigeria
14. Sugarcane	- India, Brazil	15. Sugarbeat	- Ukraine, France
16. Tobacco	- China, USA	17. Rubber	- Thailand, Indonesia
18. Cotton	- China, USA	19. Jute	- India, Bangladesh
20. Flax	- Russia, Baltic Countries	21. Hemp	- Russia, Ukraine
		22. Silk	- China, India, Japan
23. Grapes	- Italy, France	24. Banana	- India, Philippines
25. Mangoes	- India, Pakistan	26. Apples	- China, France, Italy
27. Pineapples	- Thailand, Philippines	28. Cloves	- Islands of Zemba, Zansibar
29. Pepper	- Malaysia, India	30. Potatoes	- China, Russia
31. Cork	- Spain	32. Olives	- Italy, Spain
33. Peaches	- Spain		

CHIEF CROPS PRODUCING STATES IN INDIA

1.	Bajra	-	Rajasthan, Gujarat
2.	Barley	-	Uttar Pradesh
3.	Betelnut	-	West Bengal
4.	Cardamom	-	Karnataka

5.	Cashewnut	-	Kerala
6.	Chillies	-	Maharashtra, Andhra Pradesh
7.	Cinchona	-	Tamil Nadu
8.	Cloves	-	Kerala
9.	Coffee	-	Karnataka
10.	Coriander	-	Rajasthan
11.	Cotton	-	Gujarat, Maharashtra
12.	Cotton Seeds	-	Maharashtra
13.	Gram & Pulses	-	Madhya Pradesh
14.	Groundnut	-	Gujarat
15.	Hemp	-	Chattisgarh, Madhya Pradesh
16.	Jowar	-	Maharashtra
17.	Jute	-	West Bengal, Bihar
18.	Linseed	-	Chattisgarh
19.	Mango	-	Uttar Pradesh
20.	Maize	-	Uttar Pradesh
21.	Mustard	-	Rajasthan
22.	Onion	-	Maharashtra
23.	Opium	-	Uttar Pradesh
24.	Pepper	-	Kerala
25.	Ragi	-	Karnataka
26.	Rapeseed	-	Rajasthan
27.	Rice	-	West Bengal, Andhra Pradesh
28.	Rubber	-	Kerala
29.	Sandalwood	-	Karnataka
30.	Silk	-	Karnataka
31.	Sugarcane	-	Uttar Pradesh, Maharashtra
32.	Tapioca	-	Kerala, Tamil Nadu
33.	Tea	-	Assam, West Bengal
34.	Tobacco	-	Gujarat, Andhra Pradesh
35.	Turmeric	-	Andhra Pradesh, Orissa
36.	Wheat	-	Uttar Pradesh, Punjab
37.	Saffaron	-	Jammu Kashmir
38.	Coconut	-	Kerala, Tamil Nadu

MAJOR IRRIGATION AND MULTI-PURPOSE PROJECTS

	Project	State	Rivers
1.	Nagarjuna	Andhra, Karnataka	Krishna
2.	Tungabhadra	Karnataka	Tungabhadra
3.	Pochampad	Andhra Pradesh	Godavari
4.	Gandak	Bihar, U.P.	Gandak
5.	Kosi	Bihar	Kosi
6.	Kakrapara	Gujarat	Tapti
7.	Ukai	Gujarat	Tapti
8.	Mahi	Gujarat	Mahi

	Project	State	Rivers
9.	Bhadra	Karnataka	Bhadra
10.	Upper Krishna	Karnataka	Krishna
11.	Ghataprabha	Karnataka	Ghataprabha
12.	Malaprabha	Karnataka	Malaprabha
13.	Tawa	Madhya Pradesh	Tawa
14.	Chambal	Madhya Pradesh, Rajasthan	Gandhi Sagar Dam, Rana Pratap Sagar Dam, Jawahar Sagar Dam
15.	Bhima	Maharashtra	Pawana, Krishna
16.	Jayakwadi	Maharashtra	Godavari
17.	Hirakud	Orissa	Mahanadi
18.	Bhakra Nangal	Punjab, Haryana, Rajasthan	Sutlej
19.	Mahanadi Delta	Orissa	Mahanadi
20.	Beas	Punjab, Haryana, Rajasthan	Beas, Sutlej
21.	Parambikulam Aliyar	Tamil Nadu, Kerala	Aliyar
22.	Sarda Sahayak	Uttar Pradesh	Sarda, Ghagra
23.	Ramganga	Uttar Pradesh	Ganga
24.	Farakka	West Bengal	Bhagirathi, Ganga
25.	Mayurakshi	West Bengal	Mayurakshi
26.	Kangsabati	West Bengal	Kangsabati, Kumari
27.	Damodar Valley	West Bengal, Bihar	Damodar

FIRSTS IN THE WORLD AND IN INDIA

Biggest Library	United States Library of Congress, Washington, D.C.
Biggest Museum	American Museum of Natural History, New York
Biggest Hotel	The Excalibur Hotel (Las Vegas), Nevada (USA)
Biggest Auditorium	Municipal Auditorium (Atlanta)
Brightest Star	Sirius A (Dog Star)
Biggest Planet	Jupiter
Brightest Planet	Venus
Biggest Palace	Vatican Palace
Biggest Park	Yellow Stone National Park (USA)
Biggest Waterfall	Boyoma (formerly Stanley Falls) (D.R. of Congo)
Biggest Dome	Gol Gumbaz (India)
Biggest Dam (in India)	Bhakra Dam
Biggest Dam (in the world)	Grand Coulee Dam on Columbia River (U.S.A.)
Biggest Ocean	Pacific
Biggest City (in population)	Tokyo (Japan)
Biggest Cinema House	Roxy (New York)
Biggest Telescope	Mt.Semirodriki (Russia)
Country with Largest Electorate	India

Coldest Place	Verkhoyansk (Russia) –85°C
Driest Place	Death Valley (California) (rainfall 1/2 inch)
Deepest Lake	Baikal (Eastern Syberia, Russia)
Fastest Airliner	Concord
Fastest Animal	Cheetah
Fastest Bird	Swift, Falcon
Fastest Train	Japan's mono rail (Nearly 900 kmph)
Farthest Planet	Pluto (Now Neptune)
Highest Volcano	Ojos de Salado (Argentina-Chile)
Highest Plateau	Pamirs
Highest Mountain Peak	Mt.Everest (Nepal)
Highest Rainfall (in India)	Mawsynrnam (Meghalaya)
Highest Rainfall (in World)	Mt. Waialeala (Hawaii)
Highest Waterfall	Salto Angel Falls (Venezuela)
Highest City	Wenchuan (China)
Hottest Place	Al' Azizia 136°F (Libya)
Largest Airline	Aeroflot (Russia)
Largest Airport	King Khalid International Airport (Saudi Arabia)
Largest Land Animal	African Elephant
Largest Archipelago	Indonesia
Largest Archway	Sydney Harbour Bridge (Australia)
Largest Artificial Lake	Owen Falls (Uganda)
Largest Balloon	Explorer II (USA)
Largest Church	Basilica of St.Peter (Vatican City, Rome)
Largest Clock	Big Ben
Largest Continent	Asia
Largest Country (in population)	China
Largest Country (in area)	Russia
Largest Delta	Sunderbans (8000 sq.miles)
Largest Desert	Sahara (N.Africa)
Largest Desert (in Asia)	Gobi (Mongolia)
Largest Desert (in India)	Thar
Largest Diamond	The Cullinan
Largest Diamond Mine	Kimberley (S.Africa)
Largest Gorge	Grand Canyon (USA)
Largest Forest	Coniferous Forest (Northern Russia)
Largest Fresh Water Lake	Lake Superior (North America)
Largest Gulf	Gulf of Mexico
Largest Island	Greenland (renamed Kalaadit Nunaat)
Largest Inland Sea	Mediterranean Sea
Largest Peninsula	Arabia (3,250,000 sq.km.)
Largest Sea Bird	Albatross
Largest Sea Port	Port of New York and New Jersey
Largest Stadium	Strahov Stadium (Prague, Czech Republic)
Largest Volcano	Mauna Loa
Longest Corridor	Rameswaram Temple (India) 4000 ft
Longest Thorough fare	Broadway (New York)

Longest Non-Stop Train	Flying Scotsman
Longest Road	Grand Trunk Road
Longest Road Tunnel	Laerdal Road Tunnel (Norway, 24.51 km)
Longest Railway Tunnel	Seikan Rail Tunnel (Japan, 53.85 km)
Longest Swimming Canal	English Canal
Longest Railway Platform	Kharagpur (West Bengal, 833m)
Longest Railway Run	Trans-Siberian Railway (6000 miles)
Longest River	Nile (Egypt, 6,695 km)
Longest River (in India)	Brahmaputra (2,900 km)
Longest Railway Bridge	Lower Zambezi (Africa)
Longest Saree (in the world)	1276 ft (370 m) mfd. by "POTHYS" Textile dealer of Tamil Nadu (India)
Largest Sea	South China Sea
Longest Shipping Canal	Baltic White Sea Canal (152 miles)
Longest Day	June 21
Longest Dam	Grand Coulee Dam (America), Hirakud (in India)
Longest Mountain Range	Andes (South America)
Longest Wall	Great Wall of China
Nearest Planet (to the sun)	Mercury
Smallest Planet	Pluto
Smallest Continent	Australia
Smallest Bird	Humming Bird
Shortest Day	December 22
Tallest Animal	Giraffe
Tallest Bridge	Milau road bridge (France). Road surface is 270 metres above ground, a world record and the total structure, with suspension cables added is 343 metres (1,132 ft) above ground and its highest point or 23 metres higher than the Eiffel Tower.
Tallest Office Building	Taipei Tower (Taiwan - 1667 Ft., 101 storeys)
Tallest Statue	Bronze Statue of Buddha (Tokyo)
Tallest Statue	Statue of Thiruvalluvar (133 ft. T.N., India)
Tallest Tree	Red Wood Creek Grove in Redwood National Park, California (USA)
Tallest Tower	C.N.Tower (Toronto, Canada)
Widest Waterfall	Khone Falls (Laos)

LONGEVITY TABLE (Approximate)

Animals	(in years)	Birds	(in years)
Cat	12	Canary	24
Crocodile	300	Crow	10
Elephant	100	Goose	50
Horse	30	Lark	18
Pig	25	Parrot	60

Animals	(in years)	Birds	(in years)
Sheep	12	Pelican	50
Whale	100	Skylark	30
Camel	40	Vulture	100
Cow	25	Crane	24
Dog	15	Eagle	100
Goat	15	Hen	14
Lion	40	Nightingale	18
Rabbit	5	Peacock	24
Tortoise	350	Robin	12
		Swan	16

STATES FIRST IN PRODUCTION

Betelnuts - West Bengal

Bajra - Rajasthan, Gujarat and Maharashtra

Barley - U.P., Bihar

Cashewnut - Kerala

Cinchona - Tamil Nadu (Nilgiri Hills), West Bengal (Darjeeling)

Coffee - Karnataka, Tamil Nadu (Nilgiri Hills) and Kerala

Cotton - Maharashtra, Madhya Pradesh, Tamil Nadu and Punjab

Cotton Seeds - Maharashtra, Punjab, Madhya Pradesh and Andhra Pradesh

Chillies - Maharashtra, Andhra Pradesh

Cardamom - Karnataka, Kerala, Sikkim

Pulses - Madhya Pradesh, Uttar Pradesh, Rajasthan

Groundnut - Gujarat, Andhra Pradesh, Tamil Nadu

Hemp - Chattisgarh, Madhya Pradesh and U.P

Jute - West Bengal, Assam, Bihar

Linseed - Madhya Pradesh, Orissa, Uttar Pradesh, Maharashtra and West Bengal

Maize - Uttar Pradesh, Bihar and Punjab

Mustard and Rape-seed (Sarsom) - Rajasthan, U.P., West Bengal, Punjab, Bihar and Orissa

Poppy (Opium plant) - U.P., Himachal Pradesh, Punjab, Bihar, Tamil Nadu, Orissa and Rajasthan

Rubber - Kerala, Tamil Nadu, Karnataka

Grams - Madhya Pradesh, Tamil Nadu

Silk - Karnataka, Kashmir, West Bengal, Assam & Tamil Nadu

Spices (Pepper) - Kerala, Karnataka, Tamil Nadu

Sugarcane - U.P., Maharashtra & Tamil Nadu

Tea - Assam, West Bengal, Tamil Nadu (Nilgiri Hills), U.P., (Dehra Dun), Kerala and Himachal Pradesh (Kangra Hills)

NAMES - OLD AND NEW

Countries and cities have changed their names over the years.

New Name	Old Name(s)
Ankara	Ancyra, Angora
Astana	Akmola, Tselinograd, Akmolinsk
Banjul	Bathurst (Capital of the Gambia)
Beijing	Peking, Beiping
Belize	British Honduras
Benin	Dahomey
Botswana	Bechuanaland
Burkina Faso	Upper Volta
Cambodia	Kampuchea, Khmer Republic
Cape Canaveral	Cape Kennedy
Chennai	Madras
Dhaka	Dacca
Djibouti	French Somaliland, French territory of the Afars and the Issas
Equatorial Guinea	Spanish Guinea
Ethiopia	Abyssinia
Ghana	Gold Coast
Guyana	British Guiana
Harare	Salisbury
Hawaiian Islands	Sandwich Island
Ho Chi Minh City	Saigon
Indonesia	Dutch East Indies
Iran	Persia
Iraq	Mesopotamia
Istanbul	Byzantium, Constantinople
Jakarta	Batavia
Kinshasa	Leopoldville
Kolkata	Calcutta
Lesotho	Basutoland
Madagascar	Malagasy Republic
Malabo	Clarencetown, Port Clarence, Santa Isabel
Malawi	Nyasaland
Malaysia	Malaya
Mumbai	Bombay
Myanmar	Burma
Namibia	South-West Africa
Nauru	Pleasant Island
Oslo	Christiania
Sri Lanka	Ceylon
St.Petersburg	Petrograd, Leningrad
Suriname	Dutch Guyana
Taiwan	Formosa
Tasmania	Van Diemen's Land

Thailand	Siam
Togo	Togoland
Tuvalu	Ellice Islands
Vanuatu	New Hebrides
Volgograd	Stalingrad, Tsaritsyn
Yangon	Rangoon
Zambia	Northern Rhodesia
Zimbabwe	Southern Rhodesia

SPORTS

MAJOR SPORTS AND THE TERMS ASSOCIATED WITH THEM

Badminton	Deuce, Double, Mixed doubles, Drop, Smash, Let, Fault, Love all
Basketball	Ball, Basket, Blocking, Dribbling, Held ball, Multiple throws, Pivot Free throw, Jump ball, Holding
Baseball	Pinch, Strike, Home, Bunt, Base, Battery, Catcher, Diamond, Infield, Outfield, Hitter, Pitcher plate, Pull out, Short stop
Boat Race	Cox
Boxing	Upper cut, Kidney punch, Babitt punch, Knock down, Hitting below the belt, Auxiliary point system, Defence, Down, Hook, Jab, Lying on, Seconds out, Slam, Upper cut, Win by knock out, Weight in
Bridge	Diamonds, Finesse, Hearts, Dummy, Revoke, Chicane, Grand Slam, Little slam, Vulnerable, No Trump, Rubber, Dealer, Ruff, Suit, Tricks
Chess	Bishop, Gambit, Checkmate, Stalemate, Castle, King, Knight, Rook, Queen, Pawn
Cricket	Ashes, Body-line bowling, The break, Bye, Crease, Drive, Duck, Follow-on, Googly, Hat trick, L.B.W., Legbye, Maiden over, No ball, Ranji Trophy, Rubbers, Test Matches, Caught, Chinaman, Cover drive, Hit wicket, No ball, off break, on drive, out, over, pitch, popping crease, run down, run out, sixer, silly point, square leg, straight drive, stone walling, wicket, stumped
Croquet	Mallet, Hoops, peg out
Draughts	Huff
Football	Off side, scope, drop kick, penalty kick (or goal kick), corner kick, free-kick, dribble, throw-in-touch-downs, tripping, direct free kick, hat-trick
Golf	Bunker, bet-ball foursome, bogey, foursome, caddie, fairway, dormy, fourball, greed holes, links, niblic, put, rough, par, threesome, tee, stymied

Hockey	Carried, short corner, bully, stick, offside, roll-in, penalty, striking circle, under-cutting, dribble, carry, hat-trick, off-side, tie-breaker
Horse Racing	Also ran, Dead heat, Jockey, Punter, Steeple chase
Polo	Bunker, Chukker, Mallet
Rifle Shooting	Bull's eye (Centre of target)
Rowing	Bow, Bucket, Cow, Ergo meter, Feather, Paddle, Regatta
Rugby Football	Scrum, Drop kick, A trackle, Lines, Touch, Try
Shooting	Bag, Bull's eye, Marksmanship, Plug, Muzzle
Skiing	Tobogganing
Swimming	Crawl, Butterfly stroke, Breast stroke
Tennis	Foot fault, Backhand drive, Volley, Smash, Half-volley, Hand, Deuce, Service, Let, Grand slam, Double-fault, Ground stroke,
Volley ball	Deuce, Spikersi Booster, Blocking, Doubling, Heave, Holding, Love all, Point, Service, Volley, Strike
Wrestling	Head lock, Half nelson, Heave, Hold, Scissor, Rebouts

IMPORTANT STADIA AND SPORTS

INTERNATIONAL

Epsom (England)	- Horse Race
Leeds (England)	- Cricket
Lords (England)	- Cricket
Oval (England)	- Cricket
Wembley Stadium (England)	- Soccer
Yankee Stadium (New York)	- Boxing

NATIONAL

Feroze Shah Kotla Ground	- Delhi
Nehru Stadium	- Chennai
M.A.Chidambaram Stadium	- Chennai
National stadium	- Mumbai
Brabourne Stadium	- Mumbai
Yadavindra Stadium	- Patiala
Ranjit Stadium	- Kolkata
Barabati Stadium	- Cuttack (Orissa)
Eden Gardens	- Kolkata
Green Park	- Kanpur
Shivaji Hockey Stadium	- New Delhi
Wankhede Stadium	- Mumbai

SPORTS : MEASUREMENTS

Badminton Courts: 44 ft by 20 ft. (doubles); 44 ft. by 17 ft. (singles).

Baseball: Diamond shaped ground; 90 ft.on each side and 127 ft. along the diagonal.

Billiards Table: 10 ft. long, 5 ft. wide and 3 ft.high.

Boxing Ring: 12 sq.ft to 20 sq.ft.

Basketball: 85 ft. by 46 ft. (maximum dimensions).

Cricket Grounds: Ground oval-shaped; Wickets: 22 yards apart; Ball $8\frac{13}{16}$ to 9 inches in circumference and $5\frac{1}{2}$ oz. to $5\frac{3}{4}$ oz. in weight; Width of the Bat $4\frac{1}{4}$ inches and maximum length 38 inches; Bowling crease: 8 ft. and 8 inches in length; Popping crease 4 ft. from the wicket and deemed unlimited in length; stumps 27 inches out of the ground.

Derby Course: $1\frac{1}{2}$ to 2 miles.

Football Field: Length 100 yds. to 130 yds.; Breadth 50 yds. to 56 yds.; Goal width 8 yds.; Bar 8 ft. from ground; Area 6 yds. from each goal post; Ball 27 inches to 28 inches in circumference; Duration 90 minutes maximum.

Golf: Hole $4\frac{1}{2}$ inches, Ball $1\frac{1}{4}$ oz. in weight.

Hockey: Ground 100 yds. by 55 to 60 yds.; Duration of game two periods of 30 minutes each plus extra time in case of draw or suspension of game for some reason; Goal-perpendicular posts: 8 yds. apart joined together by a horizontal cross bar 7 ft. from ground; Ball $8\frac{13}{16}$" in circumference; Weight of the ball $5\frac{3}{4}$ oz.

Marathon Race: 26 miles 385 yards.

Polo: Ground 300 yards × 200 yards.

Tennis Court: 78 feet × 28 feet (singles), 78 feet × 36 feet (doubles).

Volleyball Court: Rectangular 30 feet × 60 feet.

Water Polo: 30 yds × 20 yds.

TROPHIES ASSOCIATED WITH SPORTS

International

American Cup	- Yacht Racing
Ashes	- Cricket (Australia-England)
Canada Cup	- Golf (World Championship)
Colombo Cup	- Football (India, Pakistan, Sri Lanka and Myanmar)
Corbillion Cup	- World Table Tennis (Women)
Davis Cup	- Lawn Tennis
Derby	- Horse Race (England)
Grand National	- Horse Steeple Chase Race (England)
Holker	- Bridge
Jules Rimet Trophy	- World Soccer Cup
King's Cup	- Air Races (England)
Merdeka	- Football (Asian)
Prince of Wales Cup	- Golf (England)
Reliance Cup	- Cricket
Ryder Cup	- Golf (England)
Schneider Cup	- Seaplane Race (U.K.)
Swaythling Cup	- World Table Tennis (Men)
Thomas Cup	- World Badminton (Men)
Tunku Abdul Rahman Cup	- Badminton (Asian)
U Thant Cup	- Tennis

Uber Cup	-	World Badminton (Women)
Yonex Cup	-	Badminton
Walker Cup	-	Golf (England)
Westchester Cup	-	Polo (England)
Wightman Cup	-	Lawn Tennis (Women of U.S.A. and England)
William Todd Memorial Trophy	-	Basket ball
William Cup	-	Basket ball
Wimbledon Trophy	-	Lawn Tennis

National

Aga Khan Cup	-	Hockey
All-India Maharaja Ranjit Singh Gold Cup	-	Hockey (men)
All-India Women's Guru Nanak Championship	-	Hockey (women)
Bangalore Blues Challenge Cup	-	Basketball
Barna-Bellack Cup	-	Table Tennis (Men)
Beighton Cup	-	Hockey (Kolkata)
Mumbai Gold Cup	-	Hockey
Burdwan Trophy	-	Weight-lifting
Chakola Gold Trophy	-	Football
Cock of the Fleet Trophy	-	Regatta
D.C.M. Trophy	-	Football
Dhyan Chand Trophy	-	Hockey
Dr. B.C.Roy Trophy	-	National Football (Junior)
Duleep Trophy	-	Cricket
Durand Cup	-	Football
Ezra Cup	-	Polo
F.A. Cup	-	Football
G.V. Raja Memorial Trophy	-	Football
Gurmit Trophy	-	Hockey
I.F.A. Shield	-	Football
Irani Cup	-	Cricket
Jaswant Singh Trophy	-	Best Services Sportsman
Jayalakshmi Cup	-	National Table Tennis Championship (Women)
Kuppuswamy Naidu Trophy	-	Hockey
Lady Rattan Tata Trophy	-	Hockey (Women)
Maulana Azad Trophy	-	Inter-University Sports and Athletics
MCC Trophy	-	Hockey
Moinuddowla Gold Cup	-	Cricket
Murugappa Gold Cup	-	Hockey
Nagjee Trophy	-	Football
Nehru Trophy	-	Hockey
Nizam Gold Cup	-	Football
Obaidullah Gold Cup	-	Hockey
Prithi Singh Cup	-	Polo
Radha Mohan Cup	-	Polo
Raghbir Singh Memorial Cup	-	Football
Rajkumari Challenge Cup	-	Table Tennis (Junior girls)

Ramanujan Trophy	-	Table Tennis (Junior boys)
Ramnivas Ruia Challenge Gold Trophy	-	Bridge
Rangaswamy Cup	-	National Hockey Championship
Ranji Trophy	-	National Cricket Championship
Rene Frank Trophy	-	Hockey
Rohinton Baria Trophy	-	Cricket (Inter-University)
Rovers Cup	-	Football
Sahni Trophy	-	Hockey
Santosh Trophy	-	National Football Championship
Sanjay Gold Cup	-	Football
Sethu Cup	-	Aquatics
Scindia Gold Cup	-	Hockey
Sheesh Mahal Trophy	-	Cricket
Sri Krishna Gold Cup	-	Football
Subroto Mukerji Cup	-	Football (Inter-School)
Todd Memorial Trophy	-	Football
Tommy Emar Gold Cup	-	Hockey (Women)
Vizzy Trophy	-	Cricket
Vittal Trophy	-	Football
Wellington Trophy	-	Rowing
Winchester Cup	-	Polo
Yadavindra Cup	-	Hockey

SPORTS AND SPORTS PERSONS

ARCHERY

Cho Youn-jeong (S.Korea)
Kim Soo-Nyung (S.Korea)
Park Kyung (S.Korea)
Shyam Lal (India)
Tarundeep Rai (India)
Sabastian Flute (France)

Jay Barrs (U.S.A)
Lee Eun-Kyong (S.Korea)
Krishna Das (India)
Kim Kyung-wook (Korea)
Ms. Dola Banerjee (India)
Yun Mi-Jin (S.Korea)

ATHLETICS

K.C.Rosakutty (India)
P.T.Usha (India)
Carl Lewis (U.S.A)
Jean Galfione (France)
Maxim Tarassov (CIS)
Valsamma (India)
Shiny Abraham (India)
Marion Jones (USA)
Robert Korzeniowski (Poland)
Maurice Greene (U.S.)
Szymon Ziolkowski (Poland)
Denise Lewis (Britain)
Michael Johnson (U.S.)
Haile Gebrselassie (Ethopia)
Virgilijus Alekna (Lithuania)

Mercy Kuttan (India)
Ben Johnson (Canada)
Sergei Bubka (U.S.S.R)
Igor Potapovich (Kazakhstan)
Ji Zebiao (China)
Bahadur Singh (India)
Maurice Greene (USA)
Donovan Bailey (Canada)
Arsi Harju (Finland)
Sergey Kyyugin (Russia)
Tereza Marinova (Bulgaria)
Naomi Takahashi (Japan)
Jonathan Ewards (Britain)
Anier Garcia (Cuba)
Stacy Dragila (U.S.)

Cathy Freeman (Australi)
Maria Mutalo (Mozambique)
Elina Zvereva (Belarus)
Nils Schumann (Germany)
Konstantinos Kenteris (Greece)
Erki Nool (Estonia)
Wang Liping (China)
Naoh Kiprono Ngenyi (Kenya)
Nick Hysong (U.S.)
Heike Drechsler (Germany)
Yelena Yelerina (Russia)
Nouria Merah-Benida (Algeria)
Anju Bobby George (India)

Gabriela Szabo (Romania)
Olga Shishigina (Kazakhastan)
Irina Privalova (Russia)
Angelo Taylor (U.S.)
Ivan Pedrosa (Cuba)
Marion Jones (U.S.)
Yanina Korolchik (Belarus)
Reuben Kosgei (Kenya)
Kamila Skolimowska (Poland)
Derartu Tulu (Ethopia)
Trine Hattsted (Norway)
Million Wolde (Ethopia)
Ms. Manjit Kaur (India)

BADMINTON

Ardy Wiranata (China)
Gillian Gilks (UK)
Peter Rasmussen (Denmark)
Razif Sidek (Malaysia)
Aparna Popet (India)
Ami Ghia (India)
Arun Baidya (India)
Maureen D'Souza (India)
Radhika Bose (India)
Ji Xinpeng (China)
Gu Jun (China)

Wendy Poulton (England)
Prakash Padukone (India)
Ye Zhaoying (China)
Jalani Sidek (Malaysia)
Kirsten Larsen (Denmark)
Madhumita Bisht (India)
Camilla Martin (Denmark)
P.G. Chengappa (India)
Gong Zhicao (China)
Gu Fei (China)
Ms. Aparna Popat (India)

BALL BADMINTON

D.Rajaram (India)
A. Sam Christ Das (India)

L.A.Iqbal (India)
A. Karim (India)

BASKETBALL

Sean Kenip (U.S.A)
Suman Sharma (India)
Hanuman Singh (India)
T. Vijayaraghavan (India)

Brian Kelleybrew (Australia)
Radhey Shyam (India)
Om Prakash (India)
Surendra Kumar Kataria (India)

BILLIARDS

Geeth Sethi (India)
Yasin Merchant (India)
Ashok Sandilya (India)
Wilson Jones (India)
Madan Chandra (India)

Girish Parikh (India)
Shyam Shroff (India)
Manoj Kothari (India)
Subhash Agarwal (India)
Pankaj Advani (India)

BOWLING

Christian Nokel (Germany)
Lee Ji-Yeon (S. Korea)
Byun Yong Yong-hwan (S. Korea)

Hiroshi Yamamoto (Japan)
Masami Hirai (Japan)
Che Kuk Hung (Hong Kong)

BOXING

Mike Tyson (U.S.A)
Lennox Lewis (UK)

Oleg Mascaev (Uzbekistan)
Mike Weaver (U.S.A)

Muhammad Ali (U.S.A)
Somluck Kamsing (Thailand)
J.V. Jollyron (India)
Giovanni Parisi
Dingko Singh (India)
Manoj D. Pingle (India)
Mohd. Ali Qamar (India)
Brahim Arloum (France)
Mario Kindelan (Cuba)
Jorge Guttierrez (Cuba)
Wijan Ponlid (Thailand)
Mahamadkadz Abdullaev (Uzbekistan)
Audley Harrison (Britain)

Fabrice Tiozzo (France)
Gurbax Singh Sandhu (India)
Ariel Hernandez (Cuba)
Kaur Singh (India)
Laurent Boudouani (France)
Michael Mutua (Kenya)
Narendra Rana (India)
Guillermo Rigondeaux Ortiz (Cuba)
Oleg Saitov (Russia)
Felix Savon (Cuba)
Bekzat Sattarkhanov (Kazakhastan)
Alexander Lebziak (Russia)
Aghil Kumar (India)

BRIDGE

Jaggy Shivdasani (India)

Jimmy Mehta (India)

CARROM

Anthony Maria Irudayam (India)

CHESS

Gary Kasparov (Russia)
Viswanathan Anand (India)
Bhaghyashree Thipsay (India)
Koneru Humpy (India)
Anupama Abhyankar (India)
Manual Aaron (India)
Jayashree Khadilkar (India)
R. Sudhakar Babu (India)
Alexander Gatkin (Russia)
Krishnan Sasikiran (India)
Surya Shekhar Ganguly (India)
Harikrishna (India)

Anatoly Karpov (Russia)
Anupama Gokhale (India)
Boris Spassky (U.S.A.)
Aarthie Ramaswamy (India)
Rohini Khadilkar (India)
Dibyendu Barua (India)
Vassanti Khadilkar (India)
Praveen Mahadev Thipsay (India)
Alexander Khalifman (Russia)
Bobby Fischer (USA)
Vladimir Krammik (Russia)
Jovanka Houska (India)

CANOEING

Tony Estanguet (France)
Hnut Holmann (Norway)
Josefa Idem Guerrini (Italy)

Thomas Schmidt (Germany)
Andreas Dittmar (Germany)
Gyorgy Kolonics (Hungary)

CRICKET

Don Bradman (Australia)
Richard Hadlee (New Zealand)
Ian Botham (England)
Imran Khan (Pakistan)
Vivian Richards (West Indies)
Kapil Dev (India)
Adam Gilchrist (Australia)
Muhammed Azharuddin (India)
Anil Kumble (India)
Sunil Gavaskar (India)
Chetan Sharma (India)
Javagal Srinath (India)
Vinod Kambli (India)

Gary Sobers (West Indies)
Graham Gooch (England)
Wasim Akram (Pakistan)
Allan Border (Australia)
Sachin Tendulkar (India)
Bishen Singh Bedi (India)
Krishnamachari Srikkanth (India)
Ravi Shastri (India)
Dilip Vengsarkar (India)
Rahul Dravid (India)
Ajay Jadeja (India)
Saurav Ganguly (India)
Ajit Agarkar (India)

Allan Donald (South Africa)
Azhar Mahmood (Pakistan)
Kiran More (India)
Chris Cairns (New Zealand)
Shanta Rangaswami (India)
Craig McMillan (New Zealand)
Curtly Ambrose (West Indies)
Mark Taylor (Australia)
Debasish Mohanty (India)
Graeme Hick (England)
Inzamam-ul-Haq (Pakistan)
Zaheer Abbas (Pakistan)
Salim Malik (Pakistan)
Lance Klusener (South Africa)
Clive Lloyd (West Indies)
Tony Greig (England)
Ian Chappel (Australia)
Mark Waugh (Australia)
Malcolm Marshall (West Indies)
Virender Shewag (India)
Lakshmipathy Balaji (India)

Navjot Singh Sidhu (India)
Manoj Prabhakar (India)
Brian Lara (West Indies)
G.R. Vishwanath (India)
B.S. Chandrashekhar (India)
Nayan Mongia (India)
Sanath Jayasuriya (Sri Lanka)
Arjuna Ranatunga (Sri Lanka)
Glenn McGrath (Australia)
Gary Kirsten (South Africa)
Javed Miandad (Pakistan)
Jacques Kallis (South Africa)
David Gower (England)
Greg Chappell (Australia)
Gordon Greenidge (West Indies)
A. Kalicharan (West Indies)
Duleep Mendis (Sri Lanka)
Michael Holding (West Indies)
Jeff Crowe (New Zealand)
V.V.S. Laxman (India)
Anju Jain (India)

CYCLING

Miguel Indurain (Spain)
Clause Criquillion (Belgium)
Felicia Ballangerx (France)
Robert Barkko (Germany)
Marty Nothstein (U.S.)
Poala Pezzo (Italy)
Leontein Zijlaard (Netherlands)

Felicia Ballanger (France)
Toshinobu Saito (Japan)
Jaron Queally (Britain)
Leontien Van Moorsel (Netherlands)
Juan Ilaneras (Spain)
Miguel Martinez (France)
Vyatcheslav Ekimov (Russia)

DIVING

Dmitry Sautin (Russia)
Vera Ilina (Russia)
Xiong Ni (China)
Li Na (China)
Fu Mingxia (China)

Igor Lukashin (Russia)
Loulina Pakhalina (Russia)
Xiao Hailiang (China)
Sang Xue (China)
Tian Liang (China)

EQUESTRIAN

Isabellwerth On Gigolo (Germany)
Nicole Uphoff (Germany)
Capt. Ghulam Mohd. Khan (India)
Fateh Khan (Pakistan)
David O'Connor (U.S.)

Ludger Beerbaum (Germany)
Nadia al Mutawa (Kuwait)
Rupinder Singh Brar (India)
Konoshin Kuwahara (Japan)
Anky Van Grunsven (Netherlands)

FENCING

Alessandro Puccini (Italy)
Philippe Omnes (France)
Timea Nagy (Hungary)

Xu Xuening (China)
Pavel Kolobkov (Russia)
Kim Young-Ho (Korea)

FOOTBALL

Pele (Brazil)
Mohammad Habib (India)
Chuni Goswamy (India)
Sudhir Karmarkar (India)
Inder Singh (India)
Mukhtar Dahri (Malaysia)
I.M. Vijayan (India)
Lothar Matthaus (Germany)
Raman Vijayan (India)
Zinedine Zedane (France)

Diego Maradona (Argentina)
Baichung Bhutia (India)
Shanti Malik (India)
Prasun Banerjee (India)
Ronaldo (Brazil)
Hardeep Sangla (India)
Jo Paul Anchery (India)
Mario Kempes (Argentina)
Subroto Bhattacharjee (India)
Thierry Henry (France)

GOLF

Tiger Woods (USA)
Brian Jones (Australia)
Greg Norman (Australia)
Graham Mars (Australia)
Annika Sorenstam (Sweden)
Harji Malik (India)
Jyoti Randhawa (India)
Shruti Khanna (India)

Ali Sher (India)
Ben Crenshaw (USA)
Johny Miller (USA)
Chiranjeev Milkha Singh (India)
Simram Singh (India)
Vijyasingh (Fiji)
Robert Karlsson (Sweden)
Vijay Kumar (India)

GYMNASTICS

Li Quiling (China)
Choe Jong Sil (N. Korea)
Alexei Nemov (Russia
David Douillet (France)
Maruis Urzica (Romania)
Elena Zamolodtchikova (Russia)
Liu Xian (China)
Li Xiaopeng (China)

Shannon Miller (US)
Vikas Pandey (India)
Irina Karavayeva (Russia)
Igor Vihrous (Latvia)
Szilveszter Csollany (Hungary)
Svetlana Khorkina (Russia)
Alexi Nemov (Russia)
Yulia Barslukova (Russia)

HOCKEY

Dhyan Chand (India)
Jagbir Singh (India)
Vasudevan Bhaskaran (India)
Rupa Saini (India)
Baldev Singh (India)
Ron Steen (Holland)
Dhanraj Pillay (India)
Baljit Singh Dhillon (India)
Zafar Iqbal (India)
V.J. Philips (India)
Ajitpal Singh (India)
Mohammad Riaz (India)
Surjeet Singh (India)
Sohail Abbas (Pakistan)

Jude Felix (India)
Islahuddin (Pakistan)
Baljit Singh Chandi (India)
Pargat Singh (India)
Akhtar Rasool (Pakistan)
Richard Charlesworth (Australia)
Mukesh Kumar (India)
Baljit Singh Saini (India)
Deepak Thakur (India)
M.K. Kaushik (India)
Prithipal Singh (India)
Ramandeep Singh (India)
Thirumalvalavan (India)
Viren Rasquinha (India)

JUDO

Katsuyuki Masochi (Japan)
Zhuang Xiaoyan (China)

Nariko Annu (Japan)
Cawas Kersep Billimoria (India)

Kenzo Nakamura (Japan)
Tadahiro Nomura (Japan)
Legna Verdecia (Cuba)
Izabel Fernandez (Spain)
Severine Vandenhende (France)
Mark Huizinga (Netherlands)

Ulla Werbrouck (Belgium)
Ryoko Tamura (Japan)
Huseyin Ozkan (Turkey)
Guiseppa Maddaloni (Italy)
Makota Takimoto (Japan)
Yuan Hua (China)

KABADDI

S.Rajaratnam (India)
Ashok D.Shinde (India)
Miss Rama Sarkar (India)
Ashan Kumar (India)
Ramesh Kumar (India)

Hardeep Singh (India)
Maya Kashinath (India)
P. Ganeshan (India)
Biswajit Palit (India)

KHO-KHO

Surekha Bhagwan Kulkarni (India)
D.S.Ramachandra (India)
Hermant Mohan Takalkar (India)
Shantaram Jadhav (India)
Srirang Janardhan Inamdar (India)

S.Prakash (India)
Nilima Chandrakant Sarolkar (India)
Sushma Sarolkar (India)
Usha Vasant Nagarkar (India)
Shoba Narayan (India)

MOUNTAINEERING

Sir Edmund Hillary
Santosh Yadav (India)
Bachendri Pal (India)
Col. B.S. Sandhu (India)
Rekha Sharma (India)
Maj. Prem Chand

Tenzing Norgay
Col. D.K. Khullar (India)
Phu Dorjee (India)
Chandraprabha Aitwal (India)
Harshwanti Bisht (India)
Naik N.D. Sherpa

POLO

Lt. Col. Kuldip Singh Garcha (India)
Naveen Jindal (India)
Samir Suhag (India)

Angad Kalaan (India)
Ramiro Garros (Argentina)
Vishal Singh (India)

ROWING

Major R.S.Bhanwala (India)
Elisabela Lipa (Romania)
Steve Redgrave (Britain)
Tim Foster (Britain)
Michel Andrieux (France)
Georgeta Damian (Romania)
Luka Spik (Slovania)
Jana Thieme (Germany)
Rob Waddell (New Zealand)

Xeno Mueller (Switerland)
Surinder Singh Waldia (India)
Matthew Pinsent (Britain)
James Crackness (Britain)
Jean Christophe (France)
Doin Ignat (Romania)
Iztok Cop (Slovania)
Kathrin Bron (Germany)
Ekaterina Karsten (Belgium)

SAILING

Roman Hagara (Australia)
Christophe Sieber (Australia)
Thomas Johnson (Finland)
Jenny Armstrong (Australia)
Jom King (Australia)
Ben Ainslie (Britain)

Hans Peter Steinacher (Australia)
Alessandra Senseni (Australia)
Jyrki Jarvi (Finland)
Belinda Stowell (Australia)
Mark Turnbull (Australia)
Shirley Robertson (Britain)

SHOOTING

Ashok J.Pandit (India)
Jaspal Rana (India)
Olga Klochneva (Russia)
Kuheli Gangulee (India)
Moraad Ali Khan (India)
Roopa Unnikrishnan (India)
Sushma Rana (India)
Nancy Johnson (U.S.)
Tao Luna (China)
Daina Gudzineviciute (Lithuania)
Pia Hansen (Sweden)
Renate Mauer-Rozanska (Poland)
Maria Grozdeva (Bulgaria)
Rajmond Debevec (Slovakia)

Anja Tere (India)
Anjali Ved Pathak (India)
Kasumi Watanabe (Japan)
Manavjit Singh (India)
Mansher Singh (India)
Subhash Rana (India)
Ved Prakash (India)
Franck Dumoulin (France)
Michael Diamond (Australia)
Cai Yalin (China)
Tanyu Kiriakov (Bulgaria)
Richard Faulds (Britain)
Yang Ling (China)
Gagan Narang (India)

SQUASH

Meherwan Daruwala (India)
Chris Walker (UK)
Jahangir Khan (Pakistan)
David Palmer (Australia)

Jonathan Power (Canada)
Dan Jensen (Australia)
Cassie Campion (England)
Leilani Joyce (New Zealand)

SNOOKER

Stephen Hendry (Scotland)

Ashwini Purani (India)

SWIMMING

Xiaong Guoming (China)
Wilson Cherian (India)
Kutraleeswaran (India)
Baidyanath Nath (India)
Lisa Curry (Australia)
Michelle Ford (Australia)
Bula Chowdhury (India)
Lorraine Verghese (India)
Reza Shirazi (India)
Lt.Col. H.S. Sodhi (India)
M. Usha (India)
Rakhi Mehra (India)
Tom Dolan (US)
Ian Thorpe (Australia)
Megan Quann (U.S.)
Domenico Fioravanti (Italy)
Pieter Van den Hoogenband (Netherlands)
Brooke Bennet (U.S.)
Surie O'Neill (Australia)
Misty Hyman (U.S.)
Gary Mall (U.S.)
Olga Brusnikina (Russia)
Rehan Poncha (India)

Lu Bin (China)
Mihir Sen (India)
Arathi Saha (India)
Bhanu Sachdeve (India)
Valerie Beddoe (Australia)
Jin Montgomery (USA)
Arti Pradhan (India)
Khazan Singh (India)
Anita Sood (India)
June Croft (UK)
Nisha Millet (India)
Sebastian Zavier (India)
Zeba Wadia (India)
Yana Klochkova (Ukraine)
Diana Mocanu (Romania)
Tom Dolan (U.S.)
Lenny Krayzelburg (U.S.)
Inge de Bruijn (Netherlands)
Tom Malchow (U.S.)
Lars Froelander (Sweden)
Anthony Ervin (U.S.)
Maria Kisseleva (Russia)
Shikha Tandan (India)

TABLE TENNIS

Chire Koyama (Japan)
Vyoma Parikh (India)
Sudhir Pandhke (India)
Deng Yaping (China)
Indu Puri (India)
Andy Barden (UK)
Arup Basak (India)
Pak Yung Sun (North Korea)
Sakamoto Ryusuke (Japan)
Li Ju (China)
Yan Sen (China)

Kamlesh Metha (India)
Nandini Kulkarni (India)
Smita Desai (India)
V. Chandrasekhar (India)
Manjit Dua (India)
Anindita Chakraborty (India)
Geeta Thadani (India)
Poulomi Ghatak (India)
Subramaniam Raman (India)
Wang Nan (China)
Sowmiadeep Rai (India)

TAEKWONDO

Lee Jong-sun (S. Korea)
B.L.N. Murthy (India)
Lauren Burns (Australia)
Steven Lopez (U.S.)
Lee Sun-Hee (Korea)
Chen Zhong (China)

Han Jee-Koo (S. Korea)
Bandana Shrestha (India)
Michail Mouroutsos (Greece)
Jung Jae-Eun (Korea)
Angel Valodia Matos Feunter (Cuba)
Kim Kyong-Hun (S.Korea)

TENNIS

Monica Seles (Yugoslavia)
Boris Becker (Germany)
Jimmy Connors (U.S.A)
Martina Navratilova (U.S.A)
Ivan Lendl (U.S.A)
Jim Courier (U.S.A)
Anand Amritraj (India)
Ramesh Krishnan (India)
Chris Evert Llyod (U.S.A)
Arantxa Sanchez Vicario (Spain)
Jana Novotna (Czech)
Carlos Moya (Spain)
Enrico Piperno (India)
Pete Sampras (USA)
Pat Cash (Australia)
Henri Leconte (France)
Srinivasan Vasudevan (India)
Ramanathan Krishnan (India)
Daniel Nestor (Canada)
Sandeep Kirtane (India)
Steffi Graf (Germany)
Thomas Enqvist (Sweden)
Vishal Uppal (India)
Roger Federer (Switzerland)

Andre Agassi (U.S.A)
Stefan Edberg (Sweden)
John Mc Enroe (U.S.A)
Gabriela Sabatini (Argentina)
Leander Paes (India)
Mahesh Bhupathi (India)
Vijay Amirtraj (India)
Zeeshan Ali (India)
Gaurav Natekar (India)
Martina Hingis (Switzerland)
Lindsay Davenport (U.S.A.)
Mats Wilander (Sweden)
Yuvgeny Kafelnikov (Russia)
Michael Stich (Germany)
Bjorn Borg (Sweden)
Nandini Krishnan (India)
Nandan Bal (India)
Prahlad Srinath (India)
Premjit Lal (India)
Serena Williams (USA)
Syed Fazlauddin (India)
Venus Williams (USA)
Sania Mirza (India)
Anastasia Myskina (Russia)

VOLLEY BALL

Dalel Singh (India)
Abdul Rahim (Pakistan)
Hemlata Ursal (India)
P. Radhika (India)
Dain Blanton (U.S.)

Abhijeet Chaterjee (India)
Anu Jacob (India)
Mithu Roy (India)
Salomi Xaviour (India)
Eric Fonoimoana (U.S.)

WEIGHT-LIFTING

Karnam Malleswari (India)
Krishnan Kumar (India)
Meng Xiznjuan (China)
Newton Burrowes (UK)
Ram Chandra (India)
Pal Singh Sandhu (India)
Sandeep Kumar (India)
Nikolayn Pechalov (Croatia)
Soraya Jimenez (Mexico)
Izabela Dragneva (Bulgaria)
Lin Weining (China)
Galabin Boevski (Bulgaria)
Zhan Xugan (China)
Akakios Kakiasvilis (Greece)

Bharti Singh (India)
A.K. Pandian (India)
Andrey Chemerkin (Russia)
Nick Voukelatos (Australia)
N. Kunjarani Devi (India)
Ramesh Kumar (India)
Wilson Dhanraj (India)
Yang Xia (China)
Halil Multu (Turkey)
Chen Xiaomin (China)
Maria Isabel Urrutia (Colombia)
Ding Meiyuan (China)
Pyross Dimas (Greece)
Horrein Tavakoli (Iran)

WRESTLING

Jagminder Singh (India)
Jagdish Kumar (India)
Satpal Singh (India)
Buyanelger Bold (Mongolia)
Ashok Kumar (India)
Mahabir Singh (India)
Mukesh Kumar (India)
Sim Kwon-Hó (Korea)
Mourat Kardanov (Russia)
Armen Nazarian (Bulgaria)
Hamza Yerlikaya (Turkey)
Namig Abdullayev (Azerbaijan)
Alexander Leipold (Germany)
Alireza Dabir (Iran)
Adam Saitiev (Russia)

Rajender Singh (India)
Dara Singh (India)
Md. Hussain Mohebi (Iran)
Bob Robinson (Canada)
Ombir Singh (India)
Kripa Shankar Patel (India)
Rohtas Singh Dahiya (India)
Vateres Samourgachev (Russia)
Mikael Ljungberg (Sweden)
Filiberto Azcuy (Cuba)
Rulon Gardner (U.S.)
Mourad Oumakhanov (Russia)
Saghid Mourtasaliyev (Russia)
Daniel Igali (Canada)
Susil Kumar (India)

YACHTING

Ryan Han Wui Tan (Singapore)
Homi Motiwala (India)
Lt.Dhruv Bhandari (India)
Jose Maria Van Der Ploeg (Spain)
Kelly Subbanand Rao (India)
Farokh Tarapore (India)
Fali Unwalla (India)

Franck David (France)
Jeejee Unwalla (India)
Matensz Kusznierewicz (Poland)
Pushpendra Kumar Garg (India)
C.S. Pradipak (India)
Zarir Karanjia (India)

WORLD ATHLETIC RECORDS

Men

Athlete Name	Nat	Event	Time	Place	Date
Tim Montgomery	USA	100m	9.78	Paris	14 09 2002
Michael Johnson	USA	200m	19.32	Atlanta, Ga	01 08 1996
Michael Johnson	USA	400m	43.18	Sevilla	26 08 1999
Wilson Kipketer	DEN	800m	01:41.1	Köln	24 08 1997
Noah Ngeny	KEN	1000m	02:12.0	Rieti	05 09 1999
Hicham El Guerrouj	MAR	1500m	03:26.0	Roma	14 07 1998
Hicham El Guerrouj	MAR	1 Mile	03:43.1	Roma	07 07 1999
Hicham El Guerrouj	MAR	2000m	04:44.8	Berlin	07 09 1999
Daniel Komen	KEN	3000m	07:20.7	Rieti	01 09 1996
Kenenisa Bekele	ETH	5000m	12:37.4	Hengelo	31 05 2004
Kenenisa Bekele	ETH	10,000m	26:20.3	Ostrava	08 06 2004
Arturo Barrios	MEX	20,000m	56:55.6	La Fléche	30 03 1991
Arturo Barrios	MEX	1 Hour	21.101	La Fléche	30 03 1991
Toshihiko Seko	JPN	25,000m	13:55.8	Christchurch	22 03 1981
Toshihiko Seko	JPN	30,000m	29:18.8	Christchurch	22 03 1981
Saif Saaeed Shaheen	QAT	3000m Steeplechase	07:53.6	Bruxelles	03 09 2004
Colin Jackson	GBR	110m Hurdles	12.91	Stuttgart	20 08 1993
Xiang Liu	CHN	"	12.91	Athína	27 08 2004
Kevin Young	USA	400m Hurdles	46.78	Barcelona	06 08 1992
Javier Sotomayor	CUB	High Jump	2.45	Salamanca	27 07 1993
Sergey Bubka	UKR	Pole Vault	6.14	Sestriere	31 07 1994
Mike Powell	USA	Long Jump	8.95	Tokyo	30 08 1991
Jonathan Edwards	GBR	Triple Jump	18.29	Göteborg	07 08 1995
Randy Barnes	USA	Shot Put	23.12	Westwood	20 05 1990
Jürgen Schult	GDR	Discus	74.08	Neubranden Burg	06 06 1986
Yuriy Sedykh	RUS	Hammer	86.74	Stuttgart	30 08 1986
Jan Zelezný	CZE	Javelin	98.48	Jena	25 05 1996
Roman Šebrle	CZE	Decathlon	9026	Götzis	27 05 2001
United States	USA	4x100m Relay	37.4	Barcelona	08 08 1992
United States	USA	"	37.4	Stuttgart	21 08 1993
Santa Monica Track Club	USA	4x200m Relay	01:18.7	Walnut, Ca	17 04 1994
United States	USA	4x400m Relay	02:54.2	Uniondale	22 07 1998
Great Britain & N.I.	GBR	4x800m Relay	07:03.9	London	30 08 1982
Federal Republic Germany	FRG	4x1500m Relay	14:38.8	Köln	17 08 1977

Athlete Name	Nat	Event	Time	Place	Date
Bernardo Segura	MEX	20,000m Race Walking	17:25.6	Bergen	07 05 1994
Jefferson Pérez	ECU	20km Race Walking	1:17:21	Paris Saint-denis	23 08 2003
Maurizio Damilano	ITA	30,000m Race Walking	01:44.1	Cuneo	03 10 1992
Thierry Toutain	FRA	50,000m Race Walking	40:57.9	Héricourt	29 09 1996
Denis Nizhegorodov	RUS	50km Race Walking	3:35:29	Cheboksary	13 06 2004
Haile Gebrselassie	ETH	10km Road Race	27:02:00	Doha	11 12 2002
Felix Limo	KEN	15km Road Race	41:29:00	Nijmegen	11 11 2001
Paul Tergat	KEN	20km Road Race	56:18:00	Milano	04 04 1998
Paul Tergat	KEN	Half Marathon	59:17:00	Milano	04 04 1998
Paul Kosgei	KEN	25km Road Race	1:12:45	Berlin	09 05 2004
Takayuki Matsumiya	JPN	30km Road Race	1:28:36	Kumamoto	16 02 2003
Paul Tergat	KEN	Marathon	2:04:55	Berlin	28 09 2003
Takahiro Sunada	JPN	100km Road Race	6:13:33	Yubetsu	21 06 1998
Morocco	MAR	Road Relay	1:57:56	Litochoro	17 04 1994

Women

Athlete Name	Nat	Event	Time	Place	Date
Florence Griffith-Joyner	USA	100M	10.49	Indianapolis	16 07 1988
Florence Griffith-Joyner	USA	200M	21.34	Seoul	29 09 1988
Marita Koch	GDR	400M	47.6	Canberra	06 10 1985
Jarmila Kratochvílová	TCH	800M	01:53.3	München	26 07 1983
Svetlana Masterkova	RUS	1000M	02:29.0	Bruxelles	23 08 1996
Yunxia Qu	CHN	1500M	03:50.5	Beijing	11 09 1993
Svetlana Masterkova	RUS	1 MILE	04:12.6	Zürich	14 08 1996
Sonia O'Sullivan	IRL	2000M	05:25.4	Edinburgh	08 07 1994
Junxia Wang	CHN	3000M	08:06.1	Beijing	13 09 1993
Elvan Abeylegesse	TUR	5000M	14:24.7	Bergen	11 06 2004
Junxia Wang	CHN	10,000M	29:31.8	Beijing	08 09 1993
Tegla Loroupe	KEN	20,000M	05:26.6	Borghol zhausen	03 09 2000
Tegla Loroupe	KEN	1 HOUR	18.34	Borgho lzhausen	07 08 1998
Tegla Loroupe	KEN	25,000M	27:05.9	Mengers kirchen	21 09 2002
Tegla Loroupe	KEN	30,000M	45:50.0	Warstein	06 06 2003
Gulnara Samitova	RUS	3000M STEEPLECHASE	09:01.6	Iráklio	04 07 2004
Yordanka Donkova	BUL	100M HURDLES	12.21	Stara Zagora	20 08 1988
Yuliya Pechenkina	RUS	400M HURDLES	52.34	Tula	08 08 2003
Stefka Kostadinova	BUL	HIGH JUMP	2.09	Roma	30 08 1987
Yelena Isinbayeva	RUS	POLE VAULT	4.92	Bruxelles	03 09 2004
Galina Chistyakova	URS	LONG JUMP	7.52	Leningrad	11 06 1988
Inessa Kravets	UKR	TRIPLE JUMP	15.5	Göteborg	10 08 1995
Natalya Lisovskaya	URS	SHOT PUT	22.63	Moskva	07 06 1987
Gabriele Reinsch	GDR	DISCUS	76.8	Neubran denburg	09 07 1988
Mihaela Melinte	ROM	HAMMER	76.07	Rüdlingen	29 08 1999
Osleidys Menéndez	CUB	JAVELIN	71.54	Réthimno	01 07 2001
Jackie Joyner-Kersee	USA	HEPTATHLON	7291	Seoul	24 09 1988
Marie Collonvillé	FRA	DECATHLON	8150	Talence	26 09 2004
German Democratic Republic	GER	4X100M RELAY	41.37	Canberra	06 10 1985

Athlete Name	Nat	Event	Time	Place	Date
United States "Blue"	USA	4X200M RELAY	01:27.5	Philadelphia, PA	29 04 2000
USSR	URS	4X400M RELAY	03:15.2	Seoul	01 10 1988
USSR	URS	4X800M RELAY	07:50.2	Moskva	05 08 1984
Nadezhda Ryashkina	URS	10,000M RACE WALKING	41:56.2	Seattle, WA	24 07 1990
Olimpiada Ivanova	RUS	20,000M RACE WALKING	26:52.3	Brisbane	06 09 2001
Yan Wang	CHN	20KM RACE WALKING	1:26:22	Guangzhou	19 11 2001
Yelena Nikolayeva	RUS	"	1:26:22	Cheboksary	18 05 2003
Paula Radcliffe	GBR	10KM ROAD RACE	30:21:00	San Juan, PUR	23 02 2003
Elana Meyer	RSA	15KM ROAD RACE	46:57:00	Cape Town	02 11 1991

OLYMPIC/ASIAN/COMMONWEALTH/SAF GAMES

OLYMPIC GAMES:

It is held once in 4 years. The aims of the Olympic Movement are to promote the development of those fine physical and moral qualities which are the basis of amateur sports and to bring together the athletes of the world in a great quadrennial festival of sports. The honour of holding the olympic games is entrusted to a city and not a country or area. The choice of the city is with the International Olympic Committee.

OLYMPIC SYMBOL:

It comprises five rings or circles, linked together to represent the sporting friendship of all people. The rings represent the continents - Europe, Asia, Africa, Australia and America. Each ring is of a different colour. (i.e.) blue, yellow, black, green and red.

OLYMPIC FLAG:

The Olympic flag, created in 1913 at the suggestion of Baron Pierre de Coubertin, was solemnly inaugurated in Paris in June 1914 but it was raised over an Olympic stadium for the first time at the Antwerp Games in 1920. There is also a second Olympic flag, which is used for the Winter Games. These flags are made of white silk and contain five intertwined rings. From left to right the rings are blue, yellow, black, green and red. At least one of these colours is found on the flag of every country.

Colour of ring	Continent represented
Blue ring	Europe
Yellow ring	Asia
Black ring	Africa
Red ring	America
Green ring	Oceania

OLYMPIC FLAME:

Olympic flame was ceremonially lighted and burned at the Amsterdam Games in 1928. The modern version of the flame was adopted in 1936 at the Berlin Games. The Olympic flame symbolises the continuity between the ancient and the modern games. The torch used to kindle the flame, is first lit by the Sun's rays at Olympia, Greece, and then it is carried to the site of the games by relay of runners. Ships and planes are used when necessary. On July 15, 1976, space age technology was used to transport the Flame.

OLYMPIC MOTTO:

The Latin motto is Citius-Altius-Fortius meaning Swifter, higher and stronger composed by Rev. Father Didon on 1897. It was introduced as the Olympic motto on 1920 for first time at VII Olympic game held at Antwerpin Belgium.

OLYMPIC PRIZES, MEDALS AND CERTIFICATES

During ancient times the Olympic heroes received a crown of olive branches for their exploits. During modern times olympic champions are rewarded with medals and certificates. The winning athlete now receives a gold medal, the athlete in the second place is awarded a silver medal and the third athlete wins a bronze medal. The size of the medal is 60 mm in diameter and 3 mm thick. The first and second place medals are made of 92.5 per cent silver. The medal for the first winner is then plated with 6 gram of fine gold. The third place medal is of bronze.

Modern Olympic Games were staged at the following cities:

Summer Olympic Games

	Year	Venue	Competitors	Nations	Medal Ceremonies
I	1896	Athens (Greece)	245	14	43
II	1900	Paris (France)	1,225	24	86
III	1904	St Louis (USA)	689	13	89
IV	1908	London (Britain)	2,035	22	107
V	1912	Stockholm (Sweden)	2,547	28	102
VI	1916	Berlin (West Germany)	Not held due to World War I		
VII	1920	Antwerp (Belgium)	2,669	29	151
VIII	1924	Paris (France)	3,092	44	126
IX	1928	Amsterdam (Holland)	3,014	46	109
X	1932	Los Angeles (USA)	1,408	37	117
XI	1936	Berlin (West Germany)	4,066	49	129
XII	1940	Tokyo (Japan)	Not held due to World War II		
XIII	1944	London (Britain)	Not held due to World War II		
XIV	1948	London (Britain)	4,099	59	136
XV	1952	Helsinki (Finland)	4,925	69	149
XVI	1956	Melbourne (Australia)	3,184	67	145
XVII	1960	Rome (Italy)	5,348	83	150
XVIII	1964	Tokyo (Japan)	5,140	93	163
XIX	1968	Mexico City (Mexico)	5,530	112	172

Year	Venue	Competitors	Nations		Medal Ceremonies
XX	1972	Munich (West Germany)	7,123	121	195
XXI	1976	Montreal (Canada)	6,028	92	198
XXII	1980	Moscow (USSR)	5,217	80	203
XXIII	1984	Los Angeles (USA)	6,797	140	221
XXIV	1988	Seoul (South Korea)	8,465	159	237
XXV	1992	Barcelona (Spain)	9,367	169	257
XXVI	1996	Atlanta (USA)	10,310	197	271
XXVII	2000	Sydney (Australia)	10,321	200	300
XXVIII	2004	Athens (Greece)	10,500	202	301
XXIX	2008	Beijing (China)	(Scheduled)		
XXX	2012	London (England)	(Scheduled)		

Winter Olympic Games

Year	Venue	Country
1924	Chamonix	France
1928	St. Moritz	Switzerland
1932	Lake Placid	New York
1936	Garmisch-Partenkirchen	Germany
1948	St. Moritz	Switzerland
1952	Oslo	Norway
1956	Cortina d'Ampezzo	Italy
1960	Squaw Valley	California
1964	Innsbruck	Austria
1968	Grenoble	France
1972	Sapporo	Japan
1976	Innsbruck	Austria
1980	Lake Placid	New York
1984	Sarajevo	Yugoslavia
1988	Calgary	Alberta
1992	Albertville	France
1994	Lillehammer	Norway
1998	Nagono	Japan
2002	Salt Lake City	U.S.A.
2006	Turin	Italy
2010	Van Couver	Canada (Scheduled)
2014	Sochi	Russia (Scheduled)

33rd National Games - 2007

33rd National Games were held in Guwahati from 9th to 18th February. 11,000 athletes from 33 team participated in the event. Karate has been included as a discipline in this games. These Games were inaugurated on 9th February 2007 at the Indira Gandhi Athletic Stadium, Sarusajai, Guwahati. The closing ceremony of the event took place on February 18, 2007 at the Indira Gandhi

Athletic Stadium where the Services team were declared winners with 59 Gold medals, closely followed by Manipur that won 51 gold medals, whereas the host state Assam bagged as many as 38 gold medals only.

MEDALS TALLY

Place	Team	Gold	Silver	Bronze	Total
I	Services Team	59	46	37	**142**
II	Manipur	51	32	40	**123**
III	Assam	38	53	57	**148**
IV	Kerala	31	19	25	**75**
V	Haryana	30	22	28	**80**
XIV	Tamil Nadu	10	21	20	**51**

ICC World Cup - 2007

The 2007 (9th) edition of the ICC Cricket World Cup is being held in West Indies from March 13 to April 28, 2007. In this World Cup, there are 16 teams which are divided in four groups. **Group A**: Australia, South Africa, Scotland, The Netherlands. **Group B**: Sri Lanka, India, Bangladesh, Bermuda. **Group C**: New Zealand, England, Kenya, Canada. **Group D**: Pakistan, West Indies, Zimbabwe, Ireland. Australia beat Srilanka by 63 runs in Final.

Previous World Cup Winners : 1975 - West Indies; **1979** - West Indies; **1983** - India; **1987** - Australia; **1992** - Pakistan; **1996** - Sri Lanka; **1999** - Australia; **2003** - Australia; **2007** - Australia.

ICC World Cup-2011 will be held at India, Pakistan, Srilanka and Bangladesh.

ICC World Cup-2015 will be held at Australia and New Zealand.

15th Asian Games - 2006

The 15th edition of the Asian Games was inagurated in a colourful ceremony in Doha (Qatar) on December 1, 2006. The host country Qatar, presented a spectacular show of its history, culture and heritage at the opening ceremony. More than 13,000 athletes from 45 Asian nations took part in the games that were played for the first time in the Arab World. Koneru Humpy brought India its first Gold Medal in the 15th Asian Games by winning the individual women's rapid chess championship. She was followed by Pankaj Advani who won the Gold medal in the Billiards event. Jaspal Rana won two Gold Medals in the individual shooting events while India won the Gold in the team shooting event.

1st place China (164G, 88S, 63B) won 315 Medals, 2nd Place South Korea (58G, 53S, 82B) won 193 Medals, 3rd Place Japan (50G, 71S, 77B) won 198 Medals and 8th place India (10G, 18S, 26B) won 54 Medals.

ASIAN GAMES

Asian Relations Conference held at New Delhi decided to organise International Games for Asian Countries on the lines of the Olympics once in four years.

Year	Venue	No.of Games	No.of Athletes	No.of Countries	Ranking
1951	New Delhi, India	6	489	11	I-Japan II-India III-Iran
1954	Manila, Philippines	8	967	18	I-Japan II-Philippines III-S.Korea
1958	Tokyo, Japan	13	1422	20	I-Japan II-Philippines III-S.Korea
1962	Jakarta, Indonesia	13	1545	17	I-Japan II-Indonesia III-India
1966	Bangkok, Thailand	14	1945	18	I-Japan II-S.Korea III-Thailand
1970	Bangkok, Thailand	13	1752	18	I-Japan II-S.Korea III-Thailand
1974	Teheran, Iran	16	2357	25	I-Japan II-Iran III-China
1978	Bangkok, Thailand	19	2879	25	I-Japan II-China III-S.Korea
1982	New Delhi, India	21	3411	33	I-China II-Japan III-S.Korea
1986	Seoul, S.Korea	25	3345	27	I-China II-Japan III-S.Korea
1990	Beijing, China	27	4684	37	I-China II-Japan III-S.Korea
1994	Hiroshima, Japan	34	5300	42	I-China II-Japan III-S.Korea
1998	Bangkok, Thailand	36	8000	41	I-China II-Japan III-S.Korea
2002	Pusan, S. Korea	37	7000	44	I-China II-S.Korea III-Japan
2006	Doha, Qatar	38	8000	42	I-China II-S.Korea III-Japan

XVI Asian Games will be held in 2010 at Guong Zhou, China.
XVII Asian Games will be held in 2014 at Incheon (South Korea).

COMMONWEALTH GAMES

Conducted every four years on the lines of the Olympics but entries are limited only to Commonwealth Countries.

	Year	Venue	Countries participated	No.of disciplines	No.of players participated
I	1930	Hamilton, Canada	11	6	400
II	1934	London, England	16	6	500
III	1938	Sydney, Australia	15	7	464
IV	1950	Auckland, New Zealand	12	9	590
V	1954	Vancouver, Canada	24	9	662
VI	1958	Cardiff, U.K.	35	9	1130
VII	1962	Perth, Australia	35	9	863
VIII	1966	Kingston, Jamaica	34	9	1050
IX	1970	Edinburgh, U.K.	42	9	1383
X	1974	Christchurch, New Zealand	39	9	1276
XI	1978	Edmonton, Canada	48	10	1500
XII	1982	Brisbane, Australia	47	10	2143
XIII	1986	Edbinburgh, U.K.	26	10	2240
XIV	1990	Auckland, New Zealand	57	10	2900
XV	1994	Victoria, Canada	67	10	3350
XVI	1998	Kuala Lumpur, Malaysia	70	16	4000
XVII	2002	Manchester, (UK)	72	17	5000
XVIII	2006	Melbourne, Australia	71	24	4500
XIX	2010	New Delhi, India	Scheduled		

SAF GAMES

SAF Games rechristened

South Asian Federation Games are rechristened as South Asian Games at the 32nd meeting of the South Asian Sports Federation meeting in Islamabad (Pakistan) on April 2, 2004. The 10th edition of the Games were held in Colombo, Sri Lanka in August 2006.

10th SAF Games medals tally

India finish on the top of the medals tally with 234 medals (118 Gold, 69 Silver, 47 Bronze) followed by Pakistan and Sri Lanka at the 10th South Asian Federation Games held in Colombo (2006). Bangladesh will be the hosts for the 11th edition of the South Asian Games in the year 2008.

1st Afro-Asian Games

The first Afro-Asian Games started on October 24, 2003 in Hyderabad. The motto of the Games is "Peace Prosperity and Progress".

The next Afro-Asian Games will be held in Algiers (Algeria) in 2007.

CURRENT AFFAIRS

(NATIONAL)

Ansari elected Vice-President of India

Mohammad Hamid Ansari, the common candidate of the United Progressive Alliance and the Left parties, was on 2007, August 10 declared elected as the country's new Vice-President. In a triangular contest, Mr. Ansari scored a comfortable victory securing 455 out of the 762 votes polled.

First Woman President in India

Pratibha Devisingh Patil became the first woman and 12th President of the country when she was administered the oath of office by the Chief Justice of India K G Balakrishnan in the Central Hall of Parliament on July 25, 2007.

Red Fort added in UNESCO World Heritage List

UNESCO updated the World Heritage list by adding the Red Fort in India, the Sydney Opera House in Australia, the Iwami Ginzan Silver Mine in Japan and the Parthian Fortresses of Nisa in Turkmenistan, in Wellington (New Zealand) on June 28, 2007. The list also updated the name for the Auschwitz Concentration Camp in Poland, which will now be known as 'Auschwitz-Birkenau German Nazi Concentration and Extermination Camp (1940-1945)'.

2nd Underground Railway Corridor for Kolkata

The city is set to be the first in the country to have a second underground railway corridor. The project providing for Metro services along an east-west corridor that is to extend underwater across the Hooghly river to Howrah on the other side was ratified at a meeting of the West Bengal Cabinet on June 14, 2007. The construction work will begin in December 2008. Work is expected to be completed in 2013. The new project, which has been accepted by the Centre as a central sector project, will cost nearly Rs. 5,000 crore. It is to have 12 stations cutting across the city from Salt Lake in the east to Howrah station.

BrahMos Missile handed over to Army

Hon'ble President Dr. A.P.J. Abdul Kalam handed over a replica of the Mobile Autonomous Launcher (MAL) of the *BrahMos* missile to the Chief of the Army Staff Gen. J.J. Singh, symbolising the commencement of the delivery of the missile's version to the Army in New Delhi on June 21, 2007. BrahMos is a product of India-Russia cooperation. The *BrahMos* supersonic missile will primarily be deployed against 'value targets' near the India-Pakistan border, in the plains stretching from Jammu region to Rajasthan.

INS Jalashwa Commissioned

The Indian Navy on June 22, 2007 commissioned INS Jalashwa, a Landing Platform Dock (LPD). The ship is the first of its class to be inducted into the Navy and was acquired from the US, in the process marking a milestone in the bilateral relationship. With the induction of INS Jalashwa, formerly known as USS Trenton, India joins the selected group of countries operating an LPD, giving the Navy enhanced capability to move troops and equipments to greater distances in furthering the country's maritime interests.

Two New Districts in Karnataka State

Karnataka Cabinet on June 21, 2007 approved the formation of two new districts Ramanagara and Chikballapura to facilitate easy administration to the people. Kolar district was bifurcated to form the Chikballapura district and Ramanagara was formed as a new district consisting of four taluks after dividing the Bangalore Rural district. Chikballapura district would have six taluks with a population of 11.49 lakh in 1514 villages. The population in Ramanagara district is 10.08 lakh in 827 villages. With the formation of two more districts, the total number of districts in the state will be 29.

Goa Assembly Elections

The Congress – National Congress Party (NCP) alliance won 19 seats and emerged as the largest combination in a fractured verdict of the Goa Assembly elections. In the results declared here on June 5, 2007, the Bharatiya Janata Party bagged 14 seats. While the Save Goa Front (SGF) and the Maharashtrawadi Gomantak Party (MGP) won two seats each, the United Goans Democratic Party (UGDP) got one and Independents two. Rebel Congressman Churchill Alemao, who formed the SGF, bagged the Navelim seat by over 5,000 votes, defeating veteran Congressman and Industries Minister Luisinho Faleiro.

New Chief Minister of Uttar Pradesh

Bahujan Samaj Party (BSP) chief, Mayawati was sworn-in as the new Chief Minister of Uttar Pradesh on May 13, 2007 for the fourth time. She assumed reins of power heading a 50-member jumbo ministry inducting several persons from the upper castes, reflecting the rainbow coalition she stitched to get an absolute majority in elections, which were held to elect a 403-member Assembly in seven phases in April-May, 2007. On May 11, 2007 the results of the Assembly elections were declared. Across the populous State, BSP's elephant emerged triumphant garnering a phenomenal majority of 206 seats, smelting its rivals into surrender, Samajwadi Party came a distant second at 97 seats while Bharatiya Janata Party (BJP) folded up at

51. The performance of Congress was even worse, finishing a poor fourth with a paltry 22. The remaining 26 seats were taken by others such as the Rashtriya Lok Dal of Ajit Singh, other minor parties and the independents.

150 Years of India's First War of Independence

Reviving memories of the momentous events that resulted in the revolt of 1857, a spectacular cultural show was presented at the Red Fort here on May 11, 2007 to commemorate 150 years of the First War of Independence. On May 11, 1857, hundreds of sepoys reached Delhi from Meerut to persuade Mughal ruler Bahadur Shah Zafar to lead them in their struggle for freedom from foreign rule. Addressing the gathering, President APJ Abdul Kalam shared his vision of a developed India with them – a country where there is employment, health and food security for all, the rural-urban divide is bridged and there is a transparent and corruption-free administration.

New TV channel in Tamil

A new television channel to cater to *"the needs and desires of the people"* will be launched on August 15, 2007 Tamil Nadu Chief Minister and Dravida Munnetra Kazhagam president M. Karunanidhi confirmed. According to informed sources, Raj TV, which has two unused sets of transponders in Thaicomm satellite, will host the new channel.

India's Largest Ship Launched

The Hindustan Shipyard Limited (HSL) launched India's largest and most modern bulk carrier m.v. Good Princess on May 18, 2007. The ship is worth over Rs. 100 crore and has been built in 14 months by HSL. It will be delivered to the Chennai-based Good-earth Maritime Limited (GML) in four months. Good Princess is the second in the series of four bulk carriers with a capacity of 30,000 DWT. Its length is 178 metres and width is 28 metres.

Prithvi-I Test-fired successfully

Prithvi-I, the medium range surface-to-surface missile, was successfully test-fired in an "extended range" of more than 150 km by the Army as part of its "training module" at Chandipur-on-sea on May 9, 2007. The successful launch met all the mission objectives including terminal parameters such as velocity of impact and validated the integrated command control and communication network for the deployment of the weapon system.

"Green Giant" A-380 comes in India

Forget about it being the world's largest passenger aircraft or its wing-span giving goose bumps to even the biggest soccer field. The most gentle and quiet big daddy of all passenger jetliners, the A-380 completed its 100-minute Delhi-Mumbai flight, on May 8, 2007 with aplomb, grace and finesse. If the take-off from Delhi's Indira Gandhi International Airport showed how easy it was to manoeuvre the big bird, the landing at Mumbai's Chhatrapati

Shivaji Airport demonstrated that it could land with ease, approaching the runway with the speed of a single-aisle aircraft. On this flight, the aircraft carried about 175 passengers, including media personnel, senior Airbus officials, travel agents and Kingfisher Airlines chairman Vijay Mallya, who has placed orders for purchase of five A-380s. The first delivery is expected only in 2011, and by then Mr. Mallya hopes Kingfisher would get permission to fly abroad, so that the aircraft could be deployed on the U.S. routes. Kingfisher is the only carrier from India that has ordered the A-380, with a list price of about $ 300 million (about Rs. 1,200 crore per aircraft).

Round Table Conference on Kashmir

The third Round Table Conference on Kashmir was held in New Delhi on April 24, 2007. Addressing the conference, the Prime Minister Manmohan Singh dismissed Pakistan's claims that the two South Asian nuclear neighbours were nearing settlement on the Kashmir issue, while announcing the decision to set up the Standing Committee and Oversight and Monitoring Mechanism to implement the recommendations of the Working Groups of the Kashmir Roundtable Conference.

Supreme Court Declines in Vacate Stay on OBC Quota

The Supreme Court of India on April 23, 2007 declined to vacate the interim stay on 27 per cent reservation for Other Backward Classes (OBCs) in elite educational Institutions. A Bench of Justice Arijit Pasayat and Justice L.S. Panta held that its earlier order staying the provision of OBC Quota in a central legislation was final as far as the present academic session starting 2007 was concerned. On March 29, 2007 the two-member Bench had stayed section 6 of the Central Educational Institutions (Reservation in Admission) in so far as it related to 27 per cent quota for OBCs in institutions like IITs, IIMs and Central Universities.

PSLV-C8 successfully launches Italian Satellite 'Agile'

PSLV-C8 (Polar Satellite Launch Vehicle) was successfully launched on April 23, 2007. The launch vehicle also carried an Italian astronomical satellite, AGILE, from ISRO's Satish Dhawan Space Centre, Sriharikota. It was the first commercial launch of a foreign satellite.

New Commission on Centre-State Relations

Government has set up a Commission on April 27, 2007 to look into the issues on Centre-State Relations keeping in view the major changes that have taken place in the polity and economy of India over two decades. The Commission was headed by Justice Madan Mohan Punchhi (Retd.), former Chief Justice of India, Dhirendra Singh, IAS (Retd.), Vinod Kumar Duggal, IAS (Retd.) and Dr. N.R. Madhava Menon, former Director, National Judicial

Academy, Bhopal and former Director, National Law School of India Bangalore have been appointed as the members of the commission.

14th SAARC Summit-2007

The 14th summit of the South Asian Association for Regional Cooperation (SAARC) took place in the Indian capital New Delhi on April 3 & 4, 2007. The Indian delegation in the SAARC Council of Ministers at its two-day meeting apprised that India would host the next Council of Ministers prior to the summit meeting. Afghanistan, the eighth member of the group, also attended the 14th summit.

AWARDS

National Film Awards - 2005

These awards were announced for 2005 on August 7, 2007 in New Delhi.

❖ **Best Film for Swarna Kamal Award :** *Kaalpurush (Bengali)* ; ❖ **Best Film for Indira Gandhi Award :** *Parineeta (Hindi)* ; ❖ **Best popular Film for Swarna Kamal Award :** *Rang De Basanti (Hindi)* ; ❖ **Best Actor:** Amitabh Bachchan *(Black, Hindi)* ; ❖ **Best Actress:** Sarika *(Parzania, English)* ; ❖ **Best Director :** Rahul Dholakia *(Parzania, English)* ; ❖ **Best Audiography :** Nakul Kamte *(Rang De Basanti, Hindi)* ; ❖ **Best Editor :** P.S. Bharathi *(Rang De Basanti, Hindi)* ; ❖ **Best Male Play back Singer :** Naresh Iyer *(Rang De Basanti, Hindi)* ; ❖ **Best Female Play back Singer :** Shreya Ghoshal *(Paheli, Hindi)* ❖ **Best Feature Film for National Integration Award :** *Daivanamathil, Malayalam* ; ❖ **Best Film on Family Welfare Award :** *Thavamai Thavamiranthu, Tamil* ; ❖ **Best Film on Other Social Issues Award :** *Iqbal, Hindi* ; ❖ **Best Supporting Actor :** Nasseeruddin Shah *(Iqbal, Hindi)* ; ❖ **Best Supporting Actress :** Urvasi *(Achhuvinte Amma, Malayalam)* ; ❖ **Best Film On Environment Conservation / Preservation Award :** *Thutturi, Kannada*; ❖ **Best Children's Film :** *Blue Umbrella, Hindi* ; ❖ **Best Child Artist :** Sai Kumar *(Bommalata - A Bellyful of Dreams)* ; ❖ **Best Cinematography Award :** Madhu Ambat *(Sringaram, Tamil)* ; ❖ **Best Screenplay Award :** Prakash Jha, *Shridhar Raghavan and Manoj Tyagi (Apaharan, Hindi)* ; ❖ **Best Art Direction Award :** C.B. More *(Taj Mahal - An Eternal Love Story)* ; ❖ **Best Costume Designer Award :** Anna Singh *(Taj Mahal - An Eternal Love Story)* and Sabyachi Mukherjee *(Black)* ; ❖ **Special Jury Award :** Anupam Kher *(Maine Gandhi Ko Nahin Mara)* ; ❖ **Best Music Director :** Lalgudi Jayaraman *(Sringaram, Tamil)* ; ❖ **Best Lyrics :** Barguru Ramachandrappa *(Thaayi, Kannada)* ; ❖ **Special Effects Award :** Tata Elexi *(Anniyan, Tamil)*.

8th IIFA Awards, 2007

The 8th annual IIFA awards took place at Sheffield, Yorkshire in Northern England on June 9, 2007. The award was created seven years ago to promote Indian films to an International audience.

❖ **Best Film :** *Rang de Basanti* ❖ **Best Actor :** Hrithik Roshan *(Krrish)* ❖ **Best Actress :** Rani Mukherjee *(Kabhi Alwida Na Kehna)* ❖ **Best Director** : Rajkumar Hirani *(Lage Raho Munnabhai)* ❖ **Best Supporting Actor :** Arshad Warsi *(Lage Raho Munnabhai)* ❖ **Best Comic Actor :** Tusshar Kapoor *(Golmaal)* ❖ **Best Actor in Negative Role :** Saif Ali Khan *(Omkara)* ❖ **Best Actress in Supporting Role :** Soha Alikhan *(Rang de Basanti)* ❖ **Life Time Achievement Award :** Dharmendra. ❖ **Best Music Director :** A.R. Rahman *(Rang de Basanti)* ❖ **Best Lyrics :** Prasoon Joshi *(Chand Sifarish) (Fanaa)* ❖ **Best Male Playpack Singer :** Shaan *(Chand Sifarish) (Fanaa)* ❖ **Best Female Playback Singer :** Sunidhi Chauhan *(Beedi) (Omkara).*

Green Oscar, 2007

The seven year old Ashden Awards, also called Green Oscars, are thought to be world leaders in raising awareness of the huge potential of local sustainable energy to both tackle climate change and improve the quality of people's live. The awards have the official aim of encouraging the wider use of local sustainable energy projects to encourage its wider take-up across the world.

● An Indian company SEICO, a Bangalore-based company with the futuristic vision of a "world in which no family needs to burn oil lamps for light, where wireless digital communications are available to everyone, and where young people can see a bright future reflected in the solar cells that will power it" won the Outstanding Achievement Category of the Ashden award. ● A Kerala-based company, Biotech came first on the food security category for turning leftover food into biogas. Thereby solving two problems at one stroke-dealing with waste and generating clean cheap power.

Lal Bahadur Shastri National Award-2006

Renowned agricultural scientist Dr. M.S. Swaminathan has been chosen for the Lal Bahadur Shastri National Award for Excellence in Public Administration, Academics and Management, 2006. Dr. Swaminathan has been selected in recognition of his pioneering work in the field of agricultural research.

French Honour for Shah Rukh Khan

The French Government chose Bollywood actor Mr. Shah Rukh Khan for the 'Ordre des Arts et des Lettres' (Order of the Arts and Literature), for his exceptional career. The award is one of the most important cultural awards of France.

U.N. award for Vasundhara Raje

Rajasthan Chief Minister Vasundhara Raje received the prestigious "Women Together Award" at the United Nations headquarters in New York to join the league of Nobel laureates, social workers and celebrities from the field of music and cinema. Heba Abdul Latif of the UN Department of Political Affairs handed over the award to Ms. Raje for her pioneering initiatives among the weavers of Kota doria saris. Those who received the Third Women Together Award, along with Ms. Raje, this year included Nobel laureates Shirin Ebadi and Wangari Maathai, artiste Yoko Ono, novelist Barbara Probst Solomon, TV producer Francine Le Frank, economist Isabel Estape and journalist Rosa Maria Calaf. The award comprises a trophy and a certificate.

Kalam selected for King Charles II Medal

President Dr. A.P.J. Abdul Kalam has been selected for being awarded the prestigious King Charles II Medal by the Royal Society of London in recognition of his extraordinary contribution in the field of Science and Technology. The prestigious Medal is awarded to Foreign Heads of State for extraordinary contributions to the promotion of Science and Technology. It has only been awarded once in the past, to Emperor Akihito of Japan in 1998.

National Communal Harmony Awards

Octogenarian social activist from Assam Rabindra Nath Upadhyay and Delhi-based Institute for Socialist Education were presented the National Communal Harmony Awards for 2006 by President A.P.J. Abdul Kalam in New Delhi on May 23, 2007. The National Communal Harmony Awards comprise Rs.5 lakh for an organisation and Rs.2 lakh for an individual as well as a citation. Mr. Upadhyay is a Gandhian who played an active role in the freedom movement and is now working in the communally disturbed areas of the northeast. The Institute for Socialist Education, headed by its founder and former MP Shashi Bhushan, has been championing the cause of secularism and integration.

Dadasaheb Phalke Award - 2006

Hrishikesh Mukherjee was awarded the prestigious "Dadasaheb Phalke Award for 2006 on April 30, 2007.

Lokmanya Tilak Award - 2007

Missile technologist A. Sivathanu Pillai was awarded the Lokmanya Tilak Award for 2007 on August 2, 2007 at Pune by Union Power Minister Sushil Kumar Shinde.

Jnanpith Award - 2004

Noted Kashmiri poet, Rehman Rahi was selected for the Jnanpith Award for 2004 on March 10, 2007 for his outstanding contribution to Indian literature.

Padma Awards - 2007

The President APJ. Abdul Kalam presented to 121 names for the civilian awards in New Delhi on January 26, 2007 to the following:-

Padma Vibhushan (10): Prof. Balu Sankaran, Medicine; Fali Sam Nariman, Public Affairs; Khushwant Singh, Literature and Education; N.N. Vohra, Civil Service; Naresh Chandra, Civil Service; Justice (Retd.) Prafullachandra Natwarlal Bhagwati, Public Affairs; Raja Rao (Posthumous), Literature and Education; Dr. Raja Jesudoss Chelliah, Public Affairs; Sudarshan Erinackal Chandy George, Science and Engineering; Dr. Venkataraman Krishnamurthy, Civil Service.

Padma Bhushan (32): Prof. Bhikhu Parekh, Literature and Education; Chandra Prasad Saikia (Posthumous), Literature and Education; Ela Gandhi, Public Affairs; Rev Father Gabriel, Literature and Education; Gopaldas Neeraj, Literature and Education; Dr. Gurcharan Singh Kalkat, Science and Engineering; Ms. Indra Nooyi, Trade and Industry; Jamshed J. Irani, Trade and Industry; Javed Jan Nisaar Akhtar, Literature and Education; Prof. Jeffrey D. Sachs, Literature and Education; Justice K.T. Thomas, Public Affairs; Kavalam Narayan Panikkar, Art; Captain L.Z. Sailo, Literature and Education; Dr. Manju Sharma, Science and Engineering; Dr. N. Mahalingam, Trade and Industry; O. Suzuki, Trade and Industry; Dr. Prithipal Singh Maini, Medicine; Pandit Rajan Misra, Art; Ramankutty Nair, Art; Pandit Sajan Misra, Art; Dr. Saroj Ghose, Science and Engineering; Dr. Shiv Kumar Sarin, Medicine; Prof. (Vaidya) Shriram Sharma, Medicine; Somnath Hore (Posthumous), Art; Sunil Bharti Mittal, Trade and Industry; Syed Haider Raza, Art; Hakim Syed Mohammad Sharfuddin Quadri, Medicine; Prof. T.N. Srinivasan, Literature and Education; Prof. Tapan Ray Chaudhuri, Literature and Education; Tyeb Mehta, Art Dr. V. Mohini Giri, Social Work; Dr. Vilayanur Ramachandaran, Science and Engineering.

Padma Shri (79): A. Sivasailam, Trade and Industry; Prof. Adya Prasad Mishra, Literature and Education; Amitav Ghosh, Literature and Education; Prof. Ananda M. Chakrabarty, Science and Engineering; Dr. Ananda Shankar Jayant, Art; Prof. Anoop Misra, Medicine; Dr. Ashok Kumar Hemal, Medicine; Astad Aderbad Deboo, Art; Dr. Atul Kumar, Medicine; Dr. B. Paul Thaliath, Medicine; Dr. Bakul Harshadrai Dholakia, Literature and Education; Dr. Balbir Singh, Medicine; Dr. Baldev Raj, Science and Engineering; Shri Bharath Balachandra Menon, Art; Prof. Devindra Rahinwal (Posthumous), Social Work; Prof. Dilip K. Biswas, Science and Engineering; Gajendra Narayan Singh, Art; Geeta Chandran, Art; Giriraj Kishore, Literature and Education; Rajmata

Goverdan Kumarri, Art; Prof. Harpinder Singh Chawla, Medicine;Jeev Milkha Singh, Sports; Dr. K.R. Palani Swamy, Medicine; Khalid Zaheer, Social Work; Prof. Kharak Singh Valdiya, Science and Engineering; Kiran Karnik, Science and Engineering; Ms. Koneru Humpy, Sports; Dr. Lalit Pande, Environment Protection; Louis Remo Fernandes, Art; Dr. M. Mohan Babu, Art; Dr. Mahadev Prasad Pandey, Literature and Education; Dr. Mahipal S. Sachdev, Medicine; Dr. Manjunath Cholenahally Nanjappa, Medicine; Dr. Mayilvahanan Natarajan, Medicine; Ms. Meenakshi Gopinath, Literature and Education; Ms. Miriam L'vovna Salganik, Literature and Education; Dr. Mohsin Wali, Medicine; Mujtaba Hussain, Literature and Education; Prof. Mushirul Hassan, Literature and Education; Ms. Naina Lal Kidwai, Trade and Industry; Prof. Narmada Prasad Gupta, Medicine; Neelamani Devi, Art; P. Gopinathan, Art; P.R. Thilagam, Art; Pannuru Sripathy, Art; Prof. P. Namperumalsamy, Medicine; Prof. Pratibha Ray, Literature and Education; Pushpa Hans, Art; Rabinder Gokaldas Ahuja, Sea Cadet Corps Management; Rajinder Gupta, Trade and Industry; Dr. Ravi Narayan Bastia, Science and Engineering; Ravindra Dayal, Literature & Education; Prof. Rostislav Borisovich Rybakov, Literature and Education; Ms. Runa Banerjee, Social Work; S. Dhakshinamurthy Pillai, Art; Sister S.M. Cyril, Social Work; Shanti Hiranand, Art; Shashikala Jawalkar, Art; Prof. Shekhar Pathak, Literature and Education; Dr. Sheo Bhagwan Tibrewal, Medicine; Sonam Skalzang, Art; Sonam Tshering Lepcha, Art; Prof. Sudhir Kumar Sopory, Science and Engineering; Dr. Sukumar Azhikode, Literature and Education; Sushil Gupta, Social Work; Dr. Syeda Saiyidain Hameed, Public Affairs; T.S. Rangarajan @ Kavingar Vaali, Literature and Education; Ms. Tarla Dalal, Cookery; Ms. Teesta Setalvad, Public Affairs; Dr. Temsula Ao, Literature and Education; Dr. Thanu Padmanabhan, Science and Engineering; Dr. Thekkethil Kochandy Alex, Science and Engineering; Thingbaijam Babu Singh, Art; Lama Thupten Phuntsok, Social Work; Valayapatti A.R. Subramaniam, Art; Vijaydan Detha, Literature and Education; Vikram Seth, Literature and Education; Waman Thakre, Art; Dr. Yusufkhan Mohamadkhan Pathan, Literature and Education.

Gallantry Awards - 2007

The following persons were awarded the country's second highest peacetime award for gallantry, Kirti and Shaurya Chakra Awards on January 26, 2007.

Kirti Chakra: Col. Gulbir Singh Sarna (29 RR); Maj. Manish Hiraji Pitambare (Parachute Regiment); Capt. Vishal Bhandral (Garhwal Rifles); Lt. Natarajan Parthiban (Jammu & Kashmir); Light Havildar Manjit Singh (Sikh Regiment); Sub-inspector Dhirendra Nath Pratap Singh (CISF).

Shaurya Chakra: Of the 31 Shaurya Chakras, 12 were awarded posthumously. This included two Border Roads Organisation personnel killed while undertaking road clearance operations in hazardous conditions.

Lt. Col. Raj Kumar (Kumaon Regiment); Lt. Col. Vinay R. Chauhan (1 Gorkha Rifles, posthumous); Maj. Jung Bahadur Singh (SM Army Service Cops); Maj. Naveen Bindal (Army Air Defence); Maj. Shineesh Mukundan (Grenadiers); Maj. Virinder Sidhu; Maj. Krishnan Nishant Nair (Bihar Regiment); Maj. Manvendra Singh (20 Jammu and Kashmir Rifles); Capt. Nayanjyoti Buragohain (1 Naga Regiment); Capt. Shashi B. Singh (SM Corps of Engineers, posthumous); Capt. Ajit Anthony (Rajputana Rifles, posthumous); Lt. Thiyam Ibungochouba Luwang (21 Parachute Regiment); Subedar Samde Khan (14 Grenadiers); Naib Subedar M.A. Cruz (201 Engineer Regiment, posthumous); Havildar Santosh Kumar (14 Grenadiers); Havildar Bhag Singh (16 Sikh Regiment); Lance Havildar Sishpal Singh (Dogra Regiment); Sepoy Satnam Singh (Mahar Regiment); Subedar Sant Kumar (SM Grenadiers).

Besides the Kirti Chakras, anti-terrorist operations have won 73 Sena Medals and one Vayu Sena Medal for the armed forces personnel. The President awarded 393 medals to the uniformed personnel on the occasion of Republic Day.

Param Vishisht Seva medals

The President's honours list also includes 19 senior Army officers who have been decorated with Param Vishisht Seva Medals. This includes the new Vice-Chief of Army Staff Lt. Gen. Deepak Kapoor, Western Army Commander Lt. Gen. Daljit Singh and Director - General of Military Operations Mohan Pandey.

President APJ Abdul Kalam has also approved four Bar to Sena Medals (Gallantry), one Bar to Ati Vishisht Seva Medal, 52 Ati Vishisht Seva Medals, one Youth Seva Medal, four Bar to Vishist Seva Medals, 123 Vishist Seva Medals, two Bar to Sena Medals, 41 Sena Medals, 12 Nao Sena Medals and Vayu Sena Medals (15).

Independence Day Gallantry Awards - 2007

Three Army men have been awarded the Ashok Chakra, the country's highest award for valour during peacetime. All the three - Colonel Vasanth Venugopal, Captain R. Harshan and Naib Subedar Chunni Lal - laid down their lives while battling terrorists in Jammu and Kashmir. The President approved 140 gallantry awards for the Armed Forces, Coast Guard and Civilians.

These include six Kirti Chakras (the second highest award for valour), 20 Shaurya Chakras (the third highest award), two bar to Sena Medals (gallantry), 99 Sena Medals, four Nao Sena Medals and six Vayu Sena Medals. The last two are naval and air force equivalents of Sena Medals awarded to Army personnel.

In a "rather rare" instance, two Army battalions have won three gallantry awards each. Personnel from the 9 Maratha Light Infantry, parent unit of the Chief of the Army Staff, Gen. J. J. Singh, have won an Ashok Chakra (Col. Vasanth, posthumous), a Kirti Chakra (Capt. Abhinav Handa) and Shaurya Chakra (Lance Naib B. S. Ganpat, posthumous).

Kalpana Chawla Excellence Awards - 2007

Former captain of the Indian women's hockey team, Sita Gussain and rifle shooter Shilpi Singh were awarded the Kalpana Chawla Excellence Awards. The awards ceremony was organised by the Punjab Engineering College (Chandigarh) Old Boys Association.

Lata Mangeshkar Awards

Hridayanath Mangeshkar - 2007; singer Jayamala Shiledar - 2006; singer Manna De - 2005; singer Snehal Bhatkar - 2004. The award has been instituted by the Madhya Pradesh Government.

52nd Filmfare Awards - 2007

These awards were presented on 24 February 2007, at the Yashraj studios in Andheri, Mumbai.

◆ **Best Film :** *Rang De Basanti* ◆ **Best Actor :** Hritik Roshan (*Dhoom-2*) ◆ **Best Actress :** Kajol *(Fanaa)* ◆ **Best Director:** Rakeysh Omprakash Mehra (*Rang De Basanti*) ◆ **Best Critics Award:** Rajkumar Hirani and Vidu Vinod Chopra (*Lage Raho Munnabhai*) ◆**Critics Award for Best Actor:** Aamir Khan (*Rang De Basanti*) ◆ **Critics Award for Best Actress:** Kareena Kapoor (*Omkara*) ◆ **Lifetime Achievement Award:** Jaya Bachchan, Javed Akhtar ◆ **Special Juri Recognition:** Deepak Dobriyal (*Omkara*) ◆ **Best Dialogue:** Abhijit Joshi and Rajkumar Hirani (*Lage Raho Munnabhai*) ◆ **Best Art Direction:** Sameer Chanda (*Omkara*) ◆ **Best Editing:** P.S. Bharti (*Rang De Basanti*) ◆ **Best Screenplay:** Jaideep Sahni (*Khosla Ka Ghosla*) ◆ **Best Story:** Vidu Vinod Chopra and Rajkumar Hirani (*Lage Raho Munnabhai*) ◆ **Best Actor in a Supporting Role (Male):** Abhishek Bachchan (*Kabhi Alvida Na Kehna*) ◆ **Best Actor in Supporting Role (Female):** Konkona Sen Sharma (*Omkara*) ◆ **Best Actor in a Comic Role:** Arshad Warsi (*Lage Raho Munnabhai*) ◆ **Best Actor in a Negative Role:** Saif Ali khan (*Omkara*) ◆ **Best Music:** A.R. Rahman (*Rang De Basanti*) ◆ **Best Lyrics:** Prasoon Joshi (*Chand Sifarish, Fanaa*) ◆ **Best Playback Singer(Male):** Shaan and Kailash Kher (*Fanaa*) ◆ **Best Playback Singer (Female):** Sundhi Chauhan (*Beedi, Omkara*) ◆ **Best Cinematography:** Binod Pradhan (*Rang De Basanti*) ◆ **Best Costumes:** Dolly Ahluwalia

(*Omkara*) ◆ **Best Sound Design:** Subhash Sahu and K.J. Singh (*Omkara*) ◆ **Best Background Score Award:** Salim-Sulaiman (*Krrish*) ◆ **Best Debut (Female):** Kangana Ranaut (*Gangster*) ◆ **Powerhouse Awards:** Yash Chopra ◆ **R.D. Burman Award:** Naresh Iyer ◆ **Sony-Fairone face of the Year:** Kangana Ranaut ◆ **Best Choreography:** Ganesh Acharya, Beedi Jalayle (*Omkara*) ◆ **Best special Fx:** Krrish ◆ **Best Action:** Siu Tung Ching, Sham Kaushal (*Krrish*) ◆ **Best Costumes Award:** Omkara

Sahitya Academy Awards - 2006

The following seven poets among the 23 were awarded the Sahitya Academy Awards for 2006 on December 21. They include famous poets Darshan Darshi (Dogri), Gyanendrapati (Hindi), Shafi Shauq (Kashmiri), Banshidhar Sarangi (Oriya), Harshadev Madhav (Sanskrit), Mu. Metha (Tamil) and Makhmoor Saeedi (Urdu). Ms. Rupa Bajwa has been chosen for the Sahitya Academy Award in English 2006 for her debut novel *The Sari Shop*.

Sangeet Natak Academi Awards - 2007

President APJ Abdul Kalam presented the Sangeet Natak Academi Awards to 33 persons in New Delhi on March 1, 2007. Some of the awardees include Kuchipudi guru Pasumarthy Rattiah Sarma, Mohiniattam guru Kalamandalam Vimala Menon, Assamese dancer Gorima Hazarika for 'Creative and Experimental Dance' and D. Pasupathi, the veteran Carnatic vocal guru of dance a academy Kalakshetra in Chennai. The award has been instituted by the Ministry of Culture in 1952.

National Kishore Kumar Samman' 2007 & 2006

Popular actor and BJP leader Shatrughan Sinha was awarded for 2007 and famous film director Mr. Shyam Benegal for 2006. The Kishore Kumar award is given for direction, acting, scriptwriting and lyrics by the Madhya Pradesh Government.

Rajiv Gandhi Khel Ratna award-2007

Pankaj Advani (Billiards & Snooker) has been given the country's highest sports award. This award comprising cash award of Rs.5 lakh, a scroll of honour and a medal. Manavajit Singh (Shooter) won Rajiv Gandhi Khel Ratna award in 2007.

Arjuna Awards, 2007

It was awarded to the following persons : Jayanth Taluktar (Archery), K.M. Pinu (Athletics), Chetan Anand (Badminton), Vijayendar (Boxing), Harikrishna (Chess), Anju Chopra (Cricket), Jothi Kullu (Hockey), Navaneeth Gautam (Kabaddi), Vijaykumar (Shooting), Saurav Koshal (Squash), Subajith Shaga (Table Tennis), Geetha Rani (Weight Lifting), Keethika Jhagar

(Wrestling), Rohit Bahar (Physically Handicapped). This awards comprising a cash award of Rs.3 lakh, a statute and a scroll of honour.

Dronacharya Award, 2007

It was awarded to R.D. Singh (Athletics), Damodar Chanderlal (Boxing), Koneru Ashok (Chess). This awards comprising cash award of Rs.3 lakh, a plaque and a scroll of honour.

Dhyan Chand Award, 2007

It was awarded to Virender Singh (Hockey), Rajinder Singh (Wrestling), Samsher Singh (Kabaddi). This awards for lifetime achievement in sports and games comprising a cash award of Rs.3 lakh, plaque and a scroll of honour.

Maulana Abul Kalam Azad Trophy - 2006

Punjab University, Chandigarh has won in the All India Inter-University Sports by lifting the coveted Trophy for the year 2006.

Tenzing Norgay Adventure Award - 2006

Nawang Gombu (Lifetime Achievement), Chhering Norbu Bodh (Land), Shital Kamalakar Mahajan (Air), Mukul Asthana (Water).

SPORTS
Billiards

Geet Sethi wins World Title

Billiards ace Geet Sethi has won his fifth World professional title after seven years, defeating England's Lee Lagan by over 1000 points in a five - hour final. Sethi had lost the title in 1998, having won it four times in the 1990s.

Chess

Padma Shri for Koneru Humpy

Koneru Humpy, the youngest female player in the history of chess to achieve a men's GM title was conferred the Padma Shri on January 25, 2007. Reacting to the honour bestowed on her she said that she was delighted to receive the great civilian honour at this young age. She was an Asian Junior Champion, winner of World Junior crown and is also the first player to win a chess Gold in the Asian Games. She received the Arjuna award in 2004.

India's 12th Grandmaster

Panchanathan Magesh Chandran becomes India's 12th Grand Master when he is tied for the first place in the World Open Chess Tournament held at Philadelphia (US). Other Indian Grandmasters are: Viswanathan Anand, Dibyendu Barua, Pravin Thipsay, Abhijit Kunte, Krishna Sasikiran, S.S. Ganguly, P. Harikrishna, Sandipan Chanda, Koneru Humpy, R.B. Ramesh & Tejas Bakru.

Cricket

Tendulkar crosses another milestone - 15,000 Runs in ODIs

Master Blaster Sachin Tendulkar became the first player to reach 15,000 runs in One-Day cricket in the second ODI against South Africa in Belfast (Ireland) on June 29, 2007. Tendulkar, who is already ODI's leading scorer, reached this milestone when he hit the run that took him to his 79th half century.

India-Bangladesh Test Series

India took 15 wickets on day three at the Sher-e-Bangla Stadium at Mirpur to wrap up the two-match Test series 1-0 on May 27, 2007. Mohammad Ashraful hit the joint second fastest fifty in Tests, from 26 balls, but his efforts could not prevent defeat by an innings and 239 runs. Only Jacques Kallis, against Zimbabwe, had produced a faster Test half-century. India scored 610 for 3 and Bangladesh scored 118 and then 253. Anil Kumble distinguished himself by crossing the 550-wicket mark in Tests, taking 115 matches, 21 more than Sri Lankan wizard Muttiah Muralitharan, the fastest to reach the same target.

The Test ended in India's biggest ever victory. With it, the curtains came down on the two-Test series after the rain-influenced draw in the first Test at Chittagong, Zaheer Khan was adjudged the man of the match, while Sachin Tendulkar was declared the man of the series for his back-to-back hundreds.

Ranji Trophy - 2007

Mumbai Captain Amol Muzumdar proudly lifted the Ranji Trophy after defeating Bengal in the final played in Mumbai on February 5, 2007. This was the 37th victory for the home team in the history of Ranji Trophy. Bengal, bowled out in the second innings at 339, 132 runs short of the target, lost its second back to back Ranji final.

Hockey

16th Azlan Shah Trophy

Olympic champions Australia has won its fifth Azlan Shah Trophy, the third in four years, after defeating home side Malaysia, 3-1 in Ipoh, Malaysia on May 14, 2007. Eddie Ockenden, played his best match so far in the Australian strip, winning Player of the final and scoring twice in the win, blitzing the Malaysian defense with his pace and touch. For Malaysia, it was second time unlucky in the final. They had lost to India in 1985, the only other time the hosts had entered the final of this tournament. India finished third by defeating Asian champion South Korea 1-0 in the play-off match for third place.

★ *Player of the tournament: Andrew Smith* (Australia) ★ *Player of the Match: Ed Ockenden* (Australia) ★ *Highest Scorer: 6, Lee Sung Min* (Korea) ★ *Best Goalkeeper: Kumar Subramaniam* (Malaysia) ★ *Fair Play: Argentina;* ★ *Final Placings: 1. Australia, 2. Malaysia, 3. India, 4. Korea, 5. Argentina.*

Miscellaneous

33rd National Games - 2007

33rd National Games were held in Guwahati from 9th to 18th February. 11,000 athletes from 33 team participated in the event. Karate has been included as a discipline in this games. These Games were inaugurated on 9th February 2007 at the Indira Gandhi Athletic Stadium, Sarusajai, Guwahati. The closing ceremony of the event took place on February 18, 2007 at the Indira Gandhi Athletic Stadium where the Services team were declared winners with 59 Gold medals, closely followed by Manipur that won 51 gold medals, whereas the host state Assam bagged as many as 38 gold medals only.

First place Services team (59 Gold, 46 Silver, 37 Bronze) won 142 Medals, Second place Manipur (51 Gold, 32 Silver, 40 Bronze) won 123 Medals, Third place Assam (38 Gold, 53 Silver, 57 Bronze) won 148 Medals, Fourth place Kerala (31 Gold, 19 Silver, 25 Bronze) won 75 Medals, Fifth place Haryana (30 Gold, 22 Silver, 28 Bronze) won 80 Medals and 14th place Tamil Nadu (10 Gold, 21 Silver, 20 Bronze) won totally 51 Medals.

15th Asian Games - 2006

The 15th edition of the Asian Games was inagurated in a colourful ceremony in Doha (Qatar) on December 1, 2006. The host country Qatar, presented a spectacular show of its history, culture and heritage at the opening ceremony. More than 13,000 athletes from 45 Asian nations took part in the games that were played for the first time in the Arab World. Koneru Humpy brought India its first Gold Medal in the 15th Asian Games by winning the individual women's rapid chess championship. She was followed by Pankaj Advani who won the Gold medal in the Billiards event. Jaspal Rana won two Gold Medals in the individual shooting events while India won the. Gold in the team shooting event.

1st place China (164G, 88S, 63B) won 315 Medals, 2nd Place South Korea (58G, 53S, 82B) won 193 Medals, 3rd Place Japan (50G, 71S, 77B) won 198 Medals and 8th place India (10G, 18S, 26B) won 54 Medals.

INTERNATIONAL

Oct. 2: International Day of Non-Violence

In a tribute to Mahatma Gandhi's philosophy of brotherhood and peace, the UN General Assembly has declared 2nd October, his birth anniversary, as the "International Day of Non-Violence". MoS for External Affairs Anand Sharma introduced the resolution in the 191-member assembly. The resolution, which urged memebr states to observe the day each year in appropriate manner to disseminate the message of non-violence, was co-sponsored by 137 of the 191 members and was adopted without a vote.

Rig Veda in UNESCO list

Thirty manuscripts of the ancient Hindu test Rig Veda dating from 1800 to 1500 B.C. are among 38 new items that have been added to the United Nations heritage list to help preserve them for posterity. The list includes the world's first feature-length film, the family archives of Swedish industrialist Alfred Nobel and the proceedings of the trials of South African anti-apartheid figures such as Nelson Mandela. The items have been included in the 'Memory of the World Register' set up by the UN Educational, Scientific and Cultural Organization (UNESCO), bringing to 158, the total number of inscriptions on the register so far. UNESCO Director-General is Koochiro Matsuura.

Israel's new President elected

Mr. Shimon Peres was elected Israel's new President in Jerusalem on June 13, 2007. Mr. Peres, an 83-year-old Nobel Peace Prize winner, has held all of Israel's top civilian posts. He assumes office on July 15, 2007 for a seven-year term.

New British Prime Minister elected

Mr. Gordon Brown took over as the new British Prime Minister replacing Mr. Tony Blair who was in office for ten years, in London on June 27, 2007. He is Britain's 52nd Prime Minister.

Atlantis returns safely

Space shuttle Atlantis that carried Indian-American astronaut Sunita Williams along with six crew members landed safely at Edwards Air Force Base in California, USA on June 22, 2007 at 1.19 a.m. (IST). Though scheduled to land on June 21, 2007, but due to bad weather, NASA withheld Atlantis' landing at the Kennedy Space Centre, Florida. Atlantis commander Rick Sturckow and pilot Lee Archambault had waited for green light to fire thrusters to slow down the orbiter, which reaches speeds of more than 26,000 km per hour. Sunita, who had set off from Cape Canaveral on December 9, 2006 on space shuttle Discovery, made history by staying 195 days in space, the longest by a woman. She also set the world record for a female astronaut on spacewalks, totalling 29 hours and 17 minutes.

New World Bank President

US President George W. Bush has chosen Robert Zoellick, a former U.S. trade representative to replace Paul Wolfowitz as President of the World Bank. Zoellick, was one of 18 mostly conservative figures, including former Defence Secretary Donald Rumsfeld and Wolfowitz, who wrote a much publicized letter to former President Bill Clinton in 1998 advocating removing Saddam Hussein from power in Iraq. It also noted that any bank executive director could nominate a candidate. The United States has traditionally selected the head of the World Bank since it was founded 60 years ago, while Europe has chosen the head of its sister organization, the International Monetary Fund.

Sonia, Mittal on Time List

Congress leader Sonia Gandhi, Steel baron L.N. Mittal and Pepsico CEO Indra Nooyi figure in Time magazine's coveted list of 100 most influential people, which also includes Al-Qaeda leader Osama bin Laden. But missing from the list for the first time in four years, is United States President George W. Bush. The list also features Queen Elizabeth II, Sudanese President Mohamed Omar Hassan Ahmed al-Bashir, acting Cuban President Raul Castro, Iranian supreme leader Ayatollah Ali Khamenei, Chinese President Hu Jintao, King Abdullah of Saudi Arabia and Pope Benedict XVI, Hillary Rodham Clinton, Barrack Obama, Secretary of State Condoleezza Rice and House Speaker Nancy Pelosi are among the Americans on the list.

Huge Oil field in China

China's newly found oil field in Bohai Bay has a reserve of one billion tonnes, or about 7.35 billion barrels, the largest discovery in the country over four decades, said the China National Petroleum Corporation (CNPC). The field lies in the Jidong offfield in the Hebei Province. The block, partly offshore, covers 1,300-1,500 sq.km. and is expected to produce light crude. The company previously estimated that the reserve of the new oilfield was 2.2 billion barrels and the daily output would be 2,00,800 barrels in three years.

China's oil dependency, or net oil imports against oil consumption, went up 4.1 percentage points year on year to 47 per cent in 2006, according to the Ministry of Commerce. In 2006, the nation produced 183.68 million tonnes of crude oil, up 1.7 per cent, and imported 138.84 million tonnes, up 16.9 per cent. Its oil consumption (crude plus oil products) amounted to 346.56 million tonnes, up 9.3 per cent.

Presidential Election in East Timor

East Timor Prime Minister Jose Ramos Horta on May 11, 2007 emerged victorious in the tiny state's first presidential poll since Independence five years ago. A Nobel Peace laureate for his role in the country's struggle for independence, Horta defeated Facisco Guterres, currently leader of the Fretilin party that had fought for freedom from Indonesia.

ASEAN Foreign Ministers' Meeting

Association of South East Asian Nations (ASEAN) Foreign Ministers' Meeting was held in Jakarta, the capital of Indonesia on April 13, 2007. At the end of the meeting, the Ministers agreed to establish a task force to look into the formation of an infrastructure fund. Other priorities, covered integrated development of capital market in ASEAN with stronger support to financial supply institutions among ASEAN communities.

China joins Elite Club

China's home made new generation fighter air craft, the Jian-10, made its debut in Beijing on January 5, 2007. A five-minute-long video film revealed how the fighter takes off, lands, fires missiles and flies in formation. A single-seater model plane was also uneviled by the China Aviation Industry Corporation I (AVICI), which spent seven years developing the Jian-10, the Taihang turbofan engine and the new generation air to air missiles.

China has become the fourth country in the world to develop its own advanced fighter aircraft, aero-engines and missiles, said Geng Ruguang, Deputy General Manager of AVICI. The Jian-10 and the Taihang turbofan engine, both with proprietary intellectual property rights (IPR), herald the third generation of Chinese fighter aircraft and military aero engines, said Mr. Geng. The Jian-10 series marks a break through in China's development of heavy fighter aircraft, said Liu Gaozhuo, executive Jian-10 programme.

Putin visits Saudi Arabia in First Time

President Vladimir Putin, making the first visit by a Russian leader to Saudi Arabia, has met King Abdullah and other senior officials for talks on the situations in Iraq and the Palestinian territories. His visit to this traditional US ally comes as Saudi Arabia is opening up to other countries, particularly in Asia. Moscow represents an option for Saudi Arabia to diversify its sources and a potential ally with considerable political clout as a member of the United Nations Security Council and the club of Mideast peacemakers. The leaders met for talks on regional and international issues including the Palestinian issue, the situation in Iraq and bilateral cooperation, the official Saudi Press Agency reported.

First U.K. Hindu School

Britain's Christians, Muslims, Sikhs and Jews already have their own state-funded faith schools and now the country's 6,00,000 strong Hindu community is set to acquire one. The school which like other faith schools, will receive millions of pounds of Government funding, will be located in Harrow, a predominantly Hindu enclave in northwest London and run by Krishna-Avanti school foundation

AWARDS

Nehru Award for International Understanding:

This award carries an amount of fifteen lakh rupees in cash and a citation which is presented to the recipient at a special ceremony in India. It is awarded to those who have contributed for international peace and understanding.

The Recipients of Nehru Awards

U.Thant (former Secretary General of the UNO)	1965
Dr. Martin Luther King (Posthumous)	1966
Khan Abdul Ghaffar Khan (Frontier Gandhi)	1967
Yehudi Menuhin (Violinist)	1968
Mother Teresa (Nun)	1969
Kenneth Kaunda (President of Zambia)	1970
Marshal Tito (Ex-President of Yugoslavia)	1971
Andre Malraux	1972
Julius Nyrere (Ex-President of Tanzania)	1973
Paul Prebisch	1974
Jonal Salk	1975
Giuseppe Tucci	1976
Tulsi Mehrji Shrestha	1977
Nichidatsu Fuji	1978
Nelson R.Mandela	1979
Mrs. Barbara Ward	1980
Gunnar Myrdal and Alva Myrdal	1981
Dr. Leopold Sedar Senghor	1982
Dr. Bruno Kreisky	1983
Mrs.Indira Gandhi (Posthumous)	1985
Olaf Palme (Ex.Prime Minister of Sweden)	1986
Perez de Cuellar (former Secretary General of the UNO)	1987
Yasser Arafat (PLO Leader)	1988
Robert Mugabe (President of Zimbabwe)	1989
Helmut Kohl (Chancellor of Germany)	1990
Aruna Asaf Ali (Social Worker, India)	1991

Maurice F.Strong (Canada)	1992
Ms. Daw Aung San Suu Kyi (Myanmar)	1993
Mr. Md.Hosini Mubarak (Egypt)	1996
Gok Chok Tong (Prime Minister of Singapore)	2003
Julius Namrai (Princess of Tanzania)	2004
Wangari M. Maathai (Environmentalist, Kenya)	**2005**
Luiz Nacio Lula Da Silva (Prasident of Brazil)	**2006**

Magsaysay Awards:

The award instituted in 1957 to honour the memory of Ramon Magsaysay, the late President of the Philippines. The award consists of a gold medal, a certificate and 50,000 U.S. dollars.

The following were awarded for the year 2007: **(1) Government Service** - Jonito R. Salonga (Phillipines); **(2) Public Service** - Kin Sun-Tae (South Korea) **(3) Community Leadership** - Mahabir Pun (Nepal); **(4) Peace and International Understanding** - Tang Xiyang (China); **(5) Journalism** - P. Sainath (India); **(6) Emergent Leadership** - Chung To and Chen Guangcheng (China).

Nobel Prizes - 2006

Peace	:	**Mohamed Unnus (Bangladesh)** won the Nobel Peace Prize '2006 for his works in foundation of Grameen Bank in all over the world for poor people.
Literature	:	**Orhan Pamuk (Turkey)** for his works in Turkish, English, French and Swedish novels *Cevdet Bey Ve Ogullari (1982), Sessiz EV (1983), The House of Silence (1998).*
Physics	:	Americans **John C.Mather** and **George F. Smoot** were jointly awarded Nobel Prize for their work that helped cement the **Big Bang theory** of how the universe was created and deeper understanding of the origin of galaxies and stars.
Chemistry	:	American **Roger D. Kornberg** was awarded the Nobel Prize for Chemistry for his studies of how cells take information from genes to produce proteins, a process that could provide insight into defeating cancer and advancing stem cell research.
Medicine or Physiology	:	**Andrew Z. Fire** and **Craig C. Mello** of the US were jointly awarded the Nobel Prize for

Medicine for their work in controlling the flow of genetic information and their discovery of RNA interference-gene silencing of double-stranded RNA.

Economic Sciences : American economist **Edmund S. Phelps** won the Nobel Economics Prize for explaining how policies to deal with inflation and umemployment today can have big effects on behaviour and welfare in the future.

64th Annual Golden Globe Awards' 2006

The 64th Annual Golden Globe Awards were presented in Beverly Hills on Jan 15, 2007 to the following:

CINEMA CATAGORIES: • Best Film, Drama - *Babel;* • Best Actor, Drama - Forest Whitaker, *The Last King of Scotland;* • Best Actress, Drama - Helan Mirren, *The queen;* • Best Musical or Comedy - Dreamgirls; • Best Actor, Musical or Comedy - Sacha Boran Cohen, Borat; *Cultural Learnings of America for Make Benefit Glorious Nation of Kazakhstan;* • Best Actress, Musical or Comedy - Meryl Streep, *The Devil Wears Prada;* • Best Director - Martin Scorsese, *The Departed;* • Best Supporting Actor - Eddie Murphy, *Dreamgirls;* • Best Supporting Actress - Jennifer Hudson, *Dreamgirls;* • Best Foreign Language Film - *Letters from Iwo Jima;* • Best Original Song - *The song of the Heart from Happy Feet;* • Best Screen play-Peter Morgan, *The Queen.* TELEVISION CATAGORIES: • Best Actor, Drama - *Hugh Laurie, House*; • Best Actress, Drama - Kyra Sedgwick, *The Closer.*

UN Population Award-2006

Dr. Halida Hanum Akhter from Bangladesh, a doctor specialising in family planning, has won the UN Population Award for the year 2006. The other winner is the *Foundation Pour la Sante Reproductive el'Education Familiale, a* Haiti-based private, non-profit organisation devoted to reproductive health and the promotion of family life. The award, instituted by the UNFPA (United Nations Fund for Population Activities), goes each year to individuals and institutions for their outstanding work in population stabilisation and in improving the health and welfare of people.

60th Cannes Film Festival Awards - 2007

★ *Palm d'or (Top Cannes Award):* "4 months, 3 weeks and 2 days" by Christian Mungiu (Director) from Romania. ★ *Grand Prize (Second Top Award):* "The Mourning Forest", "Naomi Mungiu", Japan ★ *60th Anniversary Prize:* Gus Van Sant, "Paranold Park A", US ★ *Best Director:* "The Diving Bell and the Butterfly", Julian Schnabel, USA ★ *Best Actress:*

Jeon Do-yeon, "Secret Sunshine", South Korea ★ *Best Actor: Konstantin Lavronenko, "The Banishment", Russia.*

49th Annual Grammy Awards - 2007

These Awards given for excellence in music, held in Los Angeles (USA) on February 11, 2007.

★ **Best Album of the year:** *"Talking the Long Way"*, Dixie Chicks ★ **Best Record of the year:** *"Non Ready To Make Nice"*, Dixie Chicks ★ **Best Song of the year:** *"Non Ready To Make Nice"*, Dixie Chicks ★ **Best New Artist:** Carrie Underwood ★ **Best Male Pop Vocal Performance:** *"Waiting on the World to change"* John Mayer ★ **Best Female Pop Vocal Performance:** *"Ain't No Other Man,"* Christina Agullera ★ **Best Pop Vocal Album:** *"Continuum"*, John Mayer ★ **Best Rock Album:** *"Stadium Arcadium"*, Red Hot Chili Peppers ★ **Best Rhythm & Blue Album:** *"The Breakthrough, Marry J. Blige* ★ **Best Rap Album:** *Release Therapy*.

79th Annual Academy Oscar Awards - 2007

These awards were presented in Hollywood, California (U.S.A.) on February 25, 2007.

✦ **Best Picture:** *The Departed* ✦ **Best Actor:** Forest Whitaker *(The last King of Scotland)* ✦ **Best Actress:** Helen Mirren *(The Queen)* ✦ **Best Supporting Actor:** Alan Arkin *(Little Miss Sunshine)* ✦ **Best Supporting Actress:** Jennifer Hudson *(Dreamgirls)* ✦ **Best Acheivement in Art Direction:** *Pan's Labyrinth* ✦ **Best Achievement in Cinematography:** *Pan's Labyrinth* ✦ **Best Achievement in Costume Design:** *Pan's Labyrinth* ✦ **Best Director:** Martin Scorsese *(The Departed)* ✦ **Best Documentary (feature):** *An Inconvenient Truth* ✦ **Best Film Editing:** *The Departed* ✦ **Best Foreign Language Film:** *The Lives of Others* ✦ **Best Make-up:** Pan's Labyrinth ✦ **Best Music (Original Score):** Babel ✦ **Best Music (Original Song):** *An inconvenient Truth* for the song 'I need to wake up - Music and Lyrics by Melissa Etheridge ✦ **Best Sound Editing:** Letters from Iwo Juna ✦ **Best Sound Mixing:** Dreamgirls ✦ **Best Visual Effects:** Pirates of he Caribbean: Dead Man's Chest ✦ **Best Writing (Adapted Screenplay):** The Departed ✦ **Best Writing (Original Screenplay):** Little Miss Sunshine ✦ **Best Honorary Award:** Awarded to Sherry Lansing.

Pulitzer Prizes - 2007

The prestigious Pulitzer Prizes for 2007 were presented in New York on April 17, 2007 to the following:

✦ **Breaking News Photography:** Oded Balilty of AP for his image of a lone Jewish woman defying Israeli security forces as they remove illegal settlers in the West Bank. ✦ **Public Service:** *The Wall Street Journal* for its coverage of the stock-options scandal that rattled corporate America in

2006. ✦ **Fiction:** *The Road* by Cormac Mc-Carthy, published by Alfred A. Knopf. ✦ **Drama:** *Rabbit Hole* by David Lindsay - Abaire. ✦ **History:** *The Race Beat, The Press, the Civil Rights Struggle, and the Awakening of a Nation* by Gene Roberts and Hank Klibanoff, published by Alfred A Knopf. ✦ **Biography or Autobiography:** *The Most Famous Man in America: The Biography of Henry Ward Beecher* by Debby Applegate, published by Doubleday. ✦ **Poetry:** *Native Guard* by Natasha Trethewey. ✦ **General Non-Fiction:** *The Looming Tower: Al-Qaeda and the Road to 9/11* by Lawrence Wright, published by Alfred A. Knopf. ✦ **Music:** *Sound Grammar* by Ornette Coleman. ✦ **National Reporting:** *Charlie Savage of The Boston Globe* for his revelations that Bush often used "signing statement's to assert his controversial right to bypass provisions of new laws. ✦ **International Reporting:** *The Wall Street Journal* for its coverage of capitalism emerging in China. ✦ **Feature Writing:** Andrea Elliot of The New York Times for coverage of an immigrant imam striving to serve the faithful in America. ✦ **Editorial Writing:** The Daily News of New York for its editorials on behalf of Ground Zero workers. ✦ **Commentary:** Cynthia Tucker of The Atlanta Journal.

Miss India-World, Universe & Earth - 2007

The 23-year-old girl from Mumbai, Sarah Jane was crowned the Pantaloons Femina Miss India World, 2007 at the Miss India Beauty Pageant in Mumbai on April 8, 2007. Delhi girl Pooja Gupta was named the Pantaloons Femina Miss India Universe, while the 21-year-old medical professional from New Zealand Pooja Chitgopekar was adjudged the Pantaloons Femina Miss India Earth.

Miss Universe, 2007

A 20-year-old dancer from Japan, Miss Riyo Mori, was crowned Miss Universe 2007, by Miss Universe 2006, Puerto Rico's Zuleyka Rivera, at the National Auditorium in Mexico City, Mexico, where 77 delegates competed for the title. Natalia Guimaraes of Brazil is the first runner-up, while by jonaitis of Venezuela is the second runner-up. This is the second time, Japan has won the world beauty title, after 1959, when Akiko Kosima became the first Miss Universe from Asia. Also, this is the fourth time Mexico has been the host country and the second time Mexico City has hosted the Miss Universe Paegent.

Miss World-2006

Tatana Kucharova, an 18-year-old student from the Czech Repupblic, won the Miss World 2006 beauty contest on September 30, 2006. Kucharova defeated 103 other women in voting by a panel of judges in the Sala Kongresowa, Warsaw.

Mr. World-2007

Juan Garcia Postigo of Spain has been adjudged the Mr. World 2007. He got this title after defeating the competitors of 55 countries. Lucas Gil of Brazil and Jiang Legun of China came second and third respectively in the competition. The competition was organised in Sanya (China).

Man Booker International Prize - 2006

Indian novelist, Ms. Kiran Desai has won the 'Man Booker International Prize'. Her books include *The Inheritance of loss.*

Man Booker International Prize - 2007

Nigerian novelist Chinua Achebe won the 2007 Man Booker International Prize for fiction on June 13, 2007, beating nominees including Salman Rushdie, Doris Lessing, Phillip Roth, Margaret Atwood and Ian McEwan. The £ 60,000 prize is awarded once every two years for a body of fiction.

SPORTS
Billiards

World Championship

The 33-year-old woman cueist from India, Chitra Magimairaj retained the World Billiards title, defeating Emma Bonney of England 187-147. Chitra recorded an unfinished top-break of 39 in the tie in the final at Cambridge on April 3, 2007.

Car Race
Monaco Grand Prix Championship

Defending champion Fernando Alonso of Spain drove from pole position to a clear and consummate victory for Renault in the Monaco Grand Prix at Monaco on May 28, 2006. His first win in the principality, coming in the wake of extraordinary penalty that sent disgraced rival Michael Schumacher from pole to the back of the grid, enlarged his lead over the seven times German champion.

Cricket

Muttiah Muralitharan' Quickest 700 wickets in Tests

In the third Test against Bangladesh in Kandy (Sri Lanka) on July 14, 2007, Sri Lanka's ace offspinner Muttiah Muralitharan not only reached the rare mark of 700 Test wickets, but also achieved this feat in just 113 Tests. Australia's Shane Warne, the only bowler before Muralitharan to have taken 700 or more Test wickets, took 144 Tests to get to this coveted peak of achievement.

ICC World Cup - 2007

Australia won a record third successive World Cup title amid scenes of unprecedented confusion as night fell at Kensington Oval stadium on 28th April 2007.

The Australians, who scored 281 for four from 38 overs, thought they had clinched the rain-reduced match when Sri Lanka needing 63 runs from three overs to win accepted the umpires offer to go off for bad light. Australia unbeaten in 29 World Cup matches since they lost to Pakistan in 1999, are the only team to win the tournament three times in a row. It was their fourth victory overall.

Another milestone for Shane Warne

Australian spin wizard Shane Warne reached another milestone in his farewell outing as he grabbed his 1000th international wicket in the fifth and final Ashes Test. Warne became the second bowler in the history of the game to claim 1000 international wickets as he trapped Monty Panesar before the stumps during England's first innings. The leg-spinner, who is the highest wicket-taker in Test cricket, having scalped 707 batsmen so far, has claimed 293 one-day international wickets. Sri Lankan Muttiah Muralitharan was the first to claim 1000 international wickets. The off-spinner, who is the second highest wicket-taker in Test cricket with 674 scalps, has captured 1104 international wickets so far. Meanwhile, Australian paceman Glenn McGrath, who is also playing his last Test, got his 900th international wicket.

ICC Champions Trophy - 2006

Australia won their maiden ICC Champions Trophy title by beating West Indies by eight wickets in Mumbai (Maharashtra) on November 5, 2006. The Australians bundled out the West Indies for 138 runs in just 30.4 overs before overhauling the revised target of 116 with 6.5 overs to spare in the rain affected final. Shane Watson of Australia was adjudged Man of the Match while Chris Gayle of West Indies was adjudged Man of the Series. Earlier, India was knocked out of the tournament when it lost to Australia by six wickets in Mohali (Punjab) on October 29, 2006.

ICC Awards - 2006

The third ICC (International Cricket Council) Awards were presented in a glittering ceremony in Mumbai (Maharashtra) on November 3, 2006. Ricky ponting of Australia was adudged the ICC Player of the year 2006 as aksi ICC Test Player of the Year 2006. He was also named on both the ICC ODI and Test Teams of the year

❖ **ICC Player of the year:** Ricky Ponting (Aus) ❖ **Test Player of the year:** Ricky Ponting (Aus) ❖ **ODI Player of the year:** Michael Hussey (Aus) ❖ **Emerging Player of the year:** Ian Bell (England) ❖ **Captain of the year:** M. Jayawardene (SL) ❖ **Umpire of the Year:** Simon Taufel (Aus) ❖ **Woman Player of the year:** Karen Rolton (Aus) ❖ **Spirit of Cricket Award:** England Cricket Team.

Football

FIFA World Cup - 2006

★ 32 Teams ★ 64 Matches ★ 30 Billion viewers All Over The World ★ Over 31 Days ★ 1 Champion

The biggest sporting tournament of the world, the 18th FIFA (Federation International de Football Association) Football World Cup 2006, was declared open by the German President, Mr. Hort Koehler in Munich (Germany) on June 9, 2006. The spectacular event was witnessed by a 60,000 strong audience in the Allianz Arena of Munich as well as by hundreds of millions of Viewers worldwide on the television. For the first time in the history of the mega event, every living member of the past World Cup-winning teams was present at the opening ceremony. More than 100 former players took apart in a parade during the event. The opening ceremony was followed by the inaugural match between the host Germany and Costa Rica. Philipp Lahm of Germany scored the first goal of the 18th FIFA World Cup. Germany won the match 4-2 and thus, set the momentum for the month - long sporting extravaganza end with a grand final on July 9, 2006. Italy won the World Cup in a penalty shootout in final, beating France 5-3 after a 1-1 draw through 120 minutes.

World Cup Football - 2010

The World Cup Football 2010 will be held in South Africa, according to a decision taken by the executive meeting of the FIFA at Zurich (Switzerland).

Golf

US Open - 2007

Angel Cabrera of Argentina won the US Open in Oakmont (US) on June 17, 2007, giving Argentina its major championship title in 40 years.

Hockey

Women's Champions Trophy - 2007

The Netherlands beat Argentina 1-0 on an early goal by Maartje Paumen to win the Women's Champions Trophy hockey tournament at Quilmes (Argentina) for the fifth time. The Dutch forced two penalty corners in the second minute and Paumen, who scored twice in its World Cup final victory last October, slammed in the second one. The Netherlands' steely defence then made it hard work for Argentina just to cross into Dutch territory.

World Cup - 2006

Germany defeated Australia 4-3, to retain the Hockey World Cup title, in Monchengladbach (Germany), on September 17, 2006. Germany came back from behind and scored three goals in the space of nine minutes to lift the coveted trophy. In another match, Spain beat South Korea 3-2, to secure the third place in the tournament. Jaime Dwyer of Australia was adjudged 'Player of the Tournament' while Christopher Zeller and Ulrich Bubolz, both of Germany were named 'Promising Player' and 'Best Goalkeeper' respectively. New Zealand got the Fair Play Award.

Women's World Cup - 2006

The Netherlands won the women's hockey World Cup with a 3-1 win, over Australia on October 8, 2006 in Madrid, Spain. Maartje Paumen scored twice and Sylvia Karres - the tournament's top scorer grabbed her sixth goal to snap a two game losing streak at major finals for the Oranje. It was the Netherlands' first world title since 1990. Argentina claimed the bronze medal when it trounced host Spain 5-0 in the third place playoff. The Indian women's hockey team finished 11th in the World Cup.

Table Tennis

World Championships

★ *Women's Singles:* China's Guo Yue defeated compatriot Li Xiaoxia in the women's singles final at the World table tennis championship at Zagreb on May 27, 2007. ★ *Men's Singles:* Wang Liqin beat Ma Lin in an all-Chinese men's singles final at the World table tennis championships. China thus made a clean sweep of gold and silver medals for the third time. China has won the men's singles and doubles, mixed doubles, women's singles and doubles. It is the fifth time for China to clean sweep the individual golds. ★ *Women's Doubles:* Wang Nan / Zhang Yining (China) bt Guo Yue / Li Xiaoxia (China). ★ *Men's Doubles:* Chen Qi / Ma Lin (China) bt Wang Liqin / Wang Hao (China). ★ *Mixed Doubles:* Wang Liqin / Guo Yue (China) bt Ma Lin / Wang Nan (China).

Tennis

Dubai Open-2007

Men's Singles : Swiss Roger Federer won the 2007 Dubai Open Men's Singles Tennis Tournament beating Mikhail Youzhny of Russia 6-4, 6-3 in the final at Dubai on March 3, 2007. **Women's Singles :** Belgian Justine Henin-Hardenne won the 2007 in the 2007 Dubai Open Lawn Tennis beating Amelie Mauresmo of France in the final at Dubai on Feb. 24, 2007.

Davis Cup

Russia won its second Davis Cup title in Moscow (Russia) on December 3, 2006 when Marat Safin of Russia defeated Jose Acasuso of Argentina, 6-3, 3-6, 6-3, 7-6 (5), in the fifth and deciding match. The Russians beat Argentina 3-2, in the best of-five series.

Wimbledon - 2007

Men's Singles: Roger Federer of Switzerland defeated Rafael Nadal of Spain 7-6, 4-6, 7-6, 2-6, 6-2 to win the Wimbledon men's singles title, in

London (UK) on July 8, 2007. **Women's Singles:** Venus Williams of USA defeated Marion Bartoli of France, 6-4, 6-1, to claim the title. **Men's Doubles:** French duo Arnaud Clement and Michael Llodra defeated Bob Bryan and Mike Bryan, both from USA, 6-7, 6-3, 6-4, 6-4. **Women's Doubles:** Cara Black of Zimbabwe and Liezel Huber of South Africa defeated Katarina Srebotnik of Slovenia and Japan's Ai Sugiyama 3-6, 6-3, 6-2. **Mixed Doubles:** Jamie Murray of UK and Jelena Jankovic of Serbia beat Jonas Bjorkman of Sweden and Alicia Molik of Australia 6-4, 3-6, 6-1 to win the mixed doubles title.

French Open - 2007

Men's Singles : Rafael Nadal (Spain) defeated Roger Federer (Switzerland). **Women's Singles :** Justine Henin - (Belgium) defeated Ana Ivanovic (Serbia). **Men's Doubles:** Mark Knowles (Bahamas) & Daniel Nestor (Canada) defeated Lukas Dlouhy (Czech Republic) & Paval Vizner (Czech Republic). **Women's Doubles :** Alicia Molik (Australia) & Mara Stangelo (Italy) defeated Ai Suguyama (Japan) & Katarina Srebotnik (Slovenia). **Mixed Doubles:** Nathalie Dechy (France) & Andy Ram (Israel) defeated Katarina Srebotnik (Slovenia) & Nenad Zuinonjic (Serbia).

Australian Open - 2007

Men's Singles: Roger Federer (Switzerland) beat Fernando Gonzalez (Chile) (Cyprus) by 7-6, 6-4, 6-4 in the final at Rod Laver Arena on January 28, 2007. **Women's Singles:** Serena Williams (US) beat Maria Sharapova (Russia). **Men's Doubles:** Bob Bryan & Mike Bryan (USA) beat Jonas Bjorkman (Swedan) & Max Mirniyi (Belgium). **Women's Doubles:** Cara Black (Zimbabwe) & Liezel Huber(South Africa) beat Chan Yung-Jan & Chuang Chia-Jung (Taiwan). **Mixed Doubles:** Daniel Nestor (Canada) & Elena Likhovtseva (Russia) beat Max Mirnyi & Victoria Azarenka (Belgium).

US Open-2006

Men's Singles: Roger Federer (Switzerland) beat Mikhail Youzhny (Russia); **Women's Singles:** Maria Sharapova (Russia) beat Justice Henin Hardenne (Belgium); **Men's Doubles:** Martin Damm (Czech) and Leander Paes (India) beat Jonas Bjorkman (Sweden) and Max Mirnyi (Blr); **Mixed Doubles:** Martina Navratilova & Bob Bryan (USA) beat Kveta Peschke & Martin Damm (Czech).

Miscellaneous

Sochi to host 2014 Winter Olympic Games

Sochi, a Russian Black Sea resort, has been chosen as the host city of the 2014 Winter Olympics. The announcement was made in Guatemala City on July 5, 2007. Sochi beat out Pyeongchang, South Korea by a 51-47 count in the final vote from members of the International Olympic Committee. The full IOC membership voted to elect Sochi at their session in Guatemala City, with President Mr. Jacques Rogge announcing the winner at a ceremony.

Delhi to Bid for 2020 Olympics

South Korea's Incheon pip New Delhi to host the 2014 Asian Games and India's subsequent withdrawal from the race to host the 2016 Olympic Games, Indian Olympic Association (IOA) President Suresh Kalmadi on April 28, 2007 announced that India will bid for the 2020 Olympic Games.

2014 Asian Games

New Delhi's bid to host the 2014 Asian Games came unstuck as the Olympic Council Asia awarded the multi-sport event to South Korean city of Incheon. The Council presented this honour to South Korean city in its meeting held in Kuwait. Delhi was bidding to bring back the continental mega event to the Indian soil after a gap of 32 years, having last organised the same in 1982. South Korea will be hosting the Games for a third time, with Seoul and Busan having conducted it in 1986 and 2002 respectively. Incheon seemed to have clinched the bid with its offer of USD 20 million for training, equipment and other facilities for the participating nations.

Sharapova becomes UN Anti-poverty Ambassador

Tennis world number one Maria Sharapova has beome the latest celebrity appointed goodwill ambassador of the UN Development Program (UNDP), pledging to use her charisma and fame to galvanise support for the fight against world poverty. The 19-year-old US-based Russian star also donated 100,000 dollars to eight UNDP recovery projects in rural communities in Belarus, Russia and Ukraine still affected by the 1986 Chernobyl nuclear diaster. The pre-dawn blasts on 26th April 1986, at the Soviet-era Chernobyl plant, the world's worst nuclear accident, unleashed a cloud of radioactive dust that drifted over a large swath of Europe and still haunts millions of people in Ukraine and neighbouring countries. On behalf of UNDP, Sharapova will promote international efforts to achieve the poverty-reduction Millennium Development Goals in the areas of education, health, women's rights and sanitation by the target date of 2015.

ECONOMY

Monetary and Credit Policy (2007-08)

Reserve Bank of India (RBI) Governor Y.V. Reddy announced the Annual Monetary and Credit Policy for 2007-08 in Mumbai on April 24, 2007. The policy left the Cash Reserve Ratio (CRR), Repo and Reverse Repo Rates unchanged. It kept the Bank Rate unchanged at six per cent, Reverse Repo at six per cent, Repo Rate at 7.75 per cent and the CRR at 6.5 per cent. RBI also introduced measures to make interest rates attractive for housing loans upto Rs. 20 lakh. The risk weight on the residential housing loans to individuals would be reduced to 50 per cent from 75 per cent as a temporary measure, keeping in view the default experience and other relevant factors.

This step would be applicable to loans up to Rs. 20 lakh and will be reviewed after one year, the policy said. This measure will leave banks with more money to lend for the housing sector and make interest rates attractive for loans up to Rs. 20 lakh. Meanwhile the apex bank has lowered its growth forecast to 8.5 per cent from 8.5-9 per cent as it expects global GDP to decline in 2007. Inflation targets have also been revised downward to 5 per cent from last year's targets of 5-5.5 per cent.

New Foreign Trade Policy

The Union Government on April 19, 2007 announced a host of incentives to boost exports from several sectors including a new scheme covering high-technology products, as part of the annual supplement to the Foreign Trade Policy. The measures would help maintain the 25 per cent compounded growth rate in exports witnessed in the past three years, Union Commerce and Industry Minister Kamal Nath said. The highlights of the Policy are (i) Abolishes service tax on all exports; (ii) Includes more items in Vishesh Krishi and Gram Udyog Yojana for tax sops; (iii) Gives duty exemption and remission schemes to developers of SEZs; (iv) Extends the Duty Entitlement Passbook scheme till March next; and (v) Sets $160 billion target for merchandise exports in 2007-08.

Rate of Inflation

Inflation fell for the second consecutive week, reaching a level of 5.66% for the week ended April 28, 2007 amid signs of a narrowing of the demand-supply mismatch for agricultural produce in the current rabi marketing season. While prices of cereals declined by 0.2 per cent, the price of wheat fell by one per cent. Wheat production in 2006-07 is estimated to be around 73.7 million tonnes, compared with 69.35 million tonnes the previous year.

Minimum Support Price for Kharif Crops

The Union Government on May 17, 2007 announced the Minimum Support Price (MSP) for the 2007-08 Kharif crops of paddy, coarse grains and pulses, based on the recommendations of the (CACP). The MSPs have seen an increase, over the price fixed in 2006, especially of pulses, as government wanted to encourage farmers, Agriculture Minister Sharad Pawar, said announcing the approval accorded by the Cabinet Committee on Economic Affairs (CCEA), chaired by Prime Minister, Manmohan Singh.

IT Services Revenue

Worldwide IT services revenue on May 15, 2007 totalled $672.3 billion in 2007, a 6.4 per cent rise from $631.8 billion generated last year, said

Gartner, the World's leading IT research and advisory company. While India-based vendors' IT services revenue grew 33.3 per cent in 2006, these companies earned only three per cent of the revenue tracked, while US-based vendors earned 57 per cent of the total.

Target for 11th Plan

Seeking to emulate tiger economies such as China and Korea, the Planning Commission has set an ambitious 8.5 per cent growth target for the 11th Five Year Plan, commencing in 2007-08. The Plan aims to reach 9.5 per cent growth in the final year, according to the approach paper. The paper, in a break with tradition, has been circulated to Chief Ministers and Union Ministers well in advance of a formal meeting of the National Development Council (NDC).

The Commission is believed to have described the high growth path as "feasible but not inevitable," while flagging a number of hard decisions essential to achieve this objective. It has placed the focus of the next plan on agriculture, social sector and manufacturing.

SCIENCE

Hydrocarbons found on Saturn's Moon

The Cassini spacecraft has found cup-like craters filled with hydrocarbons on Saturn's moon Hyperion. According to the astronomers, the finding could indicate more widespread presence in our solar system of the basic chemicals necessary for life. The spacecraft also found water and carbon dioxide ices, as well as dark material. NASA (National Aeronautics and Space Administration) has admitted that Cassini's ultraviolet imaging spectrograph and visual and infrared mapping spectrometer captured compositional variations in Hyperion's surface.

Brightest Star Explosion

Astronomers at the University of California have spotted a cataclysmic explosion that marked the death of a huge, distant star in a blast five times as bright and powerful as any they had seen previously. According to them a similar fate may be imminent for a star in Earth's galactic neighbourhood. The size and energy of the newly record blast, 240 million light-years away, has already begun to transform scientific understanding of how especially large stars explode, and has left awestruck researchers concerned – and a little excited – about what might happen to the similarly anemones and unstable stars closer home.

Artificial Plastic Blood

Scientists in Britain have developed an artificial plastic blood, which they claim could act as a substitute, easier to store and could be a huge advantage in war zones. The new artificial blood is made up of plastic molecules that have an iron atom at their core, like haemoglobin, that can carry oxygen through the body. The researchers say they were looking for extra funding to develop a final prototype that would be suitable for biological resting.

Solar Vaccine Refrigerator

President A.P.J. Abdul Kalam on November 1, 2006 acquired the first environment friendly Solarchill vaccine refrigerator. It was installed at the President's estate clinic in the presence of Mr. Kalam. The Solarchill was conceived as a vaccine cooler for remote areas in developing countries where access to power supply is difficult. Powered by three 60-watt photovoltaic panels, it stores the energy of the sun in ice instead of batteries. In place of the chloroflurocarbons (CFC) and other ozone depleting and global warming substances, Solarchill relies on ozone and climate friendly hydrocarbon refrigerants.

Census of India - 2001 (Revised)

The census enumeration took place from 9th February to 28th February, with 00.00 hours of 1st March as the reference date, and the revisional round was over on 5 March, 2001. No developed country can match this performance. In India this is possible because of a combination of manual tabulation and use of computers, fax and e-mail.

Census coverage

The 2001 census covered the whole of India: 28 States, 7 Union Territories, 5,564 tahsils/talukas, 640,000 villages and 5,161 towns and cities.

It may be noted that in 1991 the census enumeration could not take place in Jammu & Kashmir. In 2001 the census enumeration did take place in Jammu & Kashmir in spite of the threat from militants. Another important aspect to be noted is that 2001 census data are available for the three newly formed states of Chhatisgarh, Uttarakhand (Uttaranchal) & Jharkhand. The data are adjusted for previous census years (1991, 1981 etc) in order to enable the user to study past trends.

The decennial census of 2001 is in the 21st century and deserves special attention. The census is the most important single source of information on the life of the people of India.

❖ A special postage stamp was released to commemorate the Census of 2001.

❖ A census logo with the motto 'people-oriented' was introduced by the Census organisation.

Highlights of the final census 2001 Statistics

❖ The population of India on the 1st March 2001 was 1027 million (102.7 crores) and it has reached 1028 million on 10.5.2004 (102.8 crores) with 53.2 crore males and 49.6 crore females at an annual growth rate of 1.94. This includes the population of J & K where the 1991 census could not be conducted while the enumeration was done in 2001.

❖ In the last decade (1991-2001) the population of India increased by 181 million.

❖ In percentage terms, the decadal growth rate was 21.3 per cent compared to 23.9 per cent during the previous decade (1981-91).

❖ The decline in the decadal growth rate was 2.5 percent points during 1991-2001 decade.

❖ Bihar recorded the highest decadal growth rate, which in fact increased from 23.4 per cent to 28.4 per cent. Andhra Pradesh recorded the sharpest decline in the decadal growth rate: 13.9 per cent during 1991-2001 compared to 24.2 per cent during 1981-1991 or a decline of 10.3 per cent points.

❖ The lowest growth rate was recorded by Kerala (9.4 per cent) followed by Tamil Nadu (11.2 per cent) and Andhra Pradesh (13.9 percent).

❖ Uttar Pradesh even after the new state of Uttarakhand (Uttaranchal) was carved out in 2000, continues to be the most populous state in India with a population of 166 million (Uttarakhand population is 8.5 million). Thus Uttar Pradesh as of 1991 has a population of 175 million in 2001.

❖ Uttar Pradesh has 16.2 per cent of India's population followed by Maharashtra (9.4 per cent) and Bihar 8.0 per cent. The density of India is 325 per sq km. in 2001 compared to 267 in 1991 or an increase of 57 during the last ten years.

❖ West Bengal has the highest density (903) followed by Bihar (881).

❖ The sex ratio (females per 1000 males) is 933 in 2001 compared to 927 in 1991 or an increase by 6 points during the last decade.

❖ Kerala has the highest sex ratio (1058) and Haryana the lowest (861).

❖ The child sex ratio (0-6 age group) was 927 in 2001 compared to 945 in 1991 or a decline by 18 points.

❖ The sharpest decline in the sex ratio of the child population was in Punjab, Haryana, Himachal Pradesh, Uttarakhand, Gujarat and Maharashtra.

❖ The literacy rate (for population 7 years and over) was 64.8 per cent in 2001. The male literacy rate was 75.2 per cent and the female literacy rate was 53.6 per cent.

❖ Compared to 1991 the overall literacy rate increased by 12.6 percentage points (52.2 in 1991 to 64.8 in 2001). The increase in the male and female literacy rate were 11.7 and 14.9 percentage points respectively.

❖ The gap between male and female literacy rates has decreased from 28.8 percentage points in 1991 to 21.6 in 2001.

❖ For the first time since independence there has been an absolute decline in the number of illiterate persons: the number of illiterates declined by 32 million during the last decade. Among males the number declined by 21.5 million and among females by 10.5 million.

❖ The literacy rate was highest in Kerala (90.9 per cent) and lowest in Bihar (47.5 per cent).

India is the second most populous country in the world, with a population of 1027 million (on 1st March 2001) and it had reached 1028 million (102.8 crores) on 10-5-2004, compared to China which had a population of 1,278 million (on 1st February 2000).

Railway Budget 2007-08

The Railway Minister, Mr. Lalu Prasad Yadav, presented a "people-friendly budget", for the year 2007-08 in the Lok Sabha on 26-2-2007 without increasing the passenger fares for all classes and the freight rates and parcel tariffs and still managed to shower concessions on women, rural students, farmers and milk producers.

Highlights

➢ 1st class AC fare to be cheaper by 3% to 6%. ➢ The reduced rates would be 2% and 4% in AC two-tier. ➢ Also, candidates appearing for the main written examination by the Staff Selection Commission and the Union Public Service Commission can now avail themselves of 50 percent concession. ➢ A reduction in fares would also be effected in all classes of high-capacity newly designed coaches, which would be four percent in the busy season and eight per cent in the lean season in AC three tier and AC chair car classes, and four percent in all seasons in the sleeper class. ➢ Non-suburban fare cut by Re1 per passenger. ➢ Superfast surcharge on 2nd class tickets reduced by 20%.

> Differential discounts for lean and peak seasons, as well as popular and other trains. ➢ 40 new trains, including 8 *Garib Raths*, to be introduced. ➢ AC suburban trains for Mumbai, Chennai, Kolkata; Rs.5000 cr. over 5 years for Mumbai locals. ➢ Rail tickets to be sold at post-offices, ATMs petrol pumps. ➢ All wooden berths to be cushioned. ➢ Unreserved compartments in each train to rise from 4 to 6. ➢ Quotas for elderly and women in lower berths, special coaches for handicapped.

> All classes of coaches to be redesigned to take in many more passengers. ➢ Double and triple deck freight trains on way. ➢ Smart travel cards to be introduced. ➢ Palm tops for TTEs. ➢ Feasibility study on 300-350 kmph trains. ➢ Call local number 139 anywhere and get Rly call centers, which will also provide SMS alerts. Other facilities also on the anvil. ➢ 800 more coaches, including special coaches for the physically challenged, will be attached to popular trains. ➢ 300 more stations to be developed as model stations with focus on cleanliness. 2007 has been declared 'Cleanliness Year'.

> 8,000 is the number of new unreserved ticketing facility counters that will come up in the next two years. ➢ 6,000 automatic ticket vending machines will be installed and linked to Unreserved Ticketing System (UTS) in the metros. ➢ Rs.31,000 crore is the annual, budget outlay for 2007-08, the largest annual plan ever.

The Budget addresses the needs of all economic agents concerned - Indian Railways itself, its passengers and businesses who want to move freight. In pushing a revenue model for Indian Railways that lays stress on volumes to bring in the expected returns, the Minister hopes not only to ride on the current growth wave but also rely on improved capacity utilisation, operational efficiencies and last-mile improvements. Indian Railways achieved a surplus income of Rs. 20,063 crore for 2006-07 and set an ambitious target of Rs.21,578 crore in 2007-08 riding high on the booming economic growth. In fact, there has been a marginal reduction in fares across the board, and a selection lowering of freight tariff on sensitive commodities such as a petrol, diesel and iron ore, which can also have an inflationary effect. The Railway Minister has not only pleased the passengers and trade, but also looked at expansion and competition in a new light. The Budget combines sensitivity to popular needs and sentiments with efficiency and performance.

Budget Estimates

Sharp in short-term money making, strong in medium-term strategy, but weak long-term vision, Lalu's fourth Budget chugs on the tracks he charted four years ago. It transports record-breaking profits and freight carriage; most importantly, it delivers the lowest-ever operating ratio. Lalu's budget yearned for attention in the Lok Sabha but he had to yell his way. A surplus before devidends of Rs. 20,000 crore makes Indian Railways the country's biggest profit-making entity. To put it in perspective, the Railways' profit are 25 per cent more than Rs.16,000 crore, the training 12 month profits on ONGC and almost double of Reliance Industries' Rs.10,557 crore. Keeping the speed at which it is growing and the magical "infrastructure" sector it is operating in mind, the Railways, if listed, would command a PE multiple of at least 20 times. Which means, at Rs.400,000 crore, it would be India's most valued company, beating ONGC and Reliance by a margin of 100 per cent - and we are not factoring its huge land banks.

Safety Plan

Railway Minister announced a slew of security measures, including strengthening of the Railway Protection Force (RPF), installation of CCTV's and smart video cameras at important railway stations, induction of dog squads to detect explosives and consultation with security experts to make train travel safe and sound. Besides increasing the strength of the existing dog squads in many sensitive divisions, explosive detection devices, door frames and hand-held metal detectors are being installed.

The Minister announced an allocation of Rs. 5,500 crore towards Depreciation Reserve Fund for 2007-08 compared to Rs. 2,100 crore in 2001-02. "This has had a direct impact on railways safety record," Prasad said, adding that although the gross traffic volume had increased from 724 million train km in 2001-02 to 825 million train km in 2005-06, the number of accidents is expected to be less than 200 in 2006-07 against 473 in 2001. With regard to the introduction of the much-awaited Anti-Collision Device, the Minister said as per the Corporate Safety Plan, the testing of the ACD on the Northeast Frontier Railway (NFR) is in its last phase and is likely to be completed by March 2007.

Fares and Freight Rates

Living up to his promise of presenting a "good budget", Railway Minister Lalu Prasad slashed upper class fares up to eight per cent, effected a token reduction of a rupee in second class ordinary fares, and reduced freight rates on diesel, petrol, minerals and ores while retaining from an across-the-board freight hike. In a bid to woo traffic from low-cost airlines, he announced a reduction in fares in the AC first class by three percent in the busy season and six per cent in the lean season. The reduced rates would be two per cent and four per cent in AC two-tier. Also, candidates appearing for the main writen examination by the Staff Selection Commission and the Union Public Service Commission can now avail themselves of 50 per cent concession. A reduction in fares would also be effected in all classes of high-capacity newly designed coaches, which would be four per cent in the busy season and eight per cent in the lean season in AC three-tier and AC chair car classes, and four per cent in all seasons in the sleeper class.

Railway Minister announced reductions and discounts in the freight tariff on various commodities including diesel, Petrol, steel, cement and further discounts for consignments of wheat and fertilisers. Presenting the Railway Budget for the year 2007-08 in the Lok Sabha today, the minister said that the reduction and discount schemes were being announced in the Budget to maintain the unprecedented growth in freight transportation. Yadav proposed to reduce the classification for diesel and petrol of highest class from Class 200 to Class 210, which would bring down the freight rate for diesel, petrol and ammonia, *etc., by* about five per cent thus taking the rationalisation process further. Last year fuel was reduced from Class 240 to Class 220 thereby reducing the tariff by about nine per cent.

Proposed New Trains

32 New passenger trains, 8 new 'Garib Rath' trains and 23 extension of trains have been proposed.

Garib Raths (8)

1. Secunderabad - Yesvantpur (Tri-Weekly).
2. Jaipur - Bandra Terminus via Ahmedabad (Tri-Weekly)
3. Kolkata - Patna (Tri-Weekly)
4. Bhubaneshwar - Ranchi (Tri-Weekly)
5. Thiruvananthapuram - Lokmanya Tilak Terminus (Bi-Weekly)
6. Kolkata - Guwahati (Bi-Weekly)
7. New Delhi - Dehradun (Tri-Weekly)
8. Raipur - Lucknow (2 days in a week)

32 Pairs of New Trains

1. Shri Chhatrapati Sahu Maharaj Terminus, Kolapur Ahmedabad Exp. (Weekly).
2. Howrah - Rampurhat Express (Daily)
3. Jhansi - Kanpur Express (Daily)
4. Pune - Gorakhpur Express (Weekly)
5. Delhi - Shamli DEMU (Daily)
6. Bapudham Motihari - Varanasi (Tri-Weekly)
7. Bikaner - Jaisalmer Express (Two pairs) (Daily)
8. Mumbai - Aurangabad Jan-shatabdi Express (Six days in a week).

9.   Bhagalpur - New Delhi Express (Weekly)
10. Bijapur - Bagalkot Express (Six days in a week)
11. Allahabad - Mathura Express (Daily)
12. Nasik - Pune Express (Daily)
13. Coimbatore - Nagercoil Express via Madurai (Daily)
14. Bhubaneshwar - Rameshwaram Express (Weekly)
15. Gorakhpur - Yeswantpur Express (Weekly)
16. Yeshwantpur - Chennai Express (Two pairs) (Weekly)
17. Farrukhabad - Kasganj Express (Two pairs) (Daily)
18. Indore - Amritsar Express (Weekly)
19. Chennai Egmore - Nagore Express (Daily)
20. Rewa - Jabalpur Intercity Express (Daily)
21. New Delhi - Sahibabad EMU Service (Delhi)
22. Banka - Bhagalpur Passenger (Six days in a week)
23. Chennai Egmore - Rameshwaram Express (Six days in a week)
24. Chhapra - Chhatrapati Shivaji Terminus Jansadaran Express via Siwan, Gorakhpur (Weekly)
25. Mumbai - Ajmer / Udaipur Express (Six days in a week)
26. Solapur - Bagalkot Express (Six days in a week)
27. Ajmer - Ratlam Express (Daily two pairs)
28. Vadodara - Bhilad Express (Daily)
29. Patna - Delhi - on - Sone Intercity Express (Daily)
30. Gandhidham - Palanpur Express (Daily)
31. Lucknow Jn-Saharanpur Express (Daily) in lieu of Lucknow - Saharanpur Link Express
32. Jabalpur - Delhi via Itarsi (Two days in a week)

Allocation for Tamil Nadu

New Trains

- Coimbatore - Nagercoil daily Express via Madurai
- Yesvanthpur - Chennai (weekly) Express
- Bhubaneshwar - Rameshwaram
- Chennai Egmore - Nagore (daily) Express
- Chennai Egmore - Rameshwaram (six days a week) Express

Gauge Conversion

- Quilon - Tirunelveli - Trichendur - Virudunagar
- Vellore - Thiruvannamalai stretch of Villupuram - Katpadi
- Dindugal - Pollachi - Palghat
- Pollachi - Coimbatore
- Cuddalore - Salem   • Thanjavur - Villupuram

Railway Budget at a Glance

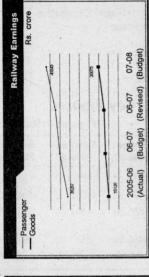

Railway Earnings

Rs. crore

4840

30297

20075

15126

2005-06 (Actual)   06-07 (Budget)   06-07 (Revised)   07-08 (Budget)

— Passenger
— Goods

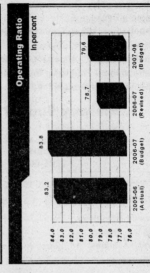

Operating Ratio

In per cent

83.2   83.8   78.7   79.6

2005-06 (Actual)   2006-07 (Budget)   2006-07 (Revised)   2007-08 (Budget)

84.0
83.0
82.0
81.0
80.0
79.0
78.0
77.0
76.0

Overall Position (Surplus)

Rs. crore

6193.32 (Actual)
6742.31 (Budget)
10627.48 (Revised)
11449.45 (Budget)

2005-06   2006-07   2006-07   2007-08

12,000.0
10,000.0
8,000.0
6,000.0
4,000.0
2,000.0

Working Results

Rs. crore

71318

54491

56687

45292

Net Traffic

— Total Working Expenses
— Gross Traffic Receipts

2005-06 (Actual)   06-07 (Budget)   06-07 (Revised)   07-08 (Budget)

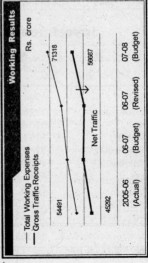

Note: Figures for 2006-07 are Revised Estimates and for 2007-08 are Budget Estimates

39

Doubling works
* Madurai - Dindugal
* Chengalpet - Villupuram - Thiruvannamalai
* Chennai Beach - Korukupet
* Chennai Beach - Atipattu fourth line
* Pattabhiram - Thiruvallur fourth line
* Thiruvallur - Arakonam third line

* Irugur - Coimbatore

Railway Budget - Key Figures

(Figures in Rs. Crore)

	Actuals 2005-06	Budget 2006-07	Revised 2006-07	Budget 2007-08
Gross Traffic Receipts	54491.38	59978.00	63220.00	71318.00
Total Working Expenses	45291.62	50124.50	49615.00	56687.00
Net Railway Revenue	10143.15	10885.54	14869.74	16021.99
Dividend Payable to General Revenues	3286.83	3480.23	3579.26	3908.54
Operating Ratio	83.2%	83.8%	78.7%	79.6%
Overall Surplus	**6193.32**	**6742.31**	**10627.48**	**11449.45**

Investment By Plan Heads

(Figures in Rs. Crore)

	2005-06	2006-07 (RE)	2007-08 (BE)
New Lines	1994.37	2525.12	1580.20
Gauge Conversion	1323.59	2045.71	2704.31
Doubling	690.53	1178.31	2002.00
Rolling Stock	5197.39	6898.35	9218.50
Track Renewal	3778.98	4206.52	4360.00
Bridge Works	410.58	517.07	602.60
Signaling	1047.79	1354.68	1607.90
Electrification	73.35	224.54	302.00
Leased Assets	1615.59	1720.12	1677.00
Passenger Amenities	256.24	401.10	493.30
Total	**16,388.41**	**21,071.52**	**24,547.81**

BE - Budget Estimates   RE - Revised Estimates

How a rupee is spent and earned

How a rupee is earned?	How a rupee is spent?

Paise

		Paise
1.	Goods Traffic Earnings	64
2.	Passenger Earnings	29
3.	Other Coaching Earnings	2
4.	Sundry: Other Earnings	3
5.	Miscellaneous Receipts	4
	Total	**100**

		Paise
1.	Staff Wages &Other Allowances	28
2.	Stores	5
3.	Lease Charges	3
4.	Depreciation Resv. Fund	7
5.	Pension Fund	12
6.	Fuel	18
7.	Dividend	7
8.	Spl. Rly. Safety Fund	1
9.	Development Fund	4
10.	Miscellaneous	8
11.	Capital Fund	7
	Total	**100**

Economic Survey 2006 - 07

- **Govt lays stress on reforms**
- **Economic Survey hints at further liberalisation**

The Economic Survey 2006-07 was presented in Parliament on 27-02-2007 by the Finance Minister P. Chidambaram.

Highlights

➲ Economy projected to grow at 9.2 per cent in 2006-07 ➲ Sustaining high growth with moderate inflation, inclusive growth and intervention in social sector recommended. ➲ Agricultural growth at 2.7 percent; total foodgrains production at 209.2 million tonne. ➲ Fiscal consolidation satisfactory. ➲ Government making efforts to ease pressure on prices.

41

⊃ FDI rises by 98.4 per cent in first half of 2006-07. ⊃ F o r e i g n exchange reserves touch $180 billion. ⊃ Buoyancy in exports. ⊃ Steady progress on infrastructure front. ⊃ Sharp rise in rate of investment' in economy. ⊃ Trade, hotels, transport and communication services continue to grow at double-digit rates for 4th successive year. ⊃ Financial services growth maintained at 11.1 percent. ⊃ Increase in savings rate expected with higher economic growth. ⊃ Need to re-visit multiplicity of poverty alleviation schemes. ⊃ Alternative mechanisms for subsidy transfers to truly needy suggested.

The Survey has two principal themes - maintaining the new growth momentum and containing inflation, have dominated all recent discourses on the macro-economy. But while the Reserve Bank of India (RBI) in its latest review of Monetary Policy has opted for price stability, the Survey suggests that maintaining the high level of economic growth would be the priority area. The biggest challenges extending to the medium term are to sustain rates of 9 percent and more while moderating inflation and simultaneously to make growth more inclusive. The surge in inflation at this juncture is no doubt a matter of serious concern. Although there is a defence of forward markets while asking for better regulation, issues like RBI's purchase of dollars, agro reforms to allow disintermediation and lower tariffs are conveniently sidestepped.

Overall, the Survey is upseat on the recent economic performance. There has been unprecedented tax buoyanc, with tax collections under all heads except excise showing robust growth. The external sector continues to be in good health with reserves adding up to nearly $185 billion. The Survey is an important document but it remains to be seen how much of its hard-headed analysis is reflected in the political economy of budget-making.

Growth Rate

Taking a cue from the spiralling inflation rates in the face of a healthy economic growth rate of 9.2 per cent in the current fiscal, the Economic Survey 2006-07 advocated "calibrated" measures, including focus on critical areas such as education, health and support for the needy to achieve the target of "inclusive growth". The government's pre-budget report card acknowledged buoyancy in all sectors of economy except agriculture, which at a 2.7 per cent growth was a cause for concern. While a sense of optimism characterised the current economic conjecture, the Economic Survey, a critical document prepared by the Chief Economic Adviser in the finance ministry and a indicator of the general Budget to be presented, interjects a note of caution in view of hardening interest rates and a high demand for credit not adequately matched by deposit growth. "Fostering the momentum of growth continues to be a top priority", the survey spelt out, in an indication that budget may continue the overall trend of moderating taxes.

Agriculture

The country's foodgrain production could fall 11 million tonnes short of the target of 220 million tonnes raising further concerns about supply side constraints of essential commodities, the primary factor behind rising inflation in recent weeks. The target for foodgrain production for 2006-07 was fixed at 220 million tonnes, but actual production could be around 209.2 million tonnes, the survey said. "Poor agricultural performance, as the current year has demonstrated, can complicate maintenance of price stability with supply side problems in essential commodities of day-to-day consumption," it said.

With a shortfall in domestic production *vis-a-vis* domestic demand and hardening of international prices, prices of primary commodities mainly food have been on the rise. "Wheat, pulses, edible oils, fruits and vegetables and condiments and spices have been the major contributors to the higher inflation rate of primary articles. As much as 39.4 percent of the overall inflation in Wholesale Price Index (WPI) on Feb, 3, 2007 came from the primary group of commodities," it said. Food articles have a high weight of 15.4 per cent in the WPI basket. The estimated actual production at 209.2 million tonnes is marginally higher than the 208.6 million tonnes in 2005-06. The target of 228 million tonnes was fixed in view of the late monsoons rains during Sept. 2006 in several States.

Inflation

Inflation has spoilt the growth party and the government is deeply worried. The country's feel-good economy-riding high on consumer spending, an industrial revival and an expanding boom in services like telecommunications and software is posed for a record 9.2 percent growth this financial year, according to the Economic Survey. But the report also reveals that inflation, measured by wholesale prices is at 6.7 percent, compared with 4.1 per cent a year ago. Finding immediate answers to inflation produced by commodity-specific supply shortfalls is difficult," says the survey. "A durable solution has to be found in increasing yields and domestic output for products such as pulses, edible oils, rice and wheat."

Foreign Direct Investment (FDI)

Indian continues to be a favourable destination for overseas investors. Be it foreign direct investment (FDI), portfolio investment by foreign institutional investors or deposits by the Non-Resident Indians (NRI) or external commercial borrowings, almost all the ingredients of overseas investments have

State of the Indian Economy

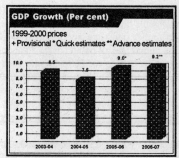

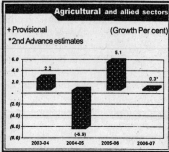

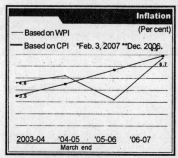

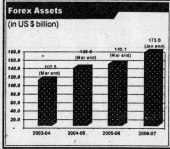

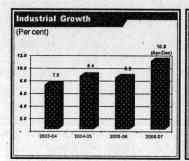

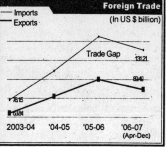

Infrastructure Performance (Growth Rates in Per Cent)
(April - December)

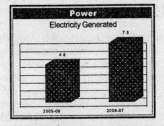

Power
Electricity Generated
4.8 (2005-06), 7.5 (2006-07)

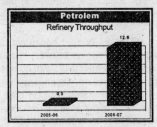

Petrolem
Refinery Throughput
0.5 (2005-06), 12.6 (2006-07)

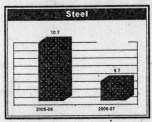

Steel
10.7 (2005-06), 9.7 (2006-07)

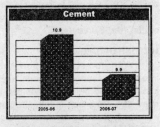

Cement
10.9 (2005-06), 9.9 (2006-07)

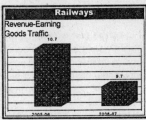

Railways
Revenue-Earning Goods Traffic
10.7 (2005-06), 9.7 (2006-07)

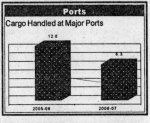

Ports
Cargo Handled at Major Ports
12.6 (2005-06), 8.3 (2006-07)

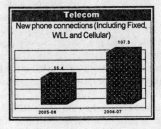

Telecom
New phone connections (Including Fixed, WLL and Cellular)
55.4 (2005-06), 107.3 (2006-07)

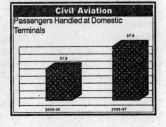

Civil Aviation
Passengers Handled at Domestic Terminals
21.3 (2005-06), 37.0 (2006-07)

witnessed a sharp upswing in 2006-07. Unlike last financial year, when the Reserve Bank of India lost five billion dollars on account of a valuation loss in foreign exchange reserves, in the first six months of the current financial year, the central bank made a killing of $5.1 billion. Forex reserves reached $180 billion as on Feb. 2007.

The pre-budget economic survey says that capital flows into India remained strong on an overall basis even after gross outflows under Foreign Direct Investment (FDI) with domestic companies seeking a global presence to harness scale, technology and market access through acquisitions overseas. Overtaking South Korea, but still behind the dragon (China), India attracted a cumulative FDI inflow of Rs. 1,81,566 crore ($43.29 billion) since August 1991 upto September 2006, the survey said. As per the latest report of UNCTAD (United Nations Conference on Trade and Development), India surpassed South Korea to become to fourth largest recipient of FDI in the region, the Survey-said.

Infrastructure

With infrastructure now showing signs of progress and providing impetus to economic growth, the Economic Survey has suggested that insurance and pension funds can be used to meet the massive investment need of $320 billion in infrastructure during the XI Plan. An indicator of the economy's progress, the document, tabled in Parliament on 27th February, 2007 says: "Outlook in infrastructure will depend on how investment in infrastructure is facilitated".

It injects a note of optimism when it observes that infrastructure - for years perceived as a constraint on growth-is showing signs of progress in areas such as power, roads, ports and airports. In this contest, it points to the fact that the overall index of six core industries, having a direct bearing on infrastructure and accounting for 27 per cent of weight in the Index of Industrial Production (IIP), registered a growth of 8.3 per cent during April-December, 2006 as against the 5.5 per cent registered a year ago. Referring to the projection of investment of Rs. 14,50,000 crore ($320 billion) required in the core sector during the XI Plan, it said investment in infrastructure required long-term funds with long payback periods, which would be possible if insurance and pension funds were utilised. The pre-budget Survey goes on to add, "Thus, success on the infrastructure front will be facilitated by the development of a vibrant bond market, and pension and insurance reforms." "A single, unified exchange-traded market for corporate bonds would help create a mature debt market for financing infrastructure," it says further, recalling that the Committee on Infrastructure, headed by the Prime Minister, has projected Rs.2,20,000 crore fund requirement for modernising and upgrading highways, Rs.40,000 crore for civil aviation, Rs.50,000 crore for ports and Rs.3,00,000 crore for the railways by 2012.

Unemployment

The overall employment rate may be on the rise, but the dip in jobs in agriculture and the organised sector is a problem, a fact that the Economic Survey acknowledges while offering higher growth as the only solution. While the rate of employment grew 2.5 per cent annually between 2000-01 and 2004-05, compared to 1.6 per cent during the preceding five years, the rate of unemployment went up to 3.1 per cent in 2004-05, as against 2.8 per cent in 1999-2000. The survey attributes the higher rate of unemployment to the growth in population. What is worrying the government is the limited scope for absorbing the growing workforce in the agriculture sector, whose share in economic activity has dipped below 20 per cent. Farm sector employment too decreased from 61.7 per cent of the total workforce in 1993-94 to 54.2 per cent in 2004-05. With the sector's share in GDP falling, it will be even more difficult for agriculture to contribute much to employment generation, the Survey notes.

Special Economic Zones

Caught in the crossfire between a country on a blazing growth path and the politically sensitive issue of acquiring farm land for industries, the government is doing a tightrope on Special Economic Zones (SEZs) and admits as much in the annual economic survey. Dwelling at length on the need for a proper policy on special economic zones, expected to generate employment, survey stresses the fact that fears about revenue losses and compensation could be alloyed only by proper policies. "The recent debate about SEZ illustrates the kind of considerations that have to be taken into account in the formulation of policies," it observed. SEZs have been in the eye of a political storm due to farm land acquisition for industrial purposes. Issues of meagre land compensation, misuse of land by real estate developers and possible impact on "food security" had caught the attention of policy makers."

Union Budget 2007 - 08

The Union Finance Minister P. Chidambaram presented the Union Budget for 2007-08 in the Parliament on Feb. 28, 2007.

The Budget is best evaluated in terms of its impact on growth, prices and rural incomes. With the allocation of 34.2 percent more money for heatlh, the Budget stands out for its thrust on the country's human development profile, which is poorer than some of the smaller neighbouring countries. The additional one per cent educationcess on all taxes is estimated to yield

Rs.5,500 crore, which will be used to fund secondary and higher education apart from expanding the intake capacity of premier Central institutions like the Indian Institutes of Technology (IITs) and Indian Institutes of Management (IIMs) to provide reservation to Other Backward Classes (OBCs).

The Budget has raised the personal income tax exemption limit by Rs. 10,000. The IT exemption limit for women in up at Rs.1,45,000 and for the senior citizens at Rs.1,95,000. The Budget has a clear focus - to curb the price rice, increase public spending on education and health and revitalise agriculture. What the Finance Minister has not done is equally significant. He has not tinkered with the Special Economic Zones, though he is concerned about the proposed loss of revenue.

Plan Outlay

The Union budget accords top priority to the social sector, followed by energy and transport that together account for nearly three-fourth of the total Plan size of Rs.3,19,992 crore, but more than half the financing would come from much maligned Public Sector Enterprises (PSEs). Social services including education, housing and nutrition have got the largest allocation of Rs.83,950.69 crore out of the total Plan allocation and the transport sector has been given the maximum increase of 43.7 per cent in the outlays.With an increase of over 15 percent in the budget allocation, the energy sector has been provided Rs.79,158.45 crore. The transport sector has been provided the third largest pool of resources of Rs.71,589.02 crore to be spent on development of railways, ports, shipping, civil aviation, roads and bridges and inland water transport. The Finance Minister has proposed a Central Plan outlay worth Rs.20,342 crore for the rural development sector, Rs.79,158 crore for the energy sector, Rs.20,434 crore for industry and minerals. He has proposed Rs.18,861 crore for the Ministry of Shipping, Road Transport and Highways, Rs.33,153 crore for the Power Ministry and Rs.28,674 crore for the Human Resource and Development Ministry.

Defence

Defence spending continued to inch towards the one lakh crore-mark with the Union budget allocating Rs.96,000 crore for the next fiscal as against this year's outlay for defence of Rs. 89,000 crore and actual spending of Rs.86,000 crore. Capital outlay on defence services (purchase of major military equipment) has been proposed at a record high of about Rs.42,000 crore and accounts for just over 40 per cent of the budget indicating that the Government's desire for a 50:50 ratio between capital equipment and revenue expenditure remains unfulfilled. Of the three armed forces, the highest outlay at about Rs. 16,500 crore was for the Indian Air Force (IAF) followed by

Rs.11,374 crore for the Army and just over Rs.10,000 crore for the Navy. This does not take into account Rs.2,700 crore earmarked for research & development, a euphemism for missiles and other strategic systems, Rs. 320 crore for the joint staff, Rs.168 crore for special projects and smaller amounts for the Rashtriya Rifles (RR) and purchase of rolling stock, mainly specially designed railway wagons for carrying missiles.

Disinvestment

The Government hopes to raise Rs.1651 crore in 2007-08 through disinvestment of a portion of its equity holdings in select PSEs. In 2006-07, the government had assumed Rs. 528.58 crore on account of bonus shares issued by Oil and Natural Gas Corporation. The disinvestment proceeds of Rs. 1651 crore in 2007-08 are on account of disinvestment of small equity in Rural Electrification Corporation (REC), Power Grid Corporation of India Ltd (PGCIL) an National Hydroelectric Power Corporation (NHPC). Provision for transfer of the same amount to National Investment Fund (NIF) has been provisioned in the Budget.

Science & Technology

Science and Technology got a major boost in the budget with the Finance Minister, P. Chidambaram, announcing plans to upgrade Industrial Training Institutes (ITIs), tax exemptions for research institutions and Rs. 50 crore for initiatives towards undertaking the first human space flight by 2014. The Government also announced Rs. 100 crore for recognising excellence in the field of agricultural research and a proposal to set up an expert committee to study the impact of climate change on India and identify the measures to be taken up in the future. The Minister said that 1396 ITIs would be upgraded into Centres of Excellence in specific trades and skills under Public-Private Partnership (PPP). The state government, as the owner of the ITI, will continue to regulate admission and fees and the new management will be given academic and financial autonomy. The Central Government will provide financial assistance by way of seed money and ITI would be encouraged to start a second shift.

Agriculture

For the first time in a Budget speech, the Finance Minister devoted a good 15-20 minutes exclusively to agriculture. While the announcements lay stress on seeds and water, there is not much in it to encourage private sector investment in areas like food processing. Most of these are seen as long-term measures that are unlikely to have an immediate impact on the present farm crisis.

This year's Budget has moved the focus away from credit and irrigation last year to seeds and extension. After little progress on the irrigation front following the announcements in 2006-07, P. Chidambaram decided to put more money into irrigation. Irrigation outlay has gone up by 35 per cent from Rs.7,000 crore to about Rs.11,000 crore. For farm credit, though the targets have already been achieved, he hiked the outlay from Rs.1,95,000 crore to about Rs. 2,25,000 crore.

Information Technology

The budget must surely have pleased Narayana Murthy, the only one who is game for software being brought under the tax net. For the rest of the software services sector, P. Chidambaram's speech served a much-evaded blow. The sector has been brought under the Minimum Alternate Tax (MAT) net and software services and IT-enabled companies will have to pay about 12 percent. Chidambaram did it with finesse, without as much as mentioning the, software sector. Quietly, he extended MAT to the income of companies that have been claiming deduction under Section 10A and 1013 of the Income Tax (read software services and BPO sector). Funds alloted for a new scheme of manpower development for the software export industry is Rs. 33 crore. The minimum alternate tax to be levied on software services and IT-enabled companies is 12 percent.

Education

The Union Budget 2007-08 has enhanced allocation for education by 34.2 percent to Rs.32,352 crore and proposes one per cent additional cess to fund secondary and higher education. The one percent additional cess would be in addition to the two per cent existing cess on all taxes to fund basic education. The additional cess would take care of 54 percent expansion of capacity for the OBC quota. The allocation for school education is proposed to be increased by about 35 per cent from Rs.17,133 crore in 2006-07 to Rs.23,142 crore in 2007-08. Out of this, the *Sarva Shiksha Abbiyan* (SSA) would get Rs.10,671 crore. The provision for strengthening teachers' training institutions would be raised from Rs. 162 crore to Rs.450 crore. Next year, two lakh more teachers would be appointed and five lakh additional class rooms built. The Mid-Day Meal Scheme, which targets to enrol more children in schools, will be provided Rs.7324 crore in the next 'financial year'.

Subsidy

The budget provides for Rs. 2,650 crore for subsiding LPG and Kerosene at the rate of Rs.22.58 per 14.2 kg domestic LPG cylinder and Re.0.82 per litre of kerosene sold through the Public Distribution System

Tax Collections

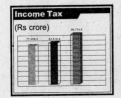

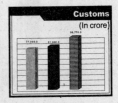

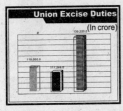

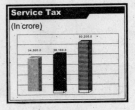

▨ 2006-07 (Budget)
■ 2006-07 (Revised)
▤ 2007-08 (Budget)

BUDGET AT A GLANCE

(Figures in Rs. Crore)

	2005-06 Actuals	2006-07 Budget Estimates	2006-07 Revised Estimates	2007-08 Budget Estimates
Revenue Receipts	347462	403465	423331	486422
Capital Receipts	158661	160526	158306	194099
Total Receipts	506123	563991	581637	680521
Non-Plan Expenditure	365485	391263	408907	475421
Plan Expenditure	140638	172728	172730	205100
Total Expenditure	506123	563991	581637	680521
Revenue Deficit	92299	84727	83436	71478
Fiscal Deficit	146435	148686	152328	150948
Primary Deficit	13805	8863	6136	–8047

Central Plan Outlay by Sectors (Rs. in crore)

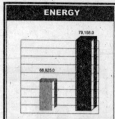

ENERGY

68,825.0

79,158.0

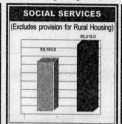

SOCIAL SERVICES

(Excludes provision for Rural Housing)

59,143.0

80,315.0

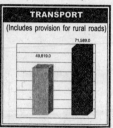

TRANSPORT

(Includes provision for rural roads)

49,819.0

71,589.0

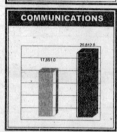

COMMUNICATIONS

17,851.0

25,812.0

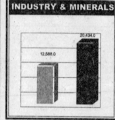

INDUSTRY & MINERALS

12,588.0

20,434.0

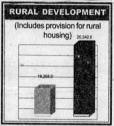

RURAL DEVELOPMENT

(Includes provision for rural housing) 20,342.0

18,268.0

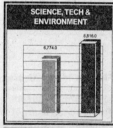

SCIENCE, TECH & ENVIRONMENT

6,774.0

6,816.0

GENERAL ECONOMIC SERVICES

2,566.0

3,632.0

AGRICULTURE & ALLIED ACTIVITIES

7,391.0

8,558.0

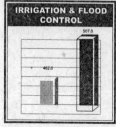

IRRIGATION & FLOOD CONTROL

462.0

507.0

GENERAL SERVICES

542.0

829.0

TOTAL

244,229.0

319,992.0

☐ 2006-07 (Revised)   ■ 2007-08 (Budget)

(PDS). Minister of State in PMO Prithiviraj Chauhan recently mooted the idea of putting in place a "dual pricing" system for LPG distribution to put an end to the misuse of domestic LPG for commercial purposes.

Income Tax

Budget 2007 has increased the basic income tax exemption limit by Rs.10,000. For individual assesses, it is now Rs.1.1 lakh, though for women assesses, it is Rs.1.45 lakh and for senior citizens Rs. 1.95 lakh. As a consequence, the total relief will be Rs. 1,000 for women and men asseses, and Rs.2,000 for senior citizens.

However, what Chidambaram has given by way of exemptions, he's taken by way of a new higher education cess of 1 per cent, which takes the total cess to 3 per cent. For higher income groups, earning a salary of Rs. 6 lakh per annum or more-this might translate into a marginally higher amount shelled out by way of taxes. This is largely due to the fact that as the income increases the percentage increase of the cess has a magnifying effect vis-a-vis a standard relief Rs.1,000. Another change has been in the hike in the withdrawl limit of the Banking Cash Transaction Tax. The exemption has been raised from Rs.25,000 to Rs.50,000 for individuals an HUFs. Now, on withdrawl from one's current account or fixed deposit exceeding Rs. 50,000 in a day, a tax of 0.1 per cent will be levied on the entire withdrawl.

Tourism

Recognising the need for 20,000 more hotel rooms for the Commonwealth Games to be held here in 2010, Chidambaram proposed a five-year holiday from income tax for new star hotels and conventions centres with a seating capacity of not less than 3,000 persons. Presenting the budget for 2007-08, Chidambaram said the work on the new two, three or four-star hotels as well as the convention centres should be completed and begin operations in Delhi or in the adjacent districts of Faridabad, Gurgaon, Ghaziabad or Gautam Budh Nagar between April 2007 and March 31, 2010. Nothing that India bid for and won for Delhi the Commonwealth Games 2010, Chidambaram recalled that the country had successfully hosted the 1982 Asian Games.

Commonwealth Games 2010

An allocation of Rs. 500 crore for the Commonwealth Games 2010 was announced in the Union budget, besides a higher allocation of Rs. 111 crore for the Sports and Youth Affairs Ministry. In a bid to make the multi-disciplinary snorting extravaganza a success, the Centre would sanction Rs. 350 crore to the Delhi government and another Rs.150 crore to the Youth

How a rupee is spent and earned	
How a rupee is earned?	**How a rupee is spent?**

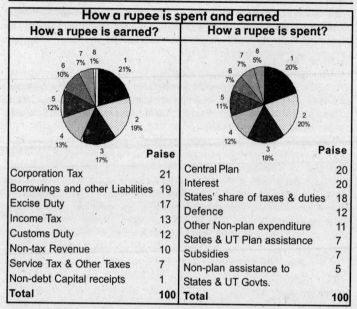

	Paise		Paise
Corporation Tax	21	Central Plan	20
Borrowings and other Liabilities	19	Interest	20
Excise Duty	17	States' share of taxes & duties	18
Income Tax	13	Defence	12
Customs Duty	12	Other Non-plan expenditure	11
Non-tax Revenue	10	States & UT Plan assistance	7
Service Tax & Other Taxes	7	Subsidies	7
Non-debt Capital receipts	1	Non-plan assistance to States & UT Govts.	5
Total	**100**	**Total**	**100**

Affairs and Sports Ministry for organising the Games. Finance Minister also earmarked Rs.50 crore for the Commonwealth Youth Games to be held in Pune next year. The Sports and Youth Affairs Ministry has been provided a budget allocation of Rs.780 crore for the year 2007-08, an increase of Rs. 111 crore from the previous year. Rs.62 crore have been earmarked for training and scouting sports talent. The scheme envisages a package of assistance to the promising sportpersons for training in India and abroad, purchase of sport equipment *etc.*

Rural Unemployment

The budget has promised to expand the National Rural Job Guarantee scheme (NREG) to 130 new districts, taking the total number of districts under the scheme to 330 with a budgetary allocation of Rs.12,000 crore. A scheme of death and disability insurance scheme for the rural landless households under the name of *Aam Admi Bima Yojana* is also on cards. Under the scheme, to be run through LIC, the centre will bear the 50 per cent of the premium of Rs.200 a year per person while the rest will have to be borne by the State governments. In order to incentivise the organised sector jobs for physically challenged persons, Rs. 1,800 crore has been earmarked. The money will be used for rewarding the employers by reimbursing their first three EPF contributions for each regularised physically challenged persons in their organization.

Industry

The industry and minerals have also seen a big jump in Plan allocation to Rs.12,588 crore in 2006-07 (revised estimates) to Rs.20,434.42 crore. The tax relief, in the form of infrastructure status, would be directly reflected in lower tariffs in the pipeline system and would make the product more affordable to consumers. The new concession would also make additional funds available as such investments would qualify for tax benefits under the new regime. Chidambaram also provided infrastructure status to the cross-country natural gas distribution network, including pipeline and storage facilities integrated with it. The status, which gives a 10-year income-tax holiday, would help bring down gas-transportation cost by 12-14 per cent. The tax break would mean a net saving of about Rs. 300 crore to fertilizer companies if they used pipelines.

Bharat Nirman Scheme

Grant to the Bharat Nirman Project has been increased by about a third to Rs.24,603 crore. The budget has increased the budgetary allocation for rural electrification scheme by about 30 per cent to Rs.3,983 crore.

STATE GOVERNORS AND CHIEF MINISTERS

STATE	GOVERNOR	CHIEF MINISTER
Andhra Pradesh	Mr. N.T. Diwari	Mr. Y.S. Rajasekar Reddy
Arunachal Pradesh	Mr. K. Sankara Narayanan	Mr. Dorjee Khandu
Assam	Lt.Gen.(Retd.) Ajay Singh	Mr. Tarun Gogai
Bihar	Mr. R.S. Gavai	Mr. Nitish Kumar
Chattisgarh	Mr. E.S.L. Narasimhan	Mr. Raman Singh
Goa	Mr. S.C. Jamir	Mr. Pratap Singh Rane
Gujarat	Mr. Nawal Kishore Sarma	Mr. Narendra Modi
Haryana	Mr. A.R. Kidwai	Mr. Bhupinder Singh Hooda
Himachal Pradesh	Justice (Retd.) V.S. Kokje	Mr. Virbadra Singh
Jammu & Kashmir	Lt.Gen. (Retd.) S.K. Sinha	Mr. Gulam Nabi Azad
Jharkhand	Mr. Syed Sibte Razi	Mr. Madhu Goda
Karnataka	Mr. Rameshwar Thakur	Mr. Kumaraswamy
Kerala	Mr. Raghunand Lal Bhatia	Mr. Aachudanandan
Madhya Pradesh	Mr. Balram Jakhar	Mr. Shivraj Singh Chauhan

STATE	GOVERNOR	CHIEF MINISTER
Maharashtra	Mr. S.M. Krishna	Mr. Vilas Rao Deshmukh
Manipur	Mr. Shivinder Singh Sidhu	Mr. Okram Ibobi Singh
Meghalaya	–	Mr. D.D. Lapang
Mizoram	Lt. Gen. (Retd.) M.M. Lakhera	Mr. Zoramthanga
Nagaland	Mr. K. Sankara Narayanan	Mr. Neiphiu Rio
Orissa	Mr. Muralidhar Chandra Kanth	Mr. Naveen Patnaik
Punjab	Lt. Genl. (Retd.) S.F. Rodrigues	Mr. Prakash Singh Padal
Rajasthan	Mr. Sylendra Kumar Singh	Ms. Vasundara Raje Scindia
Sikkim	Mr. Sudarsan Agarwal	Mr. Pawan Kumar Chamlin
Tamil Nadu	Mr. S.S. Barnala	Mr. M. Karunanidhi
Tripura	Mr. Dinesh Nandan Sahaya	Mr. Manik Sirkar
Uttar Pradesh	Mr. T.V. Rajeshwar Rao	Ms. Mayawati
Uttarakhand	Mr. B.L. Joshil	Maj. Gen. (Retd.) B.C.Kanduri
West Bengal	Mr. Gopalakrishna Gandhi	Mr. Bhuddadeb Bhattacharya

Lt. Governors/Administrators and Chief Ministers of Union Territories

Union Territory	Lt.Governor/Administrator	Chief Minister
Andaman & Nicobar	Lt. Gen. (Retd.) Bhopinder Singh	-
Chandigarh	Genl. S.F. Rodrigues (Addl. Charge)	-
Dadra and Nagar Haveli	Mr. Rajnikanth Varma	-
Daman and Diu	Mr. Rajnikanth Varma	-
Delhi	Mr. Tejendra Khanna	Mrs. Sheila Dixit
Lakshadweep	Mr. Parimal Rai	-
Puducherry	Mr. Mughul Mitti	Mr. N. Rangaswamy

COUNCIL OF MINISTERS

MANMOHAN SINGH : Prime Minister, Personnel, Public grievances & Pensions, Planning, Atomic energy, Environment , Forests and Space.

Cabinet Ministers

A.K. Antony	:	Defence
Pranab Mukherjee	:	External Affairs
Arjun Singh	:	Human Resources Development
Sharad Pawar	:	Agriculture, Consumer Affairs, Food and Public Distribution
Lalu Prasad Yadav	:	Railways

Shivraj Patil	:	Home Affairs
Ram Vilas Paswan	:	Chemicals & Fertilisers and Steel
S. Jaipal Reddy	:	Urban Development
P. Chidambaram	:	Finance
Mahavir Prasad	:	Small-scale Industries, Agro & Rural Industries
P.R. Kyndiah	:	Tribal Affairs
T.R. Baalu	:	Shipping; Road Transport & Highways
Shankersingh Vaghela	:	Textiles
Kamal Nath	:	Commerce & Industry
H.R. Bhardwaj	:	Law & Justice
Raghuvansh Prasad Singh	:	Rural Development
Priya Ranjan Das Munshi	:	Information & Broadcasting and Parliamentary Affairs
Mani Shankar Aiyar	:	Panchayati Raj, Youth Affairs, Sports & Development of North-Eastern region
Ms. Meira Kumar	:	Social Justice & Empowerment
A. Raja	:	Communication & Information Technology
Anbumani Ramdoss	:	Health & Family Welfare
Sis Ram Ola	:	Mines
Murli Deora	:	Petroleum and Natural Gas
Sushil Kumar Shinde	:	Power
A.R. Antulay	:	Minority Affairs
Vayalar Ravi	:	Overseas Indian Affairs
Ms. Ambika Soni	:	Tourism and Culture
Saifuddin Soz	:	Water Resources
Santosh Mohan Dev	:	Heavy Industries and Public Enterprises
Prem Chand Gupta	:	Company Affairs
Kapil Sibal	:	Science & Technology and Ocean Development

Ministers of State (Independent Charge)

Ms. Renuka Choudhury	:	Women and Child Development
Subodh Kant Sahay	:	Food processing Industries
Vilas Muttemwar	:	Non-conventional Energy Sources
Ms. Kumari Selja	:	Housing & Urban Poverty Alleviation
Praful Patel	:	Civil Aviation
G.K. Vasan	:	Statistics and Programme Implementation
Oscar Fernandes	:	Labour & Employment

Ministers of State

E. Ahamed	:	External Affairs
Suresh Pachauri	:	Personnel, Public Grievances & Pensions and Parliamentary Affairs
B.K. Handique	:	Chemical and Fertilisers; Parliamentary Affairs
Ms. Panabaka Lakshmi	:	Health & Family Welfare
Dasari Narayan Rao	:	Coal
Shaqeel Ahmed	:	Communications & Information Technology.
Rao Inderjit Singh	:	Defence
Naranbhai Rathwa	:	Railways
K.H. Munlappa	:	Road Transport & Highways
M.V. Rajasekharan	:	Planning
Kantilal Bhuria	:	Agriculture, Consumer Affairs, Food & Public Distribution
Manik Rao Gavit	:	Home Affairs
Sri Prakash Jaiswal	:	Home Affairs
Prithviraj Chavan	:	Prime Minister's Office
Taslimuddin	:	Agriculture, Consumer Affairs, Food and Public Distribution
Ms. Suryakanta Patil	:	Rural Development; Parliamentary Affairs
Md. Ali Ashraf Fatmi	:	Human Resources Development
R. Velu	:	Railways
S.S. Palanimanikkam	:	Finance
S. Regupathy	:	Home Affairs
K. Venkatapathy	:	Law & Justice
Radhika Selvi	:	Home Affairs
Ms.Subbulakshmi Jagadeesan	:	Social Justice & Empowerment
E.V.K.S. Elangovan	:	Textiles
Ms. Kanti Singh	:	Heavy Industries
Namo Narayan Meena	:	Environment & Forests
Akhilesh Prasad Singh	:	Agriculture, Consumer Affairs, Food and Public Distribution
Pawan Kumar Bansal	:	Finance
Anand Sharma	:	External Affairs
Ajay Maken	:	Urban Development
M.M. Pallam Raju	:	Defence
Akhilesh Das	:	Steel
Chandrasekhar Sahu	:	Rural Development

Ashwani Kumar	:	Commerce & Industries
Ms. D. Purandareshwari:		Human Resources Development
Dinshaw Patel	:	Petroleum & Natural Gas
T. Subbirami Reddy	:	Mines
Jairam Ramesh	:	Commerce & Industry
Jaiprakash Narayan Yadav	:	Water Resources

(Unallocated portfolios will be looked after by the Prime Minister)

HIGH-UPS IN INDIA

President: Mrs. Pratibha Patil
Vice-President: Mohammad Hamid Anzari
Speaker, Lok Sabha: Somnath Chatterji
Deputy Speaker, Lok Sabha: Charanjit Singh Atwal
Chairman, Rajya Sabha: Mohammad Hamid Anzari
Deputy Chairman, Rajya Sabha: K. Rahman Khan
Leader of Opposition in Lok Sabha: L.K. Advani
Leader of Opposition in Rajya Sabha: Jaswant Singh
Chief Justice of India: K.G. Balakrishnan
Principal Scientific Adviser to the Government: Dr. R. Chidambaram
Chairperson, University Grants Commission: Sukhadeo Thorat
Comptroller and Auditor-General of India: V.N. Kaul
President, Indian National Congress: Ms. Sonia Gandhi
President, BJP: Rajnath Singh
Governor, Reserve Bank of India: Y.V. Reddy
Chairman, UPSC: Subir Dutta
Chairman, Public Accounts Committee: Vijaya Kumar Malhotra
Chairman, Staff Selection Commission: B.K. Mishra
Chairman, Planning Commission: Manmohan Singh
Deputy Chairman, Planning Commission: Montek Singh Ahluwaliah
Attorney-General of India: Milon Kumar Banerjee
Solicitor-General of India: Goolam E. Vahanvati
Census Commissioner and Registrar-General of India: D.K. Sikri
Chairman, State Bank of India: O.P. Bhat
Chairman, Law Commission: Justice M. Jagannath Rao
Chairman, Oil & Natural Gas Corporation: R.S. Sharma
Chairman, Prasar Bharathi: M.V. Kamath
Chairman, National Human Rights Commission: Justice S. Rajendra Babu
Chairman, National Commission for Minorities: –
Chairman, National Commission for Backward Classes: Justice Ratnavel Pandian

Chairman, National Book Trust: Bipin Chandra
Principal Secretary to Prime Minister: T.K.A. Nair
Chairman, Securities Exchange Board of India (SEBI): M. Damodaran
Chairman, GIC: Mathew Varghese
Director-General, Indian Council of Agri. Research: Dr. Mangla Rai
Chairperson, National Commission for Women: Ms. Girija Vyas
Chairman National Commission for Scheduled Tribes: Kunwar Singh
Chairman, National Commission on Labour : Ravindra Varma
Chairman, Telecom Commission: Anil Kumar
Chairman, Telecom Regulatory Authority of India: Nripendra Mishra
Director, CBI: Vijay Shanker
Director, IB: P.C. Halder
Chairman, Indian Oil Corporation: S. Behruia
India's Permanent Representative to the UN: Nirupam Sen
Chief Vigilance Commissioner: Pratyush Sinha
Chief of Central Board of Film Certification: Sharmila Tagore
Chairman, National Forest Commission: Justice (Rtd.) B.N. Kirpal
Director-General, National Security Guards: A.K. Mitra
Director-General, Border Roads Organisation: Lt. Gen Ranjit Singh
Chairman, Press Council of India: Justice (Retd.) G.N. Ray
Director, Press Institute of India: Ajit Bhattachariya
Chairman, United News of India: Ravindra Kumar
Chairman, Central Water Commission: R. Jayaseelan
Chairperson, Children Film Society of India: Ms. Nafisa Ali
Director-General, Archaeological Survey of India: C. Babu Rajeev
Chairman, National Commission for Farmers: M.S. Swaminathan
Director, Bhabha Atomic Research Centre: S. Banerjee
President, All India Sports Council: Vijay Kumar Malhotra
President, Indian Olympic Association: Suresh Kalmadi
Director-General, Doordarshan: Naveen Kumar
Chairman, NASSCOM: N. Lakshmi Narayanan
Chairperson, Sangeet Natak Academy: Ram Niwas Mirdha
Chairman, Sahitya Academy: Gopi Chand Narang
Director, Satish Dhawan Space Centre (SHAR): M. Annamalai
Chief Information Commissioner: Wajahad Habibullah
Chairman, National Knowledge Commission: Sam Pitroda
Chairman, Research and Analysis Wing (RAW): Ashok Chaturvedi
Chairman, National Child Rights Commission: Shantha Sinha
Chancellor, Jawaharlal Nehru University : Yash Pal